AF478993

DEMOCRACY AND THE CRISIS OF INEQUALITY

DEMOCRACY AND THE CRISIS OF INEQUALITY

ZOYA HASAN

PRIMUS
BOOKS

PRIMUS BOOKS
An imprint of Ratna Sagar P. Ltd.
Virat Bhavan
Mukherjee Nagar Commercial Complex
Delhi 110 009

Offices at CHENNAI LUCKNOW
AGRA AHMEDABAD BENGALURU COIMBATORE DEHRADUN GUWAHATI
HYDERABAD JAIPUR KANPUR KOCHI KOLKATA MADURAI MUMBAI
PATNA RANCHI VARANASI

First published 2014

ISBN 978-93-80607-89-4

Published by Primus Books

Lasertypeset by Sai Graphic Design
Arakashan Road, Paharganj, New Delhi 110 055

Printed and bound in India by Replika Press Pvt. Ltd.

For

MUSHIR

Contents

Preface

Written between the late 1980s and 2012, the essays in this volume deal with a range of issues that are central to political change in India. Many of them examine important aspects of democratic evolution after Jawaharlal Nehru. Others focus on key issues pertaining to the debates over secularism, social justice, representation, and redistribution and the changing nature of state and society in the wake of globalization and liberalization. Some of the essays explore new forms of politics, identity formation, and assertions of caste, class, gender, religion, and region in the most recent phase of Indian politics.

The essays in *Democracy and the Crisis of Inequality* reflect my broader interests in the areas of state, democracy, and development, and issues of equity, social justice, and minorities. Even though there is no obvious common thread running through these essays, they do shed light on facets of the changing patterns of politics at the centre and in the states in the last three decades, focusing on the relationship between democratic politics and inequalities. The introductory chapter provides a context to the dramatic changes and critical tensions that shape the continuing transformation of the Indian democracy.

I would like to express my gratitude to Divya Kannan for her research support in preparing this volume. I am also grateful to various publishers for permission to reproduce the essays in this volume.

I couldn't have written these essays without the intellectual support and companionship of Mushir to whom I dedicate this book.

New Delhi   Zoya Hasan

Introduction

THERE ARE several important themes that define contemporary politics in India. The essays in this anthology focus on some critical aspects of Indian politics and how long-standing structures of society and the working of democracy have reconfigured state and society. Many essays here examine important aspects of democratic politics after Jawaharlal Nehru. Others look at the debates over secularism, representation, redistribution, social justice, and caste, class and gender, and the changing nature of the State in the wake of globalization and liberalization. Besides, they explore the politics and policies of group differentiated rights, regional politics, caste assertion, minority rights and women's rights and how these endeavours have made an impact on the pursuit of equality in India.

Democracy and Social Inequalities

India is known for its democracy; citizens elect its governments at regular intervals. It has consolidated a democratic system despite the absence of the preconditions often associated with democracy in the 1950s when it first became a democratic, secular republic. Apart from a period of 20 months between 1975 and 1977, when Prime Minister Indira Gandhi declared an Emergency and suspended civil rights and personal liberties, democracy has thriven and institutionalized. An increasing number of people participate in the elections and use them to influence party/government policies. This has ensured that political actors do not come only from the traditional upper caste social élite, although they continue to have a disproportionate presence in public institutions and influence over policymaking. From the late 1980s legislatures have become more socially representative, contributing to a shift in the balance of political power in the state and society. But in the process democracy has also become predominantly a means of electoral empowerment of different groups—lower castes, dalits, or even majoritarian

Hindus who claim to have been weakened by the privileges accorded to religious minorities.

While the record of representative democracy in India has been manifestly strong, that of reducing economic inequalities has been strikingly less effective. The strength of participatory democracy has not been matched with egalitarian economic development. Economic growth has averaged 8 per cent in the first decade of the twenty-first century but its benefits have gone to the top 20 per cent of the population. One key reason for this has been the growing influence of private capital and big business groups in government and policymaking. Corporate capital has gained a position of unparalleled significance within the state, middle classes, and urban society, displacing the legitimacy previously enjoyed by the developmental state. High GDP growth has seen an enormous concentration of wealth with the private corporate sector the chief beneficiary of the economic boom. It appears that the Indian state essentially serves the interests of business. India has the fifth-largest concentration of dollar billionaires in the world (after the US, Russia, China, and Germany), the third-largest middle class (after China and the US) and the single largest concentration of the world's poor. The ratio of billionaire wealth rose from less than 1 per cent of GDP in the mid-1990s to 23 per cent in 2008, and was 14 per cent in early 2010, after a fall and recovery. The increase in the number of billionaires who epitomize 'emergent India' indicates the increasing divide between the rich and the poor.

India has not been successful in reducing inequalities between its citizens. There is indeed much to be dissatisfied with: the inequalities in wealth and income have not been reduced; an unconscionably large number of people are poor even by the most modest standards of living; universal literacy is yet to be realized; a high dropout rate from schools and a very small proportion of the population go on to higher education. Basic health care facilities are inadequate. In fact, the performance in these areas compares unfavourably with many developing countries. Per capita income in India is about a quarter of China but inequality is significantly higher. This raises the broader question: how could such dramatic inequalities persist in a democracy in which voters create public pressure for improved outcomes. The logic of democracy and development are not seen to be asymmetric, and yet, asymmetries abound.

This leads into another related aspect of socioeconomic and political asymmetries: regionalism and the growing importance of states in the political system after economic liberalization. In the last twenty years or so, India's polity has become more federalized and decentralized with the introduction of democratic governance at the village and district level following the constitutional amendments of 1993. The emergence of multi-party coalitions as a regular form of government in the states and now at the Centre as well has brought about a sea change in Centre-State and interparty dynamics in India. The challenge of building and sustaining coalitions has become an issue of far greater significance in the post-Congress era. These political changes have resulted in the growth of coalition politics, increased importance of the state as the chief arena of electoral contestation and an expansion in the influence of regional and state-based political parties. The compelling need is to build federal coalitions that can reconcile regional aspirations represented by these parties with national cohesion. Significantly enough, the new realities have not been legislated or created by conscious institutional design or reform. Arguably, the deepening of democracy ties has contributed to the shift towards a more federal polity. There is also a better recognition on the part of most political leaders that accommodative approaches are essential for dealing with regions and states.

Caste, Class, Community, and the State

In India social inequality revolves around the axes of class, caste, religion, and gender. These inequalities are rooted primarily in the caste system, property, income, employment, and education. The upper castes are the most advantaged in India and Scheduled Castes and Scheduled Tribes among the poorest and most disadvantaged. However, the Indian state has made significant attempts to address these pressing concerns through constitutional provisions and above all, through the policy of mandatory reservation for these two groups since 1950 and for the Other Backward Classes (OBCs), following the implementation of the recommendations of the Mandal Commission from 1990 onwards. Post-Mandal, caste had erupted onto the political scene. Still, it can be argued that the upshot of these reservations seeking to ameliorate disadvantage was to legally entrench them, and at the same time, galvanize lower castes into active political life, transforming the landscape of democracy, but with very uneven consequences for other groups excluded from its purview. Compartmentalized identity politics has at once deepened parliamentary politics and distorted it in myriad ways.

Whilst the constitutional effort to reduce social inequalities has met with considerable success, it also created several new problems because it did not enable governments to ensure substantive equality. The political leadership is more representative but only in respect of caste. Furthermore, it is clear that the new legislative elite are no plebeians in class or economic terms. This is evident from election expenditure and declaration of assets of MPs and candidates. Moreover, most have no well defined position or progressive policy choices to offer on the major issues of our time. Most significant, then, is the remarkable ability of the political system to draft in and include the excluded but they all too soon develop stakes in the system and thus cease to be carriers of transformative politics. What's more, change is limited to the institutions of representation and to caste groups who have gained from it; it does not extend to Muslims and women, for example.

Around this idea of group sensitive policies there has, however, developed a political discourse allowing for both direct involvement in religious matters and non-involvement, where it would be better to adopt a measure of symmetry of action between groups. Religion has been politicized, but the most important issue is not the growth of religious politics per se but the inordinate play of identity politics based on caste and religion to the extent that ordinary Indians do not have access to public institutions except on the basis of social identities. Even secular parties have not hesitated in using religion for political and electoral purposes. The Congress party's effort to play the religious card calculated to undercut the popularity of its political rivals, notably, the Bharatiya Janata Party (BJP) and please the Muslim and Hindu constituency at different moments and in different ways had ended up giving a boost to the Hindu right and a phalanx of organizations associated with it.

One consequence of this ambivalence in allowing the infiltration of communal politics and prejudice into state structures was the apathetic attitude of the state during instances of mass violence against minorities, which also witnessed a rise. Mass violence has seen the state failing to uphold the law and principles of justice. The institutional apparatus has been heavily biased against the minorities, and with increasing communalization of politics, justice has often been denied to victims of communal violence. Comparative evidence from Gujarat and Mumbai points to the systematic failure of the state to provide justice, relief, and rehabilitation for the victims of communal violence. In the case of Gujarat, the state government continued to discriminate against Muslims in the aftermath of violence.

Indian secularism had never sharply separated state and religion but from the late 1980s the separation was even less noticeable. Despite its erosion in recent decades, the centrality of secularism to political life is undeniable. This is because Indian secularism is part of a broader constellation of concepts that include democracy, equality, and justice. Seen from this angle the state seeks to foster the project of secular democracy that advances justice, equality, and the rights of minorities. Hence, a leading issue in this regard is how Muslims have fared under secular developmental regimes. The Sachar

Committee appointed by the Congress-led United Progressive Alliance (UPA) Government found the condition of an overwhelming majority of Muslims to be no better than Dalits as they suffer from both discrimination and disadvantage. In fact, most Muslims are worse off because they benefit from no affirmative action. Their condition throws into sharp relief the structural dilemmas of the differentiated state policy for disadvantaged groups and the inability of the government to address the severe under-representation of Muslims in legislatures, public employment, negative stereotyping, and targeting for violence during communal riots. Six years after the implementation of the Sachar Committee Report, not enough has been done on the ground. There are serious concerns with regard to institutional capacity, poor monitoring and coordination, and delays in fund releases for some of the minority development programmes. The Sachar Report, if implemented and monitored well, has the capacity to alter the social and political position of the Muslim minority. Yet, it has failed to live up to the expectations it has created because its implementation has not been a priority of the central and state governments. Hence, the objectives of the inclusive agenda relating to the Muslim minority remains work in progress.

Another Expert Group Report in 2007 suggested the creation of an Equal Opportunity Commission (EOC), aimed at promoting diversity in education and employment by exercising the powers of a civil court to give shape to the equality jurisprudence of the constitution and ensure inclusive development. However, neither of these recommendations have been implemented. Visualized as a body to tackle all forms of discrimination, EOC faced hostility from the established social constituencies and Commissions amid fears that it would make redundant several existing commissions. The larger mandate of working for all disadvantaged sections was seen to be an encroachment on their turf and therefore they want it to be confined to minorities. A Group of Ministers (GoM) headed by Defence Minister A.K. Antony in August 2010 duly concluded that the EOC should confine itself only to minorities. This failed to resolve the jurisdiction issue. The decision faced opposition from the National Commission for Minorities, which tackles cases of violation of minority rights, over possible overlap in functions.

The middle class has grown steadily in size since independence and most conspicuously since economic liberalization initiated in the early 1990s. It has disproportionate influence on the policies finally chosen. The new middle class is very different from the middle class of the first two decades after independence, when their involvement in the national movement with its progressive commitments and values was still a living memory and an influential legacy. Despite continuity with the attitudes of that later post-independence generation, the new middle class is different in some important respects even from that of fifteen years ago, i.e. from the late 1990s. Most notably, it abhors politics as filthy and corrupt and is unsympathetic to the problems faced by the disadvantaged and poor than ever before. There is no better indicator of the character of the middle class than its response to what can be considered the landmark events of India's post-independence history—support to the Emergency, lack of concern towards the destruction of Babri Masjid, and again support to the Indo-US nuclear deal in 2008 and before that the decision to go nuclear in May 1998.

Gender and the Political Process

Identity politics has made a significant impact upon Indian politics but no area more severely than women's rights, so much so that the coherence of women as a category has come to be seriously questioned and debated. The attempts by political leaders, both secular and religiously inclined, to curry favour with religious leaders in order to marshal their support has had serious implications for women's rights and minority women's rights particularly.

The responses of government and civil society groups to the landmark Shah Bano case with the conflicting claims of personal law, identity, and gender in relation to the demand for a uniform civil code attest to both the state's compromise of its secular principles and the role of political forces in shaping women's activism at the national level. Compared to non-discrimination policies towards lower castes, the recognition of personal laws, presents a problem as state policies of accommodation reinforce inequalities and hierarchies within the community and between women of different communities. The Shah Bano case and the Muslim Women Protection of Rights on Divorce Act, 1986, which revoked the Shah Bano judgement to exclude Muslim women from the purview of the secular laws, showed the limitations of Indian secularism and pluralism, how the commitment to cultural rights can sometimes endorse practices that violate gender justice as also the constitutionally sanctioned rights of equal citizenship. By treating Muslims as a homogeneous and monolithic group and disregarding the interests of women, the state strengthened conservative Hindu and Muslim groups at the expense of Muslim women.

Commentators complain that both women's and minority rights have been used instrumentally within the politics of religion, which has sidelined the agenda of women's rights. A vital issue relates to the strategies deployed by minority groups to preserve their distinctive identity in response to threats to it, on the one hand, and how Muslim women-led networks have challenged the authority of the religious elite to represent the 'Muslim community' while re-framing the category 'Muslim women' in order to assert political agency to enhance women's rights, on the other. Although no major legal reforms have taken place with regard to women's rights as a result of these interventions, the presence of Muslim women-led networks marked a significant shift in the social landscape. It demonstrates the diversification of the women's movement as women in the Muslim communities find ways to engage with and challenge structures of power and authority within the community and the state at multiple levels. Their efforts can create a space for women to redefine their identities and reformulate relations of power within an increasingly constrained and polarized political context and one in which Muslim feminist activists have had little room to manoeuvre outside of the confines of religious boundaries.

Nothing symbolizes the male-dominated nature of Indian politics more than the controversies surrounding the Women's Reservation Bill, seeking to reserve 33.3 per cent of seats in Parliament and the state assemblies. The first bill was tabled in 1996 and has been debated ever since. Nearly every political party has endorsed the bill in their election manifestos and yet successive governments have failed to pass it. In a major step forward, it was passed in the Rajya Sabha in March 2010 which is the furthest this controversial Bill has ever got. The majority of politicians oppose women's quota because they recognize that the Women's Reservation Bill, if it is legislated, would shake the ground beneath their feet. The most visible opposition has come from caste parties who are demanding a sub-quota for backward castes but their opposition serves to obscure the unspoken and backstage hostility that is at work in most parties. The greatest fear among male Members of Parliament (MPs) is that they will lose their seats—a fear that is particularly strong among first-time MPs. This apprehension was absent when the panchayat reservations were enacted because the MPs were not going to lose their seats. This is why the 73rd and 74th Amendments to the Constitution were passed without much dissent. In 2009 women's reservation in local government was raised to 50 per cent—which went unnoticed. The bitter opposition to the extension of the same principle to state and national politics shows that despite regionalization and decentralization of politics, real power resides in the Centre and that is why the stakes are so high. Further that no party has given equal opportunities and in each party men have promoted their own interests. At the heart of the so-called stalemate over women's reservation is the decision to find a consensus among parties and parliamentarians— another stalling tactic.

Bridging the Social and Political Divide

As outlined earlier, from the early 1990s politics in India experienced tumultuous changes and began to undergo a fundamental transformation. After four decades of political stability, things started to unravel. New forms of politics, identities, and movements emerged, and old certitudes and loyalties seemed to have frayed. Ethnic politics occupied centre stage, often prompting violent conflict and major political changes. This included the rise of majoritarianism as manifested in the rise of the BJP and the growth of ethnic movements and insurgency in Kashmir and the north-east. The demolition of the Babri Masjid in December 1992 was a significant moment in this political process. The conjunction of neoliberalism in the economic sphere noted earlier along with a majoritarian turn in the political sphere defined political development in this period. These changes led to the dramatic rise to prominence of Hindu nationalism and the unmistakable decline of the Congress party that had dominated Indian politics for the greater part of the twentieth century.

These shifts in politics are best illustrated by changes in the Congress party, which was one of the most important political organizations in India's modern political history. It ruled every state until 1967. The party's hegemony was based on a concrete set of achievements: an independent model of industrial growth; considerable reduction in large-scale feudal landholdings, which benefited the upper peasantry; growth in infrastructure; expansion in educational facilities and technical personnel. This political system worked until the split in the Congress in 1969, which transformed it from a loose coalition of ideologically diverse groups into a party that was entirely dominated by the high command. The breakdown of the Congress system was starkly evident after Indira Gandhi's disastrous Emergency experiment, which resulted in a sharp and substantial drop in the vote base. Much of the responsibility for Congress decline and the weakened governmental and administrative institutions were attributed to Indira Gandhi's personal ambition and dynastic proclivities as she went about refashioning the party to suit her political interests. However, neither the need to reshape the Congress nor her capacity to do so was conceivable had the party not already been in serious and growing disarray. In short, the decline itself was not due to factors that were altogether internal to it or because of Indira Gandhi's centralizing drive but essentially the result of paradigmatic changes in the polity, economy, and society. The Congress was both shaping and being shaped by societal changes.

Two interrelated developments were at stake: one in the party system and the other, in the Congress itself and its policies with regard to the broader democratic agenda. The long-term decline of the Congress was met by three important developments: an increased focus on the interests of the lower castes; the rise of Hindu nationalism; and the growing significance of regional parties in most states. In the 1991 election, Advani's *rath yatra* and the anti-reservation sentiments among the upper castes opposed to reservation for the backward castes were the key factors in almost doubling the BJP's vote share and increasing its seats to 120, making it the single largest opposition party. The BJP's electoral success soon enabled it to overshadow the Congress as the largest party in the 1996, 1998, and 1999 elections. Several other problems were also of its own making—the increased reliance of a business-driven and market-dominated model of development from the early 1980s and the failure to implement anti-poverty programmes as the reason for the change in macroeconomic climate.

Disproving predictions that it would be reduced to double digit figures in the 2004 general elections, the Congress was back in power as the single largest party and heading the United Progressive Alliance (UPA) Government. The return to power after eight years in Opposition was a significant development from the long-term standpoint of Indian politics, as also of the Congress. The defeat of the National Democratic Alliance (NDA) in the 2004 general elections was widely interpreted as a reflection of rural disquiet and a vote for secular politics. This vote could not however be separated from the demands and concerns of the socially and economically marginalized classes and castes for an improvement in their economic condition. Ever since the Congress government began implementing economic policies from 1991 onwards designed to pursue the liberalizing agenda, it struggled to reconcile the contradiction between economic liberalization, which has benefitted the elite and upper middle classes, and its mass support among the poor who have been the losers in this process. The usual strategies depended largely on the distribution of patronage to cultivate support for winning elections was proving to be inadequate. Post-liberalization this was not working because political parties could no longer rely on incorporating voters through the usual patronage networks. Congress revival was the direct result of its renewed focus on its earlier commitments to secularism, composite nationhood, and the poor. The National Rural Employment Guarantee Act (NREGA) passed in 2005 assuring any household in the country 100 days of work on public works programme marked a major shift in government policy towards the poor. Described as the largest entitlement programme in the world for rural reconstruction and employment, it found pride of place in the President's first address to the 15th Lok Sabha in June 2009. While it is difficult to overstate the importance of such initiatives and the need for a social vision in a democratic polity, its long-term sustainability remains questionable, as the UPA is yet to prove its political stability.

Politics of Mobilization and Change in Uttar Pradesh

Uttar Pradesh (UP) was the pivot of the Congress system until 1990. This changed dramatically with the appearance of identity politics, which cracked the structure of its domination with lower castes and rich farmers, leading the rebellion that brought non-Congress governments to power and thus changed the dynamics of democracy. The consequence was to galvanize a spectrum of lower castes and rich and middle ranking farmers riding on feelings of resentment over their exclusion in policy and power under Congress rule despite having numbers on their side. The farmer's movement at one time attracted considerable attention leading to an increase in the influence of rich farmers over economic policies and the state. However, by the 1990s, the movement dissipated with the growth of caste and communal politics, as it was unable to transcend identitarian divisions. The upshot of these complex set of events was a major confrontation between the Congress and the BJP with upper castes gravitating towards the BJP and the backward castes to the Samajwadi Party (SP) and Dalits to the Bahujan Samaj Party (BSP). Before the early 1980s, the political impact of religion was limited and communal parties won few seats in the state. The change occurred in the early 1990s with the mass mobilization to demolish the Babri Masjid at Ayodhya by the BJP-RSS combine and its eventual demolition. Failure to take non-compromising stances on issues such as mass violence and communal mobilizations had eroded Congress support in UP. The Ayodhya movement entirely changed the form of electoral politics and undermined the Congress monopoly over political power it would seem forever. It decimated the Congress in UP which was critical to political power in Delhi. Prime Minister Narasimha Rao's inaction in the Babri Masjid–Ram Janmabhoomi dispute was blamed for the Congress' devastation in UP. These events inflicted severe damage on the Congress party and its political base, particularly in the Hindi heartland, and had the result of creating space for new political contenders. The BJP's influence rose exponentially while the Congress failed to devise a counter strategy to regain lost ground.

In the long-run it was two parties, the SP and BSP, and not the BJP, that managed to displace the Congress from its position of dominance. Political power had shifted decisively from the upper castes to backward castes with the SP emerging as the principal power bloc in the post-Ayodhya, post-

Mandal period. If the 1990s saw political power shift from the upper castes to backward castes, the balance of power shifted even more dramatically with Dalits posing a formidable challenge to backward caste power. From the standpoint of the disadvantaged, the growth of the BSP and its ability to form the government in 1995 and 1997 was a development of extraordinary importance. Polling over 30 per cent of the vote in 2007, the BSP won a clear majority by projecting itself as the only viable alternative to the SP, thus turning caste politics on its head to create a new social alliance of the underprivileged of great significance. UP had its first Dalit chief minister which was historic in a state where economic, political and cultural power had been the preserve of the upper castes.

The story of UP is a telling illustration of how Indian politics has changed, and with it the nature and dynamics of party politics at the state and national level. In the process, national parties were marginalized, or became adjuncts to the state parties in major states of the country. The upheaval in UP was the most spectacular expression of the new politics of caste, with caste parties and factions emerging in different parts of the country drawing lower caste forces into power play. Parties and political mobilization have overemphasized caste politics and thus hampered the development of broad-based identities and political action.

Some of the aforesaid developments have transformed the tenor and quality of democratic politics and whether this will lead to a greater social deepening of democracy broadly hinges on efforts to resolve three key issues. How will the political system, now more than ever based on egalitarian democratic values, accommodate the changes taking place in its social arrangements? How will the state balance the need to ensure social good by defining an overarching vision for a country that, on the one hand, is galloping ahead on a high growth path just as the state acts to promote private business, and on the other, is divided by huge inequalities in economy and society? And, in the face of the declining legitimacy of the state and the continuing expansion of civil society, can the state redevelop and revive its legitimacy, and if it is to do so, how should it redefine the boundaries between state and society and state and capital? These issues, with their built-in tensions, will continue to serve as sources of change in the continuing transformation of Indian democracy.

PART I

DEMOCRACY AND SOCIAL INEQUALITIES

1 | Democracy and the Persistence of Inequalities

The success of India's democracy has evoked much interest not only because India is one of the poorest countries in the world in terms of per capita income, but also because it is the world's largest democracy. Indians are not alone in celebrating their success story which was enabled by marrying political freedom with economic progress. New Western accounts speak about a rising India which can counterbalance China.[1] India is indeed rising for the aspiring as well as the already privileged classes, as is their inordinate longing for wealth and fame, and their ambition for recognition of India as a Great Power. On the other side, there are huge inequalities of income, wealth, consumption, access to education, health care, and dignified employment. This raises the broader question: how such dramatic inequalities could persist in a democracy in which voters create pressure for improved outcomes. The larger issue is the relationship between democracy and development. In India, the two can be seen as functionally related, that is each process supports the other.[2] The logic of democracy and development are not seen to be asymmetric, but how do we explain the persistent gap between the outcomes that people expect and the government's capacity to improve their well-being?

What follows is not a comprehensive account or stocktaking of India's democratic experience and its impact on inequalities or the broader relationship between democracy and development, or democracy and equality. Rather, this chapter attempts to situate social and economic inequalities, and the process of development, in the context of the transformation that has taken place in India from the 1990s, and to explore the interaction between the two processes since the early 1990s. While discussing the issue of democracy and inequalities, the focus is mainly on the state's capacity to reduce inequalities and poverty, while also paying attention to how inequalities influence Indian politics.

India remains the largest democracy in the world, and with almost 600 million voters, it is larger than the electorates of Japan, Western Europe, and North America combined. India's success in building and consolidating a vibrant democracy remains unequalled in the postcolonial world.[3] Democracy has not only survived, but has thrived and been institutionalized. The democratic process has deepened, drawing historically disadvantaged groups into the political system. This has ensured that the political actors do not come only from the traditional upper-caste social elite although they continue to have a disproportionate presence in public institutions and influence over policymaking.[4]

The key to the success of India's democracy lies in its political inclusiveness. It is one of the few countries in the developing world that took up the challenge of building an inclusive democracy in a diverse, multilingual, and multi-religious society. It is a democracy whose Constitution has given primacy to social equality and justice as a cardinal principle of governance. The freedom struggle and the social reform movements prepared some of the ground for social equality in the sense that they delegitimized the most egregious forms of oppression that characterized Hindu society. However improbable it might have seemed in 1950, the trend towards greater social equality is unmistakable.

The effort to pursue equality has been made at two levels. At one level was the constitutional effort to change the very structure of social relations: practising caste and untouchability was made illegal, and allowing religious considerations to influence state activities was not permitted. At the second level was the effort to bring about economic equality, although in this endeavour the right to property and class inequality was not seriously curbed. Moreover, the placement of the demands for economic equality into the Directive Principles of State Policy indicated clearly that the political elite did not conceive of any serious intervention to check economic inequality. Nevertheless, a discourse of economic upliftment was part of the process of development and legitimization for the postcolonial state. This discourse however did not translate into a consensus on active state intervention to bring about greater equality, except in the abolition of intermediary rights in the rural sector. Thus, the references to economic equality in the Constitution, in the courts, or from political platforms remained basically rhetorical. Besides, in legal and political arenas, most constitutional and state efforts were directed against social inequality and not against poverty.

Disadvantage and lack of opportunities are seen as unjust treatment of whole communities like lower castes, religious minorities' and tribal communities, who in time become actors and agents against social inequality. If poverty is defined as deprivation/inequality then the resentments expressed through democratic mobilization are not always against poverty per se, but rather, they are against social injustice and political exclusion. Modern Indian politics has not witnessed a struggle against poverty as such but more against historical disadvantage suffered by the poor who belong to mostly lower castes. People who participate in such mobilization are poor, but the basis and self-identification for their participation and action is not poverty, but caste discrimination. Hence, the focus has been on caste-based injustice rather than against poverty in a universal sense. People are acutely conscious of their own deprivation but completely indifferent towards parallel situations and demands emanating from others who may be equally poor and disadvantaged.

The first two decades of democracy were dominated by the elite, marked by low levels of political participation, and competition. The next two decades were more competitive, with higher political participation, an increase in non-electoral participation, and greater federalization through the emergence and growth of regional parties. Defying democratic theory, a great participatory upsurge has marked democratic politics. Since the early 1990s, India's lower orders have participated noticeably more in elections than its upper and middle classes. Thanks to the democratic upsurge, previously marginalized groups entered the political arena in large numbers, contributing to a change in the pattern of representation and a shift in the balance of political power in governments and legislatures. These trends have been doubtless helping to make democracy more inclusive, with democracy steadily chipping away at hierarchies and moving downwards. This is nothing short of a democratic revolution.

A brief comparison of the caste composition of national and state legislatures in modern day India with the situation soon after Independence reveals the significance of the democratic revolution. In the 1950s, India's national politics were dominated by English-speaking and upper-caste urban politicians who constituted two-thirds of the Lok Sabha.[5] Even the lower-level political leadership tended to come from the upper castes in north India.[6] From the 1990s, these has been a major increase in the number of lower-caste legislators and senior civil servants in influential government positions. This process of greater inclusion can be described as the 'transfer of power' from the upper castes to the lower castes and it has major political consequences for the restructuring of political power. From the turn of the twenty-first century, lower-caste chief ministers are no longer rare. The logic of 'one person, one vote' in free and fair elections has put power in the hands of the more numerous lower castes. This trend signals a social transformation that is giving voice to previously marginalized groups, and helping them to gain access to the political system.

While Indian democracy has seen a transfer of power from the upper castes/classes to the middle ranks, it has not facilitated any significant distribution of wealth and income. Rather, the vigour of electoral democracy and high levels of participation can obscure a growing concentration of power among political and economic elites. The key issue is the failure of the politics of redistributive justice to provide amelioration in the material conditions of the vast majority of people mired in poverty and economic misery. In other words, the strength of participatory democracy has not been matched with egalitarian economic development.[7]

This is the case even though both development and democracy have been declared as integral to the project of the Indian state after Independence. Until 1991, there was a broad consensus on the role of the state as a crucial player in the developmental process. State-led capitalism and various state interventions were seen as essential for a self-reliant pattern of development. This model did deliver some tangible benefits to the broad mass of the population through various kinds of development projects, the construction of the public sector, and the provision of public services such as health, education, and transport.[8] However, this model was structurally limited owing to the inability of the state to address the most basic form of inequality, that found in the countryside. Even with declarations of commitment to land reforms and curbing the concentration of economic power, relatively little was done to redress asset and income inequality. With the advantage of experience we can now see that policy measures such as land reform, that could have widened the social base of development, were never likely to take place.[9] No major land redistribution occurred after Independence, which is not to say that there were no land reforms at all, but that the net result of those reforms was to eliminate very large landholdings, to give ownership rights to the richer tenants, to create a more homogeneous class of landowners, but not to break land concentration. Attempts at land reform were thwarted by the landed interests because of their penetration of the Congress party, control over the local bureaucracy, their clout in the arena of state politics, and the legal constraints imposed by the constitutionally guaranteed rights to property.

Similarly, private asset concentration in the industrial sector was never seriously challenged. India's industrial growth did not create enough jobs to make a dent in the growing numbers of the poor. The incapacity to diffuse growth among a much wider population contributed to industrial stagnation and restricted the stimulus for domestic demand in rural areas for manufactured items of mass consumption.[10]

From the highly unequal distribution of benefits and assets, it is clear that Indian society was dominated by a ruling coalition of business interests, large landholders, and the bureaucratic elite. Although the overall power of these classes was not curbed, at the same time the broad-based interests of the people could not be completely overlooked. The solution was found in a politics of accommodation, which was strong on rhetoric and weak on substance in terms of outcomes for the poor and the dispossessed. The Congress party mastered this political strategy and it became one which helped Congress governments in the first few decades after Independence to continue to return to power. However, in the longer run this strategy also required some sort of redistributive effort to translate political accommodation into tangible legislative programmes. This was completely absent until recently when the capitalist advance necessitated government intervention to neutralize the huge vulnerabilities of the poor with regard to basic needs, especially livelihoods.

Over time, the state in India has shifted from a reluctant capitalist state to a strongly pro-capitalist state with a clear and conspicuous dominance in the relative power of the corporate sector.[11] This dominance has been achieved through an alliance of the corporate sector with the state and bureaucracy. Though the state continues to negotiate between conflicting interests, the autonomy of the state has declined as it gets increasingly intermeshed with the corporate sector.[12] The bureaucracy, which in the past was operating the social interventions of the developmental state, has gone over completely to the side of the corporate class. Significantly, the corporate sector exercises considerable influence over both central and state governments not through electoral mobilization but through political parties, bureaucracy, and the print and electronic media.[13] There is a virtual consensus among all parties regarding rapid growth led by private investment. At the state level, the dismantling of the licensing regime has opened up huge competition among state governments eager to attract capitalist investment, both domestic and foreign. This means that as far as the party system is concerned, it does not matter for the corporate sector which party or combination of parties come to power at the centre or in the states.[14] This is evidence of the major transformation that has taken place in the structure of power in recent years.

Further evidence of corporate sector domination comes from the neglect and stagnation of agriculture: per capita food consumption has fallen, and thousands of indebted farmers have committed suicide. This is a domain which has a large number of people, huge deprivation, and poverty, yet it has been ignored by the government in the past few years. Both rural and urban poor, with their livelihoods under threat from the advancing forces of corporate capital, are dependent upon direct government support for their basic needs. This challenge lies at the heart of the massive controversies in India today with regard to the acquisition of land for industry, and the plunder of natural resources by the corporate class with the help of bureaucrats and politicians.

Clearly, a significant change has taken place in thinking about development as faster economic growth, and in the translation of development objectives mainly through high growth, since the early 1990s. This has significant implications for the politics of equality in India. On the one hand, economic growth led by private investors and helped by a state-capital alliance has fuelled growth, making India among the fastest growing economies in the world. On the other hand, concentration of economic power in the corporate sector has further contributed to widening rural-urban, regional, and sectoral inequalities. Even as many Indians have benefited from the rapid economic growth of the past quarter century, the process of growth has bypassed the vast majority of the population.[15] Highly educated Indians have benefited from opportunities arising from the opening of the economy and globalization, and especially from the restructuring of industries, and the new growth areas of services and Information Technology Enabled Services. These opportunities have mostly benefited the more educated sections, while things have got worse for the majority of the rural population and a significant part of the urban population.[16]

Inequalities arise from a basic asymmetry between the growth of the national product, and the source of income of the majority, which is agriculture.[17] India's growth model is not geared to creating productive employment. Large-scale employment is the key to poverty alleviation but this might not happen under the services-led model of growth. The share of service sector has grown rapidly and most of job growth has come from this sector in hotels, restaurants, finance, and insurance. India's services-led growth depends on skilled manpower which is yet to be produced on a mass scale. Employment in the organized sector has stagnated in the face of high rates of growth, while employment in the unorganized sector has increased but not enough to absorb the rise in population.[18] The highest growth sectors are construction, trade, advertising, telecoms, and road transport. In all these sectors, what counts is privileged access to natural resources and the national commons, most critically land, mining leases, property development rights, construction permits, and spectrum allocation, which is at the core of the government's discretionary powers. Many of the new billionaires have used political patronage and influence to corner these resources.[19]

This pattern of economic growth is disequalizing and results in concentration of wealth amid impoverishment. Hence, India has the dubious distinction of having some of the richest people along with a very substantial number of the poorest people in the world as hundreds of millions of people are steeped in extreme poverty.[20] India's much talked about economic transformation illustrates the disconnection between GDP and social progress. The basic paradox is that though the GDP has been growing fast, governments have not succeeded in translating accelerated growth into inclusive development. Instead of accelerated growth positively impacting human development indicators, it seems that faster GDP/per capita growth begets slower growth in human development.[21]

The implication of poor human development and rising inequalities is impoverishment and insecurities which afflict some sections more than others resulting in acute discontent and violent clashes from time to time.[22] The growing numbers of underemployed and casual workers offer a steady source for recruitment of young men and women by extremist religious movements and by Maoist revolutionary groups in the tribal belts of West Bengal, Orissa, Jharkhand, Chhattisgarh, and Maharashtra, who are fighting to overthrow the state through violence.

These inequalities have been intensified by large-scale corruption. For example, the state exchequer has been the medium through which large-scale transfers have been made to the capitalist group and it is the most important instrument for accumulation for this class.[23] This occurs because of a high level of tolerance for tax evasion, actual reduction in tax rates and a variety of lucrative contracts, and most recently even through the privatization of public assets.[24] Disregard for the laws, including those relating to taxes, was an important dimension of the capitalist development process. Corruption and using the state as a means of accumulation are not new but the scale and ubiquity of corruption has intensified since economic liberalization. The processes vary from sale of spectrum, disposal of land and mining resources or purchases made as part of large public expenditures. The new dimension is the open business-politician-bureaucrat collusion bordering on a corporate takeover of government, and the growing plunder of natural resources. [25]

This is hardly surprising because in India there is considerable acceptance of corruption, inequality, poverty, and low levels of human development among a vast section of the population, especially in rural areas. 'The sociopolitical interests that allow the persistence of gross inequalities have ensured that public policy which would deliver basic benefits to the entire population was not made a priority.'[26] These policies in the Indian context would include: agrarian reform, food procurement, education, employment creation through public works, anti-poverty programmes, changes in governance through decentralization, and some devolution of resources. However, policy implementation when it occurs has not been universal in terms of actual effects. Beneficiary oriented anti-poverty programmes are directed to specific target groups. Since the 1990s, these have been particular caste groups and therefore exclude the poor from minority communities who need these benefits just as much as the lower castes.

Compared to the past when the Congress party was not expressly committed to any economic strategy, after 1991 it became quite strongly committed to the strategy of rapid capitalist growth. The Congress-led United Progressive Alliance (UPA) government which first came to power in 2004 and then again in 2009 firmly believes that the rapid march towards equity will depend upon achieving much higher growth of 9–10 per cent over a long period. Policymakers emphasize high growth on the grounds that everyone benefits from this for above all, it provides resources for the war on poverty. At the heart of this model was the belief that attainment of growth and equitable development are both important, but promoting both would take longer and so, in the meantime, growth has to be given immediate priority. Growth is prioritized over equity, and this is justified on the grounds that it provides resources for social welfare programmes, whereas prioritizing equity at the expense of growth leads to the redistribution of poverty. Hence, in a tradeoff between rapid growth and the pace of redistributive equity, rapid growth has to be given priority if we are to redistribute prosperity, rather than poverty.

The Bharatiya Janata Party's (BJP's) defeat on the slogan of 'India Shining' in the 2004 parliamentary elections forced the Congress to reframe its policy priorities. Although the business-driven growth model under-pinning policymaking saw no change, the Congress shifted the balance of policy from growth to inclusive growth as the centrepiece of several of its interventions. This necessitated a change in the balance between market and state in favour of a better mix between the goals of accumulation and redistribution. Therefore, within a few months of assuming office, the UPA government crafted a number of centrally sponsored government schemes designed to improve opportunities for those excluded from India's growth story, especially the rural poor and minorities. Starting in 2004 and in response to the pressures of democratic competition and coalition politics, the Congress-led UPA government began to shape a new 'welfare politics' through the introduction of rights-based legislation and large number of centrally sponsored schemes for social welfare. High on the government's agenda of greater inclusiveness were actions to address disparities in access to education, health care, water, and other public services that are necessary for people's well-being. In terms of the sheer number of policies and legislations, the UPA's focus on social welfare was impressive and indeed, unprecedented. Central budgetary outlays on such programmes have risen significantly under the UPA-1 government's higher than that under previous governments and perhaps higher in relative terms than that anywhere else in the world. Taken together these schemes and social legislations mark a significant departure in policymaking and indicate an attempt to bridge the growth-equity divide.[27]

The experience of UPA-1 from 2004 to 2009 shows that there is room for government policies to provide direct benefits to people who are unable to meet basic needs. There are a range of government policies aimed at reversing the effects of this process which could take the form of anti-poverty programmes, or guaranteed employment in public works, or subsidized food under the Public Distribution System (PDS). All these can be regarded as direct interventions to contain the excesses of inequalities. The National Rural Employment Guarantee Act (NREGA) was by far the most significant initiative undertaken by the UPA government. It was an important step towards the work security of poor rural households, given that employment as a legally enforceable right has not been granted to the citizens of any other country in the world. Of all the policy initiatives, NREGA, which is demand driven and gives 100 days of employment a year to an individual from every household, is important because it is India's first law to codify employment rights in a legal framework and, like the Right to Information Act, has begun to set an example in a global context.

However, the attempt to reconcile the goals of growth and redistribution through centrally sponsored schemes has its limitations. It faces considerable difficulty in the new political context of federalization as a substantial number of social policies are either specifically state government subjects, or are concurrently under both state and central governments. A substantial number of concerns which are particularly important from the standpoint of equality, such as land reforms, education, health, and rural infrastructure, are either specifically state government issues or are concurrently under central and state governments. The central government can devise schemes, issue guidelines for implementation, and allocate funds, but the implementation was in the hands of states. This in turn means that the effects and implications vary under different political regimes in different states.

Even though outlays on poverty alleviation and the social sector have increased, low levels of human development and high levels of inequalities persist. Outcomes are in commensurate with outlays. The real issue with these programmes is that they are not implemented properly. Beyond the amount of money spent, little attention is paid to delivery mechanisms or the quality of spending. The intended beneficiaries of these public programmes are completely dependent on the bureaucratic delivery mechanism over which they have no control.[28] The present machinery—under which centrally sponsored schemes are delivered by hundreds of mutually insulated systems of delivery set up by central government ministries, which jealously guard their turf—consumes the bulk of outlays. Convergence of these schemes at the delivery point would have a multiplier effect for the beneficiaries.[29] In short, the actual effects of the social programmes may not yield results outside of a participatory development process and inclusive growth without inclusive governance remains an unreachable goal.

If the objectives of poverty reduction are to be realized then the very content and direction of the growth process may have to change, or at the very least, a different set of organizational and institutional arrangements have to be adopted at national and state level for the delivery of these programmes. The prospects of this happening are not encouraging. After economic reforms, the scope for stepping up deliberate redistribution is limited. This is in part because the state's capacity to implement pro-poor policies has always been limited, but more so because the new ruling alliance is essentially a state-business alliance for growth which favours big business and private sector based development. The more economic growth was led by private investment, the more the benefits accrued to the rich. It is this activist role of the state in favour of business groups that has further contributed to inequalities.[30] Moreover, initial egalitarian conditions and a more labour intensive model of development, which could have been important components of combining growth with redistribution, are missing in India.[31]

In the 1980s, the singular merit of our democracy lay in providing space for political contestation and an opportunity for the expression of rights and claims, most significantly among the historically disadvantaged groups, and particularly among the lower castes. In the 1990s, democracy had to contend with the rise of Hindutva forces using extra-parliamentary movements and religio-communal politics to redefine Indian identity in majoritarian terms. In the first decade of the twenty-first century, it has had to contend with growing economic and regional disparities and inequalities which in the process, have created two economies. Indian democracy has raised the question of both social equality and majoritarian dominance. When the connection between democracy and disadvantage is made, the major form of government intervention to alleviate poverty and deprivation often centres on identity-based groups defined by demographic or social characteristics, and not the problem of poverty or conflicts between rich and poor in general. In most cases, policymakers press for equality for groups organized on the basis of caste or resentment against regional deprivation, and not equality for all communities or individuals in civil society.[32] The politics of equality is thus more concerned with external rather than internal equity, that is to say equality between caste groups rather than equality amongst group members, and rather more between some groups than all the disadvantaged groups.[33] The big losers in this process are the minorities who are excluded from this group-based discourse of development. The sharpest casualty is that the idea of equality in a more encompassing sense has fallen on bad times, and the language of markets and individual aspirations, when seen through the prism of identity, has assumed greater importance than public interest and accountability.[34] Politicians and policymakers have shifted political attention from equity and public goods for the poor to facilitating private investment.

The significance of UPA-1 lay in striking a balance between contending interests even as it took some crucial decisions and pushed through important rights based legislations. A new agenda based on rights and entitlements, which include the Right to Information, the Right to Work, the Right to Education, and the proposed Right to Food Security, represents a landmark shift in the Indian approach to issues of welfare and human development. There are real questions as to whether the blending of growth and welfare attempted by the first UPA government is feasible under the UPA-2 and the political-institutional structures of the state and capitalist growth model it promotes. Under a largely Congress dominated UPA-2 elected in 2009, calibrating the growth-equity equation appears much more difficult in view of the 'big money' which is making greater and greater inroads into the corridors of power. As is clear from data on the rising net worth of MPs elected in 2009, the dominance of the rich is getting more and more consolidated in the legislature and decision-making apparatus. The increasing monetization of the political process, backed by a state-business alliance at the apex, makes the prospect of a basic shift towards a more equitable policy regime seen more distant than before.

What has added some redistributive thrust to the growth model is that the rhetoric of social justice is deeply embedded in Indian politics even though concrete achievements have been rather limited. India is a vibrant democracy; politics, mobilization, institutions, and policy frameworks all matter, and the pressures of democratic politics do intervene to restrain rising and emerging inequalities. A strong virtue of India's democratic set-up, however electorally driven it may be, is that it is premised on the recognition of basic rights and entitlements. There is now a growing awareness of these rights and entitlements among the poor, thanks to the widening reach of the political discourse of democracy. Sections of the electorate appreciate the greater power of political institutions which can take decisions that affect the everyday and long-term distribution of opportunities. The possession of democratic rights has been a powerful weapon against poverty and an antidote to the rush to deny the importance of inequality. Greater political participation has led to a sharper sense of inequity and an attempt to use politics to rectify it. The fact that poor and marginalized groups have been vigorous in exercising their franchise, far more so than the affluent and well-to-do middle classes, is testimony to the sense of empowerment that, in their perception, democratic practices have brought them. The need for UPA-1 to change course and to accommodate the broader social interests of the poor to secure their political support, is the strongest indication yet of these pressures. India's poor continue to press their case for redistribution of growth and egalitarian strategies of growth.

Notes and References

1. Many observers in the West have begun to worry about the threats posed by the rise of India and China as evident from the remarks of Michel Rocard, a former Prime Minister of France. He shared his concerns about the place of France and the United States in the new world order with the American ambassador in Paris in October 2005: 'Speaking of the growth of India and China, along with all the other challenges confronting [the] US and France', Wikileaks quotes him as saying, 'We need a vehicle where we can find solutions for these challenges together—so when these monsters arrive in 10 years, we will be able to deal with them'. Quoted in Siddharth Varadarajan, 'Eastern promise, Western fears', *The Hindu*, 25 January 2011.

2. Sudipta Kaviraj, 'Dilemmas of Democracy and Development in India', in *Democracy and Development: Theory and Practice*, ed. Adrian Leftwich, London: Polity Press, 1996, pp. 114–38.

3. See essays in Francine Frankel et al., *Transforming India: The Social and Dynamics of Democracy*, New Delhi: Oxford University Press, 2000; Atul Kohli, ed., *The Success of India: Democracy*, Cambridge: Cambridge University Press, 2003; Niraja Gopal Jayal, ed., *Democracy in India*, New Delhi: Oxford University Press, 2001.

4. Christophe Jaffrelot and Sanjay Kumar, *Rise of Plebeians: The Changing Face of Indian Legislative Assemblies*, New Delhi: Routledge, 2009.

5. Ashutosh Varshney, 'Is India Becoming More Democratic', *Journal of Asian Studies*, vol. 59, no. 1, pp. 3–25, February 2000.

6. Ibid.

7. Atul Kohli, 'Introduction', *Democracy and Development: From Socialism to Pro-business*, New Delhi: Oxford University Press, 2009, pp. 1–20.

8. Deepak Nayyar, 'Democracy and Development', in *Democracy in India*, Niraja Gopal Jayal, pp. 361–96.

9. Francine Frankel, *India's Political Economy*, revd edn., New Delhi: Oxford University Press, 2005.

10. Jayati Ghosh, 'Social Policy in Indian Development', United Nations Research Institute for Social Development, Geneva, November 2002.

11. Atul Kohli, 'Politics and Redistribution in India', http://Princeton.edu/kohli/
    Poliiiespercent20and percent20Redistribution percent in 20 India.pdf accessed on
    27 March 2012.
12. Partha Chatterjee, 'Democracy and Economic Transformation in India', *Economic
    and Political Weekly*, 19 April 2008, p. 56.
13. Ibid.
14. Ibid.
15. Jayati Ghosh, 'Income Inequality in India', www.macroscan.com, accessed on
    24 September 2012.
16. Ibid.
17. Aseema Sinha, 'Globalization, Rising Inequality, and the New Insecurities in
    India', www.apsanet.org/imgtest/ TaskForceDifJlneqDevSinha.pdf, accessed on
    25 January 2011.
18. Ibid.
19. Ibid.
20. By contrast, China has been able to move people out of extreme poverty within
    just a generation, which has no parallel in any other country in the history of the
    world. Pranab Bardhan, *Awakening Giants, Feet of Clay: Assessing the Economic
    Rise of China and India,* New Delhi: Oxford University Press, 2010, pp. 90–103.
21. Mani Shankar Aiyar, 'The Dilemma of Development and Democracy in India',
    Centre for Media Studies, Lecture delivered at Nehru Memorial Museum and
    Library, New Delhi, 24 November 2010.
22. In 2008, attacks on Hindi-speakers and Biharis broke out in Mumbai. The
    immediate context for the violence was the recruitment by railways for Class II and
    Class IV jobs. These applicants were prevented from taking the tests by the local
    youth from Maharashtra. Indian Railways and other public sector undertakings
    are seen as providers of jobs coveted by the educated unemployed.
23. Ghosh, 'Social Policy'.
24. Ibid.
25. C.P. Chandrasekhar, 'Capital Gains', *Frontline,* 17 December 2010.
26. Ghosh, 'Social Policy'.
27. Editorial, 'On the Right Track', *The Hindu*, 8 July 2008.
28. Shankar Aiyar, 'Dilemma of Development and Democracy'.
29. Ibid.
30. Kohli, 'Politics and Redistribution'.
31. Ibid.
32. Kaviraj, 'Dilemmas of Democracy', p. 130.
33. Ibid.
34. Sinha, 'Globalization'.

2 | The Indian Polity Today and the Road Ahead

THE 2004 GENERAL elections in which 350 million people turned out to vote has produced a dramatic political upset; the greatest in Indian politics, and perhaps anywhere in the world.[1] Very few could have foreseen that the Congress-led alliance would win 30 seats more than the Bhartiya Janata Party (BJP)-led combine. Few expected the Congress to emerge as the single largest party ahead of the BJP. No one could predict the unprecedented increase in the weight of the Left in national politics, with over 60 seats in a 543-member Lok Sabha and, given these numbers, qualitatively well-placed to influence the economic, political, and foreign policies of the new government.[2] Overall, the stunning verdict signals the strong roots that electoral democracy has struck in India. Perhaps no election result, not even the defeat of Indira Gandhi and the Congress party in 1977, has been as important as that of 2004. The important difference is that the 1977 election was triggered and dominated by a crisis of regime fostered by the imposition of authoritarian rule. The 2004 elections appeared to have been taking place in relatively unexceptional circumstances without any preponderant national crisis, no overwhelming national issue, and no prior contact or countrywide mobilization among people otherwise fragmented along language, religion, and caste lines. Yet, in a remarkable demonstration of how poorly read was the electoral mood, the deep-seated anger against the pursuit of socially and politically insensitive policies, and slogans such as 'India Shining' which showcased the government's gifts to the richer segments of society, and the bruising impact of the majoritarian Hindutva campaign manifested itself in a wholesale rejection of the National Democratic Alliance (NDA).

---

* The Ninth Prem Bhatia Memorial Lecture was delivered at the India International Centre, New Delhi, on 11 August 2004.

Apart from the drama and excitement that the 2004 verdict entailed, the unanticipated defeat of the NDA represents the most remarkable turnaround in Indian politics, and is likely to be regarded by future historians of Indian democracy as a watershed; as significant, if not more so, than the election of 1977. Going by this election, the Indian democratic process is spectacularly alive and there are no signs of its slowing down as a fountainhead of change; indeed, there are signs of its quickening from the 1990s. In fact, since Independence, no trend has been more powerful and transformative than the growth and expansion of democracy. It is producing greater politicization, agency, and discourses of equality especially amongst the poor and the disadvantaged, which suggest that democracy has a wider social basis. India may be the only democracy in the world where the electoral turnout and political activism are higher amongst the poor than the upper and middle classes. The high stakes associated with elections motivates the increasing participation of these groups, but at the same time it has the effect of giving a wide range of marginal groups a high stake in the continuation and preservation of the democratic system. This is because elections are not only about the practice of democracy, the turning over of elected representatives and governments, but we see in them the opportunity of providing space for political contestation, a renewal of citizenship, and shifts in political discourse.

We can see how the discourse of politics has changed: the concept of governance has replaced development and poverty issues in the public domain; NGOs and social movements have replaced class politics; and political spin dominates public debates which are often not on substantive issues. The chapter concerns the role played by political parties in the processes of political mobilization and social transformation, and will discuss some aspects of India's democracy and the major challenges that still confront it. It will focus on the 2004 elections, and some of the key questions thrown up by the verdict. The suddenness of an election outcome very few expected and the scale of voter dissatisfaction with the BJP-led NDA should be a starting point for further questions, as well as a moment for celebration. A pressing question is whether we can see these developments as an indication that the significance of the Hindu right was waning, and whether this election outcome signified the re-emergence of secularism and tolerance as the dominant force in Indian politics.

The NDA and BJP suffered substantial losses across the country among all groups, classes, and castes. Confident of winning 200 seats on its own, the BJP lost 44 seats to shrink to just 138, and the NDA crashed from over 300 to 189 seats. The key members of the alliance suffered grievous reverses: the All India Anna Dravida Munnetra Kazhagam (AIADMK) was obliterated in Tamil Nadu; and the Telugu Desam and Trinamool Congress were decimated in Andhra Pradesh and West Bengal. The BJP suffered serious setbacks in key areas and states. Although the difference between the Congress and the BJP in terms of seats was only seven, we must remember that the Congress had 72 seats less than the BJP in the thirteenth Lok Sabha and in the election finished with seven more, which in real terms amounted to a substantial increase for the Congress which was not fully captured in a vote-and-seat-share comparison. The BJP's greatest losses came in Uttar Pradesh, Bihar, Gujarat, Delhi, and Haryana. Major figures in the government, such as Murli Manohar Joshi (Allahabad) and Swami Chinmayananda (Jaunpur), lost their seats, and they were among the key advocates of hardline Hindutva. The party's defeat in Varanasi, Mathura, and Faizabad (where Ayodhya falls) was particularly significant as these are sacred sites of Hindu nationalism, and therefore these losses had considerable symbolic significance.[3]

Notwithstanding the unambiguous defeat suffered by the NDA, there has been an intense ideological debate over interpretation of the 2004 verdict, which has been almost as passionate as the election itself. Those who were thrown off-balance by the verdict clearly wanted to minimize its significance by blaming it on anti-incumbency, state-level governance, and the NDA's choice of alliance partners. Yet, others opposed to majoritarianism nevertheless cautioned against over-reading or exaggerating the 'anti-reforms' message of the mandate.[4] Although the elections did not on the surface seem to have a single issue focus, as it transpired the verdict was a categorical rejection on the part of the electorate of both the anti-poor economic policies passing off as 'development' and the Hindu majoritarian identity politics projected as 'nationalism'. In addition to these issues, on a general level, the NDA's focus on Sonia Gandhi's foreign origin as a major campaign issue appears to have seriously misfired, with voters decisively rejecting it. The overall argument advocated here has been framed by the idea that the 2004 verdict was a mandate for tolerance, secularism, and inclusiveness delivered by a discerning electorate. In the context of this observation, it is legitimate to read this election as a battle over two different ideas of India, one inclusive and compassionate, the other homogeneous and elitist.

The first idea, backed by a wide spectrum of political opinion ranging from Gandhians, the Congress, Socialists, and the Left, has constantly underscored India's plural ethos and placed paramount emphasis on democracy, secularism, and social justice. Inspired by Nehruvian ideas, this model had ensured some level of tolerance and distributive fairness and yet, at the same time, sought to achieve economic growth, albeit slowly. The second idea is one that owes much to the flourishing, high-growth economies of East Asia. This model has little place for liberal values, secularism, social justice, and accommodation.[5] In this model, even democracy is a convenience to be used and disregarded as the need arises.

The BJP-led NDA government believed, in essence, in the second idea. Even though the right-wing BJP never won more than a quarter of the vote, its rise to power represented a paradigm shift in economic and political policy. It mounted the most potent challenge to the first model, which is closely related to the inspirations behind the freedom struggle and its progressive and modernist ideas. For the BJP, the key issue was the economic prosperity of the middle classes and the business elite, and transforming India into a Great Power by 2020. It believed that so long as the upper and middle classes were rich and happy, the bulk of the Indian population did not matter. Indeed, it allowed a miniscule economic minority to prosper at the expense of the majority and regarded the level of the Sensex as a measure of India's success. In relentlessly pursuing neoliberal economic policies, the NDA government allowed even the minimal goods that a state should provide—security of life and property, access to education, public health facilities, a minimum standard of living for large numbers of people—to become market commodities rather than entitlements.

The BJP, taken in by its own hype, which was sustained by virtually all the opinion polls, decided to advance the Lok Sabha elections by eight months, and campaigned on the slogans of 'India Shining' and the 'Feel-Good Factor' which it was convinced would pay the coalition rich electoral dividends. These slogans, however, backfired sharply. The government's so called achievements benefited only the rich, and the upper-middle class, and these sectors did not require a propaganda campaign such as this to be reminded about the escalation in their comfort levels during the past five years. By contrast, these slogans only served to remind the vast majority of the population that the benefits of reform had not reached it, and these sections of the people were determined to deny the NDA another term in office.[6] In the end, the ordinary citizen voted to puncture the illusory aspects of this success story and the perceived indifference of its champions to the plight of those excluded or adversely affected by economic reforms.[7] The Congress-sponsored advertisements captured the frustration of the majority in the simple question: *Aam aadmi ko kya mila?*

The second aspect of the electoral message of the rejection of the NDA was the repugnance that was easily discernible in relation to the Gujarat developments. Narendra Modi's continuance in office and the central government's reluctance to hold the state government accountable for the post-Godhra riots, despite the Supreme Court's indictment, seemed to influence a wide spectrum of voters across the country.[8] The communal violence and the consequent trauma for thousands of citizens, and the failure of the Modi government to fulfil its constitutional obligations were disapproved as much by the majority as the minority.

Ironically for the BJP, which would have hoped that it would be remembered by the 'India Shining' campaign and economic reforms, only the legacy of hate and divisiveness, the setting up of the minorities against the majority, rich against the poor, the upper caste against lower castes, seemed to have lingered in the minds of the voters. Although many media pundits persuaded themselves that the constraints of office would normalize the BJP, large sections of the electorate were apparently unconvinced.[9] The BJP's electoral setback in Gujarat and Hindutva strongholds in Uttar Pradesh shows that the idea of a pan–Hindu identity had very little appeal to most Hindus; and in the elections they saw themselves as Indians, preferring a multiplicity of identities vastly more consistent with secular values, recognizing that these have greater significance in a modern world. It is difficult then not to conclude that the people's verdict was a setback for sectarianism and ultra–nationalism, and an important gain for the ideas of pluralism and tolerance.[10] One of the most striking features of the 2004 elections has been the shift in the avowed position of the Congress party. The Congress strategists succeeded in giving an ideological dimension to its campaign, presenting the party as the guardian of India's heritage against the divisive politics of the Sangh Parivar. It posited the party as a champion of the *aam aadmi* against the pro–rich policies of the Hindu Right.

This shift was to a degree reminiscent of the left–of–centre reorientation of the Congress under Nehru in the early 1950s and Indira Gandhi in the early 1970s, which produced major realignments in the polity, and also played a role in reviving the party's traditional social appeal among the poor and the disadvantaged. The empathy shown by the Congress party towards the lower socio–economic groups marginalized from the 1990s by the economic reform process seems to have contributed in large measure to the return of the Congress to the centre of the political arena.[11]

This time it was the aggressive 'India Shining' slogan, agrarian distress, and rising unemployment that forced the party to challenge the cynical way in which the NDA was seeking to win another term in office by misusing manipulated indices of economic performance and celebrating the gains that a small upper crust had derived from the liberalization process. The Congress manifesto talked of revival of public investment; of emphasis on the agricultural sector; of strengthening the public distribution system for foodgrains and other essential commodities; of not privatizing profit–making public enterprises; and, above all, an employment guarantee scheme that would ensure a minimum of 100 days per year to at least one member of each household. Even though the Congress party met with limited success in the election in terms of votes and seats, it nonetheless demonstrated the power of even a partial coalition of the social majority.[12]

The Congress-led alliance worked well precisely because it happened to coincide with and express the popular mood within the political system: the need to create an alternative to the BJP's package of liberalization, privatization, and globalization tilted heavily in favour of big business, the thriving corporate sector, and middle class professionals. That seems to contain a message for the Congress that its political and governing identity would have to be firmly anchored in an egalitarian and humanistic framework, and that it would also need to unambiguously reaffirm its pluralistic democratic identity.

Another striking aspect of what proved to be a successful election campaign for the Congress was the manner in which the party and its president Sonia Gandhi took the message of the *aam aadmi* across the length and breadth of India in pointed contrast to the insensitive 'India Shining' campaign of the NDA, which dominated the cities and metropolitan centres. Sonia Gandhi's leadership and tireless personal campaigning around issues of unemployment, rural and urban distress, and the need for policies with a 'human face' struck a chord with ordinary voters. Packaged as this powerful message was in Sonia Gandhi's highly visible Jan Sampark programme, it generated large-scale voter support for the Congress. Before she made history by her unprecedented decision to decline the post of prime minister, Sonia Gandhi had the support of over 300 members of parliament. She has, by example, reintroduced the notion of morality and public service in the political domain; values that the Congress party has inherited but which, in the last three decades before 2004, it had continually disregarded or squandered. The Congress party also inherited liberal democratic and secular ideals and a deeply humanistic ethos.[13] The 2004 elections raised the question of whether Sonia Gandhi's efforts could then help renew this inheritance into a lasting force for a deepening of democracy.

One good thing that happened was the return of Indian democracy to an institutional structure based on the separation of party and government; something that had not happened since the Emergency. However, the Congress president's decision not to accept the office of prime minister and to appoint Manmohan Singh to the post provoked gratuitous concern about the Congress president emerging as a rival power centre, and about the impact of this on the institution of prime minister. The xenophobic campaign against Sonia Gandhi, first against her foreign origin and then against her as the 'super PM' was part of a concerted attempt to discredit the

Prime Minister, destabilize the UPA government, undermine the popular mandate, and marginalize the 'human face' of the Congress party. That said, the Congress faced the challenge of efficiently reworking the relationship of the government headed by Prime Minister Manmohan Singh, who was not the elected leader of the single largest party, and the party headed by Sonia Gandhi whose popularity and prestige was enhanced by her act of renunciation. Yet it is true that the fears about the party and government acting as competing power centres were not entirely new. Indeed, in the Congress party there is a long history of tension between the prime minister and the party president. Actually, from 1947 to 1976, the same person hardly ever simultaneously held the post of prime minister and party president.

The pattern changed in 1976-7 when Indira Gandhi took control of both the posts. In the case of the Congress party, two models of the prime minister-party relationship have prevailed since 1947. In the first model of 'mutuality' developed under Jawaharlal Nehru, though the prime minister's power was never in doubt, he treated the party as a vital and valuable organization for gaining power and building a nation. During Nehru's tenure, the Congress party actually formed a partnership with the prime minister and both gained from the relationship of mutuality. The prime minister was required to hold regular consultations and observe the requisite formalities. In return, hundreds of influential men and women were ready to proclaim their allegiance to the party, compete for offices under it, and campaign wholeheartedly to get its candidates elected to office besides promoting the policies of the government.[14] The party workers found emotional and material rewards in the association with a great cause and powerful government.[15] This model was supplanted during the Emergency by 'prime-ministerial domination'. In the second model, from about 1971, the prime minister began to control all-important party and government matters, and the party became a compliant and acquiescent instrument. Once the Congress returned to office in 1980, Indira Gandhi retained the office of Congress president. Later Congress prime ministers followed this pattern until the Manmohan Singh-Sonia Gandhi team decided to return to the earlier model of 'mutuality'.

In this sense, the decision of the Congress leadership to separate governance from political leadership—two equally critical tasks—and place each of them in a separate sphere, strengthens the structure of Indian democracy, ending as it does a phase of the unhealthy amalgamation of the two often competing imperatives of governance and political stewardship, which both the centrally-driven Congress and the BJP were prone to allow. A formal separation of the two functions is necessary to reinforce the institutional character of the Indian democratic and governing apparatus.

Yet, it is unimaginable and unrealistic to suggest that a democratic society and popular government can function without the mediation or the influence of political parties. In a genuine democracy, parties play a dominant and decisive role in both elections and government. The question that arises is whether there is any need for the party to maintain its distance from the government. A few clarifications might be useful. A party has three dimensions: party in government (legislators); party as an organization (branch offices and members); and party in the electorate (sympathisers and voters).[16] Indira Gandhi dispensed with the party as an organization. The party stopped articulating government policy to the people and carrying their concerns to the government, acquiring salience only during elections.[17] One immediate consequence was the plethora of unmediated demands on the government, which it was unable to accommodate. A vibrant party can act as a conduit between the government and the people by representing the interests of constituents and overseeing the working of policies to ensure that something is done about the pressing problems of the people. It increases levels of political awareness, mobilization, and participation. However, it is precisely here that Indian parties have been found wanting, failing to prioritize the fulfilment of the basic needs, welfare, and livelihood issues of the people.

Critics argue that the office of prime minister will be diminished if it remains subservient to party leaders or the UPA. However, this argument ignores the fact that the office of prime minister is an evolving one and that the power of prime ministers has waxed and waned. An exaggerated prime-ministership is the outcome of centralized politics and the growth of institutions like the Prime Minister's Office (PMO), which has acquired larger-than-life proportions in the past few years and breached the standard bureaucratic arrangements of the parliamentary system such as the cabinet secretariat or even the council of ministers.[18] Such concentration of power and centralization has created problems in the sphere of representation and a disconnect between the government and electorate, and is antithetical to effective governance. By sharing power and resources, the prime minister only enhances rather than dilutes his or her influence.[19] In addition, centralizing prime ministers found that it is not humanly possible to cope with the vast demands on their time and capacities; and such problems arise when all powers are concentrated in the person or office of the prime minister.

More to the point, the political awakening among various sections of society and simultaneous institutional decline has made it much more difficult for one institution to anticipate and respond to events, interests, and popular pressures, and to prevent things from spinning out of control.[20]

Therefore, an arrangement like the UPA Coordination Committee, consisting of representatives of all the parties supporting the government, and with someone other than the prime minister as its head, is a welcome move. Another new element is the formation of the National Advisory Committee (NAC), which will act as a watchdog of the government and oversee the implementation of the Common Minimum Programme (CMP). Thus, the institutional arrangement at the Centre has three tiers: Council of Ministers, UPA Coordination Committee, and NAC.

The political compulsions of the government aside, to assess whether this institutional arrangement is workable, one must take into account the ongoing debate about Indian democracy, especially with regard to the problem of legitimacy of political authority.[21] The basic issue is that the policies of the government have had no resonance or relationship with the needs of the people. Mediation, consultation, and continuing accountability between the government and the people have been wholly wanting. The economic policy processes seemed to bear very little relationship to the political processes and the politics of electoral and non-electoral organizations and movements which represented the aspirations and expectations of the people with regard to their basic needs. It was precisely in the area of basic needs that the policy processes had been found wanting for failing to prioritize livelihood issues. This was in part due to the insulation of economic policymaking from the political process and popular pressures since liberalization, and in part due to the high degree of centralization of decision-making on economic policy. It was also due to the fragmentation of the polity and erosion of parties, and partly because representative government had been carved up between mutually exclusive compartments. The solution in 2004 lay in building new forms and channels of articulation and representation. The UPA Advisory Council was used to help in bridging the gap and creating appropriate channels of communication and connectivity. This, in combination with Prime Minister Manmohan Singh's stress on the imperative of reforming and revitalizing public systems and institutional relations, has meant that the UPA government has brought about some important innovations and changes in the institutional arrangements for governance which could help to overcome the disjunction between the government and people.

The 2004 elections raised questions about the future of the political challenge to the BJP, and by implication, the future of the secularization project itself, particularly after the rout of the BJP in 2004. Even three months after the verdict, the BJP had failed to come to terms with its debacle. In defeat, as in victory, the central contradiction confronting the BJP was, on the one hand, the impulse towards moderation if only to become the leader of a coalition of disparate parties and, on the other, toward an aggressive anti-Muslim agenda. The electoral success of the BJP in Madhya Pradesh, Rajasthan, and Chhattisgarh demonstrated that the party could not win without the aid of the Rashtriya Swayamsevak Sangh (RSS) networks.[22] At the same time, it was a moot point whether the RSS could grow and expand without state support. The truth, which the BJP was unwilling to accept, was that the overwhelming majority of people had had more than their fill of identity politics. Although the BJP may have a future and may continue to operate as a party with significance in particular regions, its core ideology of an all-encompassing cultural nationalism and its potential to become a hegemonic ideology was seriously called into question.

This nevertheless poses a broader question about Indian democracy: namely, how can the values of mutual respect and tolerance be implemented in such a way that they govern people's real lives in a democratic nation, and cease to just represent the constitutional and legal aspirations of the nation? The core values of the Republic embodied in India's Constitution provide an admirable foundation for a society based on mutual respect, pluralism, and the protection of the basic rights of all. However, even with the elaborate protections for individual and minority rights, the experience of democracy has been one in which long-standing traditions of secular tolerance have been openly undermined, and key institutions have been pressed into the service of communal antagonism. The 2004 elections suggest that pluralism has a more hopeful future than might have been feared, opening up a great opportunity to restore the prominence of the secular discourse and promote the secularization of society. One central issue here is whether the Congress will programmatically reject soft Hindutva and work for the promotion of the secular agenda. This is no easy question to answer in relation to a party that has in numerous instances been complicit in the spread of communalism, even if it does not have the aggressively communal orientation of the BJP.[23] The big question confronting the Congress has been the separation of religion and politics, and its position in relation to secularism.

The Congress adheres, as far as it is possible, to the theoretical position of separating religion from politics. However, when it comes to practice and the application of secular principles to specific issues there does tend to be confusion between the hard line and soft line.[24] The confusion arises when communal forces raise issues which are communitarian in origin but communal in expression. The classic example is the Rama temple at Ayodhya. Only too often Congress governments have displayed ambivalence on this key problem in contemporary Indian politics. This is an issue that demands a separation of religion and politics, and a clear demarcation of party politics and democratic elections as secular matters that should not, therefore, invoke religious advocacy. The halfway measures pursued by past Congress governments principally benefited the BJP. Although the 2004 elections did not focus principally on the secular-communal divide, it became clear that what set apart the Congress from the BJP was their approach towards secularism.[25] During the election campaign, Sonia Gandhi's leadership was unsparing in attacking communalism, and this was the issue that brought the coalition together in the first place. This then could exert some pressure on the UPA to remain loyal to its secular popular mandate; and any attempt by communal forces to exert fresh pressure on the government to yield further space to their chauvinist demands should be unequivocally and unwaveringly resisted, bearing in mind the message of this verdict.

Representing, one hopes, the burial of neoliberalism and retrograde cultural nationalism, the two concepts that could have undermined the structure of the Republic, this election presented India with an opportunity to renew its original moorings as a secular democracy with strongly rooted egalitarian impulses. Both these concepts had converged to push the people and their livelihood issues into the background. The non-inclusiveness of the process of economic development in India, notably post-1991, and the uneven development between regions and between peoples, was obvious. It was the political space created by the yearning of the electorate for an India free of these dark clouds which had to be addressed and respected by the new governing formation in order to bring people's issues to the centre of the agenda.[26] The very creation of the UPA was a response to the historical need to repudiate the two flawed notions of neoliberalism and cultural nationalism. This alone can explain the phenomenon of two unlikely political formations—the Indian National Congress and the Indian Left—coming together on the same platform to shape a new governing entity that reflected the political impulses and popular aspirations that went into the rejection of the NDA in the 2004 elections. The two very distinct identities of the Congress and the Left needed to cohere to a degree that would infuse durability in the process of governance and thereby infuse the secular government formation with credibility. On both sides there was a need for accommodation: the Congress would necessarily need to steep itself in more egalitarian and pro-poor approaches; and the Left to recognise the constraints of the Congress which, as a typically centrist, catch-all political formation, lacks a strong ideological core. This required the Left to adopt a social democratic orientation for the present; and for the Congress, too, it involves reworking its understanding of economic reforms to achieve greater synchronization with its electoral support base, primarily the less well-off.

India's democratic system is well-established. There is considerable evidence that Indian democracy is deepening, and politics and elections are providing space for contestation and avenues for expression of rights and claims. While the persistence of a democratic-federal-secular polity is a major political and human achievement, formidable challenges remain in the realization of substantive democracy. One important challenge comes from the project of Hindutva, which had been seeking to redefine democracy in majoritarian terms, exposing the fragility of Indian pluralism. However, the principal challenge remains the creation of a more equal society and a reduction in the vast economic disparities that exist between regions, classes, groups, and individuals, further aggravated by globalization. This chapter has sought to emphasize the continuing disjunction between political equality and socio-economic inequality, and the problems of the legitimacy of political authority that this creates. With all its problems, India is admired worldwide as a successful democracy, as a nation-state, which has overcome threats to a united national identity, acute caste deprivation and minority weakness. It is very important that citizens do not lose their faith in the nation and the political system, and the idea of the nation-state is not superseded by a market state. For this, it is important to restore the original moorings of the Republic—secularism and social democracy—and for our identity to be rooted in an all-embracing nationhood to impart a more equitable meaning to the idea of citizenship. The strength of the CMP lies in its recognition of the progressive powers of the state and the democratic process, and an acceptance of the proposition that improving the living conditions of the social majority is the responsibility of the state, which it must immediately begin to discharge. A noteworthy aspect of the CMP is the manner in which it deals with the question of distribution. It recognises that rapid economic expansion is a necessary but insufficient condition for poverty reduction; and that this requires the creation of an appropriate enabling environment for the underprivileged that enables them to reap the benefits of more rapid economic growth through an expansion in employment.[27] By questioning 'the immanent logic of neoliberal economics' and more generally 'conservative politics' as the guiding lights of Indian democracy, the CMP created an opening for an alternative and more humane trajectory of politics and development.

The UPA sought to focus on three themes: an urgent need to address the issue of employment; the parallel urgency of increasing social spending; and the need to speak out and act openly against communalism, and the communalization of constitutional and educational institutions. By doing this, it began to reorient itself both on ethnic-religious identity issues and questions of economic and social justice. Crucial here was the reversal of past policies that have exacerbated inequality and disparities, and generated jobless growth while impoverishing the majority of the people and, above all, the need to provide justice to the victims and survivors of the Gujarat violence. The 2004 elections turned precisely on these two issues. The voters clearly exercised their franchise in favour of equity and pluralism; was the UPA government's responsibility to put into practise the original idea of India.

Notes and References

1. For analyses of the 2004 elections, see 'The Meaning of Verdict 2004', *The Hindu*, 14 May 2004.
2. For an analysis of the election results, see the articles on 'How India Voted', in *The Hindu*, 20 May 2004.
3. See 'The Problem', a Symposium on the 2004 General Elections, *Seminar*, no. 539, July 2004.
4. Vir Sanghvi, 'Two Ideas of India', *The Hindustan Times*, 16 May 2004.
5. K.C. Suri, 'Reform: The Elites Want it, the Masses Don't', *The Hindu*, 20 May 2004.
6. Yogendra Yadav, 'Economic Reforms in the Mirror of Public Opinion', *The Hindu*, 13 June 2004.
7. Praful Bidwai, 'Liberation at Last', *Frontline*, vol. 21, issue 11, 22 May–4 June 2004.
8. During the six years of NDA rule, up to 2004 reams of newsprint have been expended on demonstrating the moderate and Nehruvian credentials of Atal Bihari Vajpayee.
9. Rajeev Bhargava, 'The Magic of Indian Democracy', opendemocracy.net, 27 May 2004. www.opendemocracy.net/author/rajeev.bhargava, accessed on 5 March 2006.
10. Antara Dev Sen, 'India's Benign Earthquake', opendemocracy.net, 20 May 2004.
11. Yogendra Yadav, 'Radical Shift in the Social Bases of Power', *The Hindu*, 20 May 2004.
12. Neena Vyas, 'Silencing Her Critics', *The Hindu*, 23 May 2004.
13. Robin Jeffrey, 'The Prime Minister and the Ruling Party', in *Nehru to the Nineties: The Office of the Prime Minister in India*, ed. James Manor, London: Hurst Publishers, 1994.
14. Ibid.
15. Ibid., p. 162.
16. Ibid.
17. Kanchan Chandra, 'Elections as Auctions', *Seminar*, no. 539, July 2004.
18. James Manor, 'Introduction', in Manor, ed., *Nehru to the Nineties*.
19. Ibid.
20. D.L. Sheth, 'The Crisis of Political Authority', p. 58 and Javeed Alam, 'What is Happening Inside Indian Democracy', in *Indian Democracy*, ed. Rajendra Vora and Suhas Palshikar, Delhi: Sage Publications, 2004.

21. Manini Chatterjee, 'The Debacle and After', *Seminar*, no. 539, July 2004, pp. 20-4.
22. Praful Bidwai, 'Liberation at Last', *Frontline*, 22 May-4 June 2002.
23. Mani Shankar Aiyar, 'Can the Congress find a Future?', *Seminar*, no. 526, 26 June 2003.
24. Nilanjan Mukhopadhyaya, 'The UPA's USP', *The Hindustan Times*, 22 June 2004.
25. Prabhat Patnaik, 'On Changing Course in India: an Economic Agenda for 2004', *Social Scientist*, July 2004.
26. Editorial, 'On the Right Track', *The Hindu*, 8 July 2004.
27. Ibid.

3 | More Equal but still Not Equal?
State and Inter-Group Equality in India

In the 1950s and 1960s, it was widely believed in India as elsewhere, that the making of a successful nation-state was basically a matter of legal and political construction and policy formulation. The political and economic history of India since 1947 shows that such a constructivist picture is misleading. Historical and economic structures which underlie political processes have had a 'parametric limiting' influence on what was possible in the political world.[1] This encourages us to look beyond formal structures to the social and cultural specificities under which states operate. The focus of this chapter is on one aspect of this process: the relationship of the state to social equality in India. Instead of examining how the state reacts to given social diversity, it considers the possibility of precisely what kind of equality is produced by the state's policies, and whether such policies actually surmount, or simply subdue, the cultural/religious structure of the state. The chapter highlights the interplay of cultural pluralism and social equality in the formation and integration of the modern Indian state, focusing especially on policies of secularism, reservation, and affirmative action aimed at promoting the interests of minorities and backward classes, in relation to the goal of eliminating discrimination and equalizing opportunities for individuals. It will address the question of whether they achieve the objectives for which they are intended, and whether there are other less visible effects.

The Indian Nation-State and Minority Rights

The dominant political imagination endorsed the establishment of a modern nation-state.[2] Yet, unlike the nation-states of the modern Europe, India is not an ethnic nation; it is a nation of many ethnicities. 'Indianness' is an idea that is distinctly pluralist, but this is not an idea that could be taken for granted. The pluralist contours had to be actively designed. Mahatma Gandhi and Jawaharlal Nehru believed it was the responsibility of the nation-state to accommodate the enormous diversity of India. Values of tolerance, pluralism, and inclusion were actively encouraged and these formed a cardinal part of the self-perception of the state, with policies and institutions both projecting and building upon variety. The policy of affirmative action in favour of the Scheduled Castes (SCs) and Scheduled Tribes (STs) and the decision to desist from imposing a uniform civil code are among the important constitutional measures, legislative enactments, and government policies that upheld this perception.

Pluralism is not unique to India. Most societies in the world today are culturally heterogeneous. What is certainly unique to India though is the magnitude of diversity. There is no society in the contemporary world with such staggering cultural diversity as India.[3] A vast number of groups and communities with distinct and diverse lifestyles, languages, and religions live in India. The distinctive feature of India is the state's breadthless concern with cultural differences and its accommodation of diversity in the public domain. The national anthem is a wonderful celebration of India's diversity: India is hailed as 'Punjab, Sindh, Gujarat, Maratha, Dravida, Utkala, Banga . . .'. In this political conception, being Tamil, Malayalee, or Telugu, or Hindu, Christian or atheist, natural or naturalized citizen was not contradictory to being an Indian, as Sudipta Kaviraj observes.[4] Rather the celebration of diversity was a prelude to Indian unity.

The constitutional form of pluralism was based on secular citizenship defined by civic and universalistic criteria; it guaranteed inclusion, and at the same time, provided autonomy for communities and cultural identities. Cultural communities were accorded equal consideration in the public realm by ensuring that no group is excluded or seriously disadvantaged in the public arena. This involved an official recognition of group identity, with groups being differentiated according to caste, language, religious, and regional affiliations. The state does not, however, necessarily allow all identities to proliferate. Some identities are preferred over others. It extends constitutional/legal recognition to four specific categories—religion, language, region, and caste. Within this broad framework there is a further classification which privileged certain identities over others. The written and unwritten rules of the state recognize certain identities as legitimate and worthy of accommodation, and the rest are marginalized. The official conception entails foregrounding regional and linguistic identities at the expense of other kinds of subregional group identity, such as those formed around religion, class, and gender. Class identities have remained on the fringes except where class issues have overlapped with caste groups, such as riots related to reservations or violence against dalits. This means that demands based on language and culture will be accommodated, and other group identities can only find expression within a 'minorities discourse', that is if they are conceptualized as less than equal and therefore deserving of state protection and promotion.

In 1950, India adopted a Constitution in which provisions for equality were given great prominence. The Constitution sets forth a general programme for the reconstruction of society. Society does not however change simply with the adoption of a radical Constitution. Social relations based on caste and community, and distinctions and discrimination based on these identities persist. Two features of traditional society required special attention. The first was the predominance of collective over individual identity; and second, the unequal placement of individuals and groups in society.[5] Jawaharlal Nehru noted: 'The structure was based on three concepts: the autonomous village community, caste, and the joint family system. In all these three, it is the group that counts; the individual has a secondary role. While the state recognized the existence of different communities and different types of inequalities, its egalitarian impulse centred on the removal of inequities perpetrated by the caste system.

The consideration of collective identities in India must take into account not only caste, but also religion, and religious pluralism. It is the practice of this pluralism that has been challenged by exclusivist political parties and some major political developments from the 1990s. The principal question concerns Indian secularism and its emphasis on minority rights. The Indian state is based on a Constitution whose secular character has been reaffirmed by an amendment to its Preamble. The adoption of secularism by the state conveyed an implicit denial of religion, but in practice the state has shown great sensitivity to the imperatives of religious and group life. Unlike liberal democracies, which restrict religion to the private sphere, India devised policies by which religious communities receive equal consideration in the public realm. Acting on the assumption that providing equal rights to individuals could not ensure equal treatment to all religious communities, the Indian Constitution provided collective group rights to the minorities to protect and preserve their linguistic and cultural identity.

The provision of minority rights was influenced by the Partition of India on religious lines in 1947, and especially by the aftermath of deteriorating Hindu-Muslim relations. The spectre of communalism hung over the subcontinent when India became independent. Partition meant that Pakistan might become a homeland for Muslims, but India would remain a home for Hindus, Muslims, Christians and others, and though

Pakistan was a Muslim state, there remained more Muslims in India than in Pakistan. One way of facilitating the integration of these minorities was to recognize them as members of religious communities, and grant them collective rights; though this was a violation of liberal principles, it was seen as a necessary safeguard against larger majority groupings. In this way the state hoped to gain the trust of Muslim communities that opted to stay in their country of birth. Based on the principle of inclusion, the Indian state bestowed constitutional recognition on the rights of minority communities. These rights consisted of religious freedom, including the Right to Worship, propagate, and practise one's religion. In matters of religion, the state's non-interference was assured. These rights were also not limited to non-discrimination between various communities. They encompassed the freedom to establish religious, cultural, and educational institutions of their choice and ensured that minority institutions would not be disqualified from receiving state funding. Minority rights were granted primarily to the religious minorities and SCs on grounds of equality. For the former, minority rights would guarantee equal status in the public realm, while for the latter it would ensure non-discrimination between the upper castes and lower castes.[6]

Minority rights constrained the authority of the state to intervene in religious affairs of minority groups while the state continued to intervene in the affairs of the Hindu community. By introducing temple rights for dalits and reforming temple administration, the state intervened in religious matters of the majority community. The state also initiated legal reform in the Hindu community, introducing the Right to Divorce, abolishing child marriage, and legally recognizing intercaste marriages. Such reformist initiative was limited to the majority community and was not extended to the religious minorities owing to their opposition to any change in personal law. This created an aberration in the very notion of equal citizenship. The basic problem is obvious. If it was accepted that the state could intervene to provide equal rights to women of one community, i.e. the majority community, then what was the ground for not doing the same for others? The answer is essentially pragmatic: equality of citizenship is important, but the political leadership reckoned it was perhaps more important to respect the sensitivity of religious communities, hence the state provided a system of minority rights that would limit the possibility of cultural assimilation and safeguard against the possibility of unequal treatment. Legal reforms could be initiated only when the communities were ready to accept them. Unwilling to grant a legislature the power to reform personal laws, minority leaders saw legal reform as a fundamental encroachment on their religious identity. They have not however shunned legislative intervention altogether.

Before Independence, the ulama-led campaign culminated in the legislative enactment of a uniform set of personal laws for all Muslims in India. In 1986, it took the form of legislation to pacify their apprehensions regarding the ill-effects of the Supreme Court judgement in the Shah Bano case. Hence, the explanation for the anomaly cannot be the dispute about parliamentary competence, more likely, it centres around respecting the wishes of the minority community.[7] Thus the regime of personal laws is very much a part of secular calculation.[8] The critique of the state in this context is either that it intervenes too much as when the government passed the Muslim Women's Bill, or too little as in its reluctance to enact a uniform civil code. This is the peculiar predicament of the state to understand which we have to keep in mind not only India's composite cultural tradition, but also its demography and heterogeneity. The presence of social pluralities makes it difficult to conceive of a stable political arrangement without a regard for diversity.

Pluralism of society has given rise to an interpretation of secularism which consists of legal asymmetries between different communities with respect to personal laws. The real issue that has virtually gone unnoticed however, is whether these asymmetries really are more favourable to Muslims in general. The answer is no. What may be favourable from the Muslim male point of view is most unfavourable from the point of view of Muslim women. Minority rights thus present several problems in a multicultural polity. First, in privileging community rights over the principle of equal rights, they often reinforce existing hierarchies. Second, such rights have exacerbated gender inequalities within the group and restricted individual choice in the name of cultural integrity. Third, and most important, they underestimate the potential for cultures and communities to change and yet survive. As Bhiku Parekh argues, culture encompasses a lot of things, such as how one should live, relate to one's fellow humans, and find meaning in one's life.[9] It is perhaps a mistake to link culture solely or judge it even primarily in terms of one aspect: personal laws.[10] Above all, minority rights leave little scope for equal rights for women. With the result, one issue has recurred: what should be done when the claims of minority communities clash with the norm of gender equality that is at least formally endorsed by the state, however much it may continue to violate it in practice.

Equality in an Unequal Society

In India, inequality is historical as well as modern, horizontal as well as vertical. Historically, horizontal inequalities have been marked by the pluralism of religious, regional, linguistic, and ethnic communities, while vertical inequalities can be illustrated by reference to the hierarchically ordered caste system. In contemporary times, the picture of inequality is complicated by the existence of vast social and economic inequalities, expressed through the class structure. Thus, inequalities derive not only from caste differences, but also from class and gender, though these may often overlap with caste-derived inequalities.

The modern Indian state confronted unprecedented obstacles in the creation of an egalitarian society. It inherited the most rigidly hierarchical and compartmentalized social structure in any modern state, a structure that limited opportunities for upward mobility to an exceedingly small group. There was little concern about either the equal distribution of benefits and burdens or the consideration of interests.[11] The most striking inequalities were those with regard to caste and gender.[12] Caste was the prime symbol of social inequality and untouchability—the darkest side of this culture. It was widely viewed as an impediment to equality of opportunity and hence considered inimical to national unity, progress, and democracy. It required concerted efforts by the state to change practices embedded in society. Led by the secular and socialist-minded Nehru, the state turned its back on Hindu orthodoxy and the hierarchical order, to one based on the principle of equality: equality before law, the equal protection of laws, and the equality of status and of opportunity.

The state's determination to remove social discrimination perpetuated by the caste system was symbolized by the appointment of B.R. Ambedkar as the Law Minister. Although the Scheduled Caste Federation established by him had been defeated in his own province in the 1946 election, Prime Minister Nehru appointed him Law Minister, and he was also chosen as chairman of the drafting committee of the Constituent Assembly. Special attention was given to the SCs and STs: they were the only groupings to have legislative seats and government jobs reserved from them. This was based on the understanding that disabilities derived from caste were the most conspicuous impediment to equality. Nehru acknowledged that certain collective identities have to be emphasized as part of the general concern for equality and he supported this position in the Constituent Assembly:

Frankly I would like this proposal to go further and put an end to such reservations as there still remain. But again, speaking frankly, I realize that in the present state of affairs in India it would not be a desirable thing to do, that is to say, in regard to the Scheduled Castes. I try to look upon the problem not in the sense of a religious minority, but rather in the sense of helping backward groups in the country. I do not look at it from the religious point of view or the caste point of view, but from the point of view that a backward group ought to be helped and I am glad this reservation also will be limited to ten years.[13]

Although Ambedkar spoke strongly in support of the individual in the Constituent Assembly he pleaded for the recognition of the special claims of certain groups. What was at issue in the Constituent Assembly was not equality as a right but as a policy aimed at bringing about certain changes in society.

The policy and principles of equality were derived from the experience of types of inequality specific to the Indian social structure organized on two different axes, as caste and as class. Each type of inequality has a different structural source: social inequality is grounded in practices of the caste order whereas economic inequality is produced by the structural logic of feudalism and capitalism.

The pursuit of equality was made at two levels. At one level was the constitutional effort to change the very structure of social relations. Practising caste and untouchability was made illegal and the use of religious considerations in state activities was banned. At the second level was the effort to bring about economic equality, but in this endeavour the right to property and the legal recognition of capitalist class inequality was not seriously curbed. Moreover, the placement of the demands for economic equality into the Directive Principles of State Policy indicated that the political elite did not conceive of serious state intervention to check economic inequality. Nevertheless, a discourse of upliftment of the poor was part of the process of legitimization of the postcolonial state even though this discourse did not translate into a consensus on active state intervention to bring about greater equality, except the abolition of intermediary rights in the rural sector. Thus, the references to economic equality in the Constitution, in law courts, or from political platforms are basically rhetorical. In legal terms, much of the constitutional efforts are directed against social and not economic inequality.

The eradication of social inequality raised extremely complex problems. However, the state made remarkable efforts to tackle the basic inequalities of traditional social structures through a policy of affirmative action for historically deprived groups.[14] Sensitive to the social and cultural context in which egalitarian ideas and institutions were to be introduced, the founding fathers recognized that under Indian conditions certain exceptions to the universal criteria of the liberal state based on guarantees of individual freedoms had to be made to provide equality under the law for all groups of citizens. Social practices that violated the principle of equality were banned and policies giving access to the SCs were instituted. The scope of these policies has been expanded to cover a wide array of governmental schemes and programmes, including reserved seats in legislatures and government employment to safeguard against discrimination. These programmes permit departures from formal equality for the purpose of eliminating social discrimination.[15] The tension between these commitments to non-discrimination and to substantive equalization was expressed powerfully by Nehru when he remarked in the course of the First Amendment debate that 'We arrive at a peculiar tangle. We cannot have equality because in trying to attain equality we come up against some principles of equality.'[16]

The constitutional provisions themselves contained a number of tensions, between different conceptions of equality and divergent notions of the goals and scope of protective discrimination. Marc Galanter labels the tension as one between horizontal and vertical perspectives on equality. In the horizontal view, equality is viewed as identical opportunities to compete for existing values among those differently endowed, regardless of structural determinants of the chances of success, or of the consequences of distribution of values. In the vertical view, the transition is from a past of inequality to a future of substantive equality: the purpose of affirmative action is to promote equalization by offsetting historically accumulated inequalities.[17] In other words, given the existence of uneven capabilities among social groups, a simple application of the principle of equality can lead to inequality of outcome.

To complicate matters further, there was strong resistance to the extension of reservations to the Other Backward Classes (OBCs), leading to the fall of a central government in October 1990. It has often been said after the anti-Mandal backlash that the benefits are captured by the economically well-off OBCs or by the elite within the SCs. What is more, since the 1970s the concept of equality, both within and without the state, has undergone significant changes. By 2000, the focus shifted to appropriate representation rather than inclusion, which was the major consideration behind the system of reservations for SCs and STs. The new trend draws upon a growing preference for representation of group claims and this has been used to justify group-based representation in political institutions. This shift has emboldened more and more groups to demand better representation in legislatures and government.[18] On grounds of under-representation, religious minorities and women too could claim the same benefits. The shift from non-discrimination to under-representation marks a radical change in the conception of equality.[19] For now, self-representation by groups is the epitome of equality, and reservation the singular strategy for promoting equality.

Notwithstanding these shifts, considerable progress has been made on account of affirmative action policies.[20] These policies have produced substantial redistributive effects. Important benefits have come to thousands of SCs from reservations and the decrease in unwarranted discrimination in public employment. Reserved seats and jobs have given them a significant legislative presence and beneficiary groups have received the earnings, security, and prestige that go with government jobs. Such redistribution has not spread evenly throughout the beneficiary groups or different regions though. Only a small proportion of people could be rescued from poverty through these schemes while the number of potential claimants is huge. Not much effort was made to supplement these policies with an improvement of basic facilities that alleviate the life situation: good primary schools, better health facilities, training programmes to improve skills, etc.

Neither the Constitution nor public policy could ensure substantive equality. The aspiration for economic equality has yielded a very uneven picture of deprivation, poverty, and maldistribution. State intervention, whether in the form of affirmative action, action against adverse discrimination, or a whole host of welfare policies, has definitely not reduced vulnerability and inequity suffered by the vast majority. In virtually all the states in which SCs form a substantial fraction of the population, they continue to be over-represented among the poor, the illiterate, and casual and landless labourers.

The focus on social discrimination and subordination and not on the broader debasement on account of poverty, restricts the state's recognition of the ambit of collective disadvantages. This has meant a relative neglect of thinking and programmes directed specifically at the economic condition of the poor. One may point out, in support of such scepticism, that the Constitution declared that 'the state shall endeavour to provide, within a period of ten years from the commencement of this Constitution, for free and compulsory education for all children until they complete the age of fifteen years'. Since Independence the government of India, and all state governments have advocated ending child labour and establishing compulsory, universal, primary education for all children up to the age of fourteen. This commitment dates back to the turn of the century when Gokhale, then president of the Indian National Congress, unsuccessfully urged the British government to establish free and compulsory education. Successive governments in free India reconfirmed both goals. Over 60 years have passed since the enactment of the Constitution and the 'goal of universal primary education remains as elusive as ever before'.[21]

Despite the continuous use of the rhetoric of education for all, governments have put very little emphasis on it in practice. According to Myron Weiner, this has little to do with poverty or with economy; rather, it is simply that state leaders have chosen not to intervene. Successive governments have not made the effort to move children out of the labour force and out of their homes into the school system.[22] Of considerable importance are the attitudes of state officials, politicians, and the middle class, none of whom believe that any significant action can or should be taken to eliminate illiteracy or child labour. It is clearly a case of deliberate neglect bolstered by the lack of strong support for government intervention within the state apparatus, and a dearth of a strong political organization of the deprived outside the state, pressing the government to implement its policies.[23] Structural domination in this conception is less relevant than the belief system of the bureaucracy. The belief system is closely tied to traditional culture and to the premises that underlie the hierarchical caste system.

Of course norms and beliefs are important. They are a vital connecting element between the cultural and social systems. However, social norms are usually linked to both the politico-economic structure and the cultural edifice of society. Even the most discursive cultural practices have an irreducible politico-economic dimension, and conversely, the most material economic institutions have a constitutive cultural dimension. Thus, it is elite scepticism with regard to universal education, rather than the resource constraint, that explains why priority was not given to expanding it. This is evident from the fact that there is no provision in the Constitution for mandatory education as a right for all citizens. The ideas and values of government officials and politicians are shaped by their location in a differentiated structure of society. Even when policies on universal primary education are accepted, these are diluted by the social morphology so that they are perceived and applied differently to different sections of society.

The Political Rhetoric and the Pattern of Action

The discussions so far suggests that economic injustice and cultural values usually reinforce one another dialectically.[24] The result of this interweaving is often a vicious economic subordination as in the case of dalits. Economic disadvantages impede equal participation in public spheres and everyday life. Policies against social discrimination cannot remove inequalities rooted in the political economy. Economic injustice requires politico-economic restructuring and redistribution by the state. Hence, state intervention is a critical factor in economic and social development, but historical specificities and the class context of Indian society have influenced the limits of such action. An important institutional constraint pertains to the dependence of the state on the process of capital accumulation, and its protection of the long-term interests of capital.

Arguably, the roots of political limits can be traced back to at least the 1930s. The political leadership, along with the majority of the professional intelligentsia, opted for a statist model of modernization and agreed on the central importance of industrialization for the development of a modern nation.[25] They agreed that planning was the key instrument for poverty alleviation. Within this framework the needs of the poor received much rhetorical but very little serious attention. As a matter of fact, the political leadership was concerned mainly about the rising birth rate of the poor.[26] On the face of it the Nehruvian vision should have addressed the issue of inequity through national programmes of radical redistribution. The Nehruvian conception of industrialization, however, did not entertain the idea that radical restructuring of economic and social relations might be the precursor and foundation for industrialization and modernization.[27] Land reforms of the kind conducted in China or even in South Korea and Taiwan were not framed as a specific objective either before or after independence. Expecting that the European style of industrialization would spill into and transform agrarian relations, Nehru was slow to appreciate the importance of land reforms. When he realised that this was not happening, he did champion land reforms. However, he was defeated by the conservative landed interests which by then had acquired considerable power and clout in the Congress and in particular, in the states which were responsible for the implementation of land reforms.

With the advantage of experience we can now see that policy measures, such as land reform that could have widened the social base of development, were never likely to take place.[28] Even when the commitment was apparent as in the Sixth Five-Year Plan (1980-85), the government was more concerned about the lack of appropriate administrative machinery for the implementation of a programme of land reforms, than the constraints posed by the nexus between the policymakers, executing agencies, and landowning classes that might well be responsible for bureaucratic negligence. A state like Bihar did not acquire a single hectare of land for redistribution to agricultural labourers until the Emergency. This was not due to the lack of an administrative machinery or the failure of the administrative apparatus. On the contrary, the success of land reforms in Kerala suggests that if the state leadership had been committed to reforms and had not deliberately shunned the organization and mobilization of the rural poor, different outcomes could surely have been possible.

The needs of the poorest Indians were seriously considered only after the anti-poverty programmes introduced in the 1980s as part of a third wave of state policy. The first two phases were entirely dominated by the rapid development of heavy industry and, following the disastrous droughts of 1966-7, the increase in agricultural production. Even Indira Gandhi's winning 'Garibi Hatao' slogan of the 1971 elections, did not touch the lives of the poor until after the dalit atrocities of 1977–80 when the Integrated Rural Development Programme (IRDP), arguably the most important component of India's strategy for poverty alleviation.[29] In spite of an expenditure of considerable resources estimated at Rs. 16.61 billion in the Sixth Plan and providing support to 16.5 million beneficiaries,[30] these programmes proved ineffective in areas of concentrated poverty, while the richer states performed better than others.[31] With the introduction of liberalization in the early 1990s and a clear diminution in the state's commitment to social welfare, even this flicker of hope had all but evaporated, and there is no longer any serious belief that anti-poverty programmes can bring about a reduction in poverty or inequality. Given these trends, it is hardly surprising, that the state has failed to pursue even a non-radical strategy of supplying basic needs: health, education, and simple welfare.

The cultural and administrative limits of the state do not necessarily tell the whole story. The limits of the state derive from caste and class differences, though these may often overlap. The differentiation of society along more than one axis concurrently indicates that no one line of division is the most crucial determinant of the political processes. Political organization and collective action can be a significant mediation. The marginalized groups who are not politically organized in any meaningful sense are ineffective in compelling the state to fulfil its welfare commitments.[32] In the absence of pressure from below, the state could not pursue even a social welfare orientation in favour of the poor. This is unquestionably a case of deliberate political neglect precipitated by the lack of strong support for government intervention within the state apparatus, and the absence of a strong political organization of the deprived outside the state pressing the government to implement the state's own policies.

The Ongoing Search for Equality

After over 60 years of Independence, the most remarkable feature of India's quest for equality is the acceptance of social justice as a cardinal principle of contemporary life. However improbable it might have seemed in 1950, the trend towards greater equalization is unmistakable as democratic values have become entrenched among political elites and institutions vital to the consolidation of democracy. Nevertheless, there is still no agreement on the strategy for fostering equality. There is a coexistence of dissimilar and even conflicting strategies of realizing equality: continued assertions of the primacy of bourgeois equality and continued concessions to collective identities.[33] The strongest arguments against affirmative action as an instrument of social transformation have come out of the 1990s, yet so did the strongest assertion of caste identity.

Affirmative action policies have challenged certain common assumptions about equality. These policies sought to achieve equality by taking into account collective identities and giving them a certain primacy over individual rights. The problem is that though the basis of preferential treatment is caste, the whole group as such does not benefit, rather the individuals gain. Among them the upper crust corners the benefits. Hence, the critique of this approach, drawn from liberal principles, directs attention to a legal framework of equality that provides an alternative basis for unification and democratization where rights and norms of justice are open to a broader basis of resolution and organisation. Indeed, this has been the formal basis of the constitutional structure of the postcolonial state in India. Yet, the practical building of this structure out of the existing cultural material forced a surrender of these principles from the outset.[34] Political processes have politicized caste, in fact, state policies of reservations promoted the emergence of a vocal political leadership among lower caste groups that has used the politics of caste to enter the middle classes.[35] Using political means for upward mobility, lower caste elites operated virtually as socio-economic groups to gain educational and occupational opportunities through reservations. As a result, what has resulted is not

. . . the actualization of bourgeois equality at all but rather the conflicting claims of caste groups, not on the religious basis of dharma but on the purely secular demands of claims upon the state.[36]

What emerges then is the advancement of equality, strongly imprinted by the historical and cultural context in which the idea germinated. Although universalistic ideas remained the frame of reference for equality, India's career of equality was defined by continuous compromises between liberal principles and conditions on the ground and between individual rights and inter-group equality. This compromise produced serious legal asymmetries with respect to personal laws and women's rights. What is therefore needed is not simply an acceptance of diversities, but support of them in ways that do not violate demands of justice and equality. Just as the caste-based reservation is not a defence of traditional caste inequalities or a perpetuation of the caste system, minority rights based on religious freedom should not translate into a defence of the inequitous treatment of women.

Still, despite numerous deviations from principle and compromises in practice, social discrimination has declined in contemporary India and this has transformed historically rigid hierarchical structures, social relations, and cultural attitudes. On the one hand, this change could not have come about without the laws and programmes introduced by the state. On the other hand, these measures are too limited in scope to overcome the subordination and poverty of the people. Leaving intact the deep structures that generate disadvantge, the scope is limited for two reasons. Foremost, the progressive consensus that existed at the time of Independence has eroded, and even at that time the consensus was not sufficiently strong to become the basis for an appropriate national programme. Above all, there is lack of solidarity regarding the overall condition of the poor among those responsible for the implementation of welfare policies. Also, the single-minded focus on reservations as the sole instrument of social equality has allowed political regimes to recognize the claims of subordinate groups without having to concede to them an important share of economic power. Moreover the enhancement of social equality could not overcome the actual unequal economic structure of Indian society, reinforced by an uneven distribution of gains under a predominantly capitalist society. Yet, reservation policies have captured the attention of the public themselves. This preoccupation, however, does not reflect a social given and the emphasis on groups is not merely an expression of a community-centered social life. To a large extent, it is an effect of the centrality accorded to the idea of inter-group parity in India's quest for equality.

Notes and References

1. See 'Introduction', *Dynamics of State Formation: India and Europe Compared*, ed. Martin Doornboos and Sudipta Kaviraj, New Delhi: Sage Publications, 1997, pp. 12–14.
2. Sudipta Kaviraj, 'Crisis of the Nation-State', in *Contemporary Crisis of the Nation State?*, ed. John Dunn, Oxford: Blackwell, 1995, p. 119.
3. *The People of India* project of the Anthropological Survey of India estimated there are nearly 4,599 separate communities in India with as many as 325 languages and dialects in 12 distinct language families and some 24 scripts.
4. Kaviraj, 'Crisis of the Nation-State', p. 119.
5. Donald Eugene Smith, *India as a Secular State*, Princeton: Princeton University Press, 1963, pp. 100–34.
6. For a discussion on minority rights see Gurpreet Mahajan, *Identities and Rights: Aspects of Liberal Democracy for India*, New Delhi: Oxford University Press, 1998.
7. This was repeatedly invoked in the Lok Sabha debate to establish the legitimacy of the Muslim Women (Protection of Rights on Divorce) Bill, 1986.
8. Nivedita Menon, 'Women and Citizenship', *Wages of Freedom: Fifty Years of the Indian Nation-State*, ed. Partha Chatterjee, New York: Oxford University Press, 1998, pp. 264–5.
9. Bhiku Parekh, 'A Varied Moral World', *Boston Review*, October–November 1997, p. 36.

10. The Rudolphs have noted: The contradiction in India's concept of secularism was its simultaneous commitment to communities and to equal citizenship. Lloyd and Susanne Rudolph, *In Pursuit of Lakshmi*, Chicago: Chicago University Press, 1987, p. 39.

11. Andre Beteille, 'Equality as a Right and as a Policy', in his *Society and Politics in India*, New Delhi: Oxford University Press, 1997, p. 197.

12. Irfan Habib pointed it that India is perhaps the only country which had created, long before the advent of capitalism, through the device of serving artisan castes and semi-servile untouchables, a large landless proletariat for serving the people with hereditary rights to land or the infrastructure of the land.

13. *Constituent Assembly Debates*, 1947–9, vol. VIII, 16 May-10 June 1949, p. 331.

14. There are strong provisions for equality in the Constitution. The principal provisions are contained in Part III on Fundamental Rights and Part IV on Directive Principles of State Policy. It is, however, significant that the rights enshrined in Part III on Fundamental Rights are essentially those concerning liberty and enforceable by courts, whereas those in Part IV, concerned with welfare and distribution of material resources are not. Provisions in Part III are related to equality before the law (Article 14), prohibition of discrimination on grounds of religion, race, sex, or place of birth (Article 15) and equality of opportunity in employment (Article 16). The provisions in Part IV address disparity between classes and castes and those in Part III equality between individuals.

15. Marc Galanter, *Competing Equalities: Law and The Backward Classes in India*, New Delhi: Oxford University Press, 1984, pp. 379-80.

16. *Parliamentary Debates*, vol. XII–XIII (part II), 29 May 1951.

17. Marc Galanter, *Competing Equalities*, pp. 44–6, fn. 15.

18. I have discussed this issue in my article 'Representation and Redistribution: The New Lower Caste Politics of North India', in *Transforming India: The Socio-Political Dynamics of Democracy*, Francine Frankel, Zoya Hasan, Rajeev Bhargava and Balveer Arora, eds., New Delhi: Oxford University Press, 2002.

19. Gurpreet Mahajan, *Identities and Rights*, pp. 153–4.

20. D.L. Sheth, 'Reservations Policy Revisited', *Economic and Political Weekly*, vol. 22, no. 46; K.C. Suri, 'Competing Interests, Social Conflict and the Politics of Reservations in India', *Nationalism and Ethnic Politics*, London, 1995.

21. J.P. Naik, *Elementary Education in India: A Promise to Keep*, Delhi: Allied Publishers, 1975. What the late J.P. Naik said 25 years ago is still true.

22. Myron Weiner, *The Child and the Stale in India*, New Delhi: Oxford University Press, 1991, p. 15.

23. Ibid., p. 5.

24. On the links between economic injustice and cultural injustice see Nancy Fraser, '"From Redistribution to Recognition" Dilemmas of Justice in a "Post-Socialist Age"', *New Left Review*, July/August 1995.

25. Oliver Mendelsohn and Ivlarica Vicziani, *The Untouchables: Subordination, Poverty and the State in India*, Cambridge: Cambridge University Press, 1998, p. 157.

26. Ibid.

27. Bhiku Parekh, 'Jawaharlal Nehru and the Crisis of Modernization', in *Crisis and Change in Contemporary India*, Upendra Baxi and Bhiku Parekh, eds., New Delhi: Sage Publications, 1995.

28. D. Bandhopadhyay, 'Reflections on Land Reforms in India since Independence', in *Social Change and Political Discourse in India*, vol. 2, T.V. Suhrawardy, ed., *Industry and Agriculture in India since Independence*, New Delhi: Oxford University Press.

29. A. Vaidanathan, 'Political Economy of the Evolution of Anti-Poverty Programmes', in *Industry and Agriculture in India since Independence*, T.V. Sathyamurty, ed., fn. 28, 1995.

30. Government of India, Planning Commission (1985), Seventh Five-Year Plan, New Delhi.

31. Surprisingly, a government report admitted that poverty was the product of an economic and social system in which the pursuit of growth had led to a structural dualism; a modern elite-dominated industrial economy and marginalized poverty stricken areas. Government of India, Department of Rural Development (1985). Report of the Committee to Review the Existing Administrative Arrangements for Rural Development and Poverty Alleviation Programme, New Delhi.

32. On the differing responses of the state to the powerful and the powerless. See Niraja Gopal Jayal, *Democracy and the State: Welfare, Secularism and Development in Contemporary India*, New Delhi: Oxford University Press, 1999, chap. 2, pp. 91–100.

33. André Béteille, 'Individualism and Equality', in *Society and Politics in India*, New Delhi: Oxford University Press, 1991, p. 225.

34. Partha Chatterjee, *The Nation and Its Fragments: Colonial and Postcolonial Histories*, New Delhi: Oxford University Press, 1994, pp. 197–9.

35. D.L. Sheth, 'Secularisation of Caste and the Making of a New Middle Class', *Economic and Political Weekly*, vol. 34, nos. 34 and 35, 21–8 August 1999.

36. Partha Chatterjee quoted in Das Gasper, 'From Valued Freedoms, to Politics and Markets: The Capability Approach to Policy Practice', http://www.capability-approach.com/pub/DasGasper.pdf, accessed on 24 September 2012.

4 | Constitutional Equality and the Politics of Representation in India

IT IS WIDELY believed that an historic shift has taken place in the global forms and modes of political representation available to people seeking representation of their interests and social claims. Two changes are noteworthy. From the classic patterns of the earlier twentieth century, based on social relations forged in workplaces, organized in trade unions, and mass organizations linked to programmatic political parties, it has moved to a 'new politics' of social movements, voluntary associations, non-governmental organizations (NGOs), etc., rather than political parties, and local rather than national concerns.[1] The second change is in the process of representation marked by a greater emphasis on descriptive representation and participation in decision-making. Today, equitable and fair-minded policies can be objected to on the grounds that the processes by which they were arrived at were undemocratic and excluded women and minorities, for instance. Even when there are no laws that require it, many political parties have decided their lists are not properly representative without certain numbers of people from different groups.

These global trends are only partially applicable to India but they provide an important context for the discussion of the politics of representation in India. Most accounts of representative democracy in India indicate a deepening of democracy and place considerable emphasis on electoral politics in providing space for the expression of rights and claims by disadvantaged groups. Some political scientists have described electoral politics in the 1990s as the second democratic upsurge (the first having succeeded India's independence from colonial rule).[2] This democratic upsurge has brought political leaders from some of the historically lower and backward castes to centre stage, and significantly voter participation is higher amongst the poorer classes and the less well educated and socially underprivileged castes and classes, unlike in industrialized democracies where participation is biased in the direction of the better educated, more wealthy and advantaged citizen.[3] The increased participation in electoral politics of groups considered most peripheral has come about through political parties even though they are weakly institutionalized.

Contrary to most expectations the needs and interests of people, especially the poorer groups, are met through political parties, and not social movements and NGOs.[4] Available evidence so far highlights a substantial increase in political participation and the continuing importance of parties, both of which underline the strength and legitimacy of the political system. But this evidence also poses difficulties with regard to political representation. Political participation simply does not tell us enough about the status of political equality and citizen efficacy unless we accept the standard formulation that everyone's vote should count as one vote, which means that all are equal. Political equality implying a roughly proportionate distribution of political activity rarely extends to the sphere of representation in crucial decision-making institutions. That is to say, there is no tendency towards equality when it comes to the distribution of power or representative bodies. Political participation, in the form of voting, attending public meetings, participating in demonstrations and rallies is on the increase, but the polity that provided the genuinely equal opportunity to participate in public meetings and so on does not produce the same kind of equality among the people elected.

Representative politics has come to dominate the world of politics since the institutionalization of democracy itself. Political representation may involve either a representative acting for others by virtue of a contract or mandate between them, or it may involve descriptive representation when a person is deemed representative because of personal/social characteristics or both of these, but additionally it has a procedural character, involving the acceptance of general responsibility for the interests of people/constituents. This chapter follows this wider definition and the general principle that the representative does not represent persons as such; rather the representative is charged with the responsibility of seeing that the interests of the constituents are adequately represented in decision-making, and is obliged not only to represent interests, but also to ensure that something is done about the pressing problems of the constituency, for instance in terms of production and implementation of appropriate policies.[5] In short, the representative is accountable to his or her constituency for all acts of omission and commission.

This chapter is organized around the theme of political representation in India. Representation can be assessed in at least two ways: (a) the process of representation and (b) the quality of representation and responsiveness.[6]

Three such groups that have been historically under-represented in politics and for whom there are no electoral reservations are the Other Backward Classes (OBCs), women, and minorities (although the OBCs since 1994 have reservations in public employment).[7] The first section deals with the changing politics of representation in India in the past two decades, the growing demands for proportional representation, and for political inclusion of two influential groups: the Scheduled Castes (SCs) and Scheduled Tribes (STs) and OBCs. In the second section, representation is briefly explored in relation to women and minorities. The third section deals with some reflections on the challenges for political representation in India's diverse democracy.

The aim of the chapter is to account for the varied trajectories of caste, community, and gender in Indian politics through an analysis of the politics of representation, and to consider the limits of the dominant conception of representation as presence.[8] While the earlier form of representation with its focus on a 'politics of ideas' may be an inadequate vehicle for dealing with political exclusion, there is little to be gained by switching to a 'politics of presence'. The main argument developed here is that the politics of presence does not offer a resolution to the problems of under-representation or to the more fundamental issue of the representation of interests of constituents, especially the needs of the most vulnerable. Increasing the political representation of Muslims underscores the point that this may not bring about an equality of outcome, and is therefore not an appropriate focus for government policy. Additionally, changing the social composition of the legislature may have a minimal effect on the structure of party politics, policies and outcomes for the disadvantaged groups. The challenge of representative politics is to try to ensure a link between representatives and those represented, and this is important because it can pave the way for substantive democracy.

The Rhetoric of Representation

Electoral reservation, like job reservation, is one of a series of measures used in India for achieving greater equality of outcome across social groups. These measures are enshrined in the Constitution for the SCs and STs. In addition, reservations were extended to them in education and public employment. Though in 1950, the government's position was that only these two groups were entitled to reservations, it has been extended to the OBCs in education and public employment since 1994, but not in legislatures. More recently, the decentralization measures passed in 1992 introduced electoral reservations for a third category—33 per cent for women in local bodies.[9]

The Constitution and the dominant political discourse in the 1950s installed a specific view of representation, derived from the notion that representatives were supposed to be acting on behalf of the society taken as a whole or the constituency they represented. This was a conception widely shared by the Congress leadership; it allowed no space for descriptive representation. Of all nationalist leaders, Gandhi was the one who personified this view of representation: 'I claim myself in my own person to represent the vast mass of the untouchables. Here I speak not merely on behalf of the Congress, but I speak on my own behalf, and I claim that I would get, if there were a referendum of the untouchables, their vote, and I would top their poll.'[10] B.R. Ambedkar, in contrast, argued that representation of opinions and preferences alone was not an adequate measure for democracy for it required personal representation as well.[11] As early as 1920, Ambedkar had posed the problem of representation faced by untouchables: 'The right of representation and the right to hold office under the state are two most important rights that make up citizenship. However, the untouchability of the untouchables puts these rights far beyond their reach. They [the untouchables] can be represented by the untouchables alone.' For him clearly the general representation of all citizens would not serve the special requirements of the untouchables, because given the prejudices and entrenched practices among the dominant castes, there was no reason to expect the latter would use the law to emancipate themselves. '[A] legislature composed of high caste men will not pass a law removing untouchability, sanctioning intermarriages, removing the ban on the use of public streets, public temples, public schools. . . . This is not because they cannot, but chiefly because they will not.'[12] Gandhi reacted fiercely to the idea that upper caste Congressmen could not properly represent the untouchables, calling it 'the unkindest cut of all'. He insisted that unlike the minorities the issue of untouchability was a problem internal to Hindus and should be resolved by them.[13] Historically, the most significant political dispute with regard to representation was that between Mohammed Ali Jinnah and Jawaharlal Nehru. The differences between the two men were articulated through their very different conceptions of representation. Nehru refused the logic of Jinnah's demand that the Congress treat the Muslim League as the authoritative and representative organization of India's Muslims, a logic that placed immutable identities above changeable interests. For Nehru it was imperative that the Congress should be a movement without exclusive barriers to entry, and should be potentially open to all who subscribed to its principles.

This belief that politicians should work in favour of larger social interests that were not their own dominated the first phase of democratic politics.

Political parties throughout this period were supposed to be a crucial aggregative medium for the articulation of collective interests. Parties in office believed that they should intervene to reform the position of the socially and economically underprivileged.

Underpinning these concerns was a consensus that the state was the most important means for the promotion of public good and well-being. This conception had its origins in ideas and principles of developmental democracy, and extended to the end of the 1960s, over four general elections. Political debates were carried out in terms of conflicts between political ideals of laissez-faire and state intervention, capitalist development, and socialist redistribution. Social classes like the industrialists, managerial elites and middle classes were central to political life and representation. From the late 1970s, the conception of representation underwent very significant changes. The spread of democratic politics, in particular through the means of elections, gave rise to a new form of representation, distinct from the models associated with Gandhi and Nehru. The emerging trend pointed to a shift towards a 'politics of presence'. In this understanding, the political actor claimed to act on behalf of his or her own kind—caste, religion, or linguistic group.[14] Elected politicians saw their duty was not to act on behalf of anyone else but themselves and their own supporters linked by kin, caste, or religion. Descriptive representation by one's own group/ category has gained strength, and consequently, the political discourse has been dominated by ethnic inequalities, which dictate the pattern of mobilization while considerably weakening the earlier language of class interests, capitalism, and socialism.

The emphasis has shifted from objectively defined interests to a much greater focus on identity and distribution of patronage that openly prefers certain groups to others, and thus privileges political presence over common interests. Increased political competition in the late 1980s and 1990s led to a new wave of rhetoric, which seemed to favour the lower castes. The political and administrative importance of caste, the OBCs in particular, which took shape around the demand for reserved quotas in government set the context for these changes. The new strategy of political representation reached its apogee in the wake of former Prime Minister, V.P. Singh's, decision to implement the quota recommendations of the Mandal Commission, which changed the terms of political discourse and brought about the overriding interpretation of electoral representation as descriptive representation. Simultaneously, a range of social movements—including women's, Dalit, and minority movements—signalled similar assertions and demands for recognition and power. The main contribution of the Mandal decision was to make a broad range of castes club together under the OBC label. The new unity helped the OBCs to organize themselves as a powerful group outside the Congress system by using as leverage its main asset: its massive numbers at the time of elections.[15] By giving the lower castes large numbers of tickets and the possibility of a share in power, non-Congress parties addressed the critical issue of the representational blockage in political institutions.[16] Ultimately, the political space for OBCs increased because lower caste voters decided no longer to vote for upper caste candidates put up by parties such as the Congress. The new development lay in the fact that these groups were not content with representation by upper caste elites and they wanted personal representation.[17]

The politics of identity has doubtless contributed to the entry of these groups into the political arena. An important issue, however, is the way government policies and ethnic politics combine to manage and control political outcomes by redefining politically relevant identities and categorizations. From the beginning the definition of backwardness emphasized the centrality of caste based discrimination as the basis of affirmative action and reservation. This raises an important question regarding the extent to which backwardness and disadvantage are essentially about inequalities of the Hindu social structure and not discrimination and deprivation as such. This helps explain why some groups are advantaged more than others independently of traditional notions of political power, and how state policy can reinforce or alter such advantages. The relationship between the conception of backwardness and political power involved questions of entitlement (what are your rights?) and of classification (what group do you belong to and where does it fit the political landscape?) and political representation. It also helps explain why power sharing gets restricted to essentially upper and backward caste groups and not extended to other disadvantaged groups. At the same time, it raises the larger question of how to classify traditionally disadvantaged and under-represented groups, and where to draw the line in terms of caste versus class or caste versus community. In this latter instance it brings up questions about the status of other groups in Indian society, and the extent to which social backwardness is only about Hindu society, which automatically excludes the consideration of other axes of social stratification. The issue is straightforward: should backwardness be defined in terms of ritual and social exclusion or in terms of their social and economic backwardness? The preference was for the former, which ruled out class, community, and gender differences as decisive factors in the determination of public policies. What is more, the official identification of citizens on the basis of caste has the effect of turning caste into a tool of empowerment, even as minority identity, for instance, cannot be used to the advantage of subordinate groups.

India has become much more proportional in its approach than it was under Nehru or Indira Gandhi. This can be seen from the major increase in the number of lower caste legislators and senior civil servants in influential government positions. This has undoubtedly produced a shift in the balance of political power in governments and legislatures. Political representation has a new downward thrust, now prevalent in much of north India, which coincides with similar patterns in south and west India well established by the late 1960s. The share of upper caste legislators in all the legislative assemblies and the national Parliament has been declining and that of the lower castes rising. The backward castes with no legislative reservations constitute more than a quarter of the Lok Sabha today.[18] For parliament, 64 per cent of the north Indian MPs in the first Lok Sabha came from the upper castes and only 4.5 per cent from the OBCs; by 1996, the share of OBC MPs had increased to over 25 per cent.

Minority Representation and the Attendant Challenges

The substantial increase in the representation of backward castes has resulted in an escalation of demands for political representation from other excluded groups, notably women and minorities.[19] The space available to women within the political system has not been significant, despite the growing participation of women in elections and powerful women vying for more power.[20] From 1952 to 1999 over 1,400 women have contested elections and over 365 have been elected to parliament. The number of women candidates contesting on party tickets has fluctuated over time: it declined in the 1970s and rose again in the late 1980s, only to fall off again in the 1990s. These fluctuations correspond to changing trends and patterns of party politics and their perceptions of the women candidates, and it varies from state to state.

Of all the parties, Congress has fielded the most candidates since 1952 and therefore most of the elected candidates have been Congress members. Most parties blame women themselves for their under-representation, that is to say their low 'winnability', even though there is no evidence that women candidates represent a greater risk. For example, in the elections between 1957 and 1996, women running on party tickets won twice as often as they lost. In 1999 women contestants formed only 5.2 per cent of the total contestants but compared to men the success rate of women candidates in major political parties was better.[21] However, parties give low preference to women candidates, even though voters are not disinclined to support their candidacy. Voters have accepted women candidates no differently than a male candidate in the past, which means there are other considerations weighing against the selection of women on party tickets. These include the rising cost of running a campaign and women's capacities in marshalling the necessary resources. With elections becoming more competitive and expensive there is greater struggle for patronage and men had distinct advantages in getting it. They used their political networks and their resources to get access to tickets, party posts, and political influence. Indeed, political parties have often given tickets only to attract 'women's votes' or appeal to 'women's constituency'. It was in the light of this experience and that of several other countries that enhanced women's representation through quotas that the demand for reserved seats for women came up in the 1990s. The Women's Reservation Bill (WRB) proposes to reserve one-third of seats in legislatures for women.[22] Despite strong pressure from women's organizations to introduce reserved constituencies as a method of increasing women's representation, it encountered strong opposition from political parties. What was puzzling was the reluctance of political parties who supported the reservation of seats for women in local bodies to have a similar legislation at the parliamentary level. Doubts were raised over whether reservations of constituencies was the best route, especially given the problems relating to the rotation system. A new scheme under discussion proposes creating additional parliamentary and legislative seats by one-third as a way out of the imbroglio on the WRB. The disinclination to extend quotas to women raises important issues about the relationship of gender and representation on the one hand, and minorities and representation on the other; historically speaking, the latter has been a loaded issue since Partition, while the former gets short shrift on the ground that women do not constitute a category or group.

The controversies surrounding legislative reservations for women, however, form an interesting comparison because there are such striking parallels in their histories, as both the Mandal Commission and the WRB demonstrate. Neither women nor backward classes were entitled to preferential treatment after Independence, but in subsequent decades it became clear that the democratic goals of the nation required more attention to discrimination and exclusion. The government undertook an examination of the status of women and backward classes resulting in two government reports—'Towards Equality' and the Mandal Commission—with two very different outcomes. Both reports echoed the same position about unequal access to education and opportunities but striking differences in reaching their goal. However, the repeated deferment of the WRB shows that gender is not seen as a legitimate political category compared to caste or tribe. Even though the legitimacy of gender as a political category was never questioned, it appeared to be at odds with identity politics. Thus the main arguments against women's reservations continue to be tied to concerns about other disadvantaged groups, namely OBCs and SCs. Between the two the backward castes represent a particularly powerful constituency in democratic politics and the 1990 decision to grant reservations to OBCs in central government jobs increased their political clout.[23] Throughout the debate over women's reservations, caste groupings were given precedence over gender, which is singled out as a problematic category for group-based policies. The gender basis of backwardness is contrasted with caste backwardness, which was still considered a more legitimate political grouping. In other words, the inequalities faced by other communities outweighed those faced by the category of women. Importantly, backwardness and reservation seen as reparation are wholly defined in terms of caste origins and the historical injustice suffered by the lower castes. This national recognition has given the caste-based critiques of women's reservations a political grounding.

Although India's Constitution does not require that minorities will be included in government, there is a national consensus that the dominance of the Congress party after independence allowed minorities to gain effective representation, ensuring minority proportionality in politics, education, and government employment, and giving minorities a veto over decisions harmful to their interests.[24] While the Congress governments regularly offered positions to Muslims it was in no way proportional to their population.[25] Given the exaggerated ideas about the Muslim presence in public life it is hardly surprising that the issue of Muslim under-representation has gone unnoticed, in fact it has gone by default. Muslim representation in all spheres of public life remains far below what their numbers would warrant. On the whole the representation of Sikhs, Christians, and Jains is roughly in proportion to their population. Only Muslim representation continues to be appreciably lower than the proportion of their population, averaging 4 to 6 per cent.[26] Only 10 states have Muslim representation in parliament, and the rest have no representatives from the Muslim community.

More significantly, the success ratio of Muslim candidates slipped from 61 per cent in 1952 to 18-20 per cent in 1991–9.[27] This pattern is explained partly by the demographic distribution of Muslims as compared to other minorities, and partly by the sharply polarized intercommunal situation prevailing in the country.[28] It has also been explained by the majoritarian first-past-the-post electoral system, which helps minorities that are geographically concentrated and not those minorities that are geographically dispersed.[29] Thus, the STs manage to win seats in excess of the quotas reserved for them largely due to the concentrated nature of their population in central and north-east India where they are present in large numbers. Disaggregating constituency data shows one interesting feature and it is this: out of the 406 Muslim MPs elected from 1952 to 1999, only 24 per cent were elected from Muslim majority constituencies, whereas 76 per cent were elected from non-Muslim majority constituencies indicating that significant proportions of non-Muslims were voting for them. There is clear evidence that Muslims can and do win from non-Muslim majority constituencies despite the Hindu–Muslim polarization since 1989. This points to the importance of voting on non-ethnic party lines which means political parties can accommodate minority groups like Muslims.

Despite the striking under-representation of Muslims, the idea of promoting the representation of minorities is very controversial. Historically, the political claims of Muslims are grounded in perceptions of a distinct group identity and interest, and as such are conceived as more threatening to national cohesion. Several Muslim organizations have used the group identity argument to emphasize the need for increasing the representation of Muslims in legislatures and decision-making; they are demanding proportionate representation. This argument gives primacy to identity over differences of opinion and interests. It sees minority identity and security endangered by the lack of an authentic representative voice in legislatures.[30] The identity argument, however, would have to address the question of who the Muslim legislator represents—the people of his constituency, the people of his religious community, or the nation as a whole. According to one leading advocate of Muslim representation:

a Muslim legislator also represents the Muslim community. He acts as a channel of communication between the community and the system. When he promises to carry the legitimate and felt grievances to the powers-that-be, he builds up the confidence that justice will be done. The Muslim legislator is thus both an advocate of the community and a pillar of the system. With his presence in the corridors of power, he is the agent of history for bridging the psychological gap that still exists between the community and the administration.[31]

In this view, the community is defined as an internally coherent monolith, presumed to be devoid of internal differentiation, much less of differences of opinion and interests.

There are at least two ways of addressing under-representation of Muslims: the political and the electoral. With the climate of communalism and confrontation between the Congress party and the BJP in the 1990s and early 2000s, there was little hope that even secular parties would give a proportionate number of seats to Muslims, and so some suggested a remodelling of the electoral system.[32] This system was likely to improve the representation of minorities as political parties would be compelled to give representation to candidates from all the communities and regions on their list and also accord due priorities on it to be able to appeal to the entire electorate.[33] There were two options here: one was through a semi-proportionate system to ensure that Muslim representation in the legislature goes up substantially; the second was simply a careful delimitation of constituencies that produces Muslim plurality constituencies enabling under-represented groups to get a fair chance of election.[34] There were two objections levelled against it. First, it would engender ethnification of the party system and if this gave rise to social polarization, as for instance in Sri Lanka, then minorities would suffer isolation despite more proportional representation. In other words, the prospect of legislative majoritarianism would easily offset the gains from proportionality in representation. Second, this system though much more representative may not be effective in India in the absence of a properly institutionalized party system. Only a democratic party can ensure that candidates are given tickets on merit and seats from where they stand a good chance of winning. Also it works best in small countries with a maximum of three to four parties. It has been pointed out that even the delimitation of constituencies would achieve Muslim representation at the cost of reducing the clout of Muslim electorate in the remaining constituencies. The fear is that minority voters would become a national constituency—equivalent to a separate electorate—which will become the restricted sphere of influence of minority parties.[35] All this has to be weighed against the aggregative potential of the single-member plurality systems. Developments in the realm of communal politics in the past decade show that the protection of minorities has occurred when minorities have been able to rely on majority support, rather than acting alone as minorities. Instead of mainstreaming the community this would lead to the further segregation of Muslims. Party lists should assign fairly high priority to giving proportional representation to minority candidates. This will induce parties to internalize minority concerns and at the same time encourage minority voters to opt for mainstream parties.

The Challenges for Political Representation

We must therefore ask the implications of these shifts in the representative process are and what the representatives have been able to do with political power. Electoral competition between political parties and participation is flourishing, and political power has moved downward, a development that cannot be taken lightly. The political elite is not monolithic. To understand representation however, we need to look at how the representatives in the political system exercise power, that is, it should be judged against the criteria of both processes of participation and outcomes. Outcomes should be assessed in terms of the extent to which the well-being and interests of the constituents are advanced. Whilst backward caste mobilization has successfully challenged upper caste/class domination, the experience of the north Indian states of Uttar Pradesh and Bihar would suggest that the achievement of power was rarely translated into policy outcomes which are pro-poor in the socio-economic sense, or the implementation of policies and programmes that address the vital concerns of the disadvantaged. Lacking a broad-based social vision they often end up as sectarian struggles, which cannot challenge the structures of privilege and exploitation. Further, an over-emphasis on descriptive representation could weaken the basis for political accountability.

More compelling is the argument that it undermines a politics of general interest and shared concerns. Consequently, it has invariably resulted in promoting personal empowerment, rather than more positive outcomes. In other words, descriptive representation achieves little more than the empowerment of elites. We need to look closely at the informal structures of power and see how the actors in the political system exercise power. This entails an examination of the relationship between class power in society and political power. A number of studies of rural Uttar Pradesh have revealed clear differences regarding formal and informal access to land, access to lucrative non-agricultural jobs, and ties to the state apparatus, among caste groups. Much like the dominant castes in Andhra Pradesh, Maharashtra, and Gujarat, the Jats and the upper OBCs have achieved sufficient upward mobility since the green revolution, and used their economic advantage to gain public employment. They managed to obtain these benefits through connections with politicians often acting as intermediaries between the public and the administration.

The important point is that their political success is closely linked to their economic power, which they can leverage to secure state privileges, such as police and legal intervention in defending agricultural land or improving low wages for farm workers. They have been able to take advantage of identity politics and backward caste mobilization to advance their interests.

A recent study of electoral reservation for SCs and STs calls into question the extent to which the MPs and MLAs elected from reserved constituencies can effectively represent the interests of SCs and STs. Even though there are very few systematic attempts to measure the impact of electoral reservations in terms of their wider socio-economic and policy implications, one analysis that looks at reservations and policy outcomes shows that there is no positive relationship between the number of SC and ST legislators on government performance measured in terms of total expenditure, education spending or land reform legislation and implementation.[36] There is, however, a positive relationship between the proportion of ST legislators in a state and the amount of welfare spending targeted at the STs. There is no such relationship in the case of the proportion of SC legislators and spending on SC welfare.[37] The ST representatives are more effective due to the concentration of the tribal population in particular constituencies—their political strength is built upon local tribal support. But this study does show that the proportion of SCs and STs has a positive impact on the level of job quotas, although this would benefit the 'creamy layer' among the targeted groups. The best effect of electoral reservation has been to provide a guaranteed minimum number of legislators from the SCs and STs and that it provides representation for a group that would not otherwise get adequate representation.

Although the debate on political representation and the form it should take remains inconclusive, rival positions have marshalled arguments about the implications of different conceptions of representation, and this chapter will therefore conclude with three main arguments. The first concerns the shift from the representation of ideas and policies to representation as presence and its broader political implications. Representation as presence has always existed in India, both among and within parties. Within the dominant Congress party, particular social groups won more positions on party lists and organization but overall there was an attempt to maintain a balance between ideas and presence. Now most political parties give priority to representation as presence. This could over-politicize group differences, thereby disrupting political stability, weaken the basis for political accountability, and undermine representation aimed at promoting the general interests and shared concerns, which might also have policy implications. Such a shift towards identity politics has exacerbated social conflicts and advanced the politicization of social cleavages. Indeed, the most overtly conflictual aspects of Indian politics have in recent years been those related to ascriptive identity politics, variously, Punjab, Assam, Kashmir, Ayodhya, and Mandal. It has reduced accountability and damaged responsiveness because presence becomes a value in itself at the expense of interests, principles, and ideas.

The second concerns proportionality in the process of representation and the varied trajectories of gender and minority as categories/groups in enhancing their presence in decision-making structures. Several factors account for the problems with regard to increasing the representation of women and minorities. The comparison between women and OBCs, and between Muslims and OBCs, is useful because it shows that although women constitute half the population and Muslims are a numerically large minority, they cannot harness their numbers in the absence of political mobilization and the readiness of political parties to give them nominations.

Indeed, the political empowerment of OBCs in Uttar Pradesh is a significant reminder in this regard because it shows that they first mobilized through political formations and then went on to demand reservations. The category of women illustrates the difficulty of building a political identity based on gender, but when we look at the problem in a larger time-frame then we can see that reservations do play the role of a catalyst in the construction of political identities. In other words, SCs, STs, and OBCs have become political categories through reservations. True, women are heterogeneous and divided by caste, class, religion, and region, but so are the OBCs, and yet they have overcome this heterogeneity and dispersal thanks to political mobilization and reservations, which has been crucial to their political success along with representation.[38]

Reservations have not been extended to other disadvantaged groups because the official conceptions of backwardness draw from a representation of Indian society mainly in terms of its caste-based social stratification. The inequalities of gender and class consistently get discounted, as do the disadvantages of belonging to a particular religious minority when they are incompatible with caste. Not surprisingly, Indian politics has shown time after time that caste and caste-like groupings, such as the OBCs, tend to prevail over gender and minority identity (though the latter prevail in relation to personal laws, etc.). This has been reinforced because: 'The influx of lower orders into the field of democratic contestation has . . . (made) it respectable to talk of caste in the public domain. The emergence of social justice as a rubric to talk about caste equity (and) political representation of castes and communities. . . is a distinct achievement of this period.'[39]

The uncomfortable questions thrown up by the WRB and Muslim under-representation have been invariably located in a template of group identities. But there are difficulties in defining the exact characteristics of group identity in any coherent way.[40] The politicization of identity has worked most successfully in the case of SCs and STs because it has been used as part of a broader and more complex conception of social and economic backwardness.[41] Above all, the expression of identity takes a more practical conception of political identity in terms of government policies and programmes. Seen in these terms, political identities can be related to the ideological and social bases of parties and whether they are broadly based or based on narrower social/ethnic constituencies. Issues of group representation, therefore, should be approached in terms of their political consequences and outcomes, rather than abstract and essentially contested, conceptions of group identity and development.[42]

The third argument pertains to the substance of representation. While much of the justification for electoral reservation revolves around the need for marginalized groups to have a voice within the legislature which will otherwise get submerged, there is little systematic evidence to show that representatives elected from these seats have performed this role effectively. Special representation in governing institutions may not benefit the whole community, and it invariably results in promoting the personal empowerment of the middle classes and elites, and the transfer of resources to them. It may just create a new elite among the disadvantaged who participate with society's elite. Foregrounding group claims can result in bypassing equality in a more fundamental sense. It has the important effect of preventing fundamental change, such as land reform, because the new elite now has a stake in the existing system. However, this should not rule out measures such as electoral reservations for women or modifications in the electoral system to increase the presence of excluded groups because making political elites more representative is an important objective that stands on its own, even if it does not result in social redistribution or increasing the weight attached to the concerns of the disadvantaged. But even as proportionate presence in the higher echelons can be seen to have symbolic effects, it is only one of the strategies required to achieve substantive equality and policy outcomes. Increasing the presence of excluded groups is insufficient to ensure that these groups are better represented. There is no guarantee that changing the composition of political elites would change the substance of representation. What matters is substantive representation where representatives actually represent the interests of their constituents. Today, the limiting conditions are not social backwardness per se, or the social background of representatives, but rather the power structures themselves and materially there is no change in the power structures. It may well be that the overemphasis on electoral politics and representation as presence is producing a space that does not allow democracy to take on the radical shape of substantive democracy. By its very nature representation as presence does not have a broad transforming agenda. It is a politics of positional change, not structural reform.

Notes and References

1. John Harriss, 'Political Participation, Representation and the Urban Poor: Findings from Research in Delhi', *Economic and Political Weekly*, vol. XL, no. 11, 12 March 2005.
2. Yogendra Yadav, 'Electoral Politics in the Time of Change; India's Third Electoral System, 1989-99', *Economic and Political Weekly*, 21-8 August-3 September 1999, pp. 2393–9.

3. Membership of political parties went up between 1971 and 1998, and participation in political activities like attendance at election meetings more than doubled in the same period. According to the Centre for the Study of Developing Societies (CSDS) survey of political attitudes, the number of those who said they were members of political parties almost doubled between 1971 and 1996. For more details see Yogendra Yadav, 'Understanding the Second Democratic Upsurge', in *Transforming India: Social and Political Dynamics of Democracy,* ed. Francine Frankel et al., Delhi: Oxford University Press, 2000, pp. 134–5.

4. For example see findings of the survey reported by Harriss, 'Political Participation'.

5. Neera Chandhoke, 'Crisis of representative democracy', *The Hindu,* 19 June 2004.

6. Ibid.

7. Alistair McMillan, *Standing at the Margins: Representation and Electoral Reservation in India,* Delhi: Oxford University Press, 2005, pp. 6-7.

8. Anne Philips, *Politics of Presence,* Oxford: Clarendon Press, 1995, p. 25.

9. Stephanie Tawa Lama-Rewal, 'Fluctuating, Ambivalent Legitimacy of Gender as a Political Category', *Economic and Political Weekly,* vol. XXXVI, no. 17, 28 April 2001, pp. 1435-40.

10. Gandhi, *Autobiography,* Boston: Beacon Press, 1993.

11. For a discussion of Ambedkar's ideas on the subject see Valerian Rodrigues, 'Ambedkar on preferential treatment', *Seminar,* no. 545, May 2005, pp. 56-8.

12. Cited in Gail Omvdt, *Dalits and the Democratic Revolution: Dr Ambedkar and the Dalit Movement in Colonial India,* Delhi: Sage, 1994, p. 146.

13. Ravinder Kumar, 'Gandhi, Ambedkar and the Poona Pact, 1932', in *Struggling and Ruling: The Indian National Congress, 1885-1985,* ed. Jim Masselos, New Delhi: Sterling Publishers, 1987.

14. Sunil Khilnani, 'The Indian Constitution and Democracy', in *India's Living Constitution: Ideas, Practices, Controversies,* ed. Zoya Hasan, E. Sridharan and R. Sudarshan, Delhi: Permanent Black, 2002, pp. 73-4.

15. Khilnani, 'Constitution and Democracy', p. 98.

16. This point has been emphasized by Kanchan Chandra, 'The Transformation of Ethnic Politics in India: The Decline of Congress and the Rise of Bahujan Samaj Party in Hoshiarpur', *Journal of Asian Studies,* vol. 59, no. 1, February 2000.

17. Chandra, 'Transformation of Ethnic Politics', pp. 54-5.

18. Christophe Jaffrelot, 'The Rise of Backward Classes in the Hindi Belt', *Journal of Asian Studies,* vol. 59, no. 1, February 2000.

19. On women's representation see Tawa Lama-Rewal, 'Gender as a Political Category', pp. 1435-40.

20. Approximately 365 women MPs between 1952 and 2000 is not a bad record and is more than many comparable states. Over time India has been losing ground as other countries have increased the political representation of women quite dramatically mainly through some form of quotas. Only seven countries have achieved the critical mass of 30 per cent: Sweden, Norway, Denmark, Finland, South Africa, The Netherlands, and Germany. In all these countries quotas have ensured that women constitute a certain number on candidate lists, both parliamentary and committee.

21. Data from 'Towards Equality. The Unfinished Agenda: Status of Women in India 2001', National Commission for Women, Government of India, New Delhi, 2002, pp. 287-8.

22. The Women's Reservation Bill proposes to reserve one-third of the seats in legislatures for women. Doubts have been raised over whether reservations of constituencies is the best route, especially given the problems relating to the rotation system. Many observers have argued that the alternative of a mandatory quota of tickets for women by every recognized political party would be superior and more efficacious. However, women's organizations and many women MPs have expressed grave misgivings that this would result in party bosses limiting women to the seats they cannot win.

23. Tawa Lama-Rewal, 'Gender as a Political Category'.

24. For example, Arendt Lijphart the proponent of consociational theory makes this argument (see Arendt Lijphart, 'The Puzzle of Indian Democracy: A Consociational Interpretation', *American Political Science Review*, vol. 90, no. 2, 1996.

25. Steven Wilkinson, 'India, Consociational Theory, and Ethnic Violence', *Asian Survey*, vol. xl, no. 5, September/October 2000.

26. Niraja Gopal Jayal, 'A Malevolent Embrace? The BJP and Muslims in the Parliamentary Election of 2004', *India Review*, vol. 3, no. 3, July 2004, pp. 187-90.

27. This information is based on E. Sridharan, 'Elections and Muslim Representation in India', unpublished, mimeo, December 2004.

28. Ibid.

29. E. Sridharan, 'Does India Need to Switch to Proportional Representation: The Pros and Cons', in *Recasting Indian Politics: Essays on a Working Democracy*, ed. Paul Flather, London: Palgrave, 2006.

30. Several Muslim MPs during the debate on the Shah Bano controversy questioned the legislative competence of parliament to legislate on personal laws.

31. Syed Shahabuddin, *Muslim India*, July 1985.

32. Congress leader Salman Khurshid, President of the Uttar Pradesh Congress Committee, has been advocating a change to Proportional Representation (PR) system, *The Hindu*, 25 January 2005.

33. In the event of under-representation of particular groups, seats could be allotted from the party lists according to the percentage of votes received by parties. However, under this system the representation of the disadvantaged critically depends on whether the open or closed lists systems are followed. The former allows strategic voting and facilitates minorities getting representation for their candidates. In the open list the parties mention the names of candidates, which enables voters to give their preferences, while in the closed system the voter does not have a choice and has to exercise preferences for the party and not the candidate. In the latter, representation depends on internal democracy and the accommodative politics practised within parties. Sridharan, 'Proportional Representation'.

34. Yogendra Yadav 'Electoral Reforms: Beyond Middle Class Fantasies', *Seminar*, no. 440, April 1996, p. 20.

35. Ibid., p. 62.

36. Rohini Pande's study discussed in McMillan, *Standing at the Margins*, p. 198.

37. Ibid.

38. See Prakash Louis, 'Safeguards or Segregation? Reservations for the Scheduled Castes in Bihar'; Bhupinder Singh, 'The Policy of Reservations for Scheduled Tribes'; and K.S. Narayana, 'Reservations for Backward Classes in Karnataka's

Panchayati Raj Institutions' all in *Electoral Reservations, Political Representation and Social Change in India: A Comparative Perspective,* Stephanie Tawa Lama-Rewal, ed., Delhi: Manohar Publishers, 2004.

39. Yadav, 'Electoral Politics', pp. 2393–9.

40. McMillan, *Standing at the Margins,* pp. 310–11.

41. One recent study focusing on the role of political identity argues that the representation of Dalit interests has come not from elected representatives from reserved constituencies but from a Dalit party, the BSP. On this see Sudha Pai, 'A Quest for Identity through Politics: The Scheduled Castes in Uttar Pradesh', in Tawa Lama-Rewal, *A Comparative Perspective,* 2004.

42. Ibid.

5 | Region and Nation in India's Political Transition

During the 1990s Indian politics were marked by a struggle between two rival conceptions of the nation: one wanted to establish a unicultural nation to be governed by a strong centre; the other argued that India was a social mosaic that could be sustained by a democratic and federal structure held in place by strong states. Strains between national and regional identity, and the unsatisfactory functioning of federalism, constituted the underlying base of these differences. At the heart of these differences were varying conceptions of modern India and the struggle to reconstitute the state and society in a more secular and federal direction on the one hand, and in a more conservative and unitary direction on the other.

Scholars and journalists writing about Indian politics have paid most attention to the apex or the centre—who controls the leadership at the top—as if those at the summit of power speak and act for the entire system of state organizations and different levels of governance in the polity. Not enough attention has been paid to the political changes at the regional/state level, contestations between the states and the centre, and how the state/region rather than the centre is reshaping the polity. This chapter examines the emerging relationship between nation and region by exploring the process of regionalization as triggered by social change and upward mobility in the states, explores the shifts in the structure of party politics induced by the institutional and ideological decline of the Congress party, and assesses their impact on the political order in India. Political trends during the 1990s have shown that we should not overemphasize the centre or major battles among large-scale social classes/forces operating at some grand level. Struggles on multiple planes and especially at the regional level provide the key to understanding the major transitions in Indian politics. The political system is rapidly moving from a centralized system toward a multi-layered distribution of political and economic powers. Many aspects of the unfolding political scenario are indicative of greater democratization and empowerment, yet there are many issues of equity and growth, both regionally and individually, that the emerging polity does not necessarily have answers to.

The Changing Relationship between Centre and State

The priority of the political leadership presiding over the transition from colonialism was to weld together a unified nation-state from culturally and linguistically distinct and economically disparate regions. Consequently, the Constitution and the policymakers, especially Jawaharlal Nehru, followed ideologies of social transformation and composite nationalism to integrate all strands of the people. Religion, culture, and language were accommodated as long as the various groups did not make demands for recognition as corporate groups in state and society. The linguistic reorganization of the states was the single most important policy in this period to facilitate the process of accommodation of both national and regional identities.[1] The combination of composite nationalism and linguistic reorganization, in conjunction with a centralized state committed to the goal of planned economic development and social transformation, managed to check any reassertion of centrifugal tendencies for the first two decades after Independence. The dominance of the Congress party at the centre and in the states also helped in creating political homogeneity between the two arenas.[2] Granville Austin in his assessment of the functioning of the Constitution in the first two decades noted that 'Congress ministries had not aggrandized their authority at the expense of constitutional government either in the states or in New Delhi'.[3] In effect, the powers of the central government were not abused or misused.

However, the project of integrating the nation through the centralizing drives of the state ran into rough weather in the post-1967 period. Some of the tensions at that time related to cultural diversities, but more often, conflicts were generated by uneven economic and political development. Nevertheless, during the 1960s the centre demonstrated elements of flexibility and pragmatism in dealing with the regional opposition. As a result, Tamil nationalism—the first major expression of nationality centred opposition—was accommodated within the parameters of the Indian Union, a process no doubt facilitated by the Dravida Munnetra Kazhagam's (DMK) electoral triumph in the 1967 elections. The centre also succeeded in neutralizing secessionist movements in Nagaland and Mizoram through a combination of coercion and development funds that helped to consolidate a regional elite whose aspirations shifted from independence to autonomy to centre-sponsored development.[4]

A new dimension was added to centre-state relations in the 1980s, which had until then been dominated by differences over an interpretation of the Constitution and dissatisfaction with the distribution of powers between the centre and states.[5] Regional autonomy from New Delhi in financial, administrative, and political matters now became the key issue in confrontations between the centre and states. Regional politics acquired a new force with the rise of militancy in Punjab, Assam, and Kashmir.[6] Led by regional elites who mobilized cultural identities, rather than just economic grievances or political discrimination by the centre, these movements demanded greater autonomy from the centre and in some cases even sovereignty. At stake in all three conflicts was the varying conception of the single unified nation, which was pitted against the demands for autonomy and independence. The central government's counter-offensive, based primarily on coercion and a majoritarian ideology of national unity, complicated the political terrain in all the border states.

The operation of Indian federal politics since Independence has basically given rise to three kinds of regional assertions, all with very different implications for adaptation in the polity. The first, mentioned earlier, are the militant movements in Kashmir, Punjab, and Assam, which have been directed against an overpowering centre and have claimed varying degrees of autonomy and independence from the Indian state. In at least two of these instances of political conflict, region and nation have been on a collision course, representing a break in the accepted conception of a unified nation. The second type of regional assertion, which is grounded in the distinctiveness and underdevelopment of regions—Uttarakhand, Chhattisgarh, and Jharkhand—demands autonomy within the Indian federal framework. The third is the regional assertions of those whose area of operation coincides with the federal territorial division of the union. In this category can be grouped centre-state and inter-state conflicts, that is, tensions in which the state government is the leading agent.[7] These assertions, impelled as they are by an aspiration for a change in centre-state relations and the devolution of powers to the states are not quite autonomy movements. At the forefront of demands for a greater voice in national policy and decision-making are Tamil Nadu, Andhra Pradesh, Karnataka, West Bengal, and Assam.

The emergence of these regional pressures should be seen in the context of the defeat of the Congress in the 1967 elections and the formation of non-Congress governments in several states. To reverse this trend, Indira

Gandhi shattered the boundaries between the centre and states and sought to control the Congress and states through central domination.[8] The keystone of her political strategy was an unprecedented centralization of power, within the ruling party, within the prime minister's office, and excluding parliament and cabinet from decision-making.[9] The Emergency accelerated the concentration of power within the offices in New Delhi. The specific measures taken by Indira Gandhi to centralize political authority most crucially involved severing the link between parliamentary and legislative assembly elections, the selection of chief ministers by her advisers in New Delhi rather than by the state legislative parties, and frequent impositions of President's rule in various states to influence state politics. The principal effect of these policies was felt even by the Congress party, but its centrality in the political arena ensured that its actions nevertheless transformed the relationship of the centre to the states by decreasing their relevance and that of the districts as critical arenas of political competition and mobilization independent of the centre.[10] This strategy proved to be counterproductive in managing tensions and cleavages for it made the Congress more vulnerable by undermining the regional leadership of the party, thus eroding the foundations of the autonomy necessary for a centrist party operating in a heterogeneous society.[11] This marked a departure from past trends: since the 1930s, a combination of strong central command and relatively independent provincial leadership has been the spindle of the Congress machine.

Democratic functioning within the Congress declined all through the 1970s and 1980s, just when democracy was assuming a new importance in the polity and civil society.[12] The defeat of the Congress party in the 1977 elections brought about further changes in centre-state relations. A new feature of the post-1977 period was greater competition between political parties and also greater social polarization in the states. This reduced the room for manoeuvre for the central government since the control of the centre itself was beginning to be contested. During this period, the Congress party continued to wield power over a highly centralized state but its political authority was greatly reduced in the states. This opened up the space for new alignments to reinforce the growing opposition in the states.

Central control reached unprecedented levels in the context of worsening government-opposition relations between 1974-84. The demands of states for greater participation in policy processes were met with stiffening controls and a continuation of the centralized set-up. One effect of excessive centralization was manifest in the continually shrinking support base of national parties, and the rise of regional parties to power at the state level,[13] the most dramatic example being the electoral success of Telugu Desam in Andhra Pradesh in the 1982 Assembly elections. The rise of Telugu Desam indicated that regionalism could be kindled simply by the discernment of political discrimination or centralized decision-making by the centre.[14] Against this new development, the non-Congress chief ministers of Andhra Pradesh, Karnataka, West Bengal, and Jammu & Kashmir organized several conclaves in 1983-4 with the explicit purpose of creating a united anti-Congress front. Their chief demand was a fundamental renegotiation of centre-state relations and the vesting of greater powers in the states.

The central government however continued to intrude into spheres reserved for the states to the part that several felt aggrieved that they were getting a raw deal from the centre. By the early 1990s, there was substantial resentment towards the excessive centralization of economic and political power. Alienation and disaffection was strengthened by the failure of the central government in lessening regional disparities or levelling out economic inequalities.

The basic issue was the imbalance in the economic equation between the centre and the states which was heavily tilted in favour of the centre. States received a rather small share of the central pool of taxes.[15] In 1995-6 the states' share of the gross tax revenue of the centre was little over 20 per cent.[16] Apart from taxes, only 40 per cent of the funds given to the states are decided by the Finance Commission, a statutory body, while the larger share is decided by the Planning Commission, an executive body, which increases the scope for arbitrariness. As for resource transfer to states and central assistance to state plans, in 1996 only 30 per cent of the Rs. 62 crores set aside for this was given to state plans; the rest went to central plans.[17] Not surprisingly, states were discontented. Assam was sore it could not benefit from its own resources like coal, oil, and natural gas; Karnataka's chief minister asked for quick clearance of power projects in view of the power crisis in the state, but the centre would not oblige; Maharashtra complained that it received too meagre an amount from the central divisible tax pool; Telugu Desam chief ministers believed that poverty in Andhra Pradesh could be tackled by the Rs. 2 per kg. rice scheme whereas the centre wanted them to implement an employment generation programme like the Jawahar Rozgar Yojana.[18]

Critical changes in Indian politics generated by the expansion of democratic politics and the persistence of militant movements in the north-east, Punjab, and Kashmir prompted some rethinking on questions of regional autonomy. The centre was compelled to entertain these demands owing to the various ramifications for national unity. Attempts were made to resolve them through a series of high level 'Accords' such as the Assam and Punjab Accords.[19] Greater autonomy in decision-making was promoted with the democratic decentralization and revitalization of local self-government institutions, through the devolution of power to elected panchayats in 1991, and with the creation of autonomous councils for Jharkhand and Gorkhaland in the early 1990s.[20] On the whole the Indian state could claim considerable success in nation-building at this time—it was able to incorporate regional dissensions using the persuasive and coercive means at its disposal. These initiatives did not however mitigate the desire to create centres of autonomous power.

The Political Transformation (1989-97)

To understand why this was the case requires examination of the changes in the polity caused by the decline of Congress hegemony. At the centre of the political transformation from 1989-97 was the crumbling of the Congress system had which for over four decades occupied a position of dominance both at the national level and in the states. By the 1996 elections, the Congress party had not been able to win a national majority since 1984, and even that mandate was secured in the context of an emotional wave generated by Indira Gandhi's assassination. Realignments caused by the Ayodhya and Mandal issues had shrunk the party's social base and reduced their vote share to an unprecedented low of 28 per cent in 1996.[21] In contrast, the aspiring Bharatiya Janata Party (BJP) which won seats in 12 states in 1996, had become mainly strong in the northern states. Ironically, for a party claiming to replace the Congress at the all-India level, the principal reason for its improved performance at that time was the regional concentration of its support in Uttar Pradesh, Haryana, Rajasthan, Maharashtra, Gujarat, and Karnataka. By contrast the Congress' weakness stemmed from its national spread: it won seats in 26 of 31 states.[22]

The most striking feature of the 1996 elections was the spectacular rise of regional parties and the challenge posed by these alterations to the 'nationalization of politics' which had gained ascendancy in the previous two decades.[23] As the importance of regional and state parties began to emerge and government formation became rather dependent on them, one newspaper report in May 1996 quipped that 'the world's largest democracy now has the distinction of electing the world's largest opposition'. This summed up the dramatic political change which had occurred with the polity shifting from a dominant party system to a minority and multiparty system. Similarly, the 1998 elections also revealed how much Indian democracy had changed in the previous ten years. It confirmed the tendency towards regionalization that had been apparent since the 1989 elections which propelled the National Front coalition government of V.P. Singh to power. About 200 seats in the Twelfth Lok Sabha went to parties that had essentially local or regional support. What emerged then, was a multiparty system involving the Congress, BJP, and regional parties. However, the combination of parties differed from state to state and this not only intensified political conflict at the state level but also complicated the transition to a post-Congress polity at the national level.[24]

These momentous changes were partly an outcome of specific social and political circumstances in different states propelling the growth of contending regional formations with their own social and political agendas. The process of change was closely linked to the differential dynamics of Congress decline, and to the emergence of specific regional and vernacular discourses that have eroded centralized political authority.

This decentring of politics has shifted focus from New Delhi to the states with their distinct political cultures and discourses, and their caste-class and caste-community mobilization and alliances. The single most important source of change was the entry of hitherto peripheral groups into the political system. This was the result of the immense social awakening among the lower castes and Dalits, particularly in north India—a region that for decades constituted the citadel of the upper-caste dominated Congress system.

The centrepiece of Congress hegemony was the politics of social consensus and a strategy of mobilization which aggregated the interests of different sections of society on the basis of an inclusive ideological package of nationalism, secularism, and the Nehruvian version of socialism. The Congress operated as a centrist party, representing no single category of interest, and its coalitional character enabled it to attract a wide range of individuals and groups. The party was able to rule for so long because it deftly persuaded the lower orders to believe that existing political arrangements worked in their interests, whereupon the business of governance could be left to the Congress. From the 1980s however, its claims to ideological leadership were challenged by the counter-hegemonies that were generated by new social forces. The crucial question for them was not the failure to accommodate the claims and counter-claims of the backward and lower castes for power-sharing, but the very structure of representation and centre-state relations, which was at odds with the way groupings now wanted to conduct political business and representation. People preferred to invoke the strength of caste and community, or regional majorities on the ground; they wanted to be represented by their own community/regional leaders. However, the decline of the Congress also meant the decline of a particular type of politics organized around a universalist secular-nationalist discourse.

Marking a break from the presuppositions of this discourse were competing attempts to redefine political identity. The Hindu Right made the most infuential attempt to redefine political identity. The Ayodhya movement played a crucial part in the reconstruction. The 'Ayodhya strategy' succeeded in winning new adherents largely because the BJP and affilitated organizations seized the opportunity provided by the communal compromises made by the Congress to arrest its own decline in the 1980s. The escalation of political competition from the late 1970s saw the Congress appealing to community identities. Unable to respond to the groundswell of social discontent and opposition graving in civil society, the Congress chose the easier option of stoking majoritarian and minoritarian politics. This shift, though prompted by electoral compulsions, was part of the retreat from the central principles of the Nehruvian project and the long-term decline in the secularity of the state. The BJP took advantage of this to rework the balance of power by taking the communal issue beyond the boundaries set by the Congress, and thus forcing open the ambivalences in the relationship between secular and communal politics. Its main appeal however, was to the insecurities of those in the upper castes who were willing to switch allegiances after the decline of the Congress. The destruction of the Babri Masjid by Hindu extremists in December 1992 persuaded many in the lower castes that this was an upper caste backlash against the Mandal move by the Janata Dal government. In the post-demolition period, caste assertions signalled an attempt by marginal groups to claim the middle ground vacated by Congress decline. They combined with other subaltern groups to strengthen their own bargaining position vis-à-vis national parties and the bigger parties in the states. Consequently, the political map was dotted with regional, state, and locally-based parties. Their leaders perceived the politics of regionalization and fragmentation as the best chance to transform their control over vote banks into autonomous power at the state and at the national level.[25]

Congress and Regional Politics

The internal decimation of the Congress weakened its control over regional politics; if anything, regular central interference in regional politics bolstered disgruntlement with the Congress which fuelled regional aspirations of autonomy from Congress domination.[26] The broader impetus for regionalization could be traced to the rapid pace of socio-economic change from the 1970s giving rise to strains and pressures, and the dissatisfaction of new groups with the Nehruvian paradigm. The early contours of this challenge were epitomized in the 1970s by Charan Singh's critique of the urban–industrial–metropolitan policy of the Congress and the upper-caste dominated power structure. Initially, the sub-national and sub-state pressure directed against the Congress and the centre (or both) came mainly from the agrarian surplus producers who were the chief beneficiaries of the growing commercialization of agriculture. The new rural bloc accused the centre and state governments of being biased in favour of urban India and sought a place for its non-farming members in the government and state bureaucracies. Over the years they courted alternative political formations and resorted to mass agitations to enhance their influence, knowing full well that they stood to gain the most from the success of non-class farmers or regional movements in which all groups or classes participated.

There were other regional assertions which combined popular grievances with elements of political manipulation from above. Many of the leaders of regional movements sought to use their political authority to accumulate wealth and power in order to become part of the regional economic elite. Besides the agrarian bourgeoisie whose interests were demarcated regionally,[27] significant sections of the urban middle classes also benefited from the greater decentralization of power, greater industrialization or investment of public resources, or the state getting a greater share of central resources. State governments employ millions of people and very often, public employment exceeds that offered by large-scale industry. State-based linguistic exclusivity, articulated by the Shiv Sena type of 'sons-of-the-soil' movement in Maharashtra or the Assamese movement against the influx of foreigners' favours the urban middle classes seeking government employment.[28] This was true of linguistic politics in most states and was partly a result of the success of the regional language policy which produced new generations of youth who had no exposure to any other language except the vernacular and who as a result, could not hope to gain employment in any state except their own. The new middle classes thrown up by the two decades of economic change across the small towns of India up to the 1990s were vernacular in culture and many of them have used regionalism for the fulfilment of economic and political aspirations of upward mobility.[29]

The close connection between new regional bourgeoisie and business groups and regional parties in the 1990s demonstrated the social character of many of the regional upsurges. Parties such as the DMK and Telugu Desam became powerful advocates of regional business interests. Agrarian change and agricultural growth played a critical part in shaping the process of capitalist development in the regions and in creating the new class of regional capitalists, who in the post–Green Revolution period from the late 1970s moved into industry. Typically, such businessmen were born in agrarian merchant/trading, moneylending, or professional middle class families and invariably have agrarian and rural roots.[30] They are often first or second generation business families and have moved into areas like cement, sugar, pharmaceuticals, and electronics backed by the state governments and public financial institutions. They promote regional political parties to gain support and leverage with foreign investors and national big business.

Regional pressures certainly shifted the centre of regional gravity to the more prosperous states of southern and western India, with capital accumulating and gravitating there in new industries, new information technologies, research, and development complexes. The relatively higher level of economic development in these states demonstrated the benefits of regional assertion, which had clearly helped in building broad-based political affinities that could then make claims on the central government to augment development opportunities and public investment. Both the state and central governments intervened to support industrial enterprise in states where the regional capitalists were already influential: for example, Gujarat, Maharashtra, Karnataka, Tamil Nadu, Andhra Pradesh, Punjab, and Haryana. In contrast the four north Indian states of Uttar Pradesh, Bihar, Madhya Pradesh, and Rajasthan, though they accounted for nearly one-third of the members of Parliament, had neither singly nor collectively pulled their weight in favour of economic development at that time.

The most visible outcome of the struggle for economic and political power was an increase in government representation of the vernacular elite who established themselves at local and regional levels. It was illustrated in the strategic shift from protests against the symbols of Brahman domination, to an appropriation and consolidation of political power through an acquisition of economic clout, control over the educational system, and jobs in the government sector. The scale of the transfer of power, and indeed the social constellations which gave rise to these shifts, varied from state to state, but the unmistakable aftermath of regionalization was the displacement of upper castes from positions of power and the rise to power of intermediate classes and castes. This had already happened in Tamil Nadu, Karnataka, Andhra Pradesh, Kerala, Gujarat and Maharashtra and then began in Bihar, Madhya Pradesh and Uttar Pradesh.

One feature of this political transformation was the diffusion of power downwards and greater autonomy and power for the states.[31] The emergence of states as pathways to power marked a decisive change from Indira Gandhi's regime under which the centre was deliberately given priority over the states. Then, the centre was the most important avenue for a quick rise to power, whereas by the 1990s states were strong and new groups found that they could quickly establish their dominance through control of the state arena.

Three principal changes need to be examined the centre was not pre-eminent in the way it was during Indira Gandhi's rule; there was a growth in the power of state governments after the collapse of the centralized Congress party; and politically and ideologically, a perception took root that the state was an important arena for both political power and economic development. Meanwhile, liberalization and economic reforms accelerated the shift of power from the centre to the states as states competed with each other to attract foreign direct investment, and to establish tax structures and institutional mechanisms for the clearance of such projects.[32] Indeed, some state governments such as Tamil Nadu, Andhra Pradesh, Karnataka, Maharashtra, Gujarat, and Orissa took the lead in mobilizing investment by national enterprises and multinational corporations, with control over sanctions to acquire land, buildings, power connections, telephones, and other services. As the then Finance Minister, P. Chidambaram, pointedly remarked, the push for economic reform no longer depended upon the uncertainties of party politics at the centre as chief ministers can influence and make policies for the central government. But the fact remained that economic reform was increasing disparities between states with the flow of domestic and foreign investment channelled to the relatively developed and stable states.

The formation of the United Front government in June 1996, comprising 13 regional and state-based parties, was a forceful demonstration of the shift of power to the states.[33] Dominated by regional parties, this conglomeration sealed the fate of the short-lived BJP government, which was unable to secure the support of regional parties for the confidence vote sought by the BJP government in Parliament in May 1996.[34] The BJP had expected that once it was invited to form the government by the President, regional parties would simply gravitate towards the party at the prospect of participating in the BJP-led government, but this assumption clearly underrated the importance of the regional phenomena and misjudged the priorities of parties like the DMK, Telugu Desam, Assam Gana Parishad, and Tamil Manila Congress who were socially rooted in regions and had their own regional agendas which ran contrary to that of the BJP. Regardless of the BJP's efforts to demonstrate its federal face by making promises to revoke the arbitrary use of Article 356, the party favoured a nationalized and unified organization which combined three dimensions: the conflation of a strong state with a Hindu state, a highly centralized party apparatus, and links with the Rashtriya Swayamsevak Sangh (RSS) which was not accountable to Parliament or anyone.[35] The opposition to the BJP thus stemmed not only from a rejection of communalism, but also from the rejection of its notions of a monolithic and homogeneous India held together by a domineering centre.[36]

The appointment of Deve Gowda, a regional leader, as prime minister in 1996 signalled a most important moment in the regionalization process, because the crucial thing was not that regional leaders were playing an important role in the selection of the prime minister, but that one of them had made it to the top job in the country. Gowda's selection marked the emergence of a new cluster of non-upper caste leadership which had local roots and was unwilling to be the junior partner of national parties. Unable to speak Hindi, the official language of the Union, Gowda repeatedly emphasized the national relevance of Karnataka's development experience and his own political and administrative record as chief minister of that state. The process of replacing Gowda by Inder Kumar Gujral as the leader of the United Front in April 1997 was similarly controlled by regional leaders, notably by the chief ministers of Andhra Pradesh, Tamil Nadu, Assam, West Bengal, and Bihar. Again, no one was left in doubt of the enormity of transition from one-party dominance to regionally-driven coalition politics. Thus the United Front demonstrated the possibilities of regionally-driven coalition politics as a device for managing social and regional pluralism. The salience of both these aspects has grown as the Indian polity has become more participatory: while regional leaders played a crucial role in the choice of successors to Jawaharlal Nehru in 1964 and Lal Bahadur Shastri in 1966, on both these occasions their role was not as decisive and conspicuous as it was in the operation of the United Front.

Institutional Arrangement

It remains to be seen whether the new role played by chief ministers and regional parties signifies a substantial redistribution of power between states and centre, and more importantly, whether it will actually produce an alternative concept and structure of governance. So far little thought has been given to institutional arrangements which might provide mechanisms for communication between various parties involved in the coalition or between the centre and the states. Moreover, the crucial issue is not just a shift of power from centre to states but a change in the orientation of the state to build an institutional framework for a federal-democratic-secular state; to use the state actively to reconstitute society and maintain the balance in favour of unity and equity against incoherence and injustice. Undoubtedly, states have increased their relevance and significance, but this has happened mainly because of a regionalization of politics caused by Congress decline and the resulting redistribution of power, and not because of an energetic restructuring of the existing political system. Beyond this, the introduction of elections to municipal corporations and local panchayats, with statutory provisions for reservations to increase the participation of lower castes, dalits, and women, has been used to institutionalize grassroots popular participation. Over time this has the greatest chance of heightening political consciousness and incorporating the demands of the newly mobilized and disadvantaged groups into the state and national policymaking process. Though the shape of political arrangements is not clear yet, none the less it is evident that we are witnessing a decisive movement in the power structure: the ascendancy of previously excluded and numerically large groups will be an enduring feature of the transition to a post-Congress polity and the regional and state-based parties will be the nodal points of democratic power.

In the 1990s, much of India's regional politics was not at odds with the centre or national economic development, rather state and regional parties did well in states with the highest rates of growth. Among seven states ranked in 1996 as having had the highest rates of growth—Tamil Nadu, Andhra Pradesh, Karnataka, Arunachal Pradesh, Maharashtra, Punjab, and Assam—only Arunachal Pradesh was ruled by the Congress party and Karnataka by an officially designated national party, the Janata Dal.[37] Notwithstanding these positive trends, most importantly the increased participation of groups long considered marginal, there were serious problems of cohesion and unity of political parties in mobilizing support around issues of caste and religion that made it difficult to constitute stable alliances and governments at the state level. The complexities of these changes, and the various tendencies at work, was dramatized by the problems of ungovernability that confronted the United Front coalition and its short-lived collaboration with the Congress. The United Front's justification for cooperation with the Congress was to protect secularism, yet the Front was not able to prevent the BJP from coming to power in two states, first as an ally of the Akali Dal in Punjab and then by making a deal with the Bahujan Samaj Party in Uttar Pradesh. What is more, it was allowed to continue in power in the most crucial state even when the deal fell through in October 1997. In the event, the coalition exhausted itself in mutual bickering with the Congress repeatedly threatening to withdraw its support from outside, thus discrediting the coalitional experiment. It became clear that there was a need to put in place institutional mechanisms to maintain coordination between political parties that could provide support from outside for the effective working of coalition politics.

To conclude, in the 1990s, two conceptions of political identity—the inclusionary nationalism of the Congress and the exclusionary nationalism of the BJP—failed to either preserve or establish their supremacy across the length and breadth of the country. In contrast to the inclusiveness of the Congress, the BJP's attempts to privilege an exclusive Hindu identity and integrate all sections of society around an amorphous appeal of Hindutva produced polarization and conflict, and thus compounded the problem of putting together an alternative agenda by exacerbating communal divisions. In the 1990s, neither of the centralized parties seemed capable of dealing in any meaningful way with the increased competitiveness, rising assertiveness, and mobilization of increasing segments of the population. At the same time however, there was a need to recognize that historically the Congress filled a space in Indian politics and continued to embody a shared imagination of the nation. Beneath the surface of the struggles in the 1990s however, lay a complex network of changes in Indian society, which had as much to do with the evolution of different cultures and the uneven economic development of the regions, as with the shifting ways in which regional and national identities were formed and reformed in response to structures of centralization and processes of politico-economic inclusion and exclusion.

Notes and References

1. That Congress accepted the principle of unilingual states is evident from the fact that Congress branches from the early 1920s were known provincially by their linguistic divisions. Ashis Banerjee, 'Federalism and Nationalism', in *Federalism in India: Origins and Development*, ed. Nirmal Mukharji and Balveer Arora, Delhi: Vikas, 1992.

2. T.V. Satyamurthy, 'Introduction', in *Region, Religion, Caste, Gender and Culture in Contemporary India*, vol. 3, New Delhi: Oxford University Press, 1996.

3. Granville Austin, *The Indian Constitution: Cornerstone of a Nation*, Oxford: Oxford University Press, 1966, p. 191.

4. For a recent account see Tilottama Misra and Udayan Misra, 'Movements for Autonomy in India's North-East', in *Region, Religion, Caste, Gender and Culture*, Satyamurthy, pp. 107–44.

5. This formed the core of the reform agenda of the 1970s. It was reflected in the terms of the Sarkaria Commission.

6. Regional insurgencies in Punjab, Kashmir, and Assam have attracted much scholarly attention. There are a number of studies of the Punjab problem. See for example Rajiv Kapur, *Sikh Separatism: The Politics of Faith*, London: Allen & Unwin, 1986; Paul Brass, 'The Punjab Crisis and the Unity of India', *India's Democracy: An Analysis of Changing State-Society Relations*, ed. Atul Kohli, Princeton, 1986. On Kashmir see M.J. Akbar, *Behind the Vale*, Delhi: Viking, 1991. On Assam see Jyotirindra Dasgupta, 'Ethnicity, Democracy and Development

in India: Assam in General Perspective', *India's Democracy*, Atul Kohli, ed., Cambridge: Cambridge University Press, 1991.

7. On this pattern see Achin Vanaik, *The Painful Transition: India's Bourgeois Democracy*, London: Verso, 1990.

8. On this see Paul Brass, 'Punjab Crisis and Unity of India', in *India's Democracy*, Kohli.

9. The March 1971 parliamentary elections, the events in Bangladesh, the war with Pakistan, and the March 1972 assembly elections—all in the course of the one year—together pushed towards the creation of a consensus on nation-building through a strong central government.

10. See Chapter 6 of this work for more on these development.

11. In fact, until the late 1960s, the Congress itself was a cluster of regional power centres because the Congress organization in most states, except the northern states, functioned as an effective vehicle for regional participation. Only after the 1977 elections did it function as a national party without strong roots in regional politics.

12. For the ruling party itself, centralization was premised on the assumption of a dichotomy between governance and polity and further that institutions at the state and district level embedded in the local polity were invariably weak, inefficient and unreliable and thus required the superior wisdom of the centre. This point is made by Balveer Arora and Nirmal Mukharji in their Introduction to *Federalism in India*.

13. For an analysis of centre-state relations in this period see Paul Brass, 'Pluralism, Regionalism and Decentralizing Tendencies in Contemporary Indian Polities', *The States of South Asia: Problems of National Integration, Essays in Honour of W.J. Morris-Jones*, ed. A. Jayaratnam and Denis Dalton, Hawai: University Press of Hawai, 1982.

14. On the growth of the Telugu Desam see Atul Kohli, 'The NTR Phenomena in Andhra Pradesh: Political Change in a South Indian State', *Asian Survey*, October 1988.

15. Manoj Mitta and Smruti Koppekar, 'Centre–State Relations: Changing Equations', *India Today*, 30 June 1996, p. 81.

16. Ibid.

17. Ibid.

18. Ibid.

19. Balveer Arora, 'Adapting Federalism to India: Multilevel and Asymmetrical Innovations', in *Multiple Identities in a Single State: Indian Federalism in Comparative Perspective,* ed. Balveer Arora and Douglas Verney, Delhi: Konark, 1995.

20. The 72nd Constitution Amendment Bill was unanimously passed on 22 December 1992. Although the Panchayat Act leaves the initiative to the states, it lays down a list of 29 subjects which must be transferred by the states to the panchayats.

21. Yogendra Yadav, 'How India Voted', *India Today*, 31 May 1996.

22. The BJP's vote share of 20 per cent hid the fact that the bulk of it came from these five states where on an average its vote share was 36 per cent.

23. Yadav, 'How India Voted'.

24. For a detailed analysis of the pattern of party competition see Yogendra Yadav, 'Reconfiguration in Indian Politics: State Assembly Elections, 1993-95', *Economic and Political Weekly*, 13-20 January 1996, pp. 99-102.

25. Francine Frankel, 'The Problem: a symposium on emerging issues in centre–state relations', *Seminar*, no. 459, November 1997.

26. James Manor, 'Regional Parties in Federal Systems', *Multiple Identities*, ed. Arora and Verney, p. 125.

27. Achin Vanaik, *The Painful Transition*, pp. 123-5.

28. Ibid., chap. 3, pp. 130-1.

29. On this aspect see D.L. Sheth, 'The Great Language Debate: Politics of Metropolitan versus Vernacular India', *Crisis and Change in Contemporary India*, Upendra Baxi and Bhiku Parekh, Delhi: Sage, 1995.

30. Sanjay Baru, 'Economic Policy and the Development of Capitalism in India: The Emerging Role of Regional Capitalists and Regional Political Parties', paper presented at the conference on 'Democracy and Transformation: India's Fifty Years after Independence', organized by the Centre for the Advanced Study of India, University of Pennsylvania, November 1997.

31. On the growing importance of the state as the leading arena of contestation, see Atul Kohli, 'Power and Powerlessness', in *State Power and Social Forces: Domination and Transformation in the Third World*, ed. Joel Migdal, Atul Kohli, and Vivien Shue, Cambridge: Cambridge University Press, 1995. Also see Yadav, 'Reconfiguration of Indian Polities'.

32. Frankel, 'The Problem', p. 14.

33. The combined strength of regional parties was greater than that of the Janata Dal: regional parties had 58 seats and Janata Dal 46 seats in the 1996 Parliament.

34. Although the BJP allowed some flexibility to state units to adapt to specific political cultures of different states, the concerns of BJP's political discourse from Kashmir in the north to Karnataka and Kerala in the south were supra-regional. This is evident from the issues that formed the staple of party's campaign for power at the centre——Ayodhya, uniform civil code, ban on cow slaughter, abolition of Article 370 which accords a special status to Kashmir.

35. While itself favouring a strong centralized state, it attacked the Congress for encouraging fissiparous tendencies and corruption, that in fact were a result of centralization. Tapan Basil et al., *Khaki Shorts, Saffron Flags*, Delhi: Orient BlackSwan, 1993, p. 114.

36. Mahesh Rangarajan, 'The Politics of Transition', *Seminar*, no. 449, January 1997.

37. Frankel, 'The Problem', pp. 13-15.

6 | The Prime Minister and the Left

Modern political regimes are marked by the presence of strong central executive leadership. This feature—common to many political systems, including developing countries—arises from the enormous expansion of governmental activities and state intervention in the contemporary period. In India's parliamentary democracy, the prime minister is the main focus of power and responsibility. The office of prime minister has played a paramount role in the governance of the country which has become considerably more complex than it was in the first two decades after independence. The range of activities covered by the central government as a whole has grown and so has the remit of individual ministries. The prime minister's secretariat has risen in importance, particularly after Indira Gandhi assumed power. She increased its powers to a point of excessive centralization by shifting much of the effective power to the prime minister's office. The result was a concentration of power at the apex of the ruling party, the central government, and the federal system. This has had a considerable impact upon many institutions and political formations. In particular, the central government's actions, and those of the prime ministers, have affected the growth and strategy of Left formations, the main concern of this chapter.

This chapter neither purports to discuss in detail the approach of all prime ministers towards Left formations, nor is it exclusively focussed on the office of prime minister. Rather, an attempt is made to examine the changing state of play between the prime minister, the central government, and the Left. The analysis offered is mainly confined to the states of Kerala and West Bengal, where, by the 1990s, communists established an impressive support base and ushered in radical reforms. Such an analysis is significant not because of the electoral performance of Left parties (which in itself is not very impressive), but because of the larger interventions made by Left forces in the post-independence public debates, policies and processes of social transformation. These interventions command popular attention and prestige, and it therefore becomes imperative for the central government, the ruling party, and the prime minister to respond and react to the ideological perspective articulated by the Left parties and groups on a range of national issues. It is here that the significance of the Left parties can be located.

Before looking at the relationship between prime ministers and the Left, it is necessary to consider the central features of communist strategy and practice. The striking fact about communist practice over the years has been its emphasis on expansion through participation in parliamentary politics.[1] In the three states of Kerala, West Bengal, and Tripura, communist parties have enlarged their influence and have come to power through electoral institutions. The stress on parliamentary politics has been most marked since the Telengana insurrection. Communists organized militant mass movements in various areas in the period 1946-51. This high agitational activity extended to Telengana,[2] other parts of Andhra Pradesh, Travancore-Cochin, Malabar (Kerala), Tripura, Manipur, and parts of West Bengal, eastern Uttar Pradesh and Maharashtra. The communists mounted this series of militant actions across classes and strata at what they 'saw as a moment of revolutionary breakthrough, one which was full of transformatory possibilities'.[3]

This misreading of the historical conjuncture was compounded by their reluctance to recognise that India had become independent in August 1947.[4] According to the communist understanding of the time, the state was completely dependent on imperialism which made it all the more necessary to wage a liberation struggle for the capture of state power, and to use all forms of protest and agitation to attack and oppose the government. They thus criticized the Nehru government and launched massive opposition against the bourgeois leadership as a whole, Nehru included. The class challenge posed by the militant activities of the Communist Party of India (CPI) was very strongly resisted by the Congress government. The Telengana uprising for one, was brutally suppressed by the Indian state.[5] The CPI responded by organizing an uprising across India which was built around the railway strike of March 1949, and Nehru was condemned for a fascist offensive against the working class at the dictates of 'Anglo-American capital'.[6] Soon thereafter, however, all militant struggles declined and dissipated. Repression was justified by the central government on the grounds that militant mass movements had developed into anti-national campaigns 'worse than an open rebellion and aiming at total disruption which would result in widespread chaos regardless of consequences'.[7]

The CPI was subjected to state repression on account of its struggles and agitations against state power. This encounter led to some rethinking in the CPI which resulted in the decision in mid-1950 to pursue a parliamentary route. The end of the Telengana struggle had coincided with the announcement of the first general elections in 1952, and the CPI performed quite well and became the leading opposition party in the Indian Parliament. It embarked upon a parliamentary journey as part of the transition to socialism, with the state also playing a role in drawing the communists into this process, with the main impetus coming from Jawaharlal Nehru.[8] Yet the pursuit of the parliamentary line in the 1950s and 1960s did not lead to the abandonment of extraparliamentary agitations: the undivided CPI and later the Communist Party of India (Marxist) or CPI(M)--created in 1964--were at the forefront of numerous land seizure agitations and mass struggles. However, the structural constraints and electoral considerations combined to propel the party into the orbit of essentially redistributive policies, rather than the complex task of the revolutionary transformation of Indian society.

In 1957 the voters of Kerala elected the first Communist majority to the state assembly. It was an event of historic significance as it was the first Indian state to elect a Communist government. Described as the 'Yenan of India', Kerala became a symbol of communist triumph identified with the new strategies of peaceful transition and 'the parliamentary road to socialism'.[8] However, this historic experiment was not allowed to last very long—the central government dismissed the Communist government on 31 July 1959.

This dismissal has been widely commented upon.[9] It is mainly worth considering here because it illuminates the way in which Jawaharlal Nehru and the Congress Party dealt with the Left, and Nehru's growing disillusionment with socialism.[10] The removal of the Communist ministry led by E.M.S. Namboodiripad was extremely controversial, especially because Nehru's sympathies for the Left had indicated that the CPI government should be allowed to function freely. Initially, Nehru was tolerant and almost proud of the fact that the first instance of the communists attaining power through democratic elections had taken place in India—indeed, his tolerance annoyed the anti-communists of the day. *Time* magazine informed its readers that Nehru had conferred respectability on the communist: 'Reds have long wished to set up a Yenan in India's hinterland', and Nehru was giving them their chance.[11]

The Communist government in Kerala seized the opportunity to start radical agrarian and educational reform.[12] Land reforms threatened landed interests, most notably in Travancore, where landlords fulminated at the prospect of losing land in excess of the proposed ceiling. The new Educational

Act 'to remove corruption, communal bias and maladministration'[13] evoked strong opposition from the church, which controlled much of Kerala's largely privately-run educational system. The landlords and the church joined hands to launch a sustained and vitriolic campaign against the state government. They concentrated their ire on the Education Bill because it was more widely disliked than the agrarian reforms and even Nehru was uneasy that the Bill, which affected minority institutions, could lead to trouble.[14] The landlords organized demonstrations and appealed to New Delhi to dismiss the state government. The local Congress party actively participated in these agitations.[15] Although the Communists pressed ahead with their land reform programme, it was struck down by the Kerala High Court, and the state government was dismissed in 1959.

S. Gopal suggests that Nehru was initially not inclined to interfere in the functioning of the Kerala government. It was reports from V.K. Krishna Menon regarding the deteriorating situation in Kerala, rather than constant complaints from Congressmen, that influenced Nehru's mood.[16] He began to blame the Communists for the growing tension and conflict in the state: according to him, the CPI in Kerala was adopting the Leninist tactic of using bourgeois democracy in the struggle to establish Communist supremacy. The Prime Minister categorically disapproved of this approach, particularly the promotion of class conflict and class hatred. Nehru clearly declared 'I don't want communism here'.[17]

Nehru was not prepared to entertain Namboodiripad's plea for a non-partisan rather than a pro-Congress approach, yet he expected the Kerala government to treat all parties and groups impartially. He repeatedly advised the Chief Minister to remain above party interests when he himself was finding it increasingly difficult to do so.[18] Nehru's growing impatience with communist activities, which he held responsible for a breakdown of law and order in Kerala, was more likely influenced by the experience of Communist insurgency in Telengana and developments in Communist countries. The suppression of freedom and ideological rigidity, reflected in the Soviet Union's attitude towards Tito and the execution of Nagy in Hungary, incensed Nehru. 'Nehru turned away mentally not only from the Soviet Union, which he held responsible for the cold-blooded act, but generally from Communist parties, including that of India, which supported the Soviet government and their policies in Hungary and towards Yugoslavia.'[19] These developments led to a rethinking of 'first principles' and Nehru came to believe that democracy and socialism were not ends in themselves, but means to achieve the good of the individual.[20]

A conjunction of circumstances, local and international, weakened Nehru's reluctance to interfere in an arbitrary manner in Kerala. Indira

Gandhi's role as the President of the Congress Party agitating for a change of government in the state was also an important element in the Kerala crisis. If Nehru baulked at approving the mass agitation, Indira Gandhi had no such qualms. She appreciated the discontent among the people. In June 1959, she was reported to have said to *The Hindu* correspondent: 'As Congress President I intend to fight them [Communists] and throw them out.'[21] In the event, the Congress party in Kerala intensified its participation in the campaign, confident that the central leadership did not disapprove of their association with it. Mrs Gandhi's role was crucial in the dismissal of the Communist government to the point that one Congress leader stated that 'but for Mrs Gandhi's influence they would not have been able to convert the Central government to their way of thinking'.[22] Namboodiripad has also attributed a considerable measure of responsibility to her for the agitation.

The accepted opinion on the dismissal is that Nehru was influenced by his daughter to interfere in Kerala.[23] It appears, however, that Nehru himself was unwilling to control the activities of the Congress by subduing his party's agitation in the state, which would have contributed to the restoration of peace in Kerala. He allowed party activists in Kerala and their anti-Communist allies to increase pressure on the All India Congress Committee (AICC) and was thus 'pushed' into taking a decision to dismiss the Communist ministry.[24] Nehru subsequently justified this as unavoidable, though Gopal concludes that he 'arrived at a decision which he knew to be wrong for what he believed were the right reasons'.[25]

The question over why the Prime Minister should have acquiesced in the intervention is much debated. One explanation is that the Congress system depended heavily on the control of government and the apparatus of the state for the consolidation of the party and the survival of state governments, so when it was not in power, the party felt paralysed.[26] In other words, the Congress was a party held together by power and governance, rather than by ideology:

As long as the Congress held office, that loyalty could usually be retained by the rewards that office brought. Kerala was the first serious instance of office being lost, and Congress supporters in Kerala at once turned to the central authorities and said in effect: Do something or we will take over connections and influence at elections elsewhere.[27]

The goal was to restore the Congress to power. Hence, it was necessary for the central government to use state power to contain the CPI as a competing political force capable of forming governments by winning elections.

At the political level, there is no doubt that the success of the CPI in gaining power and governing in the interests of the poor outraged vested interests and Congress politicians. What irked the Congress most was that the CPI showed a determination to implement its policies.[28] This exposed an important chink in the Congress armour: the traditional lack of political will to implement its own policies. A wide gulf thus separated the party's rhetoric and actions. The successful development of counter-hegemony by the CPI, through a determined implementation of progressive policies, necessarily provoked strong opposition from the Congress, regardless of the ministry 'partisanship', 'failure to maintain law and order', 'promotion of conflict', etc.[29]

With the eclipse of the socialists, communists posed the only serious challenge faced by the Congress and Nehru. The Prime Minister's handling of the Kerala crisis suggests that he was not prepared to countenance the challenge posed by communists, despite the fact that their support was regionally limited and they were not strong enough to compete electorally with the Congress at an all-India level. At that level, Nehru could afford to be non-partisan because opposition was negligible in what was still a system of one party dominance. In the case of Kerala however, he found this difficult because the radical actions of the Communists threatened the legitimacy of the Congress which claimed to be building a socialist society, but was doing very little in that direction. In such circumstances, Nehru was unable to place himself or the office of the prime minister above the party: 'His obligations as Prime Minister and his inclinations as party leader came into conflict, and it became increasingly difficult to reconcile the two.'[30] He allowed the Congress party to take undue and undemocratic advantage of what was a contrived crisis, created by Congress leaders who were convinced that the only way for them to regain control was by dismissing the Kerala government.

Indira Gandhi and Communism

The experience of Kerala foreshadowed the problems faced by Prime Minister Indira Gandhi in restoring the primacy of the Congress party after its decline in the 1967 national elections. Both the survival of the party and the governance of the country became more complex after Nehru. The keystone of her political strategy was an unprecedented centralization of power within the ruling party, within the central government at the expense of Parliament, the Cabinet and the judiciary, and within the federal system. This centralization was part of a process set off by the split in the Congress in 1969, which for the first time reversed the decline in the credibility and authority of the Congress. Together, the March 1971 parliamentary elections, the events in Bangladesh, the war with Pakistan, and the March

1972 assembly elections—all in the course of one year—pushed towards the creation of a consensus on nationbuilding through a strong central government. These changes, which have been widely commented upon, led to transformations in the role of the executive and in the character of centre-state relations.[31] The specific measures taken by Mrs Gandhi to centralize political authority most crucially involved the abandonment of intra-party democracy. Most important, state chief ministers were now selected by the Prime Minister in consultation with her political advisors rather than by the ruling party in state assemblies. The centralization of power in party and government produced what Kochanek described as a 'new political process', which 'tended to centralize decision making, weaken institutionalization, and create an overly personalized regime'. [32]

Many of Indira Gandhi's most important political actions were taken with a view to concentrating power and authority in her own hands and in the prime minister's office. Consequently, the prime minister's Secretariat acquired awesome powers in the early 1970s.[33] For example, by 1970, she had brought under her personal control the most crucial departments; she assumed the key portfolio of Home which, together with the expansion of the Cabinet Secretariat, gave her complete control of all internal security and government intelligence.[34] This concentration of power created the conditions for frequent central interventions in state politics in the Indira Gandhi era, which took place through the formal machinery of government.

In the Nehru era of one party dominance, the Congress organization, an informal institution, had been deployed as a watch dog; its task was to supervise and if possible, to determine the course of events in the states. Central intervention was often not necessary then, as most state governments were under the control of powerful Congress leaders. In the post-Nehru era, central government's and frequent resources, imposition of President's Rule in various states was marshalled to influence state politics in a pro-Congress direction. After the decline of the Congress in the late 1960s and 1970s, the central government made vigorous efforts to ensure the survival of unstable Congress governments at the state level and sought to put the Congress back in power in states where it had lost the elections. The principal consequence of these policies was a further centralization of power and a decline in the importance of non-governmental mechanisms of central intervention in state politics, and concomitantly, of states and districts as critical arenas of political competition and mobilization independent of the centre.[35]

Indira Gandhi's strategy of establishing Congress supremacy was not confined to reordering the institutional sphere. It also involved crucial ideological manoeuvres through which she dramatically appropriated the Left platform. She managed to build a considerable national following by highlighting Congress government failure in redistribution and her own commitment to the upliftment of the poor. By a series of measures taken after the split in the Congress in 1969, which included the nationalization of banks, the abolition of privy purses, and the nationalization of insurance, Indira Gandhi dramatically appropriated a Left platform.

During this period, she frequently expressed her belief in socialist policies without ever defining her vision of socialism. Her attempts to identify with the underprivileged and poor—though not entirely rhetorical because of important new policies such as the nationalization of banks and insurance, the takeover of trade in foodgrains, and the reduction in land ceilings—were largely a defensive strategy born out of pragmatism. Mrs Gandhi realized that the party would lose ground to leftist forces unless it moved to the left of centre, so she often made use of leftist slogans to discredit the opposition and to contain her enemies within the party by representing the party conflict as a fight between forces of progress and reaction.

During these years she enjoyed unrivalled popularity, but she failed to use the opportunity to reorganize the Congress as a mass organization committed to socialist policies. This would have required a dramatic change in the social composition of the Congress and its methods of organization. Indira Gandhi did nothing to resolve the contradiction between an accommodative party ideology and an organization aimed at conciliating the propertied classes, and such economic plans and institutions as were required to accomplish social reform. Instead, she used populist appeals to establish her position as leader of the progressive forces. While doing so, she was careful to assure the propertied classes that their interests were not threatened by reform. She explained that her reforms were actually aimed at the containment of radicalism: 'Violent radicalism can be prevented only by convincing people through our actions that we are resolving glaring economic and social injustice and deprivation. . . .'[36] Her reforms were also designed to prevent a red revolution: 'I dislike the word contain, but if only people paused to think, I am containing communism in India. The government cannot afford to move even the slightest to the Right because this will in no time begin a move on the part of Communists interpreting my actions as anti-people.'[37]

The circumstances which made this ideological shift possible were both interesting and indicative of the wider power play in the country and the challenges faced by the Congress party. The first real challenge to the Congress system had come in 1967 when Congress lost power in eight states. The CPI(M)-led United Front came to power in Kerala and in West Bengal. As Indira Gandhi broke with the Syndicate and radicalized her government's policies, the CPI decided to support her while the CPI(M) remained opposed. The most serious challenge to the Congress by an opposition party was thus mounted by the CPI(M), the more militant of the Communist parties and the most formidable rival of the CPI for the leadership of the Indian Left.[38] The CPI, for its part, anticipated tangible benefits from an alignment with the Prime Minister and her party. Above all, the alliance held out the prospect of neutralizing the CPI(M) in the regional strongholds of Kerala and West Bengal.[39]

Similar considerations of political expediency guided Indira Gandhi's approach. She needed the support of radical socialists, including the CPI, in containing the CPI(M), while establishing her own credentials and power as the leader of the progressive forces. The CPI(M)-led United Front had already inflicted significant setbacks on the Congress in Kerala and West Bengal. The CPI(M) position in Kerala, however, depended in large measure on the support of the CPI, and this was to some extent true of West Bengal also.[40] If CPI support was withdrawn, or better still transferred to the Congress, the challenge of the CPI(M) could therefore be blunted.[41]

An opportunity for an alignment between the Congress and CPI was provided by the Kerala mid-term election of 1970. There was an uneasy alliance between the CPI(M) and the CPI in the United Front which had come to power in 1967. The state government led by E.M.S. Namboodiripad, had introduced the Kerala Land Reforms Amendment, which in conception was the most radical agrarian reform in India—particularly beneficial to tenants, hutment dwellers and agricultural labourers.[42] The Bill was passed in October 1969, but the government collapsed soon after, as a result of which these reforms could not then be implemented. In contrast to 1959, the role of external factors this time was minimal: there was no 'liberation' struggle and the central government was not a significant irritant. The government fell because of inter-party rivalries and allegations of corruption against Front partners. However, the mutual antagonism and quarrels between the CPI and CPI(M), which were responsible for the collapse of the ministry, cannot be separated from the efforts made by the Congress to wean away the CPI. At the same time the CPI(M) efforts to assert its hegemony and isolate the CPI within the Front proved to be counterproductive, as they drove the CPI closer to the Congress.

This paved the way for Congress support to the Mini-Front led by the CPI, thus signalling the end of Congress hostility towards a section of the communists. Indira Gandhi, who had played an important part in the dismissal of the first CPI-led United Front, now played an equally significant part in establishing an alliance with the CPI. The reasons for cooperation were not very different from those behind the earlier hostility for in both moments, Mrs Gandhi was driven by a desire to weaken the radical forces. Indeed, the new ministry's fundamental objective was to destroy the CPI(M) hegemony in Kerala politics.[43] For this it was imperative to implement land reforms in order to effectively neutralize the CPI(M). Consequently, the CPI ministry, claiming to be the 'residuary legatee of the United Front government', committed itself to the implementation of land reforms which were designed by its predecessor, the CPI(M).[44] The central government obliged by expediting presidential approval of the Land Reforms Bill in less than two months.

The CPI government's decision to implement land reforms placed the CPI(M) in a dilemma. Although the members of the new government had not been involved in drafting the radical Bill, they were now in a position to claim credit for its implementation and to appropriate the reform as their own. Even the Congress could claim credit for the reform. Although the CPI(M) was in the opposition, it could not oppose the measure for fear of jeopardizing the implementation of land reforms. Instead, popular pressure was mounted for speedy implementation of reforms. The point to note is that Kerala was the only state in which a 'CPI-led coalition with the Congress party's support and Central government's encouragement presided over seven years of reform on the basis of a programme drawn up by the CPI(M)-led United Front government'.[45] This helped the Congress to regain the ground lost by the party over the previous two decades.

The Congress reaped the fruits of this cooperation by winning 32 of the 56 seats it contested in the 1970 mid-term state poll in Kerala, in alliance with the CPI. In the 1971 Lok Sabha mid-term elections, the same alliance produced greater setbacks for the CPI(M) which retained only two of its nine seats.[46] The prime minister played a masterly role in marginalizing the CPI(M): she campaigned personally in as many as 50 of the 56 constituencies in which the Congress was contesting. She attacked the CPI(M) for their strategy of confrontation between the central government and the states, and for promoting conflict between the poor and rich classes. She also promised to solve Kerala's problems of poverty and unemployment by means of programmes that would accomplish great changes 'without the revolutionary costs of "cutting off peoples heads"', as she put it.[47] As noted earlier, the personal effort paid off for Congress seats jumped from 9 in 1967 to 32 in 1970, with 17 of the 27 seats gained from the opposition coming at the expense of the CPI(M). The alliance effected by Mrs Gandhi played a key part in counter-balancing and isolating the CPI(M). This alliance not only excluded the CPI(M) from power in Kerala in the 1970s, but also helped to bring Kerala into line with the dominant trends in centre-state relations and, above all, with the political economy of capitalist development.

West Bengal and the Communists

Despite the above mentioned efforts to marginalize the CPI(M), by the early 1970s, it had emerged as the more powerful force in the Indian Left. The major area of strength was West Bengal where the party first came to prominence in 1967. After the defeat of the Congress that year, West Bengal experienced a succession of coalition governments, but what differentiated it from many other states also experiencing instability and a decline in Congress support, was the critical political presence of the Left as the only viable opposition to the Congress. The First United Front of the CPI(M), the CPI, and the Bangla Congress was formed in March 1967. Within the coalition, the most significant force was the CPI(M), led by Jyoti Basu. The Front planned far-reaching agrarian reform in emulation of the Kerala pattern. The Minister for Land and Land Revenue Hare Krishna Konar, announced that the state government would recover surplus land in excess of the ceiling laws, and that the police in rural areas would not interfere with 'the democratic and legitimate struggles of the people' to identify and transfer such lands.

The state government did not believe that land distribution could be achieved without peasant mobilization from below. Hence the CPI(M) organized poor peasants and encouraged them to seize land and crops from landlords, and the Second United Front which took office in February 1969 intensified peasant mobilization. By early 1970, the CPI(M) land and land revenue minister reported that 300,000 acres of surplus land in excess of ceiling had been recovered and redistributed.[48] Undoubtedly the land seizure movements aggravated class conflicts in rural areas, resulting in the growth of the Naxalite movement led by radical dissidents from the CPI(M).[49] The growing social tensions and violence engendered dissatisfaction among the landed and middle classes, culminating in strong intervention by the central government, and eventually contributed heavily to the fall of the United Front government itself. The deterioration of law and order provided the pretext for central intervention so in a sense, 'the CPI(M) had only neutralized the "near state" and thus invited the wrath of the more distant state (i.e. invited federal intervention)'.[50]

Both United Front governments in West Bengal in 1967 and 1969 were dismissed at the behest of the central government. The dismissal of the First United Front within eight months of assuming power was done under particularly controversial circumstances by Governor Dharma Vira, who was chosen by the prime minister to control the turbulent politics of West Bengal which were slipping out of Congress hands. Dharma Vira's appointment had been opposed by the Left because of his reputation as 'Indira Gandhi's man', and, above all, because of his willingness to intervene in state politics in an unconstitutional manner. Precisely for these reasons, such an assignment suited him. He claimed in his autobiography, that he found 'life as a constitutional governor a bit too dull'.[51] The defection of P.C. Ghosh and other Bangla Congress legislators to form the Progressive Democratic Front provided the opportunity for his actions. After consultations with the Prime Minister, the Governor rejected the majority claims of the Front, even though they had not actually been tested. The Chief Minister's personal assistant felt that the 'Governor and Chief Secretary had acted in a partisan manner'.[52] Bhupesh Gupta of the CPI accused the central government of ruling West Bengal 'with a gun'.[53] The *Economic and Political Weekly* attacked the situation as a 'bureaucratic coup hatched by the governor, in league with the West Bengal Chief Secretary, Inspector General of Police, Union Home Ministry, Central Director of Intelligence Bureau, and the regional army chief, which culminated in the dismissal of the United Front Ministry'.[54]

Clearly, these events suggested that Indira Gandhi was interested in forming a Congress government without going in for mid-term polls, which she did not want to risk owing to the strong anti-Congress feelings sweeping different parts of the country, and particularly in West Bengal. As such, the United Front government was replaced by a Congress-supported coalition and then when that came apart, President's Rule was imposed. During this period, the Governor played a partisan role in helping the Congress stage a comeback to power. Unlike events in Kerala in 1959, the central government appeared not to be directly involved, the Prime Minister preferring to use the state Governor to restore Congress rule in order to deflect attacks and criticism from herself and her government. The Congress Party was keen to use available institutional means to weaken the Left. President's Rule offered the party breathing space to revive and possibly regain its lost hegemony. Despite these opportunities, however Congress failed to form a stable government, although it gained a vital foothold from which to combat the CPI(M) for a time.

After the collapse of the United Front, the Prime Minister took an even more active interest in West Bengal politics. Supposedly this became necessary on account of the state government's incompetence in dealing with the rush of refugees from Bangladesh in 1971, which compounded the law and order problem in West Bengal. The prime minister appointed Siddhartha Shankar Ray as Union Minister without Portfolio to deal with West Bengal affairs, including refugee and other problems of the state. Most important, Ray's leadership also provided a boost to the organized resistance against communists and the Congress government was able to imprison hundreds of communists. The United Front, as long as it was in power, had avoided taking action against Naxalites but now, state power was used liberally to crush their revolt.

After each of the two United Front dismissals, the central government established direct control over West Bengal. Both interregnums were marked by increasing state repression to the point that Congress leaders admitted that the government had committed atrocities between 1971 and 1977.[55] The police were let loose to capture Naxalites, aided by Congress-organized volunteer squads of hoodlums.[56] Hundreds of CPI(M) cadres were killed in the terror unleashed by the state in the early 1970s. Another equally important dimension of state repression was the cover it provided for Congress to sweep the elections in 1972 through widespread electoral fraud and violence. Terror and physical attacks made it impossible for CPI(M) members and supporters to conduct a normal campaign in the 1972 assembly elections. Jyoti Basu, the CPI(M) leader, listed 35 assembly constituencies where fair, elections were seriously endangered.[57] Congress launched a counter-attack by getting the Election Commissioner and police to assert that elections were fair; but the Commission conceded that there were 'pockets of dissidence where normal elections were circumscribed'.[58] The central government, however, supported the local Congress assessment that elections were held normally and calmly. These manoeuvres constrained the CPI(M), albeit temporarily, in its emerging stronghold of West Bengal where, as in the case of Kerala, it was prevented from converting growing popular support into governmental power. Repeated central intervention made it almost impossible for the Left to form a ruling coalition while ideological divergence and inter-party rivalries among coalition members compounded the crisis of instability. The Bangladesh War, law and order problems, and coalitional instability were used as a shield to impose President's Rule and eliminate the political rivals of the Congress. The sustained violence and terror marginalized the CPI(M) which had expanded its base during United Front experiments. It was especially important to contain the further growth of Left formations which, in the course of the United Front governments, had created conditions for peasant mobilizations that directly threatened prosperous interests. These interests had lost the protection of the state owing to the neutralization of the police as an agent of class repression.

The relentless intervention by the Centre and the prime minister in West Bengal aggravated tensions between the Centre and state government, and between the Congress and Left formations. Clearly President's Rule was the most potent instrument of central government intervention and its misuse was not confined to West Bengal. Several other states were subjected to it repeatedly,[59] and its use increased dramatically after Mrs Gandhi became prime minister. As Bhagwan Dua points out, Mrs Gandhi surpassed all prime ministers in her abuse of President's Rule which she used to resolve crises in state politics.[60]

This occurred because after the end of one-party dominance, state politics became the most important arena of conflict between alternative parties and even alternative prime ministers. Control of states became vital for the consolidation of power in New Delhi. Political competition enlarged the political arena to include centre-state relations as contested terrain where the federal machinery was used to determine political outcomes.[61] In this contest, the office of the governor assumed great significance, though in normal circumstances it does not involve the exercise of power. In times of political uncertainty, the governor's discretion becomes quite substantial.

The increasing use and abuse of President's Rule in a large number of states indicated that the mechanism was used to combat opposition, regardless of the ideological orientation of the government. This in turn suggests that the prime minister and the central government were not necessarily more antagonistic towards Left-dominated governments than they were to other opposition governments. At one level this is correct, but at the same time, it is extremely significant that the highest incidence and abuse of President's Rule occurred in Kerala and West Bengal during periods when Communist-led United Front governments were pressing ahead with radical programmes that challenged bourgeois hegemony. Both central intervention and prime ministers' involvement in the politics of these two states diminished in the late 1970s and 1980s when the Left formations were more concerned with redistributive issues, in contrast to the 1950s and 1960s, which for the Left had been a period of class politics and protracted battles for the exploited and the oppressed. Precisely because the overall trajectory of capitalist development was not jeopardized by the redistributive policies or the anti-communal politics of the 1970s and 1980s, the Left was allowed the political space to carry out these policies without much interference from the centre and the prime minister.[62]

The Emergency, 1975–7

The declaration of an Emergency on 26 June 1975 was a watershed in Indian politics, and it affected the Left in significant ways. To begin with, the suspension of normal democratic functioning changed the character of the party system and altered relations between the Congress and opposition parties. The imposition of the Emergency pitted all parties against the Congress, with the exception of the CPI. The common experience of repression brought the ideologically opposed left- and right-wing formations much closer than ever before, on the imperative need to defend democracy.

The CPI supported the Emergency in the belief that it would thwart the right reactionary conspiracy that 'is using all the rights and liberties of the parliamentary democracy set up in order to destroy the freedom of our country'. This was not all. The party approved the economic policies and measures set out by Indira Gandhi against 'the neocolonialists, monopolists, landlords, hoarders and speculators'. The Congress-CPI alliance was briefly refurbished, but very soon the CPI's expectations were belied as Indira Gandhi showed no inclination to move in the direction hoped for by the CPI. As a matter of fact, the prime minister categorically opposed the possibility of any further nationalization. This created frictions between the prime minister and the CPI. Differences widened as the central government issued a presidential ordinance to stop the minimum guaranteed bonus for industrial workers in 1974-5. The party failed in its bid to persuade the prime minister to suspend the measure, leading to further tensions and culminating in an end of the Congress-CPI alliance.

The wrath of the Emergency regime was directed against the CPI(M) and Communist Party of India Marxist Leninist CPI(ML). The CPI(ML) was banned in September 1975 and hundreds of communists were arrested and imprisoned without trial.[63] The CPI(M) strongly opposed the Emergency for according to the party, the prime minister had used the rightist challenge to establish a one-party authoritarian state. Unlike the CPI, the CPI(M) expected from the outset that the Emergency regime would destroy democracy and deprive the people of their civil liberties. However it was reluctant to join hands openly with right-wing parties in opposing it. The principal objective of the party was to safeguard its hard core support base. This the party was able to do better than the CPI, whose association with the Emergency considerably damaged its credibility. The CPI suffered heavy losses in the 1977 Lok Sabha elections, owing to its proximity to the Congress and the widely disapproved of Emergency.

The defeat of the Congress party in that Lok Sabha election brought about further changes in the party system. One important feature was freer competition between political parties and also greater social and political polarization in the states, with reduced manoeuvrability for the central government since the control of the centre itself was contested. This opened up the space for new alignments to strengthen the opposition. However, Indira Gandhi's return to power once again altered the milieu of centre-state relations although there were important differences in the post-1980 period that limited the scope of arbitrary central intervention. Although the opposition was in disarray, it had much greater potential and substance than the 1980 and 1984 election results implied. Parties like the CPI(M) and the Bharatiya Janata Party retained the support of important groups and the ideological resources to confront the Congress in the north and the east. Overall, the opposition was in a stronger position than before and was more capable of exerting pressure on the central government and of mustering support in a number of states to humble the Congress at the polls. The cohesive electoral base of opposition parties in certain regions enabled them to control state governments with clear majorities, in contrast to the 1960s when opposition coalitions were unstable and therefore much more vulnerable to central intervention.

Communism and the Prime Minister

After the Emergency, the CPI(M) emerged in 1977 as West Bengal's ruling party—leading a Left Front—it won all subsequent elections (until its dramatic defeat in the 2011 Assembly elections). Although there were no attempts on the part of the central government to dismiss the Left Front governments, this did not mean that there were no tensions between the centre and West Bengal. For example, Left Front government's relations with Rajiv Gandhi were strained. The prime minister took a keen personal interest in the 1987 state assembly elections in West Bengal and was the party's chief campaigner in the elections. He made caustic comments about the CPI(M) during the campaign, indicating the depth of his opposition to the Communist government.[64] He also blamed the policies of the Left Front for the economic stagnation in the state, while the Left Front placed the blame squarely on the central government and Rajiv Gandhi's economic policies.

Increasingly in the 1990s, tensions have arisen over the distribution of power and resources between the central government and the states. This reflects the new priorities of the CPI(M) which is much more focused on governance and development rather than radical transformation. In the 1960s, the party did not hesitate to proclaim that its purpose was to 'capture power by making the fullest use of the constitutional machinery so that it can break the constitution from within'. Later, the party strove for the restructuring of centre-state relations to expedite productivity and development. The calls for a major change in centre-state relation have also helped it to marshall considerable support from non-Congress and non-communist parties, many of whom are in power in other states and thus are equally impatient with the centre's enormous financial powers. While state governments have been assigned heavy responsibilities, the major taxation powers are with the central government. As and when the central government faces a financial crunch, it scrimps even more in sharing resources with the states, particularly with those ruled by opposition governments.

The West Bengal government has long complained that New Delhi has subjected the state to a financial squeeze. The central government has undertaken little public investment and is reluctant to grant the state industrial licences. Between 1980-1 and 1984-5, per capita central plan assistance was Rs. 132 to West Bengal and an average of Rs. 214 to other states. Added to this, 70 per cent of this allotment was in the form of loans with interest.[65] In 1984-5, the Finance Commission recommended that New Delhi give additional loans to the state, but the Commission's recommendations were not accepted.[66]

Until the regionalization of politics and the emergence of state as the principal arena of electoral competition from the 1990s, the relationship between the central and state governments was unequal, regardless of who was the prime minister. Even those items which are under state control require central approval, so New Delhi can delay the implementation of vital programmes. Between 1981 and 1983, at least seven important bills of the West Bengal government dealing with industrial and agrarian relations were withheld for presidential approval. The West Bengal Legislative Assembly in 1983 submitted an amended version of the Land Reforms Act 1979 for presidential assent, which was finally granted to a watered down Act in 1987.[67]

In Kerala, the CPI(M)-led Left and Democratic Front (LDF) returned to power in 1987, after three decades. This was the first government formed in the state without the support of any communal or casteist party or group.[68] The LDF, while consolidating the gains of the Kerala model,[69] followed the example of the West Bengal government by devoting attention to an improvement in the economic performance of the state, which was lagging behind the national average. Between 1987 and 1990, there was a distinct improvement on this front.[70] Important policy initiatives in agriculture and industry were introduced. A notable feature of industrial policy was the encouragement given to the private sector, small-scale industries, and productivity-enhancing intermediate technologies. These new policies were a radical attempt on the part of the LDF to expand the production base—a departure from the earlier understanding of the Kerala model which sought to provide a relatively high quality of life through redistributive measures, even on a low production base.[71] New Delhi nevertheless had the power to blunt this new initiative: on several occasions in the past, it had, for example, manipulated food supplies to undercut Left governments.[72]

The LDF put pressure on the central government to increase public investment in Kerala. The state's Minister of Finance complained that it was receiving 30 per cent less than the all-India average in development funds.[73] He also charged New Delhi with freezing State Bank funds and providing only half of the per capita investment in industry which the state deserved. Kerala was also subjected to control and interference in its finances and development budget by Prime Minister Rajiv Gandhi.[74] Chief Minister E.K. Nayanar complained that the Reserve Bank of India suddenly stopped payments to the Kerala government because the latter had exceeded the ceiling on overdrafts by Rs. 250 million.[75] He explained that Kerala's difficulties were related to drought and the mismanagement of the state's finances by the previous Congress government. That government had, by contrast, been allowed to convert an overdraft of Rs. 2.42 billion into loans and advance plan assistance to the tune of Rs. 1.75 billion. Clearly, as the Chief Minister observed, New Delhi's action was 'guided by considerations other than those of sound finance'.[76]

Another case of a prime minister's hostility was revealed in the course of the election campaign in Kerala in 1989. Prime Minister Rajiv Gandhi, in a reference to the LDF government's complaint that New Delhi had cut its rice quota in order to maintain its statutory rationing system, remarked: 'Why does Kerala come to us with a begging bowl always?'[77] The LDF took strong exception to this, claiming that this was a violation of the assurance given by the central government in 1964, when statutory rationing was introduced. The monthly requirement of the state was 165,000 tonnes of rice, but this was reduced to 145,000 after June 1987, and cut further to 100,000 tonnes in February 1989. Chief Minister Nayanar, in a rejoinder, said that Rajiv Gandhi's reaction to the state's request showed that he thought that 'a master servant relationship existed between the Centre and states'.[78]

These tensions notwithstanding, the prime ministers and the Left have not been locked in confrontation in the way they were in the 1960s and 1970s. The shift has come about not because of a major change in the approach of prime ministers, but mainly because the Left formations have been much stronger under Left Front governments than they were under earlier United Fronts. Furthermore, unity in the ranks of the Left forces has prevented prime ministers from exploiting inter-party quarrels, ideological divergences, and coalitional instability to undermine them. Between 1967 and 1976, Indira Gandhi had effectively used intra-communist disputes to weaken the Left. The CPI's strategic alliance with the Congress in the early 1970s had led to the disruption of the Left United Front of 1967 in Kerala and to the formation of an anti-CPI(M) front including the CPI and other minor Left parties. This alliance gave the Congress a new respectability and enabled it to contain the growth of the CPI(M). The re-establishment of Left unity after 1977 ruled out such manoeuvres.

Forces beyond the control of the prime ministers and the Left formations have also produced changes in the structure of political relations. An important development was the emergence of communal politics in the 1980s. This reshaped the agenda of Indian politics as also of Left politics. The shift profoundly affected the strategy of the Left formations. In fact, the most significant feature of Left politics after the emergence of BJP as a major force in national politics has been their opposition to the BJP's communal agenda, which has brought the Left to the forefront of the struggle against communalism all over the country. This pushed struggles for economic relief for the people into the background.

There are several other reasons why the Left formations have reoriented their strategies. The experience in an earlier period of United Front governments in Kerala and West Bengal played a part in this reorientation. Those governments had initiated the most radical changes achieved anywhere in the country. Both governments were summarily dismissed. What is more, West Bengal was the site of widespread repression in the 1970s. These experiences contributed to the adoption of basically redistributive goals. Underlying these shifts were the demands of electoral politics and the need to build up the economy of those states. The imperatives of widening and maintaining electoral support, stimulating economic growth and working with the central government strengthened the Left's commitment to the rules of parliamentary politics. The Left formations do not now subscribe to the principle of revolution or nothing. Rather they represent a radical alternative which underscores redistribution through mass mobilization, and the reorientation of mass mobilization to assist the expansion of the production base. These shifts have in one sense rendered repeated central intervention unnecessary. It is equally significant, however, that despite structural limitations and central interventions in the exercise of power at the state level, Kerala and West Bengal have demonstrated that even while functioning within the overall framework of national development, with all its consequences and contradictions, state governments can achieve some redistribution of wealth and popular participation in the political process.

Notes and References

1. T.J. Nossiter, *Marxist State Governments in India*, Oxford: Oxford University Press, 1988; K.S. Subramaniam, *Parliamentary Communism: Crisis in the Indian, Communist Movement*, Delhi: Ajanta Publications, 1987; G.D. Overstreet and M. Windmiller, *Communism in India*, Berkeley, CA: University of California Press, 1959; and V. Fic, *Peaceful Transition to Communism in India*, Bombay: Nachiketa Publications, 1969.

2. There is a considerable literature on Telengana. See, for example, G.M. Adhikari, *What is Happening in Hyderabad*, Delhi, 1949 and P. Sundarayya, *Telengana People's Struggles and its Lessons*, Calcutta: Foundation Books, 1972.

3. This reading was of decisive importance in the elaboration of the communist position in the period from 1946. What gave these upheavals a revolutionary look was the chain of actions which spread across classes and strata and social groups, extending from the armed forces and police to the peasants and workers. The Political Theses adopted in early 1948 were based on this misunderstanding. *Documents of the History of the Communist Party of India*, New Delhi, n.d.

4. The Communist Party of India (CPI) declared: 'The so-called transfer of power was one of the biggest pieces of political and economic appeasement of bourgeoisie which was necessary to strike a deal over the manpower and resources of a vast territory, though as a junior partner, was the dream of the bourgeoisie and it has realized it. From the standpoint of revolution all that it means is that henceforth the bourgeoisie will guard the colonial state.' *Documents of the History*; Also J. Alam, 'State and the Making of Communist Politics in India, 1947-57', *Economic and Political Weekly*, November 1991, pp. 2573–6.

5. Adhikari, *What is Happening in Hyderabad*, pp. 7–8.

6. CPI Statement, 2 March 1949.

7. S. Gopal, *Jawaharlal Nehru: A Biography, 1947-1956*, Delhi, Oxford University Press, 1979, p. 70.

8. Fic, Peaceful Transition.

9. E.M.S. Namboodiripad, *What Really Happened in Kerala: The Story of the Disruptive Game played by Rightwing Communist (CPI)M*, Delhi, 1966; Robin Jeffrey, 'Jawaharlal Nehru and the Smoking Gun: Who Pulled the Trigger on Kerala's Communist Government in 1959?', *Journal of Commonwealth and Comparative Politics*, March 1991; T.J. Nossiter, *Communism in Kerala*, Delhi: Oxford University Press, 1982.

10. For discussion of Nehru's disillusionment with socialism with special reference to Kerala, see Gopal, *Jawaharlal Nehru*, vol. 2, chap. 10.

11. Cited in Jeffrey, 'Jawaharlal Nehru', p. 75.

12. On the policy actions of the First Communist Ministry in Kerala, see Nossiter, *Communism in Kerala*, pp. 140-78, and K. Lieten, 'Progressive State Governments: An Assessment of First Communist Ministry in Kerala', *Economic and Political Weekly*, 6 January 1979.

13. Gopal, *Jawaharlal Nehru*, vol. 2, pp. 56-8.

14. Nehru was however more sympathetic than G.B. Pant, Central Minister for Home Affairs, who warned that the Bill might be ultra vires and that, if passed, it would discourage non-official initiative in education, Gopal, *Jawaharlal Nehru*, vol. 2, p. 56.

15. Ibid., pp. 56-62; Jeffrey, 'Jawaharlal Nehru', pp. 78-9.

16. Gopal, *Jawaharlal Nehru*, p. 57.

17. Ibid., p. 58.

18. Namboodiripad remarked: 'I think we have a right to expect from you an approach to such problems which is not strictly a Congressman's approach but an approach which would be non-partisan and national.' Ibid., p. 58.

19. Ibid.

20. Ibid.

21. Quoted in Jeffrey, 'Jawaharlal Nehru', p. 80.

22. Gopal, *Jawaharlal Nehru*, vol. 2, p. 67.

23. Ibid.

24. B.N. Pandey, *Jawaharlal Nehru*, London: Macmillan, 1976, p. 399.

25. Gopal, *Jawaharlal Nehru*, vol. 2, p. 73.

26. Jeffrey, 'Jawaharlal Nehru', pp. 72-4.

27. Ibid., p. 74.

28. T.V. Satyamurthy, *Centre-State Relations in India since Independence*, Delhi, 1985.

29. Ibid.

30. Ibid.

31. See J. Manor, 'Parties and the Party System', in *India's Democracy*, A. Kohli, ed., Princeton: Princeton University Press, 1988, pp. 62-98.

32. S.A. Kochanck, 'Mrs Gandhi's Pyramid: The New Congress', in *Indira Gandhi's India*, H.C. Hart, ed., Boulder, CO: Westview Press, 1976, pp. 104–5.

33. For a discussion of the Prime Minister's Office, see M. Limaye, *Cabinet Government in India*, New Delhi: Radiant Publishers, 1989; P.N. Dhar, 'The Prime Minister's Office', in B. Sarkar, ed., P.N. Haksar, *Our Times and the Man*, Delhi: Allied Publishers, 1989, pp. 48-61; and C.P. Bhambhri, 'The Prime Minister in Indian Politics since Independence, 1947-1987', ed. C.P. Bhambhri, Delhi: Shipra, 1988.

34. Kochanek, 'Mrs Gandhi's Pyramid', p. 104.

35. For an interesting discussion of the centralizing tendencies, see Paul Brass, 'Pluralism, Regionalism and Decentralizing Tendencies of Contemporary Indian Politics', *The States of South Asia*, ed. A.J. Wilson and D. Dalton, Honolulu and Delhi: University of Hawai Press, 1982, pp. 223-64.

37. F. Frankel, *India's Political Economy*, Delhi: Oxford University Press, 1978, chaps. 10 and 11.

38. Z. Masani, *Indira Gandhi: A Biography*, London: Hamish Hamilton, 1975.

38. Ibid.

39. The CPI split in 1964 to form the CPI and the Communist Party of India (Marxist) or the CPI(M). The CPI(M) was split in 1968 into CPI(M) and the Communist Party of India (Marxist-Leninist) or CPI(ML). CPI support was concentrated in Bihar, and CPI(M) strongholds were West Bengal and Kerala.

40. I. Malhotra, *Indira Gandhi*, London: Hodder and Stoughton, 1989.

41. Frankel, *India's Political Economy*, p. 447.

42. For details see Nossiter, *Marxist State Governments*.

43. Ibid., p. 219.

44. Satyamurthy, *Centre-State Relations*, p. 435.

45. Ibid.

46. Nossiter, *Marxist State Governments*.

47. Frankel, *India's Political Economy*, p. 448.

48. According to Marcus Franda, the CPI(M) claimed to have distributed 200,000 acres of land under the Second United Front Government. M. Franda, 'Radical Politics in West Bengal', *Radical Politics in South Asia*, ed. P.R. Brass and M. Franda, Cambridge, MA: MIT Press, 1973, p. 202.

49. See for example, S. Ghosh, *The Naxalite Movement*, Calcutta: Firma Mukhopadhaya, 1974 and B. Das Gupta, *The Naxalite Movement*, Bombay: Allied Publishers, 1975.

50. A. Kohli, *Democracy and Discontent: The Crisis of Governability in India*, Cambridge: Cambridge University Press, 1991, p. 278.

51. Dharma Vira, *My Reminiscences*, Delhi: Vikas Publishing House, 1990, p. 101.

52. Nossiter, *Marxist State Governments*.

53. B.D. Dua, *President's Rule in India*, New Delhi, 1979.

54. *Economic and Political Weekly*, 9 December 1967, p. 2118.

55. Kohli, *Democracy and Discontent*, pp. 283-5.

56. Rabindra Ray, *The Naxalites and their Ideology*, Delhi, 1986, pp. 118–19.

57. *The Times of India*, 14 March 1972.

58. Ibid.

59. President's Rule was used 61 times in the states between 1951 and 1980. Several states have undergone President's Rule five or six times since independence. Since 1967, there has never been a time when no state has been under it. Information from Brass, 'Pluralism, Regionalism', pp. 246–7.

60. Dua, *President's Rule*, p. 610.

61. Brass, 'Pluralism, Regionalism', pp. 246–54.

62. This point has been made by Prabhat Patnaik with regard to the Kerala experience in Richard W. Franke and Barbara Chasin, 'Kerala State, India: "Radical Reform as Development"', *Monthly Review*, January 1991, p. 35.

63. Ray, *The Naxalites*, p. 119.

64. Prasanta Sen Gupta, 'Politics in West Bengal: The Left Front Versus the Congress (I)', *Asian Survey*, September 1989.

65. Amrita Basu, 'Parliamentary Communism as a Historical Phenomenon: The CPI(M) West Bengal', in *Two Faces of Protest: Contrasting Modes of Women's Activism in India*, Berkeley: University of California Press, 1992, pp. 25–53.

66. Ibid.

67. Commission on Centre-State Relations Report, part II, New Delhi, 1987, pp. 600–1.

68. For details, see J.M. Thomas Isaac and S. Mohanna Kumar, 'Kerala Elections, 1991: Lessons and Non-Lessons', *Economic and Political Weekly*, 23 November 1991, pp. 2697–8.

69. 'Kerala Model' refers to the positive achievements of the policies of distribution adopted in Kerala in ensuring a relatively high quality of life to the people in the region despite its relative economic backwardness. Ibid., p. 2692. Also see R.W. Franke and B.H. Chasin, *Kerala: Development Through Radical Reform*, Delhi: Promilla & Co. Publishers, 1992.

71. Thomas Isaac and Kumar, 'Kerala Elections', pp. 2697–8.

72. Ibid., p. 2703.

73. Franke and Chasin, *Kerala*, p. 20.

74. 'Kerala's Financial Position Facts and Figures', *Text of the Memorandum presented to the Prime Minister on 28 December 1987 by Chief Minister of Kerala*, Trivandrum, 1987.

75. 'Speeches of the Chief Minister', *Voice of Kerala*, Trivandrum, 1989, pp. 158–69.

76. Ibid.

77. Ibid.

78. Ibid.

PART II

CASTE, COMMUNALISM AND THE STATE

7

The Die is Cast(e)
The Debate on Backward Caste/Class Quotas, 1990 and 2006

Introduction

IN THE LAST few decades, the expansion of group-based preferential policies has dominated public debates in India. Even as affirmative action programmes worldwide have come under fire from people advocating group-blind policies, India has persisted with, and even expanded mandatory reservations and affirmative action, which are unprecedented in their scope and extent, and radical in their content. Both central and state governments have, in varying degrees, implemented policies for reservations that aim to increase opportunities for backward classes/castes in government employment and education. The access of these castes to public institutions was traditionally low. The government's position in 1950 was that only two categories—the Scheduled Castes (SCs) and the Scheduled Tribes (STs)—were entitled to reservations in education, public employment and the legislature. A central issue has been whether to define the backward classes in terms of economic position or caste. The first attempt, by the Kalelkar Commission, was unsuccessful with many dissenting voices on the Commission, including the Chairman himself. Its recommendations were not accepted by the Congress government when it reported in 1955. However, in August 1990, Prime Minister V.P. Singh of the Janata Dal-led National Front government announced the implementation of reservations in central government jobs for the Other Backward Classes (OBCs), which for the purposes of this chapter, will be known as Mandal I. Fifteen years later, in April 2006, the Congress-led United Progressive Alliance

---

* The title of this chapter is a variation of the theme title of the *Little Magazine* issue on reservations (*Little Magazine*, vol. VI, issues 4–5).

Proceedings of the British Academy 159, 165–187. © The British Academy 2010.

(UPA) government made moves to introduce reservations for the OBCs in institutions of higher and professional education (Mandal II). The Mandal Commission, which submitted its report in 1980, had recommended 27 per cent reservations in both the government and the education sector, but V.P. Singh did not extend reservations to educational institutions because he was apprehensive that this was likely to fuel even stronger protests, and could thus dissipate the likely political gains from implementing OBC reservations in government jobs.

Both decisions have been a major source of conflict. For any understanding of why this is so, it is important to separate Mandal I and Mandal II. Mandal I essentially acted as a catalyst to open up the political and bureaucratic system for sections of the OBCs. Mandal II sought to increase educational access and opportunities for disadvantaged groups at the point when the post-Independence consensus on the Nehruvian mixed economy model and the Congress social coalition of extremes (upper castes, SCs, and minorities) had broken down.[1]

This chapter focuses on the controversy generated by the UPA government's decision to extend reservations for OBCs in higher education. Two issues have dominated Indian policy debates regarding reservations for OBCs. The first issue is whether caste is an indicator of disadvantage, especially in the case of OBCs. The key concern is whether OBCs should be identified on the basis of caste or on the basis of economic and occupational criteria. The second issue pertains to the conception of backwardness itself for backwardness, as it was widely defined, excluded non–Hindus. Both issues assume a new importance in the context of the vast social and economic changes that have taken place in the country since the 1990s which have important implications for social relations and which also raise further questions with regard to the fairness and relevance of reservation policies and their implications for excluded groups.

Mandal I: Reservations in Central Government

The Constitution provided clear policies of reservations for SCs but it did not do so in the same unambiguous terms for the backward castes, even though the OBCs as an official category gained currency during the Constituent Assembly debates in the late 1940s. After Independence the number of groups entitled to reservation was expanded to include the OBCs. When India became independent, Nehru gave them a new name— 'other backward classes'—implying classes other than the untouchables and tribes. The Constitution refers to 'backward classes' in Articles 15(4) and 16(4), under which the state is empowered to make special provision for any socially and educationally backward classes of citizens. But in its usage it was an all-encompassing category that would include the underprivileged and the marginalized castes: 'it was not a class category and it has been understood to mean certain castes'.[2]

Article 340 of the Constitution empowers the state to appoint a commission 'to investigate the condition of socially and educationally backward classes'. At the all-India level two such commissions have so far been appointed. In 1953, Kaka Kalelkar, former disciple of Gandhi, was asked to head the first Backward Classes Commission with terms of reference to:

Determine the criteria to be adopted in considering whether any sections of the people in the territory of India (in addition to the Scheduled Castes and Scheduled Tribes . . .) should be treated as socially and educationally backward classes; and, in accordance with such criteria, prepare a list of such classes setting out also their approximate number and their territorial distribution.

Investigate the conditions of all such socially and educationally backward classes and the difficulties under which they labour and make recommendations. . . .[3]

The Kalelkar Commission reported in 1955. The majority opinion in the Commission favoured identification of backward classes in terms of low social position in the traditional caste hierarchy, lack of general educational advancement among the major section of a caste or community, and inadequate representation in government services and in the fields of trade, commerce and industry.[4] The Report made two main recommendations. First, the backward classes should benefit from a 70 per cent quota in technical education institutions. Second, quotas should be reserved for them in central and state administrations: 25 per cent of vacancies in Class I, 33.3 per cent in Class II, and 40 per cent in Class III and IV.[5] There was however a dissenting, minority report and in his covering letter to the President, the Chairman himself expressed doubts:

It is only when the Report was being finalized that I started thinking anew and found that backwardness could be tackled on a basis or a number of bases other than caste. I only succeeded in raising the suspicion of a majority of my colleagues that I was trying to torpedo the recommendation of the Commission. This was another reason why I signed the Report without even a minute of dissent.[6]

The Congress government decided not to act on the Report's recommendations with regard to central government jobs, but invited the state governments to go ahead and identify lists of backward classes and fix their own quotas for reservations. The rejection of reservations in the central government was only a partial setback for the OBCs, however, as several states had already granted them extensive reservations in government employment and educational institutions.

It was left to the Second Backward Classes Commission, constituted in 1978, during the Janata Party regime at the Centre, to examine the desirability or otherwise of making a provision for reservation for those backward classes that were not adequately represented in public services. The Commission Report marked a watershed in redefining the official discourse, which had from the time of Kalelkar's dissenting covering letter sought to emphasise economic backwardness as an important factor for decisions with regard to social and educational backwardness. Disregarding Kalelkar's approach, the Mandal Commission charted its approach on the lines adopted by State Commissions which had defined backwardness in caste terms rather than socio-economic terms. It recommended a reservation of 27 per cent for OBCs in central government jobs; this would be in addition to the 22.5 per cent posts for SCs and STs already reserved in all services and public sector undertakings.[7]

When the Mandal Commission submitted its report in 1980, the Congress party was in power and it was unwilling to act on the report and Indira Gandhi did not implement any part of the Mandal Report. Neither did Rajiv Gandhi. He told his aides, 'It's a can of worms; I won't touch it.'[8] Thus it was only in 1990 when a non-Congress coalition government came to power that it proposed the implementation of the Mandal Commission recommendations. In this context, V.P. Singh's decision to implement reservations of government jobs had far-reaching implications in changing the balance of power between castes. It signified a major victory for the backward castes and the non-Congress parties advocating 'Mandalization' (a term coined to convey the upward mobility of the backward classes) of opportunity structures and politics.

The historic decision prompted widespread disturbances and violence in several parts of the country. Despite the violent protests however, the government went ahead and implemented the decision on 27 per cent reservation for OBCs in central government jobs. This was not done through legislation (as in the case of Mandal II in 2006) but through an executive order following a decision in the cabinet. As Arjun Singh was to say much later in April 2008 after the Supreme Court upheld 27 per cent reservations for OBCs in higher education, 'V.P. Singh's was a knee-jerk reaction'.[9] There was no build-up to it, there was no discussion with other political parties, and several of them criticized the government for acting hastily without consulting them. However, all of them extended support to reservations because none of them could afford to alienate the huge lower-caste constituency.

Social justice was the 'key legitimating concept in the political arguments over reservations in the Mandal debate'.[10] The Mandal position held empowerment and participation of the backward castes in public institutions as critical for the creation of a more just society. The basic issue was with regard to the importance attached to historical discrimination as against current inequalities. V.P. Singh described his decision to implement the recommendations of the Mandal Commission as 'a momentous decision of social justice'.[11] For its proponents, reservations were not a means for economic well-being and improvement in material needs; they were a means to facilitate the inclusion of OBCs in arenas of education and state power where they had been under-represented. The central rationale of OBC reservations was therefore to break the upper-caste monopoly on government jobs and professions that remained unchanged after nearly half a century of democracy. The motivation of the project was quintessentially political—the point was that it would help to erode the hold of the upper castes on public employment, and would thus enable OBCs to have a sense of participation in running the affairs of the country.[14]

Subsequently in 1991 the new Congress minority government led by Narasimha Rao proposed that 10 per cent of the vacancies in civil posts and services under the Government of India should be reserved for other economically backward sections of the people who were not covered by any of the existing schemes of reservation. This, however, was never implemented. In its judgment on the *Indira Sawhney* v. *Union of India* case on the challenges to both the Singh and Rao government decisions, the Supreme Court in a majority decision upheld the 27 per cent reservation for socially and educationally backward classes (in effect the OBCs) but struck down the 10 per cent reservation for economically backward people. The main opinion, authored by Justice Jeevan Reddy, supported the argument that, in the context of contemporary Indian society, economic criteria alone cannot be the basis of backwardness, although this may be a consideration along with or in addition to social backwardness. In deciding the constitutionality of reservations for the OBCs, however, the court mandated that the government must make use of economic considerations in helping the truly backward, by which it meant that government must find ways to disqualify the more advantaged individuals in these classes. At the same time and in the same decision, the court also forbade reservations for economically disadvantaged upper castes. In other words, the court ruling suggested that to be a member of an OBC, it was not enough to be in a lower caste if one's father was a government minister or bureaucrat in the government, just as it was also not enough to simply be poor if one was of a high caste. It is worth quoting the court's judgment in the *Sawhney* case:

Over the years caste has become synonymous with class for the purpose of reservations. Government policy has relied on courts, which have given their imprimatur of approval to the conflation and substitution of caste and class. The deliberate use of the term classes rather than castes in the constitutional text has been interpreted by the court to mean general social groupings rather than economic classes.[13]

Clearly, the judiciary has played an active role in imposing procedures for programme design and in striking a balance among the competing interests articulated in the constitutional blueprint and group interests in society. The Mandal I decision led to widespread protest and unrest but once the court approved the proposed changes, there was widespread public acceptance.[14]

The changing face of the Indian bureaucracy is in a large measure attributable to this elaborate regime of reservations. The OBCs had a negligible presence of about 2 per cent in government employment in 1990 when the Mandal recommendations were accepted, and even this small representation in employment was restricted to the lower rungs of government jobs. Upper castes constituted 37.6 per cent of the civil services.[15] Even though the full impact of the Mandal initiative will be known only after twenty years, the recent data on social profiles of the 400-odd individuals who annually clear the civil service examination to join the Indian Administrative Service (IAS), Indian Foreign Service (IFS), Indian Police Service (IPS), and other services show that 'people who had no access to the civil services are coming in. The city-born and city-bred are busy chasing a plethora of new economy options while those born and schooled in district and small towns, often from the lower castes, are flocking to the IAS'.[16]

The radical change began after the implementation of OBC reservations in government jobs. The significant increase registered by the OBCs has been made possible entirely by the 27 per cent reservations for them, and their representation in the civil services has been boosted as many have made it to the general category also. By 2000, the SCs, STs, and OBCs together accounted for more than 55 per cent of the total recruitment in the union civil services. This marked a dramatic shift from the pattern that was prevailing until the early 1990s when 60 per cent of all Hindu officers belonged to the upper castes.[17]

Mandal II: Reservations in Higher Education

In April 2006, Human Resource Development Minister Arjun Singh made an announcement that the central government was planning to extend reservations to OBCs in central educational institutions. It stirred a huge public debate even though it was not the first time that the central government was considering reservation for backward castes. Supporters called the proposal a belated move to promote social justice and inclusion in upper-caste-dominated higher education, even as opponents warned that India's edge in the knowledge economy would dwindle, competitiveness erode, and multinational companies move away.

The preceding discussion indicates that OBCs have been the subjects of preferential treatment previously because of under-representation in governmental structures. But this group, unlike the SCs or Muslims, is neither a statistical minority--in fact the OBCs are a statistical majority as they constitute roughly 40-50 per cent of the population--nor are they a minority in the sociological sense of lacking political and bureaucratic power as noted above.

Despite decades of preferential treatment in different forms, public life in India outside of politics is disproportionately dominated by upper castes. They continue to dominate public institutions, skilled professions, and the media, while the SCs, STs, OBCs, and Muslims are way behind the upper castes in all spheres of public life and in higher and professional education specifically. The spread of higher education among deprived groups is generally low; the gaps across categories remain very large. It is these large differences in educational attainment and access that state intervention in the form of reservations seeks to address.

The forerunner to the 2006 political controversy was the decision of the Supreme Court in August 2005 which made it clear that it was impermissible to enforce reservations in private educational institutions which do not receive financial support from the state. This meant that educational opportunities in the private institutions would remain outside the purview of affirmative action policies of the state for disadvantages groups. The 93rd Amendment was thus necessitated by the Supreme Court's judgement in the *Inamdar* case in 2005.[18] The seven-member bench went into all these issues, and noted that though the issue of reservation was not a central one in the *Pai Foundation* and *Islamic Academy* cases, it had to be taken into account, especially where minority institutions were involved.[19] The judges observed: '. . . [in the case of private institutions] neither the policy of reservation can be enforced by the state nor any quota of percentage of admissions can be carved out to be appropriated by the state'.[20] One of the key issues considered by the court in these judgements was the right of minority institutions to run their colleges the way they want to.

The issue of access to higher education has always been an emotive one, especially in India where the barriers to entry in higher education are still very high. Higher education has grown enormously since Independence— from 25 to 348 universities and 700 to 17,625 colleges. About eight million students in India join undergraduate studies each year, although this is only 8-9 per cent of the relevant age group between 20 and 24 years who are enrolled in these institutions, as against 50 per cent or more in some developed countries. With the changes in India over the past 25 years, especially the phenomenal economic growth of recent years, there has been an escalating demand for higher education, particularly professional and technical education, in engineering and medical colleges and management institutes. Elite institutions like the Indian Institutes of Technology (IITs), Indian Institutes of Management (IIMs), and medical colleges are in great demand from various sections, most notably the upwardly mobile middle classes, because these institutions provide heavily subsidized high-quality education which can fetch a good job anywhere in the world. The emergence of knowledge-based empowerment as a major source of income and privilege has further enhanced their significance as professional courses have become an even more important means for upward mobility.[21]

The national-level data from the 55th Round of the National Sample Survey Organization (NSSO) (1999-2000) showed in stark terms the inequalities in access to higher education. Students from the middle classes and upper castes traditionally associated with more education—comprising roughly 20 per cent of the population—dominate higher education, compared to 9 per cent or less for all other categories.[22] The Hindu upper castes formed little more than a third of the total urban population, but they accounted for two-thirds of professional and higher education—in other words, their share in higher education is twice their share in the population. The obvious consequence of the upper-caste over-representation is the under-representation of other groups.

The UPA government amended the Constitution in 2005 to permit reservations in aided and unaided educational institutions in favour of SCs, STs, and OBCs, except in institutions run by minorities. After the passage of the 93rd Constitutional Amendment Act, which was essentially an enabling provision, the supporters of OBC quotas argued that it necessitated further legislation to ensure the implementation of affirmative action in institutions of higher education. Once the demand for reservations gathered momentum, the central government had to implement the provisions of Article 15(5) in respect of all institutions and universities under its purview. Moreover, several states had either already made laws or were going to make laws to implement this provision. Treating this as an enabling legislation, the UPA government decided to introduce quotas for OBCs in publicly funded educational institutions, premier technology institutes, medical colleges, and central universities. The government was under considerable pressure from coalition partners and political parties which unanimously favoured an expeditious introduction of reservations in higher education for the OBCs.

The official argument in favour of reservations offered two principal justifications: first, extending quotas in higher education was the continuation of preferential treatment in public employment to the OBCs since 1994; and, second, it came up in 2006 mainly in the context of the legislation on private unaided institutions. The government's position was that it had already amended the Constitution; a new clause (5) had been added to Article 15 (which is a fundamental right); the constitutional amendment has been carried with near unanimity by Parliament; and there was an all-party consensus on the issue. Moreover, unlike the Mandal I decision, which was rushed through without adequate consultations, this legislation was the result of wide-ranging consultations with MPs from all political parties, and it had been routed through the cabinet and various government departments.

Acute dissatisfactions arising out of unequal representation in prestigious educational institutions, and the historical disadvantage in education of certain groups, are among the primary reasons for the institution of reservations in higher education. Therefore the principal justification was cast in terms of the need to enhance equality of opportunity for the weaker sections of society, especially under the new economy. Government reasoning regarded equality as a positive right which requires the state to minimise existing inequalities and to treat the underprivileged with special care as envisaged in the Constitution. The promotion of equality and the elimination of inequality formed an essential part of the basic structure of the Constitution, and not providing reservations to SCs, STs, and OBCs would be a violation of this basic structure. For the first time, the government put forward the basic structure doctrine in its affidavit to the Supreme Court: reservation is part of the basic structure of the Constitution and therefore the government had no option but to introduce reservations for the OBCs. Further, Clause (5) of Article 15 was inserted to enable the state to implement it.

Controversies and Protests

The UPA government decided to introduce the Central Educational Institutions (Reservation in Admission) Bill 2006 to cover central universities, institutions of national importance set up by Parliament, and institutions directly or indirectly aided by the central government, or linked to central universities or centrally created institutions. It excluded private unaided institutions and it excluded minority educational institutions. The Bill provoked a major agitation by doctors. The countrywide agitation was organised by a group which calls itself Youth For Equality (YFE). It started from the All India Institute of Medical Sciences (AIIMS) and included students from premier medical colleges and from the IITs and IIMs. Spearheaded by the doctors of AIIMS, the agitation originated in this institute, which remained its 'nodal point' throughout. A government-appointed committee headed by the University Grants Commission Chairman S.K. Thorat (to look into complaints from MPs and media reports on allegations of harassment of SC and ST students at AIIMS) noted in its report that the 'AIIMS became the venue of the protest primarily to paralyze health care for thousands of people and attract public attention against reservation. Paralysing of the health care services including emergency services would put pressure on the government'.[23]

For nineteen days, doctors and medical students were on strike, bringing essential health services to a standstill. The main support came from the corporate sector, traders associations, chambers of commerce, industry lobbies, the Indian Medical Association, executives of information technology companies, residents welfare associations in many cities, business executives, and, above all, owners of private professional colleges.[24] As in the anti-Mandal agitation of 1990-1, the students engaged in mockery of the lower castes by enacting casteist forms of protest such as the symbolic sweeping of streets, shoe-shining, and shouting slogans that lower castes are fit only for menial jobs while others are 'naturally' suited to respectable professions such as engineering and medicine.[25] The doctors called off their agitation after the court's directive that they resume work or face contempt.

The National Knowledge Commission (NKC) opposed OBC reservations and publicized its opposition through its majority (6 : 2) report in the media.[26] Two members of the NKC decided to quit in protest against OBC reservations. Despite the protests and media support for the agitation against OBC reservations, public sympathy was largely in favour of OBC quotas, except among the elites and the upper middle classes, who were clearly unhappy with the decision. The media coverage may have succeeded in making it a national and emotive issue but it does not seem to have made much difference to the strong pro-reservation position on this subject. Asked if they were in favour of reservations, 63 per cent of the respondents in the *Indian Express*-CNN-IBN poll expressed support for reservations and only 34 per cent were against them.[27] It is important to note, however, that a larger majority of respondents—67 per cent— expressed a preference for economic criteria, irrespective of caste, for the identification of beneficiaries.

Shifts in public debate

In the years since Mandal I, the political and economic landscape has changed almost completely. Market reforms have contributed to the breakdown of the Nehruvian consensus on a mixed economy and the Congress social coalition of upper castes, minorities, and SCs.[28] India's GDP has grown steadily over the past two decades, and during 2004-7 its annual growth has exceeded 8 per cent. The economy has witnessed an explosion of high finance, stock market, information technology, software exports, media, entertainment, and real-estate speculation. However, the bulk of people have not gained significantly from the paradigm shift in economic policy. Economic boom and high growth have brought benefits only to the top 20 per cent of the population, which has seen an unprecedented rise in income and job opportunities.[29]

The basic feature of the process of economic development has been exclusion—from control over assets, from benefits of growth, from education, and from income-generating opportunities. The imbalances and exclusions have led to the creation of two economies across the social and regional landscape of India. Government jobs were drying up and after economic liberalization salaries in government continue to be modest in comparison to the astronomical pay packets in the private sector and the media. Consequently, the upper castes and middle classes have flocked to the booming managerial and executive jobs in the corporate sector, but they want subsidized high-quality education to provide them with the credentials for access to such jobs. Graduates from these institutions find immediate placement in the private sector; hence the increased stakes in elite institutions, which open up opportunities for high-salaried jobs as opposed to the civil service, which has lost its sheen for the upwardly mobile middle classes. These are the groups that took an active part in the anti-quota agitation. The agitators in 1990 were primarily from the lower-middle classes interested in government jobs, whereas in 2006 the protestors were principally interested in private-sector employment.

From the 1990s, the politics around reservations for OBCs has centred on two dimensions. At one level it has been characterized by clashes between social and political forces that support and oppose reservations for OBCs in education and employment. Those who support quotas perceive reservation-based affirmative action as an instrument to uplift sections that have been oppressed for centuries and to lessen the dominance of upper castes. Those who oppose reservation look at the issue of upper-caste dominance differently. They claim that their dominance is solely due to merit, and that any attempt to undermine merit will result in the erosion of progress. This will hurt India's rise as an economic power and therefore the government would be well advised to allow market forces and merit to produce a twenty-first-century economy. The crux of the argument is that reservations militate against merit and allow degrees or qualifications to be awarded to people with less than deserving performance and aptitude. Such a system is inefficient as compared with openly competitive systems. These measures are unfair benefits given to particular caste groupings undeserving of such protection and hence pandering to vote-banks of politicians. A study by Satish Deshpande has noted however that: 'Merit in the Indian context refers to certification of competence, aptitude or knowledge acquired through examination of some kind. . . . What matters is not how well one does in the exam but how much better one does than others taking the same exam.'[31]

Supporters argue that higher education inherently involves exclusion and 'merit' legitimises such exclusions. Unlocking the gates of higher education was necessary to dilute the upper-caste monopoly. [32]

In the past fifteen years, the Mandal initiative has helped to change the face of the polity; the grammar of entitlement has become part of the new language of politics, and all parties now accept the logic of quotas. The political class, including the BJP which brought down the V.P. Singh government for implementing the Mandal Report and whose political base lies among upper-caste Hindus, seems to realise that a reversal on reservation policy is no longer possible. However, outside the political domain, the opposition to reservations amongst the intelligentsia, media, and civil society at large continues to be strong. The arguments in civil society were broadly of two types: arguments about institutions, and arguments about caste disadvantage. The institutional argument mainly focused on the importance of merit for the maintenance of institutional efficacy in the field of higher education. Merit and inclusion were interpreted as irreconcilable in the new post-economic reforms discourse.[33]

The Civil Society Debate

On the issue of caste disadvantage, two sets of arguments came up. One argument recognised that caste is associated with inequalities and discrimination, and that it is the responsibility of public policy to address these. There were however differences among those espousing this argument regarding whether quotas would be efficient in achieving these outcomes or whether alternative strategies could be devised for this. A second set of arguments highlighted the difference between SCs, who are poor and exploited, and the OBCs, who are powerful and do not deserve quotas—

a point that had been emphasized by Rajiv Gandhi in his Lok Sabha speech in September 1990. There is also the argument that the regime of reservations does not actually help the weaker sections among the deprived since the benefits are cornered by the affluent among them (this too was highlighted by Rajiv Gandhi). The argument suggests that as the OBCs were economically empowered through the democratic system in the 1960s and 1970s, they have economic and political power and are administratively empowered by reservations in government service and therefore do not require reservations in higher education as well. This line of reasoning was particularly strong among the upper-middle-class opponents of Mandal II and in regions which have had no tangible exposure to reservations in the education sector. Not surprisingly, in the four South Indian states as well as in Maharashtra and Gujarat, which have had a long experience with quotas, the opposition to OBC reservation was muted.

A third important feature of the civil society debate in Mandal II was the complete disengagement from the political process, as there was a pervasive feeling among the protestors that they were above it. The disdain towards the political class and parliament encouraged protestors to concentrate on the judiciary and the media, which they perceived as friendly towards their cause. This was evident from the tendency to arrogate powers to decide on the public policy of affirmative action rather than leave it to the state to decide. It also derives sustenance from the belief that excluded groups do not possess the intelligence or aptitude for higher education. This was palpable from the condescending attitude of the student leaders to the very policy of quotas: the state can address the problem of discrimination and disadvantage as long as state intervention through affirmative action did not reduce opportunities for them.

Mandal II sought to cut through the conceptual tangles that have besieged the issue of OBC reservations. The UPA government relied on previous court rulings which had clearly given their approval for the substitution of caste for class, and to privileged caste over other identities. It was repeatedly argued that often, caste is deemed to be a social class and so if a group was socially backward, it would be a backward class for the purposes of Article 16(4). While caste cannot be the sole criterion to determine the class of persons for whom reservation must be sought, caste can indeed be one of the factors (or even the primary factor) relevant in determining which sections of society in India require reservation in employment or in institutions of higher education. In other words, it is constitutionally justified to take caste as the social unit or class to be examined and tested for backwardness or its absence in terms of the criteria of social and educational backwardness devised by the government.

Political Response

The decision on OBC quotas in higher education was part of a plan to demonstrate the backward caste and social justice credentials of the Congress party. This party had traditionally supported the reservation principle, starting with Nehru, who introduced the constitutional amendment in 1951 to enable the state to make special provision for the advancement of socially and educationally backward classes and SCs and STs. However, the Congress leadership was ambivalent on the issue since Rajiv Gandhi questioned the scientific basis of OBC quotas in his Lok Sabha speech in September 1990 and argued for a comprehensive action plan for the disadvantaged groups. He had criticized the V.P. Singh government for thinking only 'around caste' and 'vested interests in particular castes'.[34] The 2006 move was an attempt to counterbalance the long-standing distrust of the backward castes towards the party, which was generally seen as a party favouring the upper caste. Against this perception, the reservation gamble was a crucial element in the new strategy to wean the OBCs away from regional and state-based parties which have been the preferred choice of the backward-caste voters. Even though there was disagreement within the Congress with regard to the timing of the quota proposal (and more so with Arjun Singh for trying to take credit for it), the party leadership could hardly afford to vacillate or disown the issue. Equally, the party knew that open support would alienate the upper castes. If, however, the Congress stuck firmly to its pro-reservation stand, it could hope to win some OBC support and offset the lower-caste advantage enjoyed by regional parties like the Samajwadi Party and the Bahujan Samaj Party who claimed to be the champions of the disadvantaged in north India. The Congress general secretary stated: 'The issue isn't politics alone. At its core is social justice. We will not, I repeat, we will not recant on the quota issue. That is settled and the perceived silence of the prime minister and the Congress president must not be mistaken for ambivalence or confusion. Both are supportive of this policy.'[35]

Propelled by pressures and counter-pressures, the UPA government was keen to strike a fair balance between the competing claims of the disadvantaged and the advantaged. The UPA chairperson Sonia Gandhi underscored the point that the extension of OBC quotas to central educational institutions would go hand in hand with an increase in seats for general category students. This approach found approval in the Cabinet. One newspaper reported that the Union Cabinet meeting that cleared the bill on reservation for the OBCs 'witnessed the most serious and purposeful discussion so far in the life of the UPA Government'.[36] The advocates of quotas made a strong case for a total and complete changeover to the new reservation regime for the OBCs. A senior minister cited the 'centuries of injustice' that had been the OBCs lot and argued that the backward classes were not asking for a 'backlog' compensation but were merely demanding correction of the injustice. In other words, the OBCs are demanding their legitimate, long-delayed share in social privileges like centrally funded higher education. Some ministers drew the attention of the Cabinet to the Supreme Court pronouncements on the concept of the 'creamy layer' (that is, the economically more affluent segment) and on the need to gradually phase out these strata from the reservation regime. However, opinion was firmly in favour of retaining the creamy layer. The Prime Minister urged his colleagues 'not do anything that would destroy the country's "knowledge strength"'. The final decision reflected his three main concerns: (a) there should be no dilution in the existing seats and opportunities available in the 'non-reserved' categories; (b) the extension of the 27 per cent reservation for the OBCs should be staggered to ensure that the requisite infrastructure was in place; and (c) certain institutions of 'national/strategic' importance should be kept out of the reservation regime.[37]

The UPA government decided to increase the number of seats in the general category so that the number of seats filled by 'open competition' did not shrink. Under this formula, the number of unreserved seats would be increased in proportion to the 27 per cent to be reserved for the OBCs. However, the government's plan of accommodation through expansion rather than cutting into general category seats failed to halt the protest. The opponents remained unconvinced, indeed sceptical about the government move, which according to one critic 'exemplified the way government thinks of admissions: goodies be distributed to whoever they want, a mechanism for buying out different groups'.[38]

The Lok Sabha unanimously approved the legislation for reservations for OBCs in central educational institutions by a voice vote in December 2006. Cross-party support marked the Lok Sabha debate on the Bill as virtually every speaker lauded the UPA government's initiative to introduce reservations for OBCs in higher education, which they argued was long overdue. The support for the legislation cut across parties, barring the BJP's opposition to the provision on the exclusion of minority educational institutions. Inspired by key provisions in the Constitution, namely, Article 46 and Article 15(5), the new legislation was a significant measure, as it was the first time that parliament legally recognized the reservation of seats in educational institutions for OBCs as a necessary measure to give effect to the constitutional provisions.

The most striking feature of the political response was the wide-ranging political support for Arjun Singh's proposal, in contrast to the more limited support for V.P. Singh's attempt to provide reservations for OBCs in government jobs: reservations in higher education garnered the support of all parties and MPs. In the first place, the Congress, which initiated Mandal II, had opposed Mandal I. The second noteworthy difference is that prior to this Act, reservations at the central level were the result of an executive decision implemented usually through an Office Memorandum; there was no statutory backing for these policies. This led to several court rulings interpreting constitutional provisions in a manner perceived to be against the interests of backward classes.[39] As executive actions, the court found it easy to stay the operation of such an Official Memorandum in 1990. Mandal II, however, went through a much wider consultative and legislative process. Nevertheless, the court stayed the operation of this Act too. Thus, an active role of the judiciary is a strong feature of both episodes for in both cases, the judiciary questioned procedures and methodologies for design and assumed the role of policymaking.

Judicial Intervention

The court intervened in the middle of the Mandal II agitation, staying the law and declaring that the OBC reservation issue 'requires judicial review'. This put paid to Congress-UPA quota plans of rolling out OBC reservations in 2007. Significantly however, the court had not overturned reservations for OBCs. The petitioners in *Ashoka Thakur* v. *Union of India* claimed that the Act and the Amendment violated their fundamental right to equality. The Court's two-judge bench had issued an interim order on 29 March 2007 partly staying the law, but as it involved substantial constitutional issues, the government sought the reference of the case to a Constitution Bench. This included Chief Justice K.G. Balakrishnan and Justices Arijit Pasayat, C.K. Thakker, R.V. Raveendran, and Dalveer Bhandari. The five-judge Bench heard arguments for 25 days spread over three months from 7 August 2007 to November 2007. The basic issues were whether the 93rd Amendment was unconstitutional and violative of the basic structure of the Constitution, and whether it confers on the state unbridled power to make special provision for the OBCs. On 10 April 2008, the five-judge Constitution Bench upheld the Constitution (93rd Amendment) Act of 2005, under which the state had been empowered to make special provisions for socially and educationally backward classes in admission to educational institutions, providing a 27 per cent quota for OBCs in IITs, IIMs, and other central educational institutions. The court, while declaring that the creamy layer should be excluded from the quota, held that the Act does not violate the basic structure of the Constitution. It also said that reservations should not be in perpetuity but should be revised at periodic intervals.

The judgment was in keeping with the Supreme Court's long-standing interpretation of the constitutional provisions on equality, namely that the fundamental right to equality is compatible with schemes like reservations that confer benefits on disadvantaged groups. The Chief Justice pronounced that affirmative action, though 'apparently discriminatory, is calculated to produce equality on a broader basis'. He reasoned that a constitutional amendment which 'moderately abridges or alters the equality principle' but does not abrogate it would not violate the basic structure of the Constitution.[40] The government counsel justified the identification of socially and educationally backward classes on the basis of caste in view of the societal structure of the country, while making submissions on the 27 per cent quotas in higher education for the OBCs.[41] As in Mandal I, the government counsel argued that caste should be construed as a unit leading to reservation. However, the Chief Justice, referring to the arguments made against the application of the creamy layer to educational institutions, stated that: 'They are excluded because unless this segment of caste is excluded from that caste group, there cannot be proper identification of the backward class. If the "creamy layer" principle is not applied, it could easily be said that all the castes that have been included among the SEBCs (Socially and Educationally Backward Classes) have been included exclusively on the basis of caste.'[42]

The die is cast(e)

Several important issues and concerns emerge from these controversies. From the beginning, reservations for backward castes have been haunted by questions regarding definition and identification, the relationship between caste and deprivation, its implications for the core commitment to SCs/STs, and the exclusion of minorities. A striking point with regard to the political and legislative history of affirmative action for backward castes is that caste remains the most important unit of identification in reservation policy, which in turn has intensified competition among the disadvantaged groups and caused resentment among those excluded from preferential treatment.

One issue that has been far from settled is the question of the relationship between caste and class and whether OBCs constitute a caste or class. By the time of Mandal II, caste and class had become almost inseparable to the point that caste was seen to stand for class. The 2006 OBC quota law said that 'caste is the starting point for identification of socially and educationally backward classes'. Legal jurisprudence has therefore accepted caste as a basis of classification, as is evident from the Mandal II judgement. Several court verdicts in favour of the equivalence of caste and class held that class included persons grouped on the basis of their castes. In line with the court's long-standing interpretation of the constitutional provisions on equality, the court ruling in *Thakur* reiterates that caste itself can be used as a criterion for identification.

The internal differentiation and social heterogeneity among the OBCs suggests that the creamy layer, or the privileged within the OBCs, must be excluded. However, governments have been wary of excluding the affluent sections from the ambit of reservations for fear of political repercussions. The OBC-dominated parties like Rashtriya Janata Dal, Dravida Munnetra Kazhagam (DMK) and the Pattali Makkal Katchi (PMK), which are key members of the UPA, were opposed to it. The National Commission for Backward Classes has periodically conducted social audits to determine the status of various castes, but has not excluded them.[43] The dominant castes such as Nadars and Yadavs continue to remain on the list. As a result, caste groups that have benefited from past systems of quotas, or which have disproportionate political/economic power, continue to enjoy the benefits of reservations and keep the majority still deprived.

The principle behind the creamy layer exclusion is that if the starting points in most respects for various groups are equal, then there is little justification for giving them the benefits of reservation. To put it differently, when it comes to the OBCs, caste alone cannot be a justification for treating them differently. The Supreme Court, recognizing the multiple disadvantages that characterize Indian society, was demanding that the government should provide justification for policies and balance different considerations. It felt that the exclusion of the creamy layer would imply that reservation was not based on caste alone, but on other factors such as social and economic backwardness. Without excluding the creamy layer, the affluent among these castes would stand to benefit more from reservations in higher education and in effect get more benefits than the poor.

In contrast, the supporters of OBC reservation argue that the move to exclude the creamy layer is misplaced and would negate the very purpose of reservation, which is not removing poverty but changing the social composition of higher education. Since the opportunities for higher education are generally availed by the privileged in every social group, only the creamy layer in every group is able to access higher education. 'By disqualifying those most likely to succeed in elite institutions, creamy layer exclusion undermines the very purpose of the proposed law'.[44] As a result, most of the seats reserved for the OBCs would remain unfilled. The fact remains however that group rights do not entitle all individuals in the group, which means there has to be some criterion for admitting specific members to educational institutions. Creamy layer norms could be used to ensure that the more privileged are given last preference.

Another important issue pertains to the attitude towards affirmative action for minorities. If there was one group that needed special treatment in view of its educational backwardness and under-representation in government employment, it was Muslims. Affirmative action was above all needed to tackle their educational backwardness. The chairman of the National Commission made a strong plea for greater access for Muslims in the available higher educational institutions. He suggested the need to evolve 'a suitable mechanism' to ensure an equitable share of minorities in higher education. Yet there was no serious consideration of 'suitable mechanisms' for ensuring access for educationally backward Muslims to modern higher education. This was because backwardness is only recognized in relation to caste, despite the fact that there are glaring disparities between Muslims and other groups in higher education. There is neither affirmative action nor adequate provisioning of schools and colleges in minority-concentration areas. Disadvantage is defined in such a way as to exclude non-Hindus, although theoretically the OBC category includes backward classes from all religions. Given this definitional bias, it would be natural for such groups to see themselves as objects of structural discrimination.[45] Yet, there was no agreement on a suitable mechanism for doing this, despite a recommendation of the Parliamentary Standing Committee that a suitable mechanism to ensure access of minorities should be created.

These issues highlight the unresolved tensions in regard to reservations for OBCs. Throughout the evolution of this policy there has been little philosophical or constitutional consensus on preferential treatment for the OBCs. When reservations were introduced by the new state, the idea was to tear down the barriers to social exclusion and promote the participation of historically excluded and disadvantaged groups. Policies of affirmative action were viewed as instruments which could offset the advantage enjoyed by some and equalize opportunities for others. Moreover, they were seen as complementary to the commitment to an active welfare state that would ameliorate the conditions of the masses by providing an additional boost to the hitherto excluded and poor. It must be remembered that the liberalization of the economy has resulted in widening inequalities and disparities between the rich and the poor, and that social conflicts have become more acute during the past decade of growth. In the context of the rising economic divides, reservations address only the most exclusionary aspects of one axis of exclusions. Furthermore, reservations, though politically necessary and practically helpful, are not the main instrument for the construction of a more egalitarian society. For that, far more foundational changes are required, such as a major redistribution of income and wealth-generating assets like land, better schooling and colleges, special training and skill development programmes, preferential treatment in the allocation of government licences and contracts, employment-generating policies, and so on. Once the need for foundational changes is recognized and taken forward, then there is certainly a strong case to be made for alternative, more sophisticated forms of affirmative action than reservations. It is now time to think about how to use different and new means to bridge disparities and deepen social equality so that the pursuit of equality and justice does not remain anchored in caste, and caste alone.

Notes and References

1. Jawaharlal Nehru's inaugural speech in the Constituent Assembly on 13 December 1946, 'Official Reports of the Lok Sabha Secretariat', *Constituent Assembly Debates (CAD)*, vol. I, Delhi, 1989, p. 59.
2. Quoted in *The Indian Express*, 18 May 2006.
3. Interview with Arjun Singh, *Outlook*, 22–8 April 2008.
4. V.P. Singh, Rajya Sabha Debates, 7 August 1990. Speech cited in Bajpai, 2006.
5. Government of India Report, 1955.
6. S. Patil, 'Should "Class" be the Basis for Recognizance Backwardness?', *Economic and Political Weekly*, vol. 25, no. 50, 1990, p. 2740.
7. Government of India, 'Report of the Backward Classes Commission', vol. 1, 1980, Chairman B.P. Mandal.
8. Ibid.
9. Rajiv Gandhi quoted in the *Indian Express*, 18 May 2006.
10. Interview of Arjun Singh, *Outlook*, 22–8 April 2008.
11. Rochana Bajpai, 'Redefining Equality: Social Justice in the Mandal Debate, 1990', in *Political Ideas in Modern India: Thematic Explorations*, V.R. Mehta, and T. Pantham, eds., Sage Publications, pp. 326–339.
12. V.P. Singh, Rajya Sabha Debates, 7 August 1990, cited in Bajpai, p. 329.
13. Further political reasons for V.P. Singh's decision may have been to undercut both the farmer politics and the emerging communal politics of the BJP. And one reason for the acceptance of the decision may have been because the objections were overtaken by the politics of religion, which for a while trumped the politics of caste.
14. *Indira Sawhney & Others* v. *Union of India*, AIR 1993 SC 477, 1992 Supp (3) SCC 217.
15. Rethinking Affirmative Action, Michigan Law Renew, vol. 97, March 1999, pp. 1296–1310.

16. S. Goyal, 'Social Background of Officers in the Indian Administrative Service', in *Dominance and State Power in Modern India: Decline of a Social Order*, F. Frankel and M.S.A. Rao, eds., New Delhi: Oxford University Press, 1989, pp. 425-33.

17. A. Puri, 'Meet your New DM', *Outlook*, 7 August 2007.

18. S. Goyal, op. cit., p. 430.

19. *W.P. No. 350 of 199—Islamic Academy of Education + 1 v. State of Karnataka and Ors* (2003) 6 SCC 697. Reviewing the role of private higher education providers, an 11-member bench of the Supreme Court in the *Pai* judgement had ruled that fees charged by unaided institutions cannot be regulated but no capitation can be charged. This was once again challenged in the Supreme Court, which reiterated the concept of keeping fees imposed by private education providers within 'reasonable' limits. Consequent to *Islamic Academy,* some state governments, notably Karnataka and Kerala, sought to tighten controls on the unaided private colleges, and enacted legislation to this effect. Their Acts were however stuck down by the courts and, at the Education Ministers' conferences held in 2004 and early 2005, the state ministers asked the central government to enact that which would enable them to exercise the powers they wanted.

20. *P.A. Inamdar & Ors. v. Stare of Maharashtra,* 2005 AIR (SC) 3226.

21. T. Ghosh, 'Case for Caste Based Quotas in Higher Education', *Economic and Political Weekly*, vol. 41, no. 24, 2006, pp. 2428–32.

22. For a discussion of unequal access, see S. Deshpande, 'Exclusive Inequalities Merit, Caste and Discrimination in Indian Higher Eductaion', *Economic and Political Weekly*, vol. 41, no. 24, 2006, pp. 2438–44.

23. 'Report', *Committee to Enquire into the Allegations of Differential Treatment of Scheduled Castes/Scheduled Tribes Students in AIIMS,* 2007, p. 67.

24. These colleges admit over 530,000 students and charge capitation fees upwards of Rs. 50 lakh for admission to professional colleges, such as medical and engineering colleges.

26. For instance, during the agitation, upper-caste student protestors blocked busy streets and started polishing shoes (imitating shoeshine boys) with placards that read: 'This is what we will be reduced to because of the reservation system'. The implication was that the occupation that they (the upper castes) would be reduced to was a 'Dalit occupation'. In other words, it is right for Dalits to continue to do the menial jobs, but if upper castes have to descend to this low level, it is unacceptable. Needless to add, the belief that reservations would push the upper castes down to the menial jobs was only a presumption, not supported by any evidence.

27. The National Knowledge Commission is a high-level advisory body to the Prime Minister set up with the objective of transforming India into a knowledge society.

28. CNN-IBN poll conducted by A.G. Nielsen reported in the *Indian Express,* 25 July 2006.

29. A. Heath and Y. Yadav, 'The United Colours of the Congress: Social Profile of Congress Voters 1996 and 1998', *Economic and Political Weekly*, vol. 35, nos. 34–35, 1999, pp. 2518–28.

30. J. Ghosh, 'Income Inequality in India', *People's Democracy*, vol. 28, no. 7, 2004.

31. Satish Deshpande, 2006, pp. 2442-3.

32. P. Bidwai, 'The Merit Sallacy', *Frontline*, 16 June 2006.

33. P.B. Mehta, 'Let them Have Scholarships', *The Indian Express*, 3 April 2007.

34. Rajiv Gandhi's speech on the Mandal Commission in the Lok Sabha, reproduced in the *Indian Express,* 9 June 2006.

35. As reported in *The Times of India,* 14 July 2006.

36. *The Hindu,* 23 April 2006.

37. Ibid.

38. Mehta 2007.

39. V. Venkatesan, 'Legal Backing', *Frontline*, vol. 23, no. 8, 22 April–5 May 2006.

40. Arguments in the Supreme Court and final verdict reported in *The Hindu,* 12 April 2008.

41. *The Hindu,* 11 October 2007.

42. Ibid., 11 April 2008.

43. A. Raman, 'Keep It Skinned', *Outlook*, 16 April 2007.

44. S. Deshpande, 'Quota Sans Creamy Layer in Education', *The Economic Times*, 16 April 2008.

45. B. Parekh, 'Limits of the Indian Political Imagination', in *Political Ideas in Modern India: Thematic Explorations*, V.R. Mehta and T. Pantham, eds., New Delhi: Sage, 2004, pp. 437–58.

8 | # Politics of the Middle Classes in India

CONTEMPORARY POLITICS in India provides an interesting case for the study of economic and political transitions in comparative contexts. In contrast to cases such as Eastern Europe and Latin America, which have been characterized by both the economic transition from state planning to liberalized economies and the political transition of democratization, India's transition has been initiated within the political context of a vibrant parliamentary democracy. It has generated a lively debate about political developments in India, particularly the dramatic rise to prominence of political Hinduism and its association with the middle class. To understand this association, we need to first look at the nature and size of the middle class and its dominant concerns and orientations, not abstractly, but with reference to political Hinduism. The first part of this chapter offers a brief sketch of the Indian middle class. The second part offers some comments on contemporary political change and the role of the new middle class in these dramatic changes, namely the rise of Hindu nationalism and neo-liberalism. Though discerning a pattern in contemporary political change is fraught with difficulty, future historians will notice a connection between the political sway of the Bharatiya Janata Party (BJP) and economic neo-liberalism, which has provided a major benefit to the middle classes. Assessing the implications of these trends is even more difficult, but these trends reflect the assertions of the upper castes and upper and middle classes, and have broader implications for the understanding of democracy in the post-colonial world.

The grouping of the middle class is problematic in the Indian context. The middle class in the historical context of modern Europe consisted of a hierarchy detached from inherited wealth and status and based on achievements in business, education, and the professions. The middle classes in India did not emerge, as you would expect, in the aftermath of an industrial revolution that weakened the traditional social order.[1] Compared to Europe, the Indian middle classes appeared late on the scene and were artificially formed under colonial rule, primarily because of the educational policy introduced under British rule for meeting the administrative requirements of the Raj.[2] Given these origins, members of the middle class were drawn from the upper castes having a literate tradition. Consequently, members of the civil services and the professions disproportionately filled the ranks of the middle classes.

The middle class has grown steadily in size since independence and most conspicuously after the economic reforms initiated in the early 1990s. The middle classes are differentiated in terms of occupation, income, and education, and they are the product of upward and horizontal mobility. Unlike the middle classes elsewhere, they are diverse in terms of language, religion, and caste.[3] The latter form of diversity has a recent origin because until quite recently the middle classes were entirely dominated by the upper castes.[4]

Various estimates have been made of the size of the middle class. The most widely accepted are the ones based on surveys carried out by the National Council of Applied Economic Research (NCAER). Until 1996, the NCAER used the income criteria, according to which it had set up five income tranches: above Rs. 96,000 annually, between Rs. 700,001 and Rs. 96,000; between Rs. 45,001 and Rs. 70,001; between Rs. 22,501 and Rs. 45,000; below Rs 22,500. But since there is no way of accurately judging the distribution of income and the number of households that fall into various categories, assessments have been more often than not based on consumption patterns.

In India, then, consumption patterns rather than income generally define the middle class. Trends in consumption patterns have been used to assess the size of the middle class, which is not altogether inappropriate since consumption, and the lifestyle associated with it, is the most important characteristic of this social class. Based on trends in the consumer market, the NCAER classification of consumers is simply based on the ownership of assets and consumption, and not on household income. In the advanced industrial democracies, statistical classification of groups is done with reference to employment, income, and tax liabilities. In India however, there is no equivalent way of obtaining statistics about employment patterns and income for the vast mass of people. According to Nilakanth Rath, despite the fact that the database on the Indian economy has become enormously rich, information on the distribution of income, and even more so on wealth, is still very inadequate.[5] Thus very little data is available on the distribution of the population according to the level of total household or individual income.

This is because tax evasion is widespread and tax recovery is very limited owing to the large amount of hidden income or black money. The Finance Minister had disclosed in the Winter Session of the Lok Sabha (2000) that the outstanding dues amounted to Rs. 620,000 million, of which corporate tax alone had a share of Rs. 280,000 million.[6] Even as large numbers of shopkeepers and traders simply do not fall into the tax net, the rural rich are not taxed, and the very rich are either under-taxed or the full sources of their incomes are not known.

Covering the actual trends during the years 1994–5 and 1995–6, the 1998 NCAER Report on Indian Market Demographics classifies the number of households into the 'Very Rich', the 'Consuming Class' and the 'Climbers'. These three consumer groups of households increased from 77.6 million households in 1994–5 to 87.8 million in 1995–6.[7] The most optimistic assessments of the size of the middle class put the tally at 170 to 200 million people out of India's population of 1 billion, including 13 per cent of rural and 42 per cent of urban households. Amongst the latter it has been said that there has been a 90 per cent increase in average family incomes during 1983-8 period (alone)'.[8] This estimate, which is an overstatement, still means that in India the middle class really means the top 20 to 25 per cent of the population, with more than three-fourths of the population below it. Significantly, the bulk of these three-fourths are below the poverty line. The middle classes include what has been described as the petty bourgeoisie, traders, employees in the corporate sector, the middle ranks of the professions, civil service, and government employees. In terms of absolute numbers even 170 million is very substantial, but compared to the whole population, it is not very big. Most developed societies have a much larger middle class, which constitutes the median in these societies. As a result, it can act as a significant buffer between the dominant classes and the sizeable layer of the lower classes. This large social grouping is wooed by the upper classes to stabilize their own position.

In India however, the lower classes and the poor are much larger and they are more self-assured today, especially since electoral politics is now the central arena of democratization and are dominated by high levels of participation of the lower orders of society, as compared to the relative lack of political interest of the upper middle classes and the elite. Given the nature of the middle classes, they find themselves bracketed with the elite in terms of its interests, especially because from the early 1990s the much larger layer beneath them has challenged the privileges of the upper and middle classes. The middle classes dominate the corporate world, the bureaucracy, the media, and the professions. Not surprisingly, this class has had a very considerable influence in shaping government policies as well as the values and discourses of a range of institutions from the press to the judiciary. It has a disproportionate influence on the policies finally chosen. What it does not have, however, is control over the electoral-democratic process. Threatened by the economic majority, the middle class has often identified with the elite. The middle class sees its self-interest as synonymous with, and expressive of, the national interest.

Social and Political Transition

Against the background of the growth and expansion of the middle class, consider first the shifts in political culture from the early years of the Nehruvian regime in the 1950s. Politics in the sense that Nehru or the members of the Constituent Assembly understood it has been stamped out. The whole enterprise of democracy and development owed a great deal to the debates in the Constituent Assembly, which were dominated by the nationalist elite. Development and social justice were the *raisons d'etre* of the state and the basis of its legitimacy. The first three decades of economic policy were focused on state intervention and government investment in the development of large-scale industrial units (rather than on the production of consumer-oriented commodities). Such policies were connected to the process of a modernizing India in which industrial development was linked to a political culture constituted by discourses or the need for the advancement of the poor. Political speeches of Jawaharlal Nehru to popular films such as *Mother India* and *Do Bigha Zameen*[9] shaped linkages between the ideology of development, the decrease of poverty, and the nation-state and representative democracy.[10] Universal suffrage, increases in literacy, and the growth of markets and communications all created the objective conditions for the invention and reinvention of an all-encompassing national identity.[11] The legacy of the anti-colonial movement served as the ideological cement of society and development. This agenda had the support of the professional middle classes.

Four to five decades later, the ideology of anti-colonial nationalism became insufficient for political mobilization unless replaced by a powerful anti-imperialism. The growth of such nationalism has been hindered by the rise of the BJP to national power—the most significant political change from the Nehru period. For sure, political Hinduism took shape in the political system and through sustained campaigns of the Sangh Parivar since the mid-1980s, and yet, it also found more fertile ground and an expanding base of support as a result of changes in the Indian society. These included the collapse of the Nehruvian consensus, the intensification of market relations, rapid acceleration of communications and travel facilities, and generally more mobility and exposure to the world outside. Some of these changes were fuelled by the overseas connection. A development of considerable significance is the emergence of the non-resident Indians (NRIs), especially the American NRIs. They are the richest ethnic minority in the United States and some of this wealth and clout is being recycled in the Indian economy. Sometimes their 'long-distance nationalism' has prompted them to take strong positions on nuclear weapons, Kashmir, and human rights and so they do represent a powerful new force in Indian society and politics.

The transition, which is both political and social, has centred on two trends. On the one hand, there has been a shift in public political discourse away from a focus on poverty-reduction and radical redistribution of material resources as a central objective of state policy. On the other, is the development of a growing public culture of consumption and an unabashed celebration of consumerism. This shift has been associated with a much more open display of conspicuous consumption than was generally common in Indian society. Both television and print media have contributed to the dissemination of this new culture and to making it the common aspiration of the middle classes. The new culture is increasingly presented, at least by its votaries, as the widening of choices and the proliferation of a variety of goods. Consumers can choose between many different cars, washing machines, food, clothing, and international brand names. The editor of a print magazine commented:

Free us to create wealth, not control us in the name of poverty eradication—appears to be the new mantra. In the 1960s and 1970s, accumulation of wealth was still suffering from a Gandhian hangover. Even though there were a whole lot of families who were wealthy all over India in the North and South if you noticed all their lifestyles were very low key. They were not exhibitionist or they were not into the whole consumer culture. Now I see that changed completely. . . . You want to spend on lifestyle. You want your cellphone. You want your second holiday home, which earlier as I said people would feel that sense of guilt—that in a nation like this a kind of vulgar exhibition of wealth is contradictory to Indian values. I think now consumerism has become an Indian value.[12]

This is not quite the 'Tryst With Destiny' that Nehru had spoken of. Also the perception of choice blurs the fact that liberalization and globalization have created pervasive inequalities between classes and income groups. These inequalities encompass gaps in wealth, income, access to productive employment, and a whole range of other enabling material and social opportunities.[13]

In interviews conducted by Leela Fernandes in her study on the middle class, economic reforms, and globalization, individuals from various segments of the middle class pointed to the new choice of commodities as the central benefit of liberalization and regime change.[14] Even though these interviews were conducted during the early years of economic liberalization in 1998, individuals were pleased that they no longer had to depend on relatives abroad to provide them access to various foreign commodities because 'abroad is now in India', hence there was a sense of pride that their ambitions can be realized within India's borders.[15] This sentiment was vividly captured by a television advertisement of air conditioners produced by *Air Cooling Systems.* Comfortably spread out on a sofa in the posh surroundings of his air conditioned drawing room a young man proudly announces: *'Arre wah* Switzerland is in India. Now I can spend my vacations here'.

Globalization in consequence has justified the pursuit of individual wealth as never before.[16] The enormous popularity of Star KBC show (*Kaun Banega Crorepati:* Who Wants to Become a Millionaire) summed up the aspirations and values of the new middle classes. Equally significantly, the popularity of films *Hum Aapke Hain Kaun* and *Dilwale Dulhaniya le Jayenge* and the great family sagas on television, which exemplified a combination of ostentatious living, high consumerism, and traditional family values, combined with a perpetuation of traditional gender roles in the family, amply revealed the social orientation of the middle classes to which these catered. Another related example was the way in which the print media was flaunting India as a Beauty superpower next only to being a Nuclear and Information Technology superpower. All this surely constituted a major transition in political culture in India, and signalled the ways in which the Indian nation was reimagined in the context of globalization.

The New Middle Class and the Democratic Upsurge

This section addresses the relationship of the middle classes to political Hinduism and the role it played in meeting the democratic challenge from the lower castes and classes. Consider the political preferences of the middle classes at the time in question. The findings reported in the 1999 Lok Sabha post-election survey conducted by the Centre for the Study of Developing Societies on the social basis of voters' choices—of who voted for whom—showed clearly that the privileged sections were more likely to vote for the BJP in preference to other parties, including the Congress. Significantly, this survey indicated that though religious symbolism was a trademark of the BJP's mobilization strategy, religion was not the principal basis in the creation of the new social bloc, which brought the BJP to power at the Centre. Rather the social bloc was formed by the convergence of the traditional caste and community differences and class distinctions.[17] This can be seen from the fact that the share of the BJP vote increased moving up the social hierarchy from the lower castes to the upper castes, whereas that of its allies in the coalition went up moving down the social ladder. It was clear therefore that in class terms, the BJP had a pronounced upper and middle class support base. The poorer the voter the lesser the chances of voting for the BJP.[18] In short, the new social bloc was built around the master cleavage of caste and class privilege. In this context it is no exaggeration to say that the BJP represented the rebellion of the elite and middle classes as defined by an overlap of social and economic privilege.[19]

The middle classes were keen supporters of Rajiv Gandhi in the mid-1980s, but by the 1990s many of them switched their allegiance to the BJP. A number of scholars have argued that the BJP won over their support by default. For example, Christophe Jaffrelot has written that: 'The BJP attracted support by default because the Congress was deeply unpopular. Moreover, the BJP probably won over former Congress supporters all the more easily because it appeared to be the sole proponent of a political project—the building of a strong India—which had been established and assiduously promoted by Indira Gandhi.'[20]

Did political Hinduism have a persuasive power for the middle class or was its success a purely negative triumph that came about on account of the terminal decline of the Congress and the failure of left and centrist forces to fill the vacuum?

In looking at this relationship this chapter assumes that most of the basic facts about the career and composition of the Sangh Parivar and the BJP are quite well known. I will, however, mention two moments—the Mandalization of politics following the acceptance and implementation of the recommendations of the Mandal Commission, the politics of Mandir symbolized in the destruction of the Babri Masjid in Ayodhya in December 1992, and attitudes towards nuclear tests. These three moments are related to the emergence and assertion of the middle class in the countryside and cities and to what has been called the democratic upsurge. In the 1990s, elite assertions and subaltern mobilization intersected with the politics of caste, community, and region to give shape to the reinvention of India.

These developments created a constituency among the middle class for political Hinduism. The Sangh Parivar is known to be widely associated with all the three events. On the Mandal issue, even though less than 50,000 jobs were affected the depth and scale of middle class hostility is well known.

On the demolition of the Babri Masjid the middle class was more divided. Evidence of noteworthy joy notwithstanding, there was considerable disgust at the actual demolition and the defiance of the court, constitution, and law by elements of the Sangh Parivar. Indeed some of the young men who participated in the Ram Janmabhoomi agitation belonged to the lower middle classes from the upper castes. All this has to be seen in the context of protests over the Mandal Commission and extension of reservations to the Other Backward Classes. The liberal sections of the middle classes were unhappy with the violence and vandalism surrounding the demolition of the Babri Masjid in December 1992. However, on the nuclear bomb, most of the middle classes were rather pleased with the new status acquired by India as a result of the nuclear capabilities following the nuclear explosions in 1998. The overwhelming support for the decision to go nuclear had nothing do with a change in threat perceptions, but with a search for self–esteem and respect in a world where it was felt, not enough respect was shown to India.

Hence it is often suggested that the success of political Hinduism expressed the cultural ethos of the vast majority and particularly of the middle classes, which could not be articulated under the hegemony of the secular elite. The political developments of the first quarter century after Independence, however, show that there was no such relationship. If this were so, then political Hinduism should have come to power in the aftermath of Partition, which was a moment of extreme political anxiety and communalization. Yet a secular state was established. Nevertheless, an inquiry as to why the middle classes, who had made substantial gains from the Nehruvian model of social democracy, suddenly acquiesced in the hegemony of political Hinduism is required. The political ascendancy of Hinduism in the 1980s, and the backing it has received from sections of the middle class, needs a conjunctural explanation than one located in a cultural mindset. The middle class reaction was not born out of an intrinsically conservative cultural disposition, as sections of the middle classes had defended and sustained the progressive agenda of a modern secular democracy. The change in the political conjuncture—the decline of centrist hegemony and changes in material circumstances and environment—induced a shift in the political thinking of the middle classes. As Aijaz Ahmed argues:

That in a developing society in which the structures of capitalism are fully in place but where processes of state formation are weakly developed and premised on acute unevenness of region, community and class, an ideological movement of a nationalist kind is an objective necessity and if the Left fails to provide that cement, and if the liberal Centre begins to collapse, an aggressive kind of rightist nationalism will step into that vacuum to resolve that crisis that is produced by the objective processes of state formation and capitalist development—and this right-wing nationalism is bound to take advantage of precisely that misery of the masses and the petty bourgeois strata which (the) liberal model promised to alleviate and did not.[21]

The centrist hegemony of the first few decades after independence was based on the heritage of the national movement and a concrete set of achievements: an independent model of industrial growth, the considerable reduction in large-scale feudal landholdings which benefited the upper peasantry, growth in infrastructure, and the expansion of educational facilities and technical personnel. This model of economic and political development held out the promise of redistributive justice as well as the benefits of rises in income and education for substantial sections of the population, especially the middle classes. As long as this promise remained credible, the liberal-reformist sections of the middle classes were able to hold off the challenge of the Left and the Right and command the loyalty of the poor and the marginalized sections of society.[22] They were able to do so precisely because a noteworthy feature of this project was a national definition of the polity with an emphasis on the nation-state's responsibility towards society. This model began crumbling from the late 1960s, though its hegemony was provisionally propped up by the victory in the Bangladesh war. The imposition of the Emergency strongly suggested the disintegration of the model. This called for a far-reaching redefinition of nationalism itself.

The end of the Nehruvian consensus and the collapse of liberal nationalism provided the major opening for a right-wing nationalism, which set out to exploit the failures of the earlier nationalism and to formulate a different national agenda. The proposal to reformulate the national ethos coincided with the erosion of the Congress model of earlier decades and the failure to reconcile universal citizenship with specific identities. The followers of cultural nationalism took advantage of the crisis produced by these infirmities in the objective processes of state formation and economic development and stepped into the political vacuum produced by the failings of the Congress model. Much as forces of reaction may misuse nationalism, national sovereignty remains an important concept in view of the distinctive requirements of a nation-state in a developing capitalist society and the ideological bond it provides in these societies, where state formation and political institutions are weakly developed.[23] Moreover these shifts have coincided with broader processes at work, particularly the intensification of the democratic process, overlapping networks of regional and national education systems and print media, growth of Information Technology, expansion of television and videos, and the creation of one of the largest markets for consumer goods in the world. Both the restructuring and dislocation of politics and society affected by these tendencies of integration, and the associated differentiation and fragmentation required an ideology that political Hinduism seemed to provide.[24]

In addition to the historical shift, the ideology of anti-colonial nationalism that so largely guided the Constitution was mediated by the phenomenon of democratization and the wide array of struggles and conflicts between castes, classes, and communities. The deepening of democracy cannot be associated with specific events, yet, the expansion of the democratic processes has had the effect of creating a differentiated notions of citizenship. The defeat of Indira Gandhi's Emergency regime in the 1977 elections was one such event that brought about a decisive shift in the form and content of democracy. It established the importance of the vote and representative institutions of government to give voice to popular demands of a kind that had not been able to disturb the order and tranquility of the corridors of power ever before.

The new middle classes feel apprehensive that lower caste assertions have put their privileges at risk. Indeed, the process of democratization has struck very deep roots, especially among the disadvantaged and the historically marginal groups who want a share in power. Equally important, democratic values have become ingrained among intellectuals and institutions vital to democracy.[25] However, as Yogendra Yadav suggests, the big turnout figures tends to favour the numerically large disadvantaged groups. Survey data shows this is because lower castes, Dalits, and tribals are more likely to vote than upper caste Hindus, and this is also true of the very poor relative to the upper class. The better educated and more advantaged citizens are least likely to vote since their preferences would be submerged among the votes of the 'great crowd'. For this reason, conservative attitudes are not entirely uncommon in the urban middle classes that for years was regarded as the bedrock of democracy in the country. The impatience with political protest, frequent elections, and proliferation of parties in a sharply polarized parliamentary system, together with the great desire for stability and law and order point towards a disdain for democratic processes and equally for the masses and their demands on the political system. Be that as it may. The urban middle classes blame the erosion of institutions and the civility of public culture to the induction of plebian leaders and plebian politics, which has given a fillip to a blatant pursuit of power.[26] However, they readily ignore the fact that the influx of new entrants from the lower orders and the vernacularization of political discourse have not led to an effective popular control of the policy agenda.

Though democracy has not accomplished social and economic equality to the extent desired, the achievement of democratic freedoms has created pressure for democratization in many other spheres and the ground for struggles for greater equality. After two decades of intensive political competition, caste and communal conflicts had increased in a struggle to control access to the State. The democratic upsurge concentrated in the northern heartland finally ended the domination of the upper castes and upper classes in the bureaucracy, as well as in parliamentary institutions. In the circumstances, the urban middle classes, who are the main beneficiaries of economic reforms, felt threatened by the political disorder and turned to political Hinduism to safeguard their privileges. In the light of this, Thomas Blom Hansen argued that Hindu nationalism represents a conservative revolution against the broader democratic transformation of both the political field and the public culture in post-colonial India. It promises to discipline the plebian assertiveness (Hansen's phrase) created by the democratic revolution of the past decade. He notes that it was the desire for recognition in the world combined with the simultaneous anxieties of being encroached upon by the Muslims, the plebeians, and the poor, that from the early 1990s prompted many Hindus to respond to the call for Hindutva at the polls, and to embrace the promises of order, discipline and collective strength.[27]

However, it is important to remember that political Hinduism's success did not grow out of a democratic deficit, rather it was the product of the middle class perception of 'democratic excess' manifested in the intensification of political competition, lower class-caste assertions, and the equally intense battles over religious sites and symbols of culture, and the meaning of secularism, history, and national security. In this state of affairs, political Hinduism came to the fore as a kind of 'conservative populism' that mainly attracted not only the more privileged groups who feared an infringement of their dominant positions, but also plebian and impoverished groups who were seeking recognition around majoritarian rhetoric of cultural pride, order and national strength.[28] Thus, the BJP wanted and still went to transform India into a sovereign, disciplined, powerful nation, 'based not on borrowed ideas of secularism and socialism, but on an imagined past evoking the greatness of Hindu India and yet favouring globalization and integration into an open international economy'.[29] It promised to do this not by imitating western values but by being fully Indian. Building on the argument that India's imitation of the West had failed to gain the West's respect, the BJP seeks to create a new political culture of governmentality dedicated to an overall vision of control, and a foreign policy that would end India's 'isolation' or as former Foreign Minister, Jaswant Singh, put it, the 'wasted decades' of non-alignment. Both were essential for the esteem of the middle class and were part of the BJP's attempts to position India as a Great Power. The explosion of nuclear devices can be linked to this political imagination, and the hope that the tests would fetch India the recognition and prestige the middle classes craved for. The promise of a purposeful, security-oriented law and order government, in this context, formed a critical part of this design and fit in very well with the middle class concern for authority, order, and stability. Among the broad features of the emerging political design are: strong centralization of decision-making in the Prime Minister's Office, an open licence to economic pragmatism, lobbying, machinations, a conspicuous shift from the paradigm of development to national security, disinclination to tolerate dissent and disagreement, and ultra-nationalism. The entire vision was driven by a search for an elusive homogeneity—an idea of India far removed from diversity and plurality.

The Middle Classes, Neoliberalism and Political Hinduism

It is in this larger perspective that observers have noted complementarities between political Hinduism and the policy of liberalization and globaliz-ation.[30] As argued earlier, the rise of political Hinduism as a major force demands a more general explanation, rather than one couched in terms of particular trends and relationships. To start with, it is misleading to refer to it as a tendency of the majority of the population. The rhetoric is majoritarian and nationalist but in actuality it represented the interests of the few—typically urban upper and middle classes and drawn pre-dominantly from the upper castes.[31] Right-wing politics anywhere needs the active support of a part of the liberal establishment. As part of this process of expansion Hindutva ideology made significant inroads into state structures and society thanks to the support of the liberal establishment and sections of the middle classes, which though divided over its divisive, narrow-minded, and aggressive nationalism, were prepared to support its economic reforms agenda. These interests include faster economic reforms so as to complete the transition to market economy, which BJP pursued as a one-point programme when it was in power. It did this by demonstrating its friendliness not only towards liberalization and globalization, but also towards a whole range of policies including 'second generation reforms', which would support in the United States and among NRIs, multinationals, and the Indian middle classes. The party whose anti-consumerism slogan had been 'computer chips not potato chips' did not reverse the direction of economic reforms initiated by the previous Congress governments, in fact it expanded the scope of economic reforms evident from the 2001 Budget and the ecstasy and euphoria generated across TV channels, newspapers, and corporate boardrooms at the time. No matter what the opposition within the Sangh Parivar to liberalization and globalization, the BJP political establishment actively involved itself in disinvestments and privatization.[32] Accordingly, priority was given to privatization and financial and trade policy reform, which involved an explosion in the financial sector activities and incomes of this section. Professional incomes in finance approached levels equivalent to those in the developed countries, even while wages in the rest of the economy stagnated. On the other side, the neglect of social sector investment has meant that spending on education, health, and infrastructure continued to fall short of the levels needed to empower the majority to improve their human capital.

The arguments mentioned above apply in a general sense to the resurgence of revivalist sentiments of various sorts, but they have a particular resonance with the period from the early 1990s as defined by the extension of economic neoliberalism and political Hinduism. Though the impetus for liberalization came from the top levels of the state apparatus under pressure of the balance of payments crisis and the World Bank, the main beneficiaries have been the upper middle and high income groups. For a significant section of the new middle classes who have acquired a new economic status but not corresponding social status, there is an anxiety to bring the two together through greater religious observances and congregations'.[33] For the more established upper and middle classes, among whom there is also evidence of increased religiosity, it provides a sense of security in a world of radical uncertainty clearly manifest in the challenge from rights and entitlement claims of the deprived. Though the rise in religiosity and rituals is a significant development, it does not account for the middle classes' support of political Hinduism.[34] The major impetus for the greater acceptability of political Hinduism derives from the nature of liberalization and pattern of growth, which has mediated the relationship between the middle classes and political Hinduism, rather than just religious or cultural pride.

The pattern of growth involves the spiraling incomes and extravagant lifestyles of a minority even as it leaves the vast majority untouched, or worse off. As economist Jayati Ghosh argues: 'the new growth pattern is one, which is based on the market created by (at most) the upper one-third of the population. This not only has distributive and welfare implications but also means that the market remains narrower than its potential'.[35] From the middle-class standpoint, political Hinduism is helpful and functional given that it sees no need for a transformation of political and economic power configurations. Consequently, it serves the interests of groups that are already privileged and leaves unaltered the economic conditions of the majority. Economic globalization has first and foremost served the interests of the elite and upper and middle classes who have been in revolt against the model of state-led economic development, which at one time served their interests very well, but in their perception had run its course, and, therefore, needed to be changed. The unequalizing nature of the process is revealed most dramatically in the wide gaps between the rich and the poor, which have widened even faster in the recent past. Reform agenda has eroded the incomes of salaried persons, pensioners, and the elderly. One reason why it has been iniquitous is that employment generation has been insufficient to meet the requirements of a growing population. The accelerated privatization of the public sector and the move to downsize the government would aggravate the employment situation. Despite growth rates of 7 per cent in the 1990s, the growth of employment was less than 0.67 per cent in rural areas and 1.7 per cent in urban areas. Nonetheless, the 2001 Budget has laid the foundation for an exit policy, which trade and industry had been clamouring for by making it easier for industrial firms to retrench or lay off workers in units with less than 1000 employees. In other words the exit policy has opened the labour market for 96 per cent of industrial establishments and 89 per cent of industrial labour.

Withdrawal of the state also allowed private capital to renegotiate relationships with labour in the informal economy to their advantage. In this sense reforms are very much about redefining the idea of the state and its capacity to work for groups outside the middle classes. While indulging in anti-state rhetoric to deprive the vulnerable and the destitute from getting the benefits of protection, they themselves continue to take advantage of state protection.[36] Indeed, the state protects the lifestyle and interests of the already privileged, while chastizing the working class, slum dwellers, or other marginalized people who dare to rebel.[37] Even as public spaces close themselves to those without credit cards, residential localities hem themselves in against the lower orders with boundary walls and watchmen. It is not surprising that such lifestyles on the part of a relatively small minority would have undesirable social and political consequences.

The tensions and insecurities brought about by the widening inequalities induced by the pattern of growth encourage people to seek shelter in particularities, revanchism, and lumpenism in many an urban centre. The alienation that comes from deprivation can only too easily be directed towards those who are not in competition but simply represent disadvantaged and materially weak sections that can be attacked with relative ease. This may explain why so many people are susceptible to social tendencies that blame the 'other' for the great gap between aspiration and reality.

The point to note is that the policies of liberalization could have succeeded only if Indian nationalism was redefined in cultural terms so that political energies were not consumed in opposition to imperialism, but against antagonism towards the enemy within: the subordination of minorities, particularly Muslims, which is justified by an imagined past of irreconcilable differences. During the last three years of BJP rule, therefore, the central force of the anti-reform rhetoric was concentrated in the cultural sphere, particularly in relation to television, films, and media. Sushma Swaraj, in her two stints as Information and Broadcasting Minister, launched a series of attacks on sexualized representations in the media and advertising. Similarly the resistance was directed against newly embraced western customs such as Valentine's Day, which was termed a plot by the multinationals to corrupt young minds, even as the BJP government encouraged a free run for multinationals, and emerged as the champion of privatization and disinvestments. What this showed, however, was a broader pattern in which the Sangh Parivar displaced resistance to the new economic policies of liberalization from the realm of concrete economic policy to a confrontation with the cultural politics of globalization. The handling of the Enron affair and BALCO (Bharat Aluminium Company) privatization seemed to indicate that the 'economy of politics' intrinsic to the practices of governance in India was not easily controlled or disciplined by the ideology of the Rashtriya Swayamsevak Sangh (RSS).[38]

Globalization, therefore, became a critical site in which the politics of economic liberalization was negotiated through the articulation of new cultural conceptions of the nation and visual signs of wealth and culture that represented the new symbols of national progress in relation to the global. Yet, lacking a programmatic promise of redistributive justice, in contrast to anti-colonial and anti-imperialist nationalism, the dynamic of cultural politics tended to acquire an irrational and anti-minority thrust. Thus, the renewed aggression towards those categorized as 'others', that is all those who belong to 'foreign religions', can be explained. In this worldview, the only enemies were those within the nation determined by social and cultural differences. There was no recognition of domestic economic differences and antagonisms, and, consequently, the constraining role on development that can be played by certain classes, such as landed groups or monopoly capital. However, after four years of BJP-style governance the mood in the country was unsettled. Its record in government was generally unimpressive.

The functioning of BJP-led Central and state governments made it apparent that its high-minded visions of governance remained more a 'mandate of self-righteousness' than the basis of principled policies or politics and administrative reform. The Hindu Right, and the middle class domination of it, was challenged by sections of the lower castes and classes and by a coalition of popular movements, which were opposed to the project of militant Hindutva. The liberalization agenda came into conflict with the demands of the agricultural classes. It came into conflict with other supporters of the Hindu Right, whose intentions were in some senses distinctly anti-modernist, and some of their actions—from the demolition of the Babri Masjid to stopping the shooting of *Fire* and numerous other acts of vandalism—all caused disorder. The extremist constituency was offset by a moderate tendency within the BJP, which was concerned to win power in a democratic polity. Logically this would oblige the BJP to behave as a national party by going beyond its support among the middle classes and upper castes, but this would require tangible cement that can only come from a politics of equality. Equality is the only possible ground on which social and identity claims can be reconciled with the demands of justice and dignity. Though equality moved further away from the horizon secularization and the democratization of life since Independence have impinged upon public debates surrounding the secular principle and continue to inform debates on the idea of state and society in India. This is not to say that the state has accomplished its' goals. It is rather to suggest that the pressures on the state from ordinary people, such as the demands for livelihood, minimum wages, and the right to schooling are forms of protests with reference to the promise of equality and justice imagined by the Constituent Assembly.

Notes and References

1. B.B. Misra, *The Indian Middle Classes: Their Growth in Modern Times*, New York, Oxford: Oxford University Press, 1961.

2. Francine Frankel, 'Middle Classes and Castes in India's Politics: Prospects for Accommodation', *India's Democracy: An Analysis of Changing State-Society Relations*, ed. Atul Kohli, Princeton: Princeton University Press, 1988, pp. 225–61.

3. Andre Beteille, 'The Indian Middle Class', *The Hindu*, 5 February 2001.

4. D.L. Sheth, 'Caste and the Secularization Process', in *Contemporary Transitions*, ed. Peter Ronald de'Souza, Delhi: Sage, 2001.

5. Nilakanth Rath, 'Inequality in the Distribution of Income and Wealth in India', *Contemporary India*, ed. V.A. Pai Panandiker and Ashis Nandy, Delhi: Tata McGraw Hill, 1999, pp. 67–106.

6. *The Hindu*, 17 February 2001.

7. *Financial Express*, 28 November 1998.

8. Stuart Corbridge and John Hariss, *The Reinvention of India: Liberalization and Hindu Nationalism*, London: Polity Press, 2000.

9. Madhav Gadgil, 'The State in/of Cinema', *Wages of Freedom: Fifty Years of the Indian Nation State*, ed. Partha Chatterjee, 1998.

10. Leela Fernandes, '"Nationalizing the Global": Media Images, Economic Reform and the Middle Class in India', *Media, Culture and Society*, vol. 22, 5 September 2000, pp. 611–28.

11. On this aspect see Aijaz Ahmed, 'On the Ruins of Ayodhya: Communalist Offensive and Recovery of the Secular', in *Lineages of the Present: Ideology and Politics in Contemporary South Asia,* ed. Aijaz Ahmed, London: Verso, 2000.

12. Fernandes, 'Nationalizing the Global'.

13. Jayati Ghosh, 'Perceptions of Difference: The Economic Underpinnings', *The Concerned Indian's Guide to Communalism,* ed. K.N. Pannikar, Delhi: Viking, 1999.

14. Fernandes, 'Nationalizing the Global'.

15. Ibid.

16. *The Hindu,* 27 August 2000.

17. Yogendra Yadav, 'The BJP's New Social Bloc: Analysis by CSDS based on the Electoral Outcome and the Findings of a Nation-wide Postelection Survey', *Frontline,* 19 November 1999.

18. Ibid., p. 38.

19. Ibid., p. 32.

20. Christophe Jaffrelot, *Hindu Nationalism and Indian Politics,* Delhi: Oxford University Press, 1996.

21. Ahmed, 'On the Reins of Ayodhya', p. 182.

22. Ibid., pp. 177–90.

23. Ibid., p. 182.

24. Ibid.

25. Frankel, 'Introduction', *India's Democracy,* ed. Kohli, p. 3.

26. Atul Kohli, 'Democracy and Discontent: India's Growing Crisis of Governability', Delhi: Cambridge University Press, 1988.

27. Thomas Blon Hansen, *The Saffron Wave: Democracy and Hindu Nationalism,* Delhi: Oxford University Press, 2000.

28. Ibid., pp. 8–9.

29. Kohli, 'Democracy and Dissent', p. 10.

30. Ghosh, 'Perceptions of Difference'; Blon Hansen, *Saffron Wave.*

31. Ghosh, 'Perceptions of Difference'.

32. *Outlook,* 5 March 2001.

33. Christopher Fuller has observed in Tamil Nadu, the development of an active programme for the training of Brahman priests in Sanskrit scriptures. For more details see Stuart Corbridge and John Harris, *The Reinvention of India: Liberalization and Hindu Nationalism,* London: Polity Press, 2000, p. 125.

34. Corbridge and Harris, eds., *The Reinvention of India.*

35. Ghosh, 'Liberalization Debates', p. 326.

36. Rowena Robinson, 'The Great Indian Middle Class', *The Hindu,* January 2001.

37. Ibid.

38. Blon Hansen, *Saffron Wave,* pp. 222–3.

9 | Changing Orientation of the State and the Emergence of Majoritarianism in the 1980s

THE 1980s witnessed an escalation of communalism and a consolidation of sentiments around symbols of religious identities and perceptions of threats to these identities. Communal ideologies have gained much wider social acceptance, forcing a retreat from the liberal rhetoric of secularism. What is particularly striking about this decade is the role of the state in communalizing the political process in both overt and covert ways. The reassertion of communalism is not only promoted by communal forces, but also by the institutional regime of the state itself, and by its indifference and neglect of communalism.

There were deep ideological schisms between communalists and the champions of secular and composite culture in the realm of civil society in the 1950s. Yet, there is hardly any doubt that the Indian state was conceived in a secular and non-communal mould. There was acceptance of the agenda of secularism and a broadly secular ideology as the basis of integration. Nehru had emphatically declared that the government of a country like India . . . can never function satisfactorily in the modern age except on a secular basis. The sense of complementarily and existence of diverse communities, an imprimatur of the social compact, has given place to deepening confrontations at both political and social levels.

This is something new and so to understand this new phase of communalism there are two crucial aspects, which must be explored: the first is the shift in the idiom and discourse of politics and the second is the perceptible shift in the orientation of the state. The question is whether the state had fallen prey to forces beyond its control, or whether the institutions and structures of the state apparatus tend to reinforce communalism in the sphere of civil society.

The expansion of fundamentalism and revivalism is not specific to India alone. In South Asia, a number of developments in Pakistan and Bangladesh have also led to an assertion of Islamic codes of conduct and behaviour. In India the Muslim Women (Protection of Rights on Divorce) Bill of 1986, and the decision to formally open the Babri Masjid to Hindu devotees in February 1986 were two decisions that not only marked a turning point in the history of Hindu-Muslim relations, but also accelerated the pace of communal polarisation in post-Independence India.

Communalizing the Political Discourse

Secularism in India has often meant two things. The Indian state purports either to be indifferent or neutral to religion, or professes to have equal respect for all religions. Any appeals to religion and community as a tool of mobilization should also be eschewed. The draftsmen of the Indian Constitution and the early Congress leadership were quite aware that it was necessary to avoid an overt politicization of community identities. However, this could not always be achieved because the Indian understanding of secularism failed to provide a satisfactory relationship between state and religion.[1] This resulted in the adoption of a passive line of least resistance which runs into obvious difficulties. The problem has been further compounded by the fact that the secularization process has lagged behind the well-developed electoral process. This has led to a situation where political parties use narrow caste and communal categories for political mobiilzation and shift attention away from developmental to non-developmental issues.

However, even the passive varieties of secularism are valuable and functional and can serve to influence and shift the parameters of the debate in a consensual direction based on a complementarity and coexistence of pluralities. The question therefore becomes an enquiry into why passive secularism was eclipsed and given less priority in the 1980s.

To understand the retreat of secularism requires looking at the nature and character of inter-communal relations in the 1980s. Communal riots were not entirely absent in the Nehru era, but there can be no doubt that there has been a tremendous increase in the communal violence which has, since the late 1960s, so relentlessly bloodied the Indian landscape. Communal forces, kept in check by Nehru's leadership, surged forward after his death causing serious damage to India's secular fabric. The last phase of the Indira Gandhi era witnessed a marked polarization of Indian society on communal and sectarian lines and nearly 4,000 people were killed in communal violence in the 1980s.[2] This is almost four times higher than the figure of the 1970s. The number of districts affected by communal violence increased from 61 in 1960 to 250 in 1986–7. In Uttar Pradesh (UP) alone, between February 1986 and early 1988, nearly 60 major and minor riots took place, killing over 200 people, leaving more than 1,000 injured, and causing 1.5 crore of damage to property.[3] Another notable feature was that while in the past these incidents mainly occurred in urban areas, at that time they began to spread to rural areas. Equally significant was the simultaneous growth of communal organizations: over 500 militant organizations gained an active membership which ran into several millions.[4]

At the level of the political process, the imposition of the Emergency in 1975 by Indira Gandhi, followed by the defeat of the Congress party and the election of the Janata Party in 1977, brought immense changes to the party system and strategies of mobilization. Defeat caused the Congress party to disintegrate and Indira Gandhi's answer was to reconstitute and lead the Congress in an increasingly personalized direction. There was also an attempt to move into territory on the political spectrum which was normally occupied by right-wing parties, and to draw on the social support which they received in the 1977 elections. From the late 1970s, the Congress tried to move into the terrain which was traditionally occupied by the rightist parties, a move which had significant political consequences.

The orientation was part of an overall political shift in the Congress leadership. This involved a move away from the left-of-centre values of secularism and socialism and toward an ideological discourse hitherto identified with right wing parties such as the Bharatiya Janata Party (BJP). In India's political culture, these are the two ideologies that have tended to offer alternative strategies for mobilizing support. The significant changes in political discourse, and the shift in orientation were most noticeable in the realm of communalism.

The closing years of the Indira Gandhi era were marked by the breakdown of the secular consensus moulded by Nehru during which the leading ruling class party was apprehensive that its close identification with the minorities bore the risk of alienating many of their constituents. For their part, Muslims had begun to drift away from the Congress in states like UP, Bihar, and West Bengal. In the 1980 elections in Bihar and UP, the Lok Dal carved out victories in Muslim-dominated constituencies. The gradual decline of Congress support made it possible for communally oriented groups to step into the political vacuum. The Congress responded by appropriating communal themes, especially majoritarian themes, that would appeal to the Hindi heartland. Such themes and symbols gained currency in Indira Gandhi's speeches. Sometime during 1982, Congress leaders recognized that a confrontational stance towards the National Conference and the Sikh extremists might gain them the support of many

Hindus in Kashmir and Delhi.[5] An evocative theme of a national chauvinism seemed all the more useful because the party organisation was in complete disarray. This rightward shift was even justified as a 'creative strategy' by a general secretary of the All India Congress Committee (AICC).[6] The logic of the move to the right was somewhat similar to Indira Gandhi's adoption of radical slogans after 1969. Then, it was a means of undermining the parties of the Left, while in the 1980s, her move to the right was an attempt to appropriate the symbols and appeals of the rightist parties, mainly the BJP, which posed a threat to the Congress in north India. This strategy was used extensively in the 1984 elections when the Congress leaders adopted a narrow and intolerant rhetoric of confrontation in which the opposition parties were routinely attacked as anti-national forces. This sort of strategy catalysed communal sentiments and provided the Congress with the opportunity to become the chief spokesman of majoritarian interests by curiously concluding that in doing so, Congress was protecting India from the dangers of communal strife and disunity. This political methodology was extremely dangerous, especially when placed alongside figures of the steady rise of disorder and rioting in the closing years of the Indira Gandhi regime, climaxing in the slaughter of 2,400 Sikhs in Delhi in 1984 in response to her assassination by her Sikh bodyguards.

It could be argued that the ground for this was prepared in the early 1980s as Indira Gandhi moved to the right. Her own former advisers have noted that during this phase, she was more 'pragmatic' or by implication, less ideological.[7] Whether rightist or not, what is clear is that the government's policy orientation during this phase, especially when compared to the 1970s, was distinct. The shift in orientation was evident in several policy areas: Anti-poverty programmes were given low priority; there was a change of attitude toward the International Monetary Fund (IMF); and negotiations for the largest ever loan granted by the IMF were completed during this phase.[8] Ultimately many of the economic policies adopted moved in the direction of liberalising the economy.

Four decades of development had, by the late 1980s, resulted in deepening inequalities in terms of access to food, education, health care, and productive assets. The social logic of the state and the nature of the class coalition had placed constraints on state intervention.[9] Not surprisingly the anti-poverty programmes were not successful. The Congress government was not in a position to transform recalcitrant structures or to change the patterns of policy in ways that might ease the burden on the oppressed classes and avoid the political consequences of growing inequality. The unevenness of capitalist development heightened social tensions, providing a political space for the activation of exclusivist interests and ideologies seeking to appropriate the limited opportunities for economic prosperity. This often manifested itself in social reaction against minorities in different localities and regions.

The conditions of social existence progressively worsened post-Independence, as did the alienation of the people. The uneven regional growth and continuous aggravation of inequalities of wealth and income distribution encouraged the growth of oppositional movements for land rights and regional autonomy. The agitations in Gujarat and Bihar as well as innumerable other protests in the 1970s were organized against the backdrop of governmental failure to fulfil electoral promises, growing unemployment, soaring inflation, and shortages of foodgrains and essential commodities which imposed several hardships upon different sections of society. By contrast, the discontent and dissatisfaction in the 1980s was often articulated through non-secular movement and struggles.[10]

The challenge to centrist politics until the 1970s had come from linguistic movements and class conflict in the countryside and not from communal politics. The 1980s signalled the possibility of a national resurgence of congregational politics. Religious festivals, celebrations, yatras, and movements spearheaded by the Vishwa Hindu Parishad and other Hindu organizations became more strident and militant. The proliferation of religiosity was aided by the religious serials such as the telecast of *Ramayana* on Doordarshan. Much of the social support for the resurgence of religiosity came from newly rich groups in rural areas, and from professionals and entrepreneurs in the urban areas.

The shift in the political discourse was also visible in the broader context of the legitimation crisis faced by centrist parties in any developing country. The problem of mobilizing the poor majority was very apparent at that time. Secularism and socialism offered a distinct post-Independence ideological platform which was adopted by centrist parties. However, in the absence of any serious improvement in the living conditions of the poor, very little political capital remained in the rhetoric of socialism. The question of mobilization assumed urgency in the context of the defeat of the Congress party in north India in 1977 and the subsequent defeats of the Congress in Karnataka and Andhra Pradesh in 1983. Successive failures at the hustings brought to the forefront an alternative strategy of mobilization. This strategy involved direct appeals to the majority community (often against the minorities), thus downplaying broader social issues at the expense of narrow communitarian ones. However, this strategy did not generate large-scale support for the Congress in the 1986 by-elections, so the ruling party again made renewed efforts to woo the Muslim vote, this time around the Muslim Women Bill.

The Role of the Congress Party

That which was relatively new was the role of the Congress party in communalizing the political process. The controversy generated by the Muslim Women Bill highlighted the role of the government in permitting the growth of a fundamental movement, and then their making use of it to arouse sentiment among large sections of the population against the so-called appeasement of minorities.[11]

The question that needs to be addressed therefore is why the government surrendered to fundamentalist pressures. The most important consideration was the need to stem the anger over the Shah Bano verdict, which was losing the Congress its Muslim votes. Following the Congress defeat in the by-elections in Assam, Binjor, Kishanganj, Bolapur, Kedrappa, and Baroda, and believing that it was the Muslim vote which tipped the balance in favour of the opposition parties, important Congress leaders advised the Prime Minister against the dangers of a confrontation with the fundamentalists. Syed Shahabuddin's victory in a by-election was a sharp reminder that Congress would suffer electoral reverse in other constituencies as well unless it regained Muslim support. The decision to bring in the Muslim Women Bill was part of the strategy to reverse the rising tide against the Congress party's efforts to woo the Muslims; the intervention in favour of the fundamentalists was a desperate bid to regain the Muslim constituency.

The government scorned all progressive opinion which argued against the bill, and refused to withdraw it on the dubious plea that it was framed in deference to the wishes of most Muslims. In fact, only conservative Muslim groups were consulted and they were passed off as the representative opinion of the community. Within the government, Arif Mohammed Khan opposed the bill and resigned from the union cabinet in protest against the government. He believed that the government had given credence only to the views of conservatives and had ignored secular and progressive opinion in the Muslim community.

The political considerations behind the Congress strategy were revealed in the course of the debate on the bill in the Lok Sabha. A.K. Sen, Minister of Law, defended the introduction of the new legislation by stating that it was 'the consistent policy of the government that in the matters pertaining to a community priority would be given to the leader of the community'.[12] This argument assumed that Muslims constituted a self-contained and monolithic community, whose interests were represented only by Muslim MPs and a section of the ulema.

The most pernicious aspect of the controversy was the attempt by the government to provide an All India Muslim Personal Law Board sponsored bill (which would clearly debilitate and deprive the Muslim community) and simultaneously lament the absence of reformist tendencies amongst Muslims. Contrasting the importance of reform amongst Hindus and Muslims, Shiv Shankar, Minister of Commerce, stated: 'I gave the example of various laws with reference to the Hindu Code Bill. . . . [A]t that time Hindu community was prepared to accept the law. Whatever we might say here, outside the situation is that [Muslim] people are not prepared to accept this.'[13] The social logic was unfolded more explicitly by K.C. Pant, Minister of Steel and Mines:

We cannot depend only on the law for reforms. Society has to be ready for reform. The well-springs of that reform have to come from within and then the laws that have been aroused by a certain movement, they coincide and then the society moves forward. . . . In Hindu society this process has been going on for decades. It had begun a hundred years ago. As a result of that and the efforts of so many tall leaders of this country the Hindu society has been able to regenerate itself.[14]

These arguments are significant because they exposed the contradictions of Congress-style secularism, which in effect, stifled reform in the name of 'protecting' minority interests. It served an even more important function in the complex structure of Congress politics. Responsibility for the Muslim Women Bill was transferred to the fundamentalists by arguing that the bill was introduced out of deference to the wishes of the Muslim community. The outcry against the bill forced the Congress to rework its defence strategy by shifting the blame on to the Muslims themselves. 'Indeed, it would not be an exaggeration to say that on no issue since the imposition of the internal emergency in June 1975 has there been a greater measure of agreement among educated Indians than on this. It is inconceivable that Rajiv Gandhi and his advisers have not been aware of this reaction,' opined Girilal Jain, the influential editor of *The Times of India*. Indeed, they were fully aware of the political repercussions of appeasing Muslim fundamentalism. Consequently, the ruling party tried to rid itself of the bill by making recourse to the theory that Muslims perceived the Supreme Court verdict as a threat to their religious identity. This theory enabled the Congress leaders to threaten to delink the party from fundamentalist Muslims by giving the impression that 'the government was not really in tune with the provisions of the bill but had no choice in the matter because the perception of Muslims was very different'.[15]

The subtle shifts in emphasis could not alter the fact that the government was anxious to mollify the fundamentalists. This was most strikingly revealed in the haste with which the legislation was enacted. The opinion of the Ministry of Law and Justice was ignored. The legal adviser to this ministry had categorically stated that the Supreme Court had correctly interpreted the law. The Law Secretary's advice was even more emphatic: the bill to amend Sections 125 and 127 of the Criminal Procedure Code should be opposed. Assurances given by the prime minister that wide-ranging consultations would be held were not honoured. Equally, the promise to bring out a background paper on the Muslim Personal Law was not fulfilled.[16] The pleading of the opposition parties not to push through the bill was ignored as was the groundswell of opposition within the ruling party itself.

It is undeniable that the government should not have accepted the demand for a legislation of questionable constitutionality and one which discriminated against Muslim women in relation to other women. Moreover, the bill revealed a major flaw in the pluralist theory of secularism, which in practice functions as multi-theocratic secularism, or the state protection of all religions and religious priorities.

Communalism and the Ram Janmabhoomi Controversy

Another indication of the capitulation to communal pressures and the politicians' willingness to play the communal card can be seen from the government's response to the Ram Janmabhoomi controversy. The Ram Janmabhoomi Mukti Samiti came into being on 7 October 1984 and launched a 'tala kholo' agitation and a Rath Yatra. Indira Gandhi's assassination on 31 October 1984 led to its suspension, but spearheaded by the Vishwa Hindu Parishad (VHP), campaign was revived in 25 places on 23 October 1985.[17] In February 1986, the local district judge decided to open the gates of the mosque on the basis that locking them was no longer necessary for the maintenance of law and order and the protection of the idols. Thus the temple was opened to devotees amidst much fanfare on 1 February 1986. The opening of the temple was a coup masterminded by the political authorities to appease and conciliate the VHP and the Ram Janmabhoomi Mukti Samiti who had organized a powerful movement to pressurize the Rajiv Gandhi government to accommodate Hindu sentiments. The strategy employed by VHP leaders was plainly communal: 'How can Rajiv Gandhi ignore the Hindu vote bank which gave him such a massive majority at the polls, far exceeding the votes polled by his grandfather', asked the Hindu leaders.[18] Muslim leaders on the other side of communal spectrum threatened to boycott the Congress if the Babri Mosque was not restored to Muslims. In fact, the decision to enact the Muslim Women Bill was a sequel to the pressures mounted by Hindu organizations agitating for the reopening of the Ram Janmabhoomi temple.

The government also played a key role in allowing the Shilanyas processions and campaign to become a vehicle of communalization and vitiation of the political process. Compelled purely by the interest in gaining votes, the government permitted the Shilanyas at a site described by the Allahabad High Court as disputed. Adding to this, the government's clarification that the foundation stone was laid at an undisputed site was clearly designed to confuse the issue. Equally, the state indulged in dissimulation as it argued that the Ram ceremony passed off peacefully. The issue, however, was not the peaceful nature of the ceremony, but the violence leading up to the ceremony. In Bhagalpur, for instance, hundreds of Muslims were massacred in one of the worst riots since after Partition. None of this could have happened without an acceptance of the Ram Shila message at a popular level, and a high tolerance of its consequences at the official level.

The Ram Shila processions were used by communalists to threaten the unsteady Rajiv Gandhi government. For them the Shilanyas were a power play to demonstrate the strength of the Hindu vote, which the ruling party could ill afford to lose. In spite of the Shilanyas, the Congress party failed to regain the political initiative after the criticisms it had received on the issue of corruption in high places. It failed not because it was communal, but because the Congress leaders could not have it both ways; move from secularism to communalism and vice versa without creating confusion in the mind of the electorate.

The Rise of the BJP

There is not doubt that militant communal forces seemed to attain unprecedented strength in the 1980s. At the national level, the BJP was the chief beneficiary of the increasing communalization of politics. The party improved dramatically on its 1984 performance and, gaining an estimated 15 per cent of the popular vote, the BJP won 88 seats in the 1989 elections. It became the third-largest party in the country. The BJP achieved this success after it moved away from the phase of liberalism identified with Gandhian socialism, to a clear identification with the militant Hinduism of the Rashtriya Swayamsevak Sangh (RSS). The change in orientation was strengthened by two decisions in 1989. The first was the decision to accept an alliance with the Shiv Sena and second was the decision of the national executive to fully endorse and support the Ram Janmabhoomi campaign of the VHP. According to a post-election assessment by the leadership, in at least 30 seats, it was the Ram Shila Pujan and the VHP agitation that had ensured victory for the BJP candidates in 1989.[19]

The spectacular success of the BJP in the Lok Sabha elections, and its growing respectability, was an indication of the political appeal of communal and revivalist movements in north and west India at that time: 'Saffron is no longer the colour of renunciation but that of reassertion.'[20] The real significance of the BJP's success lay in the fact that it became viewed as an alternative to the centrist formations that had previously held a monopoly of power. One reason for the BJP's success was that it could capitalize on the opportunities arising from the government backtracking on social and economic issues.[21] Initially the Rajiv Gandhi regime was eager to emphasize a break with the past in both the economic and political arenas. The overall thrust was to push the liberalization agenda forward in a short time. However, many political and social groups reacted negatively to government attempts at economic reforms. Rajiv Gandhi's declining popularity was not entirely a product of his economic approach and his attempts to liberalize the economy were also not politically neutral. As these policies were alienating the traditional supporters of the Congress party, the fear of losing electoral support forced the government to slow the pace of economic change. One possible way of recovering declining political fortunes was to adopt populist policies. The new incarnation of populism, in conformity with changing times, began to draw upon conservative elements of social consciousness. The disquiet and confusion generated by the shifting agenda of Congress politics found expression in disenchantment with the ruling party. As a cadre based party guided by a distinct ideology, the BJP became the natural beneficiary of the escalation of communalism.

Broader Impacts of Communalization

The compromises made by centrist parties such as Congress and Janata Dal to communal forces was partly guided by electoral considerations to cash in on the Muslim and Hindu vote. At the same time, it is inadequate to view the consolidation of communal sentiments as the consequence of short-term electoral strategy alone. There are underlying factors that warrant exploration in much greater detail to enable us to understand the popular response to communal propaganda, as well as the response of the state.

Social mobility and economic prosperity have contributed to the rise and popularity of 'majoritarianism' and the new generations of mobile middle castes and classes born after Independence located in both the countryside and in the cities were attracted to Hindu revitalization movements. There was a tendency on the part of many of the beneficiaries of the Green

Revolution, and professionals and entrepreneurs to channel their newly acquired wealth into temples and other religious causes. For these emerging groups, patronizing ritual practices not only earned them respect, but also provided a familiar and satisfying world view and social identity. The concern for identity was particularly important for the Indian middle class eager to find its social moorings in a rapidly changing society.[22]

This is perhaps one of the principal reasons why community identities and community-based politics were revived and intensified. They gained greater legitimacy in the context of growing competition that upset the existing status, and power hierarchies that lead to resentment and envy. The motive was to displace the emerging entrepreneurial class in crucial areas of trade and business and to reduce the possibility of keen competition. In northern India, Maharashtra, and Gujarat, where there are large concentrations of Muslims, communal violence became endemic as a result of struggles between Hindus and Muslims over land, property, and business opportunities. A particular dominant group or caste, faced by a challenge from rival groups or lower classes, tended to give a communal character to such conflicts.[23] This has happened in states like Maharashtra and Gujarat where the dominant castes have closed ranks, adopting an anti-dalit or anti-Muslim stance. This tendency gained impetus with the growing acquiescence towards communal conflicts.

Communal politics also became a form of cultural nationalism in a number of states. Several cultural organizations emerged with the aim of creating among Hindus a sense of belonging to a homogeneous and centralized entity. Among them, the VHP and Hindu Ekta Manch played a crucial role in promoting a unification of the majority community. Part of the inspiration for these tendencies came from the unprecedented accent put on national security at that time. The subtle message of a threat to Mother India beamed every night on Doordarshan succeeded in underlining the imperative need for strengthening national security to meet challenges to national unity. The political elite treated the complex issue of national unity primarily from the standpoint of a need to consolidate and legitimize a strong central authority in order to strengthen national identity. The state's strategy of excessive institutional centralization is based on the hope that this would promote an enduring system of cohesion and assimilation. However, even without the pressing requirements of national security, the idea of a strong centre as the centrepiece of Indian unity has found powerful support among the ideologies of the Indian state. The trauma of Partition provided force and urgency to the problem of national unity and above all, reinforced the need for a strong centre. The centralizing tendency of the Indian state requires an ideology of unity. Setting aside the finest traditions of Indian nationalism, the contours of this ideology became increasingly drawn from those elements of larger social consciousness that were inimical to secular nationalism. Yet, to quote Salman Rushdie, 'secularism, for India, is not simply a point of view, it is a question of survival'.[24]

Note and References

1. For a discussion of this aspect see Anil Nauriya, 'Relationship between state and religion', *Economic and Political Weekly*, vol. 24, no. 8, 25 February 1989, pp. 405–6.
2. Mushirul Hasan, 'Indian Muslims since Independence: In search of integration and identity', *Third World Quarterly*, April 1988, pp. 829–30.
3. Ibid.
4. Ibid.
5. For a discussion of the shifts in Indian politics, see James Manor, 'Parties and Party System', in *India's Democracy: An Analysis of Changing State-Society Relations*, ed. Atul Kohli, Princeton, N.J.: Princeton University Press, 1988, pp. 80–91.
6. Ibid., p. 80.
7. Atul Kohli, 'Politics of Economic Liberalization in India', *World Development*, vol. 17, no. 3, March 1989, pp. 309–11.
8. Ibid., p. 309.
9. For a discussion of the constraints on state intervention see Zoya Hasan, 'State and Identity in Modern India', in *State, Political Processes and Identity, Reflections on Modern India*, ed. Zoya Hasan et al., New Delhi: Sage, 1989.
10. See Javeed Alam, 'Political Articulation of Mass Consciousness in Present day India', in *State, Political Processes and Identity*, ed. Zoya Hasan et al., New Delhi: Sage, 1989.
11. See Chapter 18 of this volume.
12. *Telegraph*, 4 December 1985.
13. Ibid.
14. Ibid.
15. *The Times of India*, 4 March 1986.
16. Ibid.
17. For details see A.G. Noorani, 'Babri Masjid-Ram Janmabhoomi Dispute', *Economic and Political Weekly*, vols. 44-45, no. 4, 4–11 November 1989.
18. *The Statesman*, 20 April 1986.
19. *The Times of India*, 16 July 1990.
20. *India Today*, 31 March 1990.
21. Harish Khare, 'Rise of BJP', *The Times of India*, 6 December 1989.
22. Romila Thapar emphasizes the quest for identity as particularly important to the Indian middle class in the process of change from caste to class: Romila Thapar, 'Which of us are Aryans', *Seminar*, December 1989.
23. Rajni Kothari, 'Communalism', in *Slate against Democracy, In Search of Humane Governance*, ed. Rajni Kothari, New Delhi: Ajanta Publications, 1988.
24. Salman Rushdie, 'In Good Faith', *Independent*, 4 February 1990.

10 | Not Quite Secular Political Practice

THERE IS A widely held view that the rise of the Hindu right, particularly the Bharatiya Janata Party (BJP), challenged the Nehruvian consensus on political secularism with its emphasis on democracy, religious neutrality (or equal standing for all citizens, regardless of religion), and social justice. Even though the BJP may not demand a role for religious institutions or state support for religious rituals, its political vision and practices are the antithesis of secularism. It not only challenges the secular basis of the state but also seeks a communal reconstruction of national identity. It regards secularism as a code for anti-Hindu politics and derides the principle of minority rights, a key feature of Indian secularism, as an unwarranted privilege.[1] Much of what has been termed the 'secularism debates' revolves around the conceptual and normative structure of secularism, which from viewpoints such as the BJP's and communitarian scholars, is deeply flawed.[2] Very few scholars have looked at the political practices of the major political parties and how they impact secularism.

In 1998, in the twelfth general elections, a coalition of sixteen parties led by the BJP won a majority of seats in the Lok Sabha (The House of the People) and formed a government in New Delhi. This marked a crucial turning point in modern Indian politics: for the first time, the BJP, India's main right-wing political party and the front party of a family of militant Hindu organizations known as the Sangh Parivar, formed a government at the Centre, ending decades of political isolation.[3] Although the BJP set aside the most contentious aspects of its agenda, such as the adoption of a uniform civil code (which is opposed by the dominant section of minorities), to forge an electoral coalition, its growing influence nevertheless posed a threat to secular democracy and to constitutional safeguards for minority rights. This party was founded on the Hindutva ideology that upholds and espouses Hinduness. It proceeds from a conception of India as divided among majority and minority religions and equates India with a Hindu nation. Many of the party leaders belong to the Rashtriya Swayamsevak Sangh (RSS) and/or the Vishwa Hindu Parishad (VHP), and both groups support recognizing India as a Hindu nation. The ideology of Hindutva and the communalization of the polity under BJP rule convinced secularists that far from adhering to secularism, the BJP advocated an ideology that endangered India's pluralism and unity. Hence, the electoral victory of a Congress-led United Progressive Alliance (UPA) in the 2004 parliamentary elections, defeating the BJP-led National Democratic Alliance (NDA), was seen as a respite for secular politics. However, the defeat of the BJP did not spell the end of the Hindu right or for that matter the role of religion in politics and society. Rather, this phenomenon has continued to have a strong influence on the functioning of the state, civil society, and minority rights. Whether it be the communalization of the polity, the anti–Muslim pogrom in Gujarat in 2002, the communalizing of national security, their educational policy, or gender issues, the BJP's legacy is disquieting, to say the least.

Two major issues confront the secular project. The first major issue is the direct political challenge that comes from the Sangh Parivar and the BJP, stressing the centrality of an homogenizing version of Hindu culture as the defining element of both religion and nation. The BJP is not prepared to recognize in word or deed the importance of minority rights and the need to guarantee the security and rights due to them as equal citizens in a democratic and non-denominational state. Its anti–Muslim stance has turned the question of minorities into a matter of bitter conflict and controversy in India, especially when 'secularism has meant providing for substantive equality for religious minorities'.[4] The second major issue confronting the secular project in India relates to the distortions in the political practices of secular parties that have clearly done harm to political secularism. These issues, arising out of the political practice of secular parties, form the more specific focus of this chapter.

The crisis of the secularist model has been interpreted by many as a manifestation of the inadequacy of Indian model itself. Political secularism is questioned not only by right-wing politicians, civil society groups, and religious leaders, but also by academics. In fact, Indian academics were among the first to voice their disagreement with secularism.[5] For T.N. Madan, Ashis Nandy, and Partha Chatterjee, the threat to secularism comes from the conceptual structure of secularism that, they argue, is terribly flawed.[6] In different ways, each argues that secularism is 'linked to a flawed modernization, to a mistaken view of rationality, to an impractical demand that religion be eliminated from public life, to an insufficient appreciation of the importance of communities in the life of people and a wholly exaggerated sense of the positive character of the modern state'.[7]

By criticizing secularism, none of these critics mean to privilege communal ideology or the politics of either the majority or minority communities.[8] However, in denouncing secularism they share the view that it is the secular model that promotes communalism or religious intolerance. In fact, they blame the doctrine of secularism for the resurgence of communal politics in India. For them, the secularity of the state is not a bulwark against the Hindu right.[9] They see Indian secularism as promoting a false idea that 'a secular state should be one which enjoins and prescribes the showing of equal respect for all religions *sarva dharm sambhavam* rather than maintaining a basic separation of state apparatuses from religious influence and institutions'.[10] Furthermore, they see no incompatibility between the political agenda of the Hindu right and the preservation of a secular state. Supposedly, the evidence for this is that the Hindu right does not attack secularism as such, but rather attacks pseudo-secularism and the pseudo-secular state. From this one cannot however draw the conclusion that the BJP is not opposed to secularism. Even though the BJP does not oppose democracy, it claims that it is the force representing the majority of Hindus. The BJP does not oppose the principle of the democratic state, but it seeks to redefine democracy as majoritarian and secularism as tolerance.[11]

In place of Nehruvian secularism, the communitarians advocate religious tolerance as being authentically Indian and therefore more effectively secular. Tolerance, they hold, is deeply rooted in Indian tradition and therefore more 'natural' to Indian culture, and especially to Hinduism. Yet, the problem of identifying an essentialized Indianness or the essential tolerance of Hinduism is obvious, as claims of tolerance do not square with tolerance of hierarchies, inequalities, and communal violence.[12] Even today there is much intolerance and intercommunity violence over what are partly religiously driven divisions. Also, there is no evidence that secularism has sought to ride roughshod over religious sensibilities. In fact, the evidence of the past two decades suggests that the state has at times gone out of its way to accommodate religious sensibilities. It is therefore not clear why secularism is inappropriate for India, particularly when secularism has not contributed to the eradication or lessening of religious faith.

The BJP was engaged in discrediting political secularism much before the communitarian critique of secularism began to dominate academic debates on the subject. It attacked the practice of secularism, and particularly that of the Congress party as pseudo-secularism, and attempted to link secularism to a Hindu conception of tolerance via the purportedly inherent tolerance of Hinduism. This strategy is rooted in the claim that Hinduism is the most tolerant of all religions and consequently most conducive to secularism. In other words, it is not the constitutional principles and laws of a secular state but the natural tolerance of Hinduism and Hindus that can make secularism safe in India. Beyond this, for the BJP, secularism means nothing more than the strategy and practices of a non-theocratic state through which it is possible to maintain peace between communities and protect the religious liberty of individuals.[13] The BJP often cites the infrequency of violence under its' rule as further evidence of its toleration and non-partisanship.

The Hindu right's unrelenting attacks on minority rights—which are redescribed as Muslim appeasement—are an attempt to snap the links between secularism and minority rights, notwithstanding the fact that India has one of the oldest and most extensive regimes of minority rights in the world.[14] This contravenes the very idea of equality—of equal respect for religions and the equality of citizenship in a democracy.[15] Secularism and democracy are separated from each other and then presented as if they are mutually exclusive concepts, but the interconnections between them in the Indian context are obvious.[16] This can be confirmed through a brief survey of the specific provisions pertaining to secularism and fundamental rights, as well as the debates in the Constituent Assembly on the rights of religious freedom, particularly in the context of communal riots and the Partition of India on religious lines in 1947.[17] These debates underline the intrinsic link between democracy and secularism, based on the recognition that India could build national unity and survive only on the basis of secularism. Any attempt therefore to distance secularism from democracy in India could change the specific meanings of these terms. In today's circumstances it is perhaps even more important to emphasize the constellation of concepts—secularism, democracy, equality, and justice—as their interconnection is an outstanding achievement of India's freedom struggle and has defined the political agenda of independent India.

The focus here is on political secularism, one of the chief pillars of the liberal democratic state in India in order to examine political processes that have led to an erosion of political secularism; a process that has been aggravated by the rising influence of the Hindu right. The political context framing these developments has been the electoral successes of the Hindu right in the 1990s on the one hand, and the simultaneous expanding influence of community-based political groupings in India, which includes caste groups and religious minorities, on the other.[18] There are two episodes in the recent history of political secularism which are vital to understandings of the growth of majoritarianism and how that might affect secularism. Much of the public debate on the distortions of Indian secularism has drawn attention to state policy toward religious minorities and the accommodation of minority sentiment, especially regarding their identity concerns. Through a brief examination of the Sethusamudram Ship Channel Project (cutting a deep channel for ships through the shallow waters of the Palk Straits and the Gulf of Mannar), and the controversies surrounding India's most famous painter M.F. Husain and his work, this chapter will later explore some of the distortions of secular practice that are associated with the politics of majoritarianism. This chapter's principal contention is that secularism has been weakened by external forces inimical to it and aggravated by the blemished record of political parties, rather than by internal flaws in the conception of secularism. It is not the concept of political secularism per se that is responsible for the problems of secularism in India.

Over the years there has been a gradual erosion of secularism and liberal democratic discourse. Opportunism and repeated attempts by political parties to play the communal card have weakened secularism. Although committed to the ideal of secularism, there have been several instances when political parties succumbed to the easy political gains to be reaped from communalism. Secular parties have also found the idea of scoring quick electoral gains by tampering with secular principles and institutions too tempting to turn down. Political leaders are eager to curry favour with religious leaders to use them to marshal political support.[19] Parties seeking to stake out a position as pro–Hindu, or simultaneously pro–Hindu and a protector of the minorities, have given a fillip to the emergence of anti-secular politics.

In India, secularism is not an option; it is an absolute necessity in the context of extraordinary diversity and pluralism. Secularism alone can create equal rights for all citizens, regardless of religion, ethnicity, or culture. A contemporary notion of secularism is best derived from the egalitarian and universalist ideas embodied in the Constitution and closely linked to the ideals of the freedom struggle. Nehruvian secularism, for all its flaws, was an integral part of an effort to build a plural conception of nationhood in extremely difficult political circumstances. A critique of political secularism is an inappropriate ground for mounting a challenge to communalism, which is one of the most serious and dangerous problems facing India today. It is not the failure of political secularism that creates these problems, but rather, it is the failure of political parties to live up to the ideals of political secularism.

Political Secularism

Secularism in India, as elsewhere, means a separation of organized religion from organized political power. The basic constituents of this separation, however, are not exactly the same as in Western secularism.[20] The term secularism did not enter the Constitution until 1976. Despite this and serious differences of interpretation, secularism has been a central feature of the Indian project of modernity and democracy. The Constitution does not mandate a strict separation of religion and state—religion has not been disestablished. Departing from the disestablishment model, the state has chosen to interpret secularism as the responsibility to ensure the protection and equality of all religions and provide for regulation and reform, rather than the strict separation of religion and state.[21] Article 30(1) recognizes the rights of religious minorities and, unlike other articles applicable to citizens qua individuals, it is a community-based right. Second, Article 30(2) commits the state to give aid to educational institutions established and administered by religious minorities. These are significant departures from the 'wall of separation' view of the secular state. Even more significant are Articles 17 and 25(2) that permit the state to intervene in religious affairs, regulating or restricting any economic, financial, political, or other secular activity that may be associated with religious practice. The third feature is the emphasis on social welfare and reform. In pursuit of this agenda, the state abolished untouchability and threw open Hindu temples to all sections of the community.[22] Unlike the American view of disestablishment that is often thought to be based on a strict 'wall of separation' between the religion and the state, the Indian state is empowered to legislate against the 'non-egalitarian' and 'caste-ridden' prejudices legitimated by Hindu society, including temple entry to former Untouchables, abolition of child marriage, and abolition of untouchability.

Secular Consensus

The features of the Indian Constitution discussed earlier depart fundamentally from the Western model. Unlike the strict separation view that renders the state powerless in religious matters, they enjoin the state to interfere in religion. Yet, there is no mistaking the overall secular design articulated in these salient principles. It was precisely because political secularism was seen as having tremendous weight and relevance as a crucial component of the democratic project that the constitutional dispensation of secularism has remained intact. Even in the face of pressures from the Hindu right, Nehru never countenanced a political role for religion, as that would have endangered national integrity. The historical triumph of the Indian National Congress is that every political party now claims to be secular.[23] Historically, the Congress sought to balance contending interests by attempting to make room within itself for both the Hindu right and orthodox clerics at the same time as it championed the cause of modern secularism.[24] This balancing act was a part of Congress' conception of its identity 'as a self-consciously representative assembly of Indians from different parts of India',[25] with secularism as the instrument through which it sought to dissolve particularistic identities.

Overall, secularism was adapted to suit Indian conditions in ways that enabled it to combine with and respond to the demands of statecraft, while incorporating both the religious ideals of Gandhi on the one hand, and the modernist outlook of Nehru on the other. Despite its many weaknesses, this strategy worked for many decades.[26] The secular consensus held dominant sway over public life well beyond the Nehruvian era, meeting serious challenge only in the late 1980s. Two features of politics in the later period, which was marked by the escalation of communal violence, have contributed to a more generalized growth of communal prejudice. One was the routine participation of large numbers of police and paramilitary personnel in communal violence, invariably on the side of the majority community across the country, and resulting in a recurring distrust of security forces by the minority communities. The second feature was the propensity of the Congress to play the 'communal card'—making pragmatic accommodations of the backward elements of both the majority and minority communities. The Congress leadership, as demonstrated by several events mentioned below, faltered at crucial moments and failed to live up to the standards set by Nehru.

Secular Practice and the Erosion of Secularism

For more than four decades after Independence, the Congress occupied a pivotal position in Indian politics. Congress' political supremacy began to decline from the late 1960s and with it, India's secular framework began to weaken.[27] Before this period, the political influence of religion was limited and communal parties won few seats. Although Indira Gandhi retained a strong commitment to India as a secular state, her definition of secularism was premised on the equality of all religions and not on the rejection of religion or the complete separation of religion and politics.[28] The clear separation between politics and religion which was required in order to maintain the secularist polity became blurred. The readiness to overstep the bounds of constitutional propriety on matters of religion and secularism created the space for the rapid rise of an anti-secular alternative.

A series of events, some unintended, others calculated, helped anti-secular forces to gain a foothold in the political system. The unravelling of the secularist fabric began with demands for regional autonomy in Punjab and the manner in which the state responded to those demands. The Congress decided to play the 'Hindu card' to undercut the popularity of its regional rival, the Akali Dal in Punjab. Indira Gandhi refused to take stern action against Jarnail Singh Bhindranwale (a Sikh preacher turned extremist), thereby allowing him to run amok and turn his extremism against Hindus.[29] Congress expected the Hindu reaction in northern India to consolidate behind the party and also help it regain political support in the rest of the country. However, the attacks against Hindus orchestrated from the Golden Temple in Amritsar spun out of control and could only be contained after Indira Gandhi ordered the army to march into the temple to remove the militants who had taken control of it. This decision inflamed Sikhs and lead to the assassination of Indira Gandhi on 31 October 1984, by her Sikh bodyguards.

Another such event was the decision of the Congress government, led by Prime Minister Rajiv Gandhi, to revoke the Supreme Court verdict in the Shah Bano case by passing the 1986 Muslim Women's Act (MWA), denying Muslim women access to civil law in matters of marriage and divorce. The Supreme Court, in a 1985 landmark judgement, granted a small maintenance allowance to Shah Bano, a seventy-three-year-old Muslim divorcee, to be paid by her husband under Section 125 of the Criminal Procedure Code.[30] The Supreme Court was asked to pronounce on the relationship between these sections of the Criminal Procedure Code of 1973 and religious personal law. The Court ruled that Section 125, as part of criminal rather than civil law, overrides all personal law and is uniformly applicable to all women, including Muslim women. This was the final decision in a long series of suits and appeals in which her ex-husband argued that he had discharged his duty according to Muslim law. The decision to overturn the Shah Bano verdict breathed life into the ideology of the Hindu nationalists who condemned the Congress for its appeasement of Muslims though this legislation.

The third and most far-reaching in this series of events that damaged and destabilized secularism was the mishandling of the Ayodhya dispute from 1989 to 1992. During this period, the BJP and its affiliates started a nationwide campaign to construct a Ram temple in place of the Babri mosque in Ayodhya in Uttar Pradesh. Hindu activists had been claiming that the mosque stood at the spot believed to be the exact birthplace of Lord

Ram. Several decisions of the Congress party, which included unlocking the disputed site, launching the party's 1991 electoral campaign from Faizabad (a town near Ayodhya), and allowing the foundation stones of the proposed temple to be laid near the mosque, were aimed at arousing Hindu sentiment, but they ended up compromising the secular principle of the separation of religion and politics and encouraging the BJP to intensify its campaign for a Ram temple.[31] Overall, the decision to turn a dispute between two religions over a piece of holy ground into a national issue was intended to appease the majority community that was unhappy with the government's decision to overturn the Shah Bano court verdict.[32]

Both these decisions, though calculated to please communally-minded Hindus and Muslims respectively, ended up giving a massive boost to the forces of the Hindu right, reflected in the BJP's rise from a mere 2 to 89 Lok Sabha seats. Giving one concession to a particular community and then offsetting it by granting concessions to other communities was a process that left both Hindu and Muslim communities feeling that they had lost something. Not only does the constitution contain no warrant for such patronizing 'secularism', but it is also a dangerous approach that provokes a backlash from both sides of the communal divide.

Despite, or some would say because of, the concessions to religious group demands, the polity has been torn apart by competitive communalism and sectarian conflict. The social and political space that the Hindu right seized was created partly by the retreat of secularism during the six years of BJP-led NDA rule, and partly by the ambivalence and contradictions in secular political practice. In this context, the election of the Congress-led UPA at the Centre, defeating the NDA, was read by many as 'a decisive vote against communalism' and as the people's 'reaffirmation of a commitment to pluralism and secularism'.[33]

Two major decisions taken by the UPA government went some way towards restoring secular faith. The first was the decision to undo the creeping Hinduization of curricula in the educational system. Under Murli Manohar Joshi, a BJP politician with close links to the RSS and the VHP, the Human Resource Development Ministry of the NDA government launched a campaign to 'saffronize' (Hinduize) all levels of education by revising textbooks, instituting regulatory changes, and appointing sympathetic officials to key positions. The new textbooks published in 2002 and 2003 immediately became the subject of criticism for their innumerable distortions of history and, above all, the Hindutva perspective embedded in the National Curriculum Framework (NCF) 2000 for primary and secondary education that was also the basis of the new school textbooks.[34] Both the NCF and the textbooks were subsequently withdrawn by the UPA government when they came to power in 2004. The second decision was the commissioning of the landmark Sachar Committee Report that highlighted the development deficit and deprivation of the Muslim community and its neglect at the hands of successive governments, thus exposing the hollowness of the propaganda that Muslims are being appeased.[35] Despite this promising start however, the UPA government failed to provide relief or bring justice to the victims of the 2002 Gujarat violence, barring the one inquiry into the Godhra incident instituted by the Ministry of Railways. Earlier, the events in Gujarat even failed to find a mention in Prime Minister Dr Manmohan Singh's first address to the nation. Overall, the politics and strategy of the UPA government (2004-9) could not overcome the weakness of secular practice arising from its lack of political will and inability to stand up to religious politics. The task is by no means easy, as can be seen from a brief discussion of two recent episodes that underline the difficulties in attempting to disentangle politics from religion.

The Sethusamudram Project Controversy

The government's stand on the Sethusamudram project controversy is a case in point. First proposed in 1841, this project envisages dredging a coral walkway between India and Sri Lanka to reduce sailing time for ships. Currently, ships have to navigate around the Sri Lankan coast to reach destinations in the east of India. Once completed, this project is expected to boost maritime trade by providing considerable economic activity in the region and by saving crucial time and money for movement from the east and west coasts of India. All parties in Tamil Nadu, except one, have actively supported it and the major objections, which are based primarily on environmental impact, have fallen by the wayside. There were no objections to the project on grounds of religious sentiment until recent faith-based opposition by certain Hindu groups.[36] In September 2007, the Archaeological Survey of India (ASI) submitted an affidavit to the Supreme Court regarding the Sethusamudram Project arguing that dredging should continue on the grounds that Ram Setu, also known as Adam's Bridge, was not an 'essential' and 'integral part of Hindu religion', which alone would warrant protection by the Constitution. This affidavit raised doubts about the Ramayana, an epic Hindu poem, and the link between Lord Ram and Ram Setu: 'We are not destroying any bridge. There is no bridge. It was not a man-made structure. It may be superman made structure, but the same superman destroyed it. That is why for centuries nobody mentioned anything about it. It (Ram Setu) has become an object of worship only recently'.[37] These statements provoked a public outcry that led to the withdrawal of the affidavit.[38] The government accepted a court's recommendation to strike a balance between 'faith and logic' by exploring alternative routes for the shipping channel to spare any damage to the Ram Setu, considered holy by many Hindus. The Sethusamudram issue quickly moved from the margins to the centre stage of national debate after the Hindu organizations protested against the project and demanded that Ram Setu be declared an ancient monument. The BJP accused the UPA government of attempting to abuse and hurt Hindu sentiments when the government suggested that there was no proof that Ram Setu was a place of worship. The party asked whether the government would have made 'such derogatory comments about the symbols and beliefs of other faiths'.[39] According to the BJP, the UPA government, by denying the historicity of Ram, was endorsing an irreligious brand of secularism that is more anti-Hindu than anti-religion. In the words of the opposition BJP leader, L.K. Advani, 'the government has sought to negate all that the Hindus consider sacred . . . and wounded *the very idea of India*'. The contention was that real secularism, as opposed to pseudo-secularism (practiced by the Congress), cannot be irreligious or hostile to Hinduism because India is quintessentially Hindu.

The ASI's affidavit had limited itself to rejecting the claim that scriptures or mythological texts such as the Ramayana constitute historical proof that Ram Setu is a man-made structure and not to belittling the importance of Ram in Indian culture.[40] The affidavit was on strong ground when it stated that it was not a man-made structure but a natural formation made up of shoals and sandbars. However, statements that questioned the veracity of the Ramayana or the occurrence of events in the text went beyond the requirements of the case. It is these overreaching statements that sparked an outcry of protest. However, even if the ASI had been more diplomatic in its wording of the affidavit, it is highly unlikely that it would have restrained the strident protests of the Hindu Right. Clearly, the BJP leadership chose to take offence not only because they have little respect for the complexity and diversity of the Hindu tradition, but also because they believe that Hindu sensibilities, concerns, and sentiment must be accorded special respect and primacy in India because Hindus form a majority of the population.[41]

Congress, fearing a possible backlash, changed its stance on the project, despite earlier claims that opposition to this project along lines of faith was 'misconceived and unsubstantiated'.[42] It took measures to withdraw the objectionable paragraph (affirming that the bridge was a geological, not a man-made, formation) that it had submitted before the Supreme Court.[43] In so doing the Centre stated that 'it has total respect for all religions, and Hinduism in particular, in the context of the present case. The Central government is alive and conscious of the religious sensibilities, including the unique, ancient and holy text of Ramayana'.[44] The Union Law Minister went a step further to say, 'Lord Ram is an integral part of Indian culture and ethos and cannot be [the] subject matter of litigation in court. . . . We have equal faith in Ram or Shiva'.[45] In effect, he was making a case that the viability of the project should be judged not on economic or environmental grounds, but should consider mythological concerns as well. An editorial in a leading newspaper observed that 'the secular credentials of the Indian state have just taken another knock. . . . Respecting one's right to religious belief is not the same as allowing the right to override the secular character of the Indian state. Indian secularism is not irreligious. But it is also not about equating mythology and geology.'[46] None of the constituents of the UPA, with the exception of Dravida Munnetra Kazhagam (DMK) in alliance with the ruling Congress party, defended the ASI affidavit or questioned the BJP, under whose government at the Centre the Sethusamudram Project was originally approved. In fact, most of them questioned the government's wisdom of gratuitously interfering in matters of faith.

This controversy reflects the difficult balance that the Congress has had to strike between protecting secular values and trying not to hurt or offend majority sentiment, or at least the vocal segments of it. The Congress party's statement claimed that the prompt withdrawal of the affidavit reflected the party's sensitivity to matters of personal belief and faith, unmindful of the fact that this proposition violated the constitutional imperative of secularism, which requires that we attempt a basic separation of religion from politics, and more narrowly, that we do not favour or privilege any religion. This is a reflection of the fragility of the secular ethos of parties such as the Congress when it finds itself under attack from, for example, the BJP seeking to use issues that appeal to religious sentiment. Appeals to majoritarian sentiment tend to benefit the BJP, and not the Congress, yet, in this instance Congress was unable to either confront the Hindu right or its claims of tolerance.[47]

The M.F. Husain Controversy

A similar pattern can be observed in the M.F. Husain controversy. The same balancing act was evident in dealing with the attacks by right-wing Hindu organizations on Maqbool Fida Husain, one of India's most distinguished and celebrated painters whose work represents an intense engagement with modernism and popular culture. Although the issue was a relatively minor one, it has important implications for the political practice of secularism, which was increasingly torn between imperatives to sustain secular principles of cultural freedom and the compulsions of political pragmatism.

The Hindutva campaign against Husain started in September 1996, when an RSS-controlled Hindi magazine, *Vichar Mimansa*, published sections of Husain's paintings using their own provocative titles. In response, activists of the Hindu right barged into the Herwitz Gallery in Ahmedabad to destroy his paintings for allegedly offending religious sensibilities and insulting Bharat Mata (Mother India) and Hindu gods and goddesses. An earlier untitled painting by Husain, which was held in a private collection until it entered the public domain in 2006, under the title of Bharat Mata, was ostensibly the source of offence. Husain apologized, saying that it was not his intention to hurt religious feelings, even as his lawyers clarified that he had not in fact named the painting himself, and that the name 'Bharat Mata' had been given by the gallery without his knowledge.[48] The artist was threatened, his Mumbai residence was ransacked, and his exhibitions were vandalized. Gallery owners were eventually forced to withdraw the painting from the bidding process for sale of the paintings. In 2004, Bajrang Dal and VHP activists attacked an art gallery in Surat to vandalize his art works. In addition, dozens of criminal cases were filed resulting in many non-bailable warrants. The anti-Husain campaign made deft use of social intimidation tactics to harass Husain, and he was eventually compelled to seek refuge in another country, rather than risk the possibility of arrest and prolonged detention.[49]

The turning point came in May 2007 after the Home Ministry advised the police chiefs of Delhi and Mumbai to take appropriate action against the artist. This was in response to a letter from L.K. Advani accusing the UPA government of double standards in that they sought to pacify Muslims protesting against the cartoons of Prophet Mohammed in a Danish newspaper, yet they refused to pay heed to the hurt sentiments of Hindu groups offended by Husain's paintings of Hindu gods and goddesses. The Home Ministry issued an advisory that all complaints against him in any part of the country would be investigated and ensured wide publicity by having the advisory prominently published in *The Hindustan Times*. This advisory has made it impossible for Husain to return to the country. It is significant that the Home Ministry took no cognizance of the protests by liberal and secular forces against the demonization of the artist, but took immediate notice of the protestations of the BJP leader to issue an advisory. Ironically, all this was happening when the Congress was in power and Husain had always had close links to the party.[50] Even worse, on the one hand, the UPA government chose not to rally for the inclusion of Husain's works at an Art Summit in Delhi in August 2008 when the organizers decided to leave out his works for fear of a backlash and vandalism. On the other hand, in 2008, the Union Ministry of Culture supported an exhibition organized by the Safdar Hashmi Memorial Trust (SAHMAT), a platform for concerned artists and academics to protest against Husain's exclusion from the Art Summit and where Hindu extremists smashed prints and photographs on display. This fiasco, and indeed the entire approach to Husain's self-imposed exile, underline the tensions within secularism and the deeper fissures in the polity regarding the ideals enshrined in the Constitution and the politics of accommodation.

It is worth noting that the controversy was not created by Husain himself as he had been painting gods and goddesses for a long time. Rather, at some point the Hindu right decided to target him to dramatize their opposition to secular cultural hegemony. He was a prime target because he is a Muslim who had dared to produce a body of work suffused with the iconography of the Hindu pantheon.[51] The attack on him really had nothing to with his iconography or the protection of Hinduism. Rather, the protestors were using Husain's name and fame to politicize and mobilize Hindu cadres. However, the more important point is that the government, instead of providing protection, seemed to be giving in to the extremists out of fear of being branded anti-Hindu and thus seen to be appeasing Muslims. Consequently, Husain was left to the mercy of courts and police investigators while the government was not prepared to defend the rule of law. This once again underlines the government's ambivalent stand on freedom of speech and expression, and the reticence of the Congress to take a principled stand to protect the basic tenets of the Constitution. As ever, the party wants to be all things to all people, but given the opposition it faces from the BJP, it frequently tilts toward making an adjustment in favour of majority sentiments to offset the BJP's charge of minority appeasement.

Conclusion

An analysis of the Sethusamudram and Husain controversies not only highlights the ambivalence of the Congress but it also underlines important differences between Congress and BJP perspectives on secularism, pluralism, and nationalism. Although Congress is often tentative in its defence of secular principles, the party is not inherently communal or majoritarian. Congress leaders could plausibly argue that such instances of compromise and vacillation were momentary aberrations. By contrast, the BJP's brand of majoritarian nationalism organizes politics around emotionally charged religious issues and actively promotes an idea of India that conflates religious identity with national identity. The party's identity is crucially dependent on the presence of Muslims as the 'other', and a Hinduism forever beleaguered by Islam. By contrast, the Congress party has nothing in common with the homogenizing nationalism of the Sangh Parivar. Historically, the uniqueness of the Congress position lay in its near complete freedom from any mystical notions of a national essence that are the staple of narrower nationalisms which have succeeded in aligning their states with faith, as in the cases of Sri Lanka or Serbia.[52] To mobilize large masses of people under the nationalist banner, the Congress, whether by design or by default, replaced cultural notions with colonial exploitation and subjugation during the anti-colonial movement.

To say all this is not to deny that Congress has often failed to differentiate its position from that of the BJP for fear of offending Hindu sentiments. Secular parties tend to lack the political courage to tackle communal elements head-on. This includes communal elements in the minority communities as well. For example, conservative and reactionary figures among Muslims are accorded importance on the baseless assumption that they are the true representatives of the followers of their faith. Instead of reinforcing its own tradition of defending secularism and deriving strength from the support that secularism enjoys in the large mass of Indian society, a sizeable section of the Congress party has either tried to appropriate the communal discourse or has ever migrated to the communal camp.

At a deeper level, both episodes show that the separation of religion and politics requires an ideological countervailing force that the Congress party—as the principal secular political force—is sometimes unable to provide. If the oscillating strategy of the Congress offers any lesson, it is that ideas and challenges emanating from majoritarian politics cannot be countered by compromise or conciliation. Congress cannot effectively counter the Hindu right so long as it remains unconvinced that secularism is not only the right moral response, but also the winning political one. In this regard, Mani Shankar Aiyar rightly remarked when the BJP won the parliamentary elections in 1998-9 that the 'real danger before the country is not a BJP electoral victory. The real danger lies in the rest of us seeking to thwart the rise in electoral support of the BJP by becoming pale imitations of the original'.[53] However, this is again a long-term problem: so long as there are sufficient votes in such divisive politics, political parties are not going to abstain from using such tactics. Much depends upon the Congress party being able to mobilize the political will to take a firm stand against the practitioners and purveyors of polarization and violence, without fearing that it will alienate the majority community from the party. Since the emergence of the BJP as a formidable political force, the Congress has sometimes found it difficult to draw the line, especially as it tries to appropriate the positions of the BJP. In both episodes, the UPA government dithered between secular principles on the one hand, and not hurting majority sentiments on the other, erring mostly on the side of the latter. Both the Husain and Sethusamudram controversies exemplify incidents, where the failure to act decisively against communal elements has weakened the capacity of Congress to uphold the original commitment to provide secular and democratic governance. That said, it would be grossly misleading to suggest that these two episodes constitute a retreat from secularism, or that they are predictable responses arising from the conceptual structure of Indian secularism.

On the face of it, political secularism has not performed its principal function to limit the role of religion in politics and in conflicts between communities. Nonetheless, it is important to remember that a secular state has survived in a deeply religious society and in a context in which ethnic nationalism remains a powerful force in the world, especially in the South Asian region. The stunning verdict in favour of secular parties and government in two successive parliamentary elections (2004 and 2009) indicates the strong support for secularism in India. Overall, Nehruvian secularism is a resilient force and still offers the most credible and viable way of building a secular democracy in an extraordinarily diverse society such as India.

Notes and References

1. See Gyan Prakash, 'Secular Nationalism, Hindutva and the Minority', in *The Crisis of Secularism in India,* ed., Anuradha Digwaney Needham and Rajeswari Sunder Rajan, Delhi: Permanent Black, 2007, pp. 177–88.
2. See articles in Rajeev Bhargava, ed., *Secularism and Its Critics,* Delhi: Oxford University Press, 1998; also see Needham and Rajan, eds., *The Crisis of Secularism.*
3. The RSS (National Volunteers Organization) was founded in Nagpur in 1925 by Keshav Baliram Hedgewar. Also known as the Sangh, it is a Hindu revivalist organization associated with Hindu militant movements. The RSS is a conservative and reactionary organization that represents a form of militant Hindu nationalism. It suffered a severe setback in 1948–9 because of the assassination of Mahatma Gandhi by one of its members (Nathuram Godse). Jawaharlal Nehru banned the RSS in 1948.
4. Needham and Rajan, eds., *The Crisis of Secularism,* p. 21.
5. For a lucid account of political secularism see Rajeev Bhargava, 'The Distinctiveness of Indian Secularism', in *The Future of Secularism,* ed. T.N. Srinivasan, Delhi: Oxford University Press, 2007.
6. The writings of these authors are included in Bhargava, *Secularism and Its Critics.*
7. Bhargava, 'The Distinctiveness of Indian Secularism', p. 20.
8. For a critique of the positions of Nandy, Madan, and Chatterjee, see Achin Vanaik, *Communalism Contested: Religion, Modernity and Secularization,* Delhi: Vistaar Publications, 1997, pp. 152–80.
9. Ibid., p. 188.
10. Ibid., p. 153.

11. Ibid.

12. Rajeswari Sunder Rajan, 'Women between Community and State: Some Implications of the Uniform Civil Code Debates in India', *Social Text*, vol. 18, no. 4, Winter 2000, pp. 55–82.

13. Rajeev Bhargava, 'Liberal, Secular Democracy and Explanations of Hindu Nationalism', *Commonwealth and Comparative Politics*, vol. 40, no. 3, 2002, p. 92.

14. Ibid.

15. Ibid., p. 93.

16. For a discussion of this interconnection see Sumit Sarkar, 'Indian Democracy: The Historical Inheritance', in *The Success of India's Democracy*, ed. Atul Kohli, Cambridge: Cambridge University Press, 2001, pp. 23–46.

17. Ibid., p. 39.

18. K.N. Panikkar, 'Secularism in Practice', *The Hindu*, 15 March 2005.

19. Bhargava, 'Liberal, Secular Democracy'.

20. For an elaboration of the Indian model of secularism and its universality, see Bhargava, 'The Distinctiveness of Indian Secularism'.

21. Ibid., pp. 35–6.

22. The Indian courts have outlined areas in which the freedom of religion is not absolute. Article 17 abolishes untouchability and makes it an offence punishable by law. The practice of untouchability cannot be protected under Article 25. The limitations of Article 25 on religious freedom exemplifies the constitutional need to accommodate the state's provision for social welfare and reform.

23. Mukul Kesavan, 'Naming the Enemy', *The Hindu*, 16 September 2001.

24. Pratap Bhanu Mehta, 'Congress, Secularism and Freedom', *Seminar*, no. 526, June 2003, pp. 26–30.

25. Mukul Kesavan, *Secular Common Sense*, Delhi: Penguin India, 1998, p. 3.

26. Ibid.

27. Mani Shankar Aiyar, 'Can the Congress Find a Future', *Seminar*, no. 526, June 2003, pp. 14–22.

28. Francine Frankel, *India's Political Economy, The Gradual Revolution, 1947-2004*, 2nd edn., New Delhi: Oxford University Press, 2005, pp. 664–5.

29. Sumit Ganguly, 'The Crisis of Indian Secularism', *Journal of Democracy*, vol. 14, no. 4, 2003, pp. 11–25.

30. Ibid.

31. Ibid., pp. 16-20.

32. Ibid.

33. Arundhati Roy, 'Let Us Hope the Darkness Has Passed', *Guardian*, 14 May 2004.

34. See Mushirul Hasan, 'The BJP's Intellectual Agenda', in *Will Secular India Survive*, ed. Mushirul Hasan, Delhi: ImprintOne, 2004, pp. 157–76.

35. Prime Minister Dr Manmohan Singh constituted a High-Level Committee on the Social, Economic and Educational Status of the Muslim Community of India. The committee, chaired by Rajender Sachar, and charged with investigating the socio-economic status of Muslims, submitted its report to the prime minister in November 2006. The Sachar Committee Report (SCR) found stark under-representation of Muslims and systematic evidence to show that they are an underclass on par with the lowest Hindu caste groups. It showed that in the twenty-odd years since the submission of the Report of the High Power Panel on Minorities, Scheduled Castes, Scheduled Tribes, and Other Weaker Sections

(1983) appointed by Prime Minister Indira Gandhi, the central government and those of the states have done very little to rectify the backwardness and under-representation of Muslims.

36. *The Hindu,* 15 September 2007.
37. Ibid.
38. *The Economic Times,* 15 October 2008.
39. Ibid.
40. Praful Bidwai, 'The Question of Faith', *Frontline,* vol. 24, no. 18, 22 September–25 October 2007.
41. Ibid.
42. *Indian Express,* 23 July 2008.
43. *Indian Express,* 15 September 2007.
44. Associated News of India (ANI), 22 February 2008.
45. *The Times of India,* 14 September 2007.
46. Editorial, 'Myth or Reality', *The Times of India,* 15 September 2007.
47. Mahesh Rangarajan, 'A Bridge Too Far', *The Telegraph,* 18 September 2007.
48. Rajeev Dhavan, *Harassing Husain: Uses and Abuses of the Law of Hate Speech,* Delhi: Sahmat, 2007.
49. Ibid.
50. Husain's painting of Indira Gandhi as Goddess Durga earned him the title of 'court painter' during the Emergency imposed by Prime Minister Indira Gandhi between 1975 and 1977.
51. Ram Rahman, 'M.F. Hussain: Why Is He in Exile?', *Indian Express,* 15 September 2007.
52. Mukul Kesavan, 'Naming the Enemy', *The Hindu,* 16 September 2001.
53. Mani Shankar Aiyar, *Confessions of a Secular Fundamentalist,* Delhi: Penguin, 2006.

11 | Mass Violence and the Wheels of Indian (In)Justice

THE MASS killings of Sikhs in New Delhi in 1984 and the 2002 pogrom in Gujarat have rightfully acquired a place in public and political discourse as two horrific episodes of extreme violence in post-colonial India.[1] They do not however stand alone. In the years between the violence of Delhi (1984) and Gujarat (2002), several major episodes of communal violence took place in Meerut-Malliana (Uttar Pradesh) in 1987, where Provincial Armed Constabulary jawans lined up and shot dead 53 Muslim youths in cold blood; the Bhagalpur massacre of 1989 during which an overnight slaughter of the Muslim minority took place and nearly 1,000 were killed; and the mass violence in Bombay in 1992–3.

Each of these major cases of mass violence has called forth investigations by numerous commissions of inquiry and civil society groups. Despite these inquiries, there has been no systematic effort to prevent the recurrence of violence, and no fair or impartial administration of justice to punish the guilty. Indeed, the tragedy is not just that mass violence happened but that successive governments are not prepared to do anything to prevent it or to provide justice to the victims. Instead of those responsible being punished, they are frequently elected to national and stare legislatures and become ministers and chief ministers. As a result, the Indian state has acquired a reputation for not being able to cope with communal violence fairly, or to protect the minorities who are the main victims of it. States and courts alike have repeatedly shown their incapacity to deal with communal issues, even

*I most grateful to Rajeev Dhavan, Senior Advocate in the Supreme Court for discussions on the criminal justice system and for making available legal materials on riots and the criminal justice system, Amrita Basu and Srirupa Roy for editorial support, and Yasundhara Sirnate, Adnan Faruqui and Manzur Ali for providing research support for this article.

more than other social atrocities such as caste violence. Most accounts of Hindu-Muslim violence tend to focus on the event of violence, on how and why violence occurs, what factors account for its outbreak, and the agents invoked. This chapter, in contrast, is focused on the post-violence situation and, drawing upon comparative material from the mass violence of Mumbai and Gujarat, it focuses attention on the hitherto only partly examined aftermath of such episodes.

On the issue of securing justice, relief, and rehabilitation for victims of communal mass violence, this chapter poses the question of why there is no conviction and prosecution of individuals involved in organized violence in India, even when there is evidence of the active or passive involvement of influential people and personnel from the administration and police. In fact, allegations of state connivance in mass violence have been strengthened by the failure of the criminal justice system to bring those responsible to justice—a fact highlighted by the Supreme Court in a recent order which reportedly referred to 'connivance' between the government and prosecution service in Gujarat.[1] The limitations of the state's role in the post-violence period, especially the inquiry commission approach or the judicial process needs to be examined, as does the question of whether we are perhaps using obsolete legal concepts to deal with mass killings that have state backing. Equally, the issue of the constitutional responsibility of the state to prevent such mass killings needs elucidating. Finally, the larger question is concerned with the post-conflict situation and what it tells us about the equality of citizenship and justice in India's democracy.

Many social scientists, civil society groups, bureaucrats, and policemen link the state response to riots, and the overall problems of the prevention of riots, to the politicization, corruption, and institutional weakness of governments. Many argue that political interference in law and order decisions has incapacitated the police force and so it does not have the independence to take action against rioters.[2] There is no doubt that the problem of political interference is serious and has grown worse in the past two decades. However, as Steven Wilkinson points out, state capacity alone cannot account for variations in Hindu-Muslim violence across time and space, because most state governments in India possess the minimal capacity required to prevent communal conflict if political leaders treat this as a priority.[3] The issue is not that state capacity is inconsequential, rather that governments can prevent violence if there is the political will to do so. Therefore, the key issue is the political will to protect or not protect minorities. The most notable examples of this are West Bengal and Bihar in the 1990s, which had low levels of riots and deaths because political leaders made the prevention of communal violence a priority. At the other extreme is Gujarat and Maharashtra, that have had high levels of communal violence and a complete absence of political will to prevent mass violence. This is partly due to the intensification of communal politics and prejudice against minorities in these two states, and partly because of the low rates of conviction and prosecution. While there may be no direct connection between riot prevention and prosecution, prosecuting the guilty even after the event fact can prove to be a deterrent in the continuation of violence, or indeed the outbreak of fresh violence in the two most violent states, Gujarat and Maharashtra.

For those concerned about the fairness of Indian democracy, examining the aftermath of violence is crucial because it gives important insights into the lasting consequences of the politics of religious division and the resultant threat to processes of pluralism and equality. There needs to be an understanding of the post-conflict situation in order to form an adequate conception of the challenges of religious nationalism and ethnic politics, and the problems it poses for non-discrimination and equal respect for all groups. Democracy combines the rule of law and constitutional governance to ensure democratic and secular justice. Without justice, governance itself is unjust and inequitable. Failure to protect the life and property of individuals belonging to minority communities is a powerful site of discrimination in Indian society and threatens long-term democracy. The claim to be the world's largest democracy and one of the great powers will be considerably diminished if mass-level crimes and barbaric forms of collective victimization of vulnerable groups continue to go unpunished. If India is to live up to its acclaimed status as a strong and vibrant democracy, it must establish and affirm the rule of law impartially. Punishing the guilty is therefore necessary not only from the viewpoint of humanism and compassion; it is imperative for strengthening the secular foundations of our democracy.

Mumbai 1992–3 and Gujarat 2002

These two major episodes of mass violence in independent India are associated with political movements and actions of the Hindutva organiz-ations linked to the Sangh Parivar.[4] Starting in the late 1980s, the Bharatiya Janata Party (BJP), Vishwa Hindu Parishad (VHP) and Rashtriya Swayamsevak Sangh (RSS) collaborated in a militant religious mobilization to 'liberate' the Ram Janmabhoomi site in Ayodhya. In October 1990, L.K. Advani personally led the temple campaign, which took him through eight states, stoking religious emotions and leaving communal conflict and violence in his trail. The agitation provoked huge incidents of rural and urban violence, of which the Mumbai violence was the worst instance. Even states where communal violence was uncommon were unable to escape the violence engendered by the agitation. The religious fervour aroused by the *Rath Yatra* was a key factor in increasing the violence, which was clearly the product of sustained mass mobilization, and derived from a broader discourse of communalism that was the driving force behind the increase in violence. For the BJP and the RSS, the Ayodhya campaign, combined with an appeal to Hindutva, offered a strategy to mobilize popular support to replace the Congress as the dominant party. This period bore witness to a continuous pattern of violence that culminated in the destruction of the Babri Masjid by Hindu mobs, who claimed that it was built on the remains of a Hindu temple.

Riots between the Muslim demonstrators protesting against the demolition and Hindus leading victory processions sparked the riots which followed shortly after this in Mumbai. The riots took place in two phases— the December 1992 phase, lasting for five days to a week, and the January 1993 phase, which occurred between 6 January and 20 January.[5] The first was primarily a Muslim backlash as a result of the Babri Masjid demolition in the week immediately succeeding demolition. The second phase was largely a Hindu backlash occurring as a result of the widely reported killings of four Hindu Mathadi Kamdar, allegedly by Muslims, in Dongri (an area of south Mumbai). Over 1,500 people were killed in the riots and thousands were displaced.[6]

The second major episode of mass violence occurred in Gujarat in March 2002 when more than 2,000 Muslims were killed, over 150,000 displaced, and scores of women raped in one of the most brutal instances of carnage in the history of Independent India.[7] There is copious evidence that the violence was planned before the horrific burning of the Sabarmati Express at Godhra station killing 59 Hindus, and that the post-Godhra carnage was aided and abetted both by the police and by local BJP and RSS politicians. In the days and weeks that followed, further waves of violence swept across the state. The attackers were mainly highly politicized Hindus shouting slogans such as 'Jai Sri Ram' and 'Jai Hanuman' and the victims were almost all Muslims. Official information furnished to the Election Commission of India indicated that only 12 of the 25 districts in the state were affected. However, relief was distributed in 20 districts which means 20 districts had to have been affected.[8] The Additional Director General of Police, R.B. Sreekumar, further informed the Commission that 151 towns and 993 villages covering 154 out of 182 assembly constituencies in the state were affected by the violence.[9] Violence was directed against all Muslims regardless of social class. One former chief justice of the Rajasthan High Court, living in retirement in Gujarat, was forced to flee and later commented to an investigative tribunal that there was 'a deliberate conspiracy to stifle criminal law'.[10]

The Gujarat violence and the state response have been extensively examined in the press and by human rights organizations.[11] It cannot strictly be called a communal riot in the conventional sense as it was a carnage aided and abetted both by the police and by local politicians.[12] The National Human Rights Commission (NHRC) investigation into the violence reported evidence of a complete breakdown of law and order in Gujarat and also found irrefutable evidence of the government's unwillingness to control violence.[13] It is clear from all the evidence placed before the Concerned Citizens Tribunal that what began in Godhra, could have, given the political will, been controlled promptly at Godhra itself.[14]

Instead, the state government under chief minister Narendra Modi took an active part in leading and sponsoring the violence against minorities all over Gujarat.[15] His words and actions throughout the developments in Gujarat show that he was openly defying the Constitution and indulging in actions directed against Muslims. According to press accounts and human rights investigations, the Modi regime facilitated the violence in many ways. For example, the police received orders not to intervene in the carnage, and those who disobeyed were punished by demotions and transfers. In this regard, the most damaging was the testimony of the Director General of Police who headed the Criminal Investigation Department (CID).[16] R.B. Sreekumar said that political leaders had pressured the police force into not registering riot offences. He observed that: '[He] instructed that I should not concentrate on the Sangh Parivar as they are not doing anything illegal'. Other features of police behaviour included the registration of First Information Reports (FIRs) not naming the accused, the refusal to take action against VHP activists who participated in the violence, and the failure to use the Disturbed Areas (Special Courts) Act of 1976 and the Prevention of Damage to Public Property Act of 1984. Even after the arson attack at Godhra, no preventive arrests were made under Section 144 of the Criminal Procedure Code (CPC).

These patterns of state complicity continued even after the cessation of violence. State authorities discriminated against Muslims in the payment of compensation and the rehabilitation of the victims.[17] The relief and rehabilitation was inadequate, failing to provide food, shelter, or security as rations were scarce. Four years later, the majority of the family members of those killed in the Gujarat violence had yet to receive their compensation disbursements. State agencies even obstructed other agencies that were attempting to step in with relief and rehabilitation, and forced the closure of relief camps after giving people a pittance to compensate for their losses.[18] In the makeshift camps established by the Muslim community, the state government refused even to provide basic facilities, security, or a survival stipend.[19] The compensation to be paid was unfair for at first, more compensation was paid to the Godhra (Hindu) victims than to the Muslims. Later, it was equalized.[20] To access compensation required proofs of identity, which victims of arson struggled to provide. As the International Initiative for Justice in Gujarat has pointed out, the state used the term 'assistance' rather than 'compensation', indicating that the state considered these payments not as a right or entitlement of the victims but as charitable measures. Prior to Gujarat 2002 state authorities in India were not always efficient in the rehabilitation of internal refugees created by ethnic conflicts, but they did not deliberately discriminate in compensation and resettlement.[21]

State obligation, though not specifically delineated, is implied in the fundamental right to life and equality. The state's liability to pay compensation for tortuous actions has been well established in a number of cases.[22] The failure of the state in this regard is therefore even more of a grey area than its complicity in the violence. As a result, privatized relief and rehabilitation dominated the post-conflict situation in both Gujarat and Mumbai.[23] Muslim NGOs and relief organizations provided relief for the mostly Muslim victims—leading to a dangerous irony that post-conflict reconstruction efforts furthered rather than mitigated the communal divide.[24] The government hardly took any steps to dispel the notion that they were hostile to minorities and their rights as equal citizens of India. Moreover, the Gujarat violence and suffering were a direct result of either calculated state disregard, or state collusion and complicity. In such circumstances, the liability and responsibility for rehabilitation should fall squarely on the government, and NGOs should not be expected to deal with the crisis; the NGOs should at best support and supplement state efforts.

Post-Violence Investigation and the Illusion of Justice

In India, an official commission of inquiry is usually set up to inquire into riots and prepare reports on the causes of tension. The body is constituted in the aftermath of a controversial event of public importance through the supreme legislative body of the country or state. Different countries recruit members to these commissions differently. In India, inquiry commissions are set up under the Commissions of Inquiry Act, 1952.[25] It is customary to appoint an ex-judge of the Supreme Court as the head of the commission and, it is to be noted, that these commissions are only recommendatory and do not have the power to prosecute. Nonetheless they help to focus public opinion on a concrete set of 'facts' (outlined in the report of the commission) when there are a number of interpretations of the same controversial event. Commissions of inquiry perform vital tasks in the orientation of public opinion. There does seem to be a direct correlation between the rise of parliamentary democracy and the setting up of official investigations into matters of public importance. This could perhaps be due to the pressures of mass democracy and the growing importance of public opinion, which seeks answers from and holds the state accountable. Some of the most well known commissions include Jagmohan Reddy on Ahmedabad (1969), Raghubir Dayal Commission (1967), D.P. Madan on Bhiwandi (1970), Vithayathil on Tellicherry (1971), Jitendra Narain on Jamshedpur (1979), Venugopal on Kanyakumari (1982), the Srikrishna Commission on Mumbai (1998), and the Ranganath Mishra Commission inquiring into the 1984 anti-Sikh violence (1985).

The failings of state administration in dealing with violence are clear from these reports. All inquiries bring out some of the common elements in riots: planning and organization, political involvement, clear targeting, absence of state prevention, and precipitating events, etc. Each has, more or less drawn the same conclusions: the police failed to act with impartiality in every case; the top level officers rarely acted alone and almost always looked to the political leadership for direction; the miscreants exploited every such delay in action by indulging in looting and arson. These reports provide a basis for prosecuting a number of people against whom 'credible evidence' exists. Although these reports have immense relevance to the system of governance, the importance accorded to them is minimal. The government, state officials, and law enforcement agencies never take seriously the recommendations regarding responsibility even of leading policemen and none of the reports have resulted in convictions. Nevertheless, governments continue to favour the commission formula to deal with outbreaks of communal violence or any type of mass violence. In keeping with this approach, on 23 January 1993, the Congress-led government of Maharashtra appointed Justice B.N. Srikrishna, then a sitting judge of the High Court of Bombay, to head a one-man commission to investigate the riots. It is important to remember that the Srikrishna Commission was initially set up in 1993 but could submit the report only in 1998, after its Terms of Reference were expanded to include the Mumbai Bomb Blasts at the Bombay Stock Exchange and subsequent riots of early 1993.

The 800-page Report is a detailed investigation of the violent rioting that occurred in the state capital of Mumbai following the 1992 destruction of the Babri Masjid in northern India. The Commission cited the immediate causes of the riots as the demolition of the Babri Masjid, the aggravation of Muslim sentiments by Hindus due to their celebration rallies and, the insensitive and harsh handling of the protesting mobs—which initially were not violent—by the police. There is plenty of evidence of the Shiv Sena's complicity in the riots. For example, the Commission found that Shiv Sena leaders led a mob, which 'attacked Chacha Nagar Masjid and the Muslims in the vicinity'. It stated that 'There is no doubt the Sena took the lead in organizing attacks on Muslims under the guidance of several leaders,' specifically naming Shiv Sena chief Balasaheb Thackeray as the driving force behind the riots. The Report clearly blamed the Shiv Sena for the pre-planned targeting of Muslim life and property in Mumbai. In a searing indictment of the organized violence, the Report stated that the measures taken by the police were inadequate and the curfews and the statutory ban on holding assemblies of five or more people were not effectively implemented. The police force was hopelessly inadequate in dealing with the extraordinary situation that arose in the wake of the destruction of the Babri Masjid. Further, the Report held that the police responded unsympathetically to calls for help by individual members of the Muslim community, and sections of the police remained inactive or even participated in the violence.[26] The police were indicted for being biased and harsh in their treatment of Muslims during the span of the riots and the Commission documented the fact that there were also several incidents of unnecessary police firing.

The Srikrishna Report thus exposed the partiality of the state and the collusion of the Shiv Sena, which it emphatically condemned. The Report points to a 'built-in bias against Muslims, which became pronounced with murderous attacks by the Constabulary and officers'. According to the Report, this bias was manifest in their reluctance to firmly put down incidents of violence and arson: 'On occasion the attitude was that one Muslim killed was one Muslim less'.[27]

The Srikrishna Report recommendations remained unimplemented even eight years after its submission. As we have seen already, the Commission was categorical in fixing responsibility and in criticizing politicians and the government. It was unsparing in its' censure of the Shiv Sena's role in the instigation of riots and that of the police, who did nothing to stop the rampaging mobs. However, the legal process did not take any action against the persons accused in the Commission's Report. Not a single member of the Sena was brought to justice, and no action was taken against the erring officials or police. The Maharashtra Chief Minister Manohar Joshi condemned the report as 'anti-Hindu and pro-Muslim'.[28] His government rejected the Report in the legislative assembly owing to its bias in favour of one community. In short, the Srikrishna Inquiry Commission proved meaningless because of the inaction of successive governments.

The Congress, which was in power when the riots broke out, and which had set up the Commission in response to public pressure, had welcomed the Report and initially demanded the arrest of Bal Thackeray. Later however, it retracted, demanding just stern action against the guilty. After saying this, the Congress fell silent. With an eye on the elections, it wanted to win back the Muslim votes but did not want to alienate the Hindus. While the Shiv Sena openly defended its role, the BJP maintained a studied silence. For both the Shiv Sena-BJP government and the Congress party, the Report was best buried. The former rejected it because it indicted both parties for their role in the riots; the latter was reluctant to alienate the Hindu voters and the influential police force. The government found a way out of implementing the Report by filing an affidavit in the Supreme Court in January 2000 to the effect that it planned to refer the Report to the Crime Branch. Over 200,000 people had to flee the city and many of them have not returned, yet not one of the culprits has been convicted. Though cases had been registered against some of them, instead of prosecuting them, the government just decided to quietly close the cases. Nearly 3,000 cases were thus dropped.[29] The Commission indicted 31 police personnel ranging from the rank of Deputy Commissioner of Police to constables yet the Shiv Sena-BJP government promoted ten of these indicted police officers.[30] Of the indicted police personnel, the government suspended five constables. It is always easy to take some symbolic action against the lower ranks. However, the higher ranks tend to escape unscathed and are sometimes ever rewarded. The government decided to exonerate 12 of the police officers indicted by the Srikrishna Commission, as stated in the affidavit submitted to the Supreme Court.

A similar pattern can be observed in the case of the Gujarat violence. On the surface at least, a different kind of resolution appeared to be in order since a different mechanism of inquiry was activated. In the immediate post-conflict period, Justice Nanavati, a retired judge of the Supreme Court, was asked to head a commission of inquiry, submited its report in 2008. However, unlike the case of the Mumbai violence and the seemingly infinite countenancing of delay, matters were not left to stand. For a variety of reasons, in particular, the activism on the part of the civil society inquiry commissions and citizens' tribunals convened by diverse sets of local, national, and international actors, the central government announced a new institutional measure. The NHRC was authorized to carry out the major investigation, which it did with relative speed, submitting its Final Report and recommending, amongst other things, a Central Bureau of Investigation

(CBI) inquiry.[31] It was clear from all the reports, and most notably from the NHRC's that the police force in Gujarat could not be trusted with the investigation and prosecution of the case.

The NHRC's investigation was repeatedly checked and countered by the Gujarat state government. For instance, in the initial months, the government confronted the NHRC with a dilution of the issues by showing that the 'riots' were just another part of Gujarat's long history of communal riots, pointing to the earlier Commissions of Inquiry by Justice Reddy in 1969 and Justice Dave in 1985. If the Modi government had been left to its own devices, they would have followed the usual explanation of 'riot as explosion' to bypass addressing the issues of responsibility and accountability. The BJP government was keen to portray the violence as an unfortunate explosion which, despite the administration's efforts, resulted in widespread chaos and death. The projection of 'riots as explosion' enables the claim that nobody was culpable, and that the rule of law yielded to mob passions.[32]

The Final Report of the NHRC did not take cognizance of these claims. Instead, the NHRC indicted the state government on multiple courts, citing its active role in different stages of the violence. Thus, in light of the advance information available, the state government's handling of the Godhra affair was elucidated. The Commission felt that 'the facts indicate that the response was often abysmal, or even non-existent, pointing to gross negligence in certain instances or, worse still, as widely believed, to a complicity that was tacit if not explicit'.

The Report also directed attention to the post-conflict justice and rehabilitation process. Expressing deep concern about the criminal justice delivery system and the negation of the human rights of victims, the NHRC Report spoke of the massive breakdown of law and order in Gujarat. It pointed to violations of numerous fundamental rights set out in the Constitution of India, including equality before the law (Article 14), prohibition against discrimination (Article 15), protection of life and personal liberty (Article 21), and protection against arrest and detention in certain cases (Article 22). On this basis, the NHRC reiterated its submission that the CBI and not the state agencies should carry out the investigation of the various crimes, and that significant criminal trials should likewise be removed from the purview of the state courts.

Despite the NHRC's plea, neither the state nor the central government wanted an independent investigation by the CBI. On encountering resistance from Modi's government the NHRC asked the central government to direct the state government under Article 355 of the Constitution to adopt the recommendation. However, the investigation of the cases was not handed over to the CBI or supervised by a national monitoring committee, but instead, was left entirely to the Gujarat police so those suspected of transgression were effectively put in charge of investigative justice.

In the case of criminal trials, the approach was different. The NHRC filed a Special Leave Petition (SLP) in the Supreme Court seeking orders for five key cases in which individuals were accused of perpetrating communal violence, to be tried outside the state.[33] Seeking retrial of these cases in courts outside the state was consistent with the active role that the NHRC had played in bringing the perpetrators of violence to face legal action. Among these was the Best Bakery case in which fourteen people were burnt to death on 1 March 2002, in a bakery in Baroda city.[34] Despite the fact that this was among the worst cases of violence in the aftermath of Godhra, and that this was the first to come up for hearing (and therefore of considerable importance as a precedent setting case), the state court acquitted all of the accused. Of the 120 witnesses listed by the prosecution, more than a third never made it to the witness box. Of the 73 who did, more than half turned hostile. For example, the prosecution's prime witness and main complainant, Zahira Shaikh, who was escorted to the trial by the local BJP legislator, told the court that she had neither seen nor heard anything about the incident. The judgment provoked a storm of protest and a spate of critical editorials and commentary in leading newspapers.[35]

On the basis of assertions made in their SLP, the NHRC's plea to move the case outside the state did not go unheard.[36] In an historic verdict, on 12 April 2004 the Supreme Court overturned the acquittal of all the 21 accused in the Best Bakery case. It took the unprecedented step of ordering the re-investigation and retrial of the case after both the trial court and the high court had acquitted the accused. Not only this, the Court transferred the case to Maharashtra despite the fact that there are very few cases in the past where the Supreme Court has ordered the retrial of a criminal case in another state. The Supreme Court noted that 'The justice delivery system was being taken for a ride and was allowed to be abused, misused and mutilated by subterfuge'. Indeed, never before has the Supreme Court so strongly expressed its lack of confidence in the administration and the justice system of the state. The bias of the state is highlighted in the Court's view that: 'The modern day Neros were looking elsewhere when Best Bakery and innocent children and helpless women were burning, and were probably deliberating how the perpetrators of the crime could be protected.'[37] By ordering the retrial, the Supreme Court touched on the heart of the matter: the failure of the state administration to discharge its constitutional responsibilities to provide protection of the life and liberty of all citizens, without discrimination on the basis of religion.

The Gujarat state government applied for a modification of the Supreme Court's order in a review petition to which the Court gave a fitting reply. Thereafter, the stage was set for a special court to be designated and the trial to begin. Despite several attempts to block the trial in Mumbai, charges were framed and the retrial began on 4 October 2004 in Mazgaon Court, in south-central Mumbai. However, on 3 November 2004, Zahira Sheikh, the young woman whose face had somehow come to symbolize this struggle, held a press conference in the presence of two lawyers in Vadodara, and declared herself as a hostile witness and retracted her earlier testimony. Subsequently evidence surfaced that her family had been offered bribes to retract their statements. The Supreme Court later concluded that Zahira was lying. This was clearly a bid to not simply derail the ongoing Best Bakery retrial in Mumbai, but to seriously discredit the judicial and constitutional processes that had made history by ordering the retrial and transfer in the first place.[38]

In sum, the NHRC Report represented a departure from the standard 'ritual of inquiry' in two ways. The first was at the level of the Report itself, in the kinds of indictments, analyses, and recommendations that were offered in the context of the Gujarat violence of 2002. One major outcome of the NHRC intervention in the Supreme Court was that the Gujarat government was compelled to reveal to the court the specific steps it had taken to ensure the protection of witnesses in the Best Bakery and other pending cases.

Overall, both the Srikrishna Commission and the NHRC indict the state machineries of Maharashtra and Gujarat respectively for their failure to prevent violence, and their active complicity in the violence. There are however significant differences that stem from the mandate of these commissions, and from their divergent constitutions as national (NHRC) and state (Srikrishna Commission) bodies. For instance, the NHRC did not restrict itself to collecting evidence and suggesting reforms purely for the administrative machinery of the state. Therefore, its indictment of the state is stronger than that of the Srikrishna Report. Moreover, the Srikrishna Commission did not make any recommendations in the area of relief and rehabilitation of the victims, which significantly, the NHRC does in great detail. The NHRC also recommended payment of compensation to the victims, which the Srikrishna Report (did not take into account). In another significant difference, the NHRC Report directed the state government to rebuild places of Muslim worship destroyed in the violence. It gave a detailed list of all destroyed mosques and madrasas and emphasized the importance of this measure in rebuilding the lost confidence of the Muslim community. The Srikrishna Report was clinical in its assessment of casualties, reducing them to statistics, whereas the NHRC stressed the need for post-trauma counselling of victims and the provision of better facilities at relief camps.

The second difference was at the level of implementation or concrete outcome. The Srikrishna Report had confined itself to a statement about the need for speedy trials. In this context, it is interesting to consider Thomas Blom Hansen's argument regarding the role of the Commission in general, and the Srikrishna Commission specifically, in legitimating the state. He argues that the appointment of a commission helps to sustain the 'myth of the state' as sublimely sovereign and an impartial arbiter between social factions. The commission is thus a mechanism and also a site for the state to legitimize itself as the guarantor of security and justice for its citizens.[39] He argues that the commission and the court proceedings can be seen as 'state spectacles', 'public displays of the state as a producer of impartial and universal justice', as well the 'profane sides of state power in the form of brutality and misconduct by politicians, officials and police'.

In other words, it can be argued that the implementation of recommendations was never really the mandate, or indeed the intention, of the Srikrishna Commission. This statement can be extended to cover all other commissions of inquiry as well. Usually, by the time reports come to be written, after overcoming the various procedural hurdles in the way, they are far from useful. Very often commissions of inquiry into incidents of communal violence, such as the Srikrishna Commission appointed by the government in power to buy time and evade responsibility.

In this regard, the NHRC Report seemed to chart out a different path. As we have seen, the NHRC Report both recognized the need for speedy and fair trials to enable the healing of community wounds, and pursued avenues for their implementation. In the end however, implementation was confined to the singular issue of transferring (a discrete number of) cases outside the state of Gujarat. And with the dramatic turnaround of the Best Bakery case documented earlier, the 'wheels of justice' have once again ground to an all too familiar halt. In the absence of any wide-ranging restructuring of political, judicial—indeed constitutional—orders, and without a transformation in political will, the NHRC inquiry remains an isolated, exceptional intervention.

Conclusion

From the Mumbai violence in 1992-3 to the Gujarat pogrom in 2002, Hindu-Muslim riot cases have invariably *not* resulted in the conviction and prosecution of these guilty of perpetrating the violence. Over the past fifteen years, the reluctance of the party in power and the unwillingness of the administration to make timely interventions to prevent violence has become a central concern for minorities and their relationship to the state. Hindu-Muslim violence is of course not new. As we can see from the two major episodes of violence discussed in this chapter, what is new is the active (or passive) involvement of government and administration in the riots against minority communities. In the post-violence phase—from the registration of cases, to the gathering of evidence, prosecution of the accused, and delivery of justice in courts—the judicial process has been allowed to become a casualty of political processes, or executive fiat. Since episodes of large-scale communal violence are usually fomented by political elites to advance their own political agenda, shielding the guilty is an accepted part of the post-conflict political process. Not only has this alienated minorities, but it also signals to the general public that immunity for grave crimes is the rule in India; the powerful cannot be brought to book and the law is only applied against the underprivileged and powerless.

The protracted trial in the Best Bakery case raised serious questions about the capacity of the state government and legal system to punish the guilty.[40] The tragic twists and turns in this high profile case underscored the complexity of winning a court case against mass crimes, especially when the crimes were well organized and enjoyed the support of local and powerful political organizations. In the case of the Mumbai riots, a similar pattern can be observed. Thus, despite the considerable evidence of the Shiv Sena's involvement in mass crimes, legal intervention has been conspicuous by its absence. The failure to dispense justice in such cases was not an instance of justice being denied or derailed; rather there is a deeper, more complex pattern of inaction, and an incapacity on the part of the political and legal system to deal with large-scale communal violence.[41] This is not because things go wrong in one individual case, such as the Best Bakery case. Instead, the recurrent breakdown of prosecutions indicates a pattern of institutional bias against minorities that may well be responsible for the lack of justice.

There are at least three major reasons for the abysmal record of justice in cases of mass violence against minorities. Foremost is the lack of political will to stop the violence, and later, to punish its perpetrators. Comparative evidence clearly shows that large-scale rioting does not take place when there is a political will to stop it and the police force is ordered to do so. The complicity of political and administrative personnel in violence remains the primary issue, and it is this which needs to be addressed directly, for without it justice has no chance.

Independent inquiries and newspaper investigations have found that local administration and law and order agencies have had the capacity to prevent violence but have failed to take preventive action because of direct orders from the top, or because they feared retribution if they acted without seeking political approval.[42] A.S. Samra, Mumbai's former police commissioner, observed: 'Our penal code and our idea of justice revolves around the idea that individuals commit crimes and are punished, whereas political parties as a whole do politics. There might be individuals within these parties who commit crimes, even leaders, but they must be punished as individuals. What can we do to an organization? Ban it? This is difficult to do more permanently in a democracy?'[43]

The contention that it is difficult to convict murderers in riot cases is debatable. There is something wrong in suggesting that murders committed in front of a large number of people by known locals are impossible to detect and prosecute.

Both the Srikrishna and NHRC Reports indicted incumbent governments for inaction during the periods of violence. Both cases make it amply clear that violence was not just an act of failure, but part of a design.[44] Yet, the political will to uphold the rule of law was simply not there. The Mumbai and Gujarat violence and their aftermath epitomize the irresponsibility of political parties and the broader inadequacies of their engagement in the justice process. Even parties who oppose communal politics have not had the courage to propose any specific reform, systemic or otherwise, to deal with the legal and political aspects of riots, and to discourage parties from engineering mass violence for the sake of electoral advantage. This is despite the fact that the scale of death and destruction wrought by communal violence is greater than any single instance of terrorism or caste atrocities, the two recurring problems for which India has for years had special laws.[45] The principle of adopting stringent laws and provisions to deal with the scourge of terrorism and caste violence should apply to communal violence as well. This however requires a consensus that the perpetrators of violence against minorities should be brought to book in the same way as persons responsible for caste atrocities. Such a consensus is clearly not there, which is hardly surprising given the position of communal violence as an acceptable form of political violence in modern India. Indeed, communal politics and discourse have been a central pillar for the BJP and RSS for the past several decades and one that the Congress has repeatedly shown it is not above using for its own advantage either.

The second difficulty arises from the infiltration of communalism into state structures, immobilizing the state and preventing it from being able to provide justice. Compounding this, unlike caste violence, communal violence is not a structural problem, but rather, it is an institutional problem which often stems from communal biases and prejudices within society towards religious minorities. Communal prejudice is hard to identify and pinpoint and even harder to deal with and so the apportioning of blame or responsibility is extremely difficult. Thus, individuals indulging in such violence can resort to group mobilization to cover up their actions.[46] Perpetrators of communal violence can indulge in atrocities knowing that their actions are very likely to go unpunished.

This should compel us to take cognizance of a pattern of 'institutional communalism' along the lines of the 'institutional racism' that is now widely acknowledged and addressed in the United Kingdom. Such an approach is urgently needed in India because the formal right to equality before the law can only have substantive meaning if we can find ways to neutralize the legal effects of discrimination in dealing with mass violence against minorities. There are very few Muslims in positions of" authority in the police force, bureaucracy, or political parties at the national or state level. Although there is no direct relationship between minority proportionality in the administration and levels of communal violence,[47] the presence of minorities in office and the allocation of political positions both provide opportunities to incorporate the concerns and interests of minority groups in the calculations of politicians belonging to a variety of groups.[48]

The third difficulty relates to the incapacity of the legal system to work in cases of mass violence.[49] This complication might arise from using obsolete legal concepts to deal with mass killings which have the backing of the state. Though injustice is recognized, a 'nobody can really be blamed' in mob violence formula disguises the failure of the rule of law, and everyone is let off.[50]

There is a fundamental problem regarding the definition of a 'riot' for the definition is usually ambiguous and so trying to prove a rioting case is very difficult. Next is the issue of criminal punishment and responsibility. The view of a 'riot as a mob explosion' which results in a legal breakdown has dominated political thinking on communal riots. Therefore, the most important task is taken to be the restoration of peace without controversy and without blaming anyone, rather than the carriage of justice.[51] Implicit in this approach has been a repeated reluctance to use criminal law against named agents, particularly 'important people'. As Dhavan argues, 'in India political governance seeks to generalize the problem of riots out of existence in the name of peace; and legal governance, no less exactingly, seeks to individuate the problem out of existence by insisting on rigorous proof of individual complicity'.[52] Thus, the law punishes only those who give provocation for a riot (Section 153), provide the land for unlawful assemblies (Section 154), benefit from the riot (Section 155), or harbour those who participate in such unlawful acts (Section 156–7).[53] This partly explains the low conviction rate in India because proving that individuals are guilty of the crime of rioting has always been difficult, especially given the laws of evidence of hostile groups in such cases.[54] It has also encouraged the myth that no one can really be punished for what happens in a riot because riots are political acts. This is the kind of deliberately created ambiguity through which L.K. Advani and others sought to escape both the moral and legal blame arising out of their presence at the demolition of the Babri Masjid.

Along with Supreme Court Best Bakery judgement, the resignation of Jagdish Tytler from the Union Cabinet in 2005 over his alleged involvement in the 1984 violence marked the beginning of an attempt by the judicial and political process to deal with mass violence. This is a small but significant step, which has set a new benchmark for the pursuit of justice in India's democracy. For the first time since Independence, a politician who appears to have been complicit in violence has had to pay the political price for his involvement. It is a triumph of the rule of law and secular politics over moral indifference and communal injustice. No doubt much more remains to be done to bring the guilty to book and to deliver justice to the victims, yet the removal of a minister from the Union Council of Ministers is a positive gesture. Prime Minister Manmohan Singh's apology to the Sikh community in Parliament will also force the Congress and other political parties to look at communal violence and post-conflict justice issues in a way that has not been seen before.[55] Political authorities can no longer sweep all questions under the debris or get away by expressing helplessness in dealing with communal violence.

In the end however, justice is not the only issue at stake. Of equal importance is the issue of the state's responsibility to defend the citizen's fundamental right to a life free from communal depredations. Thus radical reform and corrective measures that include both police and judicial reform,[56] and witness protection schemes are necessary.[57] To ensure that such mass violence does not recur in future, the government may need to introduce a law to deal with communal violence of the kind experienced in Mumbai and Gujarat. Overall, stringent laws and preventive action on the lines of the Scheduled Castes/Scheduled Tribes Atrocities Act are in order.

With the tabling of the Communal Violence (Prevention, Control, and Rehabilitation of Victims) Bill in the Indian Parliament in 2005, it appeared that the United Progressive Alliance government was demonstrating an unusual willingness to undertake such transformative measures. However, the Bill has been widely criticized by anti-communal groups, human rights organizations, and women's groups. These citizen groups had also rejected earlier drafts of this Bill, but few of their concerns were addressed in the version of the Bill that was hurriedly tabled in the Rajya Sabha on 5 December 2005.

The basic flaw in the proposed law against communal violence is that it cannot be invoked even when communal crimes take place unless the state or the central government decides to declare an area as communally disturbed. Therefore if a state has the support of the centre, it can engage in the worst kind of communal crimes and get away with it. The Act can only be invoked in the most extreme circumstances where there is criminal violence resulting in death or the destruction of property, and where there is danger to the unity of the country. The most controversial provisions relate to granting immunity to the police and the army, despite the fact that various commissions of inquiry have found the police and civil authorities either passive or partisan.[58]

It could be argued therefore that the Communal Violence Bill continues to exceptionalize violence. Whether through the reservation of indictments for the most 'extreme' cases, or the granting of immunity or exemption to civil and police authorities, the dislocation of violence from normal political processes of governance is the main thrust of the Bill. This is in part a reflection of the structure of law itself. Finally although it is offered as an investigation of the workings of law, government, and justice in the aftermath of mass violence, this chapter concludes with a call to interrogate the limits of legal solutions to the problem of violence in India. While this does not mean that the quest for justice must be abandoned, it requires an engagement with the wider political arena of post-colonial India, and the unexceptional yet enduring social, political, and economic inequities and discrimination that continue to endure long after the fires of Gujarat, Mumbai, Delhi, Bhagalpur, or Meerut have faded from view.

Notes and References

1. 'India: Abuse of the law in Gujarat: Muslims detained illegally in Ahmedabad', Amnesty International, 6 November 2003.
2. See chapter entitled 'State Capacity Explanations', in *Votes and Violence: Electoral Competition and Communal Riots in India*, Steven Wilkinson, Cambridge: Cambridge University Press, 2005, pp. 63–96.
3. Ibid., p. 85.
4. The data released by the Home Ministry affirms that prior to the Babri Masjid demolition, the percentage of Muslim victims in communal riots was 80 per cent. Post-Babri demolition, the ratio might have become more adverse to Muslims. Cited in Ram Punyani, 'Is Riot Free India a Possibility?', *Counter Currents*, 15 September 2005.
5. Thomas Blom Hansen, *Urban Violence in India: Identity Politics, 'Mumbai', and the Post-Colonial City*, Delhi: Permanent Black, 2002.
6. According to Amnesty International, 1,788 people were killed in Mumbai.

7. The Gujarat violence has been documented in many reports: *Concerned Citizen's Tribunal Report,* 2002; *Gujarat Carnage,* 2002: *A Report to the Nation,* April 2002; *State-Sponsored Carnage in Gujarat,* March 2002: *Communalism Combat,* 2002.

8. Election Commission of India Press Note, *General Elections to the Gujarat Legislative Assembly,* 16 August 2002, no. ECI/PN/35/2002/MCPS, p. 15.

9. Ibid., p. 15.

10. The case of Justice Kadri who was forced to move out from Gujarat cited in Siddharth Varadarajan, ed., *Gujarat the making of a tragedy,* New Delhi: Penguin Books, 2002.

11. See especially the National Human Rights Commission (NHRC) Report, 2002.

12. On this aspect see cover story 'Communal Fascism in Gujarat: Appeasing the Hindu Right on Ayodhya', *Frontline,* 29 March 2002.

13. Established in 1993 under statute (The Protection of Human Rights 1993), the NHRC is an important institution for defending human rights. Headed by an ex-Chief Justice of India and including judges from the Supreme Court, High Court, and others, it is a distinguished body which has to date made significant interventions despite its limited powers.

14. For details of the Gujarat government's response to the riots, see 'We Have No Orders to Save You': State Participation and Comlicity in Communal Violence in Gujarat', *Human Rights Watch,* vol. 14, no. 3, Delhi, 25 July 2003.

15. See for example 'Modi Ties Hands of Cops Who put Their Foot Down', *Indian Express,* 26 March 2003.

16. Details in R.B. Sreekumar, 'Diary of a Police Officer', *Indian Express,* 16–17 April 2004.

17. Harsh Mander, 'State Subversion: Gujarat Victims Completely Isolated', *The Times of India,* 22 November 2003.

18. In *R. Gandhi* v. *Union of India,* the Madras High Court held the state liable to pay compensation to victims of anti-Sikh riots in the wake of Indira Gandhi's assassination. AIR 1989 Madras 205.

19. Harsh Mander, *Cry, My Beloved Country: Reflections on the Gujarat Carnage,* Delhi: Rainbow Publishers, 2004, pp. 80–2.

20. *The Hindustan Times,* 21 March 2002.

21. Amnesty International, 'A memorandum to the government of Gujarat on its duties in the aftermath of violence', 28 January 2005.

22. The State's liability to pay compensation for tortuous actions has been well established in a number of recent cases. *Union Carbide* v. *Union of India* (1991) 4 SCC 82; *D.K. Basu* v. *State of West Bengal* (1997) 1 SCC 584; *Nilabati Behera* v. *State of Orissa* (1993) 2 SCC 740; *Chairman Railway Board* v. *Chandnma Das* (2000) 2 SCC 465.

23. Report of the Forum for Fraternity and Reconciliation, *The Hindu,* 29 July 2002. In *Challa Ramkonda Reddy* v. *State of AP,* the Andhra Pradesh High Court held the state liable for constitutional tort even for inaction of its officials. AIR 1989 AP 235.

24. *Indian Express,* 22 August 2003.

25. Rules regarding these commissions are outlined in the Commissions of Inquiry Act, 1952. The 1952 Act states that 'The appropriate Government may, if it is of opinion that it is necessary so to do, and shall, if resolution in this behalf is passed by each House of Parliament or, as the case may be, the Legislature of the State,

by notification in the Official Gazette, appoint a Commission of Inquiry for the purpose of making an inquiry into a matter of public importance and performing such functions and within such time as may be specified in the notification and the Commission so appointed shall make the inquiry and perform the functions accordingly'.

26. Justice B.N. Krishna, Report of the Srikrishna Commission Appointed for Inquiry into the Riots at Mumbai during December 1992 and January 1993.

27. Srikrishna Report findings cited in Praveen Swarni, 'A Searing Indictment', *Frontline*, 11 September 1998.

28. Manohar Joshi cited in Lyla Bavadam and Praveen Swami, 'Facing the Heat', *Frontline*, vol. 15, no. 17, 15-18 August 1998.

29. Hosbet Suresh, 'And Justice for All', *The Little Magazine*, New Delhi, 25 July 2003.

30. 'India's Dismal Record in Riot Convictions', *The Times of India*, 12 May 2005.

31. NHRC 'Final Report', 21 May 2002.

32. Rajeev Dhavan, 'Criminal (In)Justice System', *Journal of the NHRC*, vol. 2, 2003, pp. 60–87.

33. V. Venkatesan, 'For a Fair Trial', *Frontline*, 29 August 2003.

34. 'Most Wanted: Gujarat Best Bakery Case Shows the Criminal Justice System at Its Worst', *Indian Express*, 30 June 2003; 'Speedy Injustice', *The Times of India*, 30 June 2003.

35. 'Charred Justice', *The Statesman*, 1 July 2003; 'Fixing Witnesses', *The Hindu*, 1 July 2003; 'Justice Blindfolded', *The Hindustan Times*, 30 June 2003; 'Half Baked Justice', *The Hindustan Times*, 4 July 2003.

36. The NHRC in its Special Leave Petition (SLP) pointed out that even though the principal witnesses turned hostile, the fast track trial court judge, Justice Mahida, made no attempt to ascertain why this was happening, the cross-examination was perfunctory, and the trial was reduced to a farce by doing away with a detailed cross-examination by the investigating officer who took the witness stand. For details see Venkatesan, 'For a Fair Trial'.

37. Supreme Court order of fresh probe and retrial of Best Bakery Case outside Gujarat, cited in 'Evil gets a new name: Modern-day Neros', in *The Times of India*, 14 April 2004.

38. Teesta Setalvad, 'Long Wait for Justice', *Communalism Combat*, October 2003.

39. Thomas Blom Hansen, 'Governance and Myths of State in Mumbai', in *The Everyday State and Society in Modern India*, ed. C.J. Fuller and Veronique Benei, Delhi: Social Science Press, 2000.

40. The Bombay High Court acquitted five accused and upheld the life term of four accused. Of the total 17 accused in the case at the trial court, nine were convicted in 2006. These nine had appealed against their conviction before the Bombay High Court. Five of these were exonerated, Reported in 'Best Bakery Case: 5 acquitted, life term for four upheld', *The Hindu*, 9 July 2012.

41. Rajeev Dhavan, 'Justice, Justice and the Best Bakery Case', *India International Centre Quarterly*, New Delhi, vol. 30, no. 2, Monsoon 2003, pp. 1–11 and 'Riots as Murder: Re-examining the Best Bakery Case'. Available online at http:// www.sabrang.coni/spaper/rajivdhavan.pdf, accessed on 4 August 2002.

42. Dhavan, 'Justice, Justice and the Best Bakery Case', pp. 94–5.

43. Quoted in Hansen, *Urban Violence in India*, p. 140.

44. Indira Jaising, '1984 in the Life of a Nation', *Indian Express*, 1 November 2004.

45. Manoj Mitta, 'In 2004, a Response to Gujarat', *Indian Express*, 20 February 2004.

46. The classic example of such group solidarity was Modi's repeated invocation of Gujarat's *asmita* (pride) in the post-violence situation, hence implicit protection for the perpetrators of criminal violence.

47. Wilkinson, *Votes and Violence*, pp. 129–32.

48. For a development of this argument, see Wilkinson, *Votes and Violence*.

49. Rajeev Dhavan, 'Is India's "Best" Justice Good Enough?' *The Hindu*, 25 July 2003.

50. Ibid.

51. Dhavan, 'Criminal (In)Justice System', *Journal of the NHRC*, vol. 2, 2003.

52. Ibid.

53. Wilkinson, *Votes and Violence*, pp. 89-90.

54. Ibid.

55. The Prime Minister in the Rajya Sabha on 11 August 2005: 'Sir, I have no hesitation in saying that what took place after Indiraji's death was a great national shame, a great national tragedy', *Indian Express*, 13 August 2005.

56. For instance, the failure of a policeman, bureaucrat, or minister to take all necessary and reasonable measures within his/her power to prevent or control mass violence must render him/her liable for punishment.

57. See Siddharth Varadarajan, 'Moral Indifference as the Form of Modern Evil', *The Hindu*, 14 August 2005.

58. There is also the concern that it would encroach on state rights and it has the potential for misuse against any state governments. On some of these aspects see Colin Gonsalves, 'The Contours of a Communal Violence Law', *Indian Express*, 12 August 2005.

12 | Muslim Deprivation and the Debate on Equality

IT IS BY now clear that discrimination in India is widespread and not confined to any single community or group. Yet, until recently, official discourse revolved essentially around issues of caste-based discrimination, by implication leaving unaddressed many other critical areas of deprivation and discrimination.[1] Caste-based reservations in employment and education have been the primary vehicle for fulfilling the constitutional promise of an egalitarian society. Since independence, we have discussed and debated eligibility of various caste groups to access and utilize the benefits of reservations. However, there are indications of a perceptible shift in academic and official thinking reflected in the recognition of the multiple axes of disadvantage that characterize our society. The recent debates on equality in the wake of the Sachar Committee Report (SCR) submitted in November 2006 give an indication of a shift beyond the caste paradigm of inclusion.

The political motivations behind the conceptual shift are clear. Winning over a large and disaffected Muslim minority—the biggest minority in the world—was essential for the Congress party to regain its primacy in Indian politics. Indeed, the implementation of social welfare programmes for Muslims over the past five years had gone a long way in marshalling support for the Congress. Undeniably, a crucial factor responsible for the spectacular verdict in favour of the Congress in the 2009 elections was the strong support of Muslims, marking an end to their post-Ayodhya estrangement from the Grand Old Party.

In addition to political considerations, the rapid transformation of India's economy and its need for a more efficient utilization of the enormous reserves of resources and manpower in the country has drawn attention to the educational backwardness of Muslims and their economic marginality.[2] They are generally not part of the ongoing economic boom; in fact, the new economic boom threatens to marginalize them further from the mainstream economy driven by knowledge and education. Service-related and IT industries recruit very few Muslims.[3] The SCR helped the government to calibrate future initiatives to incorporate Muslims into the political system and to push for a more nuanced debate on minorities that in the recent past 'largely revolved around perceptions and rhetoric'.[4]

The policy change was initially prompted by the success of the Congress-led alliance in defeating the Bharatiya Janata Party (BJP)-led National Democratic Alliance (NDA) in the 2004 elections, which signalled a repudiation of the politics of exclusion and a return to policies of inclusiveness. The UPA-I government formed with the support of Left parties had within months of assuming power set into motion a large number of proposals for the welfare of disadvantaged and deprived groups. These included the National Rural Employment Guarantee Scheme, reservations for the OBCs in higher education, the formation of the Sachar Committee, and the Prime Minister's new 15-point programme for minorities, to mention just a few. It also established new institutions to address the concerns of minorities. These included the setting up of the Ministry of Minority Affairs (MoMA), the National Commission for Religious and Linguistic Minorities, and the National Commission for Minority Educational Institutions. Besides the MoMA, the Ministry of Women and Child Development and Ministry of Human Resource Development too have earmarked funds for schemes for minorities.

The Prime Minister's new 15-point programme was recast to focus action sharply on issues linked with the social, educational, and economic uplift of minorities and to provide for the earmarking of outlays in certain schemes so that progress could be monitored. In 2006, the Union cabinet directed that 'wherever possible, 15 per cent of targets and funds be earmarked for the minorities in the schemes included in the Prime Minister's 15-point programme'. These initiatives marked a conceptual shift in favour of socio-economic development and equity issues as against the past preoccupation with identity politics and the secular-communal divide. This represented a long overdue recognition that the concept of minority rights needed an approach of substantive rather than formal equality. Following this, the government must ensure a translation of the conceptual shift into substantive policies and targeted measures with proper and speedy implementation.

The new schemes include the Area Intensive and Madrasa Modernization Scheme, setting up the National Council for Promotion of Urdu Language, leadership development of minority women, corporations to promote entrepreneurship with increased credit flows, national-level scholarships for students in professional and technical institutions, the provision of basic amenities in selected minority concentration districts, and the development of artisan clusters.

There has also been some increase in the budgetary allocations made by different ministries in the past few years for minority welfare. The plan outlay of the MoMA has been enhanced from Rs. 1,000 crore in 2008-9 to Rs. 1,740 crore for 2009-10, registring an increase of 74 per cent, though given the extent of the development deficit of the Muslim community, a greater budgetary allocation is clearly required. While most of the MoMA schemes involve the distribution of scholarships to students at different levels and coaching schemes, the multisectoral development programme for minorities in 90 minority concentration districts remains the UPAs flagship programme. However, this scheme will benefit only 30 per cent of the minority population since it has been allocated only Rs. 990 crore in the 2009–10 budget. Given its central role, however, it not only needs additional funding but should also be extended to more districts.

Evidently, framing policies to implement the conceptual shift is not easy because of a lack of political will to confront the predictable charges of minority appeasement whenever there is an attempt to introduce special measures for minority welfare. The controversy over instituting a special plan along the lines of a similar plan for the Scheduled Castes is a case in point. The Eleventh Five-Year Plan (2007–12) offered an important opportunity to correct the deficits in the empowering of minorities, bearing in mind that while 'the previous five year plans have attempted to focus on weaker sections, they have failed to include many groups, especially Muslims, in the development process'.

However, the Planning Commission did not accept the proposal for a minority sub-plan, presumably because of the political opposition from the BJP. As in the past, the BJP objected to the incorporation of any special measures, plans, or budgetary allocations for minorities and disparaged the proposal as 'communalizing the development processes'.[5] Though the Congress rejected the argument, the accusations nevertheless compelled the UPA government into taking a cautious approach with regard to the proposal for a minority sub-plan.

The question therefore is over how we assess the introduction of new initiatives to deal with Muslim deprivation in the context of a wider conception of inequalities that looks beyond the exclusive caste paradigm of reservations. The dissatisfaction with the one-dimensional model of equality embodied in caste-based reservations points to the need to think of a new model of equality applicable to a wider population. Arguably, the SCR contributed to this change in arguing that the disadvantage suffered by Muslims is the result of a larger institutional and development deficit.

This focus on Muslim deprivation and the neglect of minority development by the state touches upon the larger issues of equality and justice. This is evident from the SCR's endorsement of an equal opportunity and diversity perspective to deal with the discrimination that confronts deprived groups in India, not just Muslims.

The government set up two expert groups to design an Equal Opportunity Commission (EOC) and a Diversity Index to measure diversity in public spaces (education, employment, and housing) as a follow up to the SCR's recommendations. The EOC group was asked to 'examine and determine the structure of an Equal Opportunity Commission'. The group envisaged the EOC as a body to 'address the concerns of all deprived groups, with respect to equality of opportunity in education, employment and other sectors in a pro-active manner'. Arguing that the idea of equality was founded on the provisions relating to the Right to Equality in Part III of the Constitution of India (Articles 14-17 and 29), considerably strengthened by the Directive Principles of State Policy in Part IV, which expand the scope of the idea of equality beyond political equality to include equality in the socio-economic sphere (particularly Articles 38, 39, 41, 43, 45-47), it stressed the urgent 'need to develop a wide variety of context-sensitive, evidence-based policy options that can be tailored to meet specific requirements'.[6]

As expected, the jurisdiction of the EOC has to be wide-ranging in terms of social groups and sectors. Obviously, while it cannot limit itself to particular groups, there is the danger of it becoming too general and getting bogged down in dealing with unfair discrimination against anyone.[7] It must, therefore, be delimited in terms of domains and the nature of issues that it can take up. Moreover, the EOC should not be limited to education and employment. At the very least, it must apply to the housing sector, given the evidence of pervasive discrimination in urban housing. To what extent an EOC can help in the promotion of equality of opportunity without an anti-discrimination law that prohibits discrimination, however, remains doubtful. How much it can help eradicate structural injustice is even more debatable. The biggest issue though relates to the effectiveness of a group-driven rather than individual-driven complaints model in which redressal and adjudication of complaints will necessarily play only a minor role.

The second group was asked to propose a diversity index and work out the modalities for implementation.[8] Its report recognized that the impact of the SCR would be wider than its principal objective: 'Although the task of the Sachar Committee was to evaluate and enumerate the conditions of a specific minority group, the idea of a diversity index is floated to operationalize a broader notion of diversity, countering the tendencies of discrimination and deprivation in production, distribution and social sectors in India'.[9] Like the EOC, the Diversity Index too is not restricted to religion alone. Identification of the diversity gap and publicizing this information is expected to persuade institutions to bridge the gap.

The committee proposed a set of incentives, concessions, access to public land and resources, tenders, preferences, and advertisements to encourage institutions to bridge the diversity gap by rewarding them for enhancing participation of an under-represented community in education, employment, and housing. The implementation of the scheme is based on positive incentives; it does not propose disincentives which might be necessary to achieve diversity. One must ask then whether diversity can work without the political will to implement disincentives to ensure the fulfilment of targets.

The three expert group reports—SCR, Diversity Index, and EOC —constitute the first serious attempt to look at the multiple grounds of inequality. They deserve an integrated reading if we are to debate and critique their proposals.[10] Together these reports/proposals represent a paradigm shift in India's approach to equality, taking into account new approaches based on a broader notion of inclusion. Moving beyond an exclusive focus on caste-based reservations, they explore a combination of anti-discrimination and diversity promotion measures to pursue social justice.

Principally, they recognize that discrimination takes place on multiple grounds, and drawing rigid boundaries between beneficiaries and non-beneficiaries, between majority and minority, may produce a politics of resentment and antipathy among the excluded.[11] The new approach appears to be more holistic and has the potential to provide a fairer distribution of social advantage as it theoretically covers a larger number of people in comparison to caste-driven policies. Taken as a whole, the biggest change is a broadening of the concept of inequality to take into account contemporary discrimination.

Both the EOC and Diversity Index are in themselves extremely worthy proposals which address the first set of issues. However, neither of these proposals deal specifically with the problem of Muslim under-representation. Nonetheless, propelled by the official recognition of Muslim under-representation, both schemes are important pointers to a new model of equality which touches upon issues of justice hitherto reserved for caste groups. It takes forward the debate on equality and raises the promise of finding a way out, albeit indirectly, for increasing the representation of Muslims in the near future.

Notes and References

1. Zoya Hasan, *Politics of Inclusion: Castes, Minorities and Affirmative Action*, New Delhi: Oxford University Press, second impression, 2009; Satish Deshpande and Yogendra Yadav, 'Redesigning Affirmative Action: Castes and Benefits in Higher Education', *Economic and Political Weekly*, vol. XLI, no. 24, 26 April 2006.
2. Thomas Blom Hansen, 'The India That Does Not Shine', *ISIM Review*, International Institute for the Study of Islam in the Modern World (Leiden), vol. 19, Spring 2007.
3. Ibid.
4. Ibid.
5. Zoya Hasan, *Politics of Inclusion*, Academic Books, 2008, pp. 54–6.
6. Madhava Menon, 'Equal Opportunity Commission: What, Why and How?', Report submitted to the Ministry of Minority Affairs, Government of India, 2008.
7. Tarunabh Khaitan, 'Transcending Reservations: A Paradigm Shift in the Debate on Equality', *Economic and Political Weekly*, vol. XLIII, no. 38, 20 September 2008, p. 9.
8. Amitabh Kundu, 'Report of the Expert Group on Diversity Index', submitted to the Ministry of Minority Affairs, Government of India, 2008.
9. Ibid.
10. Ibid.
11. In particular, see Ibid.

13 | Reservations for Muslims

A FFIRMATIVE actions refer to at least three kinds of measures available to help the socially disadvantaged: affirmative action, positive discrimination, and strict quotas in school/college admissions and jobs. It can take many forms, from setting up special schools or vocational guidance facilities to declaring that the government will encourage specific groups to apply for jobs. Quota-based seats for Scheduled Castes (SCs) and Scheduled Tribes (STs) in educational institutions, legislative bodies and public offices were seen as a way of ensuring equal opportunity for people who had been excluded, subordinated, and denied social and economic resources. Caste-based distinctions, especially untouchability and forced segregation were seen as forms of discrimination that placed the excluded community in a terribly disadvantaged position. Reservations, above all, were an acknowledgement of this injustice and a means of bringing these hitherto-ostracized sections into the social and political mainstream. The policy of reservations in government jobs for the SCs and STs has to some extent guaranteed their participation in public employment.

Though the constitutionality of the use of religion as a criterion for selecting backward classes has not been explicitly under challenge, the government and courts have rejected its application in practice; hence, minority religious groups were not identified as backward for the purpose of special safeguards for the disadvantaged.[1] There are three main reasons advanced: (i) it was incompatible with secularism; (ii) in the absence of a caste system among Muslims there was no overt social discrimination suffered by them to justify special measures; and (iii) it would undermine national unity.

Secularism as defined in the Indian constitution can only mean that the state should have equal respect for all religions and/or should maintain equal distance from all religions. But this doctrine is not consistently applied to all religious collectivities, which has clear implications for the policy of reservations.

The most obvious example is the prevalent view that Muslims and Christians in India are outsiders. Both in the constitution and the Hindu Code Bill, Hindus include Jains, Buddhists, and Sikhs, while Muslims and Christians are external to this fold because their religions were born outside India. A second type of argument is derived from the perception that minority religions are different in the specific sense that they do not accept the caste system and reservations are principally a matter of social justice or reparation for those who were the victims of oppression and discrimination arising out of the Hindu caste system.[2] Since Muslims do not recognize caste there is no overt discrimination suffered by them to justify preferential treatment.

A third is the tendency to view reservation based on religion as threatening to national identity and the cohesiveness of the state. This argument had precedents in the nationalist positions articulated in the Constituent Assembly debates. The general apprehension articulated therein, and the sense of unease which continues to mark government policy, led to a concern that since any form of special representation or reservation for minorities might be divisive and had in fact led to Partition, any policy proposals aimed at increasing minority representation in government and so on might once again give an impetus to political division and separation.

Before independence, the British had inducted communities into the political process by granting separate representation to the Muslim community in various legislative bodies. The decisive shift occurred in the Constituent Assembly debates. Although the Assembly's Advisory Committee on Minorities and Fundamental Rights considered the policy of continuing reservations for Muslims, reservations were ultimately a casualty of Partition. Initially, minorities were an inclusive category encompassing religious minorities as well as the SCs and STs. It was only in the subsequent process of drafting the constitution that the term itself came to be renegotiated and redefined. It was widely agreed that only the two latter groups deserved to be the beneficiaries of a system of affirmative action. Their protection was in no small measure due to the earlier assembly resolution that had implicitly declared them Hindus. Religious minorities and lower castes were distinguished since the latter were seen as part of the Hindu community and therefore different.

The concept of minority was dropped altogether as inappropriate for the purposes of affirmative action policies. Social discrimination of a group in the Hindu caste system was considered the only legitimate ground for group-preference provisions. However, in 1956 the Sikhs fought for their rights and were included with Hindus in reservations for SCs. Again in 1990, Buddhists were accommodated along with Hindus and Sikhs in this category. Only Muslims and Christians were left outside the reservation umbrella. Conversion to Christianity or Islam legally disqualified Dalits from the benefits of reservation given to SCs.

Government policy seeks to distinguish between the political principles of minority, which are relevant for protecting cultural identities, and the social principle of backwardness to deal with issues of justice and equity. However, this distinction between the protection of identity of a social group and the promotion of its rights and interests is deeply problematic since no group can have one without the other. It creates a vicious cycle resulting in the denial of equality in one sphere and affirmation in the other. The refusal to countenance any suggestion of affirmative action is rooted in this idea of differentiated spheres of equality, which was being extended in one even as it was denied in the other. The benefits that are likely to accrue from the protection and promotion of cultural diversity are often considered adequate compensation for the disregard of substantive rights.

Despite the success of some individuals and the few highly visibile celebrities in cinema, sports, and music, Muslims on the whole have not done well since independence in such areas as education, government service, media, and the organized private sector. There is enormous documented evidence to show that on all indices—income, health, education, and employment—Muslims rated dismally lower than other communities. The 50th and 55th Rounds of the National Sample Survey Organization (NSSO) (1993 and 1999–2000) reveal that at that time Muslims faced greater deprivation in education and jobs than any other population group demarcated by religion. Even though Muslims are disproportionately urban, they are under-represented in regular salaried work in the government sector. They also have a marginal presence in the organized sector, which includes both public and private sector employment, government and legislatures.[3]

India has become much more proportional in its approach than it was under Nehru or Indira Gandhi, but Muslims have not benefited from it. The one major exception to this pattern of exclusion was the Mandal Commission, which had declared over 80 Muslims groups to be backward. The Commission drew up a list of 400 castes classified as backward, most of whom belonged to the shudra varna. It also declared over 80 Muslim groups to be backward and thus categorized half of the Muslim population as backward.[4] According to the data used, Muslims constituted a little over 8 per cent of the 27 per cent Other Backward Classes (OBC) population; backward caste Muslims were over half of the total Muslim population of 11.2 per cent; and those specified as backward included groups such as weavers, oil crushers, carpenters, and washermen.[5] In a major policy shift the Mandal Commission made provisions for reservations for these groups. Various states were directed to implement these provisions with the proportion of reserved positions that would go to them left to state governments to decide.

The Mandal Commission objected to declaring Muslims as a whole a backward community, enjoying the same status as SCs or STs.[6] The official policy was premised on the principle of social and educational backwardness of any class, with such backwardness established by certain defined criterion. It recognized specific communities cutting across religion as backward on the basis of a time-tested criterion of backwardness evolved by different states. According to this understanding, any religious community comprises both backward and non-backward sections. As in the case of Hindus, there are caste-like formations among Muslims, which the Commission recognized as the Muslim counterpart of a backward class. However, it is unclear whether the Muslim OBC category refers to the backward-forward division or whether it was meant to include all occupational groups and all converts of lower ranks known as *ajlaf* (low-born), simply excluding some advantaged groups at the top. This is important because in the case of minorities the issue is not just intra-group but also inter-group inequality.

As things stand, the Muslim OBCs have been included in backward lists at the central and state level, but arguably they are not getting the actual benefits of this provision. This should be obvious from the continued under-representation of Muslims in the central services. In 1981, they were 2.98 per cent among a total of 3,883 Indian Administrative Service (IAS) officers, while in 2000 they were marginally less at 2.83 per cent.[7] A guaranteed minimum within the 27 per cent OBC quota would increase the likelihood of Muslims getting the reserved jobs. As of now, the most prosperous among the backward castes have secured a disproportionate share of benefits and those at the bottom, including the majority of Muslims, have got very little.[8]

Thanks to the policy of a few state governments to include Muslims in the category of backward castes/classes, some Muslim groups now receive reservation most notably in Kerala, Tamil Nadu, and Karnataka, which have gone ahead to list Muslims as a backward caste. In Kerala, 12 per cent of government jobs are currently reserved for Muslims, who account for 22 per cent of the state's population. But this benefit is only available to those who come from families earning less than Rs. 2.50 lakh annually. In Tamil Nadu, Muslims are entitled to reservation under the 30 per cent category earmarked for OBCs. Karnataka brought in 4 per cent reservation for Muslims in 1994, but again the benefit is given to applicants who come from families that have an annual income below Rs. 2 lakh, or hold land below a certain ceiling, or do not have a gazetted officer as parent.

It is necessary at this juncture to move briefly to the controversy between caste and community that is frequently alluded to in the debate on reservations. Two levels of equality are at stake: intra-group and inter-group. Some Muslims are more interested in inter-group equality and hence press to be classified along religious community lines. However, the vast majority of the community demand that caste stratification be used for the classification of the Muslim community for the purpose of reservations.

One is a proposal for treating Muslims as a backward class and so entitled to the benefits of reservations. With the tacit support of the Congress, this demand was stated at a Convention on Reservation in New Delhi in 1994 where this section of Muslims asked (i) for the whole community to be declared a backward class countrywide; and (ii) that the benefits of reservations should accrue first by priority to Muslims notified as OBCs and that candidates belonging to other Muslim sub-communities (for example, *ashraf*) be admitted to those benefits only if the Muslim quotas remain unfilled.[9] Supporting a separate quota for Muslims, they emphasized the necessity of 'cutting the cake' not just horizontally by class and caste, but also vertically by religion, to evenly distribute opportunities. This was because in their view 'the entire Muslim community in the country forms a backward class'.[10]

This proposal was strongly opposed by the backward castes among the Muslims who claim that the elites of the Muslim community have monopolized the benefits of even token representation in government jobs. They claim that the marginalization of the backward caste among Muslims is of the same order as the marginalization of Muslims as a whole vis-à-vis the Hindus. As a result, the backward Muslims find themselves out of legislative assembly and government employment. They are, consequently, totally opposed to the classification of the whole community as backward and call for reservations in employment and education mainly for the backward among them.[11]

The backward classes already included in the lists of OBCs fear that the affluent and educated sections will usurp the reservation benefits under a Muslim quota and their opportunities for upward social mobility would be severely curtailed. The bottom line is that both sides to this dispute want inclusion in the backward category because they are apprehensive that unless Muslims get on the backwardness platform, they would have to compete for a diminishing proportion of unreserved seats with the larger pool of Hindu upper castes.

The case for reservations for Muslims is strong on many grounds, most explicitly, because they are discriminated against and under-represented in the public services. However, religious quotas are not an effective means of achieving the desired objective. The separate quota for Muslims is a divisive issue and is sure to provoke a communal backlash from the Hindu right which opposes the very idea of any special treatment of minorities and remains completely opposed to reservations for Muslims. It might marginally increase their representation in the state, but unleash a process that further alienates them from politics.

Moreover, the 50 per cent maximum for reservations established by the Supreme Court (1992) makes it impossible to go beyond this ceiling without a constitutional amendment. What is more, a parliamentary approval would be required to add religious groups to the list of groups eligible for reservations. On both counts it would be contentious and fraught with communally charged tensions and conflict. It makes better sense to get the backward Muslim groups on the official lists of backward classes and demand a guaranteed minimum rather than insist on a separate religious quota. There are two ways out of this impasse. First, acknowledge caste stratification among Muslims and identify the least advantaged on this basis. Second, identify disadvantaged groups on the basis of a mix of economic and social criteria. Admittedly, the first approach is more prudent and has lesser potential of alienating Hindus. Above all, it has found favour with governments willing to extend reservations to Muslims on the basis of caste, but not religion.

Kerala, Karnataka, Tamil Nadu all follow the second approach of using a mix of economic and social criteria for classification, and have already implemented reservations on this basis for Muslims. It is important to remember that these states have not given reservations to all Muslims. But they have been more successful in giving proportionate public employment and government jobs to Muslims. Most significantly, they have got around the tricky issue of caste stratification and at the same time reached out directly to the disadvantaged by circumventing the Muslim elite. Two distinctive elements of the approach are the inclusion of an economic criterion and a provision for a guaranteed minimum for Muslims fixed by the state governments.

Both approaches emphasize the constructive role of the state and its responsibility for providing some manner of substantive equality for minorities, which is imperative for redressing intra–Muslim inequality and inter-group inequality among disadvantaged groups of different communities. However, this will only be effective if supplemented with programmes that encourage and support educational progress and occupational mobility of the minorities. The key issue is the need for policy initiatives to redress disadvantage suffered by Muslims in the public sphere. Priority must be given to their inclusion in all schemes that are aimed at expanding opportunities for citizens: education, employment, and so forth. On this front the state needs to give a credible commitment, which it has not done adequately.

While affirmative action and reservations for disadvantaged groups continue to be an historical necessity, there is an urgent need to reassess the conception of backwardness to broaden it beyond castes, taking into account contemporary realities of oppression in terms of other criteria of social stratification and difference. There are two basic deficiencies in the existing conception. First, reservation policies—and the inclusiveness promoted by them—draw sustenance from a representation of Indian society exclusively in terms of its caste-based social stratification. Second, the inequalities of gender and class get discounted, as do the disadvantages of belonging to a particular religious minority. In the contemporary conception of social justice, class differences are disregarded as also those social inequalities which happen to be incompatible with caste.

Originally, the concept of backwardness was formulated on the basis of the specific experiences of institutionalized inequalities, and yet, unless it transcends that empirical context, it has limited utility. To the extent that Muslims are included in the backward class list the official notion of backwardness has been transcended, but it continues to be dominated by caste-based notions of backwardness. Yet, the pervasive discrimination of Muslims in India must compel us to re-examine facile assumptions about social backwardness stemming from historically oversimplified categories and the easy satisfaction over the secularization process going forward as a result of the provision of minority safeguards in the constitution.

Notes and References

1. Marc Galanter, *Competing Equalities: Law and the Backward Classes in India*, Delhi: Oxford University Press, 1984.
2. Laura Dudley Jenkins, *Identity and Identification in India: Defining the Disadvantaged*, London: Routledge Curzon, 2003.
3. A.R. Momin, *The Empowerment of Muslims in India: Perspective, Context and Prerequisites*, New Delhi: Institute of Objective Studies, 2004.
4. Marc Galanter, 'Group Membership and Group Preferences in India', in *Law and Society in Modern India*, New Delhi: Oxford University Press, second impression, 1994.
5. *Report of the Backward Classes Commission*, 1980; known as the Mandal Commission, pp. 60–1.

6. D.L. Sheth, 'Reservations: No Provision for Communal Quotas', *Alpjan Quarterly: A Chronicle of Minorities*, vol. 4, no. 3, April–June 2004.
7. Momin, *Empowerment of Muslims in India*, p. 63.
8. Syed Shahabuddin, 'Reservation of Muslims: Constitutional and Socially Necessary', *Alpjan Quarterly: A Chronicle of Minorities*, vol. 4, no. 4, July–September 2004, p. 8.
9. Theodore Wright Jr., 'A New Demand for Muslim Reservations in India', *Asian Survey*, vol. 37, no. 9, September 1997.
10. Ibid.
11. See the series of articles in the *Economic and Political Weekly*, 15 November 2003, especially, Anwar Alam, 'Democratization of Indian Muslims: Some Reflections'; Irfan Ahmad, 'A Different Jihad: Dalit Muslims' Challenge to *Ashraf* Hegemony'.

PART III

GENDER AND THE POLITICAL PROCESS

14 | Gender, Religion and Democratic Politics in India

I NDIA'S DEMOCRATIC politics has witnessed significant shifts that can be traced to the defining period of 1989-91, when the neoliberal restructuring of the economy and the rapid rise of political organizations that espouse Hindutva (Hinduness), a self-defined ideology of Hindu supremacy that believes Hindustan (India) is a Hindu *rashtra* (nation), changed the contours both of its economy and politics. The emergence of a Bharatiya Janata Party (BJP)-led National Democratic Alliance (NDA) government in the late 1990s marked a crucial turning point in modern Indian politics as, for the first time the BJP, India's main right-wing political party and the front party of a family of militant Hindu organizations (known as the Sangh Parivar) formed a government at the centre, ending decades of erstwhile political isolation. Be it the communalization of the polity, or the anti-Muslim pogrom in Gujarat in 2002, the communalization of national security, its educational policy, or gender issues, the BJP's legacy is, to say the least, disquieting. The electoral victory of the United Progressive Alliance (UPA) led by the Indian National Congress in the 2004 and 2009 elections, defeating the BJP-led coalition was seen in this context as a respite for secular politics.

Apart from the six years of the BJP-led coalition government in Delhi, India has not been governed by a political party or a coalition of parties that make explicit appeals to religion. Nevertheless, religious and identity politics are an important force in India's public life. They assumed greater prominence during BJP rule but that party alone has not been responsible for the increasing role of politicized religion. Even secular parties such as the Congress party, which has ruled India for more than four decades, has found the idea of scoring quick electoral gains by tampering with secular principles and institutions too tempting to resist. Political parties seeking to stake out a position as pro-Hindu, or simultaneously pro-Hindu and a protector of the minorities, have given a fillip to religious politics.

This chapter focuses on identity politics and its impact on gender equality. Identity politics, for long a part of India's political landscape, refers to movements, campaigns, party strategies, and group assertions that mobilize political support around caste and religious identities to gain access to political power and public goods, services, and resources of the state. These assertions have affected the 'woman question' so much so that the coherence of 'women' as a category has come to be seriously questioned and debated. More specifically the chapter seeks to examine the implications of the interface between politics and religion for women's rights and minority women's rights, as well as for India's democracy and political secularism. It will attempt to show how women's and minority rights are used instrumentally within the politics of religion, thereby sidelining the agenda of women's rights.

The analysis comprises three principal sections. The first section introduces the key issues of secularism and women's legal status, the second section looks at the ways in which religion and politics have been intertwined in India and the role of the Congress party and the BJP in this process, with a subsection on Hindu women's political activism. Finally, the third section examines the approach and strategies of influential political parties, women's movements, and Muslim women's groups towards legal reform and the contested issue of a uniform civil code.

Political Secularism

Secularism in India, as elsewhere, means a separation of organized religion from organized political power. The basic constituents of this separation, however, are not exactly the same as in Western European or the United States (US) secularisms. The term secularism did not enter the Indian Constitution until 1976, but despite this and serious differences of interpretation, secularism has been a central feature of the Indian project of modernity and democracy. The Constitution does not mandate a strict separation of religion and state, and religion has not been disestablished. Departing from the disestablishment model, the state has chosen to interpret secularism as the responsibility to ensure the protection and equality of all religions and to provide for regulation and reform, rather than the strict separation of religion and state.[1] Yet there is no mistaking the overall secular design articulated in three salient principles. The first is the principle of religious freedom, which covers not just the right to religious thought, but every aspect of faith, including beliefs and rituals, and also freedom from discrimination on grounds of religion, race, caste, place of birth, or gender.[2] Article 30(1) recognizes the rights of religious minorities and, unlike other articles applicable to citizens *qua* individuals, it is a community-based right. Second, Article 30(2) commits the state to give aid to educational institutions established and administered by religious minorities. The third feature is the emphasis on social welfare and reform.[3] Significantly Articles 17 and 25(2) permit the state to intervene in religious affairs and to regulate or restrict any economic, financial, political, or other secular activity that may be associated with religious practice. Unlike the US view of disestablishment, which is often thought to be based on a strict 'wall of separation' between religion and the state, the Indian state is empowered to legislate against the 'non-egalitarian' and 'caste-ridden' prejudices legitimated by Hindu society, including opening temple entry to former untouchables, abolition of child marriage, and abolition of untouchability.

Overall secularism was adapted to suit Indian conditions in ways that enabled it to combine with and respond to the demands of statecraft, while incorporating the religious ideals of Gandhi on the one hand, and the modernist outlook of Jawaharlal Nehru on the other. Despite its many weaknesses, this strategy worked for many decades. Even in the face of pressures from the Hindu right, Nehru never countenanced a political role for religion, as that would endanger national integrity.

One issue most relevant to the religion-politics relationship in India is that of minority rights. The question of whether minorities should be accorded special treatment by the state remains a matter of bitter conflict and controversy in India, especially in recent years when the Hindu right, by persistently attacking minority rights, has questioned the link between secularism and minority rights.[4] It has been particularly severe in its attack '[w]henever secularism has meant providing for substantive equality for religious minorities'.[5]

A related issue pertains to women's rights. Indeed, one of the major rationales of secularism was its promise of gender equality and support for women. Equality before the law is a principle that seeks to promote gender inclusiveness and Articles 14 and 15 of the Indian Constitution explicitly state this. One of the greatest challenges relating to gender equality pertained to the domain of personal laws.[6] After Independence, reform of personal laws became necessary to meet the needs of secularism and modernization, and to render personal laws fair, just and non-discriminatory. India's postcolonial modernist leadership demonstrated a willingness to intervene in matters of personal law, which are widely seen as the domain of religious and traditional authorities, and where religious and customary precepts (the latter often giving women even fewer rights than the former) continue to hold sway. However, only Hindu laws were singled out for reform.[7]

The Congress government under the leadership of Nehru went ahead within a year of Independence to enact a number of progressive laws in relation to marriage and divorce (1955), adoption and maintenance (1956), minority and guardianship (1956), and succession and inheritance (1956), among others. These broke away from the scriptural tradition and represented important steps in the direction of first, the liberalization and secularization of Hindu personal law and, second, the eventual formulation of a uniform civil code.[8] Nehru hailed this reform as revolutionary and 'the most outstanding achievement of his time'.[9] These changes went quite far in the direction of gender equity but not complete equality. In later years women's organizations were to argue that they did not go far enough, not in practice giving equal rights to women; most of these laws are also flouted with impunity. For example, the Hindu Marriage Act 1955 permits the marriage of a girl at 18, but not of a boy until the age of 21. Similarly the Hindu Succession Act provides for different schemes of succession for male and female intestates.

More contentious than the shortfalls of Hindu law reform was the state's reluctance to adopt a similar approach towards reform of the religious personal laws of minority communities (i.e. Muslims, Christians, Sikhs, and Parsees) to bring them into line with modern notions of gender justice. The critics have directed their energies on what they perceive as the unequal exercise of power of the state, providing for reform of the institutions and practices of Hinduism, while not deploying this power in relation to Indian Islam. This asymmetric treatment created an aberration in the very notion of equal citizenship for if it was accepted that the state could intervene to provide equal rights to members of one community, then what grounds were there for not doing the same for others?

Although Nehru considered legal reform of all personal laws necessary and a uniform civil code (for codification and the legal unification of the civil codes of different religious communities in India) for the country as a whole essential and a vital element for national development, he was apprehensive that any imposition on minorities, without their consent, would be imprudent. Hence the policy of merging the personal laws of different religious communities into a set of uniform and equal laws was indefinitely postponed until such time as the minority communities were ready for it and/or willing to initiate it. The aspiration for a uniform civil code was placed in the non-justiciable Directive Principles of State Policy (Article 35 in the draft Constitution and Article 44 in the present Constitution), leaving personal codes in place.

Post-independence the personal laws of minorities remain unchanged and unreformed. Muslim leaders, with some notable exceptions, have vocally opposed a uniform civil code, insisting that personal laws are an intrinsic part of their religion, and that therefore the state should not legislate on it. They claim protection of their personal laws under Articles 25 and 26 of the Constitution, which guarantees the right to religious freedom. Many Hindu leaders had taken the same oppositional position against reform of Hindu personal laws during the parliamentary debates in 1955-6,[10] but were overruled; this was possible because the majority in parliament comprised Hindus who were agreeable to changing these laws.[11] Equally, in regard to minorities there was reluctance to impose the will of the majority on a minority that was disadvantaged and under-represented.

The Rise of Identity Politics:
Role of the Congress and the BJP

For more than four decades after independence the Congress occupied a pivotal position in Indian politics. Congress' political supremacy began to decline from the late 1960s and with it India's secular framework began to weaken. Before this period the political influence of religion was limited and communal parties won few seats. Although Indira Gandhi retained a strong commitment to India as a secular state, her definition of secularism was premised on the equality of all religions and not the rejection of religion or complete separation of religion and politics. The readiness to overstep the bounds of constitutional propriety on matters of religion and secularism created the space for the rapid rise of an anti-secular alternative.

A series of events, some unintended, others calculated, helped anti-secular forces to gain a foothold in the political system. The unravelling of the secularist fabric began with demands for regional autonomy in Punjab and the manner in which the state responded to those demands. The Congress decided to play 'the Hindu card' to undercut the popularity of its regional rival, the Akali Dal in Punjab.[12] In addition, in a defining case delivered in 1985, the Supreme Court called for the enactment of a uniform civil code which would give all women, regardless of faith, equal rights—for example the right to alimony or maintenance once divorced. This landmark judgement granted a maintenance allowance to Shah Bano, a 73-year-old Muslim divorcee, to be paid by her husband under the Criminal Procedure Code (CrPC). The Court ruled that Section 125, as part of the criminal rather than civil law, overrides all personal law and is uniformly applicable to all women, including Muslim women.

At stake in this case was the right of a divorced Muslim woman to claim maintenance from her former husband under the CrPC. Avoiding the constitutional question of equality, the court dilated at length on the compatibility of the CrPC and the Koran. This sparked off a major political uproar which the Rajiv Gandhi government pacified by means of the Muslim Women's (Protection of Rights on Divorce) Act (MWA), which overrode the judgement and thus excluded Muslim women from the purview of the CrPC to which otherwise all citizens have recourse. Acting on the advice of the clergy, the government took the decision to nullify the court's verdict and enact the MWA in 1986, declaring that Muslim women would not have access to civil law in matters of marriage and divorce. The new law created problems not only for gender equality but also for non-discrimination on grounds of religion: Muslim women were the only ones denied this remedy under the criminal code.[13]

The reversal of the Shah Bano verdict breathed life into the ideology of the Hindu nationalists, who condemned the Congress for its appeasement of Muslims through this legislation. While it is doubtful how much Muslim support Rajiv Gandhi garnered in terms of Muslim votes in the 1989 parliamentary election, his move certainly alienated a large section of the Hindu community, especially the middle classes, who saw him as 'appeasing' Muslims. This decision was cited again and again by Hindu political activists to claim that Hindus as a majority community were discriminated against. This is an absurd charge, since the discrimination is against Muslim women, rather than Hindu men but nonetheless one that was levelled.

The most far-reaching in this series of events that damaged and destabilized secularism was the mishandling of the Ayodhya dispute. From the mid-1980s the BJP and its affiliates launched a nationwide campaign to construct a Ram temple at the site of the Babri Masjid in Ayodhya in the state of Uttar Pradesh (UP) in northern India. Hindu activists had been claiming that the masjid stood at the exact spot believed to be the birthplace of Lord Ram. Several decisions were taken by the Congress government both centrally and in UP, including unlocking the disputed site, launching the party's 1991 electoral campaign from Faizabad, a town near Ayodhya, and allowing the foundation stones of the proposed Ram temple to be laid near the mosque. All these dubious decisions were aimed at arousing Hindu sentiment in favour of the Congress for electoral purposes but ended up compromising the principle of the separation of religion and politics, and above all encouraging the BJP to intensify its campaign for a Ram temple. Overall the decision to turn a dispute between two religions over a piece of holy ground into a national issue was intended to appease the majority community, which was unhappy with the government's decision to overturn the Shah Bano court verdict.

Both the Shah Bano and Ayodhya decisions, calculated to please both communally-minded Muslims and Hindus, ended up giving a massive boost to the forces of the Hindu Right, reflected in the BJP's rise from a mere two seats in 1984 to 89 seats in the Lok Sabha (Lower House of the Parliament) in 1989. Giving one concession to a particular community and then offsetting it by granting concessions to other communities was a process that left both Hindu and Muslim communities feeling they had lost something. Despite, or some would say because of, the concessions to religious group demands, the polity has been torn apart by competitive communalism and sectarian conflict. Even as Congress flirted sporadically with the politics of religion, it was eventually to become its principal victim, paving the way for the emergence of the BJP as a major political force in the name of protecting the majority community against the excesses of minority and the vote-bank politics of the Congress.

Although Hindu nationalists have been around for nearly a century, it is only from the 1980s onwards that there has been an increase in their influence in India's public life. The Rashtriya Swayamsevak Sangh (RSS) is at the centre of a constellation of forces and organizations which includes the BJP, the Vishwa Hindu Parishad (VHP), and the Bajrang Dal. Together these organizations and their affiliates are aiming to establish a Hindu *rashtra* by playing down the horizontal divisions among Hindus; they strive for the integration of all castes, communities, and sects into a homogeneous whole. There are, however, obvious difficulties in the advancement of this project as not all Indians are Hindus. An even greater hindrance is the diversity of Hindus, who are divided into numerous castes and subcastes. In order to overcome this obstacle, Hindu nationalists have cast Muslims as 'the Other' and the enemy against whom all Hindus need to unify. The Hindutva campaigns have consistently sought to exploit a sense of anxiety about Hindu identity and the alleged partiality of the state towards religious minorities, and especially Muslims, even though upper-caste Hindus dominate all political institutions in independent India and are economically and culturally powerful. Despite this, Hindu nationalists have created a pervasive sense that Hindus have not received their due even after the Partition of India.[14] Such ideas appeal to sections of the population who need something to cling to, someone to blame, for the social and economic problems that have plagued India since independence. A distinguishing feature of this movement lies in the way this sense of vulnerability has been communicated through the claim that minorities do not condemn terrorism sufficiently. This critique posits Muslims as the adversary for all Hindus regardless of their internal differences, beliefs, and practices. It derives its charge from an external principle of coherence which is central to establishing unity among Hindus.[15] That is to say, it seeks to unite Hindus not by what they share but by what they oppose, which is the common opposition to the 'enemy within' independent India.

The growth of Hindu nationalism was aided in large measure by political opposition, especially in northern and western India, to reservations for lower castes in education and government jobs. The BJP succeeded in taking advantage of the increase in caste conflicts around redistributive policies for lower and backward caste Hindus. Middle class hostility to reservations for the Other Backward Classes (OBCs) opened up fissures between upper and backward castes, which sometimes appeared to be closely linked with communal tensions, and these at times turned caste conflicts into communal violence.[16] This happened in Gujarat in 1985 and at the national level in 1990-1. The turning point in this process came in 1989, when the central government-appointed Mandal Commission decided to implement the long-standing government report that recommended mandatory reservations of 33 per cent in government employment for the OBCs.[17] The reaction against the so-called Mandal decision proved to be violent, resulting in self-immolation of some university students, and it prompted widespread disturbances in several parts of the country. Incensed by the possibility that reservations would heighten caste consciousness and thereby undermine Hindu solidarity, the BJP organized a *rath yatra* (carriage procession) throughout the country. During the 1991 election campaign the BJP, RSS, and VHP mounted a campaign led by Lal Krishna Advani which focused on the issue of Ayodhya. Activists marched towards the disputed site carrying with them the BJP's electoral symbol (a lotus) and pressed on by loudspeakers relaying Advani's speeches and militant religious songs. Advani made a point of emphasizing that this was not a religious crusade: 'This [*rath yatra*] is a crusade against pseudo-secularism and minorityism which I regard as a political issue'.[18] 'Don't be under the misconception that I have become religious', he said, later reiterating: 'I am a politician'.[19]

The Ayodhya strategy illustrates the broader logic of the Sangh Parivar, which accords a central place to religious symbols but whose appeal ultimately has more to do with politics than religion. As mentioned above, contingent events such as the Mandal decision also gave it a fillip. The backward caste-dominated Janata Dal state governments in Bihar and UP blocked the *rath yatra*, prompting the BJP to withdraw support from the minority government led by Prime Minister V.P. Singh. The Janata Dal government at the centre collapsed in the process, as did the vote share of the party in the 1991 elections, while that of the BJP rose as it benefited from the VHP's campaign and the resentment over state action in halting the march, which was interpreted as an anti-Hindu action. The party won 120 parliamentary seats and 20 per cent of the vote, and succeeded in increasing its influence further in some states, especially UP. Many upper caste voters, embittered by the Janata Dal's decision to implement the Mandal Commission's recommendations, switched support to the BJP.

Ensconced as the major opposition party after the elections of 1990-1, the BJP faced pressure from the RSS cadres and the movement that had catapulted the BJP to centre stage, which now pressed it to focus on the Ayodhya issue. The BJP sustained the pressure by organizing Ram processions in many regions. Hindu pilgrims and RSS activists continued to flock to the site and on 6 December 1992 a large crowd of RSS and VHP members entered the disputed area and demolished the mosque. In one way the demolition of the mosque helped the BJP by showing that it was capable of uprooting what it described as a powerful symbol of humiliation, but in another way it deprived it of a focus for mass mobilization. The period was also marked by waves of communal rioting that left thousands dead across northern and western India, culminating in the election of the first ever BJP-led NDA government at the centre. In 2002 the state of Gujarat was engulfed by brutal communal violence against Muslims. It is estimated that 2,000 people were massacred. The violence in Gujarat stands out from the innumerable incidents of communal violence in India since 1947 in one particular way: the BJP government in the state was directly involved in acts of omission and commission. Gujarat was a vivid example of the politics of religion going horribly wrong, when a political party bases its appeal on ideas of religious nationalism and ethnic homogeneity, and when violence is aided and abetted at the highest levels of government and no action is taken against those who perpetrate it.

Women and the Hindu Right: Instrumentalizing Women

During the Ayodhya movement in the 1990s the Sangh combine intensified the mobilization of women with the assistance of RSS affiliated organizations—Rashtriyasevika Samiti, the VHP's Durga Vahini and the BJP-affiliated women's organization, the Manila Morcha—and of the women leaders they had thrown up. During this period it was keen to project its women leaders in public places and roles, and also its elected women members in legislative assemblies. For the first time it won recruits from educated middle-class families and professional backgrounds for the Hindutva cause. This was a major advance insofar as it succeeded in activating women and brought them into the politics of the Hindu Right. Most of these women did not come from women's organizations or movements, and therefore were indifferent to women's issues and problems. In fact, they performed mostly gender-linked roles in the public domain.[20] Their activities in the public arena re-enacted their private roles, for example preparing food packets for *kar sevaks* (Hindu volunteers) during the Ayodhya campaign.

The association of women was not, however, limited to supporting roles in the Ayodhya movement. Many of these women were also actively involved in the campaign for the demolition of the Babri Masjid in December 1992. Indeed, the most powerful voices heard in the course of the Ayodhya movement urging the destruction of the mosque were those of women goading Hindu men into violence against Muslims.[21] Another feature was the complicity and direct participation of these activists in violence against Muslims. During these incidents Hindu women were often leading processions through Muslim neighbourhoods with *trishuls* (tridents) and shouting inflammatory slogans. They were seen directing Hindu mobs towards Muslim localities and, worse still, preventing the police from helping Muslim families.[22] It is clear from these episodes that the leadership of the Hindu right does not advocate pacifism: rather, it implicitly sanctions and encourages women's participation in sectarian violence. Immunity from punishment has further emboldened and encouraged violent action as the perpetrators of violence are confident that they will never be punished or be held to account for their acts of violence.

On the face of it the Sangh Parivar appears to promote women's activism, which has helped the BJP marshal fresh support since 1989.[23] Participation in the activities of the Rashtriyasevika Samiti brings women into the public domain and this helps them to cultivate engagements beyond the confines of family and kinship. The Hindutva ideologues take pride in the fact that women were out on the streets campaigning for Hindutva and establishing a Hindu community identity through aggressive and visible religiosity. Many leaders projected the public participation of women as a sign of the emancipation of Hindu women. Tanika Sarkar remarks, however, that while the Sangh combine brought women into the public domain, it did so in ways that did not fundamentally challenge their traditional roles within a generally conservative domesticity.[24] She also notes that it permitted and encouraged education, employment, and activist politicization only on the basis of communal violence and commitment to an extremely inegalitarian social perspective. The communalized public identity of Rashtriyasevika Samiti women reinforced conservative ideas about women and their status. For Samiti women their work was different from that of other women's organizations, which educate women about their rights, for the Samiti was telling women how to sacrifice themselves to hold the family together by being a good mother: it did nothing to help them emancipate themselves as women.[25]

In other words, the ideology of the Rashtriyasevika Samiti 'is a form of surrender to patriarchy', because the primary goal is not taking forward women's issues but advancing the cause of the RSS and transmitting its ideas. Thus, while the women's movement challenged notions of women's subordination within the family and society, Hindutva ideology places them squarely within private spaces and propagates a patriarchal model even though it brings them out into public spaces.[26]

Even so, many women participants felt empowered by the experience of public activism on behalf of Hindutva. This was because many of these campaigns offered women an escape from the world of domesticity. Less noticed was the fact that the women who participated in the Ayodhya movement also quickly returned to traditional roles, working within the confines of their family and community while routinely spreading the ideology of Hindutva and the BJP. Consequently, activism did not really change women's outlook because they were not in the first place drawn to it by its advocacy of their rights; their principal attraction was Hindutva's emotional charge. Thus Hindu women's activism works in the service of Hindutva and not in support of women's interests as such.

As the BJP's primary objective is to gain power, it has encouraged women to come forward and participate in politics in different capacities, most strikingly to campaign in elections. It proudly puts up elected women members in legislative and executive bodies. The party claims to be a strong advocate of women's rights and of reserving a third of seats in parliament for women. The need to give nominations to women is self-evident in view of the steadily growing women's constituency, but the party has not given a large number of nominations to women. Indeed, the Congress party has fielded more women candidates than the BJP, although their overall performance has not been impressive. The Congress party has nominated more women to contest elections and most women elected to parliament belong to it.[27]

Even though women's empowerment is not central to the Hindutva project, the movement appears keen to promote Muslim women's rights. On the one hand, the BJP derides and decries the principle of minority rights, a key feature of Indian secularism, as an unwarranted privilege in order to decouple secularism and minority rights.[28] On the other hand, it supports Muslim women's rights if only to draw attention to the unreformed character of Muslim personal law and seek its abolition. This helps it compensate for its attack on minority rights by appearing to support Muslim women's rights. This support was staged in order to establish the party's liberal credentials even as it does little to advance Hindu women's rights.

Religion, Feminist Politics, and Uniform Civil Code

Over the years the debate on religion in the women's movement has shifted from a position that virtually ignored religion to an attempt to work for religious reform from within.[29] This shift occurred at a time when the communalization and politicization of religion was apparent in the series of events discussed in the preceding section that led to the waning of secularism and attacks on minority rights. As the issue of minorities catapulted to centre stage, Muslim women's rights became a subject of considerable debate, typically with reference to the status of Muslim Personal Law and the conflicting claims of personal law, identity, and gender. This was most clearly underlined during the Shah Bano controversy already discussed.

The BJP is the strongest advocate of a uniform civil code, while Muslim conservatives are among its strongest opponents. In 1998 the BJP promised to institute a uniform civil code if it came to power. Until then the party had raised the issue of a uniform civil code principally to embarrass the Congress party, which was reluctant to change the status quo in the face of Muslim opposition to it. The BJP has argued that leaving Muslim law untouched implies unequal and asymmetrical treatment. This asymmetry has formed the basis for the charge that secularism, especially secular practice, implies pandering to Muslims for electoral gain. Hence the party criticized the unequal exercise of the power of the state, which intervened to reform the Hindu personal laws whereas the same was not done in relation to Muslim personal law. The Muslim leadership, however fears that such laws would inevitably lead to uniform cultural practices and alien customs being foisted upon them. In this the overlaps and convergences between the Hindu and Muslim positions are striking. Both are impelled by the need to preserve gender hierarchies as well as to retain their own religious authority and autonomy.[30]

From the outset the problem with the uniform civil code debate was its gratuitous emphasis on uniformity, which found its reflection in terming it a 'uniform' civil code. Both judicial pronouncements and public debate justified it as essential for national integrity. For a long time it was rarely articulated in the public consciousness as a feminist issue.[31] It became a debate about uniformity versus minority rights, secularism versus religious laws, and modernization versus tradition in the context of the new nation-state.[32] As Tahir Mahmood, an expert in personal law, points out, the ultimate object of Article 44 (which enjoins the state to move forward towards a uniform civil code) is secularity in family law: 'the call for uniformity is merely the means'.[33]

In recent years the issue has become considerably more complicated with the changing positions of women's groups and sharp divisions on a range of issues relating to it. The decisive shift occurred in the wake of the Ayodhya conflict and the dramatic growth of the BJP and with it of Muslim fears of the imposition of a 'Hindu' code.[34] There is agreement among feminists that all religious personal laws are discriminatory and must therefore change. There are, however, disagreements over the means to achieve this objective, whether through a state-sponsored civil code or internal reform. Aware that legal change cannot be isolated from wider political conflicts and majoritarian politics, women's groups made an attempt to distance feminist positions from the Hindu Right's demand for a uniform civil code.[35] The women's movement has since moved to a more nuanced position which combines the options of reform from within personal laws, with the formulation of gender-just laws deriving from the concept of a common civil code.

For example, Kumkum Sangari argues that the opposition between a uniform civil code and personal laws is 'manichean and politically peremptory': 'The possibility of gender equality, democratic rights, and full access to equitable laws cannot be recuperated without changing the terms of the debate. The question is not whether women should come under the patriarchal jurisdiction of the state or that of the community. Such a formulation ignores feminist agency. The stake should not be the state or the community but gender justice as a principle and a social horizon.'[36]

The change is most explicit in the case of the left-leaning All India Democratic Women's Association (AIDWA), which not very long ago promoted a uniform civil code, but now favours a gradual change in personal laws in recognition of the difficulty of pushing change through state initiative. It supports a two-pronged strategy to achieve reconciliation between gender-just laws as well as reforms from within. It has actively engaged in mobilizing Muslim women and encouraging community initiatives for legal reform, codification of personal laws, and at the same time demanding legislation with regard to matrimonial property and the custody of children, among other issues.

In the context of the controversies surrounding uniform civil code, an important development over the past few years has been the emergence of Muslim women's activism seeking to promote women's rights rather than focusing all energies on changing personal laws.[37] Muslim women in India face considerable challenges as citizens and as members of the largest minority. They suffer from many disadvantages in areas such as education, employment, and access to welfare programmes. The status of Muslim women broadly indicates the shortage of three essentials: knowledge (measured by literacy and average years of schooling), economic power (captured through participation in paid work and income), and autonomy (measured by decision-making and physical mobility) as the defining features of women's low status.[38]

It is not religion or religiously-ordained customs and laws alone that affect the status of Muslim women. However, when it comes to Muslim women's rights there is an inordinate emphasis on personal laws as the stumbling block to their empowerment. Both Muslims and Muslim women continue to be defined by birth-bound identities, and consequently the notion that Muslim women's status is attributable to certain intrinsic, immutable, 'Islamic' features is widely prevalent. All the debates tend to revolve around either the desirability of reform from within, i.e. within the community and with religious sanction in order to preserve a Muslim identity, or on the need to transcend community and end the gender discrimination inherent in personal laws by working towards a uniform civil code that will govern all citizens. This preoccupation has meant glossing over the economic, political, and social problems that define the everyday experiences of Muslim women. In addition, the appropriation of Muslim women's issues by a vocal and politically influential and conservative male Muslim leadership poses a challenge to Muslim women's empowerment. The emergence from the early 2000s of forums and associations of Muslim women is an important step in facilitating a new public debate on women's rights. The alliance of Muslim women's groups with the women's movement, together with movements for secularism, democracy, and human rights, has also been crucial in broad-basing the struggle for women's rights. Two Mumbai-based groups—Women's Research and Action Group (WRAG) and Aawaz-e-Niswan—illustrate important initiatives which have gone beyond personal laws to promote gender equality.[39] They aim to provide aid and support to poor, illiterate, and marginalized women, while at the same time raising their consciousness about the gender inequities that exist in society and the need to strive to overcome them. Their engagement with legal reform is an outgrowth of these broad-based activities. Much like other women's groups, Muslim women's groups engage with a range of issues that include education, employment, and domestic violence.[40] Although these efforts have not to date inspired the development of a major reform movement among Muslims, they represent vital steps in seeking to build a rights-based movement. There is, for the first time, the beginnings of serious debate on social reform.

The project of legal reform is greatly complicated by the problems confronting the Muslim community, which remains a vulnerable minority in India. A recent high-level committee on the status of the Muslim community, known as the Sachar Committee, has shown that they are impoverished, marginalized and under-represented in public institutions.[41] They do, however, have the right to have their own personal laws and to continue to practise these under state protection. From the point of view of Muslim women this has meant that the articulation of gender interests has been tightly controlled and articulated within the terms of an identity discourse. Political negotiations over personal laws have invariably favoured conservative voices among Muslims to the detriment of women's voices and women's rights. Those who argue for reform from within of Muslim personal laws as the best strategy for enhancing the scope of Muslim women's rights ignore the fact that such an approach tends to freeze identities within religious boundaries. Very little attention has been paid to the multiple cross-cutting identities of Muslim women based on class, language, and region, among others. Implicit in this approach is the assumption of a homogeneous Muslim identity, which fails to hear the different voices within the community. Legal reform becomes tricky because the moral and legal framework on which it is based is supposed to be immutable. In addition, it is projected as an important issue for all Muslims because it supposedly defines their identity.

In the end the system of personal laws has created a legal and social quagmire. It raises the question of whether personal laws should have been allowed to continue in the first place. To have replaced the system of personal laws with a uniform civil code would have resolved and prevented many problems that haunt the country. The problem, however, was that, in the immediate aftermath of Partition it would have given a signal of inferior status to the Muslim community, which was already reeling under a sense of insecurity, no matter how neutral and how carefully framed such a code might have been. Internal reform of personal laws to bring them within the ambit of equal protection and other fundamental rights has proven to be just as complicated. It will be difficult to accomplish this goal even with the best intentions and inclinations, and even with the considerable involvement of Muslim women.

Conclusion

From the 1990s the politicization of religion has made considerable headway in India but it has not overwhelmed secular politics. Even as Hindu nationalism enabled the BJP to shift India's political agenda in the 1990s, it has so far not been able to shake the foundations of the secular state or enlarge its political support in a major way. In reality the Hindu right has encountered serious structural barriers and substantial opposition among different groups of India's diverse population. The stunning verdict in favour of a secular government in two successive parliamentary elections (2004 and 2009) is an indication of the strong opposition to the politics of religion and sectarianism. The continued existence of a secular state in a deeply religious society and in a context in which ethnic nationalism remains a powerful force in the world, and especially in India's neighbourhood, is a matter of great significance.

In India, identity politics and secularism seem to go hand in hand. The most important issue is not the growth of religious politics but the inordinate play of identity politics in public life, which has resulted in two paradoxes. The first is that India is secular and yet ordinary Indians no longer have access to public institutions except on the basis of religious and social identities. The other is the protection of conservatism among Muslims, which is the effect of a secularism that envisages state intervention in the affairs of the majority religion but strict non-intervention in that of minority religions, paradoxically in the name of secularism.

The Hindu Right has demonstrated an enormous capacity to mobilize women but this was not progressive or emancipatory politics, even though women's participation in such movements and campaigns may have helped marginally to improve the status of individual women at home. There are occasions when the BJP has supported women's rights but this was invariably to garner support for the larger goal of attaining political power. Overall Hindu women's activism provides a compelling example of the instrumentalization of women for the achievement of the political goals of the BJP and the Sangh Parivar. At the same time the resistance of minority communities to legal reform in the name of preserving their religious identities poses a serious problem for gender equality. In this regard the major issue is the eagerness of the state to put up with an enlargement in the influence of conservative leadership, which has resulted in the propping up of identity politics and strengthening the hands of forces that oppose women's rights. Even though women's groups have strongly opposed religious politics and religious patriarchies in all communities, they have nevertheless had to contend with minority vulnerability, which has often pushed women's rights aside. Muslim women frequently pushed into the conservative fold of the community have paid the price of such compromise. The irony of Indian secularism is that the protection of diversity and minority rights has resulted in a sheltered retreat into conservatism.

Notes and References

1. R. Bhargava, 'The distinctiveness of Indian secularism', 2007, pp. 28–31, http: www.vale.edumacmillan southasia events bhargava.pdf.

2. R. Dhavan, 'Religious freedom in India', *American Journal of Comparative Law*, vol. 35, no. 1, 1987, pp. 209-54.

3. R. Dhavan and F. Nariman, 'The Supreme Court and group life: religious, freedom, minority groups and disadvantaged communities', *Supreme but not Infallible: Essays in Honour of the Supreme Court of India*, ed. B.N. Kirpal et al., Delhi: Oxford University Press, 2000.

4. R. Bhargava, 'The political psychology of Hindu nationalism', *Open Democracy*, 5 November 2003.

5. A.D. Needham and R.S. Rajan, eds., *The Crisis of Secularism in India*, Delhi: Permanent Black, 2007, p. 2.

6. The term 'Muslim Personal Law', for example, refers to family law that governs the domestic relations of Muslims in India. It operates in matters relating to inheritance, marriage, divorce, maintenance, and adoption, which are regarded as personal issues because they relate to the family or personal sphere.

7. P. Chatterjee, 'Secularism and Tolerance', in *Secularism and its Critics*, R. Bhargava, ed., Delhi: Oxford University Press, 1998, pp. 345–79.

8. H.A. Parasher, *Women and Family Law Reform in India: Uniform Civil Code and Gender Equality*, Delhi: Sage Publications, 1992.

9. R. Som, 'Jawaharlal Nehru and the Hindu code: a victory of symbol over substance', *Modern Asian Studies*, vol. 28, no. 61, 1994, pp. 165–94.

10. The government succeeded in passing four Hindu Code Bills, including the Hindu Marriage Act (1955), the Hindu Succession Act (1956), The Hindu Minority and Guardianship Act (1956), and the Hindu Adoption and Maintenance Act (1956).

11. P.B. Mehta, 'Reason, tradition and authority: religion and the Indian state', *Toleration on Trial*, ed. I. Creppel, R. Hardin, and S. Macedo, Lanham, MD: Lexington Books, 2008.

12. S. Ganguly, 'The crisis of Indian secularism', *Journal of Democracy*, vol. 14, no. 4, 2003, pp. 11–25.

13. Zoya Hasan, 'Minority identity, state policy and the political process', *Forging Identities: Gender, Communities and the State in India*, ed. Zoya Hasan, Delhi: Kali for Women, 1998.

14. Bhargava, 'The political psychology of Hindu nationalism'.

15. A. Vanaik, 'The new India right: reflections on communalism and nationalism in India', *New Left Review*, vol. 9, May-June 2001, p. 183.

16. O. Shani, *Communalism, Caste and Hindu Nationalism: The Violence in Gujarat*, Cambridge: Cambridge University Press, 2007.

17. Reservations policies refers to laws, regulations, administrative rules, court orders, and other public interventions for lower and backward castes to provide government jobs and admission into schools and colleges on the basis of membership of a caste group. The access of these castes to public institutions has traditionally been low.

18. Cited in M. Nussbaum, *The Clash Within: Democracy, Religious Violence and India's Future*, New Delhi: Permanent Black, 2007, p. 175.

19. Ibid.

20. Tanika Sarkar, 'Woman, community and nation: a historical trajectory for Hindu identity polities', *Appropriating Gender: Women's Activism and Politicised Religion in South Asia*, ed. A. Basti and P. Jeffery, London: Routledge, 1998.

21. A. Basu, 'The dialectics of Hindu nationalism', *The Success of India's Democracy*, ed. A. Kohli, Cambridge: Cambridge University Press, 2001.

22. A. Basu, 'Hindu women's activism in India and the question it raises', in *Appropriating Gender*, Basu and Jeffery, pp. 167–81.

23. Ibid.

24. Tanika Sarkar, 'The gender predicament of the Hindu right', *The Concerned Indian's Guide to Commuualism*, ed. K.N. Panikkar, Delhi: Viking, 1999, p. 141.

25. Ibid., p. 150.

26. T. Bedi, 'Feminist theory and the right-wing: Shiv Sena women mobilize Mumbai', *Journal of International Women's Studies*, vol. 7, no. 4, 2006, pp. 51–68.

27. A. Basu, *Women, Political Parties and Social Movements in South Asia*, UNRISD Occasional Paper 5, July 2005.

28. G. Prakash, 'Secular nationalism, Hindutva and the minority', in *The Crisis of Secularism in India*, Needham and Rajan.

29. N. Menon, 'Introduction', *Gender and Politics in India*, ed. Menon, Delhi: Oxford University Press, 2001, p. 11.

30. R.S. Rajan, *The Scandal of the State: Women Law and Citizenship in Post-colonial India*, Delhi: Permanent Black, 2003.

31. Menon, 'Introduction', p. 30.

32. Rajan, *The Scandal of the State*.

33. Cited in R. Baird, 'Religion and law in India: adjusting to the sacred as secular', *Religion and Law in Independent India*, ed. R. Baird, Delhi: Manohar Publishers, 2005, p. 152.

34. Zoya Hasan, 'Uniform Civil Code and Gender Justice in India', *Contemporary India: Transitions*, ed. P.R. de Souza, Delhi: Sage Publications, 2000.

35. F. Agnes, 'Hindu men, monogamy and Uniform Civil Code', *Economic and Political Weekly*, 16–23 December 1995.

36. Kumkum Sangari, 'Politics of diversity, religious, communities and multiple patriarchies', *Economic and Political Weekly*, 23–30 December 1995.

37. A. Katakam, 'The divorce debate', *Frontline*, 28 August–10 September 2004.

38. Zoya Hasan and R. Menon, *Unequal Citizens: Socio-economic Status of Muslim Women in India*, Delhi: Oxford University Press, 2004.

39. Y. Sikand, 'The Muslim personal law debate: need to listen to alternative voices', 5 May 2005, http:www.islaminterfaith.org.

40. S. Vatuk, 'Islamic feminism in India: Indian Muslim women activists and the reform of Muslim personal law', *Modern Asian Studies*, vol. 42, nos. 2–3, 2008.

41. Prime Minister Dr Manmohan Singh constituted a High-Level Committee on the Social, Economic, and Educational Status of the Muslim Community of India in 2005. The committee, chaired by Justice Rajender Sachar and charged with investigating the socio-economic status of Muslims submitted its report to the prime minister in November 2006. The Report (SCR) found stark under-representation of Muslims and systematic evidence to show that they were an underclass on a par with the lowest Hindu caste groups, Government of India. *Social, Economic and Educational Status of the Muslim Community of India*, Prime Minister's High Level Committee, Cabinet Secretariat, New Delhi, 2006.

15 | The 'Politics of Presence' and Legislative Reservations for Women

Although some prominent women are at the forefront of Indian politics—Sonia Gandhi, Jayalalitha Jayaram, Mamata Banerjee and Mayawati are examples—the participation of women in governance is very small, and their presence in the political system is insignificant. This notwithstanding the fact that gender equality and political rights for women are enshrined in the Constitution. Until the reservation of 33 per cent seats for women in local government bodies came into being in 1992, the gender bias pervaded all levels of governance in India. It is against this background of the continued marginalization of women in the Indian polity that the demand to reserve one-third of the seats at various levels, particularly in local governance, marks a turning point in the debate over the political rights of women. From being acclaimed as a 'revolution' of the millions of deprived women, to being dubbed as the token *'biwi* [wife] *beti* [daughter] brigade', women's bid to challenge political monopolies and enter formal political institutions has generated much discussion, interest, and opposition.

This chapter explores the controversy over reserved legislative seats for women, and describes three key moments in the development of this

*This essay evolved from a draft of *Reservations for Women and Minorities* presented at the conference on 'Constitutional Ideas and Practice: Fifty Years of the Republic', organized by the University of Pennsylvania Institute for the Advanced Study of India, New Delhi, in January 2000. A revised version of this paper presented at a panel on 'Multiculturalism and Indian Women' at the American Philosophy Association, New York, in December 2000 and the University of Chicago Law School in January 2001. I am extremely grateful to Gurpreet Mahajan, Ritu Menon, Martha Nussbaum, and Eswaran Sridharan for their comments.

controversy since the 1930s: the negotiations over constitutional reforms during the closing years of British colonial rule; the discussions around a major government report on the status of women in 1974; and the ongoing dispute over the Women's Reservation Bill which seeks to amend the Indian Constitution to guarantee 33 per cent reservations for women in parliament and the state legislatures. This chapter offers a defence of gender quotas in legislative bodies, and to do so it on one level engages with the substantive issues raised in the debate surrounding the demand for a caste quota within the women's quota, and the arguments within the women's movement for a gender quota, irrespective of caste or community. At another level, it builds a minimalist argument for a 'politics of presence' on the ground, arguing that the presence of women in decision-making institutions can transform the political agenda.

The Nationalist Response to Quotas

The demand for women's reservation in legislatures has a long history. Legislative reservations for women were discussed in the context of constitutional reforms in the 1930s. The Government of India acts of 1919 and 1935 granted Muslims, Sikhs, and Christians separate electorates. Depressed classes were also allotted a few nominated seats in 1919 and 1925, and some elected seats in 1932.[1] The Indian National Congress, opposed to special electoral rights, argued that reserved seats would irreversibly link religious identity and political power. Following its lead, women's organizations like the All India Women's Conference (AIWC), the National Council of Women of India, and the Women's India Association, though at the forefront for female enfranchisement and civil rights for women, opposed legislative reservations for women on the grounds that 'to seek any form of preferential treatment would be to violate the integrity of the universal demand of Indian women for absolute equality of political status'.[2] Nationalists all over India made statements to this effect, arguing that guarantees of women's presence in legislatures were subsidiary to the principal goal of freedom. They demanded the right to be elected to legislatures, but with 'equality and no privileges'.[3] Sarojini Naidu, who participated in the Second Round Table Conference in 1931, opposed reserved seats for women, pointing out that she represented all Indian women, even orthodox Hindu and Muslim women.[4] The key issue was absolute equality versus preferential treatment, not only of women but also of other groups such as Untouchables, Muslims, and landholders.[5] Some women even opposed reservation for the lower castes, doubting its efficacy. However, a number of Muslim women associated with the Muslim League disagreed with the outright rejection of quotas. Unlike Congresswomen, they were eager to obtain reserved seats for Muslims. Even as Muslim men were unhappy at their quotas being diluted by women,[6] Begum Shah Nawaz Khan (who represented India at the First Round Table Conference in 1930) believed that women required special representation.

The colonial government disregarded the opposition to reservations from major women's organizations. Taking their commitment to group-based politics further, the Government of India Act of 1935 granted women 41 reserved seats in the provincial legislatures as well as limited reservations in central legislatures.[7] Yet, as women protested at the communal award which had divided their ranks, the government went ahead and, what is more, subdivided the legislative seats along religious lines. The AIWC, which was in the vanguard of opposition to the constitutional provisions, nevertheless took advantage of the provision for reservations. In the 1937 elections, 56 women became legislators, 41 in reserved seats, only ten in unreserved seats, and five in nominated seats. In the end, as Gail Pearson has argued, the reserved seats laid the ground for women's participation in politics and provided them with a very important foothold in legislatures.[8] Even as a turning point had been reached in their struggle for political participation, nationalist women continued to fight for universalization of participation in electoral politics on equal terms with men. This awareness remained paradigmatic in discussions on the nature of women's participation in politics until the 1970s.

After independence, the Congress government made partial attempts to fulfil the promises of constitutional equality it had made to women: non-discrimination on the basis of gender and the right to equal protection were included in the justifiable list of Fundamental Rights. Especially important was the acceptance of the principle of affirmative action for backward classes, in other words non-discrimination was compatible with programmes of reservations. The Constitution through Article 16(4) permits the state to make 'any provision for the reservation of appointments or posts in favour of any backward class of citizens which, in the opinion of the state, is not adequately represented in the services under the state'. Ever since, quotas have been considered the primary instrument for achieving social justice, even though Scheduled Castes (SCs) and Scheduled Tribes (STs) are the only groups to have legislative seats and government jobs reserved for them. This provision was based on the understanding that disabilities derived from caste were the most conspicuous impediment to equality, and thus state intervention was necessary to break the link between the social structures of inequality and the political reflection in levels of participation and influence.

The provision for the special representation of minorities in legislatures was extensively debated in the Fundamental Rights Advisory Committee and the Minority Rights Sub-Committee of the Constituent Assembly, but the debate was overshadowed by Partition in 1947. Most Muslim representatives supported proportional representation as a mechanism to facilitate the representation of minorities in the legislature, on the ground that as a numerical minority they would therefore become a permanent minority because they would not have sufficient numbers for election to legislatures. Despite initial backing for protected minority representation, all subsequent proposals for special representation of minority groups were opposed on the grounds that it was both inimical to national unity and incompatible with secularism. It was also feared that it would aggravate communal differences.[9] The Minority Rights Sub-Committee in the main considered the cultural and religious rights of minority groups, which were left largely untouched because of the uncertainty as to whether the will of the people articulated by a parliamentary majority carried an adequate measure of legitimacy for minority communities. In other words, even though the idea of separate representation for minorities was anathema, their religious practices received support.

Changing Attitudes to Reservation

The Constitution guaranteed women equal protection under the law, equal opportunity in public employment, and prohibited discrimination in public places. The Hindu Code Bill changed Hindu laws of marriage, divorce, and adoption to ensure that women had a measure of equal rights. The new state designed several policies to meet the needs and requirements of women. Many women were satisfied with these measures because they shared the customary view of the time that women would gain from economic growth, the principal concern of the nation. However, notwithstanding their initial promise, democracy, equality before law, and universal adult franchise failed to eradicate gender inequalities.

In 1971, the Government of India appointed the Committee on the Status of Women in India (CSWI) 'to examine the constitutional, legal and administrative provisions that have a bearing on the social status of women, their education and employment and to assess the impact of these provisions'. The CSWI in its landmark report *Towards Equality* (1974) presented a scathing critique of the political process, the worsening political position of women, and the inadequate positive impact of government-sponsored programmes and policies on the status of women:

Every legal measure designed to translate the constitutional norms of equality or special protection into practice has had to face tremendous resistance from the legislative and other elites. We are therefore forced to observe that all the indicators of participation, attitudes and impact come up with the same results—the resolution in social and political status of women for which constitutional equality was to be the only instrument, still remains a very distant objective. . . . From this point of view, though women do not lack the three recognized dimensions of inequality: Inequality of class (economic situation), status (social position) and political power, the review of the disabilities and constraints on women, which stem from the socio-cultural institutions, indicates that the majority of women are still very far from enjoying the rights and opportunities guaranteed to them by the constitution. . . . The social laws, that sought to mitigate the problems of women in their family life, have remained unknown to [the] large mass of women in this country, who are as ignorant of their legal rights today as they were before Independence.[10]

This was the first unequivocal indictment of the government's promise of gender equality. The declaration that social change and development in India had adversely affected women and the bleak picture of women's status shocked many Indians.[11] Despite indications of increased women's electoral participation, their influence on the political process was negligible. In the course of their interviews and interactions with women, the committee found that women's lack of political equality was a matter of foremost concern for women. Consequently, women's groups pressed the committee to recommend reservations for women in the legislatures. The CSWI was however divided, and hence this recommendation was never made.

A majority of the members felt that reservation would be a 'retrograde step from the equality conferred by the constitution'.[12] They argued that 'women do not constitute a community, they are not a category'; and that women's interests should not be separated from the economic, social, and political interests of other groups, strata, and classes in society.[13] Separate constituencies for women also ran the risk of narrowing their outlook. Furthermore, they expressed the concern that official policies based on distinctions between groups would harm national disunity because 'such a system of special representation may precipitate similar demands from various other communities and interests that threaten national integration'.[14] The chairperson of the CSWI, Phulrenu Guha, Union Minister for Social Welfare and the only member to have participated in the national movement, epitomized the nationalist position. Disagreeing with the proposal to reserve seats in panchayats and municipalities, she argued in her 'Note of Dissent' that such a step would help elite women and it 'would encourage separatist tendencies and hamper national integration'.[15] In short, the exigencies of national life ruled out looking at politics from a specifically gender perspective. These arguments were reminiscent of the nationalist argument personified by Sarojini Naidu's declaration: 'I am not a feminist'. Much later, Prime Minister Indira Gandhi said much the same thing when she stated: 'I am not a feminist and I do not believe that anybody should get preferential treatment merely because she happens to be a woman'.[16] Paradoxically, at the same time she referred to women as the 'biggest oppressed minority in the world' and said Indian women were handicapped from birth.[17]

On the whole, the report argued persuasively that greater opportunities needed to be given to women to actively promote their participation in the decision-making process and to recognize the social inequities and disabilities that hamper them.[18] It therefore recommended the establishment of statutory women's panchayats at the local level to ensure greater participation in the political process.[19] Two members of the committee, Vina Mazumdar and Lotika Sarkar, dissented. They did not want to limit reservations to panchayats; they favoured reservations in parliament as well. Disregarding the category versus community way of thinking, they argued that the active participation of women in the political process would help to widen equality.[20]

This signalled a break from the official discourse on women and reservations. Mazumdar explained this shift in the following words:

Over the last twenty-five years, however, the Indian women's movement, as we know it, has done a complete volte-face on this position. We have found our understanding of nation building changing radically as we sought to come closer to the life experiences, the unacknowledged wisdom and knowledge, the priorities and perspectives of the poor peasant and working women in the informal sector across the country, forcing us to raise questions about the meaning of development, of freedom, traditions, modernization, social progress and the dynamics of economic, cultural and demographic changes, that we had never asked before.[21]

The Question of Political Participation

Twenty-five years later the representation of women in India's central and state legislatures continued to be low. The average percentage of women elected to the Lok Sabha comprised between 6 and 7 per cent seats, among the lowest in the world. The percentage of women in the first Lok Sabha, which was 4.4 per cent, rose to 8.20 per cent in 1999. Within this, the number of Muslim women was extremely small. Only 7 Muslim women were elected to the Lok Sabha in the 50 years after 1947. The situation was much worse in the state assemblies. The average percentage of women in state assemblies in the 50 years after Independence was 4 per cent. The pattern was similar in the cabinets. In the council of ministers, both at the national and state levels, women were also severely under-represented. In 50 years, India never had more than one female cabinet minister at a time; in 1996, not one woman headed any of the standing committees of parliament.

Political parties have taken no initiative to reduce gender disparity in elected bodies. In 1997, the Congress party adopted a 33 per cent target for women in the selection of candidates and positions in the party organization but less than 12 per cent of tickets were actually allotted to women in the 1999 elections. Sonia Gandhi attributed the deficit to internal party pressures. Most political parties pass on the blame to women themselves (i.e. their low 'winnability') although it is well known that in comparison to that of men the performance of women candidates is better.[22] This under-representation exists despite rising women's voter turnout, which was 55.64 per cent in 1999, only 3 per cent less than the average. Political parties recognize the importance of increased female voter turnout, yet representative institutions work in ways that do not always ensure sufficient policy concern for women. Eventually, it is this policy neglect and political exclusion that provides a justification for reserved quotas, and a good reason for what Anne Phillips has described as a 'politics of presence', in which excluded groups are guaranteed fair representation, as opposed to a 'politics of ideas', in which choices between policies are made on the basis of the ideologies and programmes of political parties.[23]

Quotas in the 1990s

A gender quota in legislatures is a contentious issue. It excites and annoys the partisan and non-partisan alike. While there are major differences among women's groups on the issue of reservations and more on the question of working closely with the state, a broad cross-section has moved in that direction. There is a growing consensus that representation in decision-making is vital for women's development and an increasing acceptance of quotas as the way to do it.[24] It has been pointed out that quotas are needed to break the social barriers that prevent women from effective participation in politics. A large body of women's opinion endorsed quotas as a necessary means of encouraging women's presence in legislatures. A countrywide survey conducted by the Centre for the Study of Developing Societies in 1996 showed that 79 per cent of women supported active women's participation in politics and 75 per cent supported reservations in legislatures. Likewise an all India survey on the status of Muslim women conducted in 2000 revealed that 78 per cent of women endorsed reservations. It is significant that a high proportion of women say that they aspire to contest local elections and hold positions in local and state governments.[25] This is undoubtedly an indication of the transformative effect of reservations for women at the third tier of panchayats, because the relatively greater proximity between elected and electors promotes responsiveness and accountability.

This represents an unmistakable shift from the nationalist position, and also from the early days of the contemporary women's movement, which scoffed at the very idea of reservation and representation on the grounds that 'such representation would lead to deradicalization, and that women engaging in it would put their own political interests before the feminist cause.[26] There are two important reasons for this shift. The two decades from the 1970s saw the growth of the women's movement, with an expanding base in urban India. Questions of gender inequality were at the forefront of these movements. Spurred by the proliferation of women's groups and the socio-economic ferment and wider developments in Indian politics (the rise of communalism and religious revivalism) and society (lower-caste assertions and caste conflicts), the gender question was raised at different levels, especially regarding the caste and class basis of gender inequalities.[27] Although the women's movement addressed a range of issues, it put less effort into electoral politics and therefore did not make as much impact. Women's representation in parliament actually declined to 3.7 per cent in 1977, the lowest ever. It improved to 5.2 per cent in 1989 but was only slightly better than the 4.2 per cent of women who were elected in 1952. During this period the women's movement began to search for new ways of wielding its influence over the state and began to consider ways of increasing women's representation in politics.

This period witnessed a confluence of two trends: on the one hand, the state's attempts to foster closer links with social movements and nongovernmental organizations, and on the other, the attempt by some women's movement activists to exercise power within the state. From the 1980s, quotas in legislative assemblies became a major demand of the women's movement. The National Perspective Plan for Women prepared under Rajiv Gandhi's government in 1988 recommended that 33 per cent of seats in all elected assemblies, from village to union level, be reserved for women, and that political parties should promote women's electoral representation by alloting at least 33 per cent of their tickets to women. In 1989, the most important effort to involve women in governance was through quotas in panchayats—and this proved to be extremely significant against the background of increased women's activism and the state-backed effort to provide greater opportunities to women in local governance. Part of the wider move towards political decentralization, the promotion of panchayati raj institutions has sought to ensure adequate and active participation of women by providing quotas for various deprived groups. The 73rd and 74th Constitutional Amendments of 1992 provided reserved quotas for women in local-level institutions in India. In consequence, the number of women elected to panchayats increased to one million. At present there are 655,629 women members in gram panchayats, 37,523 in the panchayat samitis, and 3,161 in zila parishads.[28] Despite social and institutional constraints, women's participation has had a significant impact both in terms of the subjective dimension (namely, the ways in which women see themselves in their new roles), as well as the objective dimension (namely, the actual developmental impact).[29] Several studies have documented, for instance, that women representatives give greater priority to issues such as drinking water supply, installation of pumps, playgrounds, roads, community infrastructure, schooling, etc.[30] Newspaper reports highlight instances of women succeeding as panchayat leaders who have made a strong case for reservation of seats for them in the legislatures.[31] The impressive efforts of women demonstrate that panchayats are beginning to play an important role in the empowerment of women.[32] In light of this experience, the basic argument for reserved seats in legislatures is the same: that these measures are historical correctives to the under-representation of women, which is gross, and therefore structurally unlikely to be rectified in the normal course of events.

In a representation submitted to the chairperson and members of the Parliamentary Select Committee, seven women's organizations urged the committee to recommend the passage of the legislation in the Lok Sabha to reserve 33 per cent legislative seats for women. The pressure mounted both by women in panchayats and women within political parties obliged the government to table the Constitution (81st Amendment) Bill in 1996, to provide not less than one-third of the total number of seats for women in parliament and the state assemblies. Furthermore, one-third seats of the 22 per cent seats reserved for SCs and STs were to be reserved for women from these groups. Together this adds up to 33 per cent reserved seats for women in national and state legislatures.

This Women's Reservation Bill (WRB) has been listed for debate in every session of parliament since its introduction in 1996, but a handful of leaders have stalled it each time. A slightly modified version, the Constitution (85th Amendment) Bill was introduced in the Lok Sabha on 23 December 1999, but no discussion was allowed, with MPs tearing up the bill each time it was listed for discussion. The result has been that neither of the two bills has ever been discussed or voted upon.

All major political parties had professed support for women's quotas in their election manifestos and many parties still claim to support the WRB.[33]

In the event, as one newspaper headline put it, 'it is indeed a curious case of a lot of will, but no Bill'.[34] The most vocal opponents are small but powerful parties like the Rashtriya Janata Dal (RJD), Samata Party, Samajwadi Party (SP), and Bahujan Samaj Party (BSP). They contend that elite upper-caste women will monopolize reserved seats because they are better educated. Phoolan Devi, a lower-caste MP, disparaged the WRB because women with 'short hair and lipstick' would get into parliament while Other Backward Caste (OBC) women would not: 'Our [OBC] women are uneducated and cannot understand anything so unless there is reservations for them they cannot come to Parliament.' Similarly, Uma Bharati, a lower-caste leader of the Bharatiya Janata Party (BJP), underlined the limitations of backward class women and their inability to enter legislatures without quotas. These groups and the parties representing them have been most strident in opposing the WRB. Their combined strength in the Lok Sabha was not even a tenth of its total membership and yet they have managed to prevent even a debate on the bill, which means they could not have stalled the legislation without the unspoken support of MPs from other parties. In short, the relentless opposition encountered by the WRB since it was tabled in the Lok Sabha in 1999 points to a more substantial and determined opposition that goes beyond the so-called caste parties mentioned above—indeed it cuts across caste, class, and party boundaries.

Some political leaders have pushed for a sub-quota for Muslim women as well, but this is scarcely relevant at a time when the legislative representation of Muslims continues to be extremely meagre, perhaps the lowest ever. The percentage of Muslims (who make up 13.4 per cent of the population) in legislative bodies was a mere 4 per cent. Several key states have no Muslim representatives. Muslims have been a socio-economically disadvantaged group since Partition, but there were no particular efforts to improve their representation in legislatures or public employment. The principal 'privilege' they have is immunity for their personal laws, which permits multiple marriages and easy divorce. Successive governments have refused to address the problem of Muslim under-representation or shown willingness to discuss it openly, even as the decades from the 1980s are replete with all kinds of group ordering and group recognition by government for the purpose of representation.

State policy towards minorities has taken three principal forms: federal arrangements in which state and linguistic boundaries coincide, thus providing a degree of autonomy; the right of religious minorities to establish and administer their own schools fully supported by public funds; and separate personal laws concerning marriage, divorce, custody, and adoption of children. This has been the preferred way of dealing with the problem of minorities, thus conveniently sidestepping the fact that most Muslims are poor and illiterate, with very little presence either in government or in legislatures. While ways must be found to remedy this under-representation, they ought not to be tied to reservations for women as the issue of Muslim under-representation cannot be addressed piecemeal. The solution is a more generous politics aimed at accommodating a plurality of interests on grounds of gender, caste, and community.

The substantive issue is not Muslim under-representation but concerns the demand raised by backward-caste leaders for a caste sub-quota in the women's quota. The backward castes represent a powerful constituency in democratic politics. Caste-based mobilization has always been a marked feature of Indian politics, but it is much stronger today than when India became independent. Adult franchise and democracy have produced radical changes. No longer will caste groups accept Brahminical ordering of caste hierarchy and status, which implies that there is an even greater emphasis on caste identity and strategies of mobilization based on them. The positive discrimination policy culminating in the 1990 central government decision to grant job reservations to OBCs, the rise of lower-caste parties, and the realignment of the power structure on the ground have opened up opportunities for them to enter the political system.[35] Through these strategies the lower castes have succeeded in breaking the upper-caste political monopoly. By the early 2000s, the SCs and Backward Castes constituted over two-fifths of the members of the Lok Sabha, in contrast to a negligible presence in the 1950s and 1960s. However, this impressive change has not benefited lower-caste women. The political elite and particularly the lower-caste leadership remain stubbornly male: there are hardly any OBC female MPs even as OBC men have greatly increased their numbers in parliament.

The most strident opposition to women's quotas has come from male politicians who fear that their political careers would be put at risk. Some of them worry that women's reservations will dilute the lower-caste challenge to upper-caste domination. According to them, women's quotas are a means to re-establish the monopoly of the upper castes because they will corner the benefits of quotas. There is however no major conflict between gender and caste; indeed, quotas are likely to facilitate the entry of women from all castes and communities into legislatures. Unlike caste quotas, women's quotas will not alter caste equations. They will change male/female equations and give greater opportunity to women to contest elections. That is why parties would have to find suitable candidates from the same castes for seats currently held by OBC members.

Furthermore, while caste prejudice still exists in varying forms, the belief that OBC women are at a particular disadvantage appears to be misplaced, not only because it treats them as a homogeneous community, but also because it places them outside the prevailing political milieu which favours the numerically large lower castes in constituencies dominated by them. It is the sheer numerical weight of OBCs that enabled the OBC men to gain entry into state legislatures and parliament without legislative reservations. The same logic will be true for women. Moreover, it is highly unlikely that political parties, especially lower-caste parties, would give legislative tickets to upper-caste women in OBC-dominated constituencies. Male domination is more striking: male legislators completely outnumbered women within the OBC group, which suggests that the principal reason for the under-representation of OBC women in public life is gender discrimination. Thus, the conflict is not between women of different deprived groups but between men and women of the same group. This issue has become contentious because the emergence of women as a significant political grouping during the 1990s has happened simultaneously with another transformation: change in the caste composition of legislatures and the growing presence of backward castes in these institutions. These two concurrent developments—women and lower-caste assertions—have produced a political stalemate on the question of women's reserved seats in legislatures. Women's quotas are therefore aimed at correcting the denial of representation to women in decision-making by virtue of being women and the total failure of political parties to rectify this injustice.[36]

Curiously, lower-caste leaders who have so assiduously emphasized their commitment to the interests of backward-class women were prepared to break the stalemate if the 33 per cent quota were reduced to 10-15 per cent. In other words, the issue was never sub-quotas for OBC women, but a very high women's quota. A number of women leaders have correctly pointed out that reducing the proportion defeats the very purpose of quotas, as it would mean that not more than 7–8 per cent of women candidates could emerge as winners, a proportion they have already attained without reservations. However, the OBC leaders rationalize the lowering of the women's quota on the grounds of scarcity of experienced women. They argue that it would be difficult to find so many women contestants for legislative seats.[37] This argument completely ignores the leadership potential of millions of elected women in panchayats. It is even more untenable because it presumes that parties chose existing elected representatives on merit. What is more, it clearly shows that the problem is not the caste sub-quota, but the gender divide over women's quotas. More importantly, the frequent postponement and deferral in the Lok Sabha of the WRB reveals that hostility is not restricted to lower-caste politicians; rather their vociferous opposition has simply made it easier for a more diverse group of male politicians to scuttle women's quotas.

'The Politics of Presence' and Representation

Questions remain over why gender is singled out as a problematic category in the context of reservation, whether there is a basis for a distinction between women as a group, and caste and communities as a group or whether the category of women should have preference over other group identities. The debate over quotas echoes feminist debates elsewhere about the status of women as a group, given their multiple locations in the polity. In India the picture is complicated by the heterogeneity of society and the existence of numerous social groups demanding preferential treatment. There are at least two pro-women arguments and one pro-women and identity-ideology based (implicitly quota within quota) position within the women's movement. Recognizing women as a disadvantaged group, a powerful feminist case for women's reservations has justified affirmative action to redress the historical and continued disadvantages suffered by women regardless of caste and class. In short, reservations are necessary to expand equality of opportunity and to make real the formal equality given by the Constitution. The most vocal advocates of this position are the Left parties and Left groups, but this position is widely shared by women's groups and women in general. A former Left MP summed up the position in this way: "Though reservations policy per se is not democratic, it is nevertheless necessary to rectify existing imbalances. It is a partial measure, but one that is unavoidable if women are to participate effectively in politics."[38]

The second position is pro-women but against reservations. Madhu Kishwar, the editor of *Manushi* (a journal about women and society) has suggested an alternative proposal. Opposed to reservations, which according to her are unnecessary because 'our country has a well-entrenched tradition whereby any party, politician or public figure who tries to bad mouth women in public or opposes moves in favour of women's equality is strongly disapproved of',[39] she concedes that Indian democracy has failed to include women in its purview because of the Gandhian legacy that saw women's role in politics as one of self-sacrifice rather than as a bid for power, and more recently because of the corruption and criminalization of politics.[40] Concentrating on women's interests, she advocates a scheme under which parties should field at least 30 per cent women candidates.

The former Chief Election Commissioner M.S. Gill favoured the alternative of mandatory quotas of tickets by every recognized party. This requires all recognized parties to field women in one-third of the seats in every state for parliament and one-third of the seats in each region of the state (defined as a group of 15–20 contiguous assembly constituencies) for state assemblies. Parties failing to do so should lose the Election Commission's recognition. This would require an amendment of the Representation of People's Act, 1951, to make it mandatory for parties to allot one-third of tickets to women. However, given the gendered response to women's participation in politics, and the weakness of women's voices within political parties and alliances between party women and the women's movement, it is unlikely that parties will agree to an amendment that would oblige them to give one-third of their nominations to women. At most they will concede 10–15 per cent of the seats to women.

The new proposal has received the support of many parties and several smaller women's groups, as they believe that the original WRB will simply never be passed owing to the powerful opposition against it, and also partly because it is not clear that reservation of geographical constituencies is the best route, given all the problems of the rotation system. The WRB, which would only be valid for 15 years, proposes that every constituency will in the next 15 years, at least for one term, be represented by a woman. A system of lots will decide the rotation of seats and the schedule will be decided in advance to avoid uncertainties. Critics of the WRB argue that a legislator who knows that his seat will be reserved for a woman in the next election will only be interested in making a quick buck and not serve the constituency. In other words the principle of rotation would destabilize and destroy legislative careers.[41] Besides, a rotation system, it is said, will further diminish the accountability of legislators. A mandatory quota of party tickets for women, on the other hand, has the added advantage of setting in motion party reforms that will change the complexion of party politics since it will be in the interest of parties to select politically active women.

However, Left parties and the Congress party, particularly Sonia Gandhi, have opposed this proposal. Left-wing women's organizations, especially the All India Democratic Women's Association (AIDWA), the largest women's organization in the country, have criticized this proposal as a 'compromise formula' that will only ensure tickets but not seats for women. Critics fear that political parties will allot unwinnable seats to women, given the poor track record of parties in nominating women candidates. It is true that most parties in India have uneven influence at the constituency, state, and national levels so that party leaders may well farm out unwinnable seats to women.

The third position derives from a growing body of feminist politics that pays attention to group identity and the politics of competing identities of caste/community and women. There are two identifiable positions here. The first one argues that public policies must be judged in terms of their sensitivity to the identities of people for whom they are designed.[42] Therefore justifications for the women's quota must move beyond an evaluation of consequences and pay attention to identity concerns, which is a more fruitful way of understanding and ensuring the representation of women in legislative bodies. Against this, there are those who support women's quota as well as a sub-quota, who nevertheless point out that the timing of the WRB and the strong support for it cannot be explained solely in terms of women's rights. Rather, feminist and upper-caste concerns have joined together to create a general acceptability of women's reservations, which is capable of restoring upper-caste and class control of politics. Therefore the lower-caste demand for sub-quotas for lower-caste women is justified. Moreover, identity is not pre-political, it does not exist independently of ideology, and presence is constituted by a number of identifications, of which gender is only one: it alone does not guarantee representation. If the category of woman is produced by political mobilization, then quotas for women cannot be promoted in isolation from quotas for other marginalized groups in society.[43]

There are however critical questions here, in particular arguments that relate to the wider issue of 'representation versus presence' of women from lower castes and minorities. The answer to these questions must deal with the key issue of competing identities of caste, community, and women. Women are seldom, if ever, defined as a 'cultural group', despite the fact that women do have a shared history and shared experiences.[44] Given the dispersal of identities across class, caste, religion, and other axes, gender cannot be the sole rallying point for women. However, despite their numerous differences, women can be conceived of as a category on the basis of their oppression in a world defined by a sexual division of labour. Besides, notwithstanding all the differences in feminist positions as to whether the concept of women constitutes a universal category, the fact is that for some purposes and at some levels they continue to act as such and the world continues to treat them as though they represent a category. Thus, at one level, women from a particular group that has shared experiences of social discrimination can be seen as a group. At another level, these experiences cannot be taken to form a permanent cultural group with predetermined identities that necessitate quotas within quotas. As a number of critics of sub-quotas have pointed out, it is difficult to see how any sub-quota is possible without a further sub-quota for those listed as most backward within the sub-quota of OBC women. Though the claim for sub-quotas emanated from an anxiety that elite women should not be allowed to corner the benefits of reservations, it does not differentiate between privileged and less privileged women within the OBCs. It has raised neverending disputes over which groups of women should be eligible for reservations.[45] The quotas within quotas can distort the practice of representation, because in the course of redressing political imbalance it tends to valorize identity-based representation, which means, for example, that only Muslim women can represent Muslim women or that Tamil Hindus can only represent Tamil Hindus. Given India's stunning social diversity and the high level of polarization in the polity, the logic of such distinction and division can go on ceaselessly. Besides it is difficult to restrict it to excluded groups.

Conclusion

There has clearly been far greater resistance to legislative reservation for women than to reservations in panchayats and municipal bodies. This may be due to the fact that parliamentarians who passed the two constitutional amendments were not likely to be personally affected by their implementation, but legislative quotas affect them directly.[46] As noted earlier, large numbers of women support the active participation of women in politics, and reservations for women in legislative bodies might be the only way to guarantee this. A number of doubts have been raised about legislative reservations, ranging from the argument that such a provision would ghettoize women in politics, to the fear that a quota system would only result in women fighting one another in women only constituencies, which will not give them the confidence or experience to hold their own, no matter who their opponents. In effect, a measure seeking to obliterate gender divisions will end up creating new gender divisions. Then there is the widely shared uneasiness that quotas encourage proxy politics and women representatives will be pawns manipulated by vested interests in family and society. On the whole these arguments have a ring of truth, but they are in the main truer at the local and state levels than at the parliamentary level. Although the power of women MPs is generally limited, and like most MPs they are more likely to support party agendas than women's agendas, many women MPs have been influential leaders in their own right. Many of them have risen to power through institutional channels rather than as appendages of men. Of course, the power of these women to influence policy agendas would be improved if they were more closely connected with the women's movement and organizations but this will require women legislators to forge closer ties with women in office. It is probable that women will better represent women's interests as well as focus attention on such issues as poverty, housing, unemployment, and health care.

While it is quite possible that elite women are expected to outnumber poor women in election to legislatures, poor women are anyway unlikely to be elected in the absence of reservations. There is an understandable apprehension that participation and gaining entry into institutions may conservatize women, but participation in political institutions can also provide opportunities of engaging with and being able to influence state policies and agendas. As Amrita Basu has argued:

One important reason for supporting reservations in parliament, for all its inadequacies, stems from a recognition both of the state's importance to determining women's life chances and yet the dangers of becoming excessively dependent on the state. Reservations provide a way for the women's movement to engage the state while diversifying its focus from the courts and legislature to the electoral system. Working through several branches of the state simultaneously rather than focusing exclusively on one reveals the advantages and disadvantages of each.

If the purpose of legislative reservations is to alter the distribution of power and resources in elected bodies where decisions are taken which affect everyone, then surely there should be more women in these institutions. This will rectify the skewed character of representation in parliament, which does not reflect the characteristics of the total population. Reserved seats for women in legislatures will not improve opportunities for women in public employment, yet representation aimed at providing access to decision-making in elected legislative bodies can bring about a change in the norms and principles that govern the distribution of resources. As such, there is an argument to be made for the greater presence of women in legislatures and decision-making bodies on the grounds that it provides them with a very important political resource through which they can negotiate structural change. In that case, women's quotas may well transform the quality of public life. Political participation in the decision-making processes is one mechanism through which such radical change might take place, and this could undercut the force of gender in politics and alter the nature of power itself.

Notes and References

1. Laura Dudley Jenkins, 'Competing Inequalities: The Struggle for Legislative Seats for Women in India', *International Review of Social History*, vol. 44, 1999, Supplement.

2. Gail Pearson, 'Reserved Seats—Women and the Vote in India', in *Women in Colonial India: Essays on Survival, Work and the State*, ed. J. Krishnamurti, New Delhi: Oxford University Press, 1989, p. 16.

3. Ibid., p. 7.

4. Geraldine Forbes, *Women in Modern India*, Cambridge: Cambridge University Press, 1996, p. 97.

5. Ibid., p. 200.

6. Ibid.

7. *Towards Equality: Report of the Committee on the Status of Women in India*, New Delhi, Ministry of Social Welfare, Government of India, 1974, p. 356.

8. Pearson, 'Reserved Seats', p. 199.

9. Rachna Bajpai, 'Constituent Assembly Debates and Minority Rights', *Economic and Political Weekly*, 27 May 2000, p. 2000.

10. *Towards Equality*, p. 303.

11. Forbes, *Women in Modern India*, p. 227.

12. *Towards Equality*, p. 303.

13. Ibid., p. 304.

14. Ibid.

15. Phulrenu Guha, 'Note of Dissent', *Towards Equality*, p. 354.

16. Indira Gandhi, 'What Does "Modern" Mean?' in an address delivered at Miranda House, University of Delhi. Cited in Forbes, *Women in Modern India*, p. 233.

17. Ibid.

18. Ibid., p. 304.

19. Radha Kumar, 'From Chipko to Sati: The Contemporary Indian Women's Movement', in *The Challenge of Local Feminisms*, ed. Amrita Basu, Colorado: Westview Press, 1995, pp. 58-86.

20. Lotika Sarkar and Vina Mazumdar, 'Note of Dissent', *Towards Equality*, p. 357.

21. Vina Mazumdar, 'Historical Soundings', *Seminar*, September 1997, p. 15.

22. *The Statesman*, 11 September 1999.

23. Anne Phillips, *Politics of Presence*, Oxford: Oxford University Press, 1995.

24. Shirin Rai and Kumud Sharma, 'Democratizing the Indian Parliament: the Reservation for Women Debate', *International Perspectives on Gender and Democratization*, ed. Shirin Rai, London: Macmillan, 2000.

25. This information is drawn from an all-India survey on the status of Muslim women undertaken by the author and Ritu Menon for a project on the 'Diversity of Muslim Women's Lives in India', Nehru Memorial Museum and Library, New Delhi, 2000.

26. Radha Kumar, *History of Doing: An Illustrated Account of Movements for Women's Rights and Feminism in India, 1800–1900*, New Delhi: Kali for Women, 1993.

27. Semanthini Niranjana, 'Transitions and Reorientations: On the Women's Movement in India', *Contemporary India: Transitions*, ed. Peter Ronald deSouza, New Delhi: Sage Publications, 2000, pp. 268–9.

28. *Human Development in South Asia 2000: The Gender Question*, Mahbub ul Haque Human Development Centre, Karachi: Oxford University Press, 2000, p. 143.

29. Ibid., p. 42.

30. Niraja Gopal Jayal, 'Gender and Decentralization', mimeo, Delhi, 2000.

31. 'Some Good News', *The Hindu*, 29 July 2001.

32. *Human Development in South Asia 2000: The Gender Question*, p. 143.

33. ' "If 500 MPs are supporting the WRB, why is the will of 42 who are opposed to it prevailing. What's more since the relevant party—the women—want it, it is difficult to understand the reason for it not being put to vote", asked Women's Political Watch in a memorandum submitted to the Speaker of the Lok Sabha.' *The Hindu*, 8 December 2000.

34. Ibid.

35. Ibid., 21 December 1999.

36. Ibid., p. 34.

37. A recent study of 2,200 elected representatives of panchayats in Madhya Pradesh, Uttar Pradesh, and Rajasthan, by Nirmala Buch, former Secretary in the Ministry of Rural Development, demolishes the myth of ineffectiveness of women in this role. She argues that the presence of nearly one million women in panchayats and municipalities should set at rest 'the fears of proxyism and control of posts by elite women'. Among the 843 women representatives studied, the largest percentage of chairpersons and panchayat members was from the OBCs. Significantly, Uttar Pradesh had the largest number of OBC chairpersons and members. *Frontline*, 21 January 2000.

38. Malini Bhattacharya, 'Democracy and Reservation', *Seminar*, no. 457, September 1997, pp. 23–4.

39. Madhu Kishwar, 'Women and Politics: Beyond Quotas', *Economic and Political Weekly*, 26 October 1997.

40. Ibid.

41. Psephologist Yogendra Yadav made this point at a symposium on women's reservation in Lady Shri Ram College, University of Delhi, January 2001.

42. Meena Dhanda, 'Representation for Women: Should Feminists Support Quotas', *Economic and Political Weekly*, 21 August 2000, p. 2972.

43. Nivedita Menon, 'Elusive "Woman": Feminism and Women's Reservation Bill', *Economic and Political Weekly*, 28 October 2000, pp. 3837–41.

44. Uma Narayan, 'Thinking About the "Culture" in "Multiculturalism"', presentation for APA Panel: 'Multiculturalism and Indian Women', New York, December 2000.

45. Rosalind O'Hanlon and David Washbrook argue that this is precisely the trouble with the principle of self-representation enshrined in the politics of identity: the idea that there can be unitary and centred subjects who are able to speak for themselves and present their experiences in their own authentic voices. 'After Orientalism: Culture, Criticism and Politics in the Third World', *Comparative Studies in History and Society*, vol. 34, 1 January 1992.

46. Stephanie Tawa Lama-Rewal, 'Women in the Calcutta Municipal Corporation: A Study in the Context of the Debate on the Women's Reservation Bill', Centre de Sciences Humaines, Occasional Paper, New Delhi, no. 2, 2001.

16 | Uniform Civil Code and Gender Justice in India

I̴ₙ ᴛʜᴇ 1990s, religion and gender became intertwined in the political turmoil that continues to currently envelop India. One issue at the centre of this turmoil concerns the question of whether religion-based personal law should be continued or a uniform civil code (UCC) instituted. The UCC, that is, the legal unification of the civil codes of different religious communities, refers to the ideological deployment of uniformity with the double agenda of improving the status of women and of integrating communities through a set of uniform civil laws. At different historical moments, therefore, the UCC has been projected as the most salient emblem of a modern homogeneous nation in contradistinction to that of personal laws which are perceived as a symbol of difference. No other symbol than that of the UCC reconstructs with such force the contention between nation and cultural rights. The state's commitment to a UCC was expressed in the Directive Principles of State Policy in the constitution. Over six decades after Independence however, public opinion still remains sharply divided. Religious personal law in matters of marriage, divorce, maintenance, inheritance, and child custody continues to be binding on followers of different communities.

Feminist and other scholars of nationalism in post-colonial societies have drawn attention to the centrality of the 'woman question' in the transition to modernity. In India, the modernizing state, in its attempt to undertake a certain form of social transformation that would enable it to weld a nation, formulated laws that would recognize its members as part of the same nation, sharing a common nationality.[1] It would have to grant rights and guarantee equality in an undifferentiated manner to all its citizens. The institution of common laws clearly linked integration to the agenda of modern nationhood. However, as various analyses have shown, the enterprise was confounded from the outset by the dispute over the desirability as well as the feasibility of introducing legal uniformity in a socially stratified and heterogeneous society.[2] In other words, the continuing predicament over the UCC reveals the centrality of the gender question in contemporary critiques of the state. By the same token, increased women's participation and politicization engendered the formation of a public and collective identity for women which has distanced itself from definitions of separate gender roles within the private and public spheres. Instead, women's groups are focused on gender justice which cross-cuts power relations between modernity and tradition, secularism and religion, as well as between men and women, and women themselves.

This chapter explores the UCC controversy through an analysis of the changing relationship between state, communities, and the women's movement. It is an attempt to unravel some of the strands in the tangled web of interconnection between community, identity, nation, and gender. Its specific focus is on the role of the state in the promotion of gender-just laws and the various ways in which women's rights have been conceptualized.

State and Community

Until recently, scholarly works have treated gender, religious, and community identity as static and unchanging. Those studying identity construction often focus on the social and cultural domain, rather than on the state. Students of the state, however, are less inclined to examine the processes of identity formation. The debates over the UCC reveal that it is untenable to draw a sharp line of distinction between community and state on the question of religion or gender. This is on account of structural, administrative, and ideological linkages between the two.[3] The religious communities under discussion have been constituted in relation to the state and, more importantly, by political processes connected to the state. Moreover, successive governments have been involved in the internal affairs of religious communities and in the maintenance of places of worship and other kinds of religious establishments. Thus, the interface between community and the state extends to the sphere of law. This has, consequently, led to a triangular relationship between personal laws, community representatives, and the state.[4] The state has been asked to protect religious boundaries in two different ways through the demand for the exemption of minorities from the application of the Criminal Procedure Code (CrPC) made by religious spokesmen, and through the demands for a UCC made by the Hindu communalists.

The demand for a UCC, first aired by the All India Women's Conference in 1937, figured prominently in the nationalist and early feminist agendas of the 1940s and 1950s. By 2000, however, none of the major women's organizations supported it with the same degree of enthusiasm; in fact, there were serious differences of opinion on the matter. More importantly, the UCC has acquired political salience in part because gender-just laws were conspicuous by their absence, and in part because India's ruling party at that time, the Bharatiya Janata Party (BJP), a right-wing authoritarian formation, appropriated what was otherwise a feminist demand. The Congress and Left, on the other hand, opposed the demand for a UCC, though for different reasons.

The contentious issue, one that has engendered controversy, relates to marriage, divorce, maintenance, inheritance, and adoption. As is well known, Hindu family laws were changed in 1955-6 through the Hindu Marriage Act, the Hindu Succession Act, the Hindu Minority and Guardianship Act, and the Hindu Adoption and Maintenance Act. Yet, there was no attempt to secure a UCC as suggested by the Directive Principles of State Policy. Still it was argued in different circles that uniformity was essential for national unity. This argument was presented in the Minutes of Dissent submitted by Minoo Masani, Hansa Mehta and Rajkumari Amrit Kaur against the decision to postpone the UCC to the future, through its relegation to the Directive Principles of State Policy. The Minutes of Dissent argued: 'One of the factors that has kept India from advancing to nationhood has been the existence of personal laws based on religion which keeps the nation divided into watertight compartments'.[5] Hansa Mehta maintained that a UCC was more important for national unity than a national language. Similarly, the Report of the Committee on the Status of Women in India in 1972 stated that 'the continuance of various personal laws which accepts distinctions between men and women violates fundamental rights, it is also against the spirit of national integration and secularism'.[6] Likewise, Supreme Court judgements have regularly emphasized the unificatory potential of legal equality. The Supreme Court judgement in the Sarla Mudgal Case (1994), for example, said: 'In the Indian Republic, there was to be only one nation—the Indian nation—and no community could claim to remain a separate entity on the basis of religion.'

Though anxious to ensure that religion should not hinder social reform, the advocates of UCC seldom emphasized the reformist potential of the UCC. Set up invariably in terms of secular state versus religious community, the public discourse was largely silent on UCC's significance for women. From the outset the argument was always cast in terms of an opposition between legal integrity and legal pluralism. The case for legal uniformity rests on uniformity as the basis of nationhood, harmony, democracy, and individual rights for women,[7] while the case for legal pluralism rests on a presumed antagonism between the religious community and the nation-state, on the right of communities to their own laws, and on the presupposition that personal laws are tied up with religious belief.

Underlying the national integrity argument was an assumption that while the secular state has allowed minorities to carry on with their retrogressive personal laws, Hindu laws were changed and the majority community willingly accepted reform. This is a misleading argument for two reasons: Hindu laws were codified and not fully reformed, and this was done in the face of stiff opposition from Congress leaders both inside and outside parliament and from the religious elites. The major groups opposing the legislation were: the conservative hardliners within the Congress party, with leaders like Vallabhbhai Patel, Rajendra Prasad, and J.B. Kripalani, who had a completely different world view from that of Jawaharlal Nehru; Hindu fundamentalists within the Congress, including Deputy Speaker of the Lok Sabha Ananthasayanam Aiyyangar, who opposed attempts by Law Minister B.R. Ambedkar to proceed with the legislation; the Hindu Mahasabha represented by men like Shyama Prasad Mukherjee, N.C. Chatterjee and others who opposed the bills strongly for threatening the so-called religious foundations of Hindu society and subverting Hindu ideas, culture, and religion; the Sikh groups represented by men like Sardar Hukam Singh who resented being clubbed together with Hindus in the broad framework of reform; and the Muslim groups led by Nazirud din Ahmed who were clearly encouraged by the conservatives in the Congress to tilt the balance in their favour. Every single clause of the Bill was opposed and the cry of 'religion in danger' was repeatedly raised. The property clauses giving property to daughters were most vehemently opposed, as was the abolition of polygamy. Pandit Thakur Das Bhargava, a strong opponent of the Bill, summed up the opposition when he condemned the Bill as 'equality run mad'.[8]

The storm raised by the Bill took Nehru by surprise. The principle of equal rights between men and women was accepted at the Karachi Congress in 1931 and enshrined in the constitution. The easy acceptance at Karachi of the Fundamental Rights resolution ensuring gender equality, and its subsequent incorporation in the Constitution, led Nehru to believe that the Hindu Code Bill could be easily passed. He realized, however, that while accepting equality on paper, there had been no serious contemplation by his colleagues of what it implied. For Nehru, however, the Hindu Code Bill was a necessary measure which fitted into his overall perspective of national development, for which the uniformity of legal practices was a vital element.

The Hindu Code Bill was considerably watered down as Nehru came to accept that the opposition to the Bill could not be wished away and in its existing form it would never get parliamentary approval. As he explained to

B.R. Ambedkar, who resigned as Law Minister because he thought Nehru tended to compromise: 'With the best will in the world we cannot brush aside this opposition and get things done quickly. They have in their power to delay a great deal. We must, therefore, proceed with some tact'.[9] His strategy was to bide time. After the Congress victory in the 1951 elections, Nehru went ahead with the Bill, but the Bill was separated and the bills were themselves made more acceptable by whittling down the controversial points.

The Hindu Code Bill was by no means an unqualified advance for women's rights. Some provisions clearly discriminated against women.[10] Women parliamentarians criticized the Bill for not going far enough. For example, Hansa Mehta said that the Succession Bill did not go far enough, as sons were regarded as being more equal than daughters. In the case of the Hindu Succession Act, there were several compromises: the joint family system was retained as was coparcenary, whose membership was restricted to males, and which meant that sons would not only get a share of their father's property but also their own interest as coparceners in the joint family property; by excluding agricultural land from legislation relating to succession, its benefits were restricted; the unrestricted right of testation—right to make a will—which often led daughters to be dependent upon their fathers' goodwill for being provided for life. In view of these limitations, not surprisingly, the Bills were ultimately passed with the total approval of parliament, hence 'Nehru's victory was largely symbolic'.[11] Nehru himself regarded the Hindu Code Bill as 'a very moderate measure of social reform . . . indeed very largely a codification of the existing law'. He considered the symbolism important since it would be the first major shake-up of the system of Hindu personal law. In the event, he remarked that the passage of the Bill constituted the greatest advance of his career and an 'outstanding achievement of his time'. As he explained later to the chief ministers: 'They are not in any way revolutionary in the changes they bring about and yet there is something revolutionary about them. They have broken the barrier of the ages and cleared the way somewhat for our womenfolk to progress'.[12]

Minority Rights and the Constitution

The Congress government was unwilling to press for similar changes in the laws of the minority communities or to legislate a UCC. The question of personal law had come up for debate on several occasions in the Constituent Assembly. Muslim members emphasized the unchanging nature of Muslim personal law and also that it could not be changed by the state. Any changes, they argued, should be initiated by the Islamic community. As this line of reasoning confirmed government suppositions, it was effective. In the process of these negotiations Muslim political leaders represented both Islamic law and their own community as more unified than they actually were or had been. They succeeded in establishing that legal codes and religion were interlinked, and that personal laws formed an integral part of the socio-religious identity of Muslims.

In such a situation, the government refrained from interfering in the regime of personal laws. Jawaharlal Nehru was reluctant because he felt that in the aftermath of Partition his government should avoid any step that would offend the religious sensibilities of minorities, especially the Muslims. Instead, he wanted to assuage Muslim anxieties regarding their status in independent India. Nehru said: If anybody brings forward a civil code bill, it will have my extreme sympathy. But I confess I do not think the time is ripe in India for me to push through it. Although he considered a UCC for the whole country essential, Nehru was apprehensive that any imposition on minorities, without their consent, would be imprudent. Hence, the policy of merging religious communities in a single citizenship remained a pious hope enshrined in the Directive Principles of State Policy. However, given the changeable nature of cultures, Nehru, the architect of this policy, expected that these provisions and concessions to minorities would themselves be subject to change. He hoped that Muslim communities would, in the fullness of time, respond to the winds of change. Meanwhile he insisted they should have the right to decide the timing of their response.

Nehru's expectations have not yet been fulfilled. The last 60 years have witnessed little effort towards reform. By contrast, the two decades preceding independence saw considerable reformist activity, albeit of a type which stressed a return to pristine Islam and the need to observe the Shariat in everyday life. Nevertheless, there was agreement among reformers, who included a coalition of the ulama, middle-class reformers, and westernized politicians, that the status of Muslim women required amelioration.[13] Often reformers recommended eliminating custom. In some cases they advocated legislative enactments in order to bring personal law closer to the scriptures. However, a series of legal changes, which included the Dissolution of Muslim Marriages Act of 1939, led to some improvements in women's rights in the context of family relations.[14]

After independence, Muslim political leaders were able to hold off the legal advance of women's rights by taking shelter under the special provision for minorities and its overall significance in a multicultural, heterogeneous society. The Constitution provides for the religious liberty of both the individual and associations of individuals united by common beliefs, practices, and discipline. This has given rise to tensions between two different conceptions of rights: the rights of individuals and the claims of communities. Through special provisions for Scheduled Castes (SCs), Scheduled Tribes (STs) and Other Backward Classes (OBCs), the Constitution introduced the principle of positive discrimination in favour of the poorest and lowest in the social order, especially those excluded from the caste system. The grant of universal equal rights to all was offset by the recognition of injustice suffered by particular groups, especially the SCs, and thereby the recognition that preferential treatment be given in the form of reservations in government jobs and educational institutions for members of these groups.[15]

The implicit recognition in the constitution that religions have both sustained and legitimized caste and gender discrimination led the state to being at once a reformer of injustices based on religion as well as a protector of religious freedom. Hence, the minorities were granted some degree of control over their own affairs, including the right to express their cultural particularity. This took two forms: the inclusion of the freedom of religion in the fundamental rights, and safeguards for minority rights, including the right to maintain their own educational institutions.[16]

The incorporation of these rights was undoubtedly influenced by the context of partition, when the state endeavoured to gain the trust of Muslim communities that opted to stay in their country of birth. The spectre of Hindu–Muslim communalism hung over the subcontinent when India became independent. The Partition meant that Pakistan might become a homeland for Muslims, but India would remain a home for Hindus, Muslims, Christians and others, and though Pakistan was a Muslim state, there were more Muslims in India than in Pakistan. One way of facilitating the integration of minorities was to recognize them as members of religious communities. From the standpoint of universalism and egalitarianism, such group-specific rights were a violation of liberal principles, but in India they were seen not as privileges, but primarily as safeguards against larger majority groupings.

This, however, did lead to a recognition of minority identity in the legal structure of the state. Hence, personal laws, which were often disadvantageous to women, were allowed to function without any reform. While these safeguards are important, no effort has been made to ensure that they are not monopolized by the most conservative elements within the minority. The controversy over the Shah Bano judgement is a case in point.

Community Identity and Women

The turning point in the debate on gender justice was the famous Shah Bano Case. The Supreme Court, in a landmark judgement delivered in April 1985, granted a small maintenance allowance to Shah Bano, a 73-year-old divorcee, to be paid by her husband Mohammed Ahmed Khan, under the provisions of the CrPC. Ahmed Khan had argued in an appeal to the Supreme Court that since he had fulfilled his obligations under Muslim personal law by paying her an allowance for three months of the *iddat* period and *meher* as well, he was not bound to maintain her any further. The Supreme Court, however, ruled that criminal laws override personal laws and are applicable to all, including Muslim women. This judgement sparked off a political furore. To soothe ruffled feelings, the Rajiv Gandhi government enacted a legislation, the Muslim Women (Protection of Rights on Divorce) Bill, 1986, to explicitly exclude Muslim women from the purview of the CrPC, to which all citizens otherwise have recourse.

The controversy around the judgement, and the public as well as the parliamentary debate, tended to focus on the conflict between the right of the religious minority to cultural autonomy and to a separate civil code as an important guarantee of its identity on the one hand, and the claims of the state legitimized through representative institutions to articulate and realize the common good on the other.[17] The critics ignored the important question of women's rights, which remained confined to feminists and the Left parties. The Muslim leadership focused on legal issues that linked women and family life to Islamic legal identity and defended the definition of the Muslim community as a legal entity. The government defended the legislation on the ground that it conformed to the wishes of the Muslim community and should be conceded irrespective of the opinion of other communities or society at large. The law minister stated that: 'We have to tread very carefully for the Muslim personal law is linked to the Muslim religion in the mind of Muslim. We must look at it from the point of view of Muslims and then try to find out what is the law which governs the Muslims and which according to them is not merely a law of man's making as a law ordained by God. This is the belief of Muslims.'[18]

The primacy of community rights over citizenship was once again endorsed by the state which willingly limited the application of its own laws to exclude citizens from the rights available to others. The controversy signifies the important role played by official state discourse in safeguarding community identity. The Congress party legitimized it, in terms of both state policies and strategies of mobilization. In the absence of a reformed divorce law, Muslim women were unequal vis-à-vis men, and were now rendered unequal vis-à-vis women from other communities who have access to the law in respect of maintenance. To be sure, these issues raise questions that are not easily reconciled: the claims of rights of women and of individuals as against those of cultures and groups. The problem is undoubtedly compounded by the substantial purchase that community identity has on the polity.

However, community identity is not natural or primordial. Communities are constituted in distinct ways at different historical junctures. Thus, it is well known that personal laws are constructions of the twentieth century. As with the Hindu Code Bill, the Shariat Act of 1937 and the Dissolution of Muslim Marriages Act, 1939, demarcated the boundaries of the Muslim community. Nonetheless, the historicity of community construction does not deny the reality that these identities exist and that they matter to large numbers of people. Yet, it is a fact that community identity can be punitive, and there is little evidence to show that communities are committed to internal democratization of gender differences. Personal laws deny women the rights that communities claim for themselves vis-à-vis the state: autonomy, selfhood, and access to resources.

From the women's standpoint, the difficulty lies in marking the identity of the community exclusively by defining its women. Failing to define the community in broad terms, the Muslim leadership conflates religion and culture, identifying only one area as the essence of cultural identity, which boils down to personal laws. By defining community identity entirely with reference to a strict code of laws, legal change is ruled out because the survival of cultural identity depends on a codified identity. The reform of personal laws does not however mean the end of community or community identity, because there is a vast array of things which constitute the identity of the community, including language, religious rituals, pilgrimage to Mecca, fasting and prayers, etc.

Hindu Communalism, Minorities, and Women's Rights

From the 1990s, many in India have asked why action has not been taken to bring about the fulfilment of the constitutional ideal. It has become a source of political conflict and polarization between secularists and communalists, that has engaged political parties and mass media in a fierce polemic. Foremost, it has revealed deep social and political cleavages between the secular state and Hindu organizations, and between them and women in particular.

The state has had to steer a precarious course between the norm of secularism and the norm of religious pluralism. The conflicts between the two positions coexisted for four decades after independence and although there were moments when the contradictions came to the fore, not many appear to have been troubled by their disagreement. At any rate, these points of discordance were not widely contested and they did not appear to be seriously divisive.[19] However, the relative accommodation was upset in the late 1980s, which had much to do with changes in India's politics: the growth of communal politics and the controversies surrounding it.

The decision to put off consideration of legal equality created a major area of tension between the Hindu nationalists and the minority communities. Until it came to power in March 1998, the BJP had raised the issue mainly to draw a parallel between the Congress party's capitulation to Muslim conservatives in the 1950s and then again in the 1980s, in the Shah Bano Case. The lack of reform in Muslim personal law and its stout defence by the Congress party was exploited by the BJP to build a critique of secularism and of the Muslim community. It became a rallying point for communal groups campaigning against secularism and the secular practices of the state run by the Congress party.

Epitomizing a long-term tendency in politics and society, the design of the Hindu nation, in contrast to pluralistic nationalism, stands for emphasizing the distinctness of Hindu civilization, and, playing down horizontal divisions among Hindus, the integration of all castes, communities, and sects into a homogeneous whole. In some respects Hindu nationalism is, however, different from fundamentalism. Whereas fundamentalism rejects the separation of religion and state, Hindu communalism accepts this separation in principle. Partha Chatterjee argues that:

The persuasive power, and even the emotional charge the Hindutva campaign appears to have gained in recent years do not depend upon its demanding legislative enforcement of ritual or scriptuial injunctions, a role for religious institutions in legislative or judicial processes, compulsory religious instruction or state support for religious bodies, censorship of science, literature and art in order to safeguard religious dogma or any other similar demand undermining the secular character of the existing Indian state.[20]

This has crucial implications for women because the major alternative to secular law is community-based religious law.[21] By virtue of its supposed commitment to secular principles, the BJP could uphold constitutional protection of sexual equality, and in fact adopt a high moral posture to castigate secular governments for being pseudo-secular owing to their indulgence of minorities. 'Personal law', Uma Bharati argues, 'defies the spirit of the constitution'.[22]

By decrying the actions of successive Congress regimes on the issue of family law, the BJP sought to demonstrate its own commitment to constitutional principles. The BJP used the language of legal and constitutional rights to pit women's rights against minority rights. As some feminist legal scholars pointed out, it interpreted secularism to mean that Muslims and Hindus should be treated alike, thereby disregarding the vulnerabilities to which Muslims as a minority are subject.[23] This is because Hindu nationalists, unlike their counterparts in many Muslim countries, identify their principal enemies as internal rather than external.[24] By comparison, Islamic fundamentalism in West Asia, for example, is inseparable from the nationalist opposition to westernization and modernity in its various guises. Nilofer Gole notes that veiling in Turkey embodies the battleground for two competing conceptions of self and society, Western and Islamist.[25] Similarly, Valentine Moghadam observes that fundamentalists in Iran consider the veil as an antidote to the virus of 'Westoxication' and 'Euromania'.[26]

Until the BJP-led government decided to conduct a series of underground nuclear tests, Hindu nationalists had not expressed any open anti-Western sentiment. Rather, their targets were the 'outsiders' located within the nation, that is, Muslims, whom they regarded as foreign even though Indian Islam is no more derivative than Chinese, Tibetan, Thai, or Japanese Buddhism. Yet the idea that Islam is foreign is axiomatic for Hindu nationalists and for their agenda of removing the protective safeguards for communities and regions in order to produce a uniform, homogeneous code.

It is clear that the ideological consensus formulated by the state on issues of secularism and minority rights during Nehru's regime has given way to a politics of intolerance that came to pervade the culture. The opposition to the UCC provided the BJP with a crucial means of challenging the ideological legitimacy of the secular state. The compulsions of coalition politics forced the BJP government to shelve the immediate introduction of a UCC for it would have to wait until the party gained a majority in parliament to unfold its Hindutva agenda of cultural homogenization. Meanwhile, in the Hindu nationalist discourse, the UCC continues to be a touchstone of what it means to be an Indian, and a struggle over what the conditions of belonging are.

Women's Groups and Gender Justice

In the larger body politics, gender construction, identity formation, and citizenship continue to be formulated within the rhetoric of binary opposition. Salient among these are: universalism/difference, uniformity/ plurality and state/community. Rather than accepted as logical and necessary oppositions, these categories need to be historicized and subjected to closer scrutiny. Women's groups have attempted this by taking a fresh look at the process and mechanics of gender construction, especially the role of the state in this process.

From the 1940s, there was a general consensus that the state should legislate gender-just laws for all communities. This was part of the larger understanding that the state ought to play an important role in progressive social and political transformation. However, by the mid-1970s this consensus had broken down with the economic and political crisis of the state, engendered by the failures of development planning and socialism. This period saw a significant growth in women's participation in mass struggles on every front. The mass discontent brought about a radical rethinking in the women's movement on the role of the nation-state. The reluctance to universalize women's rights was illustrated by the pragmatic compromises of the state and its complicity in cashing in on religious difference, for instance through the Muslim Women's Bill. Not surprisingly, there was growing disquiet over state-initiated legislation in areas of marriage, divorce, maintenance, and inheritance, including the Hindu Code Bill.[27] The reform of Hindu laws did challenge the religious elites, but it culminated in the promulgation of laws that are not entirely just to women.

The makers of the Constitution believed that the constitutional right to equality would be reinforced by the social policy of equality. This belief informed the policy of affirmative action for the SCs which sought to reinforce equality as a right with public support for equality as a policy. When it comes to rights of women, equality as a right is enshrined in the constitution, but with no support for gender equality as a policy. Though the state is theoretically committed to ensuring the rights of its citizenry, it has been constrained by the dilemma of whether to support reforms from above or to support reforms from within. Significant initiatives to reform personal laws have been thwarted as often by the state as by pundits, mullahs, and priests. Even the strategy of reform from within in the case of the Christian community has met with prevarication from the state.[28] The legal reform of personal law becomes a bargaining counter for the state which retains the power to decide whether or not to reform the personal law of any community.

The decisive shift came in the wake of the Ayodhya movement and the dramatic growth of the BJP. The BJP's ambition was to establish a singular citizenship by obliterating the legal recognition of religious and cultural differences, hence the focus on Muslim personal law. Feminist groups are clearly uncomfortable with its appropriation of the UCC, particularly because in the hands of the BJP it became a rhetorical device to attack minorities. This created a dilemma for feminist politics, and more generally for secular democratic politics, between two conflicting norms: the norm of religious tolerance and the norm of equality between men and women. The women's movement remained committed to equality, but it did not want changes forced upon personal laws by the militant Hindu communal forces who saw the Muslim resistance to the UCC as a sign of their inability to integrate into the nation. Aware that legal change cannot be isolated from the wider political contradictions in the context of communal politics, women's groups began to seriously rethink the demand for a UCC.[29] This gave rise to two kinds of approaches: one proposed that the present historical moment of heightened religious identities requires working within them, while the other foregrounded gender justice by delinking it from national integrity.[30]

From the early 1990s, the opposition to uniform laws was marked by a simultaneous critique of the UCC and personal laws. It signalled an acknowledgement that gender justice needed to be delinked from uniform laws. Groups which earlier supported uniform legislation jettisoned it in favour of common, gender-just, or egalitarian laws, as against uniform laws. It is worth noting that the term 'uniform' was practically dropped within the women's movement, even by those groups who endorsed state legislation.[31] The change is visible in the repudiation of the UCC by all political parties, the BJP excepted. The change is most explicit in the case of the All India Democratic Women's Association (AIDWA), the largest women's organization in the country. Like other feminist groups, AIDWA has had to reckon with a political climate vitiated by communal politics and religious identities. In the 1990s, the AIDWA promoted common laws, but under BJP rule, it championed a gradual approach to legal reforms in recognition of the difficulty of pushing change in the communal climate, encouraged community initiative, and demanded fresh legislation with regard to matrimonial property and the custody of children.

A number of proposals have been mooted by women's groups to enlarge the scope for gender justice. While distancing themselves from a state-imposed UCC, feminist positions differ both from the national integrity argument and from an unqualified defence of community rights. The national integrity argument is problematic owing to its implicit and sometimes explicit rebuke of minorities as 'anti-national'. The communitarian argument is equally problematic because it endangers women's rights. Moving away from both, women's groups have given priority to the notion of women as individual citizens with inalienable rights.[32] Some groups, such as the Mumbai-based

Majlis, prefer to maximize the space for women within communities, which means reform within personal laws rather than legislation by the state. Then there are others who want to devise genuinely egalitarian or secular laws and allow people to opt for these.[33] The Forum Against Oppression of Women, Mumbai, has evolved such a code.[34] The Working Group on Women's Rights, Delhi, put forward a proposal that blends state legislation in both private and public domains and also provides the option of a return to personal laws.[35] This option would turn the regime of personal laws into something voluntary and yet leave open the possibility of transformation of a community through its own initiatives, rather than by the state.

The key to understanding these shifts lies in the specificity of the Indian discourse on secularism. Secularism in India simultaneously posits the disengagement of religion from the public arena and the need for the state to regulate religious practices, either by non-intervention, for example, declaring certain areas of jurisprudence to be the prerogative of religious leaders, or by intervention, for example, ensuring financial accountability of religious trusts.[36] The critique of the state in this context is either that it intervenes too much, as when the government passed the Muslim Women's Bill, or too little, as in its reluctance to enact a UCC. This is the peculiar predicament of the state, to understand which we have to keep in mind not only India's composite cultural tradition but also its present demography and heterogeneity. The presence of social pluralities makes it difficult to conceive of a stable political arrangement without religious tolerance and secularism. However, the definitions of secular and 'nation' take place in a political field where certain identities are privileged—even while equality is emphasized—and others subordinated. As Deniz Kandiyoti argues, whenever women serve as markers between different ethnic and religious collectivities, their emergence as full-fledged citizens with concomitant rights 'will be jeopardized'.[37]

The goal of gender equality cannot be indefinitely postponed. It is by seeking rights as citizens that women aspire to actively redefine the contours of the debate and shape new laws. 'The legitimacy of new common laws', as Kumkum Sangari argues, 'should be based on a secular and democratic horizon that seeks justice for women within a wider egalitarian project. As such it cannot be formulated by the state or the BJP, or through a consensus of religious communities'.[38] Such laws can only be made from a non-religious location, and they would have to take into account both similarities and differences, and allow the individual's right to choose where to belong. In sum, common laws have to be based on a principle of access to inalienable rights that are the same for all.

Notes and References

1. Ritu Menon, 'Reproducing the Legitimate Community: Secularity, Sexuality and the State in Postpartition India', in *Appropriating Gender: Women's Activism and Politicised Religion in South Asia*, ed. Patricia Jeffrey and Amrita Basu, New York: Routledge, 1998, pp. 15–32.

2. See Archana Parasher, *Women and Family Law Reform in India*, New Delhi: Sage, 1992; Kumkum Sangari, 'Politics of Diversity: Religious Communities and Multiple Patriarchies', *Economic and Political Weekly*, vol. 30, no. 51, 23 December 1995, pp. 3287–300.

3. Sangari, 'Politics of Diversity', pp. 3294–6.

4. Zoya Hasan, ed., *Forging Identities: Gender, Communities and the State*, New Delhi: Kali for Women, and Boulder, CO: Westview Press, 1994.

5. Parasher, *Women and Family Law Reform*, p. 233.

6. Government of India, *Towards Equality: Report of the Committee on the Status of Women in India*, Ministry of Education and Social Welfare, New Delhi, 1972, p. 142.

7. For details on this debate see Parasher, *Women and Family Law Reform*. Despite centuries of Muslim rule, the community did not adopt the Shariah as the basis of law; consequently, women's rights in the Shariah were seldom complied with or enforced. As a result, the opportunities of exercising their Koranic prerogatives, especially in claiming ownership of landed estates and property, were denied to women. Until the introduction of the Shariat Act in 1937, legal and social codes observed by Muslim communities in different parts of the country were varied and diffuse. Thus began an effort by the ulama to work for a complete supersession of non-Islamic customary practice and compulsory enactment of an Islamic legal system. The enactment of the Muslim Personal Law Shariat Application Act, 1937, signalled the acceptance by the state legal system of the principle that in all personal matters such as marriage, divorce, maintenance, inheritance, and custody, Muslims would be governed by the Muslim personal law. Similarly, the Dissolution of the Muslim Marriages Act, 1939, represented yet another attempt by the ulama to rectify what they perceived as a lacuna in the existing laws which had left Muslim women without the option of divorce, except through apostasy from Islam. For the first time, this Act gave Muslim women the right to seek judicial dissolution of marriage. For more details see A.A.A. Fyzee, *Outlines of Muhammedan Law*, Delhi: Oxford University Press, 1974.

8. Cited in Reba Som, 'Jawaharlal Nehru and the Hindu Code: A Victory of Symbol over Substance', *Modern Asian Studies*, vol. 28, no. 1, 1994, pp. 165–94.

9. Cited in Som, 'Jawaharlal Nehru and the Hindu Code', Ibid.

10. Madhu Kishwar, 'Codified Hindu Laws: Myth and Reality', *Economic and Political Weekly*, vol. 29, no. 33, 13 August 1994, pp. 2145–61.

11. Som, 'Jawaharlal Nehru and the Hindu Code', pp. 172–3.

12. Ibid., p. 178.

13. Gail Minault, 'Women, Legal Reform and Muslim Identity', *Islam, Communities and the Nation: Muslim Identities in South Asia and Beyond*, ed. Mushirul Hasan, New Delhi: Manohar, 1998, p. 139.

14. Ibid., pp. 140–2.

15. Granville Austin, *The Indian Constitution: Cornerstone of a Nation*, Oxford: Clarendon Press, 1966, pp. 50–74.

16. Donald Eugene Smith, *India as a Secular State*, Princeton: Princeton University Press, 1963, pp. 100–34.

17. Niraja Gopal Jayal, 'Secularism, Identities and Representative Democracy', in *Islam, Communities and the Nation*, Hasan, p. 161.

18. Government of India, *Lok Sabha Debates, Fifth Session, Eighth Lok Sabha*, vol. I, no. XVII, New Delhi, 1986.

19. Andre Beteille, 'Conflict of Norms and Values in Contemporary Indian Society', *The Limits of Social Cohesion: Conflict and Mediation in Pluralist Societies*, ed. Peter Berger, Boulder, CO: Westview Press, 1998, pp. 265–92.

20. Partha Chatterjee, 'Secularism and Toleration', *Economic and Political Weekly*, vol. 20, no. 28, 9 July 1994, p. 1768.

21. Basu, 'Hindu Activism in India', pp. 170–2.

22. Ibid., p. 172.

23. Ratna Kapur and Brenda Cossman, 'Communalising Gender/Engendering Community: Women, Legal Discourse and the Saffron Agenda', *Women and the Hindu Right: A Collection of Essays*, ed. Tanika Sarkar and Urvashi Butalia, New Delhi: Kali for Women, 1995.

24. Ibid., p. 171.

25. Nilofer Gole, *Forbidden Modern: Civilization and Veiling*, Michigan: Michigan University Press, 1996, p. 5.

26. Valentine Moghadam, 'Introduction: Women and Identity Politics in Theoretical and Comparative Perspective', *Identity Politics and Women: Cultural Assertions and Feminisms in International Perspectives*, ed. Valentine Mogadham, Boulder, CO: Westview Press, 1994, p. 13.

27. See for example: Anveshi Law Committee, Hyderabad 1997, 'Is Gender Justice Only a Legal Issue? Political Stakes in UCC Debate', *Economic and Political Weekly*, vol. 32, nos. 9-10, 1 March 1997.

28. In 1993, a Christian Marriage Act was proposed by the government with the approval of all Christian churches and Christian women's organizations. Despite the Christian community's support for changes in divorce laws, the Bill has not yet been debated in parliament.

29. Flava Agnes, 'Women's Movements within a Secular Framework: Redefining the Agenda', *Economic and Political Weekly*, vol. 29, no. 19, 1994, pp. 1123–8.

30. Three kinds of interventions were made with regard to legal reforms. First, there were attempts by women's groups all over the country to evolve a common package of laws that are free of gender bias. Second, there was the effort to reform from within communities. Third, a number of judicial interventions addressed themselves to discrepancies in law to reduce inequalities between men and women. For example, a recent Supreme Court judgement gave the widow and daughter of a deceased coparcener equal rights to property left by him. Another judgement granted a divorced Hindu woman the right to sell, use for income, or dispose of in any way she likes the land given to her in lieu of maintenance. In another case, the widow was granted full ownership rights of the premises given to her as part of her tenancy. Such verdicts have greatly helped to reduce the existing inequities between men and women in matters of inherited property.

31. Nivedita Menon, 'Women and Citizenship', in *State and Politics in India,* ed. Partha Chatterjee, Delhi: Oxford University Press, 1997, pp. 253–63.
32. For an explication of this argument, see Sangari, 'Politics of Diversity'.
33. This idea was put forward as early as 1945, when it was suggested that the UCC be made optional. After Independence, the Special Marriages Act or the Indian Succession Act offered a number of options. Yet the government did not endeavour to create a machinery for implementing an optional code. Had it done so, it may well have expanded the ground of secular laws, besides building up pressure for reforms within community laws.
34. The proposal includes the following: (a) the need for changes and modifications in the procedures of law to ensure effective implementation; (b) the demand for a system of social security benefits for women; and (c) the demand that the state take on the responsibility for imparting legal education to women at all levels.
35. The proposal has three features: (a) a comprehensive package of legislation providing equal rights for women in terms of access to property, guardianship, right to matrimonial home, and equal rights in the workplace as well as anti-discriminatory provisions in recruitment and promotions; (b) all Indian citizens would come under the purview of common laws at birth; and (c) all citizens would have the right to choose at any point to be governed by personal laws, if they so desire, while retaining the option to revoke this choice. See Working Group on Women's Rights, 'Reversing the Option: Civil Codes and Personal Laws', *Economic and Political Weekly,* vol. 31, no. 20, 18 May 1996, pp. 1180–3.
36. N. Menon, 'Women and Citizenship', pp. 264–5.
37. Deniz Kandiyoti, 'Identity and its Discontents: Women and Nation', *Millennium Journal of International Studies,* vol. 20, no. 3, pp. 429–43.
38. Sangari, 'Politics of Diversity', p. 3386.

17 | Minority Identity, Muslim Women Bill Campaign and the Political Process

In RECENT years, mounting social conflicts and sectarian tension in India has received considerable scholarly attention. The controversies generated by the 'liberation' of the Babri Masjid at Ayodhya and the outcry against the Supreme Court verdict in the Shah Bano Case, have brought to the fore the sharpening of social and sectarian cleavages.

In April 1985, India's highest judicial court, the Supreme Court, gave a momentous judgement—the grant of maintenance to Shah Bano, a divorced Muslim woman. Seen as a threat to Islamic Law (Shariah), the verdict evoked strong passions and led to a massive agitation among Muslims. Alarmed by its intensity, the government enacted a legislation—the Muslim Women (Protection of Rights on Divorce) Bill, 1986—to mollify Muslim opinion. But its provisions proved to be retrogressive. Article 14 of the Indian Constitution, which guarantees equality before law, was overruled by Article 15 which safeguards freedom of religion. Besides, a secular law— Section 125 of the Criminal Procedure Code (CrPC)—which guaranteed maintenance to indigent women was amended to exclude Muslim women from its purview.

The main focus of this chapter is on the movement of 1985-6 against the Supreme Court verdict. It will explore who the chief campaigners were, and what ideological spectrum they represented. It will also address questions such as why their campaign evoked such powerful responses from a wide spectrum of Muslim society, and how Muslim women in general responded to the controversy generated by the Supreme Court judgement and the Muslim Women Bill. Finally, it will question why the government introduced an amendment which curtailed the rights of Muslim women.

It is often argued that the resistance to 'change' or 'reform' is closely linked with an overriding concern to preserve the religio-cultural identity of a religious minority. However, the assertion of one's 'Muslimness' is an option available to an individual who may articulate, underplay, or stress this form of identity.[1] Identities, in general, are not simply inherited or 'givens' of the social existence; they are shaped and crystallized in a specific politics and context.[2] The outcome of a movement—fundamentalist or otherwise—is thus contingent on the social and economic circumstances of a community and the political context in which it acquires depth of support. In fact, the government's response to the well-orchestrated campaign against the Supreme Court judgement reveals how a political context, combined with a set of political considerations, can determine the outcome of many such movements.

Contextualizing the Shah Bano Verdict Opposition

In an historic judgement, the Supreme Court ruled that Shah Bano, divorced by her husband after 43 years of marriage, was entitled to maintenance from her husband. Addressing itself primarily to the issue of whether Muslim personal law imposes an obligation upon the husband, the court further ruled that a Muslim woman, unable to support herself, was entitled to take recourse to Section 125 of the CrPC which applied to all communities regardless of their separate personal laws.[3] In case of a conflict between certain provisions of the CrPC and the Muslim personal law, the former would prevail.[4]

This interpretation of the Muslim personal law triggered off a country-wide reaction; in fact, few issues after independence have evoked as strong a reaction among Indian Muslims as this Supreme Court judgement. Maulana Abul Hasan Nadvi, the president of the All India Muslim Personal Law Board (AIMPLB) compared it to the Khilafat upsurge of the 1920s.[5] A powerful section of Muslim opinion, represented by the Jamait-ul-Ulema-i-Hind, the Jamait-e-Islami, and the Muslim League denounced the judgement and organized a crusade against what they termed as interference in the Muslim personal law. The main objections were set out by Yunus Saltern, counsel for the AIMPLB. His arguments were that the Supreme Court had interfered with the Muslim personal law and had further transgressed its limits by interpreting the Koran.[6] The Muslim personal law, so ran the argument, was based on the Shariah, which is divine and immutable; hence no legislative or executive authority could amend or alter its provisions.

What was conveniently ignored in the debate was the obvious fact that many changes had already come into operation during British rule in India.[7] While family and inheritance laws were generally left untouched and unconditioned, a number of important legislations were enacted from 1827 to 1887 which sought to apply local customs and practices. Such initiatives were however vigorously opposed by various Muslim activist groups who demanded the restoration of Islamic law on the plea that Muslims should be governed by Muslim law and not by any custom which might be in the contrary.[8]

The Jamait-ul-Ulema-i-Hind took the lead in demanding restoration of the Islamic laws. Other groups also plunged into the campaign, for the issue of safeguarding the sanctity of the Shariah became a symbol for representing the Muslim identity.[9] For organizations actively involved in the mobilization of Muslims, it was part of their search for an identity so as to establish the claims to a status commensurate with its substantial minority position. In fact the demand for restoring the Muslim personal law was turned into a symbol for homogenizing the community by emphasizing the unifying symbols as opposed to the socio-economic differences which divided the Muslims of India.

Though the passing of the Shariat Act in 1937 and the Dissolution of Muslim Marriages Act in 1939 were hailed at the time as important initiatives,[10] it needs to be stated that the pre-independence legislations were not reform legislations but a restoration of Islamic law.[11] The supporters of the Shariat Act claimed that it had furthered the interests of women and unified the community at the same time. The debate on the reform of Muslim personal law has been intensified in the post-independence period. The Muslim community has resisted change of personal law on the argument that it is an integral part of the socio-religious identity of the community.

A section of the Muslim leadership has consistently tried to politicize religion as a means of safeguarding the community's separate and distinct identity. Gail Minault has pointed out that 'the political movements among Muslims in the 1920s used religious and cultural symbols which were relevant to all strata of the community'.[12] This was done to foster the unity among the 'believers' and to enhance their bargaining position in the constitutional wranglings. In the post-independence period this symbolism has come to rest entirely on laws pertaining to family and women. Invariably women are the victims of cultural distinction, because community identity is defined almost entirely in terms of family laws which tend to subordinate women. Muslim leaders displayed the dilemma that face a group using symbolic differentiation to promote cohesion because such symbolism, as Karl Marx said on the Jewish question, is not anymore the essence of the community but the essence of distinction.

The political value of the issues relating to the Muslim personal law derived largely from its importance in differentiating Muslims from other communities. What is often ignored is that Muslims do not exist in Indian society as separate and isolated entities: they operate within the social structure as segments of a composite social framework.[13] Equally significant is the tendency toward pluralism in matters pertaining to the Shariah. This is true of Muslim societies in different parts of the Islamic world. As Maxine Rodinson remarks: '. . . one is not dealing with "Islam", a single coherent doctrine, but with several ideologies, several Islams'.[14] Indian Islam is a product of the circumstances in which it emerged and crystallized and, in the process, it became necessary to adapt to the indigenous environment. However, for the ulema who were primarily concerned with Islamic norms, the maintenance of Muslim identity in a secular society required an increasing emphasis on the acceptance of these norms. Adherence to the Shariah for them became the central symbol in the preservation of Muslim identity and an idiom for integration. As a result, there is considerable opposition to change in family laws, though the community has accepted secular legislation on all other matters, including legislation on criminal laws.

Muslim personal law affects women directly and adversely. Their position under its provisions is unequal: a Muslim man can marry four wives, a woman can be divorced by unilateral pronouncement of triple talaq, a Muslim daughter inherits only half the share of the son, and a divorced Muslim wife is not entitled to maintenance. Though polygamy and unilateral divorce were not widespread as they affected only a small section of the population, maintenance, inheritance, and adoption laws affected all families and women from all classes. It was in this context that the Supreme Court judgement in favour of maintenance under the CrPC was significant because it recognized the rights of Muslim women irrespective of personal law. The reason for this is axiomatic, observed the Supreme Court:

Section 125 is part of the Code of Criminal Procedure, not of the civil laws which define and govern the rights and obligations of the parties belonging to particular religions. Section 125 was enacted in order to provide a quick and summary remedy to a class of persons who are unable to maintain themselves. What difference would it then make as to what is the religion professed by the neglected wife, children or parent. Neglect by a person of sufficient means to maintain these and the inability of these persons to maintain themselves are the objective criteria which determine the applicability of Section 125. Such provisions, which are essentially of a prophylactic nature, cut across the barriers of religion. True, they do not supplant the personal law of the parties, but, equally, the religion professed by the parties or the state of the personal law by which they are governed, cannot have any repercussions on the applicability of such laws unless, within the framework of the constitution, their application is restricted to a defined category of religious groups or classes.[15]

According to the Supreme Court verdict there is no conflict between the provisions of Section 125 and those of the personal law on the question of a Muslim husband's obligation to provide maintenance for a divorced wife who is unable to maintain herself. This conclusion was based on the understanding that Muslim personal law, which limits the husband's liability to provide maintenance for the period of *iddat*, does not countenance the situation of destitution envisaged by Section 125.[16]

Mobilizing Muslim Opposition

Conservative Muslim opinion was incensed by the Shah Bano verdict. Among the conservative sections, the Personal Law lobby was the most pronounced in berating the Shah Bano judgement. However, the Shah Bano verdict was not the first one to grant maintenance rights to Muslim women. Two important judgements by Justice Krishna Iyer in the *Tahira Bai* v. *Ali Husain Fiduli Chothia* and *Fazlunbi* v. *Khader Ali* cases in the 1970s granted maintenance to Muslim women under Section 125. Likewise in 1984 the Madras High Court conferred monthly maintenance to a Muslim woman.[17] None of these judgements evoked any protest. The Shah Bano verdict, on the other hand, provoked an outcry of massive protest. The question is therefore why this verdict is particular could spark such resistance.

To understand the success of the fundamentalist upsurge we should begin by looking at the nature and character of intercommunal relations in the 1980s. The last phase of the Indira Gandhi era witnessed an unprecedented spurt in religious fervour and a marked polarization of Indian society on communal and sectarian lines. Nearly 4,000 people were killed in communal violence.[18] Equally significant was the growth of communal organizations; there were over 500 militant organizations with an active membership which ran into several millions.[19] All these bodies, combined with Vishwa Hindu Parishad and the Virat Hindu Sammelan, were at the forefront of the campaign launched by right-wing organizations to represent and protect fundamentalist causes such as the liberation of the Babri Masjid in Ayodhya.

The intrusion of religion into politics remained unchanged under the Rajiv Gandhi regime. Innumerable examples can be listed to demonstrate the mixing of religion and politics. Indeed, over the years, the Congress has taken over the role of the protector of majority interests, a fact which encouraged the Rashtriya Swayamsevak Sangh to extend its support to the Congress.

The deteriorating economic conditions of Muslims, aggravated by systematic neglect and discrimination, made large sections of Muslims receptive to fundamentalist pressures.[20] The causes of the economic decline of Muslims are debatable, but there is no denying that they represent a picture of enormous underemployment.[21] Their problems have been compounded by the abandonment of Urdu, which is why they find it difficult to compete for government posts, and that communal riots have occurred in towns where they have attained a measure of economic well-being. This has been the pattern in Aligarh, Bhiwandi, Ahmedabad, Meerut, and Moradabad. In these towns the Hindu petty bourgeoisie, with the backing of militant organizations, have whipped up communal fervour against Muslims to displace Muslim entrepreneurs, either to reduce competition in crucial trades or to acquire land abandoned by poor Muslims fleeing from communal violence.[22] 'Hindus tend to raise their eyebrows at the assertion of equal status by a community they are used to looking down upon as their inferiors in the post-independence era', concluded a report on the Delhi riots in May 1987.[23]

Economic instability and communal riots were not entirely absent in the Nehru period but what marked out the post-Nehru period was the breakdown of the secular consensus moulded by Nehru. In the event, the leading ruling class party was apprehensive that its close identification with the minorities bore the risk of alienating many of their constituents. Indira Gandhi was quick to learn this lesson when she talked of a Hindu backlash against any further pampering of the minorities. For their part, Muslims had begun to drift away from the Congress in states like Kashmir, Uttar Pradesh (UP), Bihar and West Bengal. In Bihar and UP the Lok Dal carved out victories in the Muslim-dominated constituencies. This weakening of Congress support created a political vacuum which was exploited by the Muslim fundamentalist leadership to assert its primacy in the community. Capitalizing on the frequent riots and the discrimination against Muslims in employment, some communally-oriented Muslim organizations sought to broaden their support base by focusing on government failure to control violence and its ability to satisfy the fears of the minorities. Such fears helped the rise of Jamaat-i-Islami in Kashmir, the Itehadul Muslimeen in Hyderabad and several other bodies in northern India.

The future opposition to the Shah Bano judgement was compounded by the manner in which the verdict was framed. The previous judgements by Justice Krishna Iyer were structured in the framework of social justice; by contrast, Justice Chandrachud's judgement in the Shah Bano Case was located in the terrain of Muslim personal law. In fact, the judgement made repeated reference to Muslim personal law and Islam: 'undoubtedly, the Muslim husband enjoys the privilege of being able to discard his wife whenever he chooses to do so, for reasons good, bad or indifferent. Indeed, for no reason at all!'[24] As a result, the debate focused on the interpretation of Muslim law. This was not all. Chandrachud's critical comments on Muslim personal law were greatly resented by the ulama who condemned the judgement as an attempt to undermine the personal law of Muslims.[25] Behind the diatribe lurked the fear that if secular laws prevailed over religious laws, it would open the way for courts to modify the personal law which would weaken their stranglehold over the Muslim masses.

The Supreme Court judgement in the Shah Bano Case provided the custodians of minority identity a much needed opportunity to project their leadership and to emphasize the distinctive identity of the Muslim community. The controversy sparked off by the Shah Bano judgement injected life into Muslim organizations which were literally starved of action. For the first time after Partition, the political balance shifted in their favour as they were allowed to take the initiative in articulating the grievances of Muslims. Many of these organizations—the Muslim Majlis Mushawarat, the Muslim Personal Law Board, the Muslim League, the Jamaat-i-Islami, the Awami Action Committee and Jamait-ul-Ulema-i-Hind—widened their sphere of influence by mobilizing Muslim opinion against the Supreme Court judgement.

Spearheaded by the AIMPLB, the fundamentalists criticized the judgement as an assault on the Shariah. The principal argument put forward was that the Shariah made no provision for maintenance in the event of divorce. The written statement prepared by Syed Shahabuddin, editor of *Muslim India*, and submitted by the AIMPLB to the Supreme Court, argued that the Muslim personal law allowed a reasonable quantum of maintenance, though the period was limited to three months of *Iddat*.[26] 'The essence lies in that *Mata* has no connotation of recurrence as maintenance has.'[27] Thus, absolving the husband of all responsibilities towards his wife, the crusaders of Islam insisted that the divorced woman could claim maintenance from her paternal family rather than from her former husband.

Though a large number of Muslim organizations were involved in whipping up fundamentalist sentiments, the campaign failed to gain popular support in the first phase of the movement which focused on the issues of maintenance rights for women. The movement gained momentum towards the end of 1985 when the focus of the debate was shifted from the relatively minor issues of maintenance rights for women to the much larger issue of the status of the Muslim minority and its right to exist as a religious community in a secular society.

A crucial issue was how the judgement should be linked to the Islamic framework. For the ulama there was no ambiguity around the fact that the acceptance of the provisions of the CrPC would affect the practice of Islam. For the politicians, however, the crucial issue was how the practice of Islam could be linked to the assumption of community. As the leadership in this movement was dominated by conservative leaders, the relationship between Islamic identity and community was articulated in an essentially religious discourse. A joint statement of six Muslim organizations fused the religious and political link by expressing the fear that 'forces inimical to the Muslim community shall use this judgement as the thin end of the wedge for securing the extinction of the Muslim personal law and its substitution by a common civil code'.[28] Thus in the second phase of the campaign community identity took on a reality which was expressed in an idiom drawing heavily on religious symbols. This process of community definition had important political repercussions. In April 1985, G.M. Banatwala, a Muslim League member from Kerala, introduced a private bill in parliament to ensure the continuance of the regime of Personal Law:[29] 'The talk of the uniform civil code is an attack on the traditional spirit of tolerance and secular ideals!'[30] Minatullah Rehmani, secretary of the AIMPLB, explicitly demanded that the government should nullify the judgement by reiterating its commitment to uphold the Muslim personal law. Echoing Rajiv Gandhi's discourses on national integration and secularism, Rehmani argued that 'national integration and secularism would be strengthened when every religious denomination feels religiously secure and satisfied'.[31] The AIMPLB warned the government that 'it would be unwise and against the interests of national unity to arouse fears and apprehensions and to create a sense of religious insecurity'.[32]

From city streets and mosques, the maulvis and communal-minded politicians focused on the fear that the Supreme Court verdict was 'a death warrant of Muslim identity in Hindu India'.[33] Sidetracking the issue of Muslim women's rights, the movement concentrated attention on the imperative need to protect the Muslim personal law. Muslim organizations in UP, Bihar, Kashmir, Andhra Pradesh, and Kerala were pressed into service by the clergy and conservative leaders to rouse Muslim masses against what they dubbed as 'interference in the Muslim personal law'.[34] 'Muslim personal law is in danger' and 'Shariah is our religious right, we will die to protect it', were some of the slogans that helped to mobilize Muslims at numerous public meetings held in the course of the Shariah week launched in October 1985.[35] The campaign culminated in the observation of the All India Shariah Day, which was marked by street corner meetings and demonstrations to condemn the Supreme Court's trespass into a field which was believed to be out of bounds for it. Syed Shahabuddin, a key figure in the campaign, gave expression to the common perception that the judgement had inflamed Muslim passions because the Supreme Court had called for a common civil code mentioned in Article 14 and had thus 'arrogated to itself the function of the legislature'.[36]

One of the most striking aspects of the movement was the unity displayed by the principal protagonists of religious identity, who were otherwise opposed to each other on fundamental doctrinal matters.[37] These were the Jamaat-i-Islami, founded in 1941 by Abul Ala Mawdudidi to create a state and society based upon Islamic identity; the Jamait-ul-Ulema connected with the Dar-al-Uloom at Deoband and the AIMPLB, established in 1974. The basic aim of these groups after independence has been to oppose any change in the personal law arguing that it would be only 'the first step in the direction of erasing any symbol of a separate Muslim culture in India'.[38] The symbolic focus on Muslim personal law provided the public setting in which it became necessary to underplay the differences in doctrine in order to safeguard personal law, the only permanent guarantee for the preservation of Muslim identity. Moreover, though the perceptions of the significant issues concerning the status of the minority were not identical, they did overlap insofar as keeping intact the sanctity of the law was concerned.[39] Regional and class divisions were underplayed because the ulama, the members of the AIMPLB, and the leaders of the Muslim League came from different regions to participate in actions in defence of issues concerning the supposed Islamic identity. Perceptions came to be expressed by a shared vocabulary emphasizing symbols of Shariah and Muslim personal law as the emblem of Muslim identity.

There is no doubt that many urban based Muslim groups were apprehensive that the verdict on the Shah Bano Case violated the basic canons of Islam, a fear reinforced by the AIMPLB agitation which stirred emotions by an obfuscation of the central issue of women's rights and instead an emphasis on minority rights. This process of transfer and displacement profoundly affected the political discourse, because it raised misgivings regarding minority status and minority space in a secular society. The discourse of maintenance moved out from the law courts to the public setting, where questions were raised about the future of the Muslim personal law.[40]

The emphasis on identity was further reinforced by the enthusiastic support extended by Hindu organizations to the Shah Bano judgement. In the minds of many Muslims, this scenario created the fear that a change of personal law was being demanded by the detractors of the community. Both the petition by Shahnaz Sheikh, a Muslim woman from Bombay, challenging the validity of the Muslim Personal Law under Article 14 and the Shah Bano judgement were interpreted by vested interests as an attempt by the Indian state to impose a uniform civil code.[41] To counter such an interventionary threat, the cry of 'Islam in danger' was raised from within the community to mobilize Muslims against 'outside protection' of Muslim women.

Reaction and Government Response

Amidst growing controversies, the Indian government decided to seize the initiative. Its intervention was based on the assumption that most Muslims resented the Supreme Court verdict, viewing it as a threat to their religious identity. However, the Muslim community was divided on the issue. Large numbers of Muslims saw no conflict between the Supreme Court verdict and the Islamic principles. More significantly, large numbers of Muslim women were unaffected by the fundamentalist tide. Many of them supported the demand for maintenance rights provided under the CrPC.[42] Initially, many women were no doubt unaware of the maintenance issue, but the strong opposition against the Supreme Court judgement made them conscious of the issues involved in the debate. Muslim women's groups in Kerala, West Bengal, Bombay, and Delhi reaffirmed the right of an indigent woman to be supported by her husband, and derided the mullahs for turning religion into an instrument of injustice.

Muslim women in Calcutta, Trivandrum, Patna and Bombay condemned the AIMPLB call for a bandh to mark the Shariat Day on 4 October 1985.[43] The formation of the Committee for the Protection of the Rights of Muslim Women in Calcutta, Trivandrum, and Delhi gave organized expression to such sentiments. The committee organized public meetings and conventions in different parts of the country to highlight the issue of women's rights, submitted memoranda to the prime minister 'emphasizing the need to protect all sections of the minorities, particularly women'.[44] Its chief concern was to safeguard the rights guaranteed by the Indian Constitution. An important part of the committee's efforts was to locate Muslim women within the social domain and in the context of the community of women. It was pointed out that though laws relating to marriage and divorce form part of the civil law, maintenance was included in criminal law to prevent a divorced woman from becoming a destitute. Moreover, Section 125 of the CrPC was a mild provision. Under it a magistrate can ask a husband to provide up to Rs. 500 a month for maintenance of his wife, provided the husband has sufficient means and the wife is unable to maintain herself. What was lost in the heat of the controversy was the fact that Section 125 of the CrPC did not pertain to personal law but to vagrancy and the prevention of destitution.

The stirrings of protest by Muslim women were reinforced by the voice of dissent from within the Muslim intelligentsia. Important sections of enlightened and liberal Muslim opinion, drawn from the educated and professional classes, signed a memorandum demanding the preservation of the right of a divorced Muslim woman to claim maintenance from her former husband.[45] The list of signatories included several academicians, writers, journalists, bureaucrats, poets, painters, and theatre and film personalities. Likewise distinguished experts in Shariah laws like M.H. Beg, Murtuza Fazal Ali, Beharul Islam, S.A. Masifd, Danial Latifi and A.G. Noorani defended the rights of Muslim women. Justice M.H. Beg, chairman of the Minorities Commission, stated that granting maintenance to Muslim women under Section 125 of the CrPC 'did not interfere in any way with the Muslim Personal Law'. He also argued that those who say anything to the contrary 'neither know the Koran, nor the Muslim personal Law nor equality nor justice, nor the obligation of the Indian citizen under the constitution'.[46] Asghar Ali Engineer, a Bombay-based activist for social reforms, summed up the case of those who favoured change: 'giving more than what is stipulated by the jurists is no violation of the Shariah or the injunctions of the Quran'.[47]

Such forceful articulations refuted the claims of Muslim leaders that the community was unanimously opposed to the Supreme Court verdict in favour of maintenance. It also showed that the sentiments and feelings aroused by the fundamentalist movement were not uniform or purely religious; they were contingent on the social circumstances of the community and were very greatly inspired by the fundamentalist movement. What started as an expression of Muslim feelings and misgivings acquired the shape of significant sentiments only as a result of the intervention of specific political processes and developments in the political arena.

To begin with, the Congress party and the government welcomed the Supreme Court verdict granting maintenance to Muslim women. Arif Mohammed Khan, the then Minister Home in Union Cabinet said so and he had the backing of the overwhelming majority of the members of parliament, including the prime minister who congratulated him for his 'excellent speech' denouncing the Banatwala Bill in parliament.[48] However, the defeat of the Congress party in the by-elections in December 1985 led the government to execute a *volte face*. Fearful of further electoral reverses, the government initiated several moves to assuage Muslim feelings. Members of the AIMPLB were summoned to Delhi for consultation. Ali Mian, the alim of the Lucknow Seminary, Nadvatal-Ulma, as assidously cultivated, while the prime minister found time to attend the All-Muslim conference and to assure his audience that the Muslim personal law would not be modified or altered.[49] As such in May 1986 the Muslim Women (Protection of Rights on Divorce) Bill, 1985 was introduced in parliament.

The Bill condemned Muslim women to the status of second class citizens by denying them the option to avail of Section 125 of the CrPC. It incorporated the arguments of the AIMPLB and the Muslim League that a woman's natal family should maintain her after her divorce and not the husband as she has ceased to be his wife. It provided that the inheritors of her property would be responsible for her maintenance in accordance with the property to be inherited, without fixing the amount of property to be inherited by the divorced woman. Significant provisions of the bill introduced in parliament included:

Where a Muslim divorced woman is unable to maintain herself after the period of *iddat*, the magistrate, when approached may make an order for the payment of maintenance by her relatives who would be entitled to inherit her property on her death according to Muslim Law in Proportions in which they would inherit her property.

If any of such relatives is unable to pay her or her share on the ground of his or her not having the means to pay the shares of these relatives also.

But where a divorced woman has no relatives or any one of them has not enough means to pay the maintenance or the other relatives who have been asked to pay the shares of the defaulting relatives, the magistrate would order the State Wakf Board to pay the maintenance ordered by him on the shares of the relatives who are unable to pay.

The Muslim Women Bill was widely criticized. Even those Muslims who were dissatisfied with the Supreme Court judgement disapproved. A significant section of Muslims were of the view that a woman should have the option to be governed by their personal law or by the provisions of the civil code on maintenance. The right to maintenance was in consonance with the prevailing family laws in a number of Muslim countries which had modernized family laws. For example, the right to maintenance was available to women in Morocco, Turkey, Iraq, Egypt, Libya, Tunisia, Syria, and Algeria. In sharp contrast, Indian Muslim women were forced to depend on relatives and Wakf Boards for support. However it was also well known that the majority of Boards in UP and Bihar were either financially bankrupt or under the control of vested interests reluctant to provide maintenance to divorced women. As for the responsibility of the natal family, the provisions of the bill would give rise to tensions between a woman and her own family in case she was forced to go to court to avail of her maintenance from them. The most contentious aspect of the legislation was the transfer of the concept of maintenance from the purview of criminal and civil law to the domain of personal law. As a result, Muslim women were removed from the social domain and relocated in the domain of the family where personal law would be given primacy over their rights as citizens.

Women's organizations intervened to highlight gender identity and to safeguard the rights of women, whose identity often gets subsumed in the larger issue of community identity. Besides restoring the focus on women, their intervention exposed the subordinate and unequal position of women within the family, i.e. personal laws and in the public realm (for example, Section 125 of the CrPC), that women cannot avail because they supposedly threaten community identity.

Among the leading organizations involved in mobilizing public opinion were the All India Democratic Women's Association (AIDWA), the National Federation of Indian Women, and the Mahila Dakshata Samiti. Street corner meetings, protest marches, and signature campaigns were organized to oppose the exclusion of Muslim women from the purview of the CrPC. The AIDWA submitted 1,000,000 signatures, including those of 200,000 Muslim women, to the prime minister urging the government not to appease fundamentalists.[50] The AIDWA also organized a rally of women drawn equally from the poor and middle strata from different parts of the country. Yet the government refused to recognize strength of Muslim opposition to the bill. Instead, the sensitivity of the minority community to any form of change in the Muslim personal law was assumed. No attempt was made to reconcile the conflicting claims of minority identity and women's rights.

Government Motivations and Justifications

It is significant to question why the government surrendered to fundamentalist pressures. The most important consideration was the need to stem the anger over the Shah Bano verdict, which was losing the Congress its Muslim votes. Following the Congress defeat in the by-elections in Assam, Bijnor, Kishanganj, Bolapur, Kedrappa, and Baroda, and the belief that everywhere Muslim vote had tipped the balance in favour of the opposition parties, important Congress leaders advised the prime minister against the dangers of a confrontation with the fundamentalists. Syed Shahabuddin's victory in a by-election was a sharp reminder that Congress would suffer electoral reverses in other constituencies as well unless it regained Muslim support.[51] The decision to table the Muslim Women Bill was part of the strategy to reverse the rising tide against the Congress party's efforts to woo the Muslims. The intervention in favour of the fundamentalists was a desperate bid to regain the Muslim constituency.[52]

An important development that influenced the course of the political movement was the decision to concede the demand of the Hindu organizations to open the Babri Masjid mosque-Ram Janmabhoomi. In fact the decision to enact the Muslim Women Bill was a sequel to the communal pressures mounted by Hindu organizations agitating for this reopening in Ayodhya. The temple was opened to devotees amidst much fanfare on 1 February 1986. The opening of the temple was a coup masterminded by political authorities to appease and conciliate the Vishwa Hindu Parishad and Ram Janmabhoomi Mukti Samiti, who had organized a powerful movement to pressurize Rajiv Gandhi to accommodate Hindu sentiments. The strategy employed by these organizations was blatantly communal: 'How can Rajiv Gandhi ignore the Hindu vote bank which gave him such a massive majority at the polls, far exceeding the votes polled by his grandfather', asked the Hindu leaders?[53] Muslim leaders from other side of the communal spectrum threatened to boycott the Congress if the Babri Masjid was not restored to Muslims.

The Muslim Women Bill was an effort to pacify ruffled Muslim sentiments and the conservative objections over the reopening of the disputed Babri Masjid and the Supreme Court verdict.[54] In this way the Indian state performed a balancing act of accommodating and according protection to all religions and religious sentiments under the umbrella of multi-theocratic pluralism and an ideology of secularism that encourages and protects all religions.

It is noteworthy that the enactment of the Muslim Women Bill conferred legitimacy on the AIMPLB and the mullahs as the 'sole spokesman' of the Muslim community. The government scorned progressive opinion raised against the bill and refused to withdraw it on the dubious plea that it was framed in deference to the wishes of most Muslims. In actual fact, only conservative Muslim groups were consulted and they were passed off as the representative opinion of the community. 'All one can say at present', declared an angry Danial Latifi, a Supreme Court lawyer and an activist of the Committee for the Protection of the Rights of Muslim Women is that some Machiavelli seems to have masterminded this entire operation. That mastermind is not a friend of Islam, of the Muslims or the Republic of India. The act that preceded the bill, of the recognition of the so-called AIMPLB as the college of cardinals of Indian Muslims, is not only against Islam, but is also the most flagrant exercise of the power drunk bureaucracy.[55] Within the government, Arif Mohammed Khan raised the banner of revolt. He resigned from the union cabinet in protest against the government. His grudge was that the government had given credence to the views of only the conservatives and ignored the secular and progressive opinion in the community.

The political considerations behind the Congress strategy were revealed in the course of the debate on the bill in the Lok Sabha. A.K. Sen, Union Law Minister, defended the introduction of the new legislation by stating that it was 'the consistent policy of the government that in matters pertaining to a community priority would be given to the leaders of the community'.[56] This recognition of the so-called Muslim leadership meant that the government had no choice but to disregard the view of so many Muslim groups who had expressed their opposition to the bill.[57] A symbolic expression of their protest was highlighted on 5 May 1986, when a number of Muslim women, along with other members and supporters of the AIDWA, chained themselves to the gates of parliament to protest against the passage of the bill in Lok Sabha.[58] A fortnight earlier, a convention organized by the Committee for the Protection of Rights of Women emphatically castigated the bill as 'retrograde measure undermining the constitutional guarantees against discrimination on grounds of religion and gender'.[59]

The Congress party insisted that government was constrained to introduce the bill, because Section 125 of the CrPC was perceived by Muslims as an interference in their personal law:[60] 'We have to tread very carefully for Muslim personal law is linked to the Muslim religion in the minds of most Muslims. We might have our views, but we cannot deny the perception of the Muslims', observed government spokesman.[61] In a similar vein, Arun Nehru, former Home Minister and a confidante of Rajiv Gandhi during the period, reasoned: 'If the majority of Muslims feel that the bill is in their interest we cannot impose our views on them'.[62] This argument assumed that Muslims constituted a self-contained and monolithic community, whose interests were represented by the Muslim MPs and a section of the ulama.

The most pernicious aspect of the controversy was the attempt by the government to defend the AIMPLB sponsored bill (which would clearly debilitate and deprive the Muslim community) and lament the absence of reformist tendencies against Muslims at the same time. Contrasting the importance of reform amongst Hindus and Muslims, Shiv Shankar, Minister of Commerce, said: 'I gave the example of various laws with reference to the Hindu Code Bill . . . that at that time Hindu community was prepared to accept the law. Whatever we might say here, outside the situation is that [Muslim] people are not prepared to accept this!'[63] The social logic was unfolded more explicitly by K.C. Pant, Minister of Steel and Mines:

We cannot depend only on the law for reforms. Society has to be ready for reform. The well-springs of that reform have to come from within and then the laws that have been aroused by a certain movement, they coincide and then the society moves forward. . . . In Hindu society this process has been going on for decades. It had begun a hundred years ago. As a result of that and the efforts of so many tall leaders of this country the Hindu society has been able to regenerate itself.[64]

These arguments are significant because they exposed the contradictions of Congress-style secularism, which in effect, stifled reform in the name of 'protecting' minority interests. It served an even more important function in the complex structure of Congress politics. The responsibility of the Muslim Women Bill was transferred to the Muslim fundamentalists. When the bill was introduced on 27 February 1986 the prime minister defended it on the ground that Section 125 of the CrPC did not provide adequate protection to women and that the proposed bill 'would give her much more than was available under Sections 125 and 127 of the CrPC'.[65]

By May 1986, the government jettisoned this position in favour of the less harmful way of pandering to communalism by arguing that the bill was brought in deference to the wishes of the Muslim community. The massive outcry against the bill forced the Congress to rework its defence by shifting the blame onto the Muslims. 'Indeed, it would not be an exaggeration to say that on no issue since the imposition of the internal emergency in June 1975 has there been a greater measure of agreement among educated Indians than on this. It is inconcievable that Rajiv Gandhi and his advisors have not been aware of this reaction', opined Girilal Jain, the influential editor of *The Times of India*. Indeed, they were fully aware of the political repercussions of appeasing Muslim fundamentalism. Consequently, the ruling party tried to wash its hands of the bill by taking recourse to the theory that Muslims perceived the Supreme Court verdict as a threat to their religious identity. This theory enabled the Congress leaders to delink the party from fundamentalist Muslims by giving the impression that 'the government was not really in tune with the provisions of the bill but had no choice in the matter because the perception of Muslims was very different'.[66]

The subtle shifts in emphasis could not alter the fact that government was anxious to mollify the fundamentalists. This is most strikingly revealed in the haste with which the legislation was enacted. The opinion of the law ministry was ignored. The legal adviser to the law ministry had categorically stated that the Supreme Court had correctly interpreted the law. The law secretary's advice was even more emphatic: the bill to amend Sections 125 and 127 of the CrPC should be opposed.[67] Assurances given by the prime minister of holding wide-ranging consultations were not honoured. Equally, the promise to bring out a background paper on Muslim Personal Law was not fulfilled.[68] The pleading of the opposition parties not to hustle through the bill was ignored. What is worse, the groundswell of opposition within the ruling party was stifled by a government whip in parliament.

Conclusion

It is undeniable that the government erred in accepting the demand for a legislation of questionable constitutionality, and one which discriminated against Muslim women in relation to other women. Moreover, the bill revealed a major flaw in the pluralist theory of secularism, which functions, in practice, as multi-theocratic secularism or state protection of all religions and priority of religious sentiment over all other considerations. Finally, it is unfruitful to interpret the events connected with the enactment of the Muslim Women Bill as a simple expression of so-called Muslim feelings. Many Muslims supported the ulama's interpretation of the situation but many others did not, because their understanding of the situation did not conflict with their interests or understanding of cultural identity.

Therefore, events discussed in this chapter suggest that there was no cohesive articulation of a Muslim identity; in fact, the construction of Muslim identity has remained, as always, a product of specific political processes. An explanation of the success of certain movements in articulating a minority identity should therefore take into account the changes in the political arena, where greater attention is being given to the accommodation of the 'Hindu interests' to be counterbalanced by recognizing the religio-cultural identity of the minorities.

Notes and References

1. For a discussion of the role of socio-political factors in the formation of identity, see Peter Van der Deer, 'God Must be Liberated: A Hindu Liberation Movement in Ayodhya', *Modern Asian Studies,* April 1987; Sandria Frietag, 'Sacred Symbol as a Mobilising Ideology: The North Indian Search for a Hindu Community', *Comparative Studies in History and Society,* no. 22, 1980; Sandria Frietag, 'Ambiguous Public Arenas and Coherent Personal Practice: Kanpur Muslims 1913-1931', in *Shariat and Ambiguity in South Asian Islam,* ed. Catherine Ening, Delhi: Oxford University Press, 1988.

2. On this aspect see Chris Bayly, 'Pre-History of Communalism', *Modern Asian Studies,* no. 19, 1985; Talal Asad, 'Anthropological Conceptions of Religion: Reflections on Geertz', *Man,* no. 18, 1983; Paul Brass, 'Introduction', *Language, Religion and Politics in North India,* Cambridge: Cambridge University Press, 1974.

3. For details see C.J. Chandrachud, 'The Judgement', *The Shah Bano Controversy,* ed. Asghar Ali Engineer, New Delhi: Orient Longman, 1987.

4. The judgement also stated that according to its interpretation of the law, dowry is not the amount payable on divorce, but the money fixed on consideration of marriage and endorsed in the marriage document. Ibid., p. 31.

5. Ibid., p. 1.

6. *Muslim India*, May 1985.

7. Shahida Lateef, *The Status and Role of Women in Minority Community: The Case of Muslims in India*, Research Project, Indian Council of Social Science Research, New Delhi: unpublished, 1978, pp. 84–5.

8. 'It is significant that despite centuries of Muslim rule the Muslim community did not accept the Shariah as the basis of law. Women's rights in the Shariat were almost never compiled with or enforced, and even their right to divorce and widow remarriage suffered' notes Lateef, *Status and Role of Women*.

9. Ibid., pp. 84–5.

10. The basis of these enactments was the open approach adopted by Turkey and Egypt, which amalgamated the different schools of jurisprudence to introduce laws that favoured women.

11. On this point see Indira Jai Singh, 'Politics of Personal Law', *The Lawyers Collective*, February 1986.

12. Gail Minault, *The Khilafat Movement: Religious Symbolism and Political Mobilisation*, Delhi: Oxford University Press, 1982.

13. Imtiaz Ahmad, 'Introduction', *Modernisation and Social Change among Muslims in India*, Delhi: Manohar, 1983.

14. Maxine Rodinson, *Marxism and the Muslim World*, Delhi: Orient Longman, 1980, p. 152.

15. Chandrachud, 'The Judgement', pp. 25–6.

16. Ibid., p. 28.

17. *Indian Express*, 15 March 1986.

18. Mushirul Hasan, 'Indian Muslims since Independence: In Search of Integration and Identity', *Third World Quarterly*, April 1988, p. 830. This figure of 4,000 is almost four times that of the 1970s.

19. Ibid., p. 830.

20. Rasheeduddin Khan, 'Minority Segments in Indian Polity: Muslim Situation and the Plight of Urdu', *Economic and Political Weekly*, 2 September 1978, pp. 1514–15.

21. Mushirul Hasan, 'Indian Muslims since Independence', pp. 833–4.

22. People's Union for Democratic Rights, *Walled City Riots: A Report on the Police and Communal Violence in Delhi*, 19-24 May 1987, Delhi, p. 1.

23. 'Judgement', p. 23.

24. Ibid., see first paragraph of the judgement.

25. *Muslim India*, June 1985.

26. Ibid.

27. Ibid., May 1985, p. 195.

28. The Bill introduced by G.M. Banatwala sought to modify Article 44 of the Constitution to exempt Muslims from its purview. This was aimed against the advice contained in the judgement that government should facilitate a uniform civil code.

29. G.M. Banatwala statement in parliament, *Muslim India*, May 1985, p. 202.

30. *Indian Express*, 7 October 1985.

31. *The Statesman*, 27 October 1985.
32. *The Telegraph*, 8 March 1986.
33. *Indian Express*, 15 November 1985.
34. The outcry caused by the Supreme Court judgement and the concerted pressure mounted by the Muslim Personal Law lobby forced Shah Bano to issue a statement that the verdict be withdrawn. The retraction made seven months after the verdict was the consequence of the sustained pressure of the fundamentalists combined with the threat of social ostracism. *The Telegraph*, 22 November 1985.
35. Shahabuddin claimed that the judgement had 'injured Muslim feelings because the Supreme Court had tried to interpret the Holy Koran and in doing so had usurped the role of a social reformer and violated the basic rules of the Shariat. *The Statesman*, 1 October 1985.
36. See M.S. Agwani, *Islamic Fundamentalism in India*, Chandigarh: Twenty-First Century India Society, 1986.
37. Jamait-i-Islami statement quoted in Brass, *Language, Religion and Politics*, p. 220.
38. An AIMPLB was set up in December 1974 to monitor and resist any changes that might be brought about in the Shariat.
39. An analysis of the many discourses—legal, religious, political and feminist—that Shah Bano was drawn into and the process of discursive displacement that directly affects the formation of female identity is discussed by Z. Pathak and R. Sunderrajan in a paper on Shah Bano presented at the Indian Association for Womens Studies, Third National Conference, Chandigarh, December 1986.
40. The Urdu press, Muslim League, Jamait-i-Islami and the AIMPLB interpreted the two events as part of an attempt to impose a uniform civil code.
41. This assessment is based on the experience of women's organizations engaged in mobilizing Muslim women on the issue. It was evident from the enthusiastic participation of Muslim women from all classes in the public meetings, rallies, and signature campaigns organized in the course of the debate on Shah Bano issue.
42. *The Telegraph*, 3 October 1985.
43. 'Memorandums by Committee for Protection of Rights of Muslim Women' submitted to the prime minister on 24 February and 1 March 1986, *Mainstream*, 8 March 1986.
44. 'Stir within Muslim intelligentsia', *Mainstream*, 8 March 1988.
45. *The Statesman*, 27 April 1985.
46. *The Telegraph*, 1 September 1985.
47. At first the prime minister encouraged Arif Mohammad Khan to openly support the judgement and to denounce the mullahs who were trying to whip up agitation on the issue. A few weeks later Rajiv Gandhi allowed another minister, Zia-ur-Rehman Ansari, to speak out in defence of mullahs. *The Times of India*, 14 May 1986.
48. *The Telegraph*, 4 December 1985. The prime minister went a step further, he stated that the government was not averse to reviewing any law which came in conflict with the personal law of any religious group.
49. 'Annexure A, letter to the prime minister submitted by six womens organizations'. New Delhi, 1986.
50. Shahabuddin was elected from Kishan Ganj in Bihar. His tireless campaign against the Shah Bano verdict generated considerable support for him. From the very outset the campaign had acquired fundamentalist overtones as his

Congress rival was the secretary of the Jamait-ul-Ulema and a member of the Deoband School. However, in spite of such impeccable credentials the Congress candidate was defeated by a wide margin. The Kishan Ganj verdict strengthened the fundamentalist lobby clamouring for an amendment of Section 125 of the Criminal Procedure Code to exclude Muslims from its purview. The price that the leaders of the anti-Shah Bano agitation and the 'representatives' of the Muslim community demanded was a bill in parliament to negate the verdict and thus fortify the Muslim Personal Law from encroachment by the courts.

51. For an analysis of the sequence of developments leading to the decision to bring in the Muslim Women Bill, see Neerja Chowdhary, 'The Political Fallout', *The Statesman*, 18-20 April 1986 and 'Muslim Women Bill: A Trail of Errors', *The Statesman*, 28 April 1986.

52. *The Statesman*, 20 April 1986.

53. Ibid., 28 April 1986.

54. *Sunday*, 8-14 June 1986.

55. *The Telegraph*, 15 May 1988.

56. *The Times of India*, 28 December 1985. This recognition was implicit in the government decision to prepare the legislation in consultation with the ulama and AIMPLB.

57. Ibid.

58. *The Telegraph*, 27 April 1986.

59. Gautam, *Social Scientist*, June 1986.

60. *The Telegraph*, 15 May 1988.

61. Ibid.

62. Ibid.

63. Ibid.

64. Ibid., 28 February 1986.

65. *The Times of India*, 14 May 1986.

66. Ibid., 4 March 1986.

67. Ibid.

PART IV

Bridging the Social and Political Divide

18 | The Congress in a District, 1930–46
Problems of Political Mobilization

THE UNITED PROVINCES (UP) was the centre of nationalist activities in the 1920s and 1930s. Yet the provincial and local base of the Indian National Congress, especially in the western parts, has not been adequately investigated. This chapter seeks to fill in the lacunae by concentrating on the nature and character of the Congress movement in the Aligarh district during a crucial phase of nationalist activity: 1930–46. These years witnessed the unfolding of important political processes which influenced developments in UP at large. In a sense, Aligarh represented the very many strands which went into the making of nationalist politics in UP in particular, and the country in general. Politics in this district brought into sharp focus the problems of political mobilization as well as the interplay of communal forces which had a profound impact on the regions' social and political life.

Nationalist activity in Aligarh was sporadic and fragmented until the Rowlatt Satyagraha and the Khilafat and Non-Cooperation movements when the Congress gained a foothold in the area by mobilizing large segments of the population. Largely attended meetings, demonstrations and a massive procession of 20,000 headed by the Home Rule League were held, in connection with the Rowlatt Satyagraha. These were attended by both Hindus and Muslims, and their leaders jointly addressed meetings from common platforms in support of the satyagraha.[1] Inspired by the pan-Islamic fervour and by the charisma of Gandhi's personality, a fairly large number of students left the Muhammedan Anglo-Oriental (MAO) College in response to the Mahatma's call to boycott government aided educational

* I am grateful to Mushirul Hasan for the suggestions on an earlier draft which made this chapter much more intelligible.

institutions.[2] An otherwise respectable educational institution, the MAO College was thus turned into a vital centre of radical and nationalist activities.

Yet the response to non-cooperation outside the Muslim circles was limited—a fact which disproves the notion of the all embracing character of the movement. Only nine persons resigned their government jobs, three gave up their magistracy, and a mere twenty activists went to gaol.[3] Many of them were city Muslims associated with Khilafat Committees. In the early 1930s, however, the Congress was able to extend its base of support in the district. Its membership increased considerably, the District Congress Committee (DCC) was reactivated, and more importantly, large sections of the rural population rallied round the Congress banner. The sudden burst of nationalist activity during the Civil Disobedience movement, in particular, afforded local leaders an opportunity to play an important part in the provincial and the national arena and brought the district into the forefront of nationalist politics.

This chapter attempts to explore the cause of this transformation and to examine the nature of the Congress movement in Aligarh, whilst also bringing into sharp focus another dimension of Aligarh politics. This relates to the communal tangle which impeded the growth of the Congress and, in the 1940s, led to the emergence of the Muslim League as a powerful political force in the district. Attention is focussed briefly on the Aligarh Muslim University which became the focal point of both nationalist and separatist activity in various phases of the national movement.

In order to understand some of these political processes, it is necessary to set out the communal and caste composition and the landownership structure in the Aligarh district. In 1931 Aligarh's population was 1.3 million. Of these Muslims formed 12 per cent,[4] with a substantial concentration of their population in the Atrauli and Koil *tahsils*. Here they were also among the leading landowners. In Atrauli they were drawn entirely from Pathan Sherwani families, while in Koil they were mainly Rajput Muslims.[5] The Hindus were drawn from 18 castes, the most numerous being the Scheduled Castes who, in 1931, formed 16.05 per cent of the population. Concentrated in the *tahsils* of Koil and Hathras, the Jatavs, a Scheduled Caste, worked mostly as labourers and tenants on small patches of land. Many of them were tanners by tradition and did considerable business in leather and hides.[6] Next to them, Brahmans, Jats, Thakurs and Banias accounted for nearly one quarter of the population in 1931.[7] Of these, the Brahmans and Baraseni Banias[8] played an active role in the social and political life of the district, and were an economically powerful group.

Although the upper castes were a mere 26.6 per cent of the population, they owned and cultivated 70 per cent of the land[9] (Table 18.1). Thakurs,

TABLE 18.1: Percentage of Caste/Community and Area held in Aligarh District

Caste/ Community	1882		1943	
	Per cent of Caste/ Community to Total Population	*Per cent of Area held by Caste/ Community to Total Area*	*Per cent of Caste/ Community to Total Population*	*Per cent of Area held by Caste/ Community to Total Area*
Thakurs	7.40	27.90	7.73	22.10
Jats	8.32	22.88	7.89	17.30
Brahmans	13.82	9.14	11.04	14.50
Banias	4.99	9.29	3.84	13.60
Muslims	—	—	13.20	15.70

Source: Settlement Report (SR), 1882 and 1943.

Jats and Brahmans were the three main proprietory castes, while Banias were almost entirely absentee landlords. None of the castes had overwhelming numbers in the district, though Thakurs and Jats were economically very powerful. Their influence was magnified by their numerical strength in some *tahsils*. The Jats, for instance, were primarily concentrated in Khair and Iglas, and the Thakurs in Sikandra Rao and Hathras.[10]

Aligarh was an important commercial and industrial centre. Compared to other UP districts, its industrial population—19.7 per cent—was much higher than western UP's average of 10 per cent.[11] In addition to the lock and metal works, cotton ginning and pressing factories, stimulated by the growing cotton trade, contributed to its overall economic growth. Aligarh and Hathras, whose growth was facilitated by the expansion of commercial activity and the development of railways and communication networks, were extremely important manufacturing and trading centres; in fact, Hathras was the most important entrepot for trade in western UP.[12]

Aligarh's agrarian economy was equally dynamic, with double cropping, cash cropping, and extensive irrigation networks contributing to the prosperity of the district.[13] Yet, not all sections of urban and rural society benefited from its prosperity, for much of the wealth was concentrated in the hands of big landlords, and Bania and Brahman traders and moneylenders. Most of the small landowners, tenants and unskilled workers, though better off than their counterparts in eastern UP, lived in depressed conditions.

Aligarh's agrarian structure was different from the typical peasant proprietor areas of Meerut and Muzaffarnagar, where the distinction between the self-cultivating owner and occupancy tenant had become blurred by the last quarter of the nineteenth century,[14] and the landlord-dominated districts of eastern and central UP—areas marked by sharp

TABLE 18.2: Percentage and Area Owned by Different Size Holdings

Size of holdings	Percentage of population to total population	Percentage of area to total area	Size of average holding
Marginal 0–3 acre	56.93	16.89	1.26
Small 3–5 acre	16.15	15.44	4.07
Medium 5–10 acre	17.39	28.67	7.02
Rich 10–20 acre	7.56	23.97	13.50
Large 20–above	1.97	15.02	32.45

Source: Uttar Pradesh Zamindari Abolition Committee (UPZAC), vol. II, 1948, pp. 34–9.

landlord–tenant polarization. In many respects, its agrarian structure was similar to that of the neighbouring districts of Agra, Bulandshahr, Etah, and Mainpuri areas[15] dotted with big landowners, rich peasants and pattidars (Table 18.2).

Most of the land in Aligarh district was owned by large or small landowners: 2.2 per cent of zamindars paid as much as 62 per cent of the revenue demand, while the remaining landowners paid just over 38.6 per cent. A total of 23 estates, paying an annual revenue of Rs. 10,000, met 19 per cent of the demand.[16] Of these, most were located in Hathras, the richest *tahsil* in the district and the leading centre of Civil Disobedience activity in 1930–1. Here 270 *mahals* belonged to wealthy zamindars, Mursan as the largest, Awa, Lakhnau, Majhaula, Lalkhani, Mandir, Pahasu, Chattari, and Sadabad owned 10 or more *mahals*. This was also true of Sikandra Rao and Koil—areas that were also active during the civil disobedience. Apart from these large estates, there was also a sizeable number of rich and medium peasants. Rich peasants who formed 7.5 per cent of the cultivating population owned 24 per cent of the area while middle peasants who formed 17 per cent of the cultivators owned 28 per cent of the area.[17] Most tenants in the district held secure rights[18] and the domination of landlords was not so oppressive because the number of large estates was comparatively small. Non-occupancy tenants held a small part of the area.

In the early 1930s Aligarh was also affected by the overall spurt in political activity in UP. From 1930 and 1934 the Congress was able to enlist widespread support and establish an extensive political network in the district.[19] This was in part due to the new thrust of the party in reorienting its programme to suit the aggrieved sections in both urban and rural areas.

The revival of the Aligarh Congress in the early 1930s by Todar Singh and Malkhan Singh, combined with the decision of the UP Congress Committee (UPCC) to launch a no-tax campaign in October 1930, acted as a catalyst for working among the kisans and brought to the fore the organizational capabilities of men like Todar Singh, M.L. Gautam, Malkhan Singh, Tikam Singh, J.P. Jigyasu, Jagdamba Prasad, T.A.K. Sherwani, and A.M. Khwaja, many of whom later played a notable part in provincial and national politics. Equally vital was their ability to extend their influence in rural areas during the Civil Disobedience movement.

The Non-Cooperation movement had an essentially urban base, while Civil Disobedience, in contrast, embraced large sections of the rural population. This was largely due to a shift in Congress strategy of mass mobilization—a shift which stemmed from a recognition of the obvious: a prolonged agitation could only be sustained with the backing of the countryside. The objective basis for this shift was provided by the global depression, a fact noted by Jawaharlal Nehru who took the lead in advocating a radical approach to agrarian problems. The Civil Disobedience movement, he wrote:

happened to fit unknown to its own leaders at first with the great world slump in industry and agriculture. The rural masses were powerfully affected by the slump, and they turned to the Congress and civil disobedience. For them it was not a matter of a fine constitution drawn up in London or elsewhere, but of a basic change in the land system, especially in the zamindari areas.[20]

With the shift in the centre of activity to rural areas, village meetings, annual district political conferences, and kisan conferences assumed significance as vehicles of political mobilization and propaganda in the province. The celebration of Jawahar day, the observance of hartals against the arrest of important leaders such as Gandhi and Jawaharlal Nehru, the defiance in the act of salt-making, and the burning of the Simon Commission Report, were symptomatic of the building up of the nationalist fervour.

An extension programme of boycott was organized in Aligarh which included the burning of the Simon Report and a hartal in Koil and Hathras, followed by the salt satyagraha.[21] Thousands of people congregated in meetings and joined in enthusiastically in an effort to make salt and thereby defy the British authorities. According to the official Congress account, 177 persons were convicted for violating laws in support of the satyagraha. Most arrests took place in Hathras, Sikandra Rao, and Khair, which were fast becoming centres of Congress activity. Here the movement was built by the fervent and concerted efforts of Malkhan Singh, Jagdamba Prasad, and Gajadhar Singh. Their arrest in June 1930 led to protests and partial hartals, especially in Hathras. The extent of Congress influence in the area was further indicated by the hoisting of the Congress flag flying permanently on the municipal offices at Aligarh, Hathras, and Atrauli, and at the District Board Office in Aligarh. In contrast, there was no evidence of the Congress flag in most other districts of the Agra division.[22]

By mid-1930, however, this enthusiasm showed signs of petering out. There was increasing evidence of resistance to the boycott of foreign cloth, especially in the city, when Congress volunteers, in a bid to snuff out opposition, compelled a defiant shopkeeper to leave the city on account of his refusal not to sell foreign stocks.[23] In Sikandra Rao, Hindu merchants, emboldened by the brisk sale of foreign cloth among Muslims, resisted the Congress demand to seal their foreign stocks. In most areas Muslims were reluctant to join the boycott. This was equally true of the Baraseni wholesalers who were interested in capitalizing on the growth in the volume of Aligarh's cotton trade in order to undercut their Aggarwal rivals who had acquired great wealth by using locally produced cotton to establish ginning and pressing mills. T.A.K. Sherwani, a Congress stalwart, tried in vain to persuade his co-religionists to join the boycott. Instead, Muslim traders, merchants, and shopkeepers continued to resist picketing of their shops by Congress activists, and, on many occasions, demanded police protection.[24] Such stiff resistance compelled the district Congress to abandon the boycott campaign in the city, for its persistence would have inflamed communal passions. Interest and support thus having waned, the Congress turned their attention to rural areas in an attempt to salvage their reputation. There were many other reasons for them to do so.

The economic crisis in the early 1930s was one. The sudden drop in the prices of foodgrains, especially of cash crops, affected large sections of those dependent upon agricultural income. In Aligarh the price index fell from 221 to 117 in the slump period which led to an appreciable decrease in the area under wheat and cotton.[25] Reduced agricultural produce on account of poor rains also caused serious distress in the countryside.[26] This meant that the landlords and the *sahukars* were unable to collect rents and dues from the tenants, while the rich and middle peasants, connected to the market, became vulnerable to fluctuations in prices.[27] They were also the most heavily indebted group. The small zamindars and cultivating communities were heavily indebted; and the large amount of land transfers was a testimony to their indebtedness, observed H.R. Neville.[28] Nearly 30 per cent of the land passed into the hands of moneylenders, an indication of the declining fortunes of small zamindars.[29] Their perilous and insecure condition was also reflected in the rise in exproprietory tenancy which increased from 0.8 to 4.2 per cent of the area.[30]

Against the background of such developments, the Congress leaders tried to mobilize the peasantry in an attempt to build a broad based political movement. They laid stress on socio-political issues—the use of khaddar in preference to foreign cloth, removal of untouchability, boycott of liquor shops, swaraj and kisan unity—and their speeches described the iniquities of the British, and extolled the exemplary courage and fearlessness of Bhagat Singh and other revolutionaries in confronting the Raj. As a result, the news of Bhagat Singh's execution caused a popular outrage with thirteen meetings being held in a space of just a few weeks to condemn the execution.[31] Speakers at the Kisan Conference in 1931, extolled the sacrifices of Bhagat Singh for the sake of kisans.

Congress propaganda also focused on the economic distress of the cultivators. They were urged to support the Congress which was 'now the real force in the country capable of forcing the government to sanction their demands'[32] and the only guarantor against the excesses of the British regime. Rural meetings blamed the government for the pitiable conditions of Indian peasants and workers, and it was emphasized that although the government depended upon kisans, it was indifferent to their plight.[33] Cultivators were assured of Congress' help in ameliorating their grievances against the government as well as the zamindars. Furthermore, the campaign highlighted issues which concerned all kisans: the problem of land revenue, the demand for reduction in irrigation and canal rates, concessions, loans, and measures to end rural indebtedness. In consequence, the kisans in general, and the small zamindars and pattidars, in particular, rallied round the Congress in large numbers. Much of Congress' support in the early 1930s was thus drawn from the small zamindars, substantial peasants, pattidars among upper castes, and the cultivating caste of Jats.

Throughout the no-rent campaign much greater attention was concentrated in the landlord-dominated *tahsils* of Hathras, Sikandra Rao, Atrauli, and Koil where the anti-zamindar sentiment was strong. All these *tahsils* were marked by a proliferation of wealthy zamindars, many of whom were absentee landlords. Hathras, more than Sikandra Rao, was the heartland of the great zamindars of Aligarh as many of the big estates were located here. Landlords owned 416 out of 576 *mahals* in Sikandra Rao and the greater part of the Koil *tahsil* was owned by the large proprietors.[34] The noteworthy feature of all these *tahsils* was the high percentage of tenants and tenants-at-will. This was mainly due to widespread absentee landlordism.[35]

The Congress leaders exhorted both the zamindars and the tenants to withhold payments of revenue and enhanced rents. By the end of 1930, it went a step further by focusing on the no-rent issue. Malkhan Singh and Mohan Lal Gautam, two of the most enthusiastic and persistent no-rent campaigners, moved resolutions at the District Political Conference demanding remission of rent and other concessions to ameliorate the lot of the peasantry. K.D. Paliwal, the veteran Agra Socialist who assisted the local Congress in organizing the campaign, assured peasants that half of occupancy rents would be remitted, and that 'Congress struggles would usher in Swaraj which means Kisan raj when kisans will have the power to dismiss officials from thanedar to Governor.'[36] Such assurances had great impact on the high caste tenants in Hathras and Sikandra Rao, where Congress was able to channel their grievances against the zamindars in support of civil disobedience. The notable exception were Harijans in Hathras, who resented caste barriers and caste subordination at the hands of upper caste landowners, and showed greater interest in issues like temple entry and in programmes for their social upliftment.

Efforts to enlist the support of the tenantry, however, met with limited success. This had much to do with their secure position: they were better off than their counterparts in the eastern districts, and were well off even judging by the standards in western UP.[37] For this reason there was not much evidence of any resistance encountered by landlords in rent collection which was generally not difficult.[38] Moreover, powerful Muslim zamindars in Atrauli and Koil were able to secure the allegiance of their Muslim tenants.

The Congress encountered the opposition of Muslim zamindars, especially in Atrauli where they were dominant.[39] In Charra, which fell in the Bhikanpur estate of Nawab Muzamilullah Khan, the second-largest landlord in the district, the Nawab made no effort to conceal his distaste for Congress politics in the larger political realm as well as in his specific domain.[40] But this led to a highly-publicized Charra agitation with enthusiastic Congress volunteers hurling abuse at the Nawab for his collaboration with the British government.[41] The UP government's decision to appoint him as the Home Member in charge of Police was the last straw. This acted as a catalyst for a more sustained campaign against him which included a flurry of protest meetings, and picketing by Congress volunteers. Large numbers of volunteers collected and picketed in Charra to demonstrate their opposition to the Nawab. At the same time, attempts to intensify picketing ran into difficulty with local Muslims. Joined by their co-religionists in the city, they protested against Congress methods. When the situation got out of hand Malkhan Singh, the Congress 'dictator', sought the intervention of Jawaharlal Nehru. Eventually Sherwani was pressed into service to mediate and diffuse a potentially explosive situation.

The virtual absence of other groups among Muslims from Congress activities was described by district officials as 'the most important feature of the situation in Aligarh. . . .[42] Their absence from the local political scene was most noticeable at the Aligarh Muslim University which remained unaffected by the political ferment. The General Report on Public Instruction congratulated the University establishment on its 'control' over students, and noted with satisfaction that 'one of the gratifying features of what was in many respects a difficult year was the refusal of students to abandon their work and take part in political activities'.[43]

There were many reasons why this was so. The communal situation in the district had deteriorated rapidly from the mid-1920s, soon after the collapse of the Khilafat and Non-Cooperation movements. In 1926, the festival of Ramlila led to a communal fracas in Aligarh.[44] In 1931, there was another bloody riot in a chain of such events that took place in Kanpur, Banaras, Mirzapur, and Agra.[45]

Second, the Congress connections with the Arya Samaj and the Hindu Mahasabha alienated the Muslims. During the Civil Disobedience campaign Congress openly accepted the support organized by these groups. Both these organizations had gained considerable ground in Aligarh from the strong presence of Banias, 'the caste from which new sects such as the Arya Samaj have been chiefly recruited'.[46] Established in 1882 in the district, the Arya Samaj had grown rapidly at the turn of the twentieth century. It found vociferous support from the prosperous Baraseni Banias who were more numerous in Aligarh than in any other district in UP. The activities of the Arya Samaj were backed by commercial families of Banias and Brahmans.[47] Many Congress leaders had close connections with the Arya Samaj. It was at their instance that the Political Conference of Congress volunteers was organized in the Arya Samaj Temple in Hathras in 1934. Not surprisingly, most Muslims abstained and subsequent efforts made to persuade them to attend the District Political Conference proved unsuccessful. A few Muslims who sat through the proceedings complained about the overbearing presence of communal elements, and the use of sanskritized Hindi at the conference.[48] Such dependence upon sectional support through the use of Hindu religious symbols and Hindu organizations lent credibility to the popular Muslim perception of the Congress being a pro-Hindu organization.

Finally, the reaction of many Aligarh Muslims was also linked with the overall campaign launched by Mohamed Ali and the organizers of the All Parties Muslim Conference against the Civil Disobedience. Following his disillusionment with the Nehru Committee report, published in August 1928, Mohamed Ali stated in April 1930: 'We refuse to join Mr Gandhi, because his movement is not a movement for complete independence of India but of making the 70 million Muslims dependent on the Hindu Mahasabha'.[49] Symbolic of the collapse of the old alliance on which Gandhi had built the Non-Cooperation movement was Mohamed Ali's appeal to Muslims not to join the Civil Disobedience because its goal was 'Hindu raj'.

Such unmistakable opposition to Civil Disobedience placed the Congress leaders in a dilemma. Quickening the tempo of the agitation could potentially inflame communal passions, while abandoning it altogether was likely to widen the gulf that separated the Congress from many sections of the Muslim community. The dilemma was resolved by either minimizing political activity in areas prone to communal sensitivities or withdrawing from the scene altogether. In case of the Aligarh district, this was done at Atrauli, an area where opposition to the Civil Disobedience campaign was both intense and consistent.

The controversy generated by picketing in Charra in Atrauli provided a foretaste of things to come; it underlined the constraints involved in the Congress' attempt to extend its political base. For a while some Aligarh Congressmen pursued their struggle with the expectation of active backing from provincial leaders. But this was not easily forthcoming as the dominant section in the UP was not interested in the deepening agitations against the landlords, and was wary of conducting campaigns in areas sensitive to communal conflicts. The no–rent campaign therefore failed to make much headway in Aligarh district. The district officials gleefully recorded that 'the no rent campaign was not particularly successful in Aligarh'.[50] It was further reported:

One has only to drive through on road from Aligarh and via Ghaziabad to Meerut to realise this. The moment you enter Bulandshahr district until you leave it—you find volunteers sitting about, Congress offices in small villages, flags waving, children shouting slogans and so forth; whereas when you enter the Aligarh district on one side or the Meerut district on the other, these elements are practically absent.[51]

The official was right. There were few meetings held in Aligarh on the no-rent demand, and there was not much evidence of popular participation. The campaign was sustained by the persistence of some local Congress leaders, along with the 1,700 volunteers from the neighbouring districts of Bulandshahr and Agra where Congress had made enormous progress in the rural areas.[52] District officials attributed this to the inaction and complacence of their counterparts in Bulandshahr.[53]

The works of C.A. Bayly, Brennan, and Pandey indicate that the most important men of the Congress in Allahabad, Rohilkhand, Agra, and Rae Bareli districts throughout the 1920s and 1930s came from the ranks of the small zamindars and the upper tenants.[54] An analysis of Aligarh reveals a similar pattern. The only difference is that, unlike neighbouring Rohilkhand

TABLE 18.3: Satyagrahis Arrested

	Area-wise Breakdown of Arrests During Civil Disobedience
Hathras	63
Koil (Minus City)	60
Sikandra Rao	102
Aligarh City	46
Atrauli	11

Source: Compiled from information given in *Swatantra Sangram ke Sainik*, 1972.

or Allahabad where the Congress weilded considerable influence in district towns as well, the major support base in Aligarh was in the rural areas. This can be partially gauged from the pattern of arrests during the Civil Disobedience. Table 18.3 reveals that a large number of satyagrahis came from Hathras, Sikandra Rao, and Koil *tahsils*, while the number of those arrested in the city was comparatively small. A study of their social background suggests that they were mainly drawn from the ranks of the rich and the middle level Thakur, Brahman, and Jat peasants and small zamindars. Among them were a few wealthy Aggarwal and Brahman traders, as well as some merchants in the city.

Given the rural orientation of the Aligarh Congress, it was much harder to build the Civil Disobedience movement in the city. At the same time, its development and expansion depended largely on the organization and resources of the City Congress. In Aligarh the organization was loosely knit and faction-ridden, while its resources were meagre. This was not so in districts like Allahabad, Kanpur, Agra, and Banaras, which possessed a highly centralized and cohesive Congress organization, with no dearth of resources. They were thus able to build and sustain support for the Civil Disobedience movement. In contrast, the Aligarh City Congress was in a state of disarray as a result of perpetual conflict and rivalries within the District Congress Committee (DCC).

The Aligarh City Congress was dominated by Jwala Prasad Jigyasu, a city *rais* and leader of the wealthy Varshney trading community which had close links with communal bodies, such as the Rashtriya Swayamsevak Sangh. Jigyasu was closely associated with Madan Mohan Malaviya's Nationalist Party, founded in 1934 over the issue of the Communal Award. The DCC, on the other hand, was controlled by Todar Singh, a Thakur landowner, and Malkhan Singh who belonged to a Kirar Thakur family of tenant farmers. Both had joined the Congress during the Rowlatt satyagraha, and their active and long association established them as the foremost Congress stalwarts with a substantial following in the district. They were regarded as 'moderates' in politics, and were allied with Rafi Ahmad Kidwai and later with the C.B. Gupta faction in the UPCC.

Political rivalry and conflict between the leaders of the City and the District Congress and between Malkhan Singh and Jigyasu had been an endemic part of the Congress organization since the mid-1920s when the two leaders fought over the leadership of the DCC. They maintained a semblance of unity and set aside their internecine quarrels in the early phase of the Civil Disobedience campaign. However, their entente was short-lived. They soon began to trade charges against each other—charges of embezzlement and misuse of funds. Todar Singh levelled such accusations at Tota Ram Rathi, one of Jigyasu's trusted allies.[55] Such intra-party feuds reached a breaking point in 1932, leading to a split into two factions which operated as 'virtually different parties'.[56] Elections to the Central Legislative Assembly in 1935, and later to the UP Legislative Assembly, widened the growing schism. Jigyasu's links with Malaviya's Nationalist Party and his opposition to the Communal Award provided political ammunition to the DCC to malign him. The offshoot was that the communal controversies once again came to the fore leading to sharp division within the Congress and causing serious misgivings in Muslim circles.

In the mid-1930s, the Aligarh Congress regrouped its forces for a renewed spell of political action, with new members being recruited in the expectation of the 1937 elections. The efforts proved rewarding, for membership of the Aligarh Congress increased from 5,000 in 1934 to 10,000 in 1938, the largest in western UP and the third-largest in the province.[57] But this was small consolation, for the larger issues which had sapped the strength of the Aligarh Congress remained unresolved. Added to these were the ideological differences in the UPCC which led to two identifiable camps: Congress Socialists like Acharya Narendra Dev and Shibban Lal Saxena, and the 'Ministerialists', led by Rafi Ahmad Kidwai, Mohanlal Saxena, and G.B. Pant.[58] Congress Socialists who were active in the agrarian campaigns of the early 1930s pressed for the adoption of a socialist programme. The provincial Congress leadership, on the other hand, favoured a compromise between the zamindars and the tenants. The crystallization of these differences triggered a whole range of factional and ideological rivalries. Differences also extended to the control of the UPCC and the election of district delegates. These were heightened by the 1937 elections and the advent of the Congress ministries as various groups turned to the districts which assumed significance because control of the UPCC depended upon enlisting support at the local levels. This required influencing the election of district delegates to the UPCC: thus the electoral process established a tangible connection between provincial and district leaders.[59] While provincial leaders needed local support to ensure the election of candidates acceptable to them, the district leaders required the backing of faction leaders at the provincial level to expand and legitimize their following in local affairs.

In actual fact, the alliances forged and developed in Aligarh were made of no particular pattern, for ideology played a small part in the political processes. The conflict between Malkhan Singh, and his rival, Jigyasu, centred round the issue of control of the DCC and City Congress Committee (CCC). Attempts were also made by Jigyasu and his faction to wrest the control of the rural areas from the Malkhan Singh-Todar Singh combine, but the two sides were unevenly matched as the DCC had a much larger numerical support. This was because the bulk of Congress propaganda and policies were geared towards the mobilization of rural support. The CCC complained that Congress propaganda neglected important sections in the city, and that hardly any city leaders—with the exception of Jigyasu, Sherwani, and A.M. Khawaja—found a prominent place in the Congress organization which had become the virtual preserve of rural interests. Against this background, the UP Assembly elections added a new dimension to factional controversies as urban Congressmen were under increasing pressure to mobilize support for their group to match the resources and reservoir of support at the disposal of the DCC.

In the UP Assembly elections, Congress fielded K.D. Paliwal, the Agra Socialist, against the Nationalist Party candidate Hariday Nath Kunzru, a constitutionalist with pro-zamindar leanings, for the Agra constituency which included the Aligarh district. Paliwal was actively associated with the Civil Disobedience movement in Aligarh and was a familiar figure in Aligarh political circles. G.B. Pant, president of the UPCC, set his campaign in motion by addressing largely attended meetings. These were followed by Sardar Patel's triumphant tour of the city which terminated with a mammoth meeting in the precincts of the Lyall Library in the heart of the city. Patel called upon Aligarh citizens to reject the 'wrong course' adopted by Malaviya.[60] He asked the audience to demonstrate their solidarity with the Congress, they did so by raising their hands. In marked contrast to such a response, Malaviya encountered much opposition. He was able to draw fewer people at public meetings where his advocacy of Kunzru was widely resented. His host and local supporter, Jigyasu was embarrassed and had to apologize to Malaviya on behalf of Aligarh citizens.[61]

Such inter-group rivalries equally marred the election of district delegates to the AICC in 1936. Thakur Malkhan Singh, with the support of some members of the Parliamentary Board, managed to exclude Jigyasu and

Tota Ram Rathi from the list of district delegates to the AICC.[62] However, the UP Board of Control declared the nominations invalid on account of the innumerable charges of malpractices levelled against the local Congress. Rafi Ahmad Kidwai and N.K. Vashisht of the Aligarh Congress who had graduated to provincial politics, were asked by the UPCC to settle the contentious claims of the warring factions. Jigyasu contended that Malkhan Singh manoeuvred to keep out Tota Ram Rathi, his most trusted ally; Malkhan Singh made similar charges against his detractors. The conflict was eventually resolved by electing both Malkhan Singh and Tota Ram Rathi to the UPCC.

At another level, tension between the City and District Committees reached a head as the two groups openly traded charges and counter charges relating to financial irregularities in the course of organizing the Provincial Conference held in Aligarh in 1937. Though a Congress report had confirmed that this was so, no action was taken.[63] The *Aligarh Times* published an unsavoury account of Congress misdeeds under the provocative title: 'Aligarh Congressmen—A Gang of Free Booters; Poormen's money Misappropriated. Accounts Forged and Fabricated'.[64] The UPCC was enraged because the report was the handiwork of some local Congressmen.

The UPCC could no longer equivocate on Aligarh affairs. Jawaharlal Nehru, president of UPCC in 1939, had earlier refused to be drawn into the local squabbles of the Aligarh Congress, but he was now forced to intervene and so condemned the local leaders for bringing disrepute to the organization. Writing to the UPCC on Aligarh affairs, he observed that:

the most scandalous charge has been made to the public press. This kind of thing cannot be allowed to continue and it is time a full enquiry was made and stringent action taken against any Congressman who was guilty of this highly improper behaviour. The PCC has repeatedly laid stress on one Congressman not even criticizing another in public, either by speech or writing. He sees in Aligarh something which is infinitely worse than criticism.[65]

In the midst of such internal squabbles and political jealousies, the outcome of the 1937 elections was a redeeming feature in Congress' history in Aligarh; it demonstrated that the Congress was still the leading political organization in Aligarh. Under the broader franchise in force for the legislative assembly elections there were three general and one Muslim seat in the district. The Congress won all the three rural seats in the district with an aggregate vote of 68.5 per cent, compared to 30.4 per cent polled by the National Agriculturist Party.[66] The Muslim seat was won by Obaidur Rehman Sherwani, an independent candidate, who later joined the Muslim League.

The emergence of the Muslim League as a political force was a new phenomena with which the Congress had to contend for nearly a decade. It posed a serious challenge to Congress' claim of an all-India character and of organizing a nationalist movement to serve the interests of all sections of the community. The Congress was henceforth faced with divisions within its ranks on the communal issue, and the desertion of some important Muslim groups into the Muslim League camp. The pattern here was similar to that of the other districts in UP, except that the presence of the Aligarh Muslim University and the part played by its teachers and students in the League movement provided a new dimension to the Muslim separatist movement.

In the late 1930s, the Muslim League gained a fair measure of influence in Aligarh, extending to different parts of the city. Its flag was hoisted in Sikandra Rao in 1938 in the presence of 4,000 people amidst much condemnation by the Congress and the British government.[67] This was followed by meetings at Hathras, where it was claimed that the League alone could protect Muslim interests. Communal tension which gripped Aligarh in 1938-9, along with exaggerated reports of the so-called 'atrocities' committed by the Congress Ministries in UP and Bihar,[68] gave the Muslim League an opportunity to conduct its anti-Congress campaign effectively and to gain the adherence of certain sections of the Muslim community to its movement.

By the end of 1938, Hindu-Muslim antagonism was widespread, caused largely by the question of religious processions; the playing of music before mosques was a particularly bitter source of tension in the late 1930s. Relations remained embittered as district authorities tried in vain to convince the Arya Samaj and other Hindu organizations in Aligarh to adhere to any reasonable agreement on the issue of playing music at prayer time.[69] Symptomatic of the growth in communal assertiveness was the building of more temples to keep pace with the mushrooming of mosques. The district authorities banned further construction. The Arya Samaj, in turn, launched a Civil Disobedience with the sole aim of blowing *sankhs* and marching vociferous *jathas* in front of mosques.

W.C. Smith has pointed out that in the 1940s, the Muslim League succeeded in winning the support of the bulk of the middle and the lower middle classes in UP.[70] However, leadership of the movement remained in the hands of landlords and lawyer politicians. Muslim landlords in general supported the League in reaction to the agrarian policies of the Congress ministries, especially the UP Tenancy Bill, 1938, which they construed as 'an attack on minority culture, sustained by the patronage of Muslim landed aristocracy'.[71] The League's clause by clause attack of the Tenancy Bill in the UP Legislative Council helped it to mobilize and garner the support of landlords, including those in Aligarh who rallied round Jinnah who had emerged as a spokesman of the Muslim community.

In Aligarh, the bulk of support for the Muslim League came from the landlords and the students and teachers of the Aligarh Muslim University. Men like the Nawab of Chattari, Haji Mohammad Ismail Khan, Nawab Muzammilullah Khan, and Obaidur Rahman Khan Sherwani did not confine their activities to the preservation of class interests, but espoused overtly communal and religious causes to promote their political objectives as landlords. Their political stance aided the spread of the League in Aligarh which, along with several other districts of the Doab, became an advanced centre of Muslim League activities.[72]

The League organized several meetings in Aligarh to urge Muslims to join the newly refurbished party. Addressing a 3,000 strong meeting in the city, Khaliquzzaman condemned the Congress as 'an organization from which Muslims could not expect any benefit because it had the interest of Hindus at heart'.[73] The local Congress leaders resented such strident condemnation of their party, and took strong exception to the attacks on Gandhi and Nehru. When Maulvi Abdus Samad condemned Congress as an organization of 'kafirs', Mohan Vaish, an influential city leader, asserted that the 'harrassment' of Hindus stemmed from their own weakness in not asserting their interests.[74] In the absence of any concerted effort to bring about communal amity, such frequent communal scuffles escalated tension in the city and hardened the attitudes of both the communities against each other.

The political situation in 1938-9 was indeed a far cry from the optimistic declaration of Malkhan Singh at the 1935 District Political Conference that 'Aligarh was pro-Congress and completely devoid of communal animosity'.[75] This was certainly not the case with the bulk of the Muslims. Equally noteworthy was the fact that the Congress at all levels was reluctant to tackle the communal issue. The Muslim Mass Contact Programme petered out in less than two years because the Congress was reluctant 'to pursue it with any vigour or sense of purpose'.[76] The City Congress Committee in Aligarh, which was controlled by right-wing elements, opposed all such efforts on account of the commonly held fear that the presence of large numbers of Muslims would threaten their domination and enable the Muslims to influence Congress policies as in the days of the Khilafat and Non-Cooperation movements. Attempts to exclude Muslims from the DCC must be viewed in this light. During the 1938 elections to the DCC in 1938, Malkhan Singh, president of the DCC, joined hands with his arch rival, Jigyasu, to oppose Mohammad Usman and Kidwai, the only two Muslims who had filed nominations for the DCC.[77] Their papers were accepted only after Jawaharlal Nehru's intervention.

While the growing communal polarization impeded the Congress movement in Aligarh, it did not dampen enthusiasm for the renewal of political agitation. The launching of another round of Civil Disobedience acted as a catalyst for political activity in Aligarh. Political workers carried out a house to house campaign to condemn the government's war effort and recruitment drive. Much of this was stimulated by the socialist wing in the Congress which had become a force in Aligarh politics. Their presence was felt in the District Political Conference in May 1940 which was marked by a radical mood, evident from the fluttering Red Flag and the revolutionary names adorning the gates of the pandal.[78] Individual satyagraha which mainly consisted of the demand for the right to make anti-war speeches, elicited a fair measure of response. By June 1941, satyagrahis went to jail in large numbers. Nearly 204 persons were arrested in connection with the Quit India movement,[79] the local police found 43 cases of wire cutting in Aligarh in August 1942 and recorded two bomb explosions that occurred at the Aligarh Railway Station in September 1942 and in August 1943,[80] involving Deo Dutt, Satyamurthi, Panna Lal, Anand Mohan Rohtagi and Kishen Lal—active protagonists of revolutionary ideas in the district during the course of the Quit India movement. They had links with Congress leaders like Udaibir Singh, Srichand Singhal, Jagdamba Prasad, Malkhan Singh, and Thakur Netrapal Singh. Some, like Netrapal Singh, in fact distributed revolutionary leaflets with 'Do or Die' slogans,[81] and Srichand Singhal, who resigned as president of the Aligarh DCC in 1942, extended financial and political support.

Political developments in the Aligarh Muslim University, however underwent an unmistakable change. It is noteworthy that campus politics had for a long time been dominated by the Congress-Socialist combine. In 1936, the students had organized an impressive strike against the university's repression of nationalist activities, and had opposed the proposal to establish an All-India Muslim Students' Federation.[82] But such nationalist enthusiasm was soon replaced by an almost hysterical support for Pakistan. By 1940, there was widespread backing for the Muslim League, and Jinnah and other League leaders, who had once been spurned by the Aligarh students and teachers now turned to the same groups in order to gain a strong foothold in an institution which had served as the intellectual and political centre of the northern Indian Muslim intelligentsia.[83] The widening political base of the Muslim League was exemplified by the transition in the Aligarh Muslim University.

In the early 1940s, the staff and students of the university were busy campaigning for the newly-discovered 'causes' of the Muslim League, spreading its message, distributing pamphlets on Pakistan, and mobilizing support in favour of the two-nation theory. Jinnah made frequent trips to Aligarh, addressed several meetings at the university and in the city, and provided funds to the University City League which played a major role in disseminating the idea of a separate Muslim homeland. In the 1946 Provincial Assembly elections, large numbers of students campaigned in different parts of the country and contributed towards the victory of League candidates in several UP constituencies.[84] Aligarh, declared Jinnah, 'is the arsenal of Muslim India'.[85]

The Aligarh students' involvement in the Pakistan movement had serious political implications. It embittered communal relations in the area as evident from the outbreak of the Hindu–Muslim fracas in 1946, involving the 'university students and the city Hindus'.[86] The bitterness felt by city Hindus towards the university was reflected in the following statement:

The universal opinion of all Hindus is that the students of AMU have been allowed to illtreat the public for many years and that the present conflagration is due to the lack of control and punishment in the past. In the perception of large sections of the Hindu community, the Aligarh University was the bastion of the Pakistan movement and the symbol of Muslim communalism.[87]

The pattern of political mobilization in Aligarh was evidently different from its trajectory in the 'politically advanced areas' like Allahabad, Banaras, and Rae Bareli. The advance of political activity in some of these areas was helped by the existence of a strong Congress organization, an army of dedicated mobilizers, and the availability of a wide range of instruments of mobilization, such as the press, periodicals, and volunteer organizations. Rae Bareli, in particular, struck out a radical path 'even in opposition to the Congress leaders', by 'emphasizing the economic aspect of the agitation'.[88] Aligarh was different. There the no-tax campaign elicited little support as the non-payment of tax did not form an important part of the Congress programme. The reasons were: first, the economic aspect of the agitation did not figure prominently in Aligarh; second, attempts to intensify the agitation in certain villages by introducing an anti-landlord economic programme were frustrated by communal controversies. At the same time, the Congress in Aligarh made no serious endeavour to establish contact with the Muslim masses. Instead, as we have shown, the Congress consciously decided to minimize propaganda in areas with a high proportion of Muslims in order to avoid communal friction. It did so on account of Muslim hostility to the Civil Disobedience movement, and also because in the complex structure of UP society, agrarian and economic contradictions between groups and communities often assumed a communal dimension.[89] The Congress pressed on with Civil Disobedience with the belief that a successful anti-colonial struggle would cement the bonds of unity, and minimize friction in the long run. Such hopes were not fulfilled because the pattern of political activity and mobilization throughout the various phases of the national movement conformed to the dominant current in the Congress which laid greater emphasis on political struggles against the British Raj in its effort to build a broad based anti-imperialist movement rather than a comprehensive anti-colonial movement which could combine national and social discontent.

Notes and References

1. 'Agitation in connection with the Rowlatt satyagraha', CID Report on Aligarh, CID File no. 262, Uttar Predesh State Archives (UPSA), 1919.

2. Estimates range from 200 to 700 students who left the MAO College in support of Gandhi's call to boycott government aided institutions. Leading non-cooperators were K.G. Saiyadain, Abid Husain, Zakir Husain and K.M. Ashraf. Mushirul Hasan, 'Nationalist and Separatist Trends in Aligarh, 1915-1947', *IESHR*, vol. 22, no. 1, 1985, p. 7.

3. 'List of men who have resigned government offices on account of the non-cooperation movement, 21 October 1921', Government Administration Department (GAD), 1921, 3055, UPSA.

4. *1931 Census*, United Provinces of Agra and Oudh, vol. 18, pt. I.

5. Muslims formed 33 per cent of Aligarh city's population. Ibid.

6. *Aligarh Gazetteer*, vol. 6, 1926. H.R. Neville noted that 'Chamars were not long ago regarded as mere serfs, tied to particular holdings to such an extent that no partition was considered complete until the sharer had allotted to his share a number of Chamars in proportion to his interest in the estate', p. 77.

7. *1931 Census*.

8. Barasenis, a branch of the Banias, are generally accorded a social ranking below the Aggarwals in the Bania hierarchy. Aligarh is an important stronghold of the community, who are generally very wealthy, controlling much of the wholesale wheat, building material, and grain trade of the province. *Aligarh Gazetteer*, 1926, p. 80.

9. Area held by principal castes includes Thakurs, Jats, Brahmans, Vaish and Kayasths. The only other caste group whose population exceeds 5 per cent and also owned considerable land were Lodhs and Ahirs in Atrauli *tahsil*. Ahmad Ali, *Final Settlement Report of the Aligarh District*, 1945, Statement no. 4.

10. In terms of landownership Jats owned 57 per cent of land in Iglas *tahsil* and 34.6 per cent in Khair *tahsil*. Thakurs owned 48.7 per cent in Sikandra Rao and 24.3 per cent in Khair. *Aligarh Gazetteer*, 1926, pp. 90-100.

11. Ibid., p. 84.

12. See Francis Robinson, 'Municipal Government and Muslim Separatism in the United Provinces 1883 to 1916', *Modern Asian Studies*, vol. 7, July 1973, for a discussion on the growth of towns and trade in western UP, pp. 401-4.

13. In 1944, 51.3 per cent of the cultivated area was wet, of which more than half was canal irrigated and consequently well protected against drought. *SR*, 1945.

14. Eric Stokes, 'Structure of Landholding in Uttar Pradesh, 1860–1948', *IESHR*, vol. 12, no. 2, 1975, p. 119.

15. Aligarh had a large number of big landlords. The number of large landowners in Aligarh, Etah, and Mainpuri was comparable to many districts of Awadh which suggests that big landowners were not unique to Awadh and eastern UP. See Table 7.1 and *SR*, 1945.

16. Uttar Pradesh Zamindar Abolition Committee (UPZAC), vol. 2, Statistics, 1948, pp. 34–5.

17. Ibid., p. 34.

18. Occupancy tenants held nearly 40 per cent of the area, hereditary tenants occupied 35.2 per cent, and 13 per cent was in the hands of subtenants. The area under subtenancy was reduced as zamindars realized the importance of cultivating their own share after the UP Tenancy Act, 1938. *SR*, 1945.

19. There is very little documentary information on the organizational structure of the Aligarh Congress. This is not surprising, because the Congress organization in the district was completely eroded by the incessant factionalism and internecine struggles in the party. These disputes increased after Independence which greatly hampered the functioning of the organization. Comparing Aligarh with other districts, Paul Brass concluded that the intensity of factional conflict in Aligarh was unmatched elsewhere in Uttar Pradesh. See Paul Brass, *Factional Politics in an Indian State: The Congress Party in UP*, Bombay: Oxford, 1966.

20. Jawaharlal Nehru, *An Autobiography*, London, 1936, p. 282.

21. *Swatantra Sangram ke Sainik*, Zila Information Division, UP, Lucknow, 1972.

22. *Police Abstract of Intelligence Report of UP* (hereafter *PAI*).

23. *PAI*, 8 July and 7 September 1930.

24. *PAI*, 5 July 1930.

25. *SR*, 1945, para 36. Movement of Prices.

Statement 7: Price Index

Period	Price Index
1882-6	89
1891-5 (Base)	100
1891-1906 (excluding 1900 a year of severe drought)	117
1907-11	137
1912-16 (war years)	167
1917-21 (post-war boom)	242
1922-6	212
1927-31	192
1915-38 (preslump average)	221
1932-6 (slump period)	117

26. See Gyanendra Pandey, *The Ascendancy of the Congress in Uttar Pradesh, 1926-34*, Delhi: Oxford University Press, 1978, for a discussion of the effects of the depression in UP.

27. D.N. Dhanagre, *Peasant Movements in India 1920-1950*, Delhi: Oxford University Press, 1983, p. 120.

28. *Aligarh Gazetteer*, 1926, p. 120.

29. 'Thakurs lost 12,000 acres after the last settlement in 1904; while Jats lost 26,000 acre. Muslims were 'the greatest sufferers since the last settlement having lost 44,000 acre. Bania moneylenders rapidly gained land, the majority of them invested their capital in the mortgages which were seldom redeemed owing to the high rates of interest charged.' *SR*, 1945, paras 14-16.

30. Rich landlords were generally insulated from the debilitating process of fragmentation and transfer. The settlement officer noticed that the rich zamindars 'have on the whole gained and nearly all the loss had fallen on the small men and village communities'. Ibid., para. 6.

31. *PAI*, 4 April 1931.

32. Ibid., 10 May 1931.

33. Ibid., 2 May 1931.

34. *Aligarh Gazetteer*, 1926, pp. 291-5.

35. In Aligarh as a whole out of the total number of 1,049 single zamindari *mahals* 822 were owned by absentee landlords. *Aligarh Gazetteer*, 1926.

36. *PAI*, 2 May 1931.

37. *SR*, 1945, para. 20. High caste tenants were generally more indebted than low caste ones because they spent more on consumption, noted the *SR*.

38. *SR*, 1945, para 7, p. 2. Rents of occupancy tenants of over 20 years rose by 50 per cent and new occupancy tenants of less than 20 years rose by 8 per cent in the three decades before 1944. The rise in rents was disproportionate to the rise of prices which was 31 per cent. Yet, the proprietors did not encounter difficulties in collecting rents. The Settlement Officer attributed this to the keenness of tenants to acquire rights even at a high price.

39. Pathans occupied 55 per cent of the whole area (115,595 acre). *Aligarh Gazetteer*, 1926, p. 221.

40. *PAI*, 15 August 1931.

41. Ibid., 18 July 1931. Congress organized an intense picketing programme in Charra (Atrauli) *tahsil* largely because of the ill feeling against the powerful Nawab of Bhikanpur. In general, Atrauli landlords were extremely oppressive, they demanded *nazrana* and other *abwabs* for the letting of new holdings.

42. *PAI*, 2 May 1931.

43. *General Report on Public Instruction in the United Provinces of Agra and Oudh*, March 1931.

44. The riots during Ramlila of 1926 was the worst in the province that year.

45. Home Poll, 1930 and K.W., F. No. 249, National Archives of India (NAI) I owe this reference to M. Hasan.

46. Robinson, *Municipal Government*, p. 407.

47. *Aligarh Gazetteer*, 1926, p. 84.

48. *PAI*, 26 April 1935.

49. Quoted in Reginald Coupland, *The Constitutional Problem in India*, Oxford, 1944, p. 111.

50. *PAI*, 18 October 1931.

51. Home Poll, 1930 and K.W., F. No. 249, NAI.

52. *PAI*, 18 July 1931.

53. District officials in Aligarh and Meerut attributed the Congress movement in Aligarh to the impact of the successful campaign in Bulandshahr. The Intelligence Officer reported after a visit to Bulandshahr, Meerut and Aligarh: 'The root of the

trouble lies in Bulandshahr. I think there is a spirit of complacence in this district and that district authorities are too satisfied that all is well when it is not. There is no doubt that both Meerut and Aligarh attribute any poison which spreads over their border to the inaction of the Bulandshahr district and there is no doubt that Congress has made progress in the rural areas in Bulandshahr'. Home Poll, 1930 and K.W., F. No. 249, NAI.

54. See Pandey, *Ascendancy of the Congress*; C.A. Bayly, *The Local Roots of Indian Politics, Allahabad 1880-1920*, Oxford, 1975; Lance Brennan, From one Raj to another: Congress Politics in Rohilkhand, 1930-50', in *Congress and the Raj*, ed. D. A. Low, Arnold Heineman, 1977.

55. *PAI*, 27 September 1930. The decline of the agitation in Aligarh was attributed to the internal disputes between various factions in Aligarh Congress.

56. 'Note on Congress Affairs in Aligarh District by Jawaharlal Nehru', President of UPCC, 9 July 1939, AICC P2O Part I, 1939-40.

57. 'UPCC List of Membership in districts and cities', 25 August 1938.

58. See Brennan, 'The Raj to Another', for a discussion of ideological and factional divisions in the Congress.

59. Ibid.

60. *The Pioneer*, 8 November 1934.

61. Ibid., 10 November 1934.

62. 'UPCC: Executive Council Proceedings', 17 January 1937.

63. Jawaharlal Nehru, *Note on Congress Affairs in Aligarh District*, UPCC, 1939.

64. *Aligarh Times*, 8 June 1939 published an account of Aligarh affairs 'UPCC condemned the report: We shall no doubt enquire into all matters involving irregularities and take necessary action. PCC condemned individual Congressmen running down the Congress in public by speech or writing. Those who are responsible for such conduct are guilty of a breach of the Congress discipline as well as the code which governs the conduct of honourable men.' AICC P2O Part I, 1939-40.

65. Nehru, *Note on Congress Affairs*, UPCC, 1939.

66. P.D. Reeves, B.D. Graham, J.M. Goodman, *Elections in Uttar Pradesh 1920-1951*, Manohar, 1975, p. 266.

67. *PAI*, 13 August 1938.

68. Innumerable conflicts involving various groups, such as zamindars and moneylenders who happened to be Muslims and Hindus acquired serious communal proportions in Aligarh's highly charged atmosphere. For example a bomb attack on a Hindu moneylender who happened to hold decrees against Muslim landlords exacerbated communal tension in the city. *PAI*, 26 February 1938.

69. *PAI*, 12 November 1938.

70. W.C. Smith, *Modern Islam in India*, Lahore, 1943, p. 312.

71. Much of the understanding stemmed from the Muslim perception of decline in relation to other groups in the evolving structures of power and opportunity. Muslims did suffer a striking decline in landholdings which considerably affected their overall position because land was the economic mainstay of the Muslim upper classes. According to Brennan, in 1911, three times as many Muslims derived their income from rent of land as from services to the state. Between the last quarter of the nineteenth century and the first quarter of the twentieth

century Muslim landholdings declined quite considerably. The scale of reduction varied from 38 per cent in Sultanpur to 1 per cent in Barabanki. In Aligarh their share was reduced by 20 per cent and the loss in terms of acres involved 5 per cent of the area of the district. Lance Brennan, 'Background to Muslim Separatism in UP', *Modern Asian Studies*, vol. 18, no. 2, 1984, p. 2.

72. By the end of 1937, the Muslim League had 90 branches with 100,000 new members in the UP. Between 1938 and 1942 the League won 46 out of the 56 by-elections held in Muslim constituencies. In 1945-6 elections the Muslim League polled 75 per cent of the vote and won 460 out of the 533 Muslim seats. Hasan, 'Nationalist and Separatist Trends in Aligarh, 1915-1947', *IESHR*, vol. 22, no. 1, 1985, p. 2.

73. *PAI*, 12 February 1938.

74. Ibid., 13 May 1939.

75. Ibid., 26 April 1935.

76. Mushirul Hasan, 'Muslim Mass Contact Campaign. An Attempt at Political Mobilization', *Occasional Paper Series*, Nehru Memorial Museum and Library, 1984.

77. UPCC PZO/1621, 15 March 1938.

78. *PAI*, 11 May 1940.

79. *Swatantra Sangram ke Sainik*, 1972.

80. Aligarh Bomb Case, CID RR-26, File No. 5/3/42, UPSA.

81. CID RR-26, File No. 5/1/42, Case Diaries, UPSA.

82. Smith, *Modern Islam*.

83. M. Hasan, 'Muslim Mass Contact Campaign', p. 17.

84. By the end of 1945, 225 Aligarh Muslim University students canvassed in Punjab, 75 in UP, 25 in NWFP, and 7 in Bengal. Their numbers increased in 1946 as more funds poured into the local election committee. According to Hasan, such interventions proved rewarding in several constituencies in UP. See Ibid.

85. Jinnah to Zahid Husain, 5 December 1945 cited in Hasan, 'Nationalist and Separatist Trends', p. 21.

86. District Magistrate S.N. Pandita's Letter to Home Secretary, UP Government, 30 March 1946.

87. Ibid. They also said the police stopped Hindus from helping to put out the fire. Though the assertion was incorrect, it was widely believed in the city.

88. See Pandey, *Ascendancy of the Congress*, chapters 4 and 6 for a discussion on the strategy and level of Congress propaganda in the districts.

89. Ibid., p. 149.

19 | Bridging a Growing Divide?
The Indian National Congress
and Indian Democracy

THE SUCCESS of the Indian National Congress (INC)-led alliance in the 2004 general elections after years of terminal decline marked a critical juncture in the history of the party and Indian democracy. The 2004 elections were the outcome of a decade-long silent revolt of those who felt left out of the reform process. Efforts by its leadership to achieve organizational and political cohesion while emphasizing ideological clarity served to persuade voters that the INC could represent a more inclusive governance approach. However, ever since the INC-led government began implementing social and economic policies designed to pursue the liberalizing agenda, it has struggled to reconcile the contradiction between economic reforms that benefit the elite and upper-middle classes and its mass support among the poor who have been the losers in this process. This chapter examines the structure and pattern of transformation within the INC, both in its policy and strategy and in its organization and leadership. It considers whether the INC's dual approach of seeking to appease the powerful middle-class constituency while appealing to the economic majority has a deeper strategic purpose of achieving centrism and a broad-based social coalition. It discusses whether this shift in direction signals the arrival of more inclusive development policies to bridge the growing socio-economic divide and, if so, whether this can be sustained in the long-term.

* This paper was originally presented as the Nirman Foundation Lecture at the British Association for South Asian Studies Annual Conference held on 19–21 April 2006 at Birkbeck College, UK. The views expressed in this article are solely attributable to that of the author and not of the National Commission for Minorities of which she is a member.

For those anxious about India's future as a secular and inclusive democracy, the success of the INC-led alliance in trouncing the Bharatiya Janata Party (BJP)-led National Democratic Alliance (NDA) in the parliamentary elections of May 2004 signalled much more than a change of regimes. The rejection of the BJP was a repudiation of the NDA government's pro-rich and majoritarian politics.[1] Consequently, these two issues dominated the elections. The historical significance of this election, the fourteenth after independence, was the promise of the revival and restoration of India's democratic agenda in the context of the country's growing economic divide and unequal distribution of opportunities and wealth. The recasting of the INC as the party of *aam aadmi* (common people) in the run up to 2004 elections was a sign that it was at last serious about addressing three key issues. The first relates to the general disjunction between political inclusion and economic exclusion. The second was the divergence within the INC between its policies and programmes on the one hand, and its social base on the other. The third, somewhat of a contradiction, was between the party's largely middle-class leadership and its capacity to deliver on socially-oriented programmes and initiatives. The conscious shift in approach was an important factor in arresting the slow but steady decline of the party since Rajiv Gandhi's time. The question, however, is whether the INC can sustain this change of direction and whether this signals the arrival of more inclusive development policies to bridge the growing socio-economic divide. To advance this question, this chapter looks at the role of the INC in shaping the political and policy orientation of the United Progressive Alliance (UPA) government and the democratic agenda.

Since 1989, the leadership, constituencies, issues, and electoral strategies of political parties—including the INC—have undergone significant changes. Two interrelated developments are at stake; one in the party system, and the other in the INC as regards its commitment to the broader democratic agenda. The party system has witnessed a long-term decline of the INC and two important concomitant developments; that is, the rise of the BJP and the growing significance of regional parties, especially in southern India, but also in the states of West Bengal, Punjab, Kashmir, and the north-east. In addition to this sense of dwindling organizational base, the lack of ideological clarity and political purpose left the INC with an image of ambiguity and confusion and, more disturbingly, an impression that it lacked political direction.[2] The capacity of the INC to become an effective vehicle that could address the needs of a large section of the people alienated from the NDA's policies depended critically on its ability to sharpen its own focus on economic and political inclusion and, thereby, increase its relevance in rapidly changing circumstances. That the INC succeeded reflects the conscious efforts made by its leadership towards achieving a stronger integration of the party's organizational and social base with its programmes and policies. That was the key to its relative success in the 2004 elections. It also indicates a summoning of a greater ideological purpose and political clarity in terms of the INC's approach to the democratic agenda. This two-pronged approach of achieving organizational and political cohesion while emphasizing ideological clarity served ultimately to persuade voters that the INC could represent a more inclusive approach to governance in pursuing the economic reform agenda.

At the same time, India's democratic politics is undergoing momentous shifts, with the country's oldest party, the INC, entering into a coalition arrangement with smaller, mostly regional formations. The changes at the central level affect major shifts in the base of the body politic. The power of significant parties loosely described as regional, and the increasing electoral clout of the underclass and marginal groups is another major factor. The way in which these forces at the apex and base will combine to influence the governing pattern in the country in an era of economic reform will determine India's democratic future. Ironically, the 2004 elections can be seen as the outcome of a decade-long silent revolt of those who felt left out of the benefits of the reform process launched by the then Finance Minister Manmohan Singh in 1991.

Against this background, a crucial aspect of the transformation of the INC concerns the disjunction between its policies, framed according to middle-class aspirations, and its social base, which draws mainly from the underprivileged sections of society. Ever since the INC-led government began implementing social and economic policies designed to pursue the liberalizing agenda of economic reforms, the INC has struggled to reconcile the contradiction between economic reforms that benefit the elite and upper-middle classes, and its mass support among the poor who have been the losers in this process. This contradiction results from the effect of two factors: the change in India's social structure from an elite-mass structure to one with a substantial middle-class sandwiched between these two poles, and the need of the INC, as a catch-all party, to cater for a range of groups including the Scheduled Castes (SCs), Scheduled Tribes (STs), Other Backward Classes (OBCs), minorities, and the poor.[3]

Four key elements are essential to an understanding of the character, evolution, and strategy of any political party; that is, programmes as embodied in policies, leadership, organization and social base. At the outset it might be useful to differentiate between policies and programmes and social base on the one hand, and the leadership and the organization on the other. For a proper assessment, we must look at the interaction of all four components. It is particularly important to weave the leadership and organizational structure into an analysis of programmes and policies, since the latter are mediated through leadership and organization. The crucial issue in this regard is whether the shift in INC policies and strategy since 2002 was merely tactical, or whether it has a deeper strategic purpose. If so, the question is whether the party can effectuate structural change given its present organizational structure, and whether the shift represents a return to centrism and, therefore, an attempt to rebuild a broad-based social coalition. This chapter aims to capture the structure and pattern of transformation within the INC, both in its policy and strategy as well as in its organization and leadership. The party is pursuing a dual approach of seeking to assuage and appease the powerful middle-class constituency while, at the same time, appealing to the economic majority. The passage of the National Rural Employment Guarantee Programme Act (NREGPA) in December 2005 and the signing of the controversial Indo-US nuclear deal in March 2006 are indications of this dual approach through which the INC is seeking simultaneously to appeal to two very distinct and different constituencies in the social spectrum.

The first section of this chapter looks at the changing social base of the INC in relation to the electoral preferences of various social groupings. The second section explores attempts by the INC at a reconstitution of its policies consonant with its social support in the course of its stewardship of the UPA government. Although the jury is still out on the impact of competing pressures on the transformation of the INC, the third section attempts a limited assessment of the dualism in the INC at this critical juncture in India's democratic journey.

The INC's Decline and Changing Social Base

The INC has been the most important political institution in India's modern political history. It has dominated national politics for most period since independence. Between 1969 and 1989, however, the party changed into a centralized and family-centred political organization.[4] Whereas it once embraced a broad spectrum of ideological, caste, regional and other interest groups, the party has suffered a steady erosion of its social base since the late 1980s. Its gradual loss of what was once reliable support from significant constituencies is a process that started with the Emergency in 1975, which seriously affected the relationship between the INC and Muslim voters, lower castes, and SC constituencies.

It is worth recalling that the party last secured a majority in the Lok Sabha in 1984 under the leadership of Rajiv Gandhi. The subsequent INC government of P.V. Narasimha Rao completed its full term, and will be remembered for initiating the process of economic reform. However, Rao could not secure a majority at the elections and could only arrive at the magic mark of 272 seats in the Lok Sabha (national parliament) by a policy of 'mergers and acquisitions'.[5] Economic policy change laid the foundation for a major two-way shift towards the market internally, and towards the United States externally. These changes were quite significant. They involved a shift from a multi-class state commitment to pro-poor measures to a narrow conception of the state more closely aligned with business, capital, and middle classes avowedly supportive of capitalist development.[6]

The economic policies that have come to be adopted in India since 1991 are well known and need not be repeated here. Essentially, what this paradigm shift meant, at least in principle, was the end of an autonomous trajectory of development, and the integration of domestic businesses with globalization. But what also happened was a widening class gap as many people have not gained significantly from economic reforms. The INC, which has traditionally drawn upon the support of the poor and marginalized, and whose access to power depends largely on its capacity to continue to draw from this support, has had to deal with this hiatus in the social base more than any other party. The INC is caught between the aspirations of the middle classes, which it wants to court for the sake of political legitimacy and vantage positions in the media, and the ground realities faced by the poor, the predominant social base of support for the party. Since the 1990s India's impressive growth has captured international attention. India's Gross Domestic Product (GDP) has grown steadily, and for the past 3 years since 2003-4 has exceeded 7 per cent per annum. During this period the middle class has also grown rapidly. According to one estimate in 2004 the middle classes constituted 26 per cent of the population, or 248 million.[7] More realistic (although admittedly still imprecise) estimates suggested that the middle classes were more likely to be in the region of 150 million and primarily based in urban areas, notwithstanding prosperous commercial farmers.[8] Whatever the estimates, India's middle class is large by global standards and expanding rapidly.

Equally significant is the concomitant polarization of economy and society as a result of this generation of wealth by a minority living in the midst of a sea of deprived and dispossessed co-citizens. The increased employment opportunities and incomes arising from liberalization and new growth areas such as Information Technology and Information Technology-enabled services have mostly benefited the better-educated classes within the upper rungs of society. In relative terms, the standard of living has deteriorated for the majority of the rural population and a significant part of the urban population.[9] For nearly 600 million Indians—more than one-half of the country's total population—per capita consumption has actually declined during a decade when national incomes were supposed to be growing at around 6 per cent on average per annum.[10]

The important point is that the policymaking tilt in favour of the corporate sector and powerful economic interests has led to the creation of two economies across the social and regional landscape of India. The vast majority of Indians are poor and remain cut off from the world of mobile phones and shopping malls, yet live within a close proximity to a now very visibly rich minority. Despite the improvements of the past decade or so, a cursory look at human development indices brings home the stark divide in India's political economy, which remains unable to address the basic educational and employment needs of the majority rural population. According to official data, a large proportion of the population, namely 26 per cent or about 260 million people, lives below the poverty line.[11] The main issues are the persistence of social and economic inequities, and high rates of unemployment. These economic disparities increased sharply between 1993-4 and 2003-4 across urban–rural and gender divides.[12]

During this period, the INC suffered a significant decline in its political support. As the effects of the liberalizing economy began to be felt, the discontent of social groups became palpable.[13] The irony, however, was that the poor, despite suffering the most, continued to repose faith in the INC while the middle classes, the main gainers from the economic reforms ushered in by Manmohan Singh, did not fully trust the INC. The 1990s witnessed the rise of the BJP with considerable support among the middle classes. The central problem confronting the INC was the disjunction between the ground reality of the concentration of its social support among the disadvantaged sections and its desperate search for middle-class approval.

Historically, the success of the INC was built not just on its professed commitment to inclusive development, but also on operations of political mobilization that drew together a broad spectrum of social groups across the country under a capacious umbrella. The most notable trait in the party's building of its support base is its famous ability to draw support from across regions, classes, castes, and communities.[14] This support was recruited by regional and local leaders through a skilful balancing of local demands with wider national concerns. An intricate system of representation was worked out by what was probably the most organizationally complex political party in the world.

In the past, INC strength lay in its ability to reach out to the Rainbow Coalition and, above all, to the bottom of the social heap. This consistency and spread of support helped the party to occupy the dominant space in the political spectrum for close to four decades. However, this picture has changed significantly. For instance, the INC vote in 1991 shows the fairly even spread that one would expect from a centrist party. From 1996 to 1999, the party's voter profile underwent sharp erosion among the middle classes while the poor, the slum dwellers, the unemployed, and minorities continued to swell the ranks of the party. During this period, the upper and middle classes and/or the upper castes shifted away from the INC towards the BJP.[15]

The 2004 elections reinforced this trend; that is, the higher the class, the greater the vote for the NDA. The class slope was the opposite in the case of the UPA and the INC.[16] The profile of the new INC voter was more likely to be the socially marginalized citizen at the receiving end of social inequities. In other words, it is by and large the 'party of the underdogs',[17] especially when it faces the BJP. But the INC has to compete for this support when it is contesting against leftist parties in India—including the Rashtriya Janata Dal, the Bahujan Samaj Party and the Samajwadi Party—which muster greater support from the poor. In other words, voting patterns in 2004 confirm the picture of the BJP representing a confluence of socially and economically privileged groups, and the UPA and the INC drawing support from the underprivileged. The point to note is that the INC base in 2004 was largely among the poor, even more so than before, while its policies were, oddly enough, less pro-poor. When the party's support was more evenly distributed, it was more centrist than at present.

Even though the INC and the UPA did not succeed in creating a counter social bloc of the underprivileged, the most striking feature of the 2004 general elections was the shift in its strategy. The 'India Shining' slogan of the NDA, agrarian distress, and rising unemployment forced the INC to challenge the cynical way in which the NDA was seeking to win another term in office by misusing manipulated indices of economic performance and celebrating the gains that a small upper crust had derived from the liberalization process. The INC-led alliance worked well precisely because it happened to articulate effectively the popular mood within the political system; that is, there was an urgent need to create an alternative to the BJP's package of liberalization, privatization, and globalization tilted heavily in favour of big business, the corporate sector, and middle-class professionals.

Reconstituting the Organizational Base

Thanks to this strategy and its focus on the *aam aadmi*, the INC returned to government after a gap of 8 years.[18] The formation of the UPA Government was an historic landmark, and offered an opportunity to reverse the virtually unrestricted programme of liberalization unleashed by the NDA government and the unmistakable agenda of aligning India closely with the United States. Social conflicts had become more acute but the UPA government appeared to find a route around this conundrum by endorsing the economic reforms policies while also suggesting that, through a National Common Minimum Programme,[19] the UPA and INC had a second objective; namely, that of social justice through redistribution. Corporate India and the middle classes were quick to express their apprehensions that the two goals were incompatible and, that if it came to a choice, the government would give priority to redistribution over growth. But the INC appeared to indicate that economic reform would have to go hand-in-hand with redistributive measures to ensure that the benefits of growth reached the poor. With the enshrining of the policy to combine growth with equity, an important step was taken in strengthening Indian democracy. Singh summarized the challenge thus when he took over as Prime Minister: 'the government would have to focus on the poor, the rural, the agricultural sector. We have to provide water, schools, health facilities, jobs for the youth and a favourable environment for business and industry to flourish'.[20] Likewise, Sonia Gandhi, leader of the INC, clearly stated that 'The goal of the INC party remains one of equity and growth'.[21]

The political incentives for the INC and the UPA to act on this understanding are substantial. Presently, some of the former's policies and programmes partly reflect the demands of its social base, creating the possibility of building an enduring social coalition.[22] Yet, this is a coalition that has come about as a result of voter choices at the state level, and not because the INC had consciously set about to construct it. The coordination of a sustainable social base requires the party to rebuild its federal party organization, giving meaningful representation to the marginalized groups that have become increasingly assertive during the 1990s and thereafter.

In terms of policy, the INC and the UPA government are following a strategy that consists of a continued focus on economic reforms together with insisting that resources are made available for the implementation of social sector programmes to address inequalities. There are several policies and documents that resonate with this basic commitment, including the National Rural Health Mission, the Jawaharlal Nehru National Urban Renewal

Mission (JNNURM), new education policies, the Right to Information Act, and the proposed law for the social security for unorganized sector workers. In addition, the INC-led government has committed itself to 'ensure that all reservation quotas [for SCs and STs], including those relating to promotions, will be fulfilled in a time-bound manner'.[23] Of course, the progress has not been commensurate with expectations.[24] Similarly, the INC has set in motion a large number of proposals for minorities, especially Muslims; for example, the 15-point welfare programme, in addition to the decision to set up the National Commission for Minority Educational Institutions, which has been recast to make it monitorable and to focus action on issues linked with social, educational, and economic development of minorities.[25]

It was in the context of the rising economic divide and the climate of dissatisfaction with the neoliberal economic policies on the one hand, and the enormous opposition to state intervention on the other, that Sonia Gandhi put her weight behind the NREGPA 2005, launched on 2 February 2006 in the Anantpur district of Andhra Pradesh. The Act was the single most important promise of the INC manifesto. It would introduce legislation to guarantee at least 100 days of casual manual work at minimum wages for anyone who applied for work within a specified timeframe. While the manifesto had made the promise for both rural and urban India, the NREGPA has confined itself only to rural India, and even this is to be carried out in a phased manner starting with the 200 most backward districts. It is worth remembering that the INC had been promising rural employment guarantees since the Guwahati session of the All India Congress Committee (AICC) in May 2002. This assurance has been instrumental in marshalling popular support for the party. If properly implemented, the NREGPA will be one of the most significant pieces of legislation since Independence, with the potential to go a long way in bridging the gap between political equality and economic inequality. The scheme's critical significance lies in its promise that if the government fails to provide employment to the beneficiary families within 15 days of application, it will pay such families 25 per cent of the minimum wage for 30 days as unemployment allowance and 50 per cent of the wages for the rest of the period.[26] Even those who are concerned about implementation problems, leakages, and corruption with regard to pro-poor schemes would agree that strong pro-poor policies such as the NREGPA could have a huge impact on the ground,[27] and that the very existence of such policies set demonstrative standards and benchmarks for other parties to follow. For the INC, the NREGPA was an attempt to address the basic needs of the underprivileged sections that form the bulk of the party's social base. It is particularly significant for the party because two-thirds of the backward districts affected by the Act lie within INC-ruled states. The challenge for the party, therefore, is to effectively implement the employment scheme.[28]

Notwithstanding the NREGPA, the INC by and large fails to recognize the magnitude of widespread unemployment and agrarian distress plaguing the country. If there has been one constant preventing India from reaching its potential, it is the failure of successive governments to keep promises of implementing economic development along with a reduction in social inequalities.

Consequently, these initiatives are inadequate for dealing with inequalities and the many obstacles that stand in the way of equality. Broad-based development requires substantial investment in human resource development for enhancing people's capabilities, especially in rural areas. Instead, the approach of the UPA government—like the NDA one before it—is that the rapid march towards social justice will depend upon achieving a much higher growth rate of some 9–10 per cent over a 25-year period. In essence, the ruling policy paradigm has failed to separate the growth rate of GDP from its distributional implications for the poor. As such social sector programmes that provide education, health services or drinking water can only target the poor indirectly.[29] It is not too difficult to see what would happen to landless, small and marginal farmers under these circumstances. In 2001 in Andhra Pradesh, for instance, the high cost structure of inefficient cultivation relative to the low prices of imported products jeopardized the livelihoods of the poorest cultivators in the most backward regions.[30] In contrast, the Indian middle class appears to have a wider political and economic policy impact than its actual numbers warrant. This is because the balance of social, political, and economic power has shifted comprehensively in favour of the middle classes and global capital in comparison with all other groups. Given the political and economic weight of the middle classes, it would be unrealistic for the INC to ignore them, especially because the party may find it difficult to win over the middle castes or the OBCs that generally support regional and caste parties. Since many of these parties arose in opposition to the INC, they often built their power base around the intermediate castes—the so-called backward castes—that the latter had failed to incorporate. Thus, the party has been eager to win back the votes of the middle classes, which currently are more inclined towards the BJP. The middle classes preference for the BJP stems from a sense of alienation from the INC's image as a catch-all party, which can only survive by catering to a broader swathe of classes, castes, and communities, and is constrained from projecting predominantly middle-class interests.[31]

This ambiguity of approach indicates a fundamental tension within the INC about its self-identity. The party embraces neither the genuine politics of the poor nor can it afford to be openly elitist like the BJP. Instead, it seeks to address the needs and aspirations of both sectors. At the centre of this tension is the question of the desired policy direction that the INC leadership seeks to adopt. The policy direction that Prime Minister Singh wants to achieve is clearly in favour of a more open, liberalized economy.[32] In contrast, Sonia Gandhi is widely perceived to be pro–poor and committed to social development in the most inclusive sense. A left–of–centre perspective propels most of her important initiatives and decisions. Consequently, there is a perception of a disjunction between the 'conservative' government and the popular party, although she herself has been quick to dispel any doubt in this regard: 'The Prime Minister has taken a close personal interest in each of them [welfare goals]. And I know it has not been easy for him to balance different considerations'.[33]

In the past, the highly centralized party machine of the INC happily fell in line with Indira Gandhi when she expanded the scope of government in the economy, with Rajiv Gandhi when he launched his technology missions, and with Rao when he minimized the role of the state in the economy.[34] While this last action led to serious unrest as INC managers doubted whether the party would remain popular and electable, they did not change the policy. This time, too, the party is a little less inclined to accept the government's policy direction for the first time, a member of the Nehru–Gandhi family leads the party rather than the government. Thus, we find that overall the party is more willing to accept the new socio–political–economic agenda of the government rather than the other way round. While this is the case, it would seem that Sonia Gandhi is keen to maintain the close identification of the party with the *aam aadmi*, as reflected, for instance, in her insistence on increasing social sector allocations in development policy. The 2006 budget was an occasion to emphasize social spending in the area of anti–poverty and rural programmes and infrastructure. Overall, the eight flagship programmes in the social sector in the areas of rural employment, education, health, the midday meal scheme, and urban renewal were slated to receive a huge increase of 43.2 per cent in the 2006 Budget, although this only amounts to an allocation of Rs. 15,088 crore.[35] This is far short of the promises made in the Common Minimum Programme, in which expenditures on health and education alone amounting to 3 per cent and 6 per cent of the GDP, respectively, would require significantly more than what was given for all eight programmes. The increase in central outlay on rural employment (excluding the north–eastern areas) was only 10 per cent.[36]

The need for balance has become more pronounced in the post–reform era when the level of disparity in a society already epitomized by hierarchy and privilege has increased markedly. This is clear in regional terms, with the south and the west making the most significant gains in investment while much of north and east India lags far behind. This is even sharper in terms of social indicators of human development.[37] Even as reforms focus on cutting government spending and presence, in much of north and central and parts of eastern India the government provides only a fraction of the people with public services considered the norm in any civilized society.[38] These include access to safe drinking water and sanitation, primary health services, and schools. The cross-regional disparities have resulted in the emergence of very different socio-political and economic patterns in different parts of India. The south, with its higher rates of literacy, urbanization, human skills, and endowment as a result of decades of social reform and public action, has forged ahead of the north. Social divisions in the north, especially in the 'Hindi belt', home to over one-quarter of the total Indian population as well as the largest concentration of its poor, have contributed to this region's failure to attract commensurate investment in social welfare.[39] The bridging of these disparate elements is an extraordinary task, and one that will require closer harmonization of the centre and states, as well as of ideology and policy.

The fundamental problem is that the INC has not been able to find a way to weld its various policies into a concrete and coherent political strategy. It does not have a political and organizational strategy to connect different economic and political programmes under a central idea. The real disjuncture in the INC is not between the government and the party; it is between economic and political programmes and the second rung of leadership, who simply cannot deliver on these initiatives. With the exception of a few individuals at the top, the INC leadership is far removed from its grass roots, having more in common with the elite and middle classes than with the poor who generally vote the party to power. A rising number of powerful cabinet ministers and party leaders belong to the Rajya Sabha (upper house of parliament)—not the ideal abode for political activists—reflecting a growing disinclination to engage with the risks of mass politics. The absence of political linkages between the choice of leaders to whom party responsibilities are being delegated and the issues raised by the rough and tumble of caste battles, economic discontent and/or populism is particularly problematic. The INC, even at the level of local units, remains in the hands of individuals who have more access to the top echelons of the party than knowledge about the needs of local voters. This deep gulf is aggravated by the tendency of the party to marginalize leaders who have at least some vestiges of links between policy and politics for fear of upsetting its centralized power structure. In short, the top political leaders of the

INC have little knowledge of the issues of concern to the masses on the ground.[40]

Another important result of the expanding influence of the elite and middle classes is the change in the INC's strategic perspective in foreign policy, especially towards the United States. This marks a radical change for a party that, in the days of Jawaharlal Nehru and Indira Gandhi, took pride in the vision of India being a leader of the developing world, and adopted a policy of non-alignment that made clear its reservations about superpower hegemony. Undeniably, recent economic reforms and the growing middle-class' craving for closer business and economic ties with the United States was a driving force in the shift towards a more friendly stance with America. Since 1991, when the economy underwent a paradigm shift, the United States began to see India as an emerging market and recognized the possibility of considerable profits in doing business with it. For most of the aspiring upwardly mobile Indians, a sustained engagement with the United States is the key to the fulfilment of their lifestyle aspirations. They have bought into the American dream and its replication in India, including shopping malls, cell phones, big cars, and luxury apartments. A survey in 2006 by the US-based Pew Research Centre confirmed that India's middle class was strongly inclined towards the United States: as many as 71 per cent in this all-urban India sample had a favourable opinion of America; the highest proportion among the 16 countries surveyed.[41] This closer engagement with the United States began in the early 1990s under Rao's administration, and has been continued and accelerated by the present government. The vote against Iran at the International Atomic Energy Agency and the vote to refer Iran to the United Nations Security Council are indications of this shift. By voting for a western-sponsored resolution, India signalled the end of its independent foreign policy. The UPA government signed an historic civilian nuclear deal with the United States in 2005. Widely regarded as a breakthrough, the Indo-US nuclear deal is popular with the middle classes because it brings India and the United States closer, with its proposed separation of civilian and military nuclear sites for inspection perceived as being to India's advantage and evidence that the government did not surrender to American pressure. However, the deal comes with additional extras, including a partnership to counter China. Indeed, the principal reason the administration of George W. Bush was prepared to accept the Indian separation plan was on the basis that the Indian Government recognized the strategic significance of the partnership.[42] India's strategic location between West Asia and South-East Asia, and her emergence as a major global economic power, place it in a special league.[43] The new strategic relationship is part of a larger political arrangement premised on Washington's offer to help India become a 'Great

Power' in the twenty-first century. This has been the rationale for the Indo–US nuclear deal and defence cooperation framework, and President Bush's visit to the country in March 2006.[44]

While the new strategic relationship with the United States is not a deliberate strategy designed to win the support of the elite and middle classes, the pro-American tilt of the INC managed to wean away the middle and upper classes from the BJP. At the same time, however, this stance is likely to be detrimental to the party's Muslim support base. The huge Muslim presence in protest rallies and marches against the Bush visit took the INC by surprise. It is a matter of record that the party has been reluctant to criticize the American policy on Iraq. Its inability to speak up is inexplicable. A party that has had a long history of mobilizing world opinion against superpower domination has suddenly opted for ambivalence.

Organizationally, the INC's biggest challenge has been its inability to connect to local realities in politics.[45] A top-down political structure has hampered this task and led to organizational atrophy.[46] Time and again, the party has failed to modernize and democratize itself organizationally. Once upon a time, the INC had a strongly rooted organizational network that was the envy of political parties all over the world. It can return to this enviable state only if it brings about democracy and decentralization among its cadres at the grass roots' level. Until then, the INC will continue to be unable to engender mass mobilization or demonstrate any kind of indignation, be it on Iraq or drought, or rising prices, or farmers' suicides. The designated party spokesmen and leaders articulate the INC's position on television channels, which are deemed a sufficient recompense for any kind of mobilization of the masses. Looking up to the high command for the smallest of decisions, combined with a neglect of leaders with popular support, is now very much the party's way of practising politics.[47]

However, the INC is aware of this organizational atrophy and the risks it brings for its capacity to engage with mass politics. Rajiv Gandhi told the AICC centenary session in 1985 that 'the revitalization of our party organization is a historical necessity'.[48] Sonia Gandhi's organizational work within the party has so far mainly focused on higher levels through initiatives and adjustments within the AICC and the Working Committee. In the Hyderabad plenary in January 2006, Sonia Gandhi could have begun the task of repairing and re-energizing the 120-year-old party by announcing that elections would be held to the Congress Working Committee, breaking the now long practice of nominating members and thereby restoring a modicum of inner-party democracy. But the INC leadership fell back on the top-down device of recasting the Congress Working Committee and AICC without elections.[49]

Assessment

Since the 1990s, the INC has betrayed a lack of any coherent and consistent set of values, ideas, and policies. Heading a coalition government has made it even harder to articulate and pursue any long-term vision and perspective. The verdict of 2004 against the BJP-led NDA was a vote in favour of secularism and equitable growth. Secularism remains one of the pillars of the UPA government, and the common commitment to this principle holds the coalition together. No doubt the BJP's defeat has put a brake on the expansion of communalism and religious nationalism that were gaining ground in the 1990s. Yet the perpetrators of Gujarat violence and other riots remain unpunished, and Muslim citizens continue to lose ground. The second aspect that the INC has not addressed adequately is its ambiguity regarding economic issues. It does not sufficiently recognize that its survival depends on balancing the imperatives of economic growth with a social democratic agenda.

While the INC has continued with the NDA's economic policies, it still hankers after the label of a 'left-of-centre' party. Information and Broadcasting Minister Priya Ranjan Dasmunshi described the INC as India's greatest left party.[50] Far from taking this road, the Prime Minister and Finance Minister constantly discuss a growth target of 10 per cent per annum as the key to inclusive development. But high growth is not an automatic antidote to poverty. The issue is not the pace of growth, but the pattern of growth; in particular, the widespread unemployment that has characterized it. In addition, the much-hyped big push on agriculture and infrastructure has yet to take off. It is not enough to view the slew of social legislations or the Bharat Nirman 4-year business plan for rural infrastructure or JNNURM initiatives as panaceas. Indeed, the Bharat Nirman plan has seen only a marginal increase in allocations for irrigation and drinking water. Moreover, in seeking to finance the expansion of roads, power-generation, and telecommunications largely through reliance on 'private-public partnerships', the initiative lets the state off the hook as far as its responsibility to the public is concerned, and imposes high user-charges upon what should be low-priced services for the people. While the JNNURM plans are basically efficiency driven, the pro-poor programmes are more like add-ons or embellishments. As a result, there is no proper integration or institutionalization on the ground.

Linked to this policy disjuncture is the INC's strategic inconsistency.[51] The party lacks programmatic clarity and has no discernible appeal for the poor and disadvantaged. However, they continue to support it, presumably because of its past image and their own reservations about the BJP, perceived as more pro-rich than other parties. The INC's desire to gain the approval of the middle classes, despite its core support coming from the economically underprivileged sections, has been the single most important factor in the failure of the party to address the disjunction between its policies and politics. Its major shift in economic and foreign policies has added significance to the role of the middle classes in the arena of policymaking and public discourse, but the INC does not recognise that it performs well in elections when it can actively mobilize the socially marginalized groups. Therefore, the party must strengthen and reinforce its popular base. This underlines the need for the political leadership to harness the nation's social energy to ensure a fair and equitable process of development, shifting the balance of forces between rich and poor decisively in favour of the latter. Only in this way can it build a winning social coalition of groups as an alternative counter bloc to that of the BJP. To achieve this, it must choose between pragmatism and populism and bridge the disjunction between ideology and policy. Yet the INC is constantly vacillating between populism and liberalization. One implication of this is the bifurcation between economic policymaking and political mobilization on more people-oriented issues. Social welfare promises have become unsustainable policy packages because economic policies limit the ability of the INC to evolve a durable social base. At the same time, political mobilization during the 1980s and 1990s has made politics more competitive, heightening the welfare expectations of marginalized sections vis-à-vis the state. This is precisely the moment when party competition is on the increase, but the policy options before the voter have dramatically declined.

Nehru once wrote that 'Where there is no vision, the people perish', and his INC was a great battleground of ideas and ideologies. Even if its outcomes were below expectations, there was a clear programme and an outlook that bound together the members of the party and society. The present-day INC carries no sense of intellectual excitement however, and has ceased being at the centre of debate. This is a matter of consequence for the party and contemporary politics. It suggests that, for all its talent of leadership, the party cannot set the national agenda. A party that cannot set the agenda is unlikely to be able to break the current mould of politics, yet the stakes in breaking the current mould are very high for the INC and for the future of India's democracy. The principal problem lies in the tension between political democracy and the market economy, which surfaces at the time of elections. The voter dissatisfaction with unresponsive governments was there for all to see. Disillusionment can lead to the emergence of extremism and mobilization around religion, caste, ethnicity, and other identities. It is clear that the strategy of neoliberal economic reform has not found favour with most of the Indian electorate for the simple reason that they have not gained—and many have even lost—because of it. Yet successive governments have come in and done more of the same, disregarding all the signals that voters send out. This incapacity to influence policy is the result of a process whereby democratic choices and political processes have less and less power over the policy decisions critical to shaping people's social and material lives. This is because in India (as, indeed, in several other developing countries), a substantial section of the elites and middle classes now see their interests as more closely tied to globalization than to the rest of their own country's population. The greatest challenge of democracy today is the frustration of the majority with governments they vote in but do not control, and the self-satisfied indifference of elites towards governments they do not vote in, but control. This is the real irony. While there seems to be ample political choices available to the Indian voter, there is an absence of genuine differences, leaving the majority of the people feeling disconnected and frustrated by their inability to influence policies, especially economic and foreign policies. Until that vital connection or bridge is provided, the INC's promise to revive the democratic agenda and to become an effective vehicle of democratic aspirations and inclusive development will remain empty political rhetoric.

Notes and References

1. See Chapter 3 of this volume.
2. Malini Parthasarathy, 'INC: A new sense of purpose', unpublished paper, 2005.
3. On the size and composition of the middle class, see E. Sridharan, 'The Growth and Sectoral Composition of India's Middle Class: Its Impact on the Politics of Economic Liberalization', *India Review*, vol. 3, no. 4, October 2004.
4. Christopher Cadland, 'Congress decline and party pluralism in India', *Journal of International Affairs*, vol. 51, Summer 1997, pp 19–35.
5. Mahesh Rangarajan, 'Congress in Crisis', *Seminar*, no. 521, January 2003, pp. 34–7.
6. Atul Kohli, 'Politics of economic growth in India', unpublished paper presented at the Conference on State Politics in India in the 1990s Developing Countries Research Centre (DCRC), University of Delhi and London School of Economics, December 2004.
7. Sridharan, 'Growth and Sectoral Composition', pp. 405–28.
8. The National Council of Applied Economic Research plus other estimates of the size of the middle classes reported in *The Hindu*, 22 May 2005.
9. Jayati Ghosh, 'Income inequality in India', *People's Democracy*, vol. XXVII, no. 7, 15 February 2005.
10. Ibid.
11. Ibid.
12. *India: Social Development Report*, Delhi: Oxford University Report, 2006.

13. S.P. Gupta, 'Economic Reforms and its Impact on Poor', *Economic and Political Weekly*, vol. 30, no. 22, 3 June 1995, pp. 1295–1313.

14. Anthony Heath and Yogendra Yadav, 'The united colours of the INC: social profile of INC voters, 1996 and 1998', in *Parties and Party Politics*, ed. Zoya Hasan, Delhi: Oxford University Press, 2002, pp. 107–49.

15. Yogendra Yadav, Sanjay Kumar, and Oliver Heath, 'The BJP's new social bloc', *Frontline*, 19 November 1999, pp. 32–3.

16. Yogendra Yadav, 'The elusive mandate of 2004', *Economic and Political Weekly*, vol. 39, no. 51, 18 December 2004, pp. 5383-98.

17. Ibid., p. 5395.

18. Mahesh Rangarajan, 'The Congress–Left Relations', *The Telegraph*, January 2006.

19. *National Common Minimum Programme of the Government of India*, May 2004, http://pmindia.nic.in/cmp.html, accessed on 1 August 2006.

20. '"We will focus on the poor", Manmohan promises secular, stable Government', *The Hindu*, 21 May 2004.

21. *The Times of India*, 23 May 2005.

22. Francine Frankel, *India's Political Economy 1947-2004*, Delhi: Oxford University Press, 2nd edn., 2005, pp 786-7.

23. National Common Minimum Programme of the Government of India.

24. Even 6 months after a note by the Prime Minister reminding his colleagues of the commitment, the figures submitted to the parliamentary forum of SCs and STs by Minister of State for Personnel indicate that of the 22,157 posts identified for promotion of SC candidates, only 13,753 had been filled. Similarly, of the 12,771 posts identified for recruitment, the government had managed to fill up just 6,051. For the STs candidates, the government had 15,205 posts for recruitment but filled only 6,095. The figures for promotions were even more disheartening for the 25,809 posts identified, the ministries and departments managed only 9,950 promotions. *Outlook*, New Delhi, 27 March 2006.

25. *The Indian Express*, 26 December 2006.

26. Ibid.

27. The scheme has generated huge interest among the underprivileged. The rush of applicants shows how important this initiative has been for them. Within a week of its launch, it saw 2.7 million applicants in just 13 districts of Andhra Pradesh and close to a million in 12 districts of Maharashtra despite the fact that the wage of Rs. 60 is below the minimum of several states. See P. Sainath, *The Hindu*, 1 April 2006.

28. John Echeverri-Gent, 'Politics of development and the development of politics: an inquiry into the political means of equitable development', *Contemporary South Asia*, vol. 1, no. 3, 1992, pp. 325-49.

29. G. Krishna Reddy, 'New populism and liberalization: regime shift under Chandrababu Naidu in AP', *Economic and Political Weekly*, 2 March 2002, pp. 871–83.

30. Ibid.

31. Yogendra Yadav, 'Urban India more Polarized' and 'Economic reforms in the mirror of public opinion', *The Hindu*, 13 June 2004.

32. Harish Khare, 'A dangerous incoherence at the core', *The Hindu*, 18 January 2006.

33. Congress President Sonia Gandhi's speech at the Congress plenary session in Hyderabad, *The Hindu*, 28 January 2006.

34. Mahesh Rangarajan, 'Congress in Crisis', *Seminar*, no. 521, January 2003, pp. 34–7.

35. Or Rs. 150,880,000,000, as one crore is equivalent to Rs. 10,000,000.

36. Prabhat Patnaik, 'The budgetary non-exercise', *Frontline*, vol. 23, no. 5, 11-24 March 2006.

37. For an overview, see United Nations Development Programme, *UN Human Development Report*, Geneva: United Nations, 2003; and Jean Drèze and Amartya Sen, *Economic Development and Social Opportunity*, Delhi: Oxford University Press, 2000.

38. Mahesh Rangarajan, 'Polity in transition: India after the 2004 General Elections', *Economic and Political Weekly*, vol. 40, no. 32, 6 August 2005, pp. 3598–606.

39. Ibid.

40. Pratap Bhanu Mehta, 'Where's the party: the INC is in power. But it shows no signs of life', *The Indian Express*, 25 June 2005.

41. Only 41–5 per cent in most Western European countries have a favourable opinion, barring the United Kingdom (55 per cent). The proportion is 42 per cent in China, and only 23 per cent in Pakistan. See Pew Research Centre.

42. Siddharth Varadarajan, 'Beyond the Deal', *Frontline*, vol. 23, no. 5, 11-24 March 2006.

43. Manmohan Singh-Bush, 'Joint statement', cited in *Frontline*, vol. 23, no. 5, 11-14 March 2006.

44. Praful Bidwai, 'Nuclear deal at what price?', *Frontline*, vol. 23, no. 5, 11–24 March 2006.

45. Ibid.

46. Ibid.

47. Jyotirmaya Sharma, 'Spluttering on all cylinders', *DNA*, Mumbai, 18 May 2006.

48. James Manor, 'Organizational renewal', *Seminar*, no. 526, June 2003, pp. 23–5.

49. The INC is not the only party that does not have elections; indeed, most political parties in India do not practice internal democracy.

50. Opinion poll cited in Praful Bidwai, 'Ready to collude with empire', *Frontline*, vol. 23, no. 13, 1–14 July 2006.

51. Praful Bidwai, 'Illusory tryst with destiny: INC still groping for strategy', *Frontline*, 30 January 2006; Mahesh Rangarajan, 'The Congress-Left Relations', *The Telegraph*, January 2006.

20 | Breaking New Ground
Congress and Welfarism in India

The Congress party in the months leading to the 2004 general elections challenged the myth of the Bharatiya Janata Party (BJP)-led National Democratic Alliance (NDA) government's 'India Shining' campaign with its new slogan, 'Congress ka haath, aam aadmi ke saath' (Congress' hand (the party's electoral symbol) is with the common man). The 'India Shining' versus *aam aadmi* confrontation in the 2004 elections highlighted an apparently widespread perception that the benefits of economic growth were simply passing too many people by. Voters rejected the idea of 'India Shining', supporting instead the Congress-led United Progressive Alliance (UPA) and its promise of inclusive development. Notwithstanding several other factors that may have influenced the outcome of the elections, the discerning assessment that a pervasive feeling of exclusion contributed to its surprise win in the election went on to shape the broad policy orientation of the UPA government (2004–9). This perception was the critical catalyst that effected a policy change facilitating the introduction of welfarist policies by the UPA government at the centre which in turn had an impact on the positive verdict in favour of the Congress in the 2009 elections. This chapter tracks the processes that paved the way for a radical shift leading to the adoption of a wide range of policies that reflect a social democratic flavour; it is not, however, concerned with the outcomes of these policies. Social welfarism played a decisive role in giving substance to the inclusive policies of the Congress government and the results of 2009 elections show that voters have given a mandate for the continuation of such welfare-oriented policies.

In 2004, the electorate rewarded the UPA for its promise of pluralism and inclusion, while it rejected the BJP's politics division and of exclusion.[1] The Congress-led UPA had won 222 seats in 2004 and was able to reach a parliamentary majority with the outside support of the 61-member Left Front, which in effect meant that it did not take on the responsibilities of governance but was able to exert substantial influence on central government policies. In the circumstances, the Congress was clearly pushed by the Left parties to launch and partially implement some pro-people policies; but it can be argued that the 2009 mandate was ultimately an endorsement of Congress welfarism, albeit under political pressure from the Left. To understand this, it is important to reiterate context in which the inclusive agenda of the Congress government was forged, which was the BJP's defeat on the 'India Shining' platform. This election was a battle over two different ideas of India, one inclusive and pluralist, the other exclusivist and homogeneous. The second idea lost out in that election. The BJP's rise to power represented the most potent challenge to the first model, which is closely related to the inspirations behind the freedom struggle and its progressive and modernist ideas (the BJP or its predecessor the Jan Sangh was not a part of this struggle). For the BJP the key issue was economic prosperity of the business elite and transforming India into a Great Power by 2020.

Indeed, it allowed a small economic minority to prosper at the expense of the majority with disastrous political consequences from 1998–2004. Yet the BJP, taken in by its own hype, campaigned on the slogans of 'India Shining' and 'Feel Good' factor which it was convinced would pay the coalition rich electoral dividends. Its insensitive slogans backfired sharply. In 2004, the Congress-led UPA came to power with the understanding that growth had left behind both rural and urban India's toiling masses. It understood clearly that this inequality, particularly in opportunities, mattered hugely. It understood that India's polity was in the main secular and therefore uncomfortable with communal politics. Much of this was reflected in the UPA's National Common Minimum Programme (NCMP) agreed to between the Congress and the four Left parties, who maintained that the NCMP would be the basis for its support. For its part, the Congress fashioned its idea of inclusive growth partly out of concern for the poor and partly driven by the need to distinguish itself from its principal rival, the BJP. In power from 2004 to 2009, the Congress government took tangible action to translate this idea into some concrete measures with an emphasis on expanding the consumption driven entitlements of the poor.[2]

These shifts have to be placed in the context of enormous policy changes that had taken place since 1991. The details of these policies that came to be adopted are well known, and need not be repeated here. Economic growth and improving production was given top priority as the both the NDA and UPA governments pursued economic policies to unshackle market forces.

One key consequence was the growing influence of corporate sector and big business groups on the state which more and more acts in the interests of private players and the upper echelons of society and is getting rapidly integrated into the global economy.

From the 1990s India has witnessed an increasing convergence amongst political formations over matters of policy: economic policy (including Left-ruled state governments), foreign policy (barring the Left), security policy, issues of social justice, and environment policy, at least at a formal level. Hence, central and state governments were unwilling to roll back neoliberal policies, many of which have been pushed through without much opposition or dissent. It was this convergence which explains the longevity of neoliberalism and the remarkable continuity in economic policy-making.[3] This is despite the fact that five governments of varying political persuasions have come to power since the Congress government of Prime Minister Narasimha Rao initiated a paradigm shift towards market-led economic growth during its tenure from 1991 to 1996. For this reason, many commentators have noted that there were no longer significant differences between political formations which could influence, let alone swing electoral outcomes. What is more, the high levels of electoral participation witnessed since the democratic upsurge of the early 1990s which intensified the participation of groups that suffer from social deprivation and exclusion, has actually meant very little with regard to the policy paradigm because no matter which government comes to power there is stability and continuity in policies as these have been kept out of the democratic contestation.[4]

The Human Face of a
Neoliberal Growth Model

This argument was valid until the 2004 elections which marked a new trend not in evidence since the 1991 elections when the simultaneous rise of neoliberalism and identity politics trumped policy debates and put it beyond the pale of political and ideological differences.[5] However, the central government that came to power after the 2004 elections quickly signalled a shift in favour of greater emphasis on redistributive policies which were shaped in response to the pressures of democratic competition and coalition politics. Even though scepticism is warranted given India's poor record of implementation of distributive policies, at the same time, we must not over-emphasize ideological convergence in policymaking and, consequently, minimize the role that democratic politics has played in shaping the political agenda of the Congress government since 2004. Admittedly, there are areas of convergence between all the major parties and formations, especially in economic policy, but these too are not static or given. Here too the balance between economic and social policy can be shaped by socio-political forces, which in turn open up the possibility of democratic politics being able to shape public agenda.[6] The experience of the UPA with regard to the adoption of welfarist policies and an expenditure-driven fiscal strategy demonstrates that a more balanced approach is conceivable under democratic and civil society pressure.[7]

This shift in emphasis was clearly necessary because the benefits of India's economic boom since 2003–4 did not percolate to the vast majority who are poor and disadvantaged. In the United Nations Human Development Index (HDI) of 2007–8, India ranked a dismal 128. India then fell to 132 in the rankings of the HDI for 179 nations in 2008–9. That is the worst ever grade on the Index that decade. The HDI figures since 2002 signal a steady decline in the nation's conversion of wealth into human development—even as the numbers of its billionaires and millionaires doubled and trebled. In reality, the 'paradox of India's new prosperity',[8] has been the duality where the top 20 per cent of the population have done extremely well whereas two-thirds of the country were lagging behind. Throughout the 1990s the economy grew at a reasonably robust pace, rising to an average growth rate of 8 per cent between 2004 and 2008, since India became the tenth-largest economy globally in 2004. Despite growth acceleration and impressive economic growth, disparities remain widespread; indeed there is evidence of widening inequalities along a variety of dimensions: city versus the countryside; across regions; and along class lines.[9] The reports of the National Commission for Enterprises in the Unorganized Sector (set up by the UPA government) point out that though the unorganized sector workers account for nearly 92 per cent of the total workforce, they have been completely bypassed even as the economy's growth rates have surged. The Report on the Conditions of Work and Promotion of Livelihoods in the Unorganized Sector comes to the sobering conclusion that 77 per cent of the population, which means at least 836 million Indians, subsist on Rs. 20 or less per day.

Yet, from late 1990s to 2000s, there was too much preoccupation with growth and not enough done to reduce the rich-poor divide. Besides, the single major problem with the growth process is that it is for the most part jobless growth. Services which have fuelled the impressive 8 per cent growth account for 55 per cent of the Gross Domestic Product (GDP) and formally employ just 2 million people, or less than 0.5 per cent of the country's labour force of over 400 million (there are 190 million self-employed individuals primarily in the service sector).[10] Unemployment, a perennial problem of the Indian economy has become more serious in recent years. This is especially true of rural unemployment, which grew at an annual rate of 0.58 per cent between 1993–4 and 1999–2000, which was far below the growth of rural population.[11] Agriculture has grown at just over 2 per cent and the share of agriculture has declined from about 60 per cent at the time of independence to about 19 per cent in 2009. Nevertheless, the share of the population which is dependent on agriculture is about two-thirds. Thanks to low productivity and inconsistent growth, agriculture is not a viable option for the majority of the rural population, which has made livelihood a key issue for government intervention.

Although the growth model and 'market optimism' underpinning economic policymaking saw no change after the UPA government assumed power in 2004, it was accepted that there were serious distributional issues that needed to be addressed. It is in this regard that the UPA signalled a change of regimes as the government unveiled a slew of legislation which sought to ameliorate some of the inequalities that the process of market-led economic growth generated. Within a few months of assuming office, UPA-1 (2004–9) sought to shift the balance of policy with a focus on equity and inclusive growth as the centrepiece of several of its interventions. This shift is reflected in the Eleventh Five-Year Plan (2007-12) which underscored the theme of inclusive growth and this was to become the trademark of the Congress government with regard to social and economic development. High on the government's agenda of greater inclusiveness, therefore, were actions to address disparities in access to education, health care, water, and other public services that are necessary for people's well-being.

During its first term in office several new programmes and schemes were introduced and budgetary allocations for the social sector were increased as compared to previous years. These included a step up in public investment in agriculture and the debt relief programme for farmers. In terms of the sheer number of policies and legislations, UPA's focus on welfarism was unprecedented. This is evident from the eight flagship programmes established by the UPA government (Table 20.1).

The National Rural Employment Guarantee Act (NREGA), the Right to Information Act 2005,[12] National Rural Health Mission (NRHM), and Bharat Nirman were among the most important measures taken to transform the rural economy. In addition, the Unorganized Workers Social Security Bill 2008 which seeks to provide some health care, old age pension, and disability benefits to unorganized sector workers and to the Scheduled Tribes (STs) and the Traditional Forest Dwellers (Recognition of Forest Rights) Act 2006, that seeks to protect livelihoods and land rights of tribals and forest dwellers, were notified in January 2008. The NREGA and the Forest Rights Act were unprecedented because they represented the first time any government had recognized livelihood rights of the deprived.

TABLE 20.1: Spending on Poverty-Reducing Programmes since 2004 (in billions)

Programme	Expenditure (Rs.)
Bharat Nirman (a cluster of six infrastructure programmes)	1,14,257
Sarva Shiksa Abhiyan (education, figures only to 2008)	37,500
Midday Meals Scheme (figures only to 2008)	20,625
National Rural Employment Guarantee Scheme (NREGS)	440
Total Sanitation Campaign	2,550
National Rural Health Mission[15]	200
Integrated Child Development Services (figs, only to 2008)	160
Jawaharlal Nehru National Urban Renewal Mission	7,908
Polio Eradication	90
TOTAL	27,184 ($57.40 billion)

Source: The Times of India, 3 June 2009.

Another key initiative was the decision to establish the Prime Minister's High Level Committee (popularly known as the Sachar Committee) to inquire into the socio-economic status of Muslims in the country. It was well known that decades of anti-Muslim rhetoric, everyday discrimination, and neglect by the government had brought about a situation of economic marginality for Muslims, and a huge deficit in education and social advancement compared to most other citizens of the country.[13] The Sachar Committee Report found the most damning evidence of government neglect and discrimination against them at all levels of Indian society and by governments at the centre and in the states.[14] It reported stark under-representation of Muslims and systematic evidence to show that they are an underclass on par with the lowest Hindu caste groups.[15] The principal reason for the marginalization of Muslims has been the high level of exclusion from the mainstream employment sector. This Report set off a public debate on Muslim deprivation and under-representation which gave impetus to a new way of looking at the relationship between minorities and development and the multiple grounds of inequality in India beyond caste. It helped the government to calibrate future initiatives and policies to incorporate Muslims into the economic and political system and to push for a nuanced debate on minorities that in the recent past largely revolved around perceptions, rhetoric, and prejudice. Winning over a large and disaffected Muslim minority—the biggest minority in the world—was essential for the Congress party to regain its primacy in Indian politics. Indeed, the implementation of social welfare programmes for Muslims over the past five years have gone a long way in marshalling support for the Congress.

New welfare initiatives for minorities include the Prime Minister's New 15-Point Programme which was recast to focus action sharply on issues linked with the social, educational, and economic uplift of minorities and provide for earmarking of outlays in certain schemes so that the progress can be monitored. Important new schemes include the promotion of entrepreneurship with increased credit flows, national-level scholarships for students in professional and technical institutions, and the provision of basic amenities in selected minority concentration districts. There was also some increase in the budgetary allocations made by different ministries for minority welfare during UPA's tenure. The multi-sectoral development programme for minorities in 90 minority concentration districts remains the UPA's flagship programme for minority welfare. It was allocated Rs. 9,900 million in the Union Budget of 2009–10, but considering that the development of minorities rests largely on this flagship scheme, it needed more budgetary allocation. All in all, the UPA government needed to do a lot more to achieve the goal of inclusive development with regard to minorities.

Overall, as a percentage of the GDP, social expenditure almost doubled during the period. Central government expenditures on social services, such as health, water supply, Scheduled Castes (SCs), STs and Other Backward Classes (OBCs) came to 6.8 per cent in 2003–4; during 2004–9 it increased to almost 12.5 per cent.[16]

Needless to say the huge step up in public spending on social welfare was made possible because of an exponential increase in the magnitude of direct tax revenue from the late 1990s. By 2009, government revenues had grown to more than four times that of 2003. This enabled a fourfold increase in central government spending on the social sector. Although the social welfare spending nearly doubled by it was still less than 2 per cent of GDP, which is one of the world's lowest levels of such expenditure. Even the substantial increase in social expenditure was just not enough.[17] An even greater increase in public investment to bridge the shortfalls in the provision of public goods was necessary. The persistence of low levels of human development is one of the paradoxes of India's development experience. This despite an estimated 90 state and central level schemes that provide various kinds of social security ranging from pensions for the elderly, widows, disabled, and other vulnerable sections of society, sickness and injury benefits, and scholarships for socially and economically backward groups. However, the plethora of schemes reaches a fraction of the population that needs such support. In part this is because the present bureaucratic delivery machinery under which central sector schemes are delivered by hundreds of mutually insulated systems of delivery consumes the bulk of outlays.[18]

Assessing the Poverty Alleviation Programmes

All in all, the funds allocated to all the eight programmes was far short of what the NCMP promised on just health and education, amounting to 3 and 6 per cent of GDP.[19] The Left parties lamented that the government failed to meets its obligations under the NCMP and the threshold for a NCMP. At this point, it is important to understand the dynamics of the UPA coalition and its uneasy relationship with the Left parties which exercised major influence over the policy priorities of the government. As noted earlier, this was because the Congress was critically dependent on the support of the Left to carry on in government. The influence of the Left parties on the policy orientation of the UPA cannot be overestimated; nonetheless, it is important not to lose sight of the political perspective and strategy of Sonia Gandhi, President of the Congress party and Chairperson of the UPA. She was keen to restore her party's centre-left credentials. Most of all, she was eager to rectify an impression that the Congress was only concerned about the rich and powerful because these groups had after all gained from the economic policy paradigm shift begun by the Congress government. It was part of an all out effort to convince voters that the Congress party remains as dedicated as in the past to its central constituency, the underprivileged masses, even though the party is keen to promote the interests of the middle classes and big business in particular to increase economic growth and revenues.

In addition, the Congress leadership was apprehensive that if they were not assertive on the policy front, the Left parties would take all the credit for any policy that benefited the poor. The Left persisted in deriding the Congress for supporting the neoliberal agenda while the Congress was quick to assume the welfarist mantle to its advantage. Not surprisingly, the Congress claimed all the credit for the social democratic policies of the UPA, whereas the Left which had all along pressed for these measures was left isolated and with no political credit coming its way.

From the late 1980s the rural economy, comprising around 70 per cent of the country's population, has faced a serious crisis. Its contribution to the national income declined sharply. Apart from the declining reliance on this primary sector, inadequate rural infrastructure entailing lack of access to markets, inadequate access to proper health care and education, and above all, shrinking opportunities to gainful employment and stagnating agricultural production and growth are other important reasons for the agrarian crisis. The UPA government when it came to power in 2004 promised policies on rural employment guarantee and other infrastructural development in the rural sector. Accordingly the UPA took a number of policy initiatives of which NREGA was the most important as it promises 100 days of employment to a single individual from every household. Noteworthy also, is the UPA initiative of rural infrastructure development named Bharat Nirman which covers rural housing, rural electricity connection, telephones, road connectivity, water and sanitation, expansion of irrigation capacity, etc. The total expenditure on rural development increased from 0.58 per cent of GDP in 2004–5 to 1.2 per cent GDP in 2008–9. The bulk of this spending has been put into creating rural employment and beneficiary driven programmes for rural housing.[20] Despite the significant rise in allocation, the performance of the programmes/schemes have been below par as utilization was poor in many states, particularly in case of Bharat Nirman where progress on meeting targets was slow and none of the targets were fulfilled.

Enacted in 2005, NREGA was implemented in February 2006 in 200 districts. The passage of this legislation was clearly a major leap in the use of public policy and law as an instrument of social and economic change. Described as the 'the largest programme in the world for rural reconstruction', NREGA found pride of place in the President's first address to the Fifteenth Lok Sabha in June 2009.[21] It is probably the biggest ever demand driven guaranteed public employment initiative anywhere in the world. It ranks as the most important economic contribution of the government to the well-being of a large section of the population and a means of reviving the depressed rural economy.[22] This path-breaking piece of legislation acknowledges the fact that the state has an obligation to protect its people from unemployment and destitution, and this was indeed an important step towards ensuring some sort of economic and social security for the rural poor. Under NREGA, anyone who is willing to do manual labour at the statutory minimum wage is entitled to employment on local public works within 15 days or the state has to pay an allowance, subject to a limit of 100 days for a household in a year. As a result, employment in public works has risen to unprecedented levels in several states resulting in a 'quiet revolution in many impoverished rural districts across the country'.[23]

The NREGS is completely different from earlier government employment schemes in both conception and scale. In contrast to previous schemes, the NREGS treats employment as a right. The rights based framework entails a legal guarantee of work unlike other programmes which can be withdrawn by the government at will. In this respect, it is a new-age piece of legislation, which invokes the framework of legal rights to provide employment in rural areas and is intended to be demand driven.[24] The best guarantee of the realization of these rights lies in organized demand on the part of well-informed workers. For instance, if workers insist on payment of minimum wages, depriving them of it will be that much harder. For this to happen, of course, workers have to be aware of their rights. Furthermore, it expects substantial participation of the local people in the planning and monitoring of the scheme.[25]

Although this landmark employment programme is the most significant social welfare programme since independence, it has had an uneven record of implementation owing to a large number of problems which is only to be expected with an ambitious scheme of this magnitude.[26] It is partly because the central government had been niggardly in transferring the relevant funds to the states and partly because there were leakages and diversion of funds by some state governments. A recent survey found that NREGS workers had to put up with numerous infringements of their rights without being able to do much about it: lack of work, delays in wage payment, non-payment of minimum wages, absence of worksite facilities, to cite a few. Most of these irregularities remain unaddressed, often even unnoticed. The persistence of corruption is another aspect of this lack of accountability.[27] One important aspect of the problem is the absence of clear remedies against infringements of the Act and the lack of independent monitoring. Curiously, the NREGA talks the language of rights but there is virtual silence on available remedies when there is a violation of rights.[28]

With all its problems of implementation, it is widely recognized that NREGS has the potential to transform rural economic and social relations at many levels.[29] This is because it fundamentally challenges the prevailing power structures.[30] Progressively, it is making a difference to the lives of the rural poor, which is evident in the enthusiastic response of the local people, landless, marginal farmers, and women workers in particular. In most states, the promise of 100 days of assured employment is still a distant dream yet employment generation is much higher than under earlier public works programmes. Moreover, where employment is available, the NREGA is having an impact: wages are rising, migration is slowing down, productive assets have been created, and the power equations are changing too.[31]

Not surprisingly, the Congress party made it a point to claim NREGS as a Congress initiative to counter the Left parties' claim that UPA's pro-poor thrust, especially the implementation of NREGS, was entirely due to Left pressure to change the direction of economic policy. Congress leaders, in contrast, were eager to highlight the importance of these welfare measures in the party's scheme of policies and to make the point that it was the result of a progressive emphasis in the party strategy and its economic philosophy. To bolster this argument, one party spokesmen pointed to the Congress government in Maharashtra which had introduced the Maharashtra Employment Guarantee Scheme way back in 1977. Moreover, the party had promised at the All India Congress Committee (AICC) meeting in Guwahati in 2002 that it would enact an Employment Guarantee law if elected to power. Subsequently, this promise formed part of the Congress manifesto for the 2004 elections and was one of the key elements in the NCMP. Hence, Congress leaders insisted that the NREGS had less to do with the fact that the UPA-1 coalition was dependent on the support of the Left parties for four out of the five years it was in office, and more to do with their own rethinking.[32]

In fact, to put their imprimatur on NREGS, barely a day after assuming office as the general secretary of the Congress party, Rahul Gandhi led a delegation of office-bearers to meet Prime Minister Dr Manmohan Singh and urged him to extend NREGA to all the districts in the country. In a memorandum submitted to the prime minister, the delegation underlined the paradigm shift brought about by NREGA because it provides assured employment for 100 days to rural households. It stated: 'The key to this legislation is the word "guarantee" which makes employment a right—something that people can expect, demand and enforce.'[33] Soon thereafter it was announced that the coverage of NREGS would be extended to all 596 districts (excluding urban districts) in the country by 2008–9. In addition, when the Act was legislated in August 2005, the finance ministry's allocation was Rs. 113 billion for 200 districts which was increased to Rs. 160 billion in 2008. The budget of 2008–9 reported a quantum leap to Rs. 301 billion. However, its supporters repeatedly point out that even this amount seems be short of requirements.

On the basis of these plans and policies the Congress could project itself as a social welfarist or even a social democratic party, focused on the *aam aadmi*. The Rural Employment Guarantee and welfare programmes such as the Jawaharlal Nehru National Urban Renewal Mission (to encourage cities to improve infrastructure and basic services to the urban poor) and Bharat Nirman or what has been called the 'NREGA paradigm' created not just the much needed employment and income-raising opportunities for the poor, but also promoted 'the idea of a caring state which redistributes resources to the poor'.[34] This strategic intervention was clearly built on the frank admission by the Congress leadership that normal economic processes do not work in a situation of development deficit of regions or groups. This idea played an important part in strengthening the social democratic credentials of the Congress and these in turn helped the party to rebuild its social base among the poor and deprived and in this manner advance its political fortunes.

The Search for a Wider Social Base

There are two issues related to this political agenda that are relevant to the present discussion. First, centrism marked by a strong social welfarist thrust was the hallmark of Congress' politico-economic management of UPA-1.[35] However, in implementing this social and legislative agenda, especially NREGS, the UPA faced serious resistance from conservative elements within the ruling establishment and outside the Congress and government, especially from the corporate sector and the pro-business press. It is here that Left support and its insistence on adhering to the NCMP played a critical part in pushing the Congress to make its implementation a priority and in the end deriving huge political benefits from it. The fact that the Left parties which strongly supported such a measure were not able to translate this effort into any substantial electoral advantage for itself is ironic (they got only 24 seats in the 2009 Lok Sabha elections), but this was largely because of its doublespeak, opposing neoliberalism at the central level and doing the opposite at the state level. The unsatisfactory performance of the Left-run state governments, especially West Bengal, with regard to the implementation of these policies hampered the Left's ability to claim monopoly control over the social democratic space and any political advantage that might have ensued.[36] More specifically, its performance with regard to NREGS was very poor which greatly harmed it, whereas state governments that took it seriously and ran a decent programme gained from it.[37]

Second, these issues assumed political significance as a result of mobilization by grass roots social movements, women's groups, trades unions, lower caste groupings, and left and centre-left parties. In short, serious political mobilization had to be expended to take this agenda forward. The national campaigns for a rural employment guarantee and the right to information exemplify the extensive mobilization and public pressure undertaken around these issues. The umbrella nature of the UPA coalition and its links with several social movements meant that this mobilization could not be disregarded or overlooked as it provided a social underpinning to the UPA. It typically involved some dedicated groups, politicians, and activists who believed in the need for including rather than excluding. It shows how these campaigns, interacting with the democratic political system, shaped the development of NREGA after the 2004 elections and made it an important part of the national policy agenda.[38] Interactions and contacts between actors within the Congress party and actors in the activist network encouraged the development of guaranteed employment as a vital issue and played the most critical part in neutralizing the resistance within the government to this radical idea. Activists campaigning for guaranteed employment and powerful members of the government, particularly Sonia Gandhi and the National Advisory Council she chaired, were critical actors in pushing through the change against opposition from other actors in the government. In general, leaders in civil society and politics shaped its progress, building coalitions between them to generate support for guaranteed employment.[39]

Even as we recognize the significance of the policies introduced by the central government, it is important not to overstate the central government's achievements in this regard. One thing seems clear, however the central government and state governments that stressed welfarist measures gained in the elections.[40] Inclusive public policy and a clutch of welfare measures persuaded voters that the UPA government had made serious efforts to provide them with livelihood and inclusive development. Civil society organizations made much the same point: the government's welfare initiatives were widely recognized and appreciated in rural areas.[41] Polling data collected by the National Election Study conducted by the Centre for the Study of Developing Societies (CSDS) shows that beneficiaries were more likely to vote for Congress than non-beneficiaries who were more likely to vote for the BJP.[42] The pro-poor programmes helped the Congress to gain an advantage of 3 per cent of the vote which can prove decisive in close contests.[43] This almost certainly produced an increase in seats for the Congress and its allies in several states.

Ever since the Congress government began implementing policies designed to pursue the liberalizing agenda of economic reforms, it has struggled to reconcile the contradiction between neoliberal economic reforms, which benefit the elite and upper middle classes, and its mass support among the poor who have been the losers in this process. This challenge has been complicated by two factors: (1) a change in India's social structure from an elite mass structure to one with a substantial middle class sandwiched between these two poles; and (2) the need of the Congress party to cater for a range of groups including business interests, the middle classes, the poor and the SCs, STs, OBCs, minorities and so on. In other words, a highly elitist apex, an assertive middle class, and a mobilized majority define the new political context in which the current drama of redistributive politics is unfolding. For sure, business groups, the professional urban classes, and well–healed bureaucrats exert a great deal of influence on the state and the Congress party, but the Congress is not a party of these groups alone. Yet, its capacity to draw wide ranging social support in the aftermath of market driven economic reforms depended on its ability to sharpen its focus on economic and political inclusion and thereby increase its relevance in rapidly changing circumstances. The fact that the Congress succeeded in doing so reflects the conscious efforts made by its leadership towards achieving a stronger integration of the party's social base with its programmes and policies. It also indicates a summoning of a greater ideological purpose and political clarity in terms of its approach to the social democratic agenda.

By privileging the 'political' in the widest sense, the Congress attempted to reconcile the conflicting interests of the elites and the majority of the people by providing social safety nets to protect the marginalized from the adverse consequences of economic change. However, it has clearly not abandoned the mantra of high growth and also that of more economic reforms. This twin emphasis on social democratic policies and economic reforms is the key to the party's endeavour to satisfy both its mass base and middle class aspirations in India's changed political and policy environment. Arguably the Congress has begun to forge a new coalition of the middle classes and the poor.[44] This coalition is still a work in progress but is evidently different from the 'coalition of extremes' that defined Congress politics until the late 1980s, at least in north India, where its principal support came from the Brahmans, SCs and Muslims.[45] The new coalition is not driven by identity politics of caste or community axes which indicates that Indian politics is moving beyond the confines of narrow identity and communal politics.

This shift away from identity politics has to some extent helped to usher in a more inclusive political agenda and to bring back the poor and their concerns onto the political agenda, which is particularly important in the context of the present economic crisis. Finally, the repertoire of good policies built up by the Manmohan Singh government may not have fully impacted on the people, but they signal the possibility that political pressure might be able to force the crafting of inclusive policies that work not only for the middle classes but also for India's urban and rural poor, for lower castes, for women, for Muslims, for tribal groups and so on. It remains to be seen whether the state will continue to intervene in more supportive ways to protect the weak and whether this can be continued under UPA-2 (2009-) sans the Left push. Nevertheless, the space within which it could happen has been opened up.

Notes and References

1. See Chapter 19 of this volume.
2. Siddharth Varadarajan, 'Political Logic of Budget is that Welfarism Pays', *The Hindu*, 7 July 2009.
3. Prabhat Patnaik, one of the foremost critics of neoliberalism points out: 'The triumph of neoliberalism in India was never complete. The nationalized banks continued to remain state-owned; key public sector companies were not privatized; pension funds were not handed over to speculative finance capital; the currency was not made fully convertible; and the financial sector's holding of foreign assets, other than the foreign exchange reserves of the Reserve Bank of India (RBI), continued to remain minuscule. In short, the two interlinked and mutually reinforcing processes underlying neoliberalism, namely, the dismantling of the public sector and integration with global finance, remained arrested. 'Time for Change', *Frontline*, vol. 26, no. 7, 28 March–10 April 2009.
4. These hitherto excluded groups refer to Scheduled Castes (SCs), Scheduled Tribes (STs), Other Backward Classes (OBCs) and religious minorities. On this and the changing nature of political participation in India in the 1990s see Yogendra Yadav, 'Understanding the Second Democratic Upsurge: Trends of Bahujan Particiation in Electoral Politics in the 1990s', in *Transforming India: Social and Political Dynamics of Democracy*, ed. Francine Frankel et al., Delhi: Oxford University Press, 2000.
5. The rise of neoliberalism in India can be dated to the beginning of economic reforms in 1991. As elsewhere, it means the rule of the market, privatization, deregulation, and a cut back on public spending on social services such as health and education. Within India, the rise of identity politics acquired currency at roughly the same time—mainly in the late 1980s and the early 1990s—in the context of assertions of a range of identities, specifically identities of caste and religion. The more toxic brand of identity politics represented by the right-wing Hindu nationalists was highly influential during the 1990s culminating in the increased political support of the BJP and its coming to power at the Centre in 1998.
6. For a counter argument, see Mritunjoy Mohanty, '2009 Lok Sabha Elections: a Storm in the Teacup?', <http://tinyurl.com/p88>, accessed on 29 October 2009.
7. For a detailed assessment of the expenditure priorities of the UPA government and its resource mobilization efforts over its five-year term, from the perspective of the underprivileged sections of the population, see 'How did the UPA Spend Our Money: An Assessment of Expenditure Priorities and Resource Mobilization Efforts by the UPA Government', Centre for Budget and Governance Accountability (CBGA), New Delhi, 2009. <http://www.cbgaindia.org/>, accessed on 28 October 2009.
8. Sunil Khilnani, 'Stop Marketing India as a Brand', *The Hindu*, 24 September 2009.
9. Atul Kohli, 'Politics and Redistribution in India', <http://www.princeton.edu/~kohli/workingpapers.html>, accessed on 28 October 2009
10. Reported in Saikat Datta, Anuradha Raman, and Arindam Mukherjee, 'A Ten Foot Trench, Rs. 14.50', *Outlook*, 9 April 2007.

11. Prabhat Patnaik, 'On the Need for Providing Employment Guarantee', *Economic and Political Weekly*, vol. XL, no. 3, 15 January 2005, p. 203.

12. Right to Information Act 2005 mandates a timely response to citizen requests for government information. The Act provides a practical regime of right to information for citizens to secure access to information under the control of public authorities, in order to promote transparency and accountability in the working of every public authority.

13. Thomas Blom Hansen, 'The India that Does Not Shine', *ISIM Review*, International Institute for the Study of Islam in the Modern World, Leiden, vol. 19, Spring 2007.

14. *Prime Minister's High Level Committee, Social, Economic and Educational Status of the Muslim Community of India*, Cabinet Secretariat, Government of India, New Delhi, 2006. The Committee chaired by Rajender Sachar, a former judge of the Delhi High Court, submitted its report to the prime minister in November 2006.

15. Ibid.

16. *The Times of India*, 28 March 2009.

17. Arjun Sengupta, 'UPA has many promises to keep to India's poorest', *Deccan Chronicle*, 1 June 2009.

18. Mani Shankar Aiyar, 'Social Sector up under UPA', *The Times of India*, 28 March 2009.

19. The NCMP was the basis on which the Left parties extended support to the Congress-led UPA coalition government at the Centre, which in 2004 had won only 146 seats, which was far short of a parliamentary majority.

20. 'How did the UPA Spend Our Money', CBGA, op. cit.

21. *The Hindu*, 5 June 2006.

22. Jayati Ghosh, 'Addressing Social Concerns', MacroScan website, 10 March 2008, http://www.macroscan.com, accessed on 25 June 2008.

23. Nirmala Lakshman, 'Employment Guarantee: Signs of Transformation', *The Hindu*, 11 May 2006.

24. Jean Drèze and Siddhartha, 'The Battle for Employment: Flaws in the System', *Frontline*, vol. 26, no. 1, 3–16 January 2009.

25. Ibid.

26. 'How did the UPA Spend Our Money', CBGA, op. cit.

27. Drèze and Siddhartha, 'The Battle for Employment'.

28. Ibid.

29. Jayati Ghosh, 'Making the Employment Guarantee Work', <www.macroscan.org>, accessed on 30 June 2008.

30. Jayati Ghosh, 'Equity and Inclusion through Public Expenditure: The potential of the NREGS', paper presented at the international conference on NREGA, Ministry of Rural Development and Indian Council of Agricultural Research (ICAR), New Delhi, 21-2 January 2009.

31. Jean Drèze and Ritika Khera, 'The Battle for Employment: The NREGA is making a difference to the lives of the rural poor, slowly but surely', *Frontline*, vol. 26, no. 1, 3–16 January 2009.

32. Varadarajan, 'Political Logic of Budget'.

33. *The Hindu*, 27 September 2007.

34. Praful Bidwai, 'Aam Aadmi please, not India Inc', *Rediff.com*, 23 May 2009.

35. Varadarajan, 'Political Logic of Budget'.

36. Deepankar Basu, 'The Left and the 15th Lok Sabha Elections', *Economic and Political Weekly*, vol. 44, no. 22, 30 May 2009.

37. P. Sainath, 'Welfarist policies won the elections for parties in India', *One World South Asia*, 16 June 2009, accessed on 7 July 2008.

38. Ian Maclusan, 'India's National Rural Employment Guarantee Act: A Case Study for How Change Happens'. This case study was written as a contribution to the development of 'From Poverty to Power: How Active Citizens and Effective States Can Change the World', Oxfam International 2008. <http://www.oxfam>, accessed on 7 July 2008.

39. Ibid.

40. Sainath, 'Welfarist policies won the elections'.

41. Drèze and Khera, 'The Battle for Employment'.

42. 'How India Voted', *Report of the NES 2009, The Hindu*, 24 May 2009.

43. Ibid.

44. Suhas Palshikar, 'Tentative Emergence of a Coalition', *Economic and Political Weekly*, vol. 44, no. 21, 23 May 2009.

45. Paul Brass, 'The Politicisation of Peasantry in a North Indian State: Part II', *Journal of Peasant Studies*, vol. 8, no. 1, October 1980, pp. 3–36.

PART V

Politics of Mobilization and Change in Uttar Pradesh

21 | Power and Mobilization
Patterns of Resilience and Change in Uttar Pradesh Politics

Uttar Pradesh (UP)—in the heart of India—has been the nerve centre of Indian politics since the late nineteenth century. Banaras, Allahabad, and Aligarh, along with other towns, were at the forefront of anti-colonial struggles in the last three decades of British rule. Several of the most illustrious leaders of the Congress were drawn from the province. Similarly, the demand for a separate homeland was made by UP Muslims who were at the centre of the separatist movement. After Independence, the state became even more crucial in the calculations of the all-India political parties. The introduction of universal suffrage gave UP, with its 110,000,000 people, a share of one-sixth of the Members of Parliament which made it a political fulcrum around which much of national politics turned.

This chapter examines the historical processes through which the socio-economic and political dominance of the upper castes in UP have at once been challenged and maintained. The changing nature of dominance is explored in the context of the interaction between caste solidarity and class differentiation during the pre-colonial and post-independence periods. Particular attention is paid to regional differences, especially those between the western and eastern areas of the province/state, which are markedly distinct in social stratification, production relations, and power structure.

* I am most to Shefali Chowdhary, research scholar in the Centre for Political Studies, Jawaharlal Nehru University, for her immeasurable help in the research towards this chapter. I also wish to thank R.R. Krishan and Dr Muzaffar Alam for their comments and suggestions on an earlier draft, and my research students Jagpal Singh and Nivedita Menon for their help in preparing the tables. I am particularly indebted to N.C. Saxena for generously letting me use some of the rich data from his draft paper. 'Caste, Land and Political Power in Rural Uttar Pradesh' (1984). And finally, I am grateful to Mushirul Hasan, whose sense of style made this paper infinitely more intelligible.

As a broad generalization, the evidence reveals that in all periods, government policies have favoured rich landowners over other social classes, and that until the late 1960s, class and social issues were not effectively raised. The long-standing caste and class nexus of economic and political domination represented by the Congress was challenged only after the mobilization of the middle and backward castes in the wake of the green revolution.[1] The process was facilitated by the emergence of the Bharatiya Kranti Dal (BKD) in 1969 which attempted to build a coalition of prosperous middle castes in the western region and the more numerous backward castes in the less developed eastern region. Although significant economic differentiation had taken place as a result of the development of a capitalist tendency in agriculture, the differentiation was not reflected in class-based political mobilization. Rather, the BKD articulated the emerging conflicts primarily in a caste idiom as a struggle between the upper castes and backward castes who until then felt excluded from the arena of politics and government. Since their following was socially as well as economically divided, the BKD leadership failed to organize a cohesive new social formation which could dislodge the upper castes. They were even less successful in challenging the socio-economic roots of inequality which sustained the hierarchical social system.

This chapter considers some of the factors responsible for slowing down the process of social change and political mobilization. It argues that governmental strategies of moderate land reforms, reservations, and various anti-poverty schemes have diffused class issues, encouraged populism, and led to class accommodation. At the same time, party appeals to caste and community loyalty have also prevented mobilization based on an alliance of lower classes cutting across caste and religious lines. The limitations of this form of mobilization are best illustrated by the strategy and development of the Lok Dal. It attempted to organize middle and backward castes on social and political issues which were the main source of their grievance against Congress rule. Political mobilization of backward castes on the basis of caste rather than class has not changed the basic structures of inequality. On the contrary, overemphasis on caste as a political building block blurred economic differentiation within castes, and in this way perpetuated social divisions cross-cutting class lines.

Zamindar, Peasants, and Political Power in Pre-Colonial UP

In the pre-colonial period, the pattern of agrarian relations was more or less the same in all the regions of UP. There existed a triangular relationship between peasants, zamindars, and rulers. The ruler recognized the zamindars' right of control over their territories, including their maintenance of armed retainers, in return for which the zamindars were obliged to render certain services, such as collection of the land tax, which was generally set at half the produce.[2] The extraction of such an enormous land tax imposed a heavy burden on the peasant, while the demands on peasant production implied a certain degree of economic stratification among the peasantry. Being a regressive tax, 'land revenue would have in any case fallen more heavily on smaller peasants'.[3] Caste reinforced this stratification because after, higher castes obtained revenue concessions. It was the payment of the land tax which was at the root of much social conflict involving the peasantry.[4]

A complex hierarchy of rights are land existed in UP as indeed in other parts of the country, much before the Mughal period. The origin of the zamindars' right went back at least to the beginning of the period of Muslim kings, and the right, although recognized by the kings, was created independent of any royal action.[5] It implied a claim to a share in the produce of the soil, which varied from 10 to 25 per cent of the state revenue in the different regions of the Mughal empire. Owing to their powerful position, the zamindars were able to extend their claims beyond their specified share in the revenue records. Nevertheless, the position of zamindars could be affected by the nature of their relationship with the state. The territories of Banaras (Map 21.1) were under the control of thakurs before the eighteenth century, but were turned into a primarily bhumihar zamindari owing to the policies of Mughal jagirdars (revenue assignees) of the region. In certain other areas zamindars, with state backing, succeeded in bypassing other powerful contenders entrenched in the region.[6]

Admittedly, the caste and sub-caste divisions between different groups of dominant zamindars helped the state to augment their paramount position vis-à-vis local magnates: the Mughal rulers often manipulated caste differences to promote and strengthen one group against another. Moreover, rival factions within castes often sought external support to settle their mutual disputes. At other times, different caste groups joined together to manoeuvre or suppress contending castes.[7] From this interplay between the state on the one hand and the thakur (Rajput) clans, and their rivals on the other, emerged powerful rajas and chieftains who consolidated their power by establishing principalities which flourished in this period.[8]

The thakur dominance in the eastern districts was overwhelming. In the Banaras region, the thakurs on an average had the largest share in the zamindari.[9] According to the *Ain-i-Akbari*, in 1601 thakur zamindars paid more than two-thirds of the total revenue in the districts of middle Doab

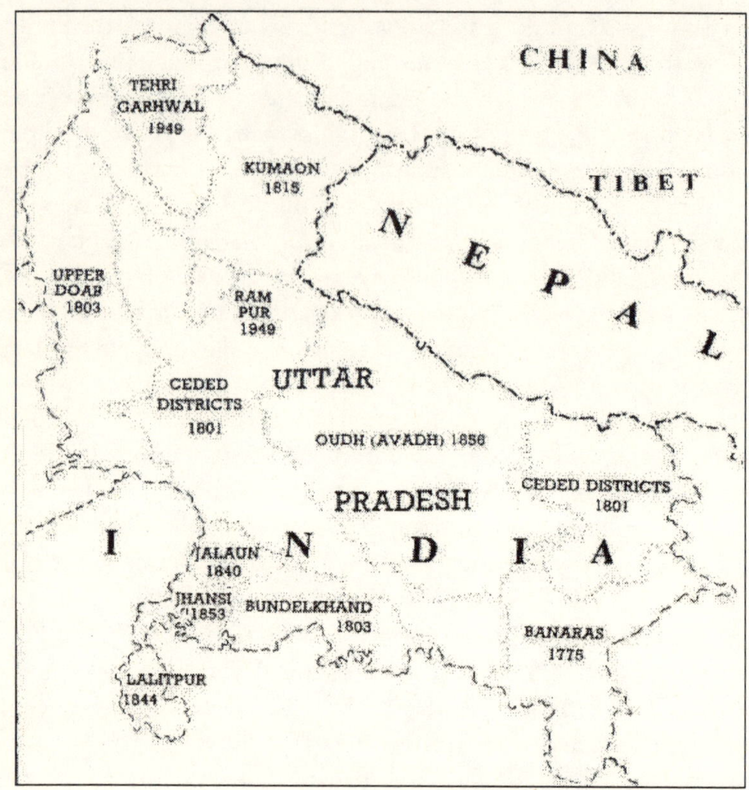

MAP 21.1: United Provinces (Uttar Pradesh): The Expansion
of British Power

Source: P.R. Brass, *Factional Politics in an Indian State: The Congress Party in
Uttar Pradesh*, Berkeley: University of California Press, 1965.

(now Agra and Allahabad divisions),[10] Awadh, and the eastern region of the
United Provinces (Maps 21.1 and 21.2).

In contrast to the eastern region, the rajput hold was relatively weak in
Rohilkhand and the upper Doab. Here they were confronted with strong Jat
chieftains on the one side, and a significant Muslim presence particularly
since the middle of the nineteenth century. Unlike the thakurs, the Jats
more frequently cultivated their own lands which encouraged a tradition
of peasant proprietorship in the western part of the province. The village
level zamindars and peasant proprietors held a much larger proportion of
land in the Doab, while in nawabi Awadh, the taluqdars, zamindars and
autonomous rajas controlled vast tracts of land. The upper Doab was also
marked by low agricultural yields and low population density conditions
which were not conducive to the production of sufficient surplus to support
a rentier class. These conditions were largely responsible for the growth of

MAP 21.2: Uttar Pradesh Districts and Divisions

Source: Statistical Diary, Uttar Pradesh, 1983.

peasant proprietors who cultivated their own land, often under a system of *bhaiyachara* tenure.[11]

The differences between the two regions were in considerable measure determined by the physical proximity/distance from the centre of Mughal power. No less important was also the fact that is the north-western part of the Mughal empire, the intermediate castes, namely the Jats and Gujars, settled and consolidated their control over agricultural production in Mughal times. Interestingly, the agrarian uprisings in the western region were led by the Jats and Gujars, while in eastern and central UP, agrarian revolts signified principally the thakurs' aspirations for social and political control in their region.

The substantial Muslim presence in the west of the province also acted as a check on rajput expansion. The influence of the Mughal power was evident in the control of land as well as in the *qasbahs* and small market towns which developed rapidly in the eighteenth century. Many of these towns originated from the seventeenth and eighteenth century Afghan settlements.[12] The Afghans consolidated their economic and political position in the region later known as Rohilkhand, initially as revenue farmers and then as nawabs and chieftains.

In Awadh the zamindars and taluqdars grew in importance in the eighteenth century as a result of the revenue functions they performed, and also because declining Mughal authority deliberately solicited their support by extending additional administrative and military powers (i.e. faujdari rights). This resulted in a state in Awadh which even though Mughal in appearance was in substance a Mughal-taluqdar political combine. The *de facto* alliance also explains why the taluqdars were anxious to defend the nawabi rule against the British in the mid-nineteenth century.

The differences between the two regions were also reflected at a social level. In the eastern region, members of higher Hindu (and Muslim) castes, i.e. rajputs, brahmans, saiyads, sheikhs, and pathans did not cultivate the land themselves. This taboo, however, was not rigidly observed in the west on account of the difficulty of obtaining labour.[13] Both brahmans and rajputs were forced to take to the plough. This accounts for the very large number of brahman cultivators in many districts of western UP.[14] Nonetheless, much of the land was cultivated through hired labour and the leasing of land. The peasant/tenants' title to permanent and hereditary occupancy of land was generally recognized as long as they paid revenue regularly. Since there was not much pressure on land, the rights of landholding tenants were respected but they could not leave the land or refuse to cultivate it. In view of the abundance of land and the relative shortage of cultivators, the zamindars often compelled them to cultivate all arable land held by them.[15] Invariably, agricultural labourers working in the fields of zamindars and peasants were from the low castes, i.e. chamars and others. It was their subjection at the hands of the upper caste peasantry, which continued unabated in the medieval period since Islam, which made almost no impression on the caste system.[16]

The Emerging Pattern of Dominance in the Colonial Period

The pattern of social relations underwent significant changes from the late eighteenth century in the wake of the declining Mughal power, and the establishment of British rule in the region. From 1801 to 1820 the British made several summary settlements in the North-Western Provinces (NWP), followed by settlements of 20 or 30 years in the 1830s and 1840s.[17]

Initially, the settlements were made with village occupants rather than with bigger landlords and revenue farmers because of the belief that settlements with village zamindars would yield higher revenue which was the driving force of the British Raj.[18] As a result, British policy disregarded the landed aristocracy and laid down that *sir* lands should be assessed at the same rates as those charged on lands of similar quality cultivated by ordinary peasants.

British policy evidently claimed to strengthen the position of the actual cultivators of land, i.e. primary zamindars. However, the execution of policy did not always create the expected results. An examination of the principles and methods of revenue assessment reveals a wide divergence between what should have happened and what actually resulted.[19] The policy was vitiated by the high land revenue demanded by the British. In the ceded and conquered provinces as a whole, excluding Banaras, Ghazipur, and Jaunpur (permanently settled), the revenue demand increased by more than 70 per cent between 1806 and 1830, while in Agra province the increase was of 15 per cent from 1835 to 1845.[20] The increase in revenue occurred at constant prices.[21] These severe assessments were based on an exaggerated notion of production, more scientific surveys which made it impossible to conceal any land so as to escape assessment, and the pressing demands for increased revenue. Furthermore, land revenue under the British was fixed on the basis of how much particular holdings ought to produce, and not on the amount of crops actually raised.[22]

Not surprisingly, many proprietors simply could not meet the heavy revenue demand, leading to accumulating arrears in revenue and forcing many zamindars to sell their shares. This happened in Allahabad where three-fourths of the district changed hands between 1842 and 1882.[23] It also happened in Aligarh where almost 83 per cent of land was alienated by the 1860s.[24] Likewise, the entire Doab was gripped by feverish sales. Here, as indeed in Rohilkhand, land alienation was closely connected to the agrarian depression, precipitated by the collapse of the indigo market and the decline in cotton exports from north India.[25] In the Agra division, depression and successive famines caused much distress to landholders. Some remissions were on occasion granted, but British officials were unrelenting in their demand for revenue, encouraging thereby alienation of land from zamindars. The tremendous pressure on zamindars can be gauged from what was officially acknowledged in 1882-3, with reference to the pre-Mutiny assessment:

The proportion of the rental left to proprietors by the old assessments in the NWP was much less than was absolutely necessary to provide for the support of themselves and their families, bad debts, expenses of management, and the vicissitudes of seasons. It is only since the late revision that they have been left a sufficient margin to live at all and count with certainty on meeting their liabilities to the state.[26]

At the same time, the evidence on land transfers does not give a uniform picture of emerging social changes. In the eastern region the main losers due to British land revenue policies were rajput landholders. Bernard Cohn has suggested that in Banaras the landed estates were transferred from rajput families to the bhumihars, brahmans and the Muslims.[27] By 1885, most of the large revenue payers in the Banaras region were those whose forefathers held administrative positions under the British, such as tehsildars and amins. In terms of caste and community most of them were Muslims, brahmans, kayasthas and bhumihars who had traditionally held landed properties in pre-colonial times.[28]

The situation was quite different in western UP, where major inroads in landed property were made by moneylenders and bankers belonging to the bania and brahman castes at the expense of some rajput and many traditional Muslim landholders.[29] In Aligarh 50 per cent of the land changed hands between 1839 and 1858 and the 'moneylending and trading classes' enhanced their share in landholding, by means of purchases, from 3.4 per cent in 1839 to 12.3 per cent in 1886.[30] The same trend was noticeable in all of western UP.

Under British rule much of the opportunity to make a fortune went to the brahmans, the khatris and the banias in the west, and to the kayasthas and the Muslims in the east, which they utilized to acquire and augment landed status so highly valued in the society of that time. The hallmark of attaining zamindar status was enough compensation for the initial difficulties the 'new men' encountered in realizing rents because many of them lacked traditional authority and were absentee landlords. From the commercial point of view, land was a profitable investment as agricultural prices were increasing rapidly while revenue demand remained almost static.

The cumulative result of these changes was a substantial whittling down in the economic position of thakur (rajput) zamindars in the eastern region and thakur and Muslim zamindars in western UP. The change did not quite amount to a 'very intensive and melancholy revolution' in the social structure of the province[31] because in a number of cases the thakur zamindars were able to hold off the new purchasers, and in some cases the upper castes retained their overall land monopoly because forfeited property was often bought by a member of the same caste.[32] This was true of Jat coparcenary communities as also brahman moneylenders who bought the landed interest of their caste brethren in the western districts.[33]

Land transfers and the concomitant change in social composition, moreover, did not lead to a diminution of large landholders. Land monopoly persisted because the great landlords were virtually insulated from the continuous process of land transfer and multiplication of landholdings.[34] Indeed, the small zamindars lost land to the big landowners.[35] The social change in the composition of the landed elite mostly affected the Muslims as they were the greatest losers from land transfers. Between the last quarter of the nineteenth century and the first quarter of the twentieth, Muslim landholdings in the province declined quite considerably. The scale of loss varied from region to region but on an average the Muslims lost 5 per cent of their holdings per district.[36] Many factors were responsible for their decline. British intervention and control of the province was one. In the 1840s, British action against the land grantees mainly affected Muslims. They suffered further losses on account of their participation in the revolt of 1857 which prompted the British to confiscate their land.

Landlords with large holdings, especially in much of western UP, were unaffected by these changes, but the change in the social composition of the elite suggests a certain fluidity in UP society which weakened the coincidence between caste/community and classes in the western districts of the province. In the eastern region, too, economic power diverged somewhat from traditional status and authority, except that the upper castes included more individuals able to purchase land rights. In contrast, western UP, the working of the market helped in the creation of a new propertied class.

The pattern of land tenure which emerged after the 1857 Revolt was distinct in each region; the one in western UP favoured owner-cultivators and the more rapid introduction of commercial cropping;[37] while the one in eastern UP encouraged absentee landlords who perpetuated status values and took no interest in commercial agriculture. After the formal annexation of Awadh in February 1866, the government's principal concern was to streamline the collection of revenue from the newly acquired province.

The developments in the last quarter of the nineteenth century must be viewed against the background of broader changes in British policy following the Revolt of 1857. After 1857, the British went out of their way to cultivate the landlords. Even while restoring the supremacy of taluqdars in Awadh, the British ensured their dependent status by completely disarming them. Though quite wrongly, that the 'large proprietors who have suffered under our rule, yet almost to a man stood by us'.[38] Consequently, Thornbill in charge of Aligarh district, urged the 'government to throw itself on the side of the larger proprietors and repress the peasantry'. As a result of this policy of propping up the landlords, revenue was not increased by government but rents were constantly enhanced by zamindars due to the increase in prices.[39]

When new settlements were undertaken, increases in the assessment were on a very limited scale, much below what would have been justified by the rise in prices.[40] The new colonial policy also reflected the shift away from dependence on land revenue for resources to the growth of a market in raw materials.

Tenants and Peasant Revolts

Before the British, cultivators were rarely evicted from the land they occupied because nothing would be gained by ousting them. Land was available in plenty and it was manpower which was scarce. As the pressure on land increased, security of tenure became a vital issue, especially in Awadh and the eastern districts of UP where land was fertile but the per capita availability of land was quite low.[41] This problem increased sharply in the eastern districts as cultivation became more profitable on account of rising prices, and increasing area under sugarcane, in the period from 1850 to 1920. As a result, landlords attempted to extend their own cultivation by ousting tenants; by 1919, more than one-third of the cultivated area in Basti had become *sir* or *khudkasht* of the proprietors.[42] Apart from eviction, tenants were exploited through enhancement of rent, *nazrana*, and *abwabs*.

By 1883, nearly 88 per cent of all cultivators tilling 77 per cent of the cultivated area in the Awadh region were tenants-at-will.[43] In Ghazipur, of the total 217,485 tenants, 65,918 were tenants-at-will in 1887; the number would have been much higher if the large class of low caste subtenants cultivating the land of high caste tenants was also taken into account.[44] The status of *koeri* and *chamar* tenants in Gonda and Bahraich was no better than the bonded slaves of high castes.[45] The *Awadh Gazetteer* noted that 'it was quite common to meet men whose fathers entered into these obligations and who still labour in their discharge'.[46] The lower caste tenants faced much greater economic disabilities than those of higher castes.

In relation to the tenantry, the districts of western UP, especially in the upper Doab and Rohilkhand, presented a different picture. For one thing, caste differences did not create a status gulf between the proprietor and occupancy tenant. In Saharanpur, by 1870 there was hardly any distinction between the rent paying tenant and the revenue paying proprietor.[47] Even upper caste zamindars generally had no inhibition towards manual labour. For the entire NWP the percentage of land cultivated by tenants-at-will was 38 per cent in 1892.

In the UP countryside as a whole, however, which was densely populated, poorly developed in terms of irrigation facilities, and with limited opportunities of urban employment, conditions were perhaps worse than

TABLE 21.1: Pattern of Holdings under Different Categories of Tenants in
Agra and Awadh 1899-1900 to 1935-36

	Percentage of total holding area under		
	Occupancy and other tenants with herediatary rights	*Statutory and heris of statutory tenants*	*Other non-occupancy tenants, including grove holders, rent-free, etc.*
AWADH			
1899-1900	5.6	–	82.2
1926-7	6.5	71.4	10.5
1935-6	6.8	69.9	11.9
AGRA			
1899-1900	35.9	–	41.9
1926-7	54.8	21.0	4.0
1935–6	49.0	23.7	6.2

Source: United Provinces Zamindari Abolition Committee (UPZAC) Report, vol. II, Statistics, 1948, p. 91.

in other parts of India. The problem was compounded by the high rental demand on the poorer classes of agrarian society.[48] Awadh, the bastion of the great taluqdars, was the worst in terms of rack renting and exploitation of tenants. Occupancy tenants formed a miniscule minority, just 2.2 per cent of the whole tenant population in Awadh. In the first two decades of the twentieth century, evictions in UP increased by over 100 per cent, and in the same period wholesale prices, rental demands, and land revenue increased in varying degrees. Revenue demand increased by 7.5 per cent, whereas rental demands went up by 12 per cent for secure tenants, and by 26 per cent for ordinary tenants.[49]

The effects of rise in prices, rents and revenue demands varied from class to class, and sometimes, even from caste to caste. The phenomenal rise in prices between 1906 and 1921 brought considerable prosperity to cultivating owners and secure tenants with sizeable holdings mainly because they were able to use a part of their holding for cash crops. The small holders and unprotected tenants were on the other hand severely affected by the rise in rents and increased prices since they had to buy some of their family's food and other requirements from the market.

Upper caste tenants were relatively better off because they had generally superior quality land under their cultivation, and what is more, the incidence of rent was lower.[50] In Rae Bareli in 1929, the *kurmi* was required to pay roughly a third more in rent than the thakur, while the *kachhi* and the *murao* tenant paid almost double.

In the years immediately after the First World War, UP experienced a severe economic crisis. Nearly half a million demobilized soldiers from the province and hundreds of workers retrenched from industrial establishments, especially tanneries and glass works, were unemployed;[51] their hardship was considerably aggravated by the rise in the prices of foodgrain and other commodities. The economic distress, in general, was concentrated in the Awadh districts where the proportion of unprotected and insecure tenants was much higher.[52] For this reason, various castes and classes coalesced and rose in protest in 1920–1 in southern and south–eastern Awadh.

Political Mobilization and Ascendancy of the Congress

The first Kisan Sabha in Awadh was initiated in Pratapgarh district, which had a large concentration of low caste, particularly kurmi tenants, who paid high rents. These were not only economically depressed compared to their counterparts in Agra and other neighbouring districts who held occupancy rights, but they were lower down in the social hierarchy. Many of them had participated in social movements from the last quarter of the nineteenth century to improve their status vis-à-vis the upper castes, and in the Kisan Sabha and the peasant movement to obtain occupancy rights. Low caste tenants, who had borne economic penalties because of their inferior caste status, were in the forefront of peasant movements.[53] They were supported by the service castes, all of whom had equally suffered from high rents and from high interest rates.

Two distinct strata of the peasantry were involved in the 1920–1 peasant agitations. One section of the peasantry had substantial holdings, but could not manage to ensure a surplus from the marketed portion of their crops because of rising rents and other exactions. They were essentially interested in pressing the government to enact legal curbs on rent enhancement. The other section of tenants had neither security of tenure nor sufficient surplus for subsistence. They engaged in a jacquerie type of activity, including attacks on landlords and looting of crops.[54] Initially, the Indian National Congress' endeavour to redress peasant grievances was confined to Allahabad district, and limited to high caste brahman and Rajput tenants and small zamindars.[55] It was only after 1920 that the UP Congress recognized the political importance of mass contact and the need to mobilize peasants by championing their cause. Still the Congress was hesitant since the agrarian movement in Awadh was not fully under its control and because it involved violent attacks on the taluqdars.[56]

At first, the Congress attempted to link the kisan agitation with the non-cooperation and Khilafat movements. Its leaders however found themselves responding ambivalently when the kisan agitation directed its ire against the landlords and developed a certain autonomy. The Congress attempted to control the movement by calling off the Non-Cooperation movement which helped to diffuse the kisan agitation. The Congress' ambivalence was a product of its understanding of the national movement as a multi-class movement whose support base should extend to all castes, classes, and communities. In view of this it is not surprising that Gandhi exhorted the peasants not to employ agitational methods against the zamindars. In 1932 when the tenants' struggle was at its height, the Congress Working Committee, presided over by Gandhi, advised Congress workers to impress upon the *ryots* that withholding of rent payment was contrary to Congress policy.[57]

Although the Awadh Rent Act of 1921 and the Agra Tenancy Act of 1926 gave greater security to tenants through a ten-year statutory tenancy and made the exaction of nazrana illegal, the agrarian structure and class relations in UP were not greatly altered. In Awadh, for instance, statutory tenants cultivated nearly 70 per cent of the area but their rights were not wholly secure because Awadh landlords generally bypassed the rental issue by resorting to nazrana which was to be paid by the tenant before being admitted or readmitted to a holding. In contrast, in the Agra province, most tenants held occupancy rights; the domination of landlords was not oppressive because the number of big estates were comparatively smaller than in Awadh.[58]

The depression of 1929-34 changed the situation quite radically.[59] The sudden drop in the price of foodgrains, especially of cash crops, affected large sections of these dependent upon agricultural income. Between 1900 and 1926 prices had increased by roughly 100 per cent: but they dropped dramatically to half in 1930–1. In Aligarh, for example, the price index fell from 221 to 117 in the slump period,[60] greatly affecting the area under wheat and cotton. Reduced agricultural produce on account of poor rains also caused widespread distress. Landlords and sahukars were consequently unable to collect rents and dues from tenants; the rich and middle peasants, selling their product in the market, were vulnerable to fluctuation in prices. They were also the most heavily indebted group because they were conscious of maintaining their status as a result of which they spent enormously on luxury consumption.

The government sanctioned remissions of rents between 1930 and 1932, but this did not uniformly improve the position of tenants. By 1932, only 25 per cent of short-term and 7 per cent of long-term loans had been repaid. Consequently, evictions for arrears of rent increased: in 1930–1 there were 31,383 suits for eviction in Awadh against 24,061 in 1926-7.[61]

Deepening economic crisis contributed substantially to the rise of political discontent and, to an extent, shaped the course of the Civil Disobedience movement. The Congress, aware of the widespread economic discontent, tried to mobilize the peasantry in an attempt to build a broad political movement; the socialist segment which was by then an important force in the Congress, took the lead in organizing the peasants.[62]

However, the response to the first phase of the Civil Disobedience movement was hardly enthusiastic by November 1930, only 6,249 Congress agitators were arrested.[63] The feeble response was partly a result of the government's initiatives in 1931 to contain peasant discontent. The Gandhi-Irwin Pact was one such effort based on the hope that landlords would offer rent remissions in return for revenue remissions. These hopes were not realized however, and by the end of 1931, the Congress paid greater attention to the economic distress of peasants by mustering support for the no-rent demand.[64] The socialists, in particular, urged peasants not to pay the full rent. In 1931-2 the UP Congress revived the no-rent campaigns in Rae Bareli and Unnao districts in Awadh and in Allahabad and Etawah districts in Agra. Between December 1931 and July 1932, over 10,000 Congress volunteers and agitators were convicted in UP. In March 1931, out of 2,004 Congress volunteers arrested, 1,397 (i.e. nearly 70 per cent) were petty tenants and landless labourers,[65] and the presence of these groups contributed considerably to the militancy of the campaign. Yet, the Congress exercised overall control over the Civil Disobedience movement. In spite of the extensive rural base built up during the Civil Disobedience movement, the multi-class character of the Congress led to its ambivalent approach to peasant problems.

In the end, the Congress' efforts to build broad-based support meant sacrificing the interests of the poorer sections. This undifferentiated approach towards political mobilization, governed by the self-conscious efforts of the Congress leadership to submerge the class issue, narrowed the agitational focus and social depth of the Congress movements in general.

The social background of the nationalist leadership exercised an influence on the policies and programmes of the Congress. The works of Bayly, Brennan, and Pandey reveal that the most important men of the Congress during the Civil Disobedience campaign were drawn from the ranks of small zamindars, pattidars and upper tenants and from a variety of upper castes and sub-castes.[66] This was also true of volunteers and activists of the Congress, which included men of considerable means, though the masses who participated in demonstrations were mostly middle and poor peasants, and tenants and subtenants of lower caste groups.

Communal Cleavages and Limitations of Congress Mobilization

Apart from the ideological limitations of the Congress strategy, the growth of communal politics militated against the mass mobilization of the peasants and tenants.[67] The Muslim response to Civil Disobedience was a case in point. In most parts of UP, Muslims absented themselves from the movement, giving credence to the charge that Civil Disobedience was a Hindu affair. There were many reasons why this was so. First, the communal situation in the province had deteriorated rapidly soon after the collapse of the Khilafat and Non-Cooperation movements in 1922-3. Symptomatic of the breakdown in the Congress-Muslim alliance was the eruption of extensive communal rioting in different parts of the country. Secondly, Congress' close connections with the Arya Samaj and the Hindu Mahasabha irked the Muslim constituents and prevented others from joining the organization. During the Civil Disobedience campaign, for instance, Congress openly accepted the support of overtly communal Hindu groups who had contributed much to the exacerbation of communal animosities.[68] Such dependence upon sectional support often lent credence to the popular Muslim perception of the Congress being a pro-Hindu organization.

This unmistakable opposition to Civil Disobedience placed the Congress leaders in a dilemma. Quickening the tempo of the agitation could potentially inflame communal passions, while abandoning it altogether was likely to widen the gulf that separated the Congress from many sections of the Muslim community. The dilemma was resolved by either minimizing political activity in areas prone to communal sensitivities or withdrawing from the scene altogether. This was done in the belief that over the long term a successful anti-colonial struggle would cement the bonds of unity, and that independence would precede and not succeed the resolution of the communal question.

The political situation changed quite dramatically after the Assembly elections in 1937. The process of political mobilization, engendered by the election itself, led various groups and parties to formulate their political strategy in relation to the demands of the new electorate which was enlarged fourfold and included the substantial tenantry and the urban petty bourgeoisie. The Congress stressed the 'mass' aspect of its policies, and formulated a political and economic programme for the consideration of the electorate. Throughout its campaign, the main focus was on the promise to reform the antiquated and repressive land tenure system. This raised widespread expectations and created a favourable impression especially among the enfranchised tenants, who hoped that under the Congress Raj they would be exempted from paying rents, and that the zamindari would be abolished altogether. Not surprisingly, the Congress did extremely well, winning all the general seats in UP for the Central Legislative Assembly and for the UP Legislative Assembly. The Muslim League's performance was less spectacular, winning 29 out of the 39 seats contested by the League.[69]

The emergence of the Muslim League as a political force was a new phenomenon which the Congress had to contend with for nearly a decade. It posed a serious challenge to the Congress claim of representing all of India and of organizing the national movement to serve the interests of all sections of the community. The Congress was henceforth faced with divisions within its ranks on the communal issue and the desertion of some important Muslim groups into the Muslim League camp. UP, in particular, became an important stronghold of the Muslim League. Until 1937, the League had been hopeful of sharing power with the Congress.[70] What accentuated the alienation of Muslims was the experience of the two years of Congress rule. When Jinnah and the Muslim League capitalized on the so-called 'wrongs' done by the Congress ministry in UP and Bihar, Jawaharlal Nehru tried to counter it by initiating a Muslim Mass Contact Campaign.[71] The campaign however petered out in less than two years because most leading Congressmen felt 'it was not necessary to lay emphasis on the Muslim mass contact and that Congress should stick to its old policy of representing the masses of India regardless of caste and creed'.[72]

By the end of 1939, Hindu–Muslim antagonism was fairly widespread enabling the Muslim League to mobilize and garner support for its crusade against the Congress.[73] The Congress–League conflict and the related Hindu–Muslim tension dominated UP politics until Partition in 1947. It overshadowed all other conflicts and in a way prevented other social cleavages from emerging. W.C. Smith pointed out that in the 1940s the League succeeded in securing the adherence of the bulk of the middle and lower middle classes.[74] However, the leadership of the movement remained in the hands of landlords and lawyer politicians.[75] The landlords decision to back the League and to rally around Jinnah's leadership was inspired by a combination of religious sentiment, the desire to preserve their privileged political position,[76] and the urge to promote their economic interests as landlords.

In spite of the growing communal controversies besetting the functioning performance of the Congress minority, it was able to push through a series of vital agrarian reforms, such as the UP Tenancy Bill, 1938. Muslims landlords attacked its provisions which they construed as 'an attack on minority culture sustained by the patronage of the Muslim aristocracy'.[77] However, given the objective circumstances in the UP countryside, tenancy reforms had to be on the agenda of any popularly elected government. Recognizing their inability to prevent such legislation, landlords tried to circumvent such proposals, and the Congress ministry was willing to extend certain concessions to them. The Congress was able to take advantage of the varying economic interests of small and large landlords and courted those who could easily be won over by concessions.[78] During the passage of the Bill and in the negotiations to amend it, an influential section in the Congress vigorously defended the rights of the '22 lakhs of so-called zamindars in our province', and more particularly of the small and medium landlords.[79]

In spite of many compromises, the Tenancy Act modified the agrarian system. By introducing a distinction between 'large' and 'small' landlords, Congress was able to protect the interests of small zamindars while condemning big zamindars. The Act considerably reduced the gains that could be made by the big landlords through the acquisition of additional *sir* and *khudkasht* lands. It thus paved the way for Zamindari Abolition by balancing the contradictory expectations of landlords interested in protecting their interests, and of socialist elements who were committed to immediate Zamindari Abolition.

The UP elections of 1945-6 were primarily a conflict between the Congress and the Muslim League over the demand for Pakistan. Although the Congress-League conflict and Hindu-Muslim hostility completely dominated UP politics in the last decade of British rule, nonetheless the abolition of zamindari figured prominently in the Congress scheme of political mobilization. The Congress and nationalist Muslim candidates exhorted the masses, including Muslims, to support the Congress which was committed to the amelioration of the socio-economic problems of the masses rather than the Muslim League which represented vested interests.

These efforts and appeals did not eventually succeed in gaining Muslim support which went overwhelmingly in favour of the League in the Muhammedan seats. Nevertheless in the general seats Congress demonstrated its supremacy. The tremendous success of the Congress was made possible in no small measure by the support of peasants who were promised a radically new system to replace the antiquated and oppressive zamindari system.

Strategy of Class Accommodation: The Social and Political Effects of Land Reforms

Towards the end of British rule in India, the rural economic structure of UP was marked by extreme inequality in the ownership of land and means of production. Approximately 8 per cent of agricultural households owned virtually all the land in the state. Moreover, within this tiny group, ownership was very unevenly distributed. At the base of the rural pyramid, 98 per cent of petty landowners paid Rs. 250 or less in land revenue;[80] at the apex, 1.5 per cent of zamindars paid Rs. 250 or more in revenue and possessed three-fifths of the land.[81] Extreme inequality was further underscored by the fact that 390 zamindars out of a total of 2 million paid 23 per cent of the land revenue.

Inequality in the distribution of land ownership was most marked in central and eastern UP. In the central districts, 11 per cent of zamindars owned three-quarters of the land; the pattern of ownership was slightly less uneven in eastern UP where approximately 11 per cent of zamindars owned 61 per cent of the area.[82] By contrast, the great majority in both these areas owned holdings of less than five acre, accounting for four per cent of the land.[83] In comparison, there was less polarization between absentee landlords and cultivating owners in western UP. In these areas, about 5 per cent of large zamindars owned 51 per cent of the land. Forty-five per cent of zamindars having holdings below five acre accounted for 4 per cent of land. More notably, western UP was dotted with a substantial class of rich and medium landowners: 36 per cent owned holdings of 5–25 acre and 18 per cent of the area, while another 13 per cent owned farms of 25–100 acre and 13 per cent of the area.[84]

Economic inequalities were reinforced by caste distinctions. There was a strong correlation between landownership and membership in the upper castes. Traditionally, the dominant landowning castes enjoyed the highest ritual status. Moreover, in UP the twice-born castes were relatively numerous and spread throughout all regions of the state.[85]

According to the 1931 Census, the brahmans and thakurs alone accounted for 16.4 per cent of the population (Table 21.2). Indeed, the brahmans, with over 9 per cent of the population represented 40 per cent of the entire Brahman caste category in India, making UP the area of maximum brahman concentration. Along with other high-ranking non-cultivatings castes, upper caste groups reached 20 per cent.

Beneath the upper strata were the elite cultivating castes (Jats, Bhumihars and Tyagis), a small category (2.1 per cent) who did not suffer caste oppression. Below them were the backward caste groups, who traditionally worked as

TABLE 21.2: Distribution of Caste and Communities in UP, 1931

	Category	Name of the caste	Percentage of total population
A.	Upper Castes	brahman	9.2
		thakur	7.2
		bania	2.5
		kayastha	1.0
		khatri	0.1
	TOTAL		**20.0**
B.	Middle Castes	jat	1.6
		bhumihar	0.4
		tyagi	0.1
	TOTAL		**2.1**
C.	Backward Castes	yadav	8.7
		kurmi	3.5
		lodh	2.2
		gujar	2.8
		kahar	0.7
		gadaria	2.3
		teli	2.0
		barhai	2.0
		kachu	1.3
		kewat	1.1
		murao	1.3
		nai	1.8
		others	10.7
	TOTAL		**41.7**
D.	Scheduled Castes	chamar	12.7
		pasis	2.9
		dhobi	1.6
		bhangi	1.0
		others	2.8
	TOTAL		**21.0**
E.	Muslims	shaikh	3.2
		pathan	2.2
		julaha	2.0
		syed	0.7
		moghul	0.1
		others (faqir, shunia, teli, nai, darzi, qasab, etc.)	6.8
	TOTAL		**15.0**

Source: 1931 Census, United Provinces of Agra and Awadh, Part 2, Provincial and Imperial Tables, 1933.

cultivators, cowherds, artisans, servants, and field labourers and who were subjected to caste disabilities. Although they accounted for the largest caste category of about 42 per cent, they also were internally divided not only along caste, but sub-caste and sub-sub-caste lines. Even the largest among them, the Yadavs, were less numerous than the brahmans, and unevenly distributed across regions, with their highest concentration occurring in the eastern districts.[86] At the bottom of the Hindu social hierarchy were the Scheduled Castes (SCs) forming 21 per cent of the population. Outside the Hindu order, but a sizeable minority were the Muslims, at 15 per cent.

Under the zamindari system, the inequalities of status and power inherent in the caste system corresponded more or less to inequalities in access to and distribution of material resources. Before independence, the thakurs formed the bulk of zamindars in the state. In Awadh and eastern UP their domination was most striking where they owned nearly 50 per cent of land in most districts.[87] In UP as a whole, thakurs and brahmans owned 57 per cent of the land, while the intermediate castes owned 32 per cent, and SCs owned a mere 0.09 per cent. Muslim zamindars owned another 11 per cent.[88]

Brahmans and thakurs had the greatest stake and share in the power structure. There was hardly any cultural distance between them largely because thakurs were extremely conscious of their high status and distance from the backward castes. In fact, their position was not threatened by the brahman-kayastha monopoly of education, professions, and government service, because wealthy thakurs did not aspire to government jobs.

The preoccupation with status among the dominant landowning castes led to widespread cultivation by tenants of Shudra rank. Roughly one-half of the cropped area was operated by low caste agriculturists, and this proportion was higher in the eastern region where the twice-born zamindars observed the ritual prohibition against touching the plough most rigorously.

The extreme disparity in the distribution of economic and political power which the British government buttressed and perpetuated in its own political interest, underwent a perceptible change after Zamindari Abolition in 1952.[89] Principally, the UP Zamindari Abolition Law was aimed against the absentee landlord who paid revenue and collected rents; and landlords who extracted *begar, nazrana* and *hari*. Zamindari Abolition was effective in removing the control of these intermediaries over land. However, though absentee landlords lost title to those areas which were in cultivating possession of tenants, they were not expropriated. The main issue which determined the fate of ex-zamindars was the criteria of definition and identification of cultivators. Owing to considerations of social status which prohibit high castes from engaging in certain kinds of manual work, performance in

TABLE 21.3: Percentage of *Sir* and *Khudkasht* by Size of Holdings

Class of Zamindars by Land Revenue Paid	No. of Zamindars	Per cent share in total LR	Total Sir and Khudkasht in lakh acre	Per cent share in total Sir and Khudkasht	Average area of Sir and Khudkasht per zamindar in acre
Less than Rs. 25	17,10,530	15.10	30.00	42.10	1.75
Rs. 25 and Rs. 250	2,76,111	27.10	28.90	40.60	10.47
Rs. 250 and Rs. 1,000	24,249	16.30	8.30	11.70	34.30
Rs. 1,000 and Rs. 5,000	5,089	14.20	2.40	3.40	47.16
More than Rs. 5,000	804	27.30	1.60	2.20	199.00
TOTAL	20,16,783	100.00	71.20	100.00	3.53

Source: UPZAC Report, vol. II, 1948.

manual labour was not considered necessary for designation as cultivator. This ancient argument bolstered the position of higher caste zamindars who were allowed to retain their *sir, khudkasht,* and grove lands. Two million zamindars were thus transformed into a privileged class of landowners.

Classification of *sir* and *khudkasht* land was crucial to Zamindari Abolition; therefore the determination of the total area under this category is important for the understanding of agrarian society in the post-independence period (Table 21.3). It is difficult to ascertain the excess area retained by landlords mainly because the prolonged process of Zamindari Abolition extending from 1946-55 offered ample opportunities for the management of abolition in a way that encouraged zamindars to use their coercive powers to evict tenants and to circumvent the law. Several field reports highlighted the massive falsification of land records which successfully dispossessed tenants of their legal rights. Patwaris, as keepers of village records, used their strategic position to falsify possession by tenants with comparatively unstable rights, particularly tenants of *sir* and *khudkasht*.[90]

At the time of Zamindari Abolition, 10,235,000 acre were recorded as *sir* and *khudkasht* land of the landlords (Table 21.4), amounting to 18 per cent

TABLE 21.4: Area held by the Ex-zamindars and the New Landowners

Category	Total area owned in lakh acre	Per cent of total area
Ex-zamindars	81.35	18.10
New owners with secure rights	362.58	80.40
Tenants with inferior rights	6.72	1.50
TOTAL	450.65	100.00

Source: Neale, 1968.

of the total area. However, before zamindari was abolished, the zamindars had resorted to legal and extra legal means to eject tenants from 66,00,000 acre of *sir* and *khudkasht*.[91] Tenants could not transfer land under law, with the result that they were forced to abandon land through eviction, gifts, and other methods. It is not surprising that the area under *sir* and *khudkasht* increased noticeably in western and central UP in the years immediately before Zamindari Abolition.[92] The increase was largely on account of resumption of land for cultivation and establishment of farms by zamindars to retain as much of their holdings as possible. Altogether, the landlords were able to secure 81,35,000 lakh acre, a 79.5 per cent of their *sir* and *khudkasht* land in UP.[93]

Initially, the UP Zamindari Abolition Committee recommended compensation of Rs. 136.15 crore but the Pant Ministry, under pressure from the landlords, increased the compensation to Rs. 150 crore.[94] Compensation was paid through a Zamindari Fund linked to a two-tier pattern proposed by Charan Singh, one of the main architects of Zamindari Abolition. Under this scheme, only the ex-zamindars acquired full ownership (*bhumidari*) rights. The bulk of tenants were designated *sirdars*. They could acquire *bhumidari* status and a 50 per cent reduction in land revenue payments to the state by depositing ten times the annual rent for their land with the Zamindari Abolition Fund.[95] The original target of the Zamindari Abolition Fund was Rs. 1.7 billion which was to be collected from 10 million tenants. The fund drive ran into difficulty as it was confronted with objections from zamindars on the one hand, and socialists on the other. Referring to the zamindars complaints, Charan Singh indignantly remarked:

No disinterested person can fail to be struck by the height of ingratitude which the zamindars have displayed. If anything, the proposal is wholly beneficial to them, on the assumption that liquidation of landlordism is agreed between us; the proposal cannot be improved upon as far as the interests of the landlords are concerned.[96]

The socialists and the UP Kisan Sabha, who were totally opposed to compensation, mobilized peasants not to make any payments. Their slogan was 'Zamindars have a lot of money, why give them more'.[97] Many tenants were willing to pay compensation, but even they were evicted, leading to agrarian riots in 1948-9.[98] In June 1951, the UP government received complaints that zamindars were ejecting tenants in spite of the fact *bhumidars* had acquired permanent legal tenure by paying 10 times their rent to the Zamindari Abolition Fund scheme. The apprehension of tenants regarding the stability of their *bhumidari* rights possibly discouraged them from paying their contribution to the fund. By 1953, after three years of collection effort the government mopped up just 21.49 per cent of the target.[99] Despite these difficulties in collection, the Pant ministry announced an increase in compensation from Rs. 135 to Rs. 160 crore.

The two-tier tenure scheme created a substantial class of rich landowners and middle peasants. In some areas, particularly in the eastern districts, the great thakur, bania, kayastha and Muslim landlords lost a good deal of land which vastly reduced their economic influence. At the same time, not all large zamindars suffered irretrievably. Many retained the major portion of their *sir* and *kludkasht* land through the eviction of tenants, along with compensation for loss of income from intermediary rights in revenue collection from their resumed estates.[100] There were also cases like that of the Raja of Mankapur (Gonda district) who retained 2,000 acre by developing an agro-based industrial complex and setting up a mango canning factory.[101] Others managed to maintain their position through political connections, spurning landlord-led parties and joining the Congress bandwagon.

In addition to this class of rich ex-zamindars, middle and small zamindars made substantial gains after Zamindari Abolition. Notwithstanding the losses suffered by some thakur landowners, they were, along with brahmans, jats and tyagis, the dominant landowners in the western region; and thakurs and bhumihars were in a dominant position in the eastern districts. In fact, their relative economic position and political influence were augmented in consequence of the decline in economic power and social prestige of former taluqdars and large zamindars.

Finally, the number of owner-cultivators increased among those who had been rich and middle peasants before Zamindari Abolition. In the western districts, tenants from among the jats, as well as Ahirs, Gujars, and other backward castes, raised the funds required to purchase ownership of land vested in the state, and become the backbone of commercial agriculture. Among the other beneficiaries from backward castes were Ahirs, Kurmis, and Lodhs in the eastern districts. They had been among the first to gain the status of occupancy tenants in the eastern region as a result of land legislation introduced by the British. Most of them acquired *sirdari* rights, and some also purchased bhumidari rights.

It can be argued that the interests of rich landowners were furthered because the Congress regarded them as the guarantor of social and political stability in the countryside. The dominant section of the party's leadership was concerned with consolidating the position of the rich and middle strata who formed the fulcrum of their political support. The importance of such considerations can be seen in the arguments put forward in favour of land reforms. Charan Singh, for instance, wrote:

Much thought was given to the political aspect of land reforms, since the drafters of the legislation were cognizant of the need to ensure political stability in the countryside. By strengthening the principle of private property where it was weakest, i.e. at the base of the social pyramid, the reforms created a huge class of strong opponents of the class war ideology. By multiplying the number of independent landowning peasants, there came into being a middle-of-the-road stable rural society and barrier against political extremism. It is fair to conclude that the agrarian reform took the wind out of the political sails of the disruptors of peace and opponents of ordered progress.[102]

The 'reordering' of agrarian society, which promoted peasant proprietors, was intended to diffuse class polarization through moderate land reforms. On the one hand, this would weaken the rightist opposition to Congress, and on the other, lessen the grievances of the peasantry which might otherwise have been mobilized by the socialists and communists. Thus, in spite of the inequalities built into the land reform and perpetuated by it, Zamindari Abolition was considered quite radical by much of the rural population. This impression enlarged the support for the Congress by depriving the lower classes of both their militant leaders and slogans; in this way it was offered as a solution to the class conflict which had threatened to erupt since 1920. In the pre-independence era, the Congress had contained this threat by making an undifferentiated appeal to all agriculturists on behalf of the nationalist movement. After independence, the Congress claimed that Zamindari Abolition would benefit all non-landlord classes; and without the parasitic landlords all classes would be able to progress under the new system. As a result both *bhumidars* who did not lose anything from Zamindari Abolition and *sirdars* who had gained some status supported the Congress.

Congress gained the support of *sirdars* even though Zamindari Abolition did not redistribute land. Moreover, the denial of ownership rights to subtenants clearly indicated that Zamindari Abolition was not intended to provide security of tenure to all tillers. Thus, in the final analysis, the agrarian strategy articulated during the first phase of land reforms buttressed the position of the landholding interests. Daniel Thorner captured this quintessential aspect of land reforms in the following observation:

UP Zamindari Abolition Act has provided for a new hierarchy of tenure holders in place of the old, but the new one is too reminiscent of the old. Zamindars have officially disappeared but the same persons have been rechristened landholders of very substantial and very high quality tracts of land. For the bulk of the peasantry classified as *sirdars*, tenure remains virtually the same and so does rent now collected by the government rather than the zamindars. At the bottom remain the mass of landless and cropsharers.[103]

The data presented earlier regarding the amount of land over which the zamindars could claim *bhumidari* tenure also underscores the immense importance of ex-zamindars in the new agrarian order who 'in the process have established themselves as a moderately progressive force at the head of rural society . . . the zamindars as individuals are still very much a power to be reckoned with in rural India'.[104]

Zamindari Abolition, which did not provide for simultaneous redistribution of land, had little effect on the inequitable distribution of holdings (Table 21.5). In fact the UPZAC rejected outright the All India Congress Committee (AICC) proposal of December 1948 which called for a ceiling on land and redistribution of the surplus.[105] Rather, the UPZAC Report suggested that no limit be placed on the maximum area held for cultivation either by a landlord or tenant. The committee justified its stand in political terms: ceilings-cum-redistribution would arouse opposition among the substantial cultivators.

In the absence of land ceilings and redistribution, Zamindari Abolition, Consolidation of Holdings Act, and other less important measures such as the Community Development Programme and Panchayati Raj could do little to help the marginal and small peasants and landless and agricultural labourers. This unfinished task was sought to be tackled by the imposition of ceilings in the 1960s and 1970s.

The ceilings programme was vigorously opposed by the UP Congress leadership and most conspicuously by Charan Singh who was Minister of Revenue and Finance.[106] Leading the crusade against ceilings, Charan Singh pleaded that ceilings were irrelevant to the land tenure system in UP because UPZAC and the Large Landholdings Act of 1957 had already forced large landholders to reduce their landholdings. Charan Singh argued that redistribution would reduce efficiency in agricultural production, which would make the state economy poorer. In view of the opposition encountered by the ceilings proposal in the UP Congress Committee and the Vidhan Sabha, any hope that ceilings would reduce land concentration and alleviate land hunger was virtually foreclosed.[107]

The Land Ceilings Act of 1960 set a high ceiling of 40 standard acre per individual which was reduced to 18 acre in 1972. In addition, grove land was excluded from the purview of the ceiling act. Moreover, land transfers in the four months before the 1960 bill was introduced reduced the potential surplus land from 688,000 acre to 437,000 acre. Even then, less than 0.4 per cent or 20,000 acre of cultivated land was actually redistributed under the 1960 Act, and one half of this was unfit for cultivation.[108] Thus, the objective of redistribution of land in favour of the landless was not ever marginally

TABLE 21.5: Comparison of Pattern of Landownership in the Period Prior to and after Zamindari Abolition

Class size of Ownership Holdings	Prior to Abolition of Zamindari		1953–4 (NSS)		1961–2 (NSS)		1971–2 (NSS)		1976–7	
	% Households	% Area Owned	% Households	% Area Owned	% Households	% Area Owned	% Households	% Area Owned	% Households	% Area Owned
Below 1 acre	37.80	6.00	39.69	2.37	44.21	1.59	50.20	4.09	50.98	5.33
Below 5 acre	81.20	39.10	78.43	31.83	75.22	19.99	86.22	42.37	84.15	35.55
Between 5 and 10 acre	12.70	26.10	14.25	29.08	12.86	20.54	9.45	27.82	9.60	24.47
Above 10 acre	6.10	34.80	7.32	39.09	11.92	59.47	4.33	29.81	6.25	39.98
Average size of holdings	3.50 acre		3.40 acre		4.39 acre		2.35 acre		2.88 acre	

Source: Figures for 1976–7 based on Shrimali, *Agrarian Change*, 1981.

achieved. The delay in eracting the bill, and the deliberate indifference encountered in Congress circles, emasculated its effects.[109] For very similar reasons, the later modification did not substantially alter the pattern of landownership. Another 4,00,000 acre should have become available under the modified legislation of 1972 if *benami* transactions and spurious sales had not taken place before and after the legislation came into force. The majority of large landholders divided their land among family members and close relatives to avoid confiscation. Government reports pointed to the impediments in the path of ceilings: a variety of loopholes remained to be exploited by skilful and politically well-connected farmers and ex-landlords, many of whom still retained thousands of acre of land by such devices as establishing bogus cooperatives or educational and charitable trusts. Altogether, only 200,000 acre could be redistributed, and of this amount, the acquisition of 60,000 acre was disputed in court cases.[110]

The agrarian strategy of the UP government indicates a deliberate effort to buttress the position of big landowners and rich peasants.[111] Their primacy in the scheme of development was strengthened by the government's failure to implement institutional change in a way that right have prevented big landowners and rich peasants from cornering the bulk of development resources. As a result, they were enabled to control local cooperative and panchayat institutions with links to higher levels of administration and government. Such ties facilitated their ability to accumulate more wealth by starting agro-industries and securing licences to trade in essential commodities like coal and kerosene.

The socio-economic domination of big landowners was reproduced in the political arena through their active participation in district and state politics. Their overall political influence was sufficient for them to direct the thrust of economic policy investment in favour of agriculture at the expense of industrial development.

The state government showed no inclination to tap agricultural surpluses for industrialization. In UP, the share of land revenue in the total state tax revenue declined from 40.8 per cent in 1952-3 to 18.8 per cent in 1968-9.[112] The continuous decline in the contribution of the agricultural sector to total taxes virtually absolved the rural rich from any responsibility of financing development.[113]

Regional Disparities and the New Agrarian Strategy

Not surprisingly, after more than three decades of economic planning, by the late 1980s UP remained industrially under-developed. Along with Bihar and Orissa, it was one of the most backward states of the country. This backwardness was evidenced in the very slow growth of the non-agricultural sector, particularly manufacturing and industry.[114] During 1960–1 and 1976-7, the economy progressed at a slow rate of 2.3 per cent per annum compared to 3.3 per cent annually for the country as a whole. Industrial growth occurred in dominantly traditional undertakings like textiles and sugar. Low productivity in the state was also due to the inadequate supply of electricity, much of which was used for agriculture rather than industry. As a result, virtually no new employment opportunities were generated. UP continued to lag behind other states, although perceptible progress was made in the 1970s when the state experienced a much publicized industrial spurt: a growth rate of 5.7 per cent in the period 1970-1 to 1978-9.[115]

However, the main breakthrough, as is well known, occurred in the production of wheat. Between 1960-1 and 1982-3, wheat production quadrupled, thus increasing its share in total food production from 27 to 58 per cent. The introduction of the 'new agrarian strategy' and a series of state sponsored schemes for extending rural credit, distributing at subsidized rates the new technological package involving fertilizer, and high yielding varieties (HYVs) was largely responsible for an increase in agricultural production.[116]

Nevertheless, until the 1980s agricultural development was unevenly distributed across the regions of the state. District-wise growth shows that at that time, the Doab not only had a consistently high rate of growth but that the absolute value of produce per hectare was about twice the state average. At the same time, in the dry districts lying south of the Jumuna, agriculture has remained virtually stagnant. The share of Bundelkhand in wheat procurement in the state fell from 15 per cent in 1967-8 to only about 0.5 per cent in 1982-3.[117] Since the successful cultivation of the HYVs depended heavily on assured supplies of water, the impact of the Green Revolution was greatest in the western districts which also happened to be the most prosperous areas in the state. Large scale irrigation canals fed by the Ganges and the Jumuna had already transformed the Doab into one of the richest tracts during the period of colonial rule.[118] The trend towards commercial farming also gained impetus from the agrarian structure characterized by peasant proprietorship. One result was that class polarization between absentee landlords and subsistence peasants did not occur to the same degree in the western region as it did in the eastern part of the state.

The Green Revolution did not have nearly the same impact in the eastern districts despite the fact that this was the region of greatest assured rainfall. In 1951, most of the area was devoted to the cultivation of rice, while commercial crops were estimated to grow over less than 16 per cent of the land. Rice cultivation in the fertile rain-fed areas seemed to have promoted a different kind of class structure and pattern of social relations. Absentee landlordism, an aversion to manual work, and apathy to innovation were prevalent. Since rice cultivation required working in knee-deep mud water, and labour was available in plenty due to high population density and the equally high impoverishment of agriculturalists, those who owned land preferred to get their crops cultivated through sharecroppers rather than cultivate it themselves.

Considering their initial advantages it was not surprising that peasants of western UP responded most enthusiastically to the new agricultural technology in the 1960s. Gilbert Etienne in a study of a Jat-lodh dominated village in Bulandshahr district found that all farmers were using fertilizers, many small farmers and landless labourers had taken to trading in milk, and of the 48 private tubewells in the village, 10 belonged to small farmers owning less than two hectare of land.[119] As against this dynamism, a village in Varanasi district dominated by thakurs, brahmans, kayasthas, and bhumihars presented a typical picture of a slow-growing backward economy. Most of the means of irrigation were either state tubewells or *moats* in wells. There were no private tubewells until 1973, although by 1979 there were 23 private tubewells. Obviously, some of the obstacles to economic improvement in the eastern districts were removed. The Gandak Command Area project vastly improved irrigation facilities, with the result that the area under wheat and sugarcane recorded higher value output per hectare.[120]

Class Differentiation and Emerging Social Conflict

On the basis of the available data on the spread effects of the new agricultural technology it is possible to assume that landowners with holdings of 10 acre and above were the greatest beneficiaries of the agrarian strategy followed from the 1970s to late 1980s.[121] A comparison of production by large and small peasants shows that where the HYVs were introduced in the case of both wheat and rice there was a tendency for both yield and cost per unit of land to be positively associated with farm size. The small peasants did not fare as well because over time, large farms accumulated more land and irrigation assets, both of which were highly productive, and capable of generating more profits and funds for further asset accumulation.[122]

As more institutional credit became available to small peasants, they were also able to marginally improve their economic position. Even so, the lion's share of the benefits from the introduction of modern methods continued to flow to the larger landowners. The disparities within the peasantry were further reinforced by the government's procurement and marketing policies. Although there is no evidence of a systematically organized agricultural lobby, the government's policies worked to the advantage of rural capitalists and agro-based industries. Cane producers, in particular, managed to exercise pressure on government to obtain higher prices for their product than the rate suggested by the centre. For this reason, the price increased from Rs. 7 per quintal to Rs. 22 in 1983. Higher profitable accounted for the substantial increase in the cane area for the 12 lakh hectare in 1980-1 to 17.3 lakh hectare in 1982-3.[123] Furthermore, the state government provided very large tax remissions to the sugar mills in order to clear the mounting debts owed by them to the rich cane growers. The purchase tax paid by the sugar mills to the government was abolished, resulting in a loss of revenue to the state of Rs. 27 crore. In addition, sugar mills were paid outright between Rs. 40 crore and Rs. 90 crore to clear their arrears. While the bureaucracy opposed the virtual subsidization of the sugar mills, the politicians preferred to appease the rich cane growers and sugar mill owners. For this reason Rs. 11 crore meant for paddy producers was diverted to sugarcane producers in 1982–3 alone.

The interests of paddy producers, most of whom were small and marginal peasants in central and eastern UP, were consistently overlooked. Indeed, they received Rs. 10 to Rs. 30 less than the recommended support price for marketed surplus. When the Department of Food and Civil Supplies, in 1980, decided to buy paddy directly from the farmers to reduce their exploitation at the hands of traders and millers who purchased 60 per cent of the produce, legislators, acting at the behest of big traders and rice millers, jettisoned the scheme. They demanded action against the Food Secretary for launching a programme which would have incurred a loss of Rs. 7 crore to the government. The much greater loss to government of providing tax remissions for sugar mills to clear cane arrears was conveniently ignored.[124]

Under the Janata government, pressures for subsidization of commercial agriculture increased substantially from the wheat and cane growers in northern India. In spite of expert advice to the contrary, the states were directed to abolish existing levies and taxes on agricultural inputs.[125] The Agricultural Prices Commission's acceptance of the parity principle—parity between the prices of inputs and procurement prices—advocated by rich farmers bears testimony to the influence of these classes at the time.[126]

The immediate impact of the 'new agricultural strategy' on the rural poor seems to have been negative since capitalist farmers, anxious to maximize profits, acted to minimize rural wages. The real income of agricultural labourers and small peasants, who made up 50 per cent of the population and were heavily dependent upon the market for food, declined in all regions of UP, including the Green Revolution areas in 1970-1. Though wages in the state varied from region to region, they were as low as Rs. 2-Rs. 3 in Banda in 1980.[127] Thus not much happened to improve the material position of the rural poor: money wages did not rise faster than the inflation rate.

The stagnation in real wages suggests that there was no necessary connection between the introduction of modern technology, which leads to greater agricultural output, and trends in wages. Wage rates, in practice, were influenced by the bargaining power of agricultural labourers, the influence and authority wielded by the landowners, the nature of contractual relations between the labourers and the landowners, and the availability of alternative employment. Moreover, employment opportunities for agricultural labour increased only if agricultural output expanded equally rapidly in all regions.[128] Otherwise, the migration of surplus labour to the regions of greater agricultural productivity, prevented the rise in wage rates in those districts which registered a higher rate of growth. The steady flow of migrant labour to the western region suggests that there was a substantial decline in real income in eastern UP. Since there was so little resistance by rural labour in the post-independence period, the exploitation and immiseration of the unorganized rural poor continues unabated. The stagnant level of rural real wage rates in UP can be contrasted with the situation in 'areas such as Thanjavur in Tamil Nadu, Kerala and West Bengal (which) have witnessed a smaller erosion in real wages than have the high-growth areas, owing to the existence of some trade union organization of labourers'.[129]

What is equally noteworthy is that the percentage of rural population living below the poverty line increased from 47 per cent in 1973 to 50 per cent in 1977-8; in terms of absolute numbers, their ranks were estimated at 510.42 lakh in 1979-80, as against 267 lakhs in 1960-1.[130] In addition, the census data indicated a dramatic increase in agricultural labourers as a proportion of all workers—from 5.80 per cent in 1951 to 19.55 per cent in 1971. The increase was most striking in the eastern districts where, according to the 1971 Census, the proportion of agricultural labour stood at over 30 per cent.[131]

As in other parts of India, the number of marginal and small peasants constituted the bulk of the cultivating population. As shown in Table 21.6, by 1980-1, approximately 87 per cent of operational holdings were less than two hectare, and accounted for 47 per cent of the area. By contrast, 13 per cent of semi-medium, medium, and large operational holdings controlled 53 per cent of the area. No less important than the overall tendency of land concentration[132] was the persisting pattern of land concentration in upper caste households as shown in Table 21.7. According to a survey conducted

TABLE 21.6: Number and Size Distribution of Operational Holdings in Uttar Pradesh

| | 1976–7 | | 1980–1 | |
	Number	Area	Number	Area
Marginal (below 1 hectare)	69.4	23.8	70.6	25.6
Small (between 1 and 2 hectare)	16.4	20.8	16.3	21.5
Semi-medium (between 2 and 4 hectare)	9.6	24.6	9.0	23.9
Medium (between 4 and 10 hectare)	4.1	23.1	3.7	20.3
Large (10 hectare and above)	0.5	10.4	0.4	8.7

Source: India, Ministry of Agriculture and Rural Development (Agricultural Census Division), All-India Estimates of Provisional Number of Operational Holdings and Area Operated 1980–1, Agricultural Census Bulletin, no. 21 (mimeo), Tables 12, 13.

in the early 1970s, 15.5 per cent of high caste households owned 40 per cent of the land, while 31 per cent of intermediate caste households controlled 27 per cent.[133] Moreover, the tendency toward concentration occurred within all caste categories. The SCs which constituted 21 per cent of the total households, operated 9.5 per cent of the area; but 1.27 per cent of SC landowners owned 15.87 per cent of the land.

Although upper caste households owned a much larger share of the cultivated area, it is too simple to link land concentration with upper caste domination as a whole. Much more important than the overall control of upper caste households, was the large area of land owned by a *small* segment of big landowners and rich peasants belonging to upper castes. This phenomenon was underscored by the greater frequency of larger sized holdings among upper castes compared with any other caste group. For example, 20 per cent of upper caste households operated holdings of over 10 acre which included more than 56 per cent of the land held by these castes.[134]

An important and not altogether unrelated consequence of the domination of big landowners and their control over most aspects of production was the persistence of a significant class of sharecroppers. Many of the landless, as indeed a number of marginal and small landowners, were forced to lease in land despite the ban on leasing. The encouragement to leasing was provided by the UPZAC which did not impose manual work as an essential qualification for the definition of a cultivator. Moreover, sharecropping was authorized by providing that any arrangement whereby a person was entitled to a right merely to share in the produce grown on the

TABLE 21.7: Percentage Distribution of Households and Area Owned by Size Class of Ownership and Caste Groups

Size/class of holdings	Landless		0–1.00 acre		1.01–2.50 acre		2.51–5.00 acre		5.01–10.00 acre		More than 10.00 acre		Total for UP	
Castes	House-holds	Area	House-holds	Area	House-holds	Area	House-holds	Area	House-holds	Area	House-holds	Area	House-holds	Area
	(1)	(2)	(3)	(4)	(5)	(6)	(7)	(8)	(9)	(10)	(11)	(12)	(13)	(14)
Higher castes	3.86	0.00	11.95	1.30	11.76	3.65	26.29	13.32	25.37	25.39	20.77	56.34	100.00	100.00
	(2.30)	(0.00)	(7.59)	(9.96)	(10.18)	(13.02)	(27.39)	(28.79	(41.44)	(42.25)	(52.07)	(57.36)	(15.63)	(40.71)
Intermediate castes	26.59	0.00	25.30	6.49	18.58	13.10	15.00	20.61	9.01	25.80	5.52	34.00	100.00	100.00
	(31.56)	(0.00)	(32.13)	(33.80)	(32.11)	(31.89)	(31.23)	(30.34)	(29.43)	(29.23)	(27.65)	(23.58)	(31.33)	(27.72)
Scheduled castes	32.68	0.00	29.89	11.41	20.01	22.29	11.21	26.08	4.94	23.65	1.27	15.87	100.00	100.00
	(56.52)	(0.00)	(55.14)	(50.78)	(20.24)	(47.84)	(33.91)	(32.84)	(23.42)	(22.90)	(9.22)	(9.41)	(45.50)	(23.71)
Scheduled tribes														
Muslim/Sikhs	33.46	0.00	16.92	3.70	18.08	10.50	15.00	19.23	7.31	17.49	9.23	49.08	100.00	100.00
	(9.53)	(0.00)	(5.41)	(5.46)	(7.47)	(7.25)	(7.47)	(8.03)	(5.71)	(5.62)	(11.06)	(9.65)	(7.49)	(7.86)
Total for UP	26.31	0.00	24.67	5.33	18.13	13.39	15.04	18.83	9.60	24.47	6.25	39.98	100.00	100.00
	(100.00)	(100.00)	(100.00)	(100.00)	(100.00)	(100.00)	(100.00)	(100.00)	(100.00)	(100.00)	(100.00)	(100.00)	(100.00)	(100.00)

Notes: 1. The main figures in the columns 1 to 12 (without brackets) are row percentages to the totals for UP in columns 13 and 14 respecitvely.

2. The figures within brackets in columns 1 to 14 are percentages with respect to column totals for UP.

Source: Shrimali, *Agrarian Change*, 1981.

land in consideration of such person assisting or, in particular, participating with the tenure holder in the actual performance of agricultural operations was not a 'lease'.[135]

According to the 26th Round of the National Sample Survey Organization (1971–2), roughly one-fourth of the farmers owning more than 10 acre were leasing out land. The total area leased out was just 7 per cent but the total number of people cultivating under tenancy arrangements was nearly 20 per cent. Dalits accounted for the largest percentage of lessors. According to the survey conducted by Kripa Shankar (in 1974–5), Chamars accounted for 40 per cent of the lessees: yadavs were the next largest group accounting for 18.61 per cent.[136] Another survey conducted by the UP government in 1980–1 revealed a much higher incidence of tenancy, mostly concealed, in the fertile Terai districts, Bundelkhand, upper Doab, and Rohilkhand, although not in the formerly zamindari dominated districts of Awadh and eastern UP. For instance, in Palanpur village in Moradabad, subtenancy and sharecropping was observed on 20 per cent of the total land.[137] In the hill and western region, absenteeism and the related phenomenon of capitalist gentleman farming, which was quite common, accounted for the greater compulsion to lease out land.[138]

Congress and the Politics of Upper Caste Hegemony

From 1952 to 1967, UP was ruled by the Congress party. It is generally assumed that the Congress in these years was essentially a coalition of district faction leaders.[139] These leaders maintained their position through control over District Congress Committees (DCCs), by helping their important members to dominate district level institutions, such as cooperative banks, zilla parishads, and panchayats. Much of the political conflict, it is argued, occurred within factions and between factions, while the absence of any popular pressure from below further encouraged personal conflicts.[140] Most of the faction leaders belonged to the dominant sections and their support at across caste and class lines.[141] Factionalism, however, does not provide an exhaustive framework for the analysis of UP politics. Much of the factional conflict within the party was between 'district bosses', who appeared to have had rather localized power bases, such as a town or party committee at the district level often consisting of constantly changing coalitions of small local bosses.[142]

At the same time, a number of important issues and policies concerned the state government and the Congress party.[143] During the early years, UP was the leading arena where the all–India conflict between the two major groups led by Jawaharlal Nehru and Sardar Patel was played out. With the exception of Patel, all the major protagonists in the epic struggle were drawn from UP. The contest between Tandon on the side of the conservatives and Kripalani, who represented the reformists, revealed that Tandon received maximum support from UP. From this conflict the conservative group led by Pant, Tandon, and Sampurnanand emerged as the dominant force. However, this group failed to establish its hegemony throughout the state. Consequently, district and city politics had their own structures of authority which were not dependent on the support and authority of the Sampurnanand–Pant group either for their survival or for the maintenance and expansion of their political base. In addition, the vastness and heterogeneity of UP, and its disparate socio-economic structures, worked against the growth of the common traditions and concerns, that characterized smaller and more homogeneous states. Indeed, a single dominant group could not represent the diverse interests of eastern and western UP and the hill regions at the same time. However, at no time during the struggle for gaining authority and support was UP politics devoid of issues. Even at the peak of Congress dominance, it was not a monolithic organization: it encompassed many groups with differing and often contradictory political orientations and policy positions.[144]

The paramount issue of whether to make the Congress an instrument of social change or to make the Congress a weapon for preserving the status quo was settled in favour of the conservatives. The conservative group was anxious to counter the radical current remaining within the Congress. The progressive elements, mainly former socialists and communists, had raised an ideological opposition to the official Congress position of restructuring social and agrarian institutions in the rural areas gradually. The Congress leadership, by contrast, was more concerned with the potential destabilizing effects of rural unrest spearheaded by the Socialists and Communists in the late 1940s. Given the ideological orientation of the dominant forces in Congress, they were particularly anxious to contain any increase in influence of the Communist Party. The Uttar Pradesh Congress Committee (UPCC) in the late 1940s and early 1950s repeatedly stressed the need to counter the communist influence on the ideological plane, because as Sampurnanand maintained, 'They were our main enemies'. Both C.B. Gupta and Sampurnanand, and a host of other Congressmen, favoured an alliance with the socialists to fight the communists. However, Pant and an equally powerful section of the Congress leadership strongly disapproved of the Socialists' decision to leave the Congress at that juncture in order to form a separate party. This view was reflected in the UPCC's April 1948 resolution which asserted:

The pace of development is not rapid as some would like it to be, but the Socialists must bear the responsibility in part. . . . The province can with justification blame them for not rendering to it a service for which they were capable, especially during the anxious time through which the province had to pass as a result of the communal passions.[145]

After the exit of the Socialists, Congress politics at the state level was marked in the early years by strategic and policy debates centring on the issues of secularism, the future of Urdu, Zamindari Abolition and the extent of compensation to zamindars, the imposition of land ceilings, and organization of cooperatives. Approaches to these issues were often coloured by varied ideological perspectives and by the political choices available to the Congress regarding the pace and content of development in general, and the role of the peasantry, in particular.

The debate on whether the Congress should act as an instrument of change was carried out between G.B. Pant, Purshottam Das Tandon, and Sampurnanand on the one side and Rafi Ahmed Kidwai and K.D. Malaviya on the other. The Pant group favoured the continuity of political traditions and structures, attempted to jettison all talk of reform, and worked to mould the UP Congress into a conservative political force. This operation was boosted by the efforts of Pant and Gupta to eliminate Rafi Ahmed Kidwai and his allies from the UP Congress when they attempted to fill the vacuum left by the exit of the Socialists in 1948. Kidwai's desire to contest the election of the Presidentship of the UPCC in 1948 was a last ditch attempt to challenge the authority of Gupta, the new conservative party boss. The Gupta-Pant faction counteract the challenge by isolating Kidwai's chief supporters on the left, including K.D. Malaviya, who argued that Congress could only succeed as a platform and should be tolerant of different positions.[146] The Gupta-Pant faction, who had by then virtually outmanoeuvred their detractors, were not prepared to countenance any ideological opposition.

Two forces—conservative and reformist—were therefore at work in the UP Congress, sometimes proceeding on parallel lines and sometimes in opposite directions. Often, differences were governed by loyalty to Nehru and the policies with which he was identified. On other occasions, they were expressed as a conflict between the party and the government. On the one hand, the organizational bosses were insistent on the primacy of the party over the government, and wanted it to act as a check on elected leaders. Their critics, on the other hand, wanted the party to play a supportive role. These tensions were complicated by the fact that many of Nehru's ardent supporters did not share his ideological commitment; rather, they attempted to influence Congress politics through invocation of the Prime Minister's name and prestige. The rivals to such 'loyalists' resented these tactics because opposition to Nehru in the structure and idiom of early UP politics was construed as conservatism. Reformists, in contrast were critical of the conservative domination of Congress. The *National Herald*, the voice of reformist Congressmen in the 1950s, bluntly condemned the UP Congress as a haven for reaction.[147] In spite of Nehru's obvious sympathies for the Kidwai–Malaviya group, the Congress High Command used its authority to strengthen the dominant conservative faction.[148]

In the 1960s, major differences erupted between the Gupta group and Charan Singh, who was gradually emerging as the principal voice of dissent. Their political disputes underscored the presence of two distinct policy positions in the state Congress. Gupta, despite all his antipathy towards planning and the public sector, was interested in the growth and expansion of modern industry. Complaining that Chief Ministers of UP, particularly Pant, had not exerted pressure on Nehru for the industrialization of the state, he sought vainly to promote industrial development by extracting resources from agriculture through taxation. Charan Singh and the majority of UP's legislators, by contrast, favoured increasing the prosperity of rich peasant proprietors by maximizing investments in and subsidies for agriculture.

The dominant group, led by Gupta, was quite influential, and virtually controlled both the government and the organization. However, their social support and core leadership was narrowly based, drawn mainly from the urban areas, and from the bania caste. Gupta's lieutenants—Banarsi Das, Ram Murti, and Jugal Kishore—were banias, giving credence to the popular belief that he represented the interests of banias.[149] In contrast, the influence of Tripathi, Gautam, and Charan Singh was concentrated in rural areas and among the upper castes. The caste base of these leaders did not, however, mean that they were deliberately trying to activate political support along caste lines since the major caste groups were spread across the state, and no single caste predominated in any region.[150]

The Congress party built its electoral support by directing its appeal to all sections of society. In its early years, it paid generous compensation to zamindars and channelled a substantial part of agricultural investment to rich farmers. At the same time, it also set up special agencies to assist small farmers, supported a minimum wages policy for the landless, and provided reservations in educational institutions and the administrative services for the SCs. In addition, it appealed to Muslims by offering them positions in the party and government, and by putting up Muslim candidates in constituencies with a large Muslim population. For its core social base the Congress relied on a coalition of brahmans, SCs, and Muslims, who together constituted 44 per cent of the state population. Indeed, this political combination enabled the Congress to outflank the opposition in many electoral contests.

Nevertheless, the party's leadership was much narrower than its electoral support. It was drawn from among the locally dominant classes in rural society and from the professionals and businessmen in the towns. An analysis of the social background of the Members of the Legislative Assembly (MLAs) in the UP assemblies from 1952 to 1967 reveals a preponderance of ex-zamindars. Meyer's study of the state's political elite stresses the overwhelming importance of class and wealth as against the caste background of legislators.[151] The class dimension was striking even among legislators elected from reserved seats: notwithstanding the reservation of one-fifth of the Assembly segments for the SCs, the majority of whom worked as agricultural labourers, only 3 per cent of MLAs came from this class. In the final analysis what emerged was a strong convergence of wealth and high caste, Meyer concludes:

the extent to which MLAs are drawn from the upper segment of rural society is phenomenal. Traditional, financial and status resources seem to have greater potency in this earlier process of democratic experience . . . of the two hierarchical factors, financial status and ritual status, the former seems to have been the most effectual in recruitment. The over representation of the high castes was by a factor of 2 or 3, whereas the factor for the wealthy would certainly have been at least 30, perhaps 300, depending upon whether the very rich comprised 1 per cent to 0.1 per cent of the society.[152]

After the creation of only one type of tenurial right in 1974, the distinction between ex-zamindars and new proprietors became increasingly blurred. Using the criterion of landownership—an important element of differentiation in rural areas—Saxena found that the majority of legislators and Block *Pramukhs* elected in 1983 were still from among the rich landowning classes.[153] Though Meyer's data on the social background of MLAs in the first three Assemblies is not comparable to the data collected by N.C. Saxena for local politicians in 1983, it was nevertheless evident that political leaders continued to be recruited from the upper reaches of rural society.

Similarly, in terms of caste, leadership positions in the Congress tended to be occupied mainly by upper castes, mostly by brahmans, banias and thakurs, while the middle and backward castes were under-represented. In fact, not more than 6 per cent of the Congress Legislature Party was drawn from the backward castes in the first three assemblies[155] (Appendix, Table VII). More than one-fifth of Congress MLAs were brahmans, and almost 50 per cent belonged to the upper castes, with little noticeable change until

1974. In 1971, 42 of the 70 Congress presidents were either brahmans or thakurs. The representation of the backward castes was reduced to six.[155] The six UP Cabinets formed between 1952 and 1974 were also dominated by the brahmans, the thakurs and the vaishyas. In the Sampurnanand, C.B. Gupta, and Sucheta Kripalani ministries, nearly half of the ministers belonged to the upper castes.[156] Yadavs and kurmis found no place in the Cabinet until 1967 (with the exception of a Yadav deputy minister in 1957-62). In Kamlapati Tripathi's government, 50 per cent of ministers in 1971-5 were brahmans.[157] The dominance of brahmans increased under the chief ministerships of Bahuguna, Sripat Misra and N.D. Tiwari (Appendix, Table A.3).

The Emergence of Political Challenge

The political ascendancy of the upper castes for over 20 years inevitably led to the exclusion of middle and backward castes which was a source of much disenchantment (Table 21.8). In addition, even the prosperous Jats, who were not considered to be members of the backward castes, were aggrieved because of their limited access to positions of power both in the public services and in the ruling party. Their experience and perceptions, as indeed of other groups, encouraged the crystallization of social cleavages that eventually posed a threat to Congress dominance in the state.

Charan Singh was the first Congress politician to recognize the political potential of mobilizing the discontent of the backward castes, most of whom belonged to the cultivating classes. As early as 1947, he had proposed reservation of 60 per cent jobs in public services for sons of cultivators[158] on the plea that 'due to the town and village contradiction, towns and urban middle classes suck all the resources and wealth while passing on the burden of taxation to the villages, the only producers of wealth'. The All India Jat Mahasabha supported Charan Singh's proposal.[159] In 1956 he presided over a Backward Classes Conference—the overt expression of the backward castes' coming of age in the post-independence period.

Such activities angered the dominant group within the Congress led by Sampurnanand and later by Gupta, which was averse to any change or even rearrangement in the structure of power. During Pant's long period of pre-eminence over the UP Congress, which extended from 1937 until his elevation to the Centre in 1954, 'there was no question of the Congress leaders resorting to competitive and controlled induction of the backward caste leaders into Congress circles'.[160] Gupta was stridently opposed to giving concessions to the backward castes. During his tenure as chief minister, he opposed the relaxation in the upper age limit for recruitment to the administrative services for backward castes by three or four years, which had been granted by the earlier Pant ministry.[161]

Sampurnanand supported more strongly the 'continuation of the upper classes coalition in the Congress which will ensure its influence in rural areas.' He opposed,

opening the doors to the backward classes because it will let loose an unplanned revolution which will blow up the whole social structure. A real clash between castes and classes will be a bloody fight and much of the work which we have done so far will go up in smoke.

He went on to assert that the

Brahmans, rajputs, kayasthas, bhumihars and vaishyas have in general been the people from whom the Congress has derived the maximum support in the past and the Congress must fulfil their expectations. Because the upper castes have been culturally affiliated to the Congress leadership, the backward classes instinctively distrust the Congress leadership. Consequently, whatever advantages are conferred upon the backward castes, they are unlikely to join the Congress fold.[162]

Such views reflected the determination to keep out the backward castes from the Congress coalition. It should be noted that efforts by the upper castes to deflect a challenge by the backward classes to their social and political dominance were reinforced by their determination to avoid the class issue. Such was the motive in dissuading Charan Singh from organizing and attending the first Backward Classes Conference held in 1956, and in issuing a circular asking Congress members not to attend the conference.[163]

TABLE 21.8: Caste Composition of the MLAs in the UP Legislative Assembly 1952–80 (by percentage)

Caste	1952	1957	1962	1967	1969	1974	1980
Brahman	27	21	21	21.46	19.05	16.25	23
Thakur	14	17	20	13.92	16.23	15.59	20
Bania, Kayastha and Khatri	15	14	12	4.95	3.76	6.95	4
Jat, Bhumihar and Tyagi	5	6	5	4.95	4.94	6.95	5
Ahir, Kurmi, Lodh and Gujar	6	10	10	16.51	17.64	23.26	13
Other Backward Castes	3	2	3	12.74	9.17	5.10	5
Scheduled Castes	20	21	22	19.81	20.94	16.31	20
Muslims	10	9	7	5.66	8.23	9.60	10
TOTAL	100	100	100	100	100	100	100

Charan Singh, along with many other backward caste Congressmen, defied the leadership, and the conference was quite a success.

Charan Singh's subsequent efforts to mobilize the backward castes, however, did not prove very successful largely because his own claim of being the natural leader of all the peasants prevented him from mobilizing the backward castes alone.[164] Besides, he belonged to the cultivating caste of the Jats which had not suffered caste oppression in the past. Indeed, Charan Singh's identification with their interests led to charges of casteism against him which the Congress leadership exploited to neutralize his appeal. For his part, Charan Singh greatly resented the Jat label; he was concerned about charges of casteism persistently raised against him since 1948 and was anxious to deny the title of the Jat leader which restricted his influence.[165]

By 1967, however, there were indications of an approaching political change in state politics. The foundations of this change had been laid by the Backward Classes movement in UP in the 1920s and 1930s, when Yadav and Kurmi elites joined hands with cognate groups in Bihar to claim Kshatriya status. Their consciousness assumed a sharper focus after the formation of the All India Yadav Mahasabha in 1923 which also had many adherents among the Ahirs of northern India. In the forties the Yadavs, Kurmis, Ahirs and Jats developed a high level of affinity. From this affinity arose the AJGAR (acronym for Ahir, Jat and Gujar) movement whose caste association meetings were marked by anti-upper caste rhetoric, which sometimes provoked agitations against these groups.[166] In a somewhat similar effort, leaders like Swami Achutananda, Swami Ram Charan Mallah, and S.D. Singh Chaurasia, attempted to mobilize and politicize the backward castes.

Also in the 1920s, Swami Bodhananda Mahasthir formed the Adivasi Hindu League. However, the backward castes failed to forge links with the SCs in any common political action.[167] This was largely due to the influence of the Arya Samaj movement which was particularly strong among the Jats in western UP and the Yadavs in eastern UP. Both of these groups were attracted by the process of Sanskritization as a means of attaining equality with the upper castes. This preoccupation excluded the SCs who could not 'dig into the puranas or remote history to adduce proof that their caste once upon a time held a higher status. To the extent upper peasant castes resorted to Sanskritization, they have generally been unable to make common cause with the lower, backward scheduled castes'.[168]

The introduction of universal suffrage and the promise of reservations, however, opened up new possibilities for the backward castes in the secular arena of politics. In the changed political context the Yadavs took the lead in demanding the adoption of the caste criterion for the purpose of defining the backward classes. The Kakasaheb Karlekar Commission, appointed by the Government of India in 1959, endorsed this approach to the definition of backwardness, leading to 2,399 castes being declared socially and educationally backward.[169] However, the recommendations of the Commission were not implemented, though some state governments established their own commissions to facilitate reservations for backward classes in government employment. No reservation scheme was proposed by the UP government.

Politicization and Mobilization of the Middle and Backward Castes

The period from 1967 to 1977 witnessed a variety of changes in UP politics that affected dominance relations. During this period the Congress party broke down as an election machine and several unstable coalition were formed. Even after the Congress returned to power in 1971, the party leadership could no longer function autonomously from the Centre. Moreover, in this period the struggle for power between the Congress and the opposition at the all-India level came increasingly to centre on north India, and especially on the key state of UP. The most striking phenomenon to emerge during this period was the mobilization of backward castes and the middle peasantry arrayed against the political power of the twice-born castes of brahmans and Thakurs in the countryside, and the Banias and Kayasthas in the urban areas. The mobilization of backward castes was spurred on by the Lohia socialists, who emphasized their social grievances in raising the issue of reservations to create a base among the upwardly mobile Ahir, Kurmi and Lodh castes. Ironically, many of these groups had supported the radical Kisan Sabhas in the pre-Independence period, but after having prospered from development programmes in the 1950s and 1960s, they shifted their support to political parties which could bring them a larger share of state power.

The implementation of land reforms, though half-hearted, helped in creating the conditions for the emergence and politicization of middle and backward caste peasants. By making former tenants economically independent of upper caste landlords, Zamindari Abolition itself led to the mobilization of lower social categories which gradually asserted themselves against upper castes. The process of political mobilization gained momentum after the growth of class differentiation in the wake of the new agricultural policies pursued by the government since the 1960s. Inequalities and disparities increased between the wheat growing western region and the rice producing eastern region and between groups within the wheat growing region. Rich and middle level peasants doubled their output and increased their income in many cases by 70 per cent. In addition, the rich peasants benefited greatly from the central government's new agricultural prices policy. During 1967-9 the procurement prices in UP increased by 31 per cent over the 1965 levels.[170] The increase raised the price of wheat to such high levels that many big producers inundated government procurement agencies with their stocks. The resulting drain on government finance led them to reconsider the system of procurement and distribution of foodgrains and to introduce price controls. This angered the market-oriented rich peasants of the upper Doab. They were especially annoyed by the Congress policy of selling imported wheat at below prevailing market rates to reduce the burden on the consumer. The enforcement of compulsory procurement of foodgrains and the imposition of restrictions on inter-state movement of stocks prevented the surplus farmers from maximizing their returns.

Many of the rich peasants, who belonged to backward and middle castes, also resented the dominance of upper castes among the Congress leadership. The Jats in western UP, for instance, had made a great deal of progress in agriculture, similarly, the former tenant and sharecropping castes of Yadavs, Kurmis, Lodhs, Gujars, and Koeris, became owner cultivators and made use of the new opportunities to adopt modern agriculture. However, they had remained largely outside the ambit of party politics. In the 1950s the Ahirs and the Kurmis gained some representation in the socialist parties. The Socialist Party, in particular, gave important positions to members of these caste groups, which enhanced its reputation as the champion of backward classes and helped it to establish a firm base among the small peasant proprietors, and among the upwardly mobile Ahirs, Kurmis and Lodh castes.

The overall participation of the backward castes in state politics increased markedly after Charan Singh left the Congress in 1967. Though the immediate provocation for his decision was the denial by C.B. Gupta of the much coveted agriculture portfolio, the more important reason was his identification with rural peasant as against urban industrial interests.[171] At the same time, ideological differences alone do not explain his parting with Congress colleagues, for the peasant proprietors whose interests Charan Singh championed had benefited from Congress' economic policies. According to his own account he resigned because he was convinced that although he was the most qualified person for the chief ministership, the upper castes would never consent to the appointment of a Jat.

Thus, after the 1967 elections, when the Congress was in a precarious position, Charan Singh resigned from the party to form a coalition of all non-Congress opposition parties. From 1967 to 1971, Congress and non-Congress coalitions took turns in power.[172] It was during this period that

Charan Singh launched the Bharatiya Kranti Dal (BKD) to articulate the discontent of the rich and middle peasants in the upper Doab, which, with its high voter turnout, was the most politicized region in the state. He formed innumerable alliances all of which were aimed at challenging Congress supremacy. The common goal of removing Congress from power encouraged him to align on the one hand with his arch rival, C.B. Gupta, who after the 1969 Congress party split joined the Congress(O), and on the other with the socialists.[173]

Immediately after its formation in 1969, the BKD articulated the interests of peasant proprietors who had prospered through the Green Revolution and were then seeking political power on their own to raise their standing and further increase their gains. The social significance of the rise of the BKD was reflected in its growing influence among the upwardly mobile peasant castes.[174] Before 1969 their discontent against the Congress had been expressed by voting for Independent candidates.[175] The formation of the BKD offered them an organizational alternative for asserting their political interests which they believed had been hitherto neglected by the Congress; and the increased prosperity of the large owner cultivators in the western districts provided them with the means to make an independent bid for power. They were not only dissatisfied with government's failure to provide subsidies for capital inputs and incentive prices for foodgrains, but were also irritated by the revised irrigation and cess rates, and development levies, sanctioned by the Congress government, on the recommendation of the Economic Advisory Council, which favoured augmenting untapped agricultural resources.[176] In consequence, the Congress suffered a major electoral reverse in the western region and its traditional hold over several backward caste groups was seriously eroded in the late 1960s.

Backward caste peasants responded to the appeal by the BKD because for them political participation signified both a search for recognition of social status and an assertion of political power to protect their economic gains. Even Charan Singh who was initially reluctant to mobilize the backward castes soon settled for an alliance with them in order to extend his support beyond western UP. However, the groundwork for the backward castes entry into politics had been prepared by the Socialist leader Ram Manohar Lohia who proposed an alliance of all backward castes to challenge Congress hegemony.

The new political formation was buttressed by Charan Singh's party. The BKD promoted their political aspirations by offering them a large number of assembly tickets: 115 candidates from middle and backward castes were put up in the 1969 assembly elections as against 23 nominated by the Congress.[177] Charan Singh's move paid off handsomely—the BKD was second to the Congress in UP, and emerged as the leading party in the western region.[178] It won the majority of seats in the western districts: 61 of the 99 successful BKD candidates came from the region, particularly Meerut, Agra, and Rohilkhand. In the districts of the upper Doab the Congress vote declined from 55 per cent in 1952 to 30 per cent in 1969. BKD support in this area was so extensive because the upper Doab had become the domain of the prosperous peasantry. More than 54 per cent of the area was controlled by peasants with a minimum holding of seven acre, making the prosperous peasantry much stronger here than in the eastern districts, where, quite predictably, the BKD won only 16 out of 96 seats. The disintegration of the socialist movement, and the subsequent decision to merge the BKD with the Socialist Party (SSP), in 1974 led to the formation of the Bharatiya Lok Dal (BLD) and helped to enlarge its base among Ahirs (or Yadavs) the largest cultivating caste in eastern and central UP.

In its programme, the BLD accorded the highest importance to agriculture, followed by small scale and cottage industry. Heavy industry was deliberately downgraded in an attempt to reverse Jawaharlal Nehru's policies and priorities. By contrast, the BLD tried to cast itself in a Gandhian mould, demanding that the government[179] should be run on Gandhian principles. The 1974 manifesto made the positions explicit: 'We favour Gandhism, not Socialism'. It called for the abolition of food zones and an end to planning and state regulation of the economy.[180] What appealed most to the rich peasantry was Charan Singh's opposition to Congress proposals for collective or cooperative farming on the grounds that it did not offer any incentives for higher production.

Thus, Charan Singh did develop a distinctive rural-oriented economic policy by promising measures to increase agricultural production, although his policies would have mainly benefited larger proprietors as against small peasants and landless labourers.[181] This was clearly evident from his 'firm' handling of the land grab movement launched by the SSP and Communist Party of India (CPI) in 1970.[182] Charan Singh severely condemned the land grab[183] which he felt was redundant since 'land reforms in UP were superior to even those in Kerala'.[184] In fact, he was convinced that 'with the abolition of zamindari, the task of "bourgeois democratic revolution" in UP had been completed non-violently'.[185] His opposition to the imposition of reduced ceilings was governed by similar considerations. He pleaded that the self-sufficient peasantry, which was the backbone of agricultural development and prosperity, should be allowed to hold 30 acre of land. By also opposing the abolition of privy purses, nationalization of the sugar industry, and the takeover of wholesale trade in wheat by the Congress government in 1971, the BLD was clearly identified with the substantial landed interests.

Its class outlook, however, could only appeal to a small proportion of the peasantry, the prosperous proprietors. However, such an appeal does not fully account for the success of the party in establishing a firm base of support in the western region and its subsequent extension to eastern UP. This pattern suggests that the party was not just recruiting support of the peasantry as a class, but was following a strategy similar to the Congress, of mobilizing rich peasants from among middle and backward castes, who in turn could deliver the votes of the poor peasants to the party. In a sense, then, the BKD's class appeal was directed towards the rich and middle peasants, while its caste appeal attracted the large number of small holders among the backward castes. In areas where the peasant proprietor and backward and intermediate caste sets overlapped, 'the party was strikingly successful in garnering the support of the peasantry as a class because it could enlist the recruiting agents (who helped) in the direct recruitment of specific support'.[188]

By concentrating attention on the backward castes, the BKD sought to draw upon the reserves of caste consciousness of backward castes, and in assembly elections from these groups. The effect of this strategy was revealed in the course of the 1969 assembly elections as large numbers of backward caste members volunteered as party workers.

Given the underdeveloped conditions in the state as a whole, it was also essential to mobilize the lower castes on the social issues which were the major source of their shared grievances. In the event, the BLD appealed to those groups which had been generally neglected by the Congress, emphasizing their unique and distinct economic interests and claiming for them proportionate representation in politics and in government.[187] The BLD applied the SSP model of concentrating on castes that were economically backward, while denouncing upper caste hegemony in politics and in administration. Thus, the political alliance moulded and promoted by Charan Singh included the Jats, who were officially not Backward, but who identified themselves with the backward castes.

The backward caste appeal enabled the BLD to challenge the political; dominance of the brahmans and thakurs by competing for the support of substantial chunks of the Other Backward Classes (OBCs) who formed nearly 26 per cent of the state's population. The bulk of them were mostly small landholders, tenants, agricultural labourers, and impoverished village artisans. Apart from caste discrimination at the hands of the upper castes, they were subjected by them to informal economic control which came mainly from moneylending, leasing out small bits of land, and providing house sites to small peasants. The result was that notwithstanding their numerical preponderance, the small peasants of lower castes lived under conditions of social and political servitude.

Charan Singh, although not a member of a listed backward caste, made consistent efforts to identify with the backward castes by appealing for votes as an 'old Yadav'. During his stint as chief minister, he promoted the backward castes on the plea that they were 'hardly represented in the senior postings in the entire administration of UP'.[188] For the first time, three ministerships went to members of the middle and backward peasant castes in the 1967 Samyukta Vidhyak Dal (SVD) Ministry headed by him. The second Charan Singh ministry in 1970-1 also gave considerable representation to middle and backward castes.[189] This led the Congress to accuse him of deliberately favouring Jats and the backward castes. The caste issue, moreover, was linked with Charan Singh's policies of high produce prices and subsidies on modern inputs, both of which benefited the rich peasants who were drawn from the middle and backward castes.[190] The coalescence of caste and economic issues was thus closely linked to the evolving support base of the BLD and the Congress among identifiable caste and classes in UP. The BLD sought to combine horizontal and vertical mobilization; its success lay in combining caste and class with regional issues and interests in a manner which maintained its appeal and attractiveness to specific groups.

The Lok Dal thus effectively used the traditional caste idiom for political and economic ends.[191] Demands for cheaper inputs and subsidies were articulated in terms which appeared to transcend class interests. It was not however always easy to downplay the rich proprietor image. The party tried to do so by addressing its political appeal to the undifferentiated category of kisans whose interests it championed against the urban–industrial interests.

In contrast, Congress relied on a combination of a general political appeal which was derived from a populist ideology, and specific appeals which were directed at the SCs and the minorities. From the perspective of various castes and classes, the Congress was more clearly identified with the poorer peasantry and the SCs, especially during the restoration of Congress rule between 1971 and 1977. These years were consequently marked by the growing antagonism of sections of the rich peasants against the Congress. Such feelings were intensified by the land legislation in 1972 which reduced land ceilings to 18 acre per family; enabled the state takeover of the wholesale trade in wheat; and the effort to provide surplus land to the landless and house sites to the SCs. Many of these policies were criticized by Charan Singh, the leader of the BLD, then the principal opposition in the Legislative Assembly.[192] He opposed state trading in wheat because it would hurt the growers, and according to him, indicated the government's scant regard for agricultural development. In a similar vein he argued that redistribution of surplus land was no substitute for promoting rural and cottage industries.

The strident protests marked a shift from the first two decades after independence which were dominated by the more generalized concerns for promoting agriculture rather than industry. By contrast, the central issue became how to promote the interests of rich and medium landowners against those of the small peasants and landless. Consequently, the major demand was not just for greater attention to agriculture, but for greater allocations to power and irrigation. Indeed, investment in agricultural production, particularly under the heads of water and power, increased quite considerably from 36 per cent in the First Plan to 57.84 per cent in the Fifth Plan, while investment in community development and social services was drastically reduced from 29.17 per cent to 12.66 per cent in the same period.[193] The conflicting demands of the dominant landed proprietors, interested in maximizing their economic and political control over resources of production, and the rural poor interested primarily in survival was reflected in increasing social contradictions that heightened the struggle for power in UP society.

Conflict and Co-Option: The Limitations of Caste Mobilization

From the mid-1970s, the crystallization of political conflict was manifested in increasing opposition by middle and backward castes to Congress rule. Between 1967 and 1974 the percentage of upper castes in the state legislature declined from 40 per cent to 37 per cent, while the share of peasant castes increased from 20 per cent to 30 per cent in 1974[194] (Table 21.9). The BLD received the core of its support from Jats, Yadavs and Kurmis. In the 1977 elections its share of support from middle, and backward castes increased further. Against this background, the victory of the Janata Party in 1977 (a hastily assembled coalition of the BLD, Jan Sangh, and Socialists) was interpreted by some as the triumph of the middle and backward castes who had finally succeeded in breaking the opposition of the upper castes centred in the Congress. The decline of the Congress was most pronounced in areas of the upper Doab which had a large concentration of peasant castes. The social base of the Janata in this region rested on the rich and middle peasantry who were dissatisfied with the Congress governments' failure to provide further subsidies and higher procurement prices.

Nevertheless, the disaffection with the Congress and the victory of the Janata Party was mainly attributable to widespread resentment against the

TABLE 21.9: Caste Composition of MLAs in the UP Legislative Assembly by Party
(Percentage share)

Caste	1967			1969			1974		
	Congress	Jan Sangh	Lok Dal	Congress	Jan Sangh	Lok Dal	Congress	Jan Sangh	Lok Dal
Brahmans	25.25	25.77	–	16.79	23.53	6.02	22.75	9.44	3.88
Thakurs	16.34	11.34	–	36.00	21.57	13.04	17.54	22.95	9.71
Bania, Kayastha and Khatris	4.95	10.37	–	3.81	7.84	1.09	6.16	16.49	3.89
Jat, Tyagi and Bhumihar	3.96	3.04	–	1.88	1.96	14.60	6.16	4.92	11.65
Yadav, Kurmi, Lodh and Gujar	11.88	15.46	–	10.50	13.73	24.59	15.17	24.79	35.92
Other Backward Castes	4.95	8.25	–	6.21	5.88	8.10	3.79	4.92	6.80
Scheduled Castes	23.76	25.77	–	20.04	25.49	22.13	17.53	16.49	18.45
Muslims	8.91	–	–	4.77	–	10.07	10.90	–	9.70
TOTAL	100.00	100.00	–	100.00	100.00	100.00	100.00	100.00	100.00

Source: Compiled from fieldwork, 1985.

national Emergency proclaimed by the Congress government in 1975. The Janata leadership therefore still faced the task of creating an enduring base of social support among the backward castes. A first step was taken with the nomination of Ram Naresh Yadav as chief minister. Under his tenure, the state government took several measures which served the interests not only of rich farmers but of the middle and backward castes. The Janata government supported high sugarcane prices to offset losses caused by the poor monsoons in the summer of 1979[195] and increased the procurement price of wheat to Rs. 115.[196] At the same time, when the UP Backward Classes Commission, appointed in 1975, submitted its Report in 1977, the Janata government reacted in an accommodating manner.

The Chief Minister Ram Naresh Yadav, followed up the Report by reserving 15 per cent of positions in government and technical institutions for backward castes.[197] Comprising about 40 per cent of the total population, 3,521 castes were declared eligible for reservation. The principal beneficiaries were Ahirs, Kurmis, Gujars and Muslim weavers who possessed the means to gain education and the social consciousness to avail of these opportunities.

The BLD group within the Janata Party, fully supported reservations for backward castes on the argument that 'ideas and tests about merit, competitive selection and equal opportunities are bogus and irrelevant in an unequal society.[198] By contrast, the Jan Sangh constituent expressed the disapproval of the upper castes toward a potential challenge to their power. Some sections of the upper castes swung away from the Janata Party on the issue of reservations. Many of them supported the agitations against reservation in some areas of UP, demanding that class and not caste should be the criterion of social and economic backwardness.[199] Ram Naresh Yadav had misinterpreted the importance of the rising political participation of backward castes to mean that they had also experienced a substantial increase in their real social power. The upper caste opposition to reservations and the election results of 1980 quickly disproved the assumption of a basic change in the correlation of strength between the upper castes and the backward castes.

The Janata coalition broke down precisely because of the perpetual struggle over the distribution of benefits to various castes and classes which beset the government from the beginning of its tenure. At the national level, the denial of Charan Singh's claim to the prime ministership in 1977 embittered the middle and backward castes, thus setting the stage for a political struggle between them and the upper castes. In addition to the omnipresent caste conflict, the Janata Party was also plagued by the resurgence of communal violence. The development of these social contradictions, which led to the breakdown of the Janata coalition, betrayed the limitations of middle and backward caste political mobilization in UP.

The issue at stake was the status of rich peasants who had achieved a dominant economic position during the Green Revolution. Their support, first for Charan Singh's BKD then for Charan Singh's BLD faction within the Janata, and finally for Charan Singh's Lok Dal, formed in 1979 after the Janata Party break up, helped them to increase their political representation at the state level. During the 1980 elections, Congress won only 2 of the 14 seats in the upper Doab; the Lok Dal won 11 and Janata won 1.[200]

Nevertheless, the Congress leadership was still dominated by upper castes. Of the Presidents DCCs and City Congress Committees in 1973, 38 of 75 were brahmans: 40 of the 45 Zila Parishad chiefs were either brahman or thakur.[201] By contrast, Jats, Yadavs and Kurmis, were virtually absent in the Congress organization. They were also grossly under-represented in the bureaucracy: for example, nearly 70 per cent of Indian Administrative Service (IAS) and Indian Police Service (IPS) officers in 1980 were members of the upper castes while 52 per cent of the Provincial Civil Services were drawn from the ranks of the high castes. The upper echelons of the bureaucracy were more noticeably dominated by brahmans, who had been actively promoted by successive brahman chief ministers of the ruling Congress party. During Sripat Misra's tenure as chief minister in 1982 at least 17 of the senior secretaries in government departments were brahmans.[202]

Given the predominantly upper caste character of the UP government, it is not surprising that over the years implementation of reservations policy was resisted. This had encouraged the protagonists of the backward castes to level allegations of discrimination against the so-called brahman government. In June 1985 the State Backward Classes Federation and the state unit of the Lok Dal had threatened to launch an agitation for 'true implementation of the government's reservation policy and genuine acceptance of the Mandal Commission, otherwise their followers would come to the streets to settle the issues'.[203]

The evidence, however, showed that the SCs were most adversely affected by failures to fill the reserved quota: only 5.8 per cent of Class I officials, and 6.23 per cent of Class II officials were SCs, against the 18 per cent positions reserved for them. Only the reservation quota for Class IV positions (peons) was completely filled.

Divergent class interests within the middle and backward castes, between rich and middle peasants on the one hand, and marginal farmers and agricultural labourers on the other, as well as status rivalries and social barriers within and between backward castes and SCs prevented the Lok Dal from fully mobilizing the backward castes, and middle and small peasants. A host of other obstacles complicated the task, including the low level of political consciousness among them: they were still illiterate and non-politicized compared to the upper and middle castes,[204] making it easy for other parties to split the 'caste-community' vote by fielding their own backward caste candidates. Moreover, backward caste politicians, particularly the younger leaders, wanted a share in political power and patronage; the opposition parties offered them important party positions but could not provide government power. Consequently, backward caste leaders, after demonstrating their political influence in a constituency, were often drawn into the Congress fold. Thus, in the late 1970s, the Congress leadership succeeded in weaning away sections of the Yadavs by promoting and appointing them to important positions in the party, thereby undercutting the monopoly of ranks of backward castes by weaning away Kurmis and Gujars in the central region. It did so, once again, by gradually increasing the representation of these groups in the Congress. As part of this strategy Jai Ram Verma and Narendra Singh (both of backward castes) were appointed cabinet ministers in the UP government in 1985. Besides, the Congress offered tickets to Yadavs particularly in those constituencies in which Charan Singh's Lok Dal had not given them tickets.[205] In these ways Congress drew away a part of the backward caste vote from the Lok Dal.

The horizontal divisions within the middle and backward castes helped the Congress to stave off the challenge posed by the apparent political cohesion of these castes under Charan Singh's leadership. The innumerable vertical divisions among their ranks also worked against the possibility of any caste group forming the base of political support for the Lok Dal. Ironically, the greatest effect of the challenge from the Jat-led backward castes was to unite the upper castes. This was apparent from the renewed cooperation between brahmans and thakurs since 1980. Prior to this, the thakurs were not an important component of the Congress coalition; they were inducted when Congress extended its base beyond brahmans, SCs, and Muslims to counter the aggressive unity of Jats, Ahirs, Kurmis and Yadavs in many parts of the state.[206]

Caste Congruence and the Oppression of the Rural Poor

The politicization of middle and backward castes, which coincided with the Janata Party split, underscored the importance of caste in UP politics. Political articulation on caste lines, which was clearly divisive, more frequently took on a confrontational and communal character. The highly politicized groups of Jats and Yadavs when faced by a challenge from lower classes, particularly lower caste agricultural labourers, often adopted an extremely aggressive posture against the Dalits.

In fact, the rise of middle and backward castes, such as the Jats, Ahirs, Kurmis and Gujars in a number of districts intensified conflicts between the new Yadav and Kurmi landowners and the landless agricultural labourers. The new rural rich treated the dalit labourers worse than they did other poor peasants because the very fact of dalit status traditionally entailed social abuse which was not practised against the pauperized peasantry of other castes. The Crash Scheme for Rural Employment launched in October 1971 especially irked caste Hindu landowners: under the programme, UP was allotted Rs. 7 crore to provide a job to at least one member of a family with a monthly income of Rs. 100. This opened the possibility of additional employment for some of the 18 million landless workers of the state, mostly dalits. The social relations of superordination and subordination characteristic of landlord-labourer ties were thus upset. The possibility that dalits might now refuse begar galled the big landowners who evicted dalits from house-sites allotted to them.[207] The traditional centre-based relations of domination were not only to be preserved, but were deliberately used by big landowners to ensure the availability and submission of the labour force.

The extent to which modern rural capitalists were prepared to go to maintain their socio-political dominance was revealed in the increasing incidents of violence ending in dalit burnings. UP recorded the highest number of violent incidents against dalits in the 1980s, much higher compared even to Bihar where the level of social violence was generally high. According to official estimates, in 1979 there were at least 191 murders as well as the burning of hundreds of houses. It should be noted that in 1981, 1,429 cases of crimes against dalits were registered in UP as against 8 in West Bengal and 94 in Kerala. Also, the number of cases *challaned* was much lower than the cases registered: in UP out of 4,120 cases registered, only 1,674 cases were *challaned*.[208] The coercion and brutality was at its worst in western UP, particularly in Meerut, Bulandshahr, and Muzaffarnagar. The extent of terror unleashed by landowners can be guaged from the fact that the Janata government was compelled to set up a monitoring cell in Meerut to deal with complaints of brutalities against dalit rural labour.[209] The apparent middle and backward caste bias of the Janata government exacerbated the insecurity of the dalits; their leaders complained of inadequate protection and representation given to dalits in UP and Bihar.[210]

In some cases, a section of the rural poor belonging to the backward castes were in fact used in perpetrating crimes against SCs. It was from the relatively poorer sections of their own kinsmen that the landlord recruited his goons and musclemen to terrorize and oppress the weaker sections, unlike earlier days when the zamindars belonging to the upper castes recruited their retainers and musclemen from almost all castes for the purpose of subduing their tenants and subtenants. This increasing reliance on musclemen of one's own kinship group was one of the reasons why such cases of atrocites easily tended to acquire the appearance of caste conflicts. The economically exploited among the upper and middle castes remained intent on preserving the status differences between them and the SCs. On that account, they also resented government policy on reservations for the Scheduled Castes and other programmes that were interpreted as 'pampering' dalits.

One of the most inflammatory issues was the demand by rural labour for the implementation of minimum wages established by the state government.[211] Behind the facade of many caste conflicts lay economic issues of minimum wages and access to land. Attempts by agricultural labourers to press for minimum wages or efforts to raise crops on land allotted to them were seen as threats to the domination of big landowners accustomed to maximizing their profits through control over a docile labour force. There were large-scale evictions in UP after land allotments were made to landless families under the 20-Point Programme, even though the allotments were just two or three *biswa* (one *biswa* is one-thirtieth of an acre). Generally, two types of land were available for allotment to the landless—one was common and vacant land of the *gaon sabha* and the other was the land acquired as surplus under ceilings laws.[212] The conflict was exacerbated by the election of dalit *pradhans* as heads of village panchayats who had defeated their high caste rivals and thus provided a centre of support to the demand for minimum wages, the denial of *begar*, and finally to the demand for the implementation of the declared policy of giving preference to them in the distribution of land at the disposal of the state.

The Reports of the Commission for Scheduled Castes and Scheduled Tribes revealed that the atrocities against dalits were invariably instigated by the affluent sections of the middle caste peasantry who were themselves victims of social discrimination at the hands of upper caste big landowners. The new elite, capable of guiding production operations with more direct and active participation than the upper castes was 'equally sensitive to any change in the semi-feudal relations in the agrarian sector. They along with some forward class peasantry were the gainers of the added surplus accruing to their land'.[213]

Besides, social relations were further embittered by the stand of the middle caste big landowners on reservations. Before the fall of the Janata government, the Chief Minister, Banarsi Das, responding to anti-reservation agitations in western UP, had decided to scrap the reservation policy for the SCs as far as promotions were concerned (a decision which was not implemented by the successor Congress government). Charan Singh himself felt that the Union Government should reconsider Ambedkar's suggestion that reservations for the SCs would not continue beyond the 1960s. Observing that for political reasons the Union Government had been extending reservations decade after decade, he noted that the

reservations for scheduled castes in promotions should be withdrawn, [as] it has led to heart-burning and great inefficiency in services. Such reservations in favour of scheduled castes is beyond the intention of the founding fathers. I understand the High Court of Allahabad has also ruled to this effect in a recent judgement. I would therefore suggest that reservation so far as promotions are concerned should he withdrawn. Nor should there be any reservation in education, particularly of Medicine and Engineering.[214]

The opposition to reservations by sections of rich and middle peasants intensified the political offensive against landless agricultural labourers. The fact that many of the newly rich landowners were drawn from middle and backward castes while the labourers and small peasants were predominantly dalits and other more backward castes lent this struggle a single-dimensional appearance of caste conflict. Both the Lok Dal, which defended the middle castes, and the Congress which highlighted the atrocities against dalits, emphasized the caste dimension to undermine the potential development of class polarization. As the dalits constituted a very significant bloc of votes, the Congress courted them to claim the allegiance of landless and rural labour.

Apart from protective reservation in scholarships, jobs, and legislatures, the Congress government in UP drew up an economic programme to benefit the SCs. For example, of the total 12,00,000 acre (2,00,000 surplus from ceiling plus 10,00,000 barren *gaon sabha* 'village panchayat' land) distributed in 1979-89, roughly half was given to SC households.[215] Similarly 14,00,000 rural house sites were provided to SCs. Equally, they benefited by an amendment to the Land Reforms Act in 1973 which stipulated that agricultural labour households be given the highest priority in the distribution of surplus land and house sites. For an essentially conservative government which was dependent upon the electoral support of SCs, it was much more rewarding to protect the interests of the aspiring elite within these castes than to carry out poverty alleviating programmes which would benefit the masses regardless of caste and community.

Problems and Constraints of
Class Mobilization

Overall, the major parties in UP, including the Socialists, did not show a great concern for class issues after 1969. Indeed, the Socialists also concentrated political attention on language and caste as vehicles of political mobilization. A few of the movements organized by them, for example, the Nijai Bol movement in Basti district, were class movements, but in general they eschewed class mobilization. Inspired by Ram Manohar Lohia, they directed attention towards social issues, the most important of which was reservations. As early as 1962, the Socialist Party advanced the promise of 60 per cent reservation for backward castes, but the new emphasis placed on mobilization of low castes/classes did not open up new arenas of political support. The untapped potential of class as a basis of political mobilization was underscored by the Socialists failure to develop a popular base after resorting mainly to caste appeals. Their support in central and eastern UP diminished after the mid-1960s when they actively pursued social issues which appealed to specific caste groups, particularly Kurmis and Yadavs. Eventually, the emergence of the Lok Dal eroded the distinctive identity of the Socialists whose political strategy became indistinguishable from that adopted by the new party. Subsequently, the Lok Dal easily took over the base of the Socialists.

There was little evidence of marginal farmers and agricultural labourers acting on class lines. Economic homogeneity among large sections of the disadvantaged population, cross-cutting caste lines, was not reflected in class-based political polarization. This did not happen for a variety of reasons.

Despite the penetration of capitalist agriculture, the process of differentiation by which rich farmers expanded their land base and poor peasants became landless had not occurred on a large scale in UP. The land market continued to be rigid because of tenancy laws, and because of the tenacity of small producers who clung to their little plots against all odds. Moreover, the small peasant was dependent on rich landowners for goods and services such as credit, inputs, kerosene, and licences. Besides, their dependence on the rural economy was almost complete because the slow growth of the urban industrial sector offered very limited alternative sources of employment.

Though land concentration in UP had not markedly decreased by the late 1980s nonetheless the series of land legislations, by providing a measure of security to tenants, attenuated agrarian conflict, reducing both the number and power of large landlords. The removal of big zamindars weakened opposition to Congress rule, and lessened the grievances of sections of the peasantry which might have been mobilized by socialist and communist parties. In spite of all its flaws and shortcomings in implementation, Zamindari Abolition was considered by many to be quite radical. This impression was sustained by subsequent land reform legislation which renewed the support for the Congress by depriving potential class movements and organizations of some of their slogans.

Another important factor which militated against class polarization was the ability of middle peasants to draw away sections of poor peasants and rural labour to their side by arousing caste loyalty, which often impelled them to act against their best interests. Arguments were frequently made that all peasants benefited equally from high procurement prices. This had some element of truth to the extent that commercial crops, like sugarcane and potato, were also cultivated by small peasants, although to a lesser degree. However, the prices of such cash crops seldom kept pace with the large increases in the price of foodgrains, and in particular, of wheat. Since poor peasants lack resources to introduce the package of modern methods necessary for cultivation of the HYVs of wheat. The high prices for foodgrains did not bring them substantial benefits. Moreover, rising prices might have adversely affected agricultural labourers because the level of employment did not significantly increase.

The rich peasants, with their favourable position in relation to the ownership of the means of production, cornered much of the benefits of the commercial expansion of agriculture. They also used their political power for consolidating their position in relation to poor peasants and rural labour.[216]

The class interests of middle peasants were not vastly different from those of the rich peasants. They shared a virtually similar outlook on major economic issues: wages, inputs, subsidies, output prices, and better facilities for irrigation and marketing. The expansion of the cooperative and commercial credit structure also contributed to integrating the middle and rich peasantry. Consequently, middle peasant dissatisfaction was more generally directed against the government to extract input subsidies, higher output prices, better marketing facilities, and lower irrigation cesses, and much less against rich landowners who benefited most from the satisfaction of such demands. The anti-government dimension was strengthened after the emergence of the Lok Dal which articulated both the economic grievances of middle peasants and their demand for greater political representation. The chief beneficiaries of the failure of middle peasants to organize for themselves a distinct position was the large landowners and rich peasants, particularly the thakurs who aligned themselves with brahmans to consolidate their power.

The common economic interests of rich and middle peasants, which cut across caste, prevented the crystallization of social cleavages along caste lines. Moreover, lower backward castes and classes lacked the political consciousness and numerical concentration necessary to facilitate their mobilization. Since the economically disadvantaged classes were not necessarily the same as the socially and educationally backward castes,[217] the insistence on using caste as the criterion for determining backwardness actually served to accentuate social divisions under the reservations policy and perpetuated the fragmentation of the poor.

The exploitation of caste feelings by the affluent among caste Hindus preempted the possibility that the poor among SCs, the backward castes, and the upper castes, might join together on the basis of their common class interests. The politicization of the middle castes further widened the gulf separating the SCs from the middle and backward castes. Both the Congress and the Lok Dal turned caste and communal categories into voting blocs in order to create stable bases of support. The populist policies of the Congress claimed the allegiance of the marginal farmers and agricultural labourers, most of whom were drawn from the backward castes, by offering them subsidized loans, employment schemes, and house sites, while the Lok Dal attracted the upwardly mobile backward castes by promising them reservations in educational institutions and the administrative services, as well as agricultural development programmes to increase their gains from the Green Revolution. The emerging class formation and the attendant social conflict were distorted by the double process at work—the hardening of caste distinctions along with the acceleration of economic differentiation.

Meanwhile, the majority of the lower backward castes who laboured as poor peasants, sharecroppers, agricultural labourers, and village artisans remained locked in exploitative relations marked by caste distinctions and subordination. The Backward Classes movement which sought to mobilize the lower castes who suffered from double oppression in no way diminished their awareness of separate identities defined in terms of relative status within the vertical hierarchy. Many of the backward castes who shared a common experience of exploitation with the SCs were diverted by caste and community appeals from discovering their common identity as the exploited. This is perhaps the reason why leaders of the Backward Classes movement were easily seduced by the blandishments of office at the disposal of the Congress government. Without recognizing the duality of economic and social inequality that sustained upper caste power, the Lok Dal attempted to mobilize the lower castes on socio-political issues, especially their shared grievance against the Congress party which excluded them from high position in the administration and government. However, the emphasis on social issues, which was necessarily articulated in a caste idiom, only led to increasing conflict between the upper castes and backward castes, leaving the basic structure of inequality unchanged.

Notes

1. Backward castes refers to those castes which have been officially identified as backward by the UP government. Backward classes refers to those groups who have been subject to inequality associated with the social and economic structure, with particular emphasis on social and educational backwardness.
2. The fundamental difference between the Mughal and British revenue system was that revenue in the Mughal system was determined as a share of actual produce, while under the British it was drawn on the basis of what the land ought to produce. See Irfan Habib, 'The Peasant in History', Presidential Address, Indian History Congress, 43rd Session, Kurukshetra, 1982 on this point.
3. Ibid., p. 42.
4. Ibid.
5. Ibid., p. 159.

6. The brahmans and bhumihars were encouraged by the Mughal jagirdars to unite against the rajputs. 'The policy of the local agent of the Mughal jagirdar to promote the bhumihars contributed to the conditions leading to the rise of Banaras Raj in the eighteenth century.' In Awadh as well, the Mughals appointed zamindars and encouraged them to buy zamindaris of rajputs in their own bastions. In this way Saiyad zamindaris were established, for example, in Unnao and Sandila. M. Alam, *The Crisis of Empire in Mughal North India: Awadh and the Punjab 1707-1748*, Delhi: Oxford University Press, 1986, pp. 122–4.

7. Ibid., chap. 3.

8. T. Metcalfe, *Land, Landlords and the British Raj: Northern India in the Nineteenth Century*, Berkeley and Los Angeles: University of California Press, 1979, p. 13.

9. Thakur and rajput have been used interchangeably to refer to castes of Kshatriya rank.

10. K.K. Trivedi, 'Changes in Caste Composition of the Zamindar Class in Western UP, 1595-1900', *Indian Historical Review*, vol. 2, no. 1, July 1975.

11. Under the *bhaiyachara* system most of the land was partitioned among the members of the proprietary body, each member cultivating his own share. According to Asiya Siddiqi and Irfan Habib there is no evidence of communal ownership. Communal property, in so far as it existed at all, was not held and cultivated by the village community. The land was divided into fields and partitioned among members of the proprietary body, each member cultivating his own share. See A. Siddiqi, *Agrarian Change in a Northern Indian State, UP, 1819-1833*, Oxford: Clarendon Press, 1973, p. 17.

12. The Rohilla Afghan chief, with the aim of establishing himself as a prince within the Mughal diplomatic system, sought to create urban centres, which commanded the labour and tribute of a designated number of surrounding villages. In this way several towns, for example, Aonla under Ali Mohammed Khan, Pilibhit under Hafiz Rehmat Khan, Moradabad, Sambhal, Shahjahanpur, Najibabad. Etawah and Rampur were established in different phases during the eighteenth century by families of pedigree Muslim lineages. For details on the growth and decline of towns and *qasbahs* see C.A. Bayly, *Rulers, Townsmen and Bazaars: North Indian Society in the Age of British Expansion, 1770-1870*, Cambridge: Cambridge University Press, 1983, chap. 3, pp. 110-25.

13. In general, higher castes among Hindus and Muslims did not themselves cultivate the land, though Buchanan-Hamilton observed that this was not rigidly followed in most of the province. See Siddiqi, *Agrarian Change*, pp. 49-50 .

14. The ritual status of brahmans who 'were forced to take to the plough' was evidently eroded in many parts of UP. There is evidence to suggest that brahmans, in eastern UP, for example, had to employ brahmans for the performance of the ritual observance which they could have formerly performed themselves.

15. S.N. Hasan, 'Zamindars under the Mughals', in *Land Control and Social Structure in Indian History*, ed. R. Frykenberg, Delhi: Manohar, 1969, p. 28.

16. Habib, 'The Peasant in History', p. 31. Habib notes that except for Alberuni's low key disapproval of the caste system, medieval Islam produced no critique or condemnation of the caste system.

17. The directors of the East India Company were dissatisfied with the Permanent Settlement, under which Cornwallis had selected the zamindars as the future proprietors. There was much debate between H. Mackenizie, R.M. Bird and W.

Bentinck about the mode of assessment and the need to supersede the taluqdars by the 'actual proprietors' and village communities where they existed. Ultimately, British policy was governed by a variety of factors, such as the strength of landholders, the government's financial requirements, and the reliability of the subordinate staff. It is not surprising that eventually in a large number of cases, land was settle with hereditary taluqdars. See Siddiqi, *Agrarian Change*, chap. 3.

18. R. Mukherjee, *Awadh in Revolt 1857–1858*, Delhi: Oxford University Press, 1984, pp. 43-4.

19. I. Habib, 'Colonization of the Indian Economy, 1857-1900', *Social Scientist*, Delhi, March 1975, p. 131.

20. Ibid., p. 32.

21. For this point see Siddiqi, *Agrarian Change*, pp. 187-94 and Habib, 'Colonization of the Indian Economy', pp. 32-3. Both discount the possibility of large scale increase in prices after 1820.

22. The land revenue under the preceding Indian regimes was fixed as a shore of the crop and varied according to the crop cultivated, 'while the Anglo-Indian tax, whether directly imposed on the raiyats or assessed on the zamindars was a "true tax on land"'. The actual incidence of demand per acre would increase simply because of the more efficient surveys and the resumption of land hitherto held revenue free. Habib, 'Colonization of the Indian Economy', pp. 31-2.

23. B.S. Cohn, 'Structural Change in Indian Rural Society', in *Land Control and Social Structure*, ed. Frykenberg, p. 70.

24. Aligarh Settlement Report (SR), 1903.

25. Metcalfe, *Land, Landlords, and the British Raj*, p. 56.

26. Quoted in E. Stokes, *Peasant and the Raj: Studies in Agrarian Society and Peasant Rebellion in Colonial India*, Cambridge: Cambridge University Press, 1978, p. 133.

27. Cohn, 'Structural Change', p. 70.

28. In addition, Kayasthas and Banias were also buying land in the Banaras region by transferring income from public service and legal practice into land. Though Rajputs lost much land, they continued to live as before, dominating lower caste cultivators. In effect, they did not lose their social and political position. For this point see ibid., pp. 111–12.

29. F. Robinson, *Separatism among Indian Muslims: Politics of the UP Muslims, 1860–1923*, London: Cambridge University Press, 1974, pp. 119–20.

30. Stokes, *Peasant and the Raj*, p. 120.

31. Ibid., p. 121.

32. Aligarh SR, 1882.

33. Cohn, 'Structural Change', pp. 111–12.

34. The relatively secure position of big landlords was noted by H.K. Gracey, settlement officer of Kanpur: 'The fact is that the only zamindar for whom the Indian economy has a proper place is the big taluqdar governed by the law of primogeniture and owning so large an estate that he can afford to be generous, or the peasant proprietor cultivating his own land. For the small middleman who tried to live on his rents and whose property is being constantly split into smaller shares under the rules of Hindu or Mohammedan heirship, there is no niche . . .' (Kanpur SR, 1907, para 25).

35. For example, W.J. Burkitt observed that in Aligarh over the previous 30 years, 'the rich zamindars have on the whole gained, and nearly all the loss has fallen on the small men and the village communities' (Aligarh SR, 1903). The same process was at work in Mainpuri, Azamgarh, Budaun, etc. In all these areas the big estates were unaffected. Furthermore, the worst affected were small Muslim landholders in western UP. For this point see Stokes, *Peasant and the Raj*, pp. 120–4.

36. L. Brennan, 'The Illusion of Security: The Background to Muslim Separatism in UP', *Modern Asian Studies*, vol. 18, no. 2, Cambridge, 1984, p. 252.

37. Stokes suggests that the occupancy cultivator in western UP was better off than the small zamindar and on an average possessed a larger holding. The absence of a gulf separating the proprietor and occupancy tenant was also because caste differences were not so marked in the *bhaiyachara* tenures in western UP. See Stokes, *Peasant and the Raj*, p. 118.

38. Stokes, *Peasant and the Raj*, p. 196.

39. As a result of this policy the zamindars' share of the rental compared with land revenue increased considerably. The Saharanpur Rule set the minimum share of the proprietor at 50 per cent. Habib, 'Colonization of the Indian Economy', p. 45.

40. Ibid.

41. N.C. Saxena, 'Caste and Zamindari Abolition in UP', *Mainstream*, Delhi, 15 June 1985.

42. Basti SR, 1919.

43. Saxena, 'Caste and Zamindari Abolition', p. 16.

44. Ghazipur SR, 1887.

45. Gonda SR, 1887.

46. *Awadh Gazetteer*, vol. 1, 1877, p. 145.

47. Stokes, *Peasant and the Raj*, p. 118.

48. G. Pandey, *Ascendancy of the Congress in UP, 1926-34: A Study in Imperfect Mobilization*, Delhi: Oxford University Press, 1978, p. 165.

49. D.N. Dhanagare, *Peasant Movements in India 1920-1950*, New Delhi: Oxford University Press, 1983, p. 115.

50. Saxena, 'Caste and Zamindari Abolition', p. 16.

51. Pandey, *Ascendancy of the Congress*, p. 22.

52. Occupancy and secure tenants formed just 2.2 per cent of the tenants in Awadh according to Pandey, *Ascendancy of the Congress*, pp. 22–3.

53. For detail discussion of peasant revolts in Awadh, see Kapil Kumar, *Peasants in Revolt: Tenants, Landlords, Congress and the Raj in Awadh, 1886-1922*, Delhi: Manohar, 1984; M. Siddiqi, *Agrarian Unrest in Northern India: The United Provinces, 1918-22*, Delhi: Vikas Publishing House, 1978; Dhanagare, *Peasant Movements in India*.

54. Dhanagare, *Peasant Movements in India*, pp. 118–19.

55. C.A. Bayly, *Local Roots of Indian Politics, Allahabad 1880-1920*, Oxford: Clarendon Press, 1975, pp. 325–6.

56. The autonomy of the *kisari* agitation is emphasized by Dhanagare in his description of the agitation:

Sizeable groups of kisans—ranging between 3,000 and 10,000 in number—were engaged in disturbances. They attacked talukdars' crops and property and looted bazaars particularly the shops owned by notorious merchants and moneylenders.

At some places they attempted to force the release of their arrested leaders and fellow kisans. . . . In Tanda tehsil in Faizabad district there was looting in some 15 villages by evicted tenants. They moved in batches of about 500 and attacked both petty zamindars and substantial tenants. Dhanagare, *Peasant Movements in India*, p. 118.

57. Pandey, *Ascendancy of the Congress.*

58. Several districts in western UP had a large number of big landlords. For example, the number of large landowners in Aligarh, Etah, and Mainpuri was comparable to many districts of Awadh, which suggests that big landowners did not hold a monopoly in Awadh and eastern UP.

59. For a detailed discussion of the effects of the depression, see Dhanagare, *Peasant Movements in India*, and Pandey, *Ascendancy of the Congress*, 'No other period of such short duration in the history of Indian pieces shows such a violent change', commented a government official cited in Pandey, *Ascendancy of the Congress*, p. 162. Insufficient rain and drought in many areas reduced food production all over UP. In Agra division, the cultivated area decreased by 37.6 per cent in *rabi* in 1930; in UP as a whole, the cut back was 8 per cent.

60. Aligarh SR, 1944.

61. Dhanagare, *Peasant Movements in India*, p. 120.

62. On the role of socialist minded leaders, see Pandey, *Ascendancy of the Congress.*

63. Dhanagare, *Peasant Movements in India*, p. 121.

64. Pandey, *Ascendancy of the Congress.*

65. Dhanagare, *Peasant Movements in India*, p. 21.

66. See Bayly, *Local Roots of Indian Politics*; L. Brennan, 'From One Raj to Another: Congress Politics in Rohilkhand 1930-50', *Congress and the Raj*, ed. D.A. Low, Delhi: Arnold Heinemann, 1977; and Pandey, *Ascendancy of the Congress*, for a discussion of the class base of the Congress.

67. For example, in Aligarh the no-rent ran into difficulty owing to the strong opposition of Muslim landlords. For a detail discussion of this point see Zoya Hasan, 'The Congress in a District, 1930–46: Problems of Political Mobilization', *Indian Economic aand Social History Review*, Delhi, January-March 1986, p. 50.

68. In many areas of UP the Hindu Sabhas and the Congress worked in close association. Other Hindu communal institutions like religious fairs and festivals were frequently used for nationalist mobilization. In 1929 and 1930 the Arya Samaj and the Hindu Sabha issued statements in support of the Civil Disobedience movement. The Congress often sought support from these organizations, and supported, for example, the efforts of the Hindu Sabha in imparting physical training to youth. See Pandey, *Ascendancy of the Congress*, pp. 124–37.

69. P.D. Reeves et al., *Handbook of Elections in UP 1920-51*, Delhi: Manohar, 1975.

70. Since the revival of the League in the post-1937 period was centred in the United Provinces, the Congress rejection of a coalition in UP was regarded as decisive. On this point see P.R. Brass, *Language, Religion and Politics in North India*, Delhi: Oxford University Press, 1974 and Brennan, 'From One Raj to Another'. The rejection of the coalition offer was justified on the grounds that it would render impossible socio-economic reforms since the League was opposed to land reforms. Instead, the Congress preferred to win over the Muslim masses through a mass contact campaign. For more on this point see Mushiral Hasan, *Muslim Mass*

Contact Campaign, Occasional Papers on History and Society, Nehru Memorial Museum and Library, vol. XIV, 1984, pp. 32–4.

71. The plan for a Muslim Mass Contact Campaign was conceived after the Congress defeats in Muslim constituencies in 1936. Many of the protagonists of the campaign were drawn from the professional groups sharing Marxist and socialist ideas. It has been shown that Muslims did not reject the campaign; it failed because of the limited nature of Congress mobilization in rural areas. See Hasan, *Muslim Mass Contact Campaign*, pp. 26–7.

72. Ibid., p. 32.

73. The widening political base of the League was exemplified in the transition of the Aligarh Muslim University. It is noteworthy that campus politics until 1936 had been dominated by the Congress Socialists. The students had organized a strike against the government's repression of nationalist activities and had opposed the proposal to establish an All India Muslim Students Federation. However, such nationalist enthusiasm was soon replaced by almost hysterical support for the Muslim League and Jinnah. See Mushirul Hasan, 'Nationalist and Separatist Trends in Aligarh, 1915-47', *Indian Economic and Social History Review*, vol. 22, no. 1, Delhi, 1985, p. 8; and W.C. Smith, *Modern Islam in India*, Lahore: Minerva Bookshop, 1943, p. 312.

74. Smith, *Modern Islam*, p. 312.

75. In spite of the predominantly pro-landlord orientation of the League, it managed to gain adherents among a wide range of Muslim groups in the 1940. This was noted by W.C. Smith in his study of *Modern Islam in India* in the 1940s. The expansion of the League can be gauged from the fact that by the end of 1937, the League had 90 branches and 100,000 new members in the United Provinces. Between 1938 and the end of 1943 the Muslim League won 46 out of 56 by-elections in the province. See M. Hasan, 'Nationalist and Separatist Trends', p. 2.

76. For example, the Nawab Mohammad Yusuf of Jaunpur wrote to Jinnah: 'I and Muslim zamindars look to you to protect our fundamental interests and save them from economic ruination or elimination in UP'. There were many other taluqdars committed to the idea of an Islamic republic. See M. Hasan, 'Nationalist and Separatist Trends', p. 17.

77. Brennan, 'The Illusion of Security'.

78. Not surprisingly, the Governor, Harry Haig, greeted the legislation with relief, noting that it enabled the Congress ministry 'to liquidate their election promises . . . without either the agrarian revolution foretold by many or the destruction of the zamindari system'. Quoted in Reeves, *Handbook*, pp. 4–5.

79. G. Pandey, 'A Rural Base for the Congress: the United Provinces 1920-40', *Congress and the Raj*, ed. D.A. Low, Delhi: Arnold Heinemann, 1977, p. 217.

80. The majority of small landowners were subsistence farmers holding less than 5 acre each and an average holding of 1.3 acre; they owned less than 5 per cent of the land. B. Singh and S. Misra, *A Study of Land Reforms in UP*, Calcutta: Oxford Book Company, 1984, pp. 27–9.

81. Uttar Pradesh Zamindari Abolition Committee (UPZAC) Report, vol. II, 1948.

82. Singh and Misra, *A Study of Land Reforms*, p. 216.

83. Ibid., pp. 215–17.

84. Ibid., p. 215.

85. UP's case structure is different from that of south India in one important respect. In south India, brahmans were the only representatives of the twice-born castes which increased their distance from the rest of the population. In UP, there is a greater sharing of social status and political power across a larger number of upper castes, for example, brahmans and thakurs. Furthermore, brahmans in UP were not the leading landlords. As a result, there was frequent disjunction between ritual status and economic control. Thus the social configuration in UP is characterized by a more gradual and continuous social hierarchy which is strikingly different from the southern states which were marked by steep and discontinuous traditional social hierarchies.

86. No single caste is numerically more than a quarter of any district's population. Most of the larger castes (brahmans, kayasthas, thakurs, khatris, and banias) are widely dispersed and there is no region in UP in which one caste predominates.

87. Brass, *Factional Politics*, p. 16.

88. Singh and Misra, *A Study of Land Reforms*, pp. 24–7.

89. The passage of the UP Zamindari Abolition Bill in the UP Legislature was marked by sharp differences in the Congress on several issues relating to the abolition policy. Socialists in the Congress insisted on speedy abolition and 'social ownership of land and produce through collective farming'. A powerful section led by G.B. Pant played a decisive role in diluting the radical content of the Bill by 'wily management of the Committee and its discussions'. Reeves, *Handbook*, p. 8.

90. D. Thorner and A. Thorner, *Land and Labour in India*, Bombay: Asia Publishing House, 1965, p. 47.

91. P.D. Shrimali, *Agrarian Change, Agrarian Tensions, Peasant Movements and Organizations in Uttar Pradesh*, Lucknow: University of Lucknow, Department of Economics, mimeographed, 1981.

92. Singh and Misra, *A Study of Land Reforms*, p. 216.

93. Shrimali, *Agrarian Change*, p. 186.

94. *New Age*, monthly, January 1953. Major differences occurred in the Congress on the amount of compensation to be paid to intermediaries. In spite of the Committee's generous compensation offer it raised a furore of protest among zamindars who took recourse to all means, fair and foul, to get their compensation increased. They also demanded a uniform level of compensation payable to all classes of intermediaries as against the graduated scheme of compensation recommended by the government. See *Amrita Bazar Patrika*, 14 October 1948.

95. Not many tenants availed of this opportunity. By 1960 only one-third of the cultivated area was under ownership rights, 65 per cent under *sirdari* and 0.8 per cent under *asami* holdings. Of the total area under bhumidari, 45 per cent was acquired through conversion and 55 per cent through payment of multiple rental. See Singh and Misra, *A Study of Land Reforms*.

96. *Amrita Bazar Patrika*, 20 March 1949. Pandit Pant was equally amazed at the opposition of the landlords. He appealed to them to take a generous view of the Bill which had been conceived in a liberal spirit. *National Herald*, 1 April 1949.

97. F.J. Moore and C.A. Freydig, *Land Tenure Legislation in UP*, Berkeley, 1955, p. 31.

98. The total number of agrarian riots up to 15 July 1949 was 2,057 as against 1,878 for the corresponding period in 1948. A spokesman of the UP government said at Lucknow: 'Agrarian riots in UP have shown an upward trend as a result of increasing class consciousness among tenants and zamindars'. *New Age*, monthly, January 1953.

99. Moore and Freydig, *Land Tenure Legislation*, p. 33.

100. U. Patnaik, 'Reflections on the Agrarian Question and the Development of Capitalism in India', *First Daniel Thorner Memorial Lecture*, Delhi, 1986, p. 67.

101. Brass, *Factional Politics*, p. 70.

102. Charan Singh, 1958, unpublished personal papers, p. 42.

103. D. Thorner and A. Thorner, *Agrarian Prospect in India*, 2nd edn., Delhi: Allied Publishers, 1973, p. 27.

104. T. Metcalfe, 'UP Zamindars Today', *Pacific Affairs*, Honolulu, Spring 1971, p. 18.

105. The UPZAC Report proposed that 'no limit be placed on the maximum area held in cultivation either by a landlord or a tenant. Everybody now in cultivatory possession of land, will continue to hold his whole area', cited in Thorner and Thorner, *Agrarian Prospect*.

106. By distributing surplus land, Charan Singh argued, the number of uneconomic holdings would increase, which was hardly desirable. However, the majority of landholdings in UP—55 per cent—were anyway less than two acre; even these tiny holdings would yield sufficient foodgrain for a landless family.

107. For details of Congress opposition to ceilings see R.S. Newell, 'Ideology and Realities: Land Redistribution in UP', *Pacific Affairs*, Honolulu, Summer 1972; and R.C. Meyer, *Political Elite in an Underdeveloped Society: the Case of UP*, unpublished Ph.D. dissertation, University of Pennsylvania, 1969.

108. In contrast, for example in West Bengal, the United Front Government in 1969 recovered 300,000 acre from landlords and distributed 230,000 acre to poor peasants. See Newell, 'Ideology and Realities', pp. 90–4.

109. Not only politicians but also senior civil servants were hostile to land reforms. Several factors accounted for their hostility: (a) their belief in the inviolability of private property; (b) their faith in the capitalist strategy of development based on rich farmers; (c) their lack of faith in the capability of the delivery system which made them divert time and capital to such areas where short-term gains could be maximized; and (d) their ignorance of revenue laws. Very few officers bothered to grasp even the most important provisions of the Land Reforms or Ceiling Act which affected the quality of supervision. Finally, high priority was given in the state to the maintenance of law and order. As removal of illegal possession over lands allotted to the weak, and the implementation of the Minimum Wages Act entailed apprehensions of breach of peace, such programmes often were neglected.

110. Newell, 'Ideology and Realities', p. 96.

111. In an article 'Class Differentiation within the Peasantry: An approach to the Study of Indian Agriculture', Utsa Patnaik put forward the criterion of labour exploitation for demarcating classes within the peasantry: 'While no single index can capture class status with absolute accuracy, the appropriation of surplus through the use of hired labour and leasing relative to family labour was suggested as criteria of demarcation'. On this basis five classes consisting of landlords, rich peasants, middle peasants, poor peasants, and agricultural labour have been identified. Rich peasants hire outside labour and own holdings above 7.5 acre; middle peasants rely mostly on family labour and own holdings of three to seven acre and frequently work on the fields of big landowners. For more details see Joan Mencher, 'Problems of Analysing Rural Class Structure', *Economic and Political Weekly*, Bombay, 31 August 1974; and U. Patnaik, 'Class Differentiation within the Peasantry; An Approach to the Study of Indian Agriculture', *Economic and Political Weekly*, vol. 2, no. 39, Bombay, 1976. Rich peasants frequently use

hired labour owing to its relative profitability compared to renting out land to sharecroppers. With their control over sources of political and economic power, they dominate major institutions. On the merits of the rich peasant model as against the dominant caste model for understanding the power structure in rural India, see J. Macdougall, 'Two Models of Power in Contemporary Rural India', *Contributions to Indian Sociology*, vol. 14, no. 1, Delhi, 1980. At times big landowners and rich peasants have been used interchangeably to refer to the dominant strata of rural society.

112. The proportion of total agricultural tax to total tax declined from 68 per cent in 1960-1 to 58 per cent in 1965-6, while in the same period the percentage of non-agricultural taxes to total taxes increased from 32 to 42 per cent. See the *Economic and Political Weekly*, 11 September 1971.

113. Ibid. Also, in India as a whole, all direct taxes on agriculture, taken together, amounted to less than 1 per cent of NNP from agriculture. See Patnaik, 'Class Differentiation', p. 16.

114. UP's problems were compounded because not much investment was made by the centre. There were no central projects in UP during the Second Plan; in the Third Plan, however, the investment in centrally sponsored projects increased to Rs. 71 crore. Of the total central investment between 1951 and 1977, only Rs. 376 crore or 4.2 per cent was invested in UP.

115. T.S. Papola and Fahimuddin, 'Industrial Spurt in UP', *Economic and Political Weekly*, Bombay, 16 February 1985.

116. Most of the state sponsored schemes, such as subsidized inputs, guaranteed remunerative procurement prices, and expenditures on the National Rural Employment Programme (NREP) and Intensive Rural Development Programme (IRDP) directly transferred enormous resources to the rural rich. NREP and IRDP, although intended for the rural poor, also benefitted the rural rich, through the building of infrastructure facilities such as roads and transport.

117. N.C. Saxena, 'Caste, Land and Political Power in Rural Uttar Pradesh', Draft paper presented at the conference on Class, Caste and Dominance, University of Pennsylvania, May 1984, p. 85.

118. F. Frankel, 'Problems of Correlating Electoral and Economic Variables: An Analysis of Voting Behaviour and Agrarian Modernization in UP', in *Electoral Politics in the Indian States: The Impact of Modernization*, ed. John Osgood Field and Myron Weiner, Delhi: Manohar Book Service, 1977.

119. G. Etienne, *Studies of Indian Agriculture*, Bombay: Oxford University Press, 1968.

120. Saxena, 'Caste, Land and Political Power'.

121. Several studies have show this. See for example, Biplab Das Gupta, *The New Agrarian Technology and India*, Delhi: Macmillan, 1977; Biplab Das Gupta, 'India's Green Revolution', *Economic and Political Weekly*, 1 February 1977; C.R. Wharton, 'The Green Revolution: Cornucopia or Pandora's Box', *Foreign Affairs*, April 1969; and J. Mecher, 'Conflicts and Contradictions in the Green Revolution: The Case of Tamil Nadu', *Economic and Political Weekly*, February 1974.

122. Das Gupta, *The New Agrarian Technology*.

123. The section on cane growers is based on information provided by S.K. Tripathi, during an interview on 24 March 1985.

124. Saxena, 'Caste, Land and Political Power'.

125. K. Leiten, 'The Janata as a Continuity of the System', *Social Scientist*, Delhi, December–January 1980–1.

126. *Economic and Political Weekly*, 2 December 1979.

127. According to Shrimali, *Agrarian Change*, p. 259, even the minimum wages, officially fixed, were never paid.

128. R. Nayyar, 'Wages of Agricultural Labourers in UP', *Economic and Political Weekly*, Bombay, 6 November 1976.

129. Patnaik, 'Reflections on the Agrarian Question', p. 19.

130. The figures are based on the estimates given in the draft Seventh Five-Year Plan, 1985–90:

1967–73   60.2 per cent
1973–4   47.3 per cent
1977–8   50.1 per cent

131. The rise is generally regarded as an over-estimation owing to the changing definitions of the cetegory in the census. However, the largest increase in the percentage of agricultural labourers occurred in the eastern districts. The percentage of agricultural labourers, when seen in relation to cultivators, was very high. See Kripa Shankar, 'Agricultural Labourers in UP', *Uttar Pradesh Arthik Patrika*, January–June 1980.

132. It is important to emphasize this aspect of land concentration in UP, because it was commonly believed that UP was dominated by small landowners. Charan Singh, for example, used this fact to argue against land redistribution.

133. Shrimali, *Agrarian Change*.

134. Ibid.

135. Saxena, 'Caste, Land and Political Power', p. 30.

136. Kripa Shankar, *Concealed Tenancy and its Implications for Equity and Economic Growth*, Delhi: Concept, 1980, p. 124.

137. C.T. Bliss and N.H. Stern, *Palanpur: The Study of an Indian Village*, Oxford: Clarendon Press, 1982.

138. The UP government carried out a district survey in 1980–1 to estimate the number of absantee landowners. It revealed that absenteeism was most common in the Terai and in the districts south of the Jamuna—not in eastern UP and Awadh. See Saxena, 'Caste, Land and Political Power', pp. 40–1.

139. Brass, *Factional Politics*. It should be noted that factionalism was an inherent part of the transitional phase of politics where personalized networks were needed for building support. This formed an essential ingredient in the first phase of institution building in UP, as indeed in many other states.

140. In 1947, the Congress Socialists, who formed a group of nearly 50 members in the Legislature Party, were forced to leave the Congress owing to the party's decision not to allow separate organizations within the Congress. The departure of the Socialists marked the end of an era in Congress history, which had begun with the active participation of the Socialists in the agrarian campaigns of the 1920s and 1930s.

141. For a detailed discussion of factionalism and factional systems in UP, see Brass, *Factional Poiltics*, and B.D. Graham, 'The Succession of Factional Systems in Uttar Pradesh Congress Party, 1937–66', in *Local Level Politics*, ed. Marc J. Swartz, London: University of London Press, 1969.

142. D. Hardiman, 'The Indian Faction: A Political Theory Examined', *Subaltern Studies*, ed. Ranajit Guha, vol. 1, Delhi: Oxford University Press, 1982.

143. For a systematic critique of the Brass framework of factionalism, see Hardiman, 'The Indian Faction'.

144. *National Herald* of 1951-2 provides a detailed account of the issues and debates on policies in the early years of UP politics.

145. UPCC Resolution, April 1948.

146. *National Herald*, 3 August 1951.

147. Ibid., 27 September 1951.

148. Graham, 'The Succession of Factional Systems', p. 328.

149. Five on the nine cabinet members who resigned in support of Gupta in November 1953 were of his caste. Graham, 'The Succession of Factional Systems', p. 338.

150. Gupta did not depend solely on Bania support because to be successful in UP politics, a group had to rely on a number of castes as no caste was concentrated in any region.

151. Meyer, *Political Elite in an Underdeveloped Society*.

152. Ibid.

153. It should be noted that only 2 per cent Block Pramukhs, MLAs, and Rajya Sabha MPs belonged to the SCs. Saxena, 'Caste and Zamindari Abolition'.

154. A. Burger, *Opposition in a Domination Party System: A Study of the Jan Sangh, the Praja Socialist Party and the Socialist Party in Uttar Pradesh*, India, Bombay: Oxford University Press, 1969, Appendix, Table VII.

155. *The Hindustan Times*, June 1971.

156. R.K. Hebsur, 'Uttar Pradesh: Belated and Imperfect Mobilization of the Backwards', Report of the Backward Classes Commission, pt. 2, 1980, p. 160.

157. Charan Singh, unpublished personal papers, New Delhi.

158. This proposal was made in 1947 and supported by the meeting of 'Backward Classes' in western UP.

159. Charan Singh, unpublished personal papers, file no. 142, New Delhi.

160. Hebsur, 'Belated and Imperfect Mobilization', p. 160.

161. Charan Singh, unpublished personal papers, file no. 504.

162. Ibid.

163. Interview with Chandrajit Yadav, 19 June 1985.

164. The leaders of the backward castes were reluctant to leave the Congress organization. Their preference to struggle within the Congress greatly restricted the growth of the backward caste movement in UP. This was in marked contrast to Bihar where the backward castes supported the socialists. Also, in UP many of the Socialist leaders such as Prabhu Narain, Raj Narain, Chandrasekhar, and Bisram Rai, belonged to the upper castes. Interview with Chandrajit Yadav, 19 June 1985.

165. Charan Singh, unpublished personal papers, file no. 214.

166. M.S.A. Rao, *Social Movement and Social Transformation: A Study of Two Backward Class Movement in India*, Delhi: Macmillan, 1979, p. 141.

167. Hebsur, 'Belated and Imperfect Mobilization', p. 159.

168. Ibid., p. 160.

169. *The Economic Times*, 18 April 1983.

170. Frankel, 'Problems of Correlating Electoral and Economics Variables', p. 339.

171. Charan Singh strongly opposed the decision of the C.B. Gupta government to impose a surcharge of 50 per cent on the land revenue in UP.

172. For a graphic account of instability and defection in the UP government in this period see Subash Kashyap, *Politics of Power, Defections and State Politics in UP, India*, Delhi: National, 1974.

173. Before independence, the socialists were a major force in the UP Congress. However, the socialist current began to decline from the mid-1950s owing to a series of splits and mergers which eventually led to its disintegration. The 1972 split in the Socialist Party further weakened the socialists. Having failed to put forward a cohesive ideology, they concentrated attention on political mobilization through caste and language issues.

174. R.I. Duncan, *Levels, the Communication of Programmes and the Sectional Strategies in Indian Politics: BD and the Republican Party in India in UP and Aligarh District*, Ph.D. thesis, University of Sussex, 1979.

175. M. Johnson, Relation between Land Settlement and party Politics in UP, India, 1950-69, Ph.D. thesis, University of Sussex, unpublished, 1975.

176. Interview with P.D. Shrimali, 19 March 1985.

177. Charan Singh, Personal Papers.

178. Frankel, 'Problems of Correlating Electoral and Economic Variables'.

179. L. Fickett, 'Politics of Regionalism', *Pacific Affairs*, Honolulu, Summer 1971.

180. Ibid., p. 201.

181. Mankind, September 1969.

182. *The Pioneer*, 8 August 1970.

183. *The Times of India*, 25 June 1968.

184. *The Pioneer*, 8 August 1970.

185. Charan Singh, unpublished personal papers.

186. Johnson, *Relation between Land Settlement and Party Politics*.

187. Fickett, 'Politics of Regionalism'.

188. P.R. Brass, *Caste, Faction and Party in Indian Politics*, vol. 2, Delhi: Chanakya Publications, 1985, p. 322.

189. Hebsur, 'Belated and Imperfect Mobilization', p. 160.

190. *Patriot*, 25 February 1969.

191. *Economic and Political Weekly*, 3 February 1979.

192. P.R. Brass, *Caste, Faction and Party in Indian Politics*, vol. 1, Delhi: Chanakya Publications, 1984, p. 309.

193. *Draft Seventh Five-Year Plan 1985-90*, Planning Department, Government of UP, September 1983.

194. *The Statesman*, 15 October 1974, see also Table 12.9.

195. *Economic and Political Weekly*, 2 December 1979.

196. Leiten, 'The Janata as a Continuity of the System'.

197. Hebsur, 'Belated and Imperfect Mobilization', p. 161.

198. Charan Singh, unpublished personal papers. Also see the 'Lok Dal and Reservation', *The Statesman*, April 1981. The Lok Dal suggested an expanded system of reservation in services in terms of the following broad categories: (a) scheduled castes and tribes; (b) all backward communities irrespective of religion; (c) kisan communities; and (d) upper castes such as brahmans, bhumihars, kayasthas and thakurs, and some advanced sections among the minorities. Competition and merit tests were suggested only within the category and not between different categories.

199. Hebsur, 'Belated and Imperfect Mobilization', p. 161.

200. *The Pioneer*, 8 January 1980.

201. Brass, *Caste, Faction and Party*, vol. 1, p. 305.

202. *Hindi Saptahik*, 8 November 1982. 'After Sripat Misra took over as Chief Minister, most of the thakur officers were transferred to inconsequential posts. Now all important posts are manned by brahmans. Consequently, all thakur officer have rallied round Vir Bahadur Singh.' *The Telegraph*, 1 December 1982.

203. *The Statesman*, 25 June 1985.

204. Hebsur, 'Belated and Imperfect Mobilization', p. 140.

205. Not surprisingly the All India Yadav Sangh and the UP Backward Classes Front meeting pledged their support to the Congres. *The Pioneer*, 28 January 1977.

206. Interview with S.K. Tripathi, 21 March 1985.

207. *The Times of India*, 14 August 1972.

208. Government of India, 1979-81.

209. *The Times of India*, 19 August 1977.

210. A meeting of 50 Scheduled Caste MPs held on 9 July 1977, expressed unhappiness at the inadequate protection given to dalits. The meeting was presided over by Ram Dhan, and held under the auspices of the Scheduled Castes and Scheduled Tribes Forum. Intelligence Bureau, Ministry of Home Affairs; Charan Singh, unpublished personal papers.

211. *The Statesman*, 19 May 1981.

212. *Economic and Political Weekly*, 23-30 December 1978.

213. Government of India, 1979-81.

214. Charan Singh, 'Reservations for Backward Castes', unpublished personal papers, 1979.

215. Saxena, 'Caste, Land and Political Power'.

216. Saith and Tankha, 'Agrarian Transition and the Differentiation of the Peasantry: A Case Study of a West UP Village', *Economic and Political Weekly*, 1 April 1972.

217. I.P. Desai, 'Caste, Class and Reservation', *Economic and Political Weekly*, Bombay, 14 July 1984.

References

Alam, M., *The Crisis of Empire in Mughal North India: Awadh and the Punjab 1707-1748*, Delhi: Oxford University Press, 1986.

Anonymous, 'UP Zamindari Abolition', *New Age*, monthly, New Delhi, January, 1953.

Appu, P.S., *Ceiling on Agricultural Holdings*, New Delhi: Government of India, Ministry of Agriculture, 1972.

Baxter, C., 'The Rise and Fall of the Bharatiya Kranti Dal in UP', in *Studies in Electoral Politics in the Indian States*, John Osgood Field and Myron Weiner, eds., vol. 4, Delhi: Manohar Book Service, 1977.

Bayly, C.A., *Local Roots of Indian Politics, Allahabad, 1880-1920*, Oxford: Clarendon Press, 1975.

———, *Rulers, Townsmen and Bazaars: North Indian Society in the Age of British Expansion 1770-1870*, Cambridge: Cambridge University Press, 1983.

Bliss, C.T. and Stern, N.H., *Palanpur: The Study of an Indian Village*, Oxford: Clarendon Press, 1982.

Brass, P.R., *Factional Politics in an Indian State, The Congress Party in Uttar Pradesh*, Berkeley: University of California Press, 1965.

————, *Language, Religion and Politics in North India*, Delhi: Oxford University Press, 1974.

————, Congress, the Lok Dal and the Middle Peasant Castes—An Analysis of the 1977 and 1980 Parliamentary Elections in UP', *Pacific Affairs*, Honolulu, Spring, 1981.

————, *Caste, Faction and Party in Indian Politics*, vol. 1, Delhi: Chanakya Publications, 1984.

————, *Caste, Faction and Party in Indian Politics*, vol. 2, Delhi: Chanakya Publications, 1985.

Brennan, L., 'From One Raj to Another: Congress Politics in Rohilkhand 1930-50', in *Congress and the Raj*, D.A. Low, ed., Delhi: Arnold Heinemann, 1977.

————, 'The Illusion of Security: The Background to Muslim Separatism in the UP', *Modern Asian Studies*, vol. 18, no. 2, Cambridge, 1984.

Burger, A., *Opposition in a Dominant Party System: A Study of the Jan Sangh, the Praja Socialist Party and the Socialist Party in Uttar Pradesh, India*, Bombay: Oxford University Press, 1969.

Census of India, 1931, United Provinces of Agra and Oudh, pt. II, A.C. Turner, Allahabad, 1933.

————, United Provinces of Agra and Oudh, vol. VIII, pt. II, Allahabad, 1933.

Cohn, B.S., 'Structural Change in Indian Rural Society', *Land Control and Social Structure in Indian History*, in Frykenberg, ed., Delhi: Manohar.

Das Gupta, B., 1977, *The New Agrarian Technology and India*, Delhi: Macmillan.

Desai, I.P., 'Caste, Class and Reservation', *Economic and Political Weekly*, Bombay, July 1984.

Dhanagare, D.N., *Peasant Movements in India 1920-1950*, New Delhi: Oxford University Press, 1983.

Duncan, R.I., *Levels, the Communication of Programmes and the Sectional Strategies in Indian Politics—BKD and the Republican Party of India in UP and Aligarh District*, Ph.D. thesis, University of Sussex, 1979.

Etienne, G., *Studies in Indian Agriculture*, Bombay: Oxford University Press, 1968.

Fickett, L., 'Politics of Regionalism', *Pacific Affairs*, Honolulu, Summer 1971.

Frankel, F., 'Problems of Correlating Electoral and Economic Variables: An Analysis of Voting Behaviour and Agrarian Modernization in UP', in *Electoral Politics in the Indian States, The Impact of Modernization*, John Osgood Field and Myron Weiner, eds., Delhi: Manohar Book Service, 1977.

Galanter, M., *Competing Equalities: Law and the Backward Classes in India*, Delhi: Oxford University Press, 1984.

Ghosh, A., 'Caste Idiom for Class Conflict—The Case of Khanjawala', *Economic and Political Weekly*, Bombay, 3-10 February 1979.

Graham, B.D., 'The Succession of Factional Systems in the Uttar Pradesh Congress Party, 1937-66', in *Local Level Politics*, Marc J. Swartz, ed., London: University of London Press, n.d.

Gupta, Sulekh, *Agrarian Relations and Early British Rule in India*, Delhi: Asia Publishing House, 1963.

Habib, I., *The Agrarian System of Mughal India, 1556-1707*, Bombay: Asia Publishing House, 1963.

————, 'Colonization of the Indian Economy, 1857-1900', *Social Scientist*, Delhi, March 1975.

————, 'The Peasant in History', Presidential Address, Indian History Congress, 43rd Session, Kurukshetra, 1982.

Hardiman, D., 'The Indian Faction, A Political Theory Examined', in *Subaltern Studies*, Ranajit Guha, ed., vol. 1, Delhi: Oxford University Press, 1982.

Hasan, M., *Muslim Mass Contact Campaign*, Occasional Papers on History and Society, Nehru Memorial Museum and Library, vol. XIV, 1984.

————, 'Nationalist and Separatist Trends in Aligarh, 1915-47', *Indian Economic and Social History Review*, vol. 22, no. 1, Delhi, 1985.

Hasan, N., 'Zamindars under the Mughals', in *Land Control and Social Structure in Indian History*, R. Frykenberg, ed., Delhi: Manohar Publications, 1969.

Hasan, Z., 'The Congress in a District 1930-46: Problems of Political Mobilization', *Indian Economic and Social History Review*, Delhi, January-March 1986.

Hebsur, R.K., 'Uttar Pradesh: Belated and Imperfect Mobilization of the Backwards', in *Report of the Backward Classes Commission*, 2nd part, 1980.

————, Report of the Commission for Scheduled Castes and Scheduled Tribes, Part I, 27th Report, 1979-81, New Delhi.

Johnson, M., *Relation between Land Settlement and Party Politics in UP, India 1950-69*, unpublished Ph.D. dissertation, University of Sussex, 1975.

Kashyap, Subash, *Politics of Power, Defections and State Politics in UP, India*, Delhi: National, 1974.

Kumar, Kapil, *Peasants in Revolt, Tenants, Landlords, Congress and the Raj in Awadh, 1886-1922*, Delhi: Manohar Publications, 1984.

Leiten, K., 'The Janata as a Continuity of the System', *Social Scientist*, Delhi, December-January 1980-1.

Lynch, O.M., *The Politics of Untouchability: Social Mobilization and Social Change in a City of India*, New York: Columbia University Press, 1969.

Macdougall, J., 'Two Models of Power in Contemporary Rural India', *Contributions to Indian Sociology*, Delhi, vol. 14, no. 1, 1980.

Mencher, Joan, 'Conflicts and Contradictions in the Green Revolution: The Case of Tamil Nadu', *Economic and Political Weekly*, Bombay, Annual Number, February 1974.

————, 'Problems of Analysing Rural Class Structure', *Economic and Political Weekly*, Bombay, 31 August 1974.

Metcalfe, T., 'UP Zamindars Today', *Pacific Affairs*, Honolulu, Spring 1971.

————, *Land, Landlords and the British Raj: Northern India in the 19th Century*, Berkeley and Los Angeles: University of California Press, 1979.

Meyer, R.C., *Political Elite in an Underdeveloped Society, the Case of UP*, University of Pennsylvania, unpublished Ph.D. dissertation, 1969.

Moore, F.J. and Freydig, C.A., *Land Tenure Legislation in UP*, Berkeley, 1955.

Mukherjee, R., *Awadh in Revolt 1857-1858*, Delhi: Oxford University Press, 1984.

Nayyar, R., 'Wages of Agricultural Labourers in UP', *Economic and Political Weekly*, Bombay, 6 November 1976.

Neale, W.C., *Land Reforms in UP*, Washington DC: AID, 1970.

Newell, R.S., *Congress Agrarian Reform*, Philadelphia: University of Pennsylvania Press, 1966.

————, 'Ideology and Realities: Land Redistribution in UP', *Pacific Affairs*, Honolulu, Summer 1972.

Pandey, G., 'A Rural Base for the Congress: the United Provinces 1920-40', in *Congress and the Raj*, D.A. Low, ed., Delhi: Arnold Heinemann, 1977.

————, *Ascendancy of the Congress in UP, 1926-34: A Study in Imperfect Mobilization*, Delhi: Oxford University Press, 1978.

Papola, T.S. and Fahimuddin, 'Industrial Spurt in UP', *Economic and Political Weekly*, Bombay, 16 February 1985.

Patnaik, U., 'Class Differentiation within the Peasantry', *Economic and Political Weekly*, Bombay, vol. II, no. 39, 1976.

————, 'Reflections on the Agrarian Question and the Development of Capitalism in India', *First Daniel Thorner Memorial Lecture*, Delhi, 1986.

Ranadive, B.T., *Caste, Class and Property Relations*, Calcutta: National Book Agency, 1982.

Rao, M.S.A., *Social Movements and Social Transformation, A Study of Two Backward Class Movements in India*, Delhi: Macmillan, 1979.

Robinson, F., 'Municipal Government and Muslim Separatism in the United Provinces 1833-1916', *Modern Asian Studies*, Cambridge, July 1973.

————, *Separatism among Indian Muslims: Politics of the UP Muslims, 1860-1923*, London: Cambridge University Press, 1974.

Saith and Tankha, 'Agrarian Transition and the Differentiation of the Peasantry, A Case Study of a West UP Village', *Economic and Political Weekly*, 1 April 1972.

Saxena, N.C., 'Caste, Land and Political Power in Rural Uttar Pradesh', Draft paper presented at the conference on Class, Caste and Dominance, University of Pennsylvania, May 1984.

————, 'Caste and Zamindari Abolition in UP', *Mainstream*, Delhi, 15 June 1985.

Settlement Reports, SR, published in the years stated and for the following districts: Aligarh, 1882, 1903, 1904; Basti, 1919; Kanpur, 1907.

Shankar, Kripa, *Concealed Tenancy and its Implications for Equity and Economic Growth*, Delhi: Concept, 1980.

Shrimali, P.D., *Agrarian Change, Agrarian Tensions, Peasant Movements and Organizations in Uttar Pradesh*, University of Lucknow, Department of Economics, mimeographed, 1981.

Siddiqi, A., *Agrarian Change in a Northern Indian State, UP, 1819-1833*, Oxford: Clarendon Press, 1973.

Siddiqi, M., *Agrarian Unrest in Northern India, The United Provinces, 1918-22*, Delhi: Vikas Publishing House, 1978.

Siddiqui, N., *Land Revenue Administration under the Mughals 1700-1750*, Bombay: Asia Publishing House, 1970.

Singh, B. and Misra, S., *A Study of Land Reforms in UP*, Calcutta: Oxford Book Company, 1984.

Singh, Charan, unpublished Personal Papers, New Delhi, .

————, *Land Reform in UP and the Kulaks*, Delhi: Vikas Publishing House, 1981.

Singh, R., 'Caste, Land and Power in UP 1775-1970', *Teaching Politics*, Special Number on Land, Caste and Politics in Indian States, 1980-1.

Smith, W.C., *Modern Islam in India*, Lahore: Minerva Bookshop, 1943.

Srivastava, S., 'UP: Politics of Neglected Development' in *State Politics in India*, Iqbal Narain, ed., Meenakshi Prakashan, 1976.

Stokes, E., 'Structure of Land Holding in UP, 1866-1948', *The Economic and Social History Review*, Delhi, vol. XII, no. 2, April–June 1975.

————, *Peasant and the Raj: Studies in Agrarian Society and Peasant Rebellion in Colonial India*, Cambridge: Cambridge University Press, 1978.

Thorner, D. and Thorner, A., *Land and Labour in India*, Bombay: Asia Publishing House, 1965.

————, *Agrarian Prospect in India*, second edn., Delhi: Allied Publishers, 1973.

Trivedi, K.K., 'Changes in Caste Composition of the Zamindar Class in Western UP, 1595-1900', *Indian Historical Review*, vol. II, no. 1, July 1975.

Uttar Pradesh, *Agricultural Census In Uttar Pradesh 1970–71*, Lucknow: Board of Revenue, 1973.

————, *Draft Seventh Five Year Plan 1985-90*, Lucknow: Planning Department, 1983.

Wharton, C.R., 'The Green Revolution: Cornucopia or Pandora's Box', *Foreign Affairs*, April 1969.

Whitecombe, E., *Agrarian Conditions in Northern India*, vol. 1, New Delhi: Thomson Press, 1971.

APPENDIX

TABLE A.1: Uttar Pradesh Assembly Results, 1952–80

Political Party	1952		1957		1962		1967		1969		1974		1977	
	% of vote	No. of seats	% of vote	No. of seats	% of vote	No. of seats	% of vote	No. of seats	% of vote	No. of seats	% of vote	No. of seats	% of vote	No. of seats
Congress	47.93	390	42.42	286	36.33	249	32.20	198	33.70	211	32.29	208	31.95	46
Congress(O)	(Founded in 1969)										8.36	9		
BKD	(Founded in 1967)								21.29	98	21.22	104		
SP	12.03	20	7.45		8.21	24					2.90	5		
KMPP	5.70													
PSP			14.47		11.52	38	4.09	11	1.72	3	–	–		
SSP	(Founded in 1964)						9.97	44	7.82	32	–	–		
KMP	(Founded in 1969)								0.48	1	–	–		
UPRSP	0.40										0.69		0.31	
SSD	(Founded in 1969)													
Jana Sangh	6.45	22	9.84	17	16.46	49	21.67	97	17.93	49	17.12	60		
HMS	1.43				1.06				0.29	1	0.30	1	0.04	
Swatantra Party	(Founded in 1959)				4.60	15	4.73	12	1.25	5	1.13			
UPPP	1.87													
CPI	0.93		3.83	9	5.08	14	3.23	14	3.05		2.45	15	2.56	
CPM	(Founded in 1964)						1.27	1	0.49	1	0.71	3	0.58	
SCF/RPI	1.49				3.73	8	4.14	9	3.48	1			0.07	
Muslim League											1.38	1	0.20	
Janata	(Founded in 1977)												47.84	351
Unsuccessful parties and Independents	21.77		21.99		13.01		18.70		8.50	19	11.45	5	16.45	16

Source: P.R. Brass, *Caste, Faction and Party in Indian Politics,* vol. II, 1985, pp. 166–7.

TABLE A.2: Share of Castes in Land and Political Power in Uttar Pradesh (Percentage Shares)

Caste	Population	Pre-Independence zamindari rights	Post-Independence ownership of land	1952 MLAs	1957 MLAs	1980 MLAs and Lok Sabha MPs	1983 Block Pramukhs, MLCs and Rajya Sabha MPs*
Brahman	9.2	17	18	27	21	22	20
Thakur	7.2	34	19	14	17	19	44
Bania, Kayastha and Khatri	3.6	16	2	15	14	5	5
Jat, Bhumihar and Tyagi	2.1	4	6	5	6	5	6
Ahir, Kurmi, Lodh and Gujar	15.1	6	20	6	10	13	16
Other Backward Classes	26.8	2	18	3	2	5	4
Scheduled Castes	21.0	1	9	20	21	20	2
Muslims	15.0	20	8	10	9	11	5
TOTAL	100	100	100	100	100	100	100

* Indirectly elected.
Source: Saxena, 1985.

TABLE A.3: Composition of UP Council of Ministers by Caste
(Information given in this table is incomplete since the
caste of some ministers could not be confirmed)

Caste	1974	1977	1980	1984	1985
Brahman	6	6	10	11	8
Thakur	3	2	10	10	10
Scheduled Castes	4	3	8*	8	7
Muslims	6	3	5*	4	4
Kayastha, Bania, and Khatri	–		–	3	2
Yadav, Kurmi, Gujar and Lodh	2	3	–	5	3
Other Backward Castes	6	5	10 *	2	1
Jat, Bhumihar	–	5	–	1	1
Sikh	–	–	–	–	1

* This figure includes intermediate and backward castes.
Source: Compiled from fieldwork.

22 | Communal Mobilization and
Changing Majority in
Uttar Pradesh

THE ELECTORAL TRIUMPH of the Bharatiya Janata Party (BJP) in the northern states in 1991 highlighted the latent possibilities of religious activism and communal mobilization in forging political majorities. This was an unlikely scenario only a few years before. As recently as the 1984 elections, the BJP could not win a single Lok Sabha seat from Uttar Pradesh (UP). In 1991, BJP was elected to power in UP. No political party has received such remarkable support in so short a time. The question to be explored is, therefore why there was the sudden spurt in electoral support and political appeal of the BJP in Uttar Pradesh.

Recent analyses of these striking changes have attributed the achievement to the activities of the BJP and its affiliates, particularly Vishva Hindu Parishad (VHP) propaganda, its armoury of symbols and modes of transmission in underpinning the support for the Hindutva movement.[1] While it is important to explore the ideological activities of the Sangh combine (the Rashtriya Swayamsevak Sangh (RSS), BJP, VHP, Bajrang Dal, and associated organizations) in spreading the influence of Hindu nationalism, it is equally necessary to consider the role played by caste and communal issues, and the tactics and strategies of political parties in the rise of Hindutva.

In this chapter these complex developments are unravelled through an examination of social and political processes in UP and of how these factors might have contributed to making this key state politically Hindu in 1991.

* This is a revised version of a paper delivered at the South Asia Seminar at the University of Pennsylvania in December 1993. I am grateful to Mushirul Hasan, David Ludden, Ritu Menon, K.N. Panikkar, and Achin Vanaik for their comments and suggestions.

It emphasizes the crucial importance of political context, party strategies, and mobilization tactics in heightening the salience of community identities and in creating conditions conducive to the growth of the Sangh combine. This process was aided by the communal compromises and the decline of the Congress in the 1980s, but the electoral successes of the Sangh combine cannot be attributed to the political conditions and the vacuum created by Congress failures alone. Communal mobilization and the political violence engendered by the activities of the Sangh combine played a crucial part in buttressing Hindu support. This in turn altered political relationships and paved the way for an alliance of Backward Castes, Scheduled Castes, and Muslims, thus creating the problems faced by the BJP in retaining power in 1993.

The Rise of Political Hinduism

Previously a weak electoral force, political Hinduism acquired unprecedented strength in the late 1980s. While religious mobilization was not a new phenomenon in UP, the electoral triumph of the BJP through a political movement of Hindu self-assertion represented a new trend. This was a surprising development. Unlike Rajasthan, Madhya Pradesh, and Himachal Pradesh, political competition in UP centred until the Ram Janmabhoomi movement, on the Congress and various Janata Party formations. However, BJP's seat adjustments with the Janata Dal, by which the two parties agreed on seats to contest, assisted the rise of the BJP in 1989, which allowed the BJP to make inroads quickly in non-traditional areas and among its non-traditional supporters. At no point before 1991 did the BJP win even a quarter of the votes or seats in the UP State Assembly. The highest vote of 21 per cent was achieved in 1967, but the party could not maintain this level in subsequent elections; the average vote (excluding 1967) was around 10 per cent. It is noteworthy that BJP's area of strength even in the 1989 Lok Sabha was not UP, where it won only 8 seats against the 52 of the Janata Dal and Left Front, but rather Madhya Pradesh. Moreover, its victory in these 8 UP assembly seats was due largely to the absence of the Janata Dal in the contest. The important point is that the 1989 elections did not reveal strong evidence of a Hindu vote in UP, despite attempts by the Congress and BJP to marshal support on those lines.

In the early 1990s, the UP scene was in sharp contrast to Madhya Pradesh, for example, where the BJP had maintained a high vote percentage of 30 per cent since 1967, rising to 40 per cent in 1989-90. Christophe Jaffrelot's study highlights the specificity of the party building pattern in Madhya Pradesh, which relied heavily on the RSS party discipline and network from the early 1950s.[2] In UP, the BJP's expansion was more recent—its impressive political presence in the 1990s was linked strongly to the Ram Janmabhoomi movement and the erosion of the Congress base—though a long-term trend was clearly accelerated by it. The BJP's rise was so significant here because there were other alternatives, namely the Janata Dal and the socialists. This was not the case in other north Indian states where the BJP was vying for power. Yet the BJP prevailed in UP largely by harvesting gains from political mobilization around the Ram Janmabhoomi issue.

The most important actor in the temple movement was the VHP and its assortment of priests and religious leaders. The party gained enormous strength from the ideological and religio-cultural actions of the VHP and street power of the Bajrang Dal, formed in 1984. Political mobilization concentrated on ideological issues and a subjective articulation of histori-cal grievances, memories, and cultural differences specially engineered for the purpose of mobilization. Three themes characterized this mobilization: the intrinsic tolerance of Hinduism, the destruction of Hindu temples, and state repression of kar sewa (action by kar sevaks) in Ayodhya.[3] Events surrounding the first attempt in October 1990 to demolish the Babri Masjid were consecrated to highlight the 'heroic' saga of Hindu warriors fighting against the state. Opposition to the state was dramatized by the police action ordered by the chief minister, but barring one single instance of opposition from Mulayam Singh Yadav, there is no evidence of opposition from the state. In fact, a great deal of the Ayodhya movement's strength derived from its ability to draw upon the cooperation of state machinery in UP. The administration and security personnel were more than willing to oblige the kar sevaks whom they recognized as partners in forging the advancement of Hindu nationalism.

Forefronting the narrative of death and bloodshed against the Hindus, supposedly perpetrated by the state, had an extensive impact on middle-class Hindu audiences.[4] Their response however was not influenced by religious faith or religious opposition to the state, but by the cumulative failure of successive governments on material issues of everyday life. The anti-state rhetoric allowed the Sangh combine to draw upon the festering dissatisfaction and discontent of the people. Popular reactions were linked more to anti-government sentiment than to religious hurt or communalism.[5] Harping on the Ayodhya issue and on historical injustices done to Hindus could not have led to the consolidation of political Hinduism but for one very important factor: the steady deterioration of political authority and governance. The political appeal of Hindu nationalism was feeding on the crisis of the state and governance dominated by the Congress for four decades. Relentless violence and collapsing government and alienation and despair among the middle classes enabled the BJP to protect itself as the one party that was attentive to cultural identity and good governance. Political Hinduism was thus a symptom of the state's degeneration and weakening, and more markedly of the long-term decline of the Congress. It was not the novelty of its project but the failure of political rule embodied by the Congress that explained the rise of the BJP.

Congress and the Changing Face of UP Politics

From the 1920s, UP was a Congress stronghold. While its support was drawn from across the country, it was the party's influence in UP that symbolized the essence of Congress politics. In 1991, for the first time in four decades, the Congress was voted out of power in the state in two successive elections. In 1993, its representation was reduced to 28 seats in the state assembly.

The 1980s were a crucial phase in the transformation of UP politics. Four factors dominated the process of change: the alienation of rural producers, discontent of marginal groups in rural society, growing assertion of the backward castes, and the challenge of communalism. Widespread social and economic disaffection was manifested in two different ways: by the decline of the Congress as the principal actor in UP politics, and by its inept manipulation of social and political tensions. As is well known, the stability of the Congress party had rested on the accommodation and cooptation of a wide range of classes, castes, and communities. In UP, its capacity to accommodate groups and contain conflicts was restricted by the limited success of state intervention and opportunities for economic development. It was even less effective in the 1980s on account of the growth of a highly differentiated party system, dividing the electorate into clearly defined and separated social sectors. Poor governance, ineffective leadership, and severe infighting cost the Congress heavily in popular support. The consequences of such failures were heightened socio-political tensions, conflicts, and cleavages, a climate of political violence, and a growing dislocation and alienation in civil society. Social and political changes have been most marked in western UP, which has experienced two interrelated developments.[6] The first development was economic: the crystallization of an agricultural transformation that begin in the 1960s with the Green Revolution. A major breakthrough in agricultural production was achieved with new technology. The most significant improvements occurred in wheat, maize, and sugarcane. For example, average wheat yields increased from 15.5 quintals per hectare in 1979 to 18.9 quintals in 1985. The annual growth rate in foodgrain production rose by 2.78 per cent from 1969 to

1979. The second development was political: the growing assertiveness of surplus-producing farmers as a major political force. Significant opposition to government policies has come from the farmers movement, which came to the forefront from 1986 to 1990, demanding higher prices and cheaper inputs for agriculture. The growing influence of surplus-producing farmers is linked to increased food production in north-western India, in Punjab and Haryana as well as UP.[7] From this region comes the great bulk of the foodgrains procured by the government to be sold through the Public Distribution System at low, government-subsidized prices to a quarter of India's total population in urban centres; this has naturally boosted the importance of surplus-producing capitalist farmers vis-à-vis the central government and state governments. The alienation of the surplus producers from the Congress was more political than economic. The process began in 1977, with the formation of the Janata Party, which forefronted agrarian ideology and policy. Their alienation was accentuated by their perception that the price regime was tilted against them principally because of the urban domination of politics.

At the other end of the spectrum, the rural poor were clearly disillusioned with the failure of anti-poverty programmes. Available data indicates that rural inequalities remained virtually unaltered in the 1980s.[8] Unemployment and poverty were the distinct features of the state's political economy. According to the Seventh Five-Year Plan, the physical quality of life index in UP was at the 'abysmal lowest' level. In the 1980s, unemployment remained high, and moreover, opportunities for employment were confined to agriculture and government. Power, transport, irrigation, and industry that generate employment were underdeveloped. One of the reasons why the Congress regime was so singularly unsuccessful in tackling the specific problems of social and economic change lies in the low levels of economic development and the slow rates of growth in the state. Economic stagnation was responsible for the unemployment and under-employment of agricultural workers, which in turn were the major causes of the state's underdevelopment.

The transformative capacities of the Congress government were limited by the absence of an organized party capable of generating support for its policies. Gaining political power through appeals to the poor and disadvantaged worked well for some time, but in order to ensure that such support was not eroded, the much publicized socio-economic policies had to be implemented. The pro-poor policies did not work in UP as compared to the more developed states where social changes were much more visible. The public disillusionment that followed from slow economic growth was therefore charged to the Congress leadership. The government's failure to ensure social justice gave rise to social discontent and compounded cynicism among various groups regarding the efficacy of state intervention or, at any rate, about the political capacities of the Congress to effect social transformation.

At the heart of these changes was the failure of the Congress to rebuild the party after the 1969 split. The main challenge to the Congress domination was from the backward castes.[9] The Congress tried to mobilize the lower castes and classes through antipoverty programmes, but made no attempt to include the backward castes in the new coalition forged in the 1970s.[10] Though a few symbolic gestures of accommodation were made, the leadership did not restructure the party to give it a different base, as it had in Karnataka in the 1970s or in Gujarat in the early 1980s. In UP upper-caste representation in the Congress ministries and also in the state and district leadership remained high in the 1970s and 1980s. Congress leadership was dominated by upper castes: 38 per cent of the 75 presidents of District Congress Committees and City Congress Committees in 1973 were Brahmans, and 40 of 45 zillah parishad chiefs were either Brahman or Thakur. Backward castes were under represented in Congress, and in the early 1980s, Brahman representation in the leadership actually increased.[11]

It is therefore important to examine why the UP Congress resisted the political arrival of backward castes. One reason is that except during brief intervals, the Congress remained a crisis-ridden and vulnerable entity throughout Indira Gandhi's tenure. Election results in 1967, 1977, and 1989 brought no comfort to party managers. This left the Congress less room to manoeuvre change and also made party reorganization difficult in the 1970s and 1980s. Second, 40 per cent of Brahmans in India live in UP, the heartland of *Aryavarta*. They form 10 per cent of the state's population as against Maharashtra and Tamil Nadu, where they constitute just 3 per cent. No political formation could have ignored such a powerful group or disregarded the fact that it enjoyed a high ritual status, controlled land, and dominated the professions.

From the 1970s, however, the political domination of Brahmans was seriously contested by the backward castes, who came into their own with ever more political influence. Individuals from Yadav and Kurmi backgrounds who have had access to education but have, at the same time, seen their prospects thwarted by upper-caste dominance, asserted their position and staked their claims for adequate representation in the power structures. The backward castes also used both their newly gained economic power and their numerical strength to challenge the stranglehold of the upper castes over the government.[12]

Increasing power conflicts and endemic political instability led to social disorder and widespread violence. This was exacerbated by the criminalization of politics and the steady influx of the underworld into elected bodies, from the 1960s onward. It became pronounced in the 1970s and even more noticeable in the 1980s. Both the Congress and opposition parties accused each other of working with criminals. As one newspaper editorial put it:

In Uttar Pradesh no area is safe from dacoit gangs. Never before, not even in the turbulent days of the eighteenth century was the life and property as unsafe in Uttar Pradesh as it is today. Pride of place for a government that just cannot govern even its own citadel now goes not to Bihar, rated till the other day as the most mismanaged and inept state in the Indian Union, but to the stately state of Uttar Pradesh, allegedly the home state of the Prime Minister.[13]

The communal situation deteriorated sharply. Symptomatic of the growing intercommunity feuds was the extraordinary spurt in Hindu-Muslim rioting. The incidence of communal riots from the early 1980s registered sixfold increase between 1954 and 1985. A spate of communal rioting took place in UP from February 1981 to 1987, with a significant spread to rural areas. Nearly 26 conflagrations took place between February 1986 and June 1987. More than 200 people, mostly Muslims, were killed and a 1,000 injured. Damage to property was to the tune of Rs. 15 million. It is noteworthy that nearly all major riots during the 1980s occurred in towns with a spatial concentration of Muslims or in areas where Muslims had attained a measure of economic stability through their traditional artisan and entrepreneurial skills. This is a lesson drawn from Aligarh, Varanasi, Moradabad, and Meerut in the 1980s.

Communal politics and violence played a decisive role in weakening the Congress base. Yet the secular agenda was accorded low priority with the Congress party, even contributing to its decline. Congress was not inclined to stem the rot set in from the 1960s, because it comfortably held the reins of power. However, as political pressures mounted from non-Congress coalitions, there was a decisive break from the previous decades in terms of party and government identification with patronage of religious symbols, traditions, and institutions.

To sum up, political developments in UP during the 1980s and early 1990s were the byproduct of two interrelated developments: a bitter political struggle for the control of the state, pitting upper castes and classes against the backward and lower castes; and an intensification of intercommunity conflicts, which had the potential of displacing upper castes from positions of power. These structural underpinnings and social stirrings, combined with various political developments, resulted in a serious crisis of regime in the late 1980s. This crisis reshaped politics in new ways, especially conducive to Hindutva mobilization.

The underlying tensions of such socio-political conflicts could not be curbed or diffused by the Congress party in the absence of extensive district and local networks. Indira Gandhi's 1975 declaration of a national state of emergency and the party's defeat in the 1977 elections seriously strained this capacity. By the 1980s there was very little left of the organization at the state or district levels. Ram Dhan, a former general secretary of the All India Congress Committee, denounced the Congress as an entirely 'nominated structure headed by a bogus leadership. . . . In Uttar Pradesh the ruling party functions more on paper than in the field, the office bearer at various levels enjoying the spoils of office and shies away from the people. Office bearers appointed from above without any consideration to contact with grass roots or their capacity to organize and mobilize the people'.[14] The growing frustration was partly because of the failure of state government to organize elections to fill positions in local government bodies and cooperative societies. These bodies were customarily ideal platforms to engage and involve party workers. The decline in UP was striking because the Congress, though highly factionalized in the 1950s and 1960s, was nevertheless well organized. Rapid centralization of power in the 1980s accelerated its decline thereafter.

The political importance of the state played a pivotal role in the process of centralization and concomitant degeneration of the Congress organization. Delhi had the final say in the appointment of chief ministers and senior ministerial colleagues. Such an imposition produced the embarrassing and unedifying spectacle of a crop of chief ministers appearing or disappearing from the scene 'like quick change artists'.[15] In the case of UP, the prime minister and inner coterie were disinclined to appoint state leaders who enjoyed a strong political base to the high office in Lucknow. Consequently, the mantle was invariably passed on to leaders with no popular backing. In addition, state leaders were kept on a leash, their politics monitored and their activities kept under close vigil. It is not without significance that from 1980 to 1984, UP had three chief ministers and the party unit had eight ministers. Not one chief minister completed the full five-year term; in fact the average tenure of a chief minister in UP was less than 30 months.

Until the mid-1980s, Hindu nationalism had remained a weak electoral force, but there had always been a conceptual space for it in UP society provided by the strong influence of Hindu revivalism, and memories of inter-religious conflict and the Muslim separatist movement which culminated in the country's Partition in 1947. The state had a poor record in providing the healing touch after the Partition trauma. Even the state government was not immune to communal activity; despite repeated directives from Jawaharlal Nehru, it took little action to curb Hindu communalism. Many senior Congress men remained sympathetic to commonly perceived Hindu interests.[16] The first three chief ministers of UP in the 1950s and early 1960s—G.B. Pant, Sampurnanand, and C.B. Gupta—were extremely conscious of 'the northern origins of Hinduism' and were committed to a right of centre consensus. Some of their major concerns, such as the Hindi-only language policy in government and education and the exclusion of Urdu, were incorporated in Congress politics. In the area of language and minority rights, the Congress offered few opportunities to right-wing parties to build a social base. Consequently political Hinduism could not produce any significant uprising of Hindu nationalist sentiment and was unable to replace the Congress in the affections of the Hindu majority. This was the main reason for the Jan Sangh's inability to achieve a decisive electoral breakthrough in UP. However, the political culture of conservatism nurtured by the Congress clearly shaped the growth of the BJP in later decades.

Communal Politics and the 'Ayodhya Strategy'

Many new factors were responsible for reactivating communal sentiment in the 1980s. One catalyst was the alarm over the conversion to Islam of a group of low-caste Hindus in Meenakshipuram in southern Tamil Nadu. This stimulated the revival of the VHP, which specifically built upon the activities of Hindu organizations campaigning against conversions. The opposition to conversions was very strong in UP; the VHP and the BJP organized numerous meetings and demonstrations in major cities to highlight the dangers of conversions to Islam. BJP members walked out of the assembly to protest what they alleged to be the indifference of the government to conversions to Islam in eastern UP. During this period the Hindi-Urdu controversy was once again revived in response to the government's half-hearted proposal to make Urdu the second language of the state. Much of the communal politics centred around these two issues. It is noteworthy that the Congress did not oppose the protest actions.

From 1983 onward, the VHP organized a series of elaborate processions to foster Hindu unity. UP figured prominently in the *ekatamata yajna* programmes.[17] During these processions, VHP leaders repeated the theme of 'save Hinduism' and condemned conversions, the concessions to Urdu, and politicians who pampered Muslim vote banks. In many districts yatras were accorded 'a historic reception'.[18] District Congress Committees welcomed processions with arches and *pandals* (covered stages) and support for the yatra was fairly strong at the *tahsil* (subdistrict) levels.

During this period, the UP Congress had clearly begun to experiment with different methods of gaining legitimacy. The Congress first changed its strategy in the early 1980s, especially when it faced the prospect of losing power. The new design for regaining support was clearly majoritarian—best understood as a political idiom that seeks to build electoral majorities on the basis of a majority defined by ascriptive factors such as religion and language. UP provided an active field for the trial of this project as a long period of plural and communal/segmented existence was leading to a sense of unease with mainstream politics. The growth of revivalism was a reaction to the coalition built by Indira Gandhi consisting of the religious minorities and the large majority of India's deprived and marginalized peoples in the 1970s. Following the party's virtual rout in the south and the growing evidence that it was losing support among Muslims, Indira Gandhi, in an astute move, completely reversed the strategy in the north, especially in UP, building upon the confrontations in Punjab and Jammu & Kashmir, and indirectly against Pakistan and the foreign hand, 'to give to the Hindus a big boost and a firm stake in the Congress'.[20] The strategy formed the centrepiece of the Congress election campaign in 1984 held in the aftermath of Indira Gandhi's assassination, which had created a 'wave of unprecedented gloom' in Kanpur, Lucknow, Varanasi, Allahabad, Ghaziabad, and Shahjahanpur.[21]

The 1984 elections played upon two themes: national unity and the need to save the country from internal and external enemies. Assassination and opposition betrayal were the leitmotifs of the Congress crusade. The message of national unity explicitly appealed to Hindu voters; for the first time, the Congress tried to distance itself from Muslims, and consequently no effort was made to solicit their support. This catalysed communal sentiments and provided the Congress with an opportunity to emerge as the chief advocate of majoritarian interests, the only party capable of protecting India from the dangers of communal strife and disunity. Rajiv Gandhi's slogan 'Not Kashmir Desham, not Assam Desham, not Telugu Desham, but Bharat Desham' elicited a fervent response and reached a climax in the 1984 Lok Sabha elections, creating a 'tidal wave' of support for the Congress.[22] Transcending caste calculations and local considerations, the Congress routed the BJP, which had espoused the same line of national unity.

It is significant that much before the Babri Masjid imbroglio led to a serious communal polarization, the Congress government was already devising an 'Ayodhya strategy'. The 'Ayodhya strategy' was not specifically designed for UP, but it dramatically changed the agenda of this state, perhaps more than anywhere else. Designed to reverse the weakening and waning of the Congress, it contributed profoundly to the party's downfall. Given the Congress party's hegemonic position in the state, its decline opened the space for communal and caste assertions. The popular appeal of the Ram Janmabhoomi issue and the BJP success derived from it serve to spotlight the importance of the Ayodhya movement in catapulting the BJP to the centre stage.

During Congress rule, the 'Ayodhya strategy' unfolded in several different ways. For example, places mentioned in the *Ramayana* were developed, the Ayodhya *ghats* (banks) and the *parikrama* procession route around the town of Ayodhya were beautified, and a *Ramayana* study centre was established. The government announced that the *Hindi Bhasha Nidhi* (Hindi Language Trust), a government organization, would publish low-priced editions of Tulsidas' *Ramcharitmanas*. The state government was instrumental in facilitating the unlocking of the Babri Masjid in 1986. The 'Ayodhya strategy' was crafted by the government to appease and conciliate the VHP–BJP combine that had mounted an emotive movement to pressure the prime minister to accommodate Hindu sentiments. The hallmark of Congress strategy, however, was not just the appeasement of the VHP, but equally the accommodation of Muslim fundamentalism. A former associate and minister in the government of Rajiv Gandhi stated that he had unimpeachable evidence that a deal had been struck between the prime minister and Maulana Ali Mian, a noted and influential theologian of Lucknow. Rajiv Gandhi agreed to concede to his demand on revoking the Shah Bano verdict on the express assurance that he and the All India Muslim Personal Law Board would not involve themselves with the Babri Masjid dispute.[23] The deal was that Muslims would get the revocation of the court verdict through parliament while the Hindus would be granted *darshan* (viewing) at Ram Janmabhoomi by unlocking the gate. So in May 1986, Rajiv Gandhi's government introduced the retrograde Muslim Women's (Protection of Rights on Divorce) Bill. In retrospect, the bill accorded considerable legitimacy to the communalization of Indian polity on the one hand, and gave the Sangh combine a unique opportunity to press its claims on the disputed site in Ayodhya on the other. As the 1989 elections approached, the Congress government in UP capitulated to the rising Hindu sentiment by allowing the VHP to lay the foundation stone of the proposed Rama temple at the disputed site. The UP government put pressure on the VHP to go ahead with its Ram shilan puja on 9 November despite continuing Hindu–Muslim violence in different parts of the county. The agreement worked out at a meeting in Lucknow, convened by the chief minister of UP with representatives of the VHP in the presence of the union home minister, allowed the VHP to carry the 'sanctified bricks' to Ayodhya for laying the foundation stone of the Rama temple on 9 November 1989. The agreement enabled the BJP vice-president, S.S. Bhandari, to claim that whatever was happening at Ayodhya was with the full knowledge and approval—both legal and administrative—of the state government.[24]

The Congress government clearly underestimated the intensity of communal feeling aroused by the Ayodhya movement. An important consequence of the strategy was the escalation of communal violence and the polarization of communities, contributing to a groundswell of support for Hindu nationalism. However, this upsurge was not a spontaneous phenomenon; it crested during a period of crisis caused by the decline of the Congress. The opening of the locks on gates protecting the Babri Masjid sparked violence in Barabanki, Varanasi, Lakhimpur Kheri, Meerut, Rampur, Moradabad, Kanpur, and Allahabad. Indeed the Meerut riots in April 1987 signified a sharp escalation of communal conflict. Government action provoked strong protests from Muslim leaders who vitiated the communal atmosphere by launching a strident campaign for the restoration of the status quo in the Ayodhya dispute. Janata Dal leader and editor of *Muslim India*, Shahabuddin warned the Muslim community in Lucknow that 'if they do not raise themselves from slumber the day is not far off when each and every masjid will be snatched away from us'.[25] The VHP quickly stepped up its campaign emphasizing that Muslims were insensitive to Hindu sentiments. Clearly the Congress had ignored the fact that the communal energy released by divisive symbols would create the most widespread friction and strife in UP because of the growing social segregation that fostered distrust and because these disputed shrines were located there.

For several years, the Congress frittered away opportunities to prevent the spread of communalism in the state, for it believed that its 'Ayodhya strategy' could be a winning political gamble. This assumption hinged on an escalating series of compromises. In the end it was a process that the Congress could not control. The encroachment into Hindu political territory intensified communal politics and threatened the structural stability of the political system. Attempts to occupy both the secular and communal spaces left an imprint of ambiguity on Congress politics. Indeed the 1989 election strategy was a summation of this, even as the Congress claimed to have successfully accommodated the interests of the majority and minority communities. Nevertheless, the way this was accomplished caused a decisive shift in the Muslim vote, while the party's attempt to garner a Hindu vote shifted the balance of power decisively in favour of political Hinduism.

BJP and the Communal Mobilization

From this point on, politics was marked by increasing pressures from the Sangh combine on the political structures of the state. A concerted bid was made by the Sangh combine to change the political discourse by making disputed shrines an emotive focus for mobilization. It was concentrated on a single symbolic issue—the continued existence of a mosque on the site in Ayodhya venerated by the Hindus as Ram Janmabhoomi.[26] The BJP made masterly use of religious symbolism to mount the most ambitious programme of socio-religious mobilization.

The upheaval created by the Ram Janmabhoomi movement in UP was strongest there because all three disputed shrines—Ayodhya, Mathura, and Varanasi—are located in that state. The Sangh combine also gained enormously from its ties with the VHP and the numerous social, cultural, and religious organizations associated with the RSS, which appeared to link the party with the traditional values and concerns of popular Hindu culture in UP. It used these ties to amplify the friction between the state and a public increasingly dominated by the RSS–VHP through its congregational politics linking the home, the street, and the temple.[27] This new style of politics was specifically built around religious festivities requiring public participation and culminating in processions winding through major streets and towns. Insistence on taking processions through communally charged towns intensified pressure on the state as any denial of public space was interpreted as anti-Hindu.[28]

At the heart of the Sangh combine's project was the goal of creating a Hindu political majority with a distinctive cultural dimension. In addition, in UP the effort was by no means confined to an internal consolidation of the Hindu community alone. The cohesion of the community was based on a rejection of cultural pluralism and the exclusion of Muslims who had formed an important part of UP's social and cultural milieu for centuries and who have contributed significantly to the high culture of Awadh. This is why the Hindutva project was divisive: it privileges exclusiveness. This polarization along religious lines was bolstered by the high concentration of Muslims in Meerut, Moradabad, Bulandshahr, Ghaziabad, Rampur, and Aligarh, some of whom had been eager to defend the symbols of their religious identity. The 1970s have seen the economic advancement of some sections of Muslim weavers, artisans, and craftsmen who benefited from the rising demand for handicrafts and the expansion of exports. Muslim economic prosperity in the 1970s and 1980s threatened Hindu domination of trade and industry and bred resentment and anger among those Hindus accustomed to the Muslims' invisibility and deference. This infuriated the

VHP, which castigated the new markers of Muslim affluence, especially when it found expression in the mushrooming of mosques and *madrasas* (Islamic schools).

As a social phenomenon, political Hinduism derived strength mainly from the ranks of the upper-caste, middle- and lower-middle-class population in smaller cities and semi-urban areas of the state.[29] The majority of volunteer workers (kar sevaks) who assembled in Ayodhya for the demolition of the Babri Masjid in December 1992 were urban, partly modernized, and educated men.[30] The growth area of the Sangh combine was western and central UP, where Muslims are either economically prosperous or culturally visible. In both it made significant inroads into rural areas.

The Hindutva movement ran into difficulties on the issue of caste, especially the policy of reservation, which was the centrepiece of the Janata Dal's strategy to counter the politics of Hindu communalism. Formed in 1989, the Janata Dal government in New Delhi decided to reserve 27 per cent of the posts in the central government for the members of the backward castes, in accordance with the recommendations of the Backward Classes Commission, headed by Bindeshwari Prasad Mandal, which identified 3,743 castes as 'backward' and needing affirmative action measures by government. In addition to this, the UP government passed an ordinance to raise the reserved quota for backward castes in the state government by 12 per cent. The reservation policy provided significant new opportunities for social mobility to the backward castes, who were under-represented in the central and UP government. Precisely for this reason, the reservation policy was rejected by the upper castes who dominated the bureaucracy and public institutions. Accordingly, the issue of reservation polarized the backward and upper castes in towns and villages throughout the state, resulting in widespread violence. The most vehement opposition to the reservation policy came from the universities of Allahabad and Lucknow, the Indian Institute of Technology, Kanpur, and Benares Hindu University, the leading universities for recruitment into the civil services.

As long as the Congress party remained dominant in UP and was the main vehicle for social mobility and political self-expression for the upper castes, they were secure. Its defeat in 1989 heightened their anxieties as they sensed a political and economic threat to their domination. Mandal created the impression of an imminent transfer of power from upper to backward castes, and made visible all the pre-existing social divisions and tensions of Hindu society, which could not be wished away by the Ayodhya movement. For the BJP, the political fallout of Mandal was damaging to its project of Hindu nationalism and its unifying symbol. The problem was compounded as the party made significant inroads among the backward castes in major parts of the state and thus could not afford to alienate them by openly opposing Mandal. However, for the BJP—as a party that tried to project the notion of an undifferentiated Hindu society—the legitimation of caste as a basis for political organization could be highly problematic because it undermined Hindu consolidation by reinforcing alternative social allegiances.

At this time, the VHP decided to send kar sevaks to Ayodhya for the construction of the Ram temple. This diverted attention from the radical possibilities implicit in Mandal at the moment when UP was set to join the backward caste axis and instead focused attention on the urgent need for unity and cohesion. The unifying content of the symbol of Rama provided a rallying counter-ideology against both the supposed divisiveness of Mandal and the pseudo-secular state's policy of minority appeasement. Community conflict was at this juncture significant because it took the heat off the Mandal issue; it shifted attention away from intra-Hindu divisions into communal discourse. Very soon, caste conflict was turned into Hindu-Muslim polarization and rioting in which Muslims were the main victims. The escalation of community conflicts sparked off an upsurge of violence and frenzy. It is important to note that high communal frenzy was most evident in 1990, and not before or after that. Inflammatory pamphlets and provocative slogans raised during VHP marches were instrumental in unleashing violence geared toward achieving political ends. There was a spate of rioting for two months preceding the 1989 elections, a pattern repeated in 1990 and 1991. Most of these riots took place during or after major chariot processions (rath yatras) that created a tense atmosphere in the towns they traversed. From November 1990 onward, the greater proportion of violence was concentrated in UP: 34 towns were under curfew in November. The proposal to bring a second round of kar sevaks to Ayodhya in December after the fall of the Janata Dal government saw another round of widespread violence.[31]

The disorder in UP from August 1990 to June 1991 contributed to the fall of the Janata Dal government in New Delhi as well as in UP. Championed and nurtured by the BJP, the UP farmers' movement and the Congress, the anti-Mandal agitation played a crucial part in dislodging the Janata Dal government in New Delhi. From October 1990 onward, as anti-Mandal agitation slid into violence between Hindus and Muslims, intensifying social conflicts and confrontations between various groups and identities, hitherto peaceful towns and surrounding rural areas were incorporated into the ambit of communal violence.

On the face of it, the 1991 elections seemed to turn overwhelmingly on the Ayodhya controversy. The crucial issue to assess is whether the voters supported the BJP simply based on emotive, religious appeal or whether they were favourably disposed to the BJP because of the unprecedented political mobilization mounted by the Sangh combine to highlight the state repression of the kar sevaks in Ayodhya. Most accounts of elections clearly show that the Hindutva propaganda and its demonization of the state—and not merely the innate religiosity of people—played a vital part in turning the tide in favour of the BJP.[32] The BJP exploited the prevailing opinion against Chief Minister Mulayam Singh Yadav, turning it into a broad-based sentiment against the state. As the Janata Dal led by Mulayam Singh Yadav provided a viable alternative to the Congress in UP, unlike in Rajasthan and Madhya Pradesh where political contestation alternated between the Congress and BJP, the BJP discredited and decried Mulayam Singh Yadav's leadership.

The Ram Janmabhoomi issue provided the charge for the BJP's battle to control UP. The BJP successfully used non-parliamentary means to win elections in 1991. The party's high success was clearly based on the appropriation of public space that it transformed into communal space.[33] Violence played an important part in the enlargement of the political base of the BJP.[34] Overall, the Sangh combine seized the opportunity provided by the unlocking of the gates around the Babri Masjid to rework the balance of advantage in its favour. The important point is that the situation out of which these conflicts and opportunities arose was not inherently communal: its transformation into communal conflict depended upon the activities of state authorities, political parties, and politicians.

Notes and References

1. Pradeep Chibber, and Subhash Misra, 'Hindus and the Babri Masjid: The Sectional Basis of Communal Attitudes', *Asian Survey,* vol. 33, July 1993, pp. 665–72; Christophe Jaffrelot, Ashutosh Varshney, 'Contested Meanings: India's National Identity, Nationalism, and the Politics of Anxiety', *Daedalus,* vol. 122, June 1993, pp. 227–61.
2. Chistophe Jaffrelot, 1993.
3. Ashis Nandy, Sikha Trivedi, Shail Maryam and Achyut Yagnik, *Creating a Nationality: Ramjanmabhumi Movemnt and the Fear of the Self,* Delhi, 1993.
4. P.K. Datta, 'War over Music: The Riots of 1926 Bengal', in *Communalism in India: History, Politics and Culture,* ed. K.N. Pannikar, New Delhi, 1991.
5. Amrita Basu, 'Mass Movement or Elite Conspiracy? The puzzle of Hindu Nationalism', in *Contesting the Nation: Religion Community, and the Politics of Democracy in India,* ed. David Ludden, Philadelphia: University of Pensylvania Press, 1996, pp. 55–80
6. Zoya Hasan, 'Party Politics and Communal Mobilization in Uttar Pradesh', *South Asia Bulletin: Comparative Studies in South Asia, Africa and the Middle East,* vol. 14, 1994, pp. 42–52.

7. Patnaik 1991.

8. Montek Ahluwalia, 'Rural Poetry and Agricultural Performance in India', *Journal of Development Studies*, vol.8, April 1987, pp. 289–324.

9. Brass, 1984, 1989.

10. Zoya Hasan, 'Power and Mobilization Patterns of Resilience and Change in Uttar Pradesh Politics', in *Dominance and State Power in Modern India: Decline of a Social Order*, ed. Francine R. Frankel and M.S.A. Rao, New Delhi, 1989.

11. *India Today*, 30 December 1983.

12. Francine R. Frankel, 'Middle Classes and Castes in India's Politics: Prospects for Political Accommodation', in *India's Democracy:An Analysis of Changing State-Society Relations*, ed. Atul Kohli, Princeton and Delhi, 1991.

13. *The Pioneer*, 30 November 1992. (All *The Pioneer* references to the Lucknow edition).

14. Ibid., 11 August 1987.

15. Ibid., 4 August 1981.

16. Graham, 1990.

17. Richard H. Davis, 'The Iconography of Rama's Chariot', in *Contesting The Nation*, Ludden, pp. 27–54.

18. *The Pioneer*, 31 May 1984.

19. Ibid., 17 May 1984.

20. Ibid., 12 November 1984.

21. Ibid., 1 November 1984.

22. Ibid., 18 December 1984.

23. Mushirul Hasan, 1993.

24. *The Statesman*, 16 October 1989.

25. *The Pioneer*, 25 March 1986.

26. Ashis Nandy, Sikha Trivedi, Shail Maryam and Achyut Yagnik, *Creating a Nationality:Ramjnmabhumi Movemnt and the Fear of the Self*, Delhi, 1993.

27. Uma Chakrabarti, Prem Chaudhury, Pradip Datta, Zoya Hasan, Kukum Sangari and Tanika Sarkar, 'Khurja Riots, 1990–91: Understanding the Conjuncture', *Economic and Political Weekly*, 2 May 1992, pp. 951–65.

28. Sandria Frietag, 'Contesting in Public: Collonial Legacies and Contemporary Communalism', in *Contesting the Nation*, Ludden, pp. 211–35.

29. Pradeep Chibber, and Subhash Mishra, 'Hindus and the Babri Masjid: The Sectional Basis of Communal Attitudes', *Asian Survey*, vol. 33, July 1993, pp. 665–72.

30. *The Times of India*, 2 February 1993.

31. Amrita Basu, op. cit., pp. 250–69.

32. Ibid.

33. Ibid.

34. Peter Van der Veer, 'Writing Violence', in *Contesting the Nation*, Ludden.

23 | Representation and Redistribution
The New Lower Caste Politics of North India

A COMPLEX SCENARIO has been unfolding in India: the state has been in retreat, institutions have been in decline, caste and communitarian assertions have grown, and political instability has increased. The 1998 elections was the twelfth since 1952, but fourth since the last decade—a sign of the fragmented state of the polity. At the same time, there is evidence of the vitality of Indian democracy: throughout the 1990s, turnouts for elections to parliament and state assemblies have risen steadily and significantly. The data collected by the Centre for the Study of Developing Societies (CSDS) in Delhi make it clear that the steadiest increases in participation came from those in the lower social order, from the poor and illiterate. This process was aided by the regionalization of the polity, the emergence of a coalition of regional groups/parties, and the entry of hitherto marginalized groups into the political system.

Still there remains a central contradiction at the heart of Indian democracy: an inclusive polity has so far not made for a more just and equal society. This raises many questions regarding the meaning and significance of greater political participation, the relationship between democracy and social and economic equality, and the consequences of appealing to the electorate in ethnic or group terms, or making group demands on the state. One might ask whether political parties merely mirror divisions, or whether they help to deepen and extend them. In 1949, B.R. Ambedkar noted an incongruity between political equality and social and economic inequalities that would

* This is a slightly edited version of the original article which appeared in Francine Frankel, Zoya Hasan, Rajeev Bhargava and Balveer Arora, eds., *Transforming India: Social and Political Dynamics of Democracy*, New Delhi: Oxford University Press, 2000.

effectively exclude sections of the population from the democratic process. He stated in the Constituent Assembly:

On the 26th of January, we are going to enter a life of contradictions. In politics we will have equality and in social and economic life we will have inequality. In politics we will be recognizing the principle of one man one vote value. In our social and economic life, we shall, by reason of our social and economic structure, continue to deny the principle of one man one value. How long shall we continue to live this life of contradictions? How shall we continue to deny equality in our social and economic life? If we continue to deny it for long, we do so only by putting our political democracy in peril.[1]

Fifty years later, the contradiction persisted. In fact, it came to the fore in competitive politics from the 1980s. Seen from the vantage point of the 1998 elections, democratic politics is distinguished by a fundamental transformation: a dramatic upsurge in political participation in north India. That, of course, is not the whole story: the upsurge was most marked among the socially underprivileged in the caste and class hierarchy. Moreover, the downward thrust of participation was entwined with struggles of groups who mobilized under banners of ethnicity, caste, and religion. In these processes, group identity supplanted class interest as the chief vehicle of political mobilization; hence, the increasing dependence of all major political parties on ethnic appeals. Ethnic strategies of political mobilization have drawn new groups into the political arena; yet, these struggles occur in a world of great material inequality—staggering inequalities in income and property ownership, and in access to employment, education, and health care. In fact, material inequality is on the rise in India and the socially privileged remain economically powerful. This chapter focuses on the relation between the two transformations: the upsurge in participation of hitherto marginal groups and the increasing dependence of political parties on ethnic appeals to facilitate participation. Opening up the institutional space to greater participation by marginal groups is vital; equally crucial however, is how this can be achieved and the terms on which it has been taking place. In part, this means looking at the relationship between the 'struggle for recognition' of marginal groups, and social and economic equality. In addressing this problematic, this chapter focuses on axes of injustice that are simultaneously cultural and socio-economic, and paradigmatically, caste and class. In what follows, it considers only one aspect of the problem: the circumstances under which the 'politics of recognition' can foster participation and empowerment, whether such politics can help to promote redistribution, and when it is likely to be undermined?

These questions are addressed through an examination of the career of a lower caste political party, notably the Bahujan Samaj Party (BSP), and which is based on secondary sources and interviews with political leaders in Uttar Pradesh (UP), India's largest state. The BSP made rapid progress on the electoral front from the 1980s. During the 1989 general elections it received 2.07 per cent of the votes and obtained three seats in the Lok Sabha. By 1996, its growth enabled the party to obtain the status of a national party, winning 20 per cent of the vote and five seats. The questions therefore centre on how and why the BSP's mobilization strategy succeeded in attracting voters, and how successful it has been in achieving its goals from the standpoint of equality.

The location of UP is important, notably because this mega-state of 140 million people, located in the northern Hindi heartland, is one of the most backward in India. It is also one of the most deprived economically, giving its citizens less than some of the worst performing economies in sub-Saharan Africa. However, it sends 85 members to the Lok Sabha, out of a total of 545. This makes it politically the most crucial region in terms of determining the formation of the central government in New Delhi. It is also the chief locale for the transition to a post-Congress polity, and is the pivotal site of contestation between non-Congress groups. Inter-caste conflict, assertive lower castes, and Hindutva politics all manifest themselves in UP. Potentially, the most radical challenge to upper caste hegemony, the outcome of which would affect the overall structure of social inequality, has been taking place in UP. The way in which conflicts between castes and communities are played out in UP influences the course of democratic politics in north India and alters the ways of wresting and sustaining political power at the national level.

Political Realignments

The impetus for political transformation originated in the rapid realignments that began to take place in the late 1980s. The state was controlled by the Congress party until 1989, with its social base drawn from the Brahmans, the Muslims, and the Scheduled Castes (SCs). Operating as a centrist party, Congress attracted the support of a wide range of groups. As elsewhere, the centrepiece of its hegemony was a strategy that vertically aggregated the interests of different sections of society. It was an aggregation based on an inclusive ideological package of nationalism, secularism, and Nehruvian socialism. Congress succeeded in retaining its hold because it deftly persuaded the lower orders to believe that the existing political arrangements worked in their interest. It was quite a while before the Congress was challenged by the counter-hegemonies created by new social forces.

The main social conflict in UP, apparent since 1977, has been between the upper castes, represented by the Congress, and backward castes, backed by the socialists who had been a major political force in UP from the days of the anti-colonial struggle. Eventually, the backward castes were mobilized under the aegis of the Janata Dal formed in 1989 by V.P. Singh (who had left the Congress in 1988 to establish his own party), and included some of the older socialists. Dedicated to moral probity and social justice, he promised the backward castes reservations in education and government services. During the brief period from 1989 to 1990, the Janata Dal-led government in New Delhi carved out a distinctive ideology based on the dual demands of the rural majority. One was for greater opportunities through investment in agricultural infrastructure and employment, and the other for higher social status through quotas for lower castes and Other Backward Classes (OBCs) in recruitment to the elite all-India services. Ironically, the Janata Dal itself was the major victim of its political mobilization strategy. Subsequently, state and local leaders of the backward classes and dalits rejected the mediation of national parties such as the Janata Dal, even though it was essentially a party of OBCs. Instead, they attempted to enhance their access to public resources of the state through direct participation in the bargaining process that preceded the formation of governments at both the central and state levels.

The political pattern that emerged in the early 1990s demonstrated that the Hindu nationalists rather than the Janata Dal or its successor, the Samajwadi Party, had displaced the Congress as the dominant party. The growth of the Bharatiya Janata Party (BJP) which had not won even a quarter of the votes or seats in the UP Assembly before 1991, was an extraordinary development. It changed the dynamics of electoral competition and facilitated the emergence of the BJP as a national contender to the Congress. The decisive electoral battles of this period were fought in UP, where Congress fortunes declined dramatically. The most significant factor responsible for its electoral defeat was the party's inability to retain its traditional support base that had cut across caste, class, and community lines. Furthermore, Congress' actions regarding Ayodhya, the disputed site of the Babri Masjid, claimed by Hindus as the birthplace of Lord Ram, alienated devout voters among both Hindus and Muslims, accelerating the party's decline.

In 1986, a dispute about the status of the Babri Masjid, built centuries earlier by Babar on or near an ancient site sacred to Hindus, took an unexpected political turn. The district judge, presumably on instructions from Congress authorities at the Centre, allowed the padlock to be removed to allow Hindus to worship at the site. An unprecedented Ram

Janmabhoomi movement organized by the Vishwa Hindu Parishad (VHP), an organization affiliated to the BJP, and the Rashtriya Swayamsevak Sangh (RSS) demanded the building of a new Ram Mandir at the site of the mosque. The Congress, in November 1989, allowed the foundation-laying ceremony of the Ram Mandir to take place on the disputed site. Although it later prohibited the construction of the mandir, pending a court decision on the rights of each community to the area, the foundation-laying ceremony emboldened militant Hindus associated with the BJP. This helped the VHP-RSS to start a popular movement which significantly changed India's political agenda. Designed to reverse the dwindling appeal of the Congress by buttressing the 'Hindu' vote, the leadership's permissiveness in allowing the foundation-laying ceremony, while holding the line against building the temple, alarmed Muslims and disappointed Hindus, ironically contributing to the party's downfall.

At the national level, the political ground shifted in 1990 when the central government adopted the recommendations of the Mandal Commission to establish reservations. The initiative, motivated by V.P. Singh's effort to strengthen the Janata Dal's influence on the backward castes, intensified divisions among Hindus. This confrontation spurred the BJP to support the movement led by the VHP, and aim at reintegrating lower castes into the Hindu hierarchy through a religious appeal to all Hindus to demolish the Babri Masjid and replace it with a Ram mandir.

In UP, the BJP provoked stiff resistance from the Samajwadi Party led by Mulayam Singh Yadav, UP Chief Minister from 1989 to 1991. Mulayam Singh was busy consolidating his own power base by extending reservations for the backward castes in state educational institutions and administrative services. Once the new reservation policy was set in motion, the upper castes reacted violently. The conflict between the Mulayam Singh government and the upper castes in 1990 spilled into a communal conflagration that engulfed UP from October 1990 to March 1991. The disaffected upper castes, who had traditionally voted for the Congress, transferred their support to the BJP. They resented the rise of backward-caste parties and leaders in the state, and the patronage extended by the central Congress leadership in New Delhi to Mulayam Singh. He maintained his hold on UP, even after the minority Janata Dal-led National Front government collapsed at the Centre, once the BJP withdrew its support in the wake of the Mandal-Mandir controversy. The conflict between Mulayam Singh's government and the upper castes became the most enduring confrontation in UP's contemporary political history.

Political leaders and party strategies played the determining role in instigating caste and communal crusades, and in supporting political mobilization around issues of caste discrimination, social recognition, and religious identity. However, the two mobilization strategies in question, caste and community, are quite different in the outcomes they produce, even though both speak to particularistic interests. By polarizing castes into blocs and demanding representation on a bloc basis, the politics of caste identity disrupts the traditional definitions of caste-based hierarchy in Hindu society. Using political rather than religious criteria, caste-based political mobilization converges on control of the state. Such strategies of caste polarization can destabilize the political system, but appear necessary to achieve justice for lower caste groups. In other words, what may be seen as destabilizing political process from one perspective, can be seen as deepening democracy by those groups who capture state power for the first time. By contract, the politics of communalism practised by the BJP attempted to unify all Hindus within a traditional and hierarchical social order. The BJP is not known for its commitment to justice or democracy and the very concept of pluralism, which is at the heart of India's democracy, was challenged by its project to privilege a singular, majoritarian identity.

Growth of Backward and Lower Caste Politics

Although the OBCs and SCs constitute more than half its population, and just over 20 per cent of UP's population belong to upper castes, it is this 20 per cent that has dominated UP society and politics. In recent decades, however, the entry of OBCs into the political system has made a profound difference. Even more important than the rise of Hindu nationalism for the transformation of politics in the state, is the growth of backward and lower caste politics. Caste politics, admittedly, are not new. For several decades, inter-caste conflicts have furnished the principal cleavage in electoral mobilization and played a key part in structuring inter-party competition. Caste calculations have affected most aspects of social and political relations in rural and urban UP. They set the terms of political competition for entitlement and status among groups who see themselves as having equal claims to rights and power. The Hindi satirist, Harishankar Parsai, captured this centrality in a literary piece. He claimed to have persuaded Lord Krishna to contest for a seat in the state assembly:

We talked to some people active in politics. They said, 'Of course Why shouldn't you? If you won't run in the election, who will? After all, you are a Yadav, aren't you?' Krishna said, 'I am God. I don't have a caste.' They said, 'Look, sir, being God won't do you any good around here. No one will vote for you. How do you expect to win if you don't maintain your caste?'[2]

What is new is the heightened political awakening among the lower castes and dalits, a process hastened by the fragmentation of the old Congress coalition into constituent groups of upper castes, Muslims, and dalits. What is also new is the formation of local and regional parties that represent marginal groups hitherto under the Congress umbrella. The structure of representation and power-sharing conceived and practised by the Congress was at odds with the way the new groupings wanted to represent themselves. The drift has unmistakably been towards seeking direct control over the state by hitherto excluded groups.

Among these disadvantaged groups, the SCs constitute more than 20 per cent of the population of UP. After independence, policy measures for their upliftment were designed to moderate the harshness of the caste system. Reservation for them in elected legislatures and in recruitment to educational institutions and government services, as set out in the Constitution, were justified on grounds of the extreme social discrimination they had suffered for centuries, resulting in educational and economic backwardness. Most remained poor and illiterate either casual or landless labour. Despite reservations in 1991, only 22.92 per cent of SCs were literate. Their level of urbanization was 11.80 per cent compared to 22 per cent for others. As many as 81.59 per cent were engaged in the agricultural sector, as against 69.42 per cent for others; and only 18.59 per cent were employed in non-agricultural occupations, while for others the proportion was 30.58 per cent. Although the disparity in literacy between groups had narrowed since 1971, as of the early 1990s only 14.43 per cent of the SCs population had received any kind of formal education.[3] Again, while blatant forms of caste discrimination have disappeared, more subtle forms remain widespread especially in rural areas.[4] Compared to their upper caste peers, SC legislators seemed to have very little influence over the day to day implementation of public policies, underlining the real constraints on political empowerment. They could not bring about a substantial change in the distribution of agrarian assets, the most important determinant of the material condition of the rural population.[5]

In theory, zamindari abolition and land reforms should have empowered the dalit community in UP. However, it is widely accepted that these reforms, which were only partially successful, merely undermined the power of the upper caste landlords. The wider benefits of reform reached out to the former tenants or the intermediate and backward castes, not to the untouchable communities or agricultural labourers and agrestic serfs.[6] In fact, the growing power of the backward castes in the wake of the Green Revolution obliged the states in north India, most notably UP, to initiate the

Mandal Commission reforms. These translated the increasing political and economic influence of the backward castes into bureaucratic power.

Despite the limitations of land reforms, the logic of extending the franchise to all adults and allowing democratic politics, finally created a social milieu in the 1990s in which dalit voters at last confronted the dominance of the upper and backward castes. Aware of the logic of democratic politics in which a majority is won on the basis of the first-past-the-post-system, the numerical strength of lower caste groups gives them an advantage. It is important to note that dalit voters had already been mobilized by the democratic upsurge of the 1970s: the odds of the dalits turning out to vote became as high as those of the upper castes. Since then, the odds of dalit voter turnout is 70 per cent higher than that of the upper castes. This encouraged dalit leaders to launch their own platforms. According to social anthropologist, R.S. Khare, the impact of the democratic culture is unmistakable when a dalit, 'who customarily has a non-competitive subjugated status', discovers through experience, especially of other groups, that competition is one of the major mechanisms of social recuperation.[8] To compete is to claim a political right.

In the forefront of dalit politics are the new professional and administrative elites, a group that is still very small but quite aware of its prestigious social placement. Politically conscious, better educated, and assertive towards the hierarchy of caste and class, members of this group have contributed to strengthening the processes of socio-political change. The striking feature of this agenda is the belief that real improvement in their lives can only come through a discourse that focuses on political power and organization as the key to their social advancement. The logic of dalit politics, they argue, involves three major themes: a challenge to the very definition of Hinduism as the majority religion and the core of Indian tradition; an extension of this theme beyond dalits to include all sections of those oppressed and marginalized by the process of caste exploitation; and a synthesis of economic and political issues with the need for cultural recognition. At the heart of the matter is whether it is more important to change state policy outcomes, or the processes that produce them. The strategy of dalit assertion clearly indicates it is more important to acquire power as a means of changing state outcomes, than to change structures that produce them.

Given the dual inequalities of status and income/occupation built into the caste system, the dominant tendency among dalit leaders has favoured a change in the power structure, so that opportunities could be channelled to the deprived sections of society. The OBC-dominated Janata Dal, led by Laloo Prasad Yadav in neighbouring Bihar, came to power on such a platform: 'smash the upper castes, destroy the Bhura-bal'. An example of his rhetoric is the following: 'Just as peddlers visit your villages saying, choose what you like for four annas, the officers of my government will come to you with whatever you want. Free sarees, free dhotis. They will camp in your villages. They are your servants. Take what you want.'[10]

The centrality accorded to power was just as clear in the remarks of the former prime minister, V.P. Singh, the chief architect of the social justice platform: 'Through Mandal I knew we were going to bring in changes in the basic nature of power. I was putting my hand on the real structure of power. I knew I was not giving jobs, Mandal is not an employment scheme, but I was seeking to place people in the instrument of power through the use of governmental power'.[11]

The most remarkable characteristic of lower caste politics is the pursuit of power. Like the OBC leaders, the dalit leaders are preoccupied with the question of who governs and how the new political order should be established and maintained. Both attach great importance to gaining government positions, and measure social and economic progress by their groups' share in public life: education, professions, and public employment. Kanshi Ram, the pioneer of the movement to politically organize the bahujan samaj (which simply means the non-upper caste majority, Muslims included), puts the matter bluntly: 'we have a one point programme—take power'.[12] The BSP's principal slogans underscore this thrust: 'mat hamara raj tumhara, nahi chalega nahi chalega or, vote se lenge PM/CM, arakshan se SP/DM.'[13] In contrast, in the 1970s, Kanshi Ram's activities were focused on welfare and reform. By the late 1970s his strategy had changed and he no longer believed in the primacy of social reform; rather it would be a share in political and administrative power which would bring about the desired social change.[14]

Opposed to this argument stand the not so desirable structures of social dominance within north Indian society that traditionally compelled dalits to vote in accordance with the wishes of upper caste landlords. Ambedkarite in ideological inspiration, the new leadership wants to invert this structure and instead construct a new political order based on the active participation of hitherto deprived groups in government and public administration. Through controlling power, they hope to ensure that members of lower castes secure jobs and places in educational institutions. Although reservations have secured some upward mobility, dalits have a major grievance that the reservation quota is seldom filled. In the early 1980s, only 5.8 per cent of Class I officials, and 6.23 per cent Class II officials were SCs, although 18 per cent positions were reserved for them. Even when the quota was filled, the SCs complained of social discrimination in promotions and postings. Hence the dalit upsurge was stirred principally by the upwardly mobile middle strata among the SCs, who were powerless to secure important postings and proper recognition in government and society. The origins and support of the party among educated government employees is crucial for understanding both the institutional nature of its strategy and its success, a success that was limited to elite incorporation into state institutions.

The Rise of the BSP

A development of critical importance in UP has been the rise of the BSP which was able to form the government in 1995 and 1997. The BSP benefited crucially from the collapse of the Congress in UP. Its rise to prominence was partly due to the vacuum caused by the decline of the Congress, partly because of its own appeal, and also because the Congress discouraged highly assertive advocates of the oppressed castes and classes within its ranks. More importantly, the disintegration of Congress rule transformed the manner in which ethnic identities were catapulted onto the political arena. The waning of the Congress coincided with an escalation of direct caste-community appeals made by non-Congress parties, which led to an exodus of groups that were under the Congress umbrella towards the Samajwadi Party and the BSP. These two parties picked up additional support as they gathered momentum.

A crucial step in this direction was the formation in 1978 of an organization called the Backward and Minority Classes Employees Federation (BAMCEF) by Kanshi Ram. Established in Punjab, it was later extended to UP. Its chief aim was to organize the elite of the bahujan samaj who had benefited from quotas in government services. They became the chief ideologues and workers of the organization that eventually became the BSP. By the early 1990s, BAMCEF had almost 200,000 members.[15] It mobilized government officers on the assumption that their further individual progress was closely linked to the collective standing of their group.[16] It prepared the ground for the formation of the BSP in 1984; its goal was to create a coalition of minorities that actually constituted a majority: the SCs, Scheduled Tribes, OBCs, Muslims, Christians, and Sikhs, that is, all those included in the Hindu upper castes. Unable to establish itself as a party of all the minorities, the predominant base of the BSP came from the politicized dalits who were receptive to its radical message of political empowerment. In contemporary politics, its core support comes from those castes who have been the main beneficiaries of the state's reservation policies. The nucleus of its support comes from the Chamar caste, by far the largest and most politicized lower caste in UP. Backed by the BSP, dalit assertiveness succeeded in undermining the domination of upper castes and, by the mid-1990s, they were beginning to supplant them in elected government bodies.[17]

The ascent of Mayawati to the powerful office of the chief minister of UP in less than a decade of SC mobilization, highlights the success of this strategy in UP. Mayawati, a Yadav woman, became the chief minister in 1995. She was the first dalit woman to have reached the highest office in an Indian state, but gender was not the most important aspect of her accession. Its significance arises from the mobilization strategy of the BSP, centred on dalits themselves. The control of the government by a dalit had a stirring effect on dalits, who felt that they had unexpectedly pulled the ground from beneath the feet of upper castes, so that those at the bottom ruled over those at the top. This event established the dalits as a central political force in their own right and not as a vote bank to be exploited by upper castes.

Before the 1993 assembly elections, Kanshi Ram had entered into a winning alliance with Mulayam Singh. Against the background of the Mandal-Mandir controversies this alliance assumed a new relevance for the bahujan samaj's access to power. It helped the BSP and the Samajwadi Party to improve their support in the 1993 elections: the Samajwadi Party won 109 seats out of 425 and 25.83 per cent of the vote, and the BSP won 67 and 11.11 per cent of the vote, and together they formed the government which lasted nearly two years. The alliance was however dogged by differences over the distribution of benefits. This was by no means a natural alliance, since the two communities were engaged in sometimes violent conflict over land and wages in the villages. The BSP was worried by advances made by the Yadavs under Chief Minister Mulayam Singh Yadav's dispensation, while backward castes used every opportunity to tease and torment dalits and also to check the latter's efforts towards social mobility. The alliance fell through amidst considerable bickering and bitterness over atrocities towards dalits in May 1995, and the BSP quickly moved on to form a new alliance with the BJP which helped Mayawati to become the chief minister in June 1995. This alliance was however just as expedient as the previous one, its chief purpose being to control Mulayam Singh Yadav, whose increasing political influence both partners wished to curb. More importantly though, it helped the BSP to be in government. Given the overwhelming importance of acquiring power in the BSP scheme, its leadership was willing to enter into an alliance with the BJP or any other party to form a government.

The BSP's approach is fundamentally different from other parties. For it, political society is constituted by groups, and not individuals. It treats group identity as the defining one and does not consider class, gender, or occupation as relevant. Hence, its political strategy hinges on activating this identity. Implicit is a belief that universalist ideas associated with the post-colonial politics of the state were unjust, because they favoured the dominant groups without making adequate allowance for the inequities from which the lower castes suffer. Seen invariably in collective terms, disadvantage and inequity are regarded as the unfair treatment of whole caste groups, by the state or others. The new lower caste politics therefore draws upon a growing preference for the recognition of group claims on grounds of social discrimination. This has been used to increase group-based representation in existing political institutions.[18]

In accordance with this strategy, the BSP advocates a one-point programme: proportional representation for all groups in government, bureaucracy, and educational institutions. This system appealed to dalits precisely because it addressed their political aspiration, an aspiration neglected by the Congress. It effectively superseded the welfarist approach of the Congress that stressed material benefits such as jobs, houses, and sanitation for dalits, minorities, and women, but did not offer them a share in power. It treated dalits primarily as an underprivileged group requiring a programme of action to ameliorate poverty. Quite deliberately breaking from this policy, the BSP defined dalit as a 'community of humiliated' who could be liberated only by gaining political power of their 'own', and not just material gains.[19] Under Congress rule, despite the importance of the dalit vote, they achieved very little representation in the government and party organization, and the few positions that they did get were due to the benefaction of the upper castes. In a word, the significance of the dalit vote did not translate into perceptible influence for individual members in the organization or government. By contrast, Mayawati's rise to the office of chief minister was the result of the autonomous mobilization of dalits, itself the product of democratic politics, and the politics of reservation, which has made available to them new forms of political self-definition. Dalits, as much as the OBCs, are a category of political action. Political action has been an important means of affirming their political equality vis-à-vis upper castes, and a way of regaining self-esteem and self-respect.

Although Mayawati's first stint in power did not entail any structural changes in the economy or polity to benefit the vast numbers of the subaltern classes, the BSP nevertheless commanded crucial support among the dalits throughout its period in office and even thereafter. By the 1996 election it had emerged as an important political force: it notched up an impressive 20 per cent of the vote and managed to get 59 seats in the Vidhan Sabha. This was an improvement of 8 per cent on the 1993 elections, a significant development because it derived not from militant mass mobilization, but from capturing state power via anti-high caste propaganda. An additional reason was Mayawati's distinctive style and culture of administration and her determination to promote SC officers. For example, all the upper castes holding important positions, such as chief secretary and chief minister's private secretary were replace by SC officers. This change provoked resentment and, correlatively, the dalits assertion polarized the upper and lower castes.

During her two terms in office, and especially her second term, Mayawati succeeded in building a new political presence for dalits. She tried to make good the promise of political empowerment by filling the reserved quota for SCs and appointing them to important positions in the government. This was accomplished through large-scale transfers of bureaucrats: for example, 1,350 civil and police officials were transferred during her six-month tenure in 1997. As many as 467 members of the Indian Administrative Service (IAS), 380 officers of the Indian Police Service, 300 members of the Provincial Civil Service, and 250 Provincial Police were transferred. Dubbed as a 'transfer industry' by the Allahabad high court, the large-scale transfers placed dalits in key positions in the state and local administration. At the end of Mayawati's second term in office, a quarter of the district magistrates and superintendents of police and more than a quarter of the principal secretaries in 1997 belonged to the SCs.

In terms of new policies or programmes there was little to show from her two terms of government, but it could be argued that the BSP had not been in power long enough to initiate major development programmes. Mayawati, however, claimed that her government had done some indispensable work for dalits during their two short stints in power. These achievements were: (a) sharpened emancipatory campaigns among the dalits; (b) confronted the existing upper caste bias of the state apparatus in order to make way for lower castes; (c) accelerated the passage of resources and funds via government programmes for the SCs; and (d) secured dalits' access to some government land. Serious land reform was not on the BSP agenda. It limited itself to efforts that enabled dalits to take possession of land they had already been allotted. Nonetheless, land reforms have given a measure of land security to the dalits: 158,000 dalits were given possession over 120,000 lakh acres of land. In addition, unauthorized possession by dalits of Gaon Sabha land prior to June 1995 was regularized, benefiting 1,500 SC families.

The most significant programme of her second term was the Ambedkar Village Development Scheme, which provided development funds and infrastructure to 15,000 Ambedkar villages, with a 30 per cent dalit population. Basically, model villages were built by transferring funds and resources from other programmes spread over large areas, and concentrating them in smaller pockets. As many people have benefited from the programme, there is no denying that the initiative generated considerable enthusiasm among BSP cadres and the masses, even as it kindled the hostilities of other castes, particularly those who are just as poor as the dalits. Though modest, some of these measures—such as doubling the amount of scholarship money to high school students belonging to the SCs, or the decision to double the scholarship allowed to children belonging to the families engaged in unhygienic occupations—have boosted dalit confidence simply by the preference given to them by a dalit-led government.

Within the larger administration of the state, Mayawati offered her constituency the greatest possibilities of obtaining access to jobs, offices, and power. In a state where caste politics is deeply entrenched, the BSP's caste-based analysis of dalit deprivation was bound to appeal to them. Benefits in UP were distributed on the basis of patronage; consequently, dalits supported their 'own' elites in the expectation that they would share the spoils of power and wealth once they obtained government positions. The BSP has however succeeded in retaining dalit support without always delivering material benefits or political office.[20] It could be argued that its success owed much to the radical emphasis placed by the party on contesting upper-caste oppression. This aspect of its mobilization programme is critical because the party did not subscribe to any economic programme or ideology and hardly ever proposed new policies. In these circumstances, the politics of symbolism and recognition has been given priority to encourage the growth of their own constituency. An enormous amount of the BSP's energy has been spent in the politicization of dalits through symbolic acts of dalit empowerment and resisting upper caste hegemony, rather than in securing material benefits. As one IAS officer put it: 'The dalit fight is not for economic emancipation, it is a battle for social recognition. If the dalit assertion was for economic rights then we would back the communist parties. We are struggling for dignity and participation in government which gives us social status.'[21]

Towards this end, the BSP emphasized the themes of recovering dignity and status. In this connection the most flamboyant gesture of Mayawati's government was to build a Parivartan Chowk in the centre of Lucknow that would have statues of the great anti-Brahman leaders: Jyotiba Phule, Penyar E.V. Ramaswamy Naicker, Ambedkar, Shahu Maharaj. This was supplemented by the installation of Ambedkar statues in every village and town, organization of Ambedkar melas, development of Ambedkar parks in every district, carving out new districts and naming them after dalit leaders, and instituting awards in memory of a pantheon of dalit heroes. These symbolic measures were meant to challenge upper caste political and cultural hegemony. Indeed it had an electrifying effect on the collective social status of the dalits.

Although gains in dignity and self-respect are important, they make sense because they were linked to the more tangible promise of political empowerment for the SCs, as well as some improvement in economic opportunities.[22] Ultimately the principle of proportional representation played a key role in helping the party retain its hold on dalit loyalties. Mayawati achieved an increased representation of SCs by an overt focus on caste identity as the sole criterion for distributing tickets and posts. This resulted in a political empowerment of dalits in UP greater than in any other state. It is certainly true that the stable vote of SCs for the BSP was the principal reason why it could promote dalit empowerment. The preferential treatment given to dalits in turn contributed to its durability, and undoubtedly, this was because they had 'their' party and their 'own' chief minister, and power was exercised for their benefit. In other words, UP's political experience indicates that dalits used their votes to simultaneously affirm identities and avenge past humiliations, as well as to secure instrumental benefits.

Political Power versus Structural Change

The significant political transformation brought about by the dalit assertion should not, however, be allowed to mask the inequalities that continue to exist for the majority of dalits within UP. Benefits have flowed to a privileged minority within the lower castes; the dalits still remain the most dispossessed and disadvantaged group.[23]

A point worth noting is that low levels of incomes and education, rather than just under-representation and non-recognition, are the major constraints on access to, and spread of, social opportunities. Yet, most of the newly mobilized people in UP continue to see themselves as members of castes and communities anxious to preserve their group, rather than individual or class interests. Even though political competition is interwined with an intensification of social conflict at the class level, the tendency is to use mobilization as a means for winning political power, and not as a condition for intra-group equality and development. Redressing disadvantage and deprivation within this framework of empowerment from above prevented the rectification of inequalities of class, especially at the lower rungs of the social order. The strategy of the Samajwadi Party and the BSP certainly enhanced the political power of the OBCs/dalits and their ability to influence state politics, but this cannot substitute for radical social and economic change that is imperative in UP. It is difficult to imagine how the abbreviation of the political power of dominant castes could be limited to the government sector. It is hardly possible for the BSP to preside over governance without addressing the land question or without doing something about the economic and extra-economic oppression of agricultural labourers, for example. The BSP faces a strategic predicament: its autonomous politics raised the political profile of dalits at the local level, which required the government to support local resistance. However, tackling local problems entails a class approach to pressurize the government for implementation of economic redistribution, which a caste-based following cannot achieve and which the party wants to avoid.

Far from generating social and political dynamism, caste mobilization and sectional governance tend to block much-needed structural change. The failure to address inequalities in education, health, and employment opportunities, which are in fact a reflection of inequalities in the social and economic powers of different groups, is not a unique feature of lower caste parties. Equity in distribution was never the priority of any government. The political importance of the state notwithstanding, UP remains one of the poorest and least developed states in the Union. This is reflected in its high levels of mortality, fertility, undernutrition, illiteracy, social inequality, and the slow pace of poverty decline.[24] Most striking is the high degree of inequality experienced by women in terms of life expectancy, literacy, access to health facilities, and property in land. Even the redistributional programmes introduced in the early 1970s, at the height of the 'Garibi Hatao' campaign have produced insignificant results because the state lacked both the commitment and institutions required for their implementation.[25] These institutions include the Public Distribution System, the Integrated Rural Development Programmes, and the Integrated Child Development Schemes. These programmes—which involve transfers of various kinds to target groups and no redistribution of assets between different classes— are easier to implement and yet the gap between promise and delivery is very wide. There were no significant initiatives—comparable to health care in Kerala, social security in Tamil Nadu, land reforms in West Bengal, employment guarantee schemes in Maharashtra, and panchayati raj in Karnataka—to promote social development. No serious social reform, after zamindari abolition in the early 1950s, ever made headway in UP.

Social and economic development have been stymied by an unbridgeable chasm between the rhetoric of development and the ground realities of implementing socio-economic policies which required structural changes in the pattern of social relations. In this context an important impediment has been the nature of agrarian politics. These have revolved around the interests of surplus producers in receiving input subsidies and procurement prices for foodgrains. The leadership of political parties and farmer's movements has been firmly in the hands of this class and distributive policies could not be sustained in the absence of significant public action from below. The state machinery, police, and village-level bureaucracy were tilted in favour of landed groups, not least because the bureaucracy, which was recruited from the upper castes, shared the concerns of the rural rich. The privileges of governmental control have been exploited for the sectional benefit of those with political and bureaucratic power, or those with the opportunity to influence political action to challenge the oppressive patterns of caste, class, and gender relations.

Historically, the new groups in UP have had a more difficult time achieving what non-Brahmans achieved in south India, at least partly because lower caste politics in UP lacked ideological content. In the south, the non-Brahman movement institutionalized participation at an early stage, and developed gradually enough to allow upper castes time to adjust to their loss of power; this small minority moved into the commercial and industrial sectors. In UP, the upper castes form 20 per cent and the Brahmans nearly 10 per cent of the population. Besides, the organized sector was not monopolized by Brahmans alone. Diverse groups such as Kayasths, Banias, and elite sections of the Muslims community shared power. The wider range and large proportion of upper castes made it harder to organize a non-Brahman movement to displace them.[26] The upper castes dominated the government and political organizations. While the reservation of government jobs was the principal channel of upward mobility for the OBCs and the SCs, government jobs remained the most attractive career option for the upper castes as well because in contrast to the south, alternative avenues of employment in UP's stagnant industrial economy were limited. An opportunity for political change in UP arose only when the upper castes abandoned the Congress in favour of the BJP. This led to the disintegration of the Congress vote, creating a crucial opening for the disadvantaged groups to rally behind caste-based parties committed to social justice for deprived groups.

Eventually, such a group empowerment strategy cannot bring about substantive change. The two issues that have the greatest capacity to influence the well-being of subordinate groups—land reform and education—cannot be addressed without structural reform. In fact, the BSP as also the SP are parties that could push land reform legislation in UP since both draw support from the lower castes and classes. However, the BSP has rarely spelt out policies on these basic issues; they consider them irrelevant to the bigger project of winning power. Though the party has attempted to implement the existing policy of redistribution in favour of dalits, it cannot energetically and purposefully pursue this without a majority of its own. This is clearly ruled out in the fragmented party system of UP, which is structured by rough parity in numbers between the most privileged upper castes, the bloc of backward castes, and the dalits. In reality both the strength and weakness of the BSP stems from its caste-bloc politics. Its strength is that the SCs are evenly spread across the state and a dalit vote gives the party a chance in a large number of constituencies, but it also makes it logically impossible to win even a single seat without strong support from other groups. It has not however been able to attract significant support from backward castes and Muslims. It has received their support only when it fielded candidates and gave organizational responsibilities to cadres from among them.

Political Transformations

Although the benefits of empowerment have been captured only by a small elite among the subordinate groups, UP's political system has been transformed. The emergence of the BSP has added a vital dimension to the ground level economic and political development of the lower castes. The new entrants see electoral triumph as the necessary means to gaining power and challenging the domination of the established elite. I have argued elsewhere that with all its limitations, caste-based mobilization has proved to be a successful vehicle for the political empowerment of the populous backward castes.[27] It has generated a shift in the balance of political power in the government and legislature: the gap between the upper and lower castes has been steadily narrowing since 1989, when the Janata Dal came to power. This is evident from the significant increase in the number of lower caste legislators and senior civil servants in influential government positions. At the same time, the rise of the lower castes has provoked the hostility of upper castes, especially in UP, where the Samajwadi Party and the BSP emerged as major political forces. In reaction, the votes of these upper castes were transferred en bloc to the BJP to neutralize the lower caste challenge to their dominance. Even before these controversies came on to the political centre stage, the predominant conflict was between the backward and upper castes. The rise of dalits and their consolidation behind the BSP intensified this conflict, but it is clear that caste-based mobilization alone cannot continue to win mandates for lower caste leaders.

In the event two possible strategies were available to lower caste leaders. One was a form of all-embracing distributional politics committed to channelling state resources towards the improvement of all, regardless of particularism. This was conspicuous by its absence from UP. The difficulties of this policy under present political conditions was evident from the Congress performance in the 1998 elections, when the party failed to win a single seat from the state. In 1998, its vote fell below 8 per cent and a majority of its candidates forfeited their deposit.

The second alternative was an unlikely a coalition of the lower castes and minorities led by the Samajwadi Party-BSP combine. Such a broad-based social coalition, or even an electoral adjustment between the Samajwadi Party and the BSP, would seriously dent the power of the upper castes, in the process, they could emerge as important players in state and national politics. This was the lesson of the 1996 elections. The absence of an understanding between secular parties helped the BJP to win 52 seats. The Samajwadi Party and BSP together polled 45.6 per cent of the vote but only won eighteen and six seats respectively. In 34 of the 52 seats that the BJP won, its share of popular vote was less than the combined vote of the Samajwadi Party and BSP. Yet, backward and lower caste leaders are averse to the formation of a broad alliance. Rather, they were engaged in a bitter struggle for power as both compete for scarce state resources. The increasing importance of the BSP and the assertiveness of its leaders has complicated patterns of social conflict and the possibility of making such alliances. Their autonomy and independence have no doubt increased the political consciousness of dalits and promoted their empowerment, but they have also brought them into conflict with both the upper and backward castes. This is also why the BJP was relatively successful in breaking the Samajwadi Party-BSP alliance.[28]

Even after the BJP's rise to power, the Samajwadi Party and the BSP persisted with their rhetoric over which one authentically represented the lower castes. Although the break-up of the BJP-BSP alliance in October 1997 was a good opportunity for the non-upper castes to come together, they did not. This was due partly to ground level OBC-dalit hostility, and partly to the power struggle between the two groups which has moved from being a contest between unequals to a struggle for power between near equals, facilitated by the BSP's pursuit of a dalit empowerment agenda since 1993.[29]

Even as caste interests proliferate, there is however no simple dualism of upper castes versus lower castes; rather, lower caste parties can act as a brake on upper caste domination only when they are united on a common platform. Should the Muslims, more than half the backward castes, and the SCs be united behind the Samajwadi Party, the BSP, and what remains of the Janata Dal, the BJP could not win electoral majorities. It came to power by capitalizing on the divisions between these competing castes and parties. This was the central point of the 1998 parliamentary elections, when the BSP won only four seats, despite winning more than 20 per cent of the vote. In reality, the consolidation of dalits behind the BSP has been advantageous for the BJP. By refusing to form an alliance with any party the high vote of the BSP clearly establishes its electoral clout, making an alliance with it imperative. It is with this clout that BSP leaders hope to be in a position to dictate outcomes at the national and state levels.

Presumably, the lower caste leaders recognize the damage caused by these divisions but are not prepared to subdue them because they can still obtain political office, and hence do not feel an urgent need to forge coalitions. Undoubtedly, caste constituencies help them to bargain with national parties, but it also limits their political reach, and especially the prospect of extending their political influence to other states.[30] There must still be room to navigate between these constraints to find new ways that do not altogether abandon self-empowerment, and to pursue them within coalitions. Surely, lower caste parties need caste constituencies to gain access to government, as well as a broader coalition to uphold and stabilize their access. In the absence of such coalitions their support has remained limited to the specific castes they seek to represent.

There is little doubt that the growth of political consciousness around caste issues and related strategies of empowerment has provided a discursive vehicle for the mobilization of what has clearly been a progressive social and political force. It has also underwritten a new argument for secularism, one that opposes caste to communalism. It has however left behind a legacy in which caste has been bolstered as a focus of political identity and affiliation, one that may exclude broader social commitment and collective action.

North India's recent history, and that of UP in particular, indicates that for collective action to become a real force. political parties must go beyond caste. The challenge is to accommodate interests and identities which are electorally disagregated into a negotiable frame of governance. In the meantime, lower caste parties have managed to fragment, the legacy of the Congress; they have also rebutted the BJP's claim of Hindu unity by facing it to negotiate separately with competing Hindu groups, rather than with Hindus as constituents of a single homogeneous community. Although the lower caste parties do not have an agenda of structural reform, they have managed to bring formerly marginal groups into the government and diverted public resources and a flow of benefits to them. Unlike in the past, it is now difficult for any government to ignore the interests of dalits. Significantly, this has opened new spaces for the lower castes to enter the urban middle classes. This could well be the beginning of a more radical democratization of north Indian society, as the majority of dalits and OBCs begins to realize that its economic and social condition has not improved much as a result of proportional representation in the state.

Notes and References

1. *Constituent Assembly Debates*, vol. X, Official Report, New Delhi, 1989, p. 979.

2. Harishankar Parsai, *Selected Satire*, Delhi: Manas Publications, 1996.

3. *Primary Census Abstract for Scheduled Castes and Scheduled Tribes*, Paper 1, 1993.

4. For example, in Palanpur female literacy varies from zero for Scheduled Caste females to 100 per cent for Kayasths. Jean Drèze and Haris Gazdar, 'Uttar Pradesh: The Burden of Inertia', *Indian Development: Selected Regional Perspectives*, ed. Jean Drèze and Amartya Sen, New Delhi: Oxford University Press, 1997, pp. 83–6.

5. Barbara Joshi, 'Whose Law, Whose Order? "Untouchables", Social Violence and the State in India', *Asian Survey*, no. 7, July 1982, p. 684.

6. For a discussion of the impact of land reforms on different groups, see Zoya Hasan, *Quest for Power: Oppositional Movements in Uttar Pradesh*, New Delhi: Oxford University Press, 1998, chap. 2.

7. For details of the democratic upsurge, see Yogendra Yadav, 'Understanding the Second Democratic Upsurge: Trends of Bahujan Participation in Electoral Politics in the 1990s', *Transforming India: Social and Political Dynamics of Democracy*, ed. Francise Frankel et al., New Delhi: Oxford University Press, 2000, pp. 120–45.

8. R.S. Khare, *The Untouchable as Himself: Ideology, Identity and Pragmatism among the Lucknow Chamars*, Cambridge: Cambridge University Press, 1984, p. 129.

9. Gail Omvedt, *Dalit Visions: Tracts for the Times*, Delhi: Orient Longman, 1995, p. 87.

10. Vijay Nambissan, *Bihar is in the Eye of the Beholder*, 2003, p. 21.

11. Quoted in Seema Mustafa's biography of V.P. Singh, *The Lonely Prophet: A Political Biography of V.P. Singh*, Delhi: Wiley Eastern, 1996, p. 191.

12. The Bahujan Samaj Party's most popular slogan is: 'Brahman, bania, thakur chor, Baki sab DS4' (Dalit Shoshit Samaj Sangharsh Samiti). It has gone much beyond other dalit organizations by projecting itself not as a 'dalit party' but as a bahujan party of dalits, non-Brahmans, and minorities. See Gail Omvedt, 'The Anti-Caste Movement and the Discourse of Power', *Region, Religion, Caste, Gender and Culture in Contemporary India*, ed. T.V. Sathyamurthy, New Delhi: Oxford University Press, 1996, pp. 344–6.

13. Translation: 'We vote you rule, this cannot go on. Through the vote we will take the posts of prime minister and chief minister; through reservations we will take the posts of district magistrate and superintendent police.'

14. Oliver Mendelsohn and Manca Vicziam, *The Untouchables: Subordination, Poverty and the State in India*, Cambridge: Cambridge University Press, 1998, p. 223.

15. Gail Omvedt, 'Kanshi Ram and the Bahujan Samaj Party', in *Caste and Class in India*, ed. K.L. Sharma, Jaipur: Rawat, 1994, p. 163.

16. Interviews with dalit IAS officials in August 1997 in Lucknow highlighted this point.

17. The OBCs and dalits comprised 231 Members of the Legislative Assembly (MLAs) in the 422-member Uttar Pradesh Assembly in 1993. By contrast, Brahman MLAs declined from 23 per cent in 1980 to 10 per cent in 1993. Their participation expanded with the extension of reservations to the panchayats in 1993 after a rapid census ordered by Mulayam Singh Yadav to estimate the

caste-wise configuration. Equally significant is the changing composition of the Cabinet. The percentage of upper castes which, according to a study conducted by a member of the Uttar Pradesh Backward Classes Commission, was as high as 64.7 per cent at the time of Chief Minister Sripat Misra, had come down to 50 per cent under Mulayam Singh Yadav in 1990, while non-upper caste representation increased from 35 per cent to 50 per cent. See H.S. Verma, Ram Singh, and Jay Singh, 'Power Sharing: Exclusivity and Exclusion in a Mega State', Monograph presented to a panel on 'Deprivation, Backwardness and Social Transformation of the Backward Classes', Twentieth All-India Sociological Conference, Bangalore, 1993, p. 14.

18. On this, see Marc Galanter, 'Group Membership and Group Preferences in India', in his *Law and Society in Modern India*, New Delhi: Oxford University Press, 1989, p. 133.

19. Kanchan Chandra, 'Why does the Bahujan Samaj Party Succeed? A Case Study of the BSP in Hoshiarpur', Paper presented at the annual meeting of the Association of Asian Studies, Washington DC, March 1998.

20. Interview with S.R. Darapuri, Inspector General of Police, Economic Intelligence Wing, UP government.

21. This points was emphasized in a number of interviews with SC officers in Lucknow. The point was repeatedly made by S.R. Lakha, Cane Commissioner, UP Government in an interview in Lucknow, 22 August 1997. He is also the Secretary of the Uttar Pradesh IAS Association.

22. Interview with Rohit Nandan, Director of Information, UP Government, 22 August 1998.

23. Caste differences in educational levels are even now very marked. Widespread illiteracy makes it difficult for disadvantaged groups to ensure that their needs receive due attention in public debates and resource allocation. Education is an important tool for effective participation in democratic politics. Yet, there were no political campaigns or bold initiatives to improve basic education in the state. On the contrary, there is evidence of a serious decline in real per capita expenditure on education by 20 per cent between 1991-2 and 1993-4. See K. Seeta Prabhu, 'Structural Adjustment and Financing of Elementary Education: The Indian Experience', *Journal of Educational Learning and Administration*, no. 9, 1995, p. 37.

24. For instance, child survival, mortality, and literacy levels are below almost all other states, Jean Drèze and Haris Gazdar point to three social failures: low levels of education, the restricted role of women in society, and the poor functioning of public services. See Jean Drèze and Haris Gazdar, 'Uttar Pradesh: The Burden of Inertia', pp. 40–61.

25. Ibid.

26. For a discussion of caste mobilization based on a critique of caste hierarchy, see Nandini Gooptu, 'Caste Deprivation and Politics: The Untouchables in UP Towns', in *Dalit Movements and the Meaning of Labour in India*, ed. Peter Robb, New Delhi: Oxford University Press, 1993.

27. See Hasan, *Quest for Power*, especially chap. 4.

28. Mulayam Singh Yadav argues that his party suffered too much under Mayawati's chief ministership for him to consider a patch-up with her. Mayawati feels that Yadav's open opposition to the Atrocities Against Dalits Act during her term in office would harm the party's attempts to consolidate its political base.

29. Interview with Director of Information, UP Government, Lucknow, 22 August 1997.
30. Kanchan Chandra and Chandrika Parmar, 'Party Strategies in Uttar Pradesh Assembly Elections, 1996', *Economic and Political Weekly*, vol. 32, no. 5, 1997, pp. 219–20.

24 | Transfer of Power?
Politics of Mass Mobilization in
Uttar Pradesh

T WO STORIES are being told about India. One focuses on the changes in the state and the political system. This is a story of the erosion of political institutions and a crisis of governance. Political parties, parliament, and the public sector are all in a state of decline and disrepair. The solutions proposed often stress the necessity of strengthening the relative weight of civil society vis-à-vis the state.[1] The second storyline concentrates on the extension of democracy, participation, and inclusion. This line tends to emphasize the dramatic surge in participation of the lower orders of society signalling the expansion of democracy.[2] The changes in the institutional realm that are linked to the democratic surge are, therefore, not an indication of failed modernization; rather, they point to the vernacularization of politics and the entry of the beliefs and interests of lower orders of society that could not be articulated under the ideological hegemony of the urban and English-educated politicians of the Nehru era.[3] Thus it has often been argued that the new phase marks the coming of age of Indian democracy. It indicates the different character of India's democratic experiment from that of the west. Espoused by many scholars, this account has stressed that changes brought about by the dissemination of the ideas of social justice and rights from the 1980s.[4] Different versions of this storyline note the defeat of Indira Gandhi's emergency regime in the 1977 elections as a turning point which brought about a decisive shift in the form and content of democracy. It established the importance of the vote and representative institutions of

* I am grateful to N.C. Saxena and Ravi Srivastava for suggestions of materials; to Imtiaz Ahmad, John Harris, and Craig Jeffrey for extremely helpful comments on an earlier version of this paper; and to Adil Tyabji for his excellent editorial advice.

government to give voice to popular demands of a kind that had not hitherto been able to disturb the order and tranquility of the corridors of power. This notwithstanding, the influx of new entrants from the lower orders has not led to effective control of the agenda of elections.

In an attempt to understand the growth of political democratization, this chapter critically examines the trajectories of mass mobilization in Uttar Pradesh (UP), which has been the site of the most recent phase of political democratization in India, the so-called second democratic upsurge.[5] In UP, lower castes/classes have been mobilized politically in at least three different ways: peasant politics, reservation politics, and the 'social engineering' strategy of Hindu nationalism. The rise of the Janata Dal (1977-89), Samajwadi Party (SP), and Bahujan Samaj Party (BSP) in the 1990s transformed the political landscape. From the late 1980s a significant political churning was under way, which brought into play the numerous lower castes to restructure the power and caste and class privileges of the upper castes. It became difficult to conceive of a political regime that can deny them representation. At the same time, the BJP's growth and its ability to win power by exploiting divisions between lower caste parties had profound implications for the course of mass politics and development in this keystone state. The state of UP sends 85 MPs to the Lok Sabha, making it politically the most crucial state for the formation of the central government in New Delhi. The success of the BJP in UP was central to its realization of political power when it formed the coalition government in 1998, and its ability to maintain support there was of great assistance throughout its term in government.

This chapter looks at the three competing, and at times, intersecting strategies of mass mobilization already mentioned (peasant politics, reservation politics, and the 'social engineering' strategy of Hindu nationalist politics) in order to situate the lower caste challenge to upper caste control of the state and public power, and the upper caste counter-resistance to contain the effect of this challenge to their dominance. Political democratization in UP has created a situation in which new forms of mobilization, while enabling the emergence of new constituencies, finds those engaged in it unable to deal with the effects. Drawing substantially on studies of politics and society in UP, this chapter explore the nature and contradictions of mass mobilization, the extent of which is significantly influenced by caste and community identities, and the effect of these contradictions on governance and development. The argument is constructed around a broad question that has two parts: (a) can lower-caste politics and the entry of lower castes into educational institutions and administrative services, and their claims for growing share of political power, lead to social and political change? (b)

Can greater participation of the lower castes in legislature and government push government policy to address the concerns of the poor?

The process of political democratization in India is historically diverse. This diversity leaves scope for several patterns of interconnected political and social change within a similar framework of institutions resulting in differences in the democratic functioning of different states. A contextual approach would be useful in understanding the regional dynamics of democratization, most importantly, the timing and approach through which marginalized groups are incorporated into the political arena, the political alliances and alignments that are available, and the transformations these can work on the patterns of stable governance.[6] These configurations differ across regions. In south India the mobilization of the non-brahman castes happened earlier than in the north. Though backward caste movements in Tamil Nadu and Karnataka were not radical, the political mobilization of lower castes was an important vehicle for social transformation, the consequent decrease in social indignities, and the rapid displacement of upper castes from positions of power in the administration and legislatures. The establishment of a political community, based on a single language, and the transformation of its non-brahman ideology into an anti-northern Tamil nationalism facilitated these changes. Lower caste parties in northern India were unable to adopt this strategy and therefore the trajectory of lower caste politics in the north had to be different. This phenomenon needs to be understood in terms of specific histories, including the distinct social histories of mass politics.[7]

Conditions in Uttar Pradesh

Uttar Pradesh is India's largest state, and one of the most socially and economically backward in the northern heartland. Most of the states in north India are comparable to medium-sized countries. Indeed, the population of UP, which is believed to have crossed 160 million in 1997, is equal to the most populous countries of the world. Only six countries, China, India, the US, Indonesia, Russia, and Brazil have populations larger than that of UP, yet the state has lagged behind in terms of economic and social development. In the 1990s the annual growth rate of gross domestic product was estimated to have been 3.5 per cent, the third lowest amongst the major states, as against the combined state domestic product growth of 5.94 per cent per annum.[8]

The caste and class structure of UP is distinct. The twice-born upper castes account for 20 per cent of the population, indeed, the brahmans alone account for over 10 per cent of the entire brahman category in India.

Dominated by brahmans, the caste hierarchy here is the most elaborated. Caste status, economic position, and political power historically overlapped in most parts of the state. The backward castes or Other Backward Classes (OBCs) in contemporary UP, which account for 35–40 per cent of the population, span a wide cultural and structural arch, including at one extreme the dominant landowning peasant castes, and at the other extreme, the many poor artisan and service castes living just above the pollution and poverty line. The poorer jatis among them are described as the Most Backward Classes (MBCs), which constitute 26 per cent. At the bottom of the hierarchy are the former untouchables, officially known as the Scheduled Castes (SCs). They perform the most menial and arduous jobs and the majority continues to depend upon wage labour. Lower caste parties have been successful in incorporating some members of the lower castes into government.

Though there have been no major popular actions or mobilization of the poor, UP is a highly politicized state where politics means capture and control of power. By the early 2000s, two forces wielded an important influence in state politics: Hindu nationalism and parties that represent the lower castes and classes. The Congress dominated party competition for close to three decades, but since its decline in 1989 the BJP benefited considerably. Even though a mainstay of Hindu revivalism and the citadel of the Ayodhya movement, the BJP failed to establish its political supremacy in UP, notwithstanding its being in power at the centre from 1998 to 2004 and having had several stints in power in all the other states of north India except Bihar.

Strategies of Mass Politics

Historically, UP was a stronghold of the upper castes. Forming nearly 20 per cent of the population, the upper castes were over-represented in the political sphere. Their domination was particularly strong in education, the professions, and the Congress. In most parts of the state, these castes controlled business, professional, and white-collar employment. The politicization of caste identities, the increasing participation of the lower castes in the political process, and the dramatic decline of the Congress party therefore marked the history of democratic politics. These processes may be traced back to economic and political shifts occurring since the late 1960s. At that time, the central government shifted the direction of development policy from a state-led model of industrial growth to a more dedicated drive to improve agricultural production. This was the beginning of the Green Revolution technologies associated with an emphasis in increasing agricultural production through price incentives and technological change. One of the effects of this shift in policy was the rising prosperity of sections of the peasantry in the fertile areas of the state. This upwardly mobile peasantry belonged principally to the intermediate and backward castes. The initial change occurred in the 1970s when these groups began to enter the legislative assemblies in large numbers with the backing of the socialists. These groups posed the first serious challenge to Congress power, questioning too, for the first time, the upper caste monopoly of the public sphere.

The two principal forms of mass mobilization, symbolized by peasant politics and reservation politics, worked to displace the upper caste urban establishment from its positions of power. The first, initiated in the late 1960s under the leadership of Charan Singh, sought to mobilize the cultivating classes and the second was initiated by the socialist leader Ram Manohar Lohia who focused on caste identities and reservations for the lower castes in public employment and political parties. Restructuring state power and institutions was the principal concern of both initiatives. The proponents of a rural strategy mobilized all those engaged in cultivation primarily on the basis of socio-economic demands, while the strategists of reservation politics forged an alliance of the non-elite groups on the basis of caste quotas to dislodge the upper castes. Lohia's line cut through the urban-rural sectors as well as the caste system. The social groups targeted by both came from the ranks of peasants and OBCs, but significantly both treated them as an economically undifferentiated social category. Initially the two strategies complemented each other, though in the end caste identities trumped peasant politics. Together, from the 1980s these, two strategies contributed to the rise of lower castes in north Indian politics.[9]

From the 1970s, the peasantry of north India emerged as a major constituency in state and national politics. Rich farmers and surplus producers exerted a strong influence over government policy, and Charan Singh himself employed the growing power of the peasant lobby to great effect in struggles within the Janata coalition after it assumed power in 1977.[10] Shortly after Charan Singh's death in 1987, farmer politics in north India was to find its resurgence under the Bharatiya Kisan Union (BKU), a non-party organization led by Mahendra Singh Tikait, a rural jat leader from the prosperous cane and wheat growing region of western UP.[11] Of the various features of Charan Singh's peasant discourse, the one most emphasized was the rural-urban dichotomy.[12] This dichotomy was intended to highlight the urban bias of development policies that have resulted in a gap between urban people who work for the state and industrial sectors, and rural people who work in the agricultural sector. This duality succeeded in combining a variety of discontents experienced by different classes of the rural population into a unitary framework. Their actions and agitations caused a modification of agricultural policies in many states, and several of their demands soon became part of official policy.

Even so, there were other fault lines in rural society that were ignored. The strategy was not designed to include all sections of rural society, and in actuality the structural tensions and conflicts between the rich farmers and lower classes could not be resolved. Some of these tensions overlapped with the conflict between backward castes and dalits. Moreover, it was not just the divide between owner-cultivators and agricultural labourers that caused tension. Even within the category of landowners there were differences between large farmers and small and medium ones. Then, amongst the rich farmers there were differences between Jats and OBCs: the latter saw the BKU as a means for Jat assertion of their power in the countryside. Notwithstanding these contradictions, which were a common feature of farmers' movements in different parts of the country, they were able to achieve some of their aims, as ruling parties found it easy to accommodate such demands as they made than to deal with larger issues of structural reform. However, the package of policies included price guarantees of output and subsidies or inputs, which principally benefited rich farmers. At the same time, it also made them more dependent upon government policies and programmes.

The second approach to mass mobilization took shape around the demand for reserved quotas in government. From the 1960s, caste and caste quotas were seen as an instrument for social equality and self-respect.[13] Reservation was seen as the only way of securing representation for groups who might otherwise have no presence in the political process and public employment. Historically, UP has had the shortest history of caste-based positive discrimination policies. A modest quota scheme was introduced in 1978, but it was discontinued owing to objections over the criteria for identification of beneficiaries. The stimulus for change came between 1989 and 1991, a conjuncture defined by three major changes in Indian politics: Mandal, Mandir, and Market. The almost simultaneous occurrence of these three events congealed the scale and complexity of transition even as it provided, at the same time, an opportunity for realignments in state and national politics. All three offered the prospect of creating a new cleavage structure and thus new forms of mobilization.[14] In the end, all the three cleavages could not be activated and caste remained the epicentre of political change.

The turning point was V.P. Singh's decision to implement the Mandal Commission Report, which had in 1980 recommended extension of the system of reserved jobs in central government from only the SCs and Scheduled Tribes (STs) to a broader collection of socially and economically backward classes. There was little public response in south India where the battle against reservations had already been fought and lost.[15] However, in north India, upper caste students fought a high profile campaign against the extension of reservations to lower castes. At the same time, the students feared that their hopes of gaining government jobs would be thwarted by a coalition of lower castes, which they were largely shaping themselves by provoking a new cleavage between the upper and lower castes. They wanted to abolish all reservations including reservations for SCs. They protested against the new quota that would deprive them of government jobs. As employment opportunities are extremely inadequate, and conflicts have been amplified because of rising levels of education that add to the force of competition, government jobs are sought after as they provide much needed security and decent wages or salary. Hence, it is considered a desirable path of upward mobility in an underdeveloped state.

The alternative strategy, associated with the second form of mobilization, that is, caste politics, arrived with the growing influence of the BSP founded in 1984, which attempted to mobilize the lower castes by promising them a share of political power by their own caste/community members. Following the breakdown of the Congress in the 1980s, the BSP became a major partner in an anti-upper caste coalition government in 1992–5 and the BSP-led government which was established in 1995 and 1997 under the leadership of Mayawati. By 1996, the BSP had managed to win 59 seats in the legislative assembly and notched up an impressive 20 per cent of the vote, which was much higher than the Congress vote.

At this point, it seems useful to draw a distinction between elites that mobilize support through particularistic, local, or regional strategies and those that mobilize a mass base in national society, either by appealing to the citizenry in general or to a particular class. Since independence, the SCs supported the Congress party, which historically mobilized the needs and aspirations of the lower castes within an overarching framework of philanthropic compromise such that their potential antagonism was neutralized. The Congress focused on general economic issues and ignored cultural and social ones. The BSP criticized these features of Congress politics. First, the BSP promised political representation to dalits, an aspiration neglected by the Congress. Under Congress rule, despite the importance of the dalit vote, they achieved very little representation in the government and party organization. In other words, the significance of the dalit vote did not translate into perceptible influence for individual members in the organization or government. This approach was noteworthy because its success was not contingent on mass mobilization, but derived from capture of state power via anti-high caste propaganda, emphasizing the fulfilment of the reserved quota and demanding more positions for members of the SCs in government. Its aim was to capture state power for the oppressed majority by opposing caste oppression rather than setting out social and economic policies of redistribution.

The ascent of Mayawati to the office of chief minister in less than a decade of SC mobilization changed the situation for dalits.[16] During her two stints in office, and especially her second term, Mayawati succeeded in building a new political presence for them. She sought to make good the promise of empowerment by filling the reserved quota and appointing members of the SCs to important positions in government. For example, SC officers replaced all the upper castes functionaries holding important positions, such as those of chief secretary and the chief minister's private secretary. This change provoked resentment and, correlatively, the dalit assertion polarized the upper and lower castes. Through this strategy the BSP launched a new phase in the mobilization of lower castes in the region. It did however fail in terms of its own stated objective of creating a wider alliance of the 'bahujan samaj' (majority).[17] It succeeded in consolidating dalits but appeared to depend excessively on the support of a single caste.

Nonetheless, it changed state policy in a number of other ways. The programme of 'Ambedkarization' and the introduction of the Ambedkar village schemes to provide special government assistance to villages with a high proportion of dalits appear to have been significant policy initiatives in this particular context. Local studies of the BSP have reported a substantial enhancement in the access of SC members to education and basic services. The enrolment rate in higher education of SCs in 1995 was higher than the general population.[18] Reservation for SCs in public employment has increased local employment opportunities for the poorest castes.[19] Though the BSP's stint in power did not entail any structural changes in the economy to benefit the vast numbers of rural poor, it improved their political confidence, living standards, and representation of certain SCs within local bureaucracies.[20] Their efforts to marshal government intervention to settle disputes over land rights or social abuse and violence were taken more seriously when they renegotiated their relationship with state officials through a SC officer or the pradhan.[21] It forced government officers to pay more than lip service to the needs of the low caste poor.

Undeniably, the rise of lower castes has altered UP's stagnant politics. As lower caste leaders expressed increased unhappiness with the widespread practice of not filling reserved vacancies because there were no 'qualified candidates', governments have had to find ways of reducing these blockages.

Rules were introduced at the central and state levels so that every seventh or eighth new recruit had to be from a SC or ST.[22] Not surprisingly, the gap between the upper and lower castes narrowed and the share of lower castes shot up during the 1980s and 1990s when lower caste parties began to grow and acquire power. This can be seen from the major increase in the number of lower caste legislators and senior civil servants in influential government positions. The share of upper caste legislators in all the legislative assemblies and national parliament has been declining while that of the lower castes rising.[23] In the early 2000s, the lower caste legislators formed the single largest group in the state assemblies of UP and Bihar. At the same time, the rise of lower castes provoked strong hostility of upper castes, and to counter their growth, the upper castes rallied behind the BJP.[24]

The BJP-led Ayodhya movement, the greatest mass mobilization in UP's post–independent history, epitomizes the third form of mass politics.[25] The BJP was the principal gainer at the cost of the Congress and the divisions among lower caste parties. The rise of the BJP occurred between 1989 and 1991 when the BJP projected itself as a pro-Hindu party that supported the 'imagined community' of Hindus. Since the destruction of the Ayodhya mosque, the BJP shifted its strategy from ethnic mobilization to 'social engineering' in order to mobilize broad-based support. The principal targets of this strategy were the backward castes and dalits. However, its core support comes from the members of the upper castes, the majority of whom had rallied behind the BJP since 1990: its support among the backward castes was comparably weaker in this period.

Until the late 1990s, the BJP had chosen not to use caste explicitly as an organizing category that divides Hindus. It opted for what Christophe Jaffrelot called 'indirect mobilization', that is, forging alliances with parties representing the lower castes.[26] An attempt to mobilize the lower castes as a part of the Hindu constituency was made during the Ayodhya movement, which in the words of L.K. Advani 'succeeded in sublimating caste tensions'. However, the support gained then was lost after the demolition of the Babri Masjid in December 1992. Many among the lower castes looked at the assault as an upper caste backlash against the Mandal move initiated by the Janata Dal government. This resulted in an alliance of the SP and the BSP that compelled the BJP leadership to concentrate its attention on splitting the lowest castes. This strategy succeeded in 1995, breaking the SP–BSP alliance forged in the 1993 elections and bringing down the Mulayam Singh government. The BJP then threw its weight behind the BSP, which allowed Mayawati to come to power as chief minister. This proved important in checking the consolidation of the lower castes, as the cooperation of the backwards and dalits presented a formidable challenge to the BJP which could have potentially prevented it from coming to power.

Working in small town upper caste milieus, the BJP on the whole kept away from caste reform. However, the upper caste bias was a handicap in the wake of lower caste mobilization, the party being unable to ignore the lower caste phenomenon that was conspicuous in its strongholds. To endorse it would however have compromised its traditional support among upper castes and would have implied an acceptance of internal divisions in the Hindu nation, which the Rashtriya Swayamsevak Sangh (RSS) had laboured against for 70 years. In the years after the Mandal Commission, they had to make gestures of accommodation towards the lower castes, practicing their own brand of 'Mandalization', inducting a growing number of lower caste cadres in important party positions, and assigning them assembly constituency nominations. Several OBC leaders of the BJP have espoused social engineering: bringing upper caste members and backwards on a common platform. While this policy has enabled the BJP to broaden its base, the leaders of the RSS have opposed it, even though it helped the party to extend its support base, but this opposition was limited to the upper castes. There is undoubtedly a tension between the BJP leadership's advocacy of social engineering and the traditional RSS view based on 'varna' hierarchy, which questioned the notion of social engineering.[27]

On the whole, Hindu nationalists were increasingly caught between giving a greater share of power to the OBCs and emphasizing Hindu unity over caste interests.[28] Though the BJP commanded considerable support from sections of OBCs, it remained a bastion of upper castes. The upper castes' votes constantly polarized in favour of the BJP from the time when the lower caste parties became key players subsequent to the Congress' terminal decline.

As a predominantly upper caste party, whose leaders had little sympathy for lower caste aspirations, the interests of the upper caste middle class had been over-represented within Hindu nationalism. From the late 1980s, the BJP received its greatest support from the middle classes who disapproved of the reservation system and wanted to defend their control over the government and, above all, government jobs, which had been traditionally held by brahmans and banias. Arguably the Mandal decision was as important as the Ayodhya movement in rallying the upper caste middle class support around the BJP in the 1990s.[29] This group, which included all the upper castes, shared the BJP's disquiet about the rise of dalits and OBCs: that is, its unease with the social depth of democracy. The major appeal of the BJP for this group was that it ensured the status quo and thus their sustained domination over government in the face of the stiff lower caste attack on their supremacy. The extent of its support for lower castes and caste quotas varied, depending upon calculations relating to the maximization of support, even though some of its local leaders were in the forefront of the anti–Mandal agitations that had rocked UP towns in 1990. While the BJP did not downplay the divisions in its ranks, it managed to weaken them by winning over some sections of the lower castes to its side. It is well known that the kurmis, lodhs, and jats have previously backed the party. Faced with tough competition from the SP and the BSP, both of which have given the lower castes a share of power in proportion to their population, the BJP government in July 2001 proposed a quota within the quota (15 per cent) of reservations for the MBCs and scheduled to win them over with the promise of government jobs.

Impact of Mass Mobilization

This chapter now turns to the question of whether the rise of the lower castes has significantly changed democracy. Electoral competition between parties and political participation is flourishing, and political power has moved downward, developments that cannot be dismissed lightly.[30] As a result, the political elite is not monolithic. In consequence, politics and movements of the Right are as active as those of lower castes and this has counterbalanced and defused the gains made by the lower castes. This aspect has often been ignored in discussions of the dalit upsurge.

The politics of 'presence' has undoubtedly produced a shift in the balance of political power in governments and legislatures in UP.[31] Within this form of representation, the political actor claims to act on behalf of his own caste, religion or linguistic group, or even simply for himself. This is distinct from the earlier elite form of representation in which the elite self-consciously acted on behalf of a larger group of whom they were not a part and whose identity or interests they did not share. But checkmating the further advance of this strategy and its capacity to shape the polity is the disunity breaking their ranks. Castes classified as OBCs came together in the early 1990s in response to the upper caste opposition against Mandal, but such unity has vanished.[32] This is partly because the rise of the OBCs has been in effect the rise of the yadavs and to some extent the kurmis, as their share in public employment and MPs and MLAs bear witness. This is not entirely surprising because the yadavs are more numerous and relatively more educated than other OBCs, and were also the most favoured by the government of Mulayam Singh Yadav.[33] A number of authors have noted the ability of yadavs to manipulate the process of recruitment in government employment,[34] and several other reports highlighted the yadavization of the police in UP in the mid-1990s and argued that they were being systematically favoured in recruitment.[35]

Such manoeuvring was not surprising even as in the past Charan Singh's 'kisan' strategy was perceived by jats as a means of promoting their interests. Still, there is a basic difference. Parties and campaigns led by Charan Singh had seen the construction of a farmer identity, which both made use of and at the same time transcended caste cleavages to create a commonality of rural interests. This was why the ideological and intellectual direction given by Singh's critique of the dominant models of development succeeded in mobilizing a coalition of rural groups under an anti-government populism.[36] The fundamentals of this discourse posited a sharp difference between Bharat and India, and this in turn was built on a critique of the urban bias of development. However, the proponents of peasant politics came primarily from the ranks of rich peasants who deployed this discourse to promote their own interests and held back lower castes. This edifice was weighed down by the social strains that permeate north Indian society and was built on prevailing exclusions and intersection of caste and class rule.[37] In consequence, these rural coalitions broke down on caste lines, and in time were outstripped by the quota politics of socialists who ascribed inequality entirely to caste and promoted reservation in government jobs as the solution to all forms of deprivation and inequality. To put the point differently, quota politics succeeded because political under-representation tends to aggravate economic deprivation in a highly politicized state such as UP. Furthermore, the Janata Dal government implemented the reservation policy, and thus established the capacity of these parties to offer political representation in contrast to their opponents who were unable to do so. By giving lower castes a share in power, caste politics addressed the critical issue of the representational blockage in political institutions.[38]

However, political gains do not correspond to the substantial caste-based mobilization during the past two decades. It has not given lower castes the leverage and political advantage that they have gained in south India. In comparison with UP, the non-brahmin movement in the south Indian states institutionalized participation at an early stage, and developed sufficiently gradually to allow upper castes time to adjust to their loss of power: this small minority of upper castes moved into the commercial and industrial sectors, central government jobs, and many of them migrated to US, while the erstwhile backwards rapidly rose to become the dominant community and the vast majority of the population were covered by reservations. In contrast, in UP the members of the upper castes form a fifth and the brahmans nearly 10 per cent of the population. The large proportion of upper castes made it harder to displace them completely and they have stayed to fight back. Furthermore, upper castes, particularly brahmans, regard government jobs as their bequest, especially since alternative opportunities of employment in UP's sluggish economy are limited.

Challenges of Development and Governance

What has been the impact of lower caste mobilization on development and governance, especially in the area of poverty alleviation? The inseparable links between social and political structures and inadequate development during the Congress era I have detailed elsewhere.[39] Principally, Congress governments failed to establish a developmental state (an issue that deserves a separate analysis). On the other hand, the post-Congress governments have not been able to reverse this tendency. The incorporation into the political system of lower caste elites and members of the scheduled castes has apparently done little to reduce the enormous social and economic disparities that persist in the unequal social order. This raises a basic question: if there are so many lower caste politicians and bureaucrats, why is this not reflected in state policies to promote the well-being of lower castes and classes?

As far as the development effort is concerned, facts speak for themselves. UP is the largest state where growth has been slowest.[40] A chronically disadvantaged state, UP is home to five of India's 14 most backward districts. It has the largest concentration of poor and the worst infrastructure and social indicators of development. UP's per capita income is below the national average: the third lowest ahead only of Orissa and Bihar. Though foodgrains production in the state has decelerated sharply in the 1990s, UP is the largest producer of foodgrain and oilseeds, and grows about 50 per cent of the total sugarcane, with agriculture accounting for 40 per cent of the state's gross domestic state product and 75 per cent of its total employment.

In understanding the question of public policy and distribution of public goods, it is important to note that the persistence of poverty is in part a consequence of UP's poor economic performance. Economic growth has decelerated in UP since 1991, even as growth has accelerated in other states. In 1950, UP's per capita income was almost equal to the all-India average, and since then it has declined to 65 per cent of that of the country. According to the World Bank, 'The gap between UP and the rest of India widened substantially in the 1990s as annual growth in per capita income slowed down to less than 1 per cent.'[41] Employment and growth depends upon factors such as the level of human resource development, the quality of infrastructure, and the public policy environment, all of which are poorly developed in UP. The state government has failed to raise the revenue to match the growing needs of the population: development expenditure has declined whereas non-developmental expenditure on administrative services rose from Rs. 3,399 crore in 1999–2000 to Rs. 4,282 crore in 2000–1. Significantly, the administrative expenditure in the state is equal to the combined expenditure on agriculture and allied activities, irrigation and flood control, rural employment, special areas programme, industries, minerals, water supply and sanitation. Consequently, there is an absolute reduction in expenditure on industries, irrigation, water supply, sanitation, and urban development.[42]

The state has made little progress in reducing poverty since the late 1980s, and in 2001, over 41 per cent of the 160 million population still lived below the poverty line. Between 1957–8 and 1987–8, UP achieved a reduction in poverty of 13.6 per cent (from 55 per cent to 41.6 per cent). This process slowed down to 0.2 per cent from 1987–8 to 1993–4 whereas the rest of the country achieved a reduction in poverty of 3.2 per cent.[43] The accelerated economic growth in some states from the early 1990s has left UP lagging behind the rapidly developing states of Gujarat, Maharashtra, West Bengal, Tamil Nadu, Madhya Pradesh, and Rajasthan, its growth actually decelerating.[44] As per capita income growth continued to be very low, poverty may not have declined at all but the low economic growth meant that employment did not keep pace with population growth, wages remained low, and opportunities for social mobility for the lower classes were limited. In general, development policies have not substantially reduced inequalities in terms of food, education, health care, and productive assets.[45]

This has meant that resources for the investment in public goods— schools, health services, drinking water—expanded slowly. There is substantial evidence that public services and programmes, particularly those meant for the poor, work hopelessly in this state. The Comptroller and Auditor General of India (CAG) Report of 1999 highlighted numerous irregularities in the implementation of anti-poverty programmes, such as the Employment Assurance Scheme (EAS), Jawahar Rozgar Yojana (JRY), and the Million Wells Scheme. A review of implementation of programmes by Audit, as well as a survey carried out by ORG-MARG, revealed that the funds available for the programme were grossly inadequate.[46] These irregularities included the diversion of funds, a lower wage component than prescribed, and delayed payment of wages. It was noted too that these were below the prescribed minimum wages, in many cases there was improper engagement of contractors and maintenance of muster rolls, diversion or misutilization of the grain component of EAS wages, etc.[47] The upshot of these irregularities and corruption was lower employment than planned, lower remuneration to labourers than justified, and non-employment of female labourers. Unsurprisingly, the state's performance in the JRY was not up to scratch. Provision for rural employment through schemes such as the JRY forms only 1 per cent of the revenue budget.[48] This is clearly the case in rural development programmes where leakage is estimated to be between 20 and 70 per cent. Micro-studies reveal similar leakages, a lower wage labour component than stipulated, and panchayats playing a negligible role in project planning and supervision.[49] Kripa Shankar's study of JRY in two districts reports leakage to the extent of 40 per cent and that the wage component was as low as 29 per cent when it should have been 60 per cent.[50]

It was the same story with the Public Distribution System (PDS). Conceived of as a measure to ensure availability of essential commodities, PDS 'failed to function optimally'. In spite of the high incidence of poverty, the state government did not fully utilize PDS on account of tardy implementation. It did not lift even half of all that was allocated to it.[51] According to the CAG Report (1999), slum dwellers in four of the ten test checked districts were not targeted thus depriving them of the benefit of the scheme. Food security could not be ensured because of 'poor offtake and poor per capita distribution, financial mismanagement and inadequate enforcement'.[52] It was estimated that there were at least 20 per cent bogus cards. A number of other inefficiencies and issues of mismanagement were noted in the report, which also documents extensive losses due to storage, embezzlement, theft, and misappropriation. This is confirmed by a study conducted by the Tata Economic Consultancy Services, which also found extensive leakage due to the diversion of a significant portion of the subsidized foodgrain to the open market.[53] The leakages were estimated to be 46 per cent in wheat, 49 per cent in rice, and 36 per cent sugar. Some of these findings have been corroborated by other studies.[54]

As is well known, UP ranks low with regard to human development. A few demographic and development characteristics will indicate the nature of challenges that confronted the state. UP's performance in female literacy was abysmal, and after Rajasthan, it had made the least progress in narrowing the gender gap by 2001.[55] In 1991, 74.7 per cent suffered the indignity of illiteracy in UP. If UP were treated as a separate country for the gender development index, it would rank 123rd out of the 137 countries on the index, which adjusts for human development index.[56] The midday meal scheme designed to increase enrolments and reduce dropouts failed to set any target for enrolment and attendance during the implementation from

1995 to 1999 of the Nutritional Support for Primary Education Scheme.[57] The scheme envisaged distribution of foodgrains directly to schools after being lifted from the Food Corporation of India (FCI) godowns. The CAG Report (1999) found that the state government introduced a middle level of stocking of foodgrains at transport agency godowns resulting in misuse and diversion of grains.[58] Poor governance, increased corruption, declining performance, and lack of concern for the poor all of which manifested in ineffective public programmes and delivery, and inept and wasteful public expenditure, were the key factors impinging on UP's growth and development.[59]

In Salman Rushdie's novel *The Moor's Last Sigh*, one of the characters offers his definition of modern Indian democracy ('one man one bribe') and of what he calls the Indian Theory of Relativity ('everything for relatives'). Like many things written about India, this is an exaggeration, but it would appear that the second part of the definition provides a fitting description of UP's contemporary political culture where political representatives do everything for themselves and their supporters. Several commentators have documented and criticized UP's record of governance. While doing fieldwork in western UP, Akhil Gupta was struck by how frequently the theme of corruption cropped up in the everyday conversations of villagers.[60] He writes:

Most of the stories the men told each other when the day's work was done and small groups gathered at habitual places to shoot the breeze, had to do with corruption and the 'state'. Sometimes the discussion dealt with how someone had managed to outwit an official who wanted to collect a bribe, at other times with 'the going price' to get an electrical connection for a new tube well connection or to obtain a loan to buy a buffalo, at still other times with which official had been transferred or who was likely to be appointed to a certain position and who replaced, with who had willingly helped his caste members without taking a bribe, and so on.[61]

Paul Brass reached the same conclusion in his exploration of social violence: the increased importance of political brokers located outside the state. Brass takes this argument further in charging that:

. . . rule in the countryside is not based on abstractions but on control over resources and safety. It is a Hobbesian world, in which security and safety are not provided by the state, but are themselves values—that is valued objects—integral to and inseparable from the struggle for power and influence.[62]

Since the 1980s, the expansion of state functions has increased bureaucratic control of the various schemes of production and distribution, even as the control over the IAS has gradually shifted to politicians.[63] As N.C. Saxena makes clear: 'to individuals who wanted to share the spoils and patronage, however, a price had to be paid in terms of obeisance to political bosses. Thus this period was characterized by both enhanced role of the state and enhanced control of politicians over bureaucracy'.[64] The politician–bureaucrat nexus has exploited the state machinery through rent-seeking behaviour for partisan ends.

Corruption and inefficiency is rampant. Corruption has overrun virtually every institution, including institutions such as the police and judiciary, which are supposed to take action against it. According to an *India Today* and ORG-MARG survey, UP was perceived to be the second most corrupt state after Bihar in 1997.[65] A report submitted to the UP Academy of Administration in 2000 found that UP was seen to be more prone to corruption than the rest of the country.[66] People rated the police department and the department of electric supply as the biggest problems facing the state because they were the most corrupt. Most importantly, citizens believed that corruption began at the top.[67] The well-deserved reputation of poor governance and insidious corruption was one of the causes for the persistence of backwardness and appalling implementation of anti-poverty schemes.[68] This is also why the state is seen as an unattractive destination for capital and investment.

The existence of widespread sleaze that favour the locally dominant groups in economic transactions and recruitment procedures are an important consequence of partisan governance. Speed money to get one's work done is so commonplace that it is not even thought to be a corrupt practice, it is money given 'to spur into action, a perfectly legal process that would not take place unless a monetary incentive was given'.[69] Corruption is hardly new; the new aspect is its 'brazenness and openness' .[70] Politics has become increasingly dependent on the manipulation of state patronage, electoral machines, and deals between different factions and groups within parties. In short, 'parallel authority structures and mafia gangs have emerged'.[71] Craig Jeffrey's research in the upper Doab region of western UP points to the existence of a 'shadow state', or informal networks of intermediaries, in establishing influence with politicians and the police force, and as a result, the richer strata coopt the local state to legitimate their access to state institutions and employment within state institutions.[72] It reveals clear differences regarding formal and informal access to land, access to lucrative non-agricultural jobs, and ties to the state apparatus, for instance, between the Jats and other groups. Meanwhile, the poorer strata find it impossible to buy police protection or assistance or to pay bribes to secure government jobs. While nearly everyone feels insecure, the poor are the most insecure owing to their vulnerable social and economic situation.

Despite mounting popular resentment against dismal governance and corruption there is not much popular pressure or many movements in civil society demanding greater accountability. It appears as though people have resigned themselves to their fate, preferring instead to approach politicians and legislators for favours. Indeed, politicians are important intermediaries between people and officials and links with a politician can help in obtaining assistance from government officials, or jobs or assistance from the constituency development funds at the disposal of Members of Parliament (MPs). There is thus very little ground-level mobilization outside the party system which could push the government and political leaders to adopt more responsive strategies towards the powerless; the very few initiatives for political and social reform which exist include the struggle for the Right to Information in Rajasthan or the Right to Education campaign in Madhya Pradesh. Evidently the emergence of broader social solidarities is impeded by the absence of non-electoral social mobilization and action.

Conclusion

This paper has advanced two principal arguments. By looking at electoral history and the growth of parties representing middle and lower castes it is clear that UP politics has become more competitive and democratic. The salience of caste identities and their role in political and electoral mobilization has been rightly recognized as a crucial element in the success of farmers' politics.[73] However, the rise of Hindu nationalism has been seen as a powerful force breaking peasant and caste solidarities. More recently, caste came to dominate politics; indeed, caste boundaries became more important than the Hindu-Muslim boundary (notwithstanding the pervasive influence of Hindu nationalist politics) or peasant solidarities. This was in part due to the electoral success of political parties representing backward and lower castes, which enlisted members of caste groups as part of caste coalitions. To that extent, lower caste politics succeeded in drawing hitherto disadvantaged groups into the political mainstream, and by giving them a share of political power they developed a vital stake in the democratic system. Owing to the success of these coalitions even BJP politicians had to cut deals with the SCs and OBCs by offering them a growing array of job reservations, special economic programmes, and sub-quotas within caste quotas rather than the mere promise of a grand Ram temple in Ayodhya.

Empirically, the reservations strategy has worked more effectively than its critics would have expected. As in many other states, there is greater emphasis on 'proportionality' in government employment than ever it was under Congress regimes, and a new emphasis on enforcing existing job reservations and proportional allocation of government resources such as the new 'Special Component Plans', which explicitly set aside a proportion of government expenditure for SCs and STs.[74] Large numbers of lower castes have gained government jobs through reservations, and an even larger number have the opportunity to participate in democratic politics. This is not just due to the large number of groups now eligible for reservations, but also due to better enforcement. Nevertheless, in its own terms it is flawed in three respects. It is not working to the advantage of lower caste women. OBCs form the single largest group in the UP legislative assembly, but there are hardly any OBC female MPs or Members of the Legislative Assembly (MLAs) even as OBC men have greatly increased their numbers in legislatures. Second, it is working to the benefit of the lower caste middle classes. It is clear that the communities as a whole have not benefited; rather, the members of some families who have managed to take advantage of what are, after all, still a very small number of jobs for a very large number of aspirants have benefited.[75] Finally, it has given rise to resentment among Muslims and the MBCs, who have been excluded from the emphasis on proportionality in government employment. Although the central government and UP government resisted extending the principle of proportionality in government employment and spending to Muslims, non–BJP governments have made some efforts to ensure that Muslims receive a share, if not their 'fair share', of jobs and economic programmes. The MBCs have not asserted their claims against the upper OBCs even as the Yadavs have benefited more than any other lower caste group from the policies pursued in UP.[76] They can make gains only when they are united on a common platform or when they unite to gain their share of power against the dominant OBCs. This is the major challenge ahead for the lower castes.[77]

The second argument relates to regime change and the impact of mass mobilization on governance and development. While the two models of peasant and caste mobilization have challenged upper caste/ class domination, this has not necessarily promoted policies or public expenditure for services that benefit the lower castes or implementation of development policies and programmes that address the vital concerns of the poor. There are three likely reasons why the incorporation of members of lower castes into governments and legislatures has not been accompanied by a corresponding increase in the welfare of deprived groups. First, conflicts between disadvantaged groups and the social fragmentation following the collapse of the Congress created circumstances in which the Congress strategy of domination and accommodation based on a 'grand-coalition' that included representatives of all groups broke down. This was not to be replaced by an alternative type of middle caste/class regime on the lines of Andhra Pradesh or Karnataka or alternatively political regimes in Tamil Nadu, Kerala, or West Bengal where lower castes/classes are strongly represented.[78] More crucially, the upper castes, heavily represented in the BJP, staged a comeback and continued to wield considerable power and influence in state politics. Second, lower caste politics entailed targeting particular caste groups rather than a broad-based mobilization to create a rainbow coalition of the disadvantaged. UP's lower caste parties have been focused on specific groups and aggregated well-established interests that have assumed the form of political monopolies. These groups have not developed horizontal solidarities, as they are caught up in rivalries based on status and economic competition. Third, the conditions of scarcity have generated cut-throat competitive politics that is averse to structuring and regulating power to serve social ends, or to sustain a larger sense of politics. As a consequence, various groups and parties look upon the political system as a vehicle for serving particular claims and therefore work firmly within the old state project. Thus, the tendency is to make use of mobilization as a means of winning political power, and not as a provision for intra-group or inter-group equality and economic development. In brief, UP is passing through a somewhat extreme version of what Sunil Khilnani has called the 'pure politics' that he suggests India is passing through: that is, intense struggles over the access, capture, and exercise of power in ways that show little concern for procedures that regulate the exercise of power and much less using political power for public ends.[79] The intense competition for power and 'loaves and fishes of offices and jobs', as Asoka Mehta once put it, generates a politics of proximity and convenience where elected politicians see it their duty not to act on behalf of everyone or anyone except themselves and their supporters.[80]

In comparison to regional parties, which incorporated caste and language within the idea of a political community, UP's parties made no attempt to combine caste with other social categories to build broader coalitions. Historically, the Dravidian community was conceived primarily in terms of a coalition of mega-castes, that is, the non-brahman Hindu, who was neither brahman nor SC. Narendra Subramanian's analysis shows this was a layered identity, and processes of mobilization led to the emergence of an inclusive political arena based on a political discourse that transcended caste cleavages, and included all Tamils/south Indians in the formation of a homogeneous Tamil political community.[81] Though the Dravida Munnetra Kazhagam (DMK) made no effort at structural reform, despite the sharp rural inequalities and income disparities, it substituted for reform a set of social welfare policies which, combined with almost 70 per cent reservations for the backward castes in education and government, satisfied popular aspirations.[82] Social welfare programmes, ranging from massive urban housing developments for the lower middle classes to rural programmes for construction of village roads, school buildings, promotion of clean drinking water supply, the installation of one electric light connection in every hut and the free midday meal scheme for eight million children, has given substance to the government image of generosity and accommodation.[83] Such a public discourse is virtually absent at the level of UP's party politics, and where it exists, it is frequently used to serve particular interests.

Even as UP's democratic politics has shifted from the earlier conception of representation dominated by an elite acting on behalf of a larger group to a numerical one in which elected politicians act on behalf of their group, it has been unable to deal with its effects. Anchored in a politics of identity and interests that link representation and rights chiefly to reservations, this politics is generally uninterested in procedures and policies. None of the political parties are committed to a change in the structures that generate class, gender, or community inequalities. Rather, they only seek to redistribute the spoils of office to favour one group over another. At best, this can broaden the avenues of upward mobility without greatly changing the norms and structures of distribution.

Notes and References

1. Atul Kohli, *Democracy and Discontent: India's Growing Crisis of Governability*, Cambridge: Cambridge University Press, 1991.
2. Yogendra Yadav, 'Electoral Politics in the Times of Change: India's Third Electoral System, 1989-99', *Economic and Political Weekly*, 21-8 August and 3 September 1999, pp. 2393-9; Yogendra Yadav, 'Understanding the Second Democratic Upsurge: Trends of Bahujan Participation in Electoral Politics in the 1990s', *Transforming India: Social and Political Dynamics of Democracy*, ed. Francise Frankel et. al., New Delhi: Oxford University Press, 2000; Ashutosh Varshney, 'Is India Becoming More Democratic?' *Journal of Asian Studies*, February 2000, pp. 3–25; Atul Kohli, ed., *The Success of India's Democracy*, Cambridge: Cambridge University Press, 2001.
3. Yadav, 'Understanding the Second Democratic Upsurge', pp. 120–5.
4. Partha Chatterjee, *The Nation and Its Fragments: Colonial and Postcolonial Histories*, Delhi: Oxford University Press, 1993; Partha Chatterjee, 'Democracy and the Violence of the State: A Political Negotiation of Death', paper presented at a conference on 'Globalization and the State', Paris, June 2000 (mimeo); Sudipta Kaviraj, 'A Critique of the Passive Revolution', *Economic and Political Weekly*, vol. 23, nos. 45–7, 1988, and 'Modernity and Politics in India', *Daedulus*, Winter 2000; Akhil Gupta, 'Blurred Boundaries: the Discourse of Corruption, the Culture of Politics and the Imagined State', in *State and Politics in India*, Zoya Hasan, ed., New Delhi: Sage Publications, 2000.

5. The OBCs rise to power has been described by Yogendra Yadav as a 'second democratic upsurge': 'Reconfiguration in Indian Politics: State Assembly Elections 1993-95', *Economic and Political Weekly*, 13 January 1996.

6. Francine Frankel, 'Introduction', *Transforming India*, ed. Frankel et al., pp. 4–5.

7. John Harriss provides a classification of regimes by comparing regime differences across states at both the structural level and that of party-dominated government. There are differences between states in terms of the organization of agriculture, development of capitalism, the extent of industrial development, etc. These differences may then be reflected in terms of the nature of political mobilization. See 'Comparing Regimes across Indian States: A Preliminary Essay', *Economic and Political Weekly*, vol. 34, no. 48, 27 November 1999, pp. 3667-77.

8. Estimates from Montek Singh Ahluwalia, 'Economic Performance of States in Post-Reforms Period', *Economic and Political Weekly*, 6 May 2000, p. 1638.

9. Christophe Jaffrelot, 'The Rise of Other Backward Classes in the Hindi Belt', *Journal of Asian Studies*, February 2000, pp. 86–108.

10. T.J. Byres, 'Charan Singh (1902-87): An Assessment', *Journal of Peasant Studies*, vol. 15, no. 2, 1988; Ian Duncan, 'Party Politics and the North Indian Peasantry: The Rise of the Bharatiya Kranti Dal in Uttar Pradesh', *Journal of Peasant Studies*, vol. 16, no. 1, 1988; Ian Duncan, 'Agricultural Innovation and Political Change in North India: The Lok Dal in Uttar Pradesh', *Journal of Peasant Studies*, vol. 24, no. 4, 1977.

11. See articles in Tom Brass, ed., *New Farmers Movements in India*, London: Frank Cass, 1995.

12. Akhil Gupta, *Postcolonial Developments: Agriculture in the Making of Modern India*, New Delhi: Oxford University Press, 1998, p. 69.

13. Ram Manohar Lohia, *The Caste System*, Hyderabad: Ram Manohar Lohia Samata Vidyalaya, 1979; Madhu Limaye, *Birth of Non-Congressism*, New Delhi: B.R. Publishing Corporation, 1988.

14. Yadav, 'Electoral Politics in Times of Change', p. 2398.

15. Roger Jeffery and Patricia Jeffery, *Population, Gender and Politics*, Cambridge: Cambridge University Press, 1997.

16. Zoya Hasan, 'Representation and Redistribution: The New Lower Caste Politics in North India', *Transforming India*, ed. Francine Frankel et al., pp. 146–75.

17. Ian Duncan, 'Dalits and Politics in Rural North India: The Bahujan Samaj Party in Uttar Pradesh', *Journal of Peasant Studies*, vol. 27, no. 1, October 1999, pp. 54–5.

18. Government of India, *Report of the National Commission for the Scheduled Castes and Tribes*, New Delhi, 1996, p. 77.

19. Craig Jeffrey, 'Dcmocratisation without Representation? The Power and Political Strategies of the Rural Elite in North India', *Political Geography*, vol. 19, 2000, p. 1033.

20. Ibid.

21. Craig Jeffrey and Jens Lerche, 'Stating the Difference: State, Discourse and Class Reproduction in Uttar Pradesh India', *Development and Change*, vol. 31, no. 4, pp. 857–78.

22. In the 1970s and 1980s, Congress governments introduced new rules to enforce job reservations as the government was worried that they were losing the support

of SCs and STs. Steven Wilkinson, 'India, Consociational Theory, and Ethnic Violence', *Asian Survey*, vol. XI, no. 5, September/October 2000, pp. 767–91.

23. According to Christophe Jaffrelot's calculation, 64 per cent of the north Indian MPs in the first Lok Sabha came from the upper castes and only 4.5 per cent from the OBCs; by 1996, the share of OBC MPs had increased to over 25 per cent. Rajasthan is the only exception to this trend. *Journal of Asian Studies*, February 2000.

24. V.K. Rai, 'Caste, Region and Community in Uttar Pradesh', *Economic and Political Weekly*, 21-8 August 1999.

25. Shail Mayaram, Ashis Nandy, Shikha Trivedy and Indulal Yagnik, *Creating a Nationality*, New Delhi: Oxford University Press, 1995.

26. Jaffrelot, 'Rise of Backward Classes', p. 105.

27. Jasmine Zèrinini-Brotel, 'The BJP in Uttar Pradesh: From Hindutva to Consensual Politics?', *The BJP and the Compulsions of Politics in India*, ed. Thomas Blom Hansen and Christophe Jaffrelot, New Delhi: Oxford University Press, 1998, p. 72.

28. Christophe Jaffrelot, 'The Sangh Parivar between Sanskritisation and Social Engineering', *BJP and the Compulsions of Politics*, ed. Blom Hansen and Jaffrelot.

29. Christophe Jaffrelot, 'Hindu Nationalism and Democracy', *Transforming India*, ed. Frankel et al., p. 369.

30. Ashutosh Varshney makes this point about lower caste politics in his 'Is India Becoming More Democratic?'

31. Zoya Hasan, *Quest for Power: Oppositional Movements and Post-Congress Politics in Uttar Pradesh*, New Delhi: Oxford University Press, 1998.

32. Jaffrelot, 'Rise of Backward Classes', p. 101.

33. Of 900 teachers appointed by Mulayam Singh Yadav's second government, 720 were Yadavs. In the police, of the 3,151 newly selected candidates, 1,223 were Yadavs. Ibid., p. 102.

34. Jeffrey, 'Democratisation Without Representation', p. 21.

35. *Sunday*, 25 October 1994; *India Today*, 15 November 1994.

36. Gupta, *Postcolonial Developments*, p. 75.

37. Ibid., p. 74.

38. This point has been emphasized by Kanchan Chandra, 'The Transformation of Ethnic Politics in India: The Decline of Congress and the Rise of Bahujan Samaj Party in Hoshiarpur', *Journal of Asian Studies*, February 2000, pp. 12-14.

39. See Hasan, *Quest for Power*, especially chap. 2.

40. World Bank Report, *Uttar Pradesh Fiscal and Governance: Poverty Reduction and Economic Management*, No. PID8711, 29 January 2000.

41. World Bank Report No. PID8711.

42. Information from Kripa Shankar, 'In a Debt Trap', *Economic and Political Weekly*, 22 July 2000.

43. Nisha Srivastava, 'Social Security in Uttar Pradesh: Moving beyond Policy to Governance', *Social and Economic Security in India*, ed. Mahendra Ved et al., Institute for Human Development, New Delhi, 2001, p. 440.

44. Ahluwalia, 'Economic Performance of States', p. 1638.

45. Jean Drèze and Haris Gazdar, 'Uttar Pradesh: The Burden of Inertia', *Indian Development: Selected Regional Perspectives*, ed. Jean Drèze and Amartya Sen, New Delhi: Oxford University Press, 1998.

46. Report of the Comptroller and Auditor General of India (CAG) for the year ended 31 March 1999, no. 3 (Civil), Government of Uttar Pradesh.

47. Ibid.

48. Ibid., p. 2619.

49. Srivastava, 'Social Security in Uttar Pradesh', p. 445.

50. Kripa Shankar, 'Jawahar Rozgar Yojana', *Economic and Political Weekly*, vol. 29, no. 29, 1994.

51. Madura Swaminathan, *Public Distribution System*, New Delhi: Leftword, 1998.

52. Report of the CAG (Civil), p. 63.

53. Ibid., pp. 84-5.

54. Ravi Srivastava, 'Rural Labour in Uttar Pradesh: Emerging Features of Subsistence, Contradiction and Resistance', *Journal of Peasant Studies*, vol. 26, issues 2-3, 1999, pp. 263-315; Jens Lerche, 'Politics of the Poor: Agricultural Labourers and Political Transformations in Uttar Pradesh', *Rural Labour Relations in India*, ed. T.J. Byres et al., London: Frank Cass, 1999.

55. Lori McDougall, 'Gender Gap in Literacy in Uttar Pradesh: Questions for Decentralised Educational Planning', *Economic and Political Weekly*, 6 May 2000, p. 1650.

56. Ibid.

57. Report of the CAG (Civil).

58. Ibid.

59. Doubtless the 1990s post-Congress politics, with its instabilily and succession of minority governments, added to the problems of governance. Then again, the BJP government had a full five-year term. This government did very little for the poor and the marginalized even as its period in power saw a further deterioration of governance, a rise in crime, and total neglect of development.

60. Gupta, 'Blurred Boundaries', p. 331.

61. Ibid.

62. Paul Brass, *The Theft of an Idol: Text and Context in the Representation of Collective Violence*, Princeton: Princeton University Press, 1997, pp. 92-3.

63. N.C. Saxena, 'Administration and the People: Higher Bureaucracy Needs Radical Reforms', *Management in Government*, October-December 2000, p. 14.

64. Ibid., p. 12.

65. *India Today*, 24 November 1997.

66. Report on Uttar Pradesh Academy of Administration, *Perceptions and Experience of Corruption*, June 2000, p. 7.

67. Ibid.

68. The incidence of corruption at the top led members of the Indian Administrative Service (IAS) to take up cudgels against corruption with the IAS Officers Association in the state: in 1996 they launched a move to identify the most corrupt officers in their ranks through a ballot, promising to undertake an independent inquiry against corrupt officers.

69. Ibid., p. 20.

70. Ibid.

71. Saxena, 'Administration and the People', p. 12.

72. Jeffrey, 'Democratisation without Representation'.

73. Duncan, 'Agricultural Innovation and Political Change in North India'.

74. Steven Wilkinson, 'India, Consociational Theory and Ethnic Violence', p. 782.

75. Marc Galanter estimates that between 6 and 10 per cent of all SC families had benefited in the first 25 years of reservations.
76. Forming 8.7 per cent of the population, Yadavs are the third-largest caste group and they had over a quarter of the MLAs in the 1993 Assembly. Jaffrelot, 'Rise of Backward Classes', p. 102.
77. Jaffrelot, 'Rise of Backward Classes', p. 106.
78. John Harriss, 'Comparing Regimes', p. 3371.
79. Sunil Khilnani, 'The Indian Constitution and Democracy', *India's Living Constitution: Idea, Practices, Controversies*, New Delhi: Permanent Black, 2005.
80. Ibid., p. 7.
81. Narendra Subramanian, *Ethnicity and Populist Mobilisation: Political Parties, Citizens and Democracy in South India*, New Delhi: Oxford University Press, 1999.
82. Francine Frankel, 'Middle Classes and Castes in India's Politics: Prospects for Political Accommodation', *India's Democracy: An Analysis of State-Society Relations*, ed. Atul Kohli, p. 246.
83. Ibid.

<table><tr><td>25</td><td>Shifting Ground
Hindutva Politics and the Farmers'
Movement in Uttar Pradesh</td></tr></table>

Shifting Ground
Hindutva Politics and the Farmers' Movement in Uttar Pradesh

THE DECADE of the 1980s witnessed the emergence of two interrelated changes in Uttar Pradesh (UP). The first represented an unfolding and crystallization of agricultural transformation initiated in the 1980s, and the second was the growing momentum of surplus-producing farmers as a major political force in UP.[1] Both these developments heightened the growth of a powerful farmers' movement during the 1980s, when farmers mobilized to demand remunerative prices for agricultural commodities and cheaper inputs, demands that raised the broader issue of the terms of trade between the agricultural and industrial sectors.[2] All in all, farmers' politics and the agricultural sector have attracted the attention of political parties across a wide spectrum, leading to an increase in the influence exercised by surplus producers over economic policies and the state. The rapidity with which the farmers' movement gained ascendancy deserves closer analysis.

This chapter examines the growth and dynamics of the farmers' movement in UP. It explores the political and economic conditions that contributed to the rise of the movement and the ideological and social resources that made it possible. Analysis focuses on the structural contradictions in the polity and economy of UP that generated grievances and thus enhanced the assertion of farmer power and a willingness to act politically through the farmers' movement. The movement, however, became largely quiescent by the early 1990s. There were several reasons for this decline. First, class divisions prevented the maintenance of rural unity that was necessary for pushing through public policies in favour of the agrarian sector. Accordingly, the sectorally-based farmers' mobilization which flourished in the 1980s was unable to transcend its class differences. Second, and more importantly, the intensification of communal politics in UP during the 1990s undermined a sustained farmers' mobilization. In short, the farmers' movement encountered difficulties with the politics of identity (religion, caste, and ethnicity).

The Rise of the Farmers' Movement

At the forefront of the farmers' movement in UP was the Bharatiya Kisan Union (BKU), formed in 1978, with units established in Delhi, Haryana, and western UP. In 1980, the Punjab Khetibari Zamindar Union, a farmers' organization, was converted into a Punjab unit of the BKU. This gave a big fillip to the movement in north-west India. The UP branch failed to show much activity at the time of its formation. In fact the BKU came to prominence only 1987, when a concerted effort was made to resurrect the organization in order to fill the political vacuum left by the death of Charan Singh, the leading protagonist of rural interests, Chief Minister of UP, Prime Minister and Minister of Finance in the Janata Dal government (1977-9).

Largely because of the Lok Dal's failure to extract any major concessions from the Congress government on the issue of higher prices for agricultural produce, farmers' politics were in abeyance at this juncture. This was compounded by fissures in the Lok Dal itself, in which two leading factions emerged headed respectively by Ajit Singh, son of Charan Singh, and H.N. Bahuguna, the erstwhile chief minister of UP. The revival of the BKU was thus an attempt to fill the vacuum created by the decline of the Lok Dal, and hence an expression of the desire to create a strong organization for the articulation and assertion of the growing demands of farmers.

Under the leadership of Mahendra Singh Tikait, the BKU captured national attention in the winter of 1988, when its supporters laid siege to Meerut in western UP, in pursuit of demands for higher sugarcane prices, lower farm input prices, waiver of loans, higher rural investment, and a lowering of electricity and water rates.[3] Thousands of farmers thronged the Commissioner's office in Meerut for over three weeks, dramatically placing the farmers' demand before government, media, and the public at large. This was followed by a massive rally in Delhi in October 1988. Both agitations were militant in nature and received widespread support; they lasted for days, roads were blocked, and villages were closed to government officials and politicians. Farmers refused to pay taxes and electricity bills, or to clear their interest on loans from banks and credit cooperatives.[4]

It quickly became apparent that the farmers' movement had struck a responsive chord in western UP's rural areas, and captured the imagination of large sections of the rural community. Political leaders of all political parties were anxious to associate themselves with the movement in order to be seen as champions of the farmers. Both Congress and the Lok Dal tried to jump on to the BKU bandwagon and share its platform.[5] In 1989, V.P. Singh, leader of the newly-formed Janata Dal, travelled to Meerut to express his support, and Congress leaders from western UP mounted pressure on the government to open negotiations with the BKU. What worried the Congress was the escalation of rural pressure in western UP; this was an area markedly hostile to the Congress from 1967 onwards, when Charan Singh left the Congress to establish numerous rural political formations and alliances so as to challenge Congress supremacy. Several Congress leaders made concerted efforts to associate themselves with the movement because of their concern at the success of the campaign and also its usefulness in embarrassing Bir Bahadur Singh, Chief Minister of UP, in the ongoing factional struggle in the UP Congress. Government ministers severely criticized Bir Bahadur Singh's inept handling of the agitation and demanded his resignation. Prime Minister Rajiv Gandhi pressed a number of influential national leaders known for their sympathy towards the farmers of north India to negotiate with Tikait.

It was clear from all this activity that the Congress could not afford to ignore the farmers' demands because this would have isolated it from the mainstream of rural politics. To be sure the government was anxious to buttress its political standing with surplus-producing farmers, but at the same time it was not prepared to yield to farmers' pressure because the party believed that 'this would disturb the social equilibrium in rural areas besides leading to town and country polarization'.[6] This kind of ambivalence displayed by the Congress leadership heightened the alienation of farmers from the government. It was compounded by the concessions made by the Haryana government, in the form of an upward revision of sugarcane prices, above those proposed by the Commission on Agricultural Costs and Prices (CACP). Similarly, the Punjab government agreed to lower rates for tubewells and threshers, reduce reconnection charges and line service charges for new connections, and postpone payment of electricity bills for tubewells.[7] Gradually, the UP government too became more conciliatory. The most compelling reason for these concessions was the forthcoming Lok Sabha and Assembly elections in 1989. The cabinet reshuffle was used by the Prime Minister to indicate a visible shift in priorities: five ministers were designated to look after Krishi Bhavan, which in itself was significant. This was followed by a package of concessions notable for highlighting a general emphasis on agriculture. One significant feature was the rescheduling of farm loans in the drought affected areas.[8]

At the state level, these policy measures were perceived as a sign of the Centre's willingness to concede to farmers' demands. The new chief minister, N.D. Tiwari, who had in the meanwhile replaced Bir Bahadur Singh, entered into an agreement with Tikait. Several demands made by the farmers' movement were conceded by the UP government: a judicial inquiry into a police firing which killed six farmers in Aligarh district in June 1990, the waiver of electricity bills for 1987-8, the lifting of inter-district restrictions on the movement of agricultural products, the opening of polytechnics in villages, and permission for construction on farm land.

From the standpoint of the farmers, the major gain of the agitations was not the concessions but the emergence of Tikait as a powerful leader with a formidable ability to mobilize the peasantry of western UP. It is important to note that he succeeded in maintaining the momentum of the movement, despite the fact that it did not achieve its major demand of higher prices for sugarcane. Moreover, there was no disillusionment with Tikait, even after the Meerut and Delhi sit-ins were withdrawn. Rather, he succeeded in gaining considerable media attention by dramatically spurning the efforts of political parties to participate in the farmers' movement. The BKU did not allow the Lok Dal or even members of Charan Singh's family to share their platform, despite the fact that this region was the base of Charan Singh's power, and the place where farmers consistently favoured Lok Dal/Janata Dal candidates in elections.

Charan Singh, whom Tikait acknowledged as his mentor, was deeply involved in party politics. He pursued power within the existing system and through the party system, with the object of bringing about a shift in the balance of economic power from cities to the rural areas. He challenged Congress supremacy by constructing an alliance of middle and backward castes, and succeeded in marginalizing the Congress in western UP during the 1970s. By contrast, the leadership of the farmers' movement calculated that its effectiveness would be greatest when it acted as a pressure group outside the established party system.[9] Neutrality was perceived as crucial for establishing the credibility of the BKU in the eyes of the government, and also because Tikait had moved farmers' politics on to the streets.[10]

Overall, democratically induced rural pressure exercised by farmers in the 1980s pushed the state and economic policy in their favour, signalling clearly that agricultural prices and higher investment of public resources in the countryside would be the centrepiece of agricultural policy (just as land reforms used to be in the 1950s and 1960s). Furthermore, the existence of political parties with an overwhelming rural base, such as the Janata Dal, added to the pressure on the Congress to reorient policies in favour of rural development and agriculture. The fact that the majority of UP's legislators had a rural background was another reason why the government took notice of rural mobilization. Yet another reason for appeasing farmers was the rapid decline in the position of Congress throughout the 1980s. The UP government recognized the need to increase rural investment to appease farmers especially because Congress fortunes in UP were declining so rapidly in the 1980s. However, the concessions offered by government were much below what farmers' groups demanded on the price issue, and were thus were not sufficient by themselves to alter the anti–Congress orientation of western UP farmers.

Economic and Social Context

It is now important to examine the developments in Indian politics and economy that caused the farmers' movement to emerge, and to assess what kind of a movement the BKU was, and the nature of its appeal. An editorial in the *Economic and Political Weekly* in 1980 attributed the rise of farmers' movements since the late 1970s to the terms of trade having moved against the rural sector.[11] Although this was an important factor in the rise of the farmers' movement, it does not fully explain the specific determination, social support and outcome of the UP movement. To understand that we need to turn our attention to the overall economic and social context of UP itself. As is well known, the impact of the farmers' movement was greatest in those areas of UP where the new agricultural technology had brought about a rapid increase in production and incomes. Productivity levels in UP were quite low until the early 1980s, when a major breakthrough in agricultural production was achieved as a result of the introduction of new technology. The most significant improvements occurred in wheat, maize, and sugarcane production; average yields increased, for wheat from 15.50 quintals per hectare in 1978-9 to 18.69 quintals in 1984-5, and for maize from 6.85 quintals per hectare to 15.17 quintals in the same period. Fertilizer consumption in the state rose to 52 kg. per hectare in 1980-1, and the number of tractors in use to 107 per 1,000 hectares.[12] All this contributed to an annual growth rate in foodgrain production of 2.79 per cent from 1960-1 to 1978-9, a period during which the average foodgrain yield per hectare was 1,068 kg.[13] The growth rate of UP's economy throughout the 1980s was 3.5 per cent.

Within UP itself, the western region, comprising 19 districts, witnessed a markedly faster growth than other parts of the state. Along with Haryana and Punjab, the region of UP covering Meerut, Agra, Bareilly, and Moradabad divisions experienced the largest growth of rural capital investment, processing, and small-scale industries in the Green Revolution era. On virtually all the indices of growth and modernization western UP achieved considerable progress, and by the early 1980s this region was substantially ahead of other regions of the state. The impact of the Green Revolution was greater in this region partly because the western districts were well endowed with canals and irrigation works established at the turn of the century, as a result of which the Doab was transformed into one of the richest tracts during the colonial period. This process of regional growth also manifested itself in the emergence of an infrastructure and the expansion of market towns; commercial farming also gained impetus from the tradition of peasant proprietorship, a prominent feature of the agrarian structure in this part of the state. More importantly, class polarization between absentee landlords and peasant producers did not occur to the same degree in the western region as it did in the eastern parts of the state.[14]

The UP Agricultural Census of 1980-1 grouped landholdings into five broad categories: marginal holdings of less than a hectare, small holdings of one to two hectares, semi-medium holdings of two to four hectares, medium holdings of four to ten hectares, and large holdings of ten hectares and above. Farmers with semi-medium, medium, and large holdings could produce wheat surpluses, and the bulk of these were concentrated in western UP (Table 25.1). Only a quarter of the holdings in western UP were in the marginal category, compared with 48.7 per cent in the eastern region.[15]

A significant change in production technology facilitated rapid increases in output. Although accounting for less than three-tenths of all holdings in UP and 27.3 per cent of the total land area, the western region possessed 74 per cent of all private tubewells, 54.5 per cent of all improved threshing and chopping machines, and 50.1 per cent of all diesel and electric pumps. On average, the number of these modern machines per unit of area was about double the level in the eastern region, with a slightly larger total area and population than the western region.[16]

TABLE 25.1: Percentage Distribution of Holdings by Size Class
in Various Regions of Uttar Pradesh

| | Size Class in Hectares | | | | |
Region	Up to 1 %	1-2 %	2-4 %	4-10 %	10 and above %
Western	25.0	34.0	39.4	41.3	28.8
Central	18.2	20.5	17.8	13.8	10.5
Eastern	48.7	33.0	27.5	23.2	26.3
Bundelkhand	3.4	7.9	10.9	17.7	30.6
Hill	4.0	4.3	4.4	3.7	3.6
TOTAL	100.0	100.0	100.0	100.0	100.0

Source: Government of Uttar Pradesh, *Agriculture Census in Uttar Pradesh, 1980-1*, Lucknow: Board of Revenue, 1981.

An important indicator of the capitalist character of the investment taking place was the concentration not only of physical production and asset formation, but the class-concentration of land itself. Landlords and rich peasants who were becoming agrarian capitalists, responded to profitable conditions by investing more intensively on the land they already had when this reached a plateau, they looked for more land to augment their farms. This was particularly the case with the rich peasant Jat cultivators who started with a much smaller land base than the ex-zamindars.[17] A more rapid process of land transfers from small farms to the well-to-do was to be expected in the faster-growing areas, and this is indeed what was revealed by a study of land transfers spanning the period 1952-3 and 1982-3 based on a 0.2 per cent sample of Nyaya panchayats in the state.[18]

A significant finding of the study was that on average it was the smallest landholders with less than 2.5 acre who had sold land; 7.3 per cent of the land owned by them was sold, compared to around 3 per cent or less by other size-groups of farmers. In western UP the extent of land transfer was higher than the state average; those with less than 2.5 acre had transferred up to 10 per cent, and the landless had transferred 35 per cent of the total land that was sold.[19] Most of these transfers had taken place during the last five years, 1978-9 to 1982-3, out of a total of the three decades covered. The households which became totally landless after transferring land accounted for nearly 42 per cent of the total land transferred.

In contrast, of the total land that was purchased, some 60 per cent went to owners of more than 5 acre, of which 28 per cent went to those with over 10 acre. There was a net loss of land by those owning below 2.5 acre and a net gain by all others with the largest gains recorded by owners of 10 acre and more.[20] The study found that more land transfers had taken place in the post-Green Revolution period than earlier; the trends of net transfer from poorer cultivators to the well-to-do were confirmed by the income and asset-wise analysis, which showed that 56 per cent of total area sold came from farmers with below Rs. 10,000 annual income, while 61 per cent of all land purchased was by farmers with over Rs. 10,000 income. As usual, the Green Revolution area, in the western region of UP, showed a more marked picture of concentration, with 75 per cent of area purchased going to the well-to-do (Table 25.2). Within western UP, the fastest growing districts were Meerut, Muzaffarnagar, Saharanpur, Bulandshahr, Aligarh, Moradabad, Bareilly, Bijnor and Pilibhit, with productivity of major crops ranging from Rs. 1,459 per hectare in Bareilly to Rs. 2,397 per hectare in Muzaffarnagar in 1980-3 (Table 25.3). Overall, by the early 1980s nearly 42 of UP's 57 districts had productivity levels exceeding Rs. 1,000 per hectare, and the majority of these were in western UP. This increase was

TABLE 25.2: Land Transfer Matrix in Western Uttar Pradesh According to Size of Owned Holding (Size and Area in Acres)

Sellers	Buyers				
	Less than 2.5	*2.5–5*	*5–10*	*10 & above*	*Total*
Landless	10.83	37.25	53.04	154.32	255.44
	(4.25)	(14.58)	(20.76)	(60.41)	(100.00)
	(17.58)	(26.01)	(26.18)	(47.10)	(34.75)
Less than 2.5	16.62	22.46	21.88	11.76	72.72
	(22.95)	(30.89)	(30.09)	(16.17)	(100.00)
	(26.98)	(15.69)	(10.80)	(3.59)	(9.90)
2.5–5.0	15.36	48.72	23.99	14.85	103.92
	(14.78)	(46.88)	(23.09)	(15.25)	(100.00)
	(24.93)	(34.02)	(11.84)	(4.84)	(14.14)
5.0–10.0	6.09	22.84	73.54	50.59	143.06
	(3.98)	(14.92)	(48.05)	(33.05)	(100.00)
	(9.88)	(15.95)	(36.29)	(15.44)	(20.82)
10.0 & above	12.71	11.93	30.16	95.09	149.89
	(8.48)	(7.96)	(20.12)	(63.44)	(100.00)
	(20.63)	(8.33)	(14.89)	(29.03)	(20.39)
TOTAL	61.61	143.20	202.61	327.61	735.03
	(8.38)	(19.48)	(27.57)	(44.57)	(100.00)
	(100.00)	(100.00)	(100.00)	(100.00)	(100.00)

Note: Figures in first parenthesis are percentages of land sold to different categories while figures in the second parenthesis are percentage of land purchases by different categories.
Source: Shankar, *Land Transfers.*

mainly due to the extensive irrigation and cropping intensity (Table 25.4), nearly 85 per cent of the area under wheat in UP is irrigated.[21] Almost the entire area under wheat in Meerut, Muzaffarnagar, Bulandshahr, and Aligarh was irrigated. Likewise the intensity of cropping was higher than the average for the country in 1980–1. Similarly, the yields of sugarcane, the most important commercial crop in the state, improved vastly because of better irrigation and chemical fertilizers. Farmers recorded yields of around 456.55 quintal per hectare in 1982–3. UP accounted for half the total area under sugarcane in the country in 1985–6 and 84 per cent of the area under sugar was irrigated. The western region accounted for 64 per cent of the total sugarcane area in the state in the mid-1970s, and maintained the lead even though important concentrations of cane production exist in the more populous eastern region. Of the total tonnage of sugarcane crushed, as high as 57 per cent was in the western region; it also accounted for 57.5 per cent of sugar produced—owing to a marginally better juice recovery rate.

Along with Punjab and Haryana, UP has registered a significant rise in food production, and north India has emerged as the sole area producing

TABLE 25.3: Average and Value of Output of 41 Crops by District, 1980–3

District	Area	Value of Output	Value per Hectare
	('000 Hectares)	('000 Rs.)	(Rs)
Agra	463	550,901	1,189
Aligarh	645	887,293	1,376
Bulandshahr	577	978,641	1,696
Etah	473	582,062	1,230
Etawah	473	537,964	1,137
Farrukhabad	411	479,205	1,168
Mainpuri	415	480,350	1,157
Meerut and Ghaziabad	810	1,734,059	2,141
Mathura	430	569,934	1,325
Moradabad	707	1,219,688	1,725
Muzaffarnagar	515	1,234,514	2,397
Rampur	296	508,936	1,719
Saharanpur	599	1,158,756	1,934
Shahjahanpur	492	711,198	1,445
Budaun	560	657,000	1,173
Bareilly	485	707,402	1,459
Bijnor	458	901,995	1,969
Pilibhit	345	601,308	1,743

Source: G.S. Bhalla and D.S. Tyagi, *Patterns in Indian Agricultural Development: A District Level Study*, Delhi: Institute for Studies in Industrial Development, 1989.

a genuine food surplus. Within this region, Punjab-Haryana has recorded a phenomenal 134.4 per cent rise in per capita output, while UP shows a 31.5 per cent increase. The share of the northern region in the country's total food production has risen from around one-quarter to two-fifths, thus making a very significant contribution to the urban food economy. Between 1985 and 1988, 98 per cent of the total wheat procurement came from the northern region, while 67 per cent of the total rice total procurement was from this region.[22]

The bulk of foodgrains procured by the government was used to feed the urban and semi-urban population, as over 60 per cent of fair price shops were located in cities and towns or in their rural periphery, serving a quarter of the country's total population. Government procurement operations were a very important part of total sales of cereals: during the period 1981–5, for example, procurement of wheat and rice amounted to an annual average of 16.73 million tonnes, which made up 16.5 per cent of average annual production of these crops.[23] All in all, the public distribution system[24] which played a crucial role in offsetting inflation and minimizing urban discontent,

TABLE 25.4: Net Cultivated Area, Net Irrigated Area, and its Percentage
in Western Uttar Pradesh by District 1984 (Hectares)

Districts	Net Cultivated Area	Net Irrigated Area	Percentage of Net Irrigated Area to Net Cultivated Area
Saharanpur	380,732	279,708	73.47
Muzaffarnagar	334,889	294,892	88.96
Meerut	312,685	297,621	95.18
Ghaziabad	188,220	173,682	92.28
Bulandshahr	341,074	328,376	93.34
Aligarh	390,237	364,243	93.34
Mathura	308,899	225,957	84.16
Agra	345,700	229,834	66.48
Mainpuri	283,867	240,534	84.73
Etah	295,259	247,965	83.98
Bijnor	344,149	213,649	62.08
Moradabad	484,160	377,901	78.05
Rampur	189,983	140,721	74.07
Bareilly	331,120	205,465	62.05
Budaun	405,903	244,308	60.19
Shahjahanpur	347,249	253,881	73.11
Pilibhit	220,824	186,045	84.25
Farukhabad	279,095	189,492	67.90

Source: Statistical Diary, Uttar Pradesh, Economics and Statistics Division, State Planning Institute, 1986.

became increasingly dependent on government procurement of foodgrains from this region. This in turn boosted the importance of the surplus-producing capitalist farmers of the north-western region, and consequently their bargaining position vis-à-vis the state and state governments in different regions was much greater than that of farmers in other parts of the country.

The BKU: Aspirations, Participation, and Ideology

The economic discontent fuelling the farmers' movement was generally the result of increasing aspirations frustrated by the deterioration in the agriculture industry terms of trade.[25] The prices of foodgrains relative to manufactured goods rose by 50 per cent from the late 1950s to the mid-1970s.[26] From the mid-1970s, however, there was an adverse flow in terms of trade for the agricultural sector, as reflected in the wholesale prices of agricultural and manufactured products.[27] This meant that, though prices of agricultural produce were rising, they did not keep pace either with those of non-agricultural operations or with rising consumption levels. Although rich farmers were affected because the scale of profits was reduced, middle farmers with modest quantities of surplus to dispose in the market suffered more due to the sharp rise in prices of essential manufactured goods. The worst affected were the poor peasantry, which had to buy foodgrains to sustain itself and was squeezed by the rise in prices of agricultural as well as non-agricultural commodities. In this context, rich farmers who gained the most from higher output and lower input prices rallied other sections of the peasantry who objectively may have had little or no reason to identify with the demands of the farmers' agitation. The discontent over prices was located within a more generalized resentment over the large disparity in urban and rural standards of living, especially with regard to public goods and services such as drinking water, energy, roads, communications, health, and education. Accordingly, the BKU spokesmen made their case by contrasting the rate of return on their investment in agriculture and that achieved by those engaged in urban occupations in general, and government service, trade, and professions in particular.

Ignoring the social differentiation in the countryside, the leaders of the farmers' agitation claimed to speak on behalf of the entire peasantry and tried to give the issues raised by them in the discourse of agriculture versus industry, urban versus rural. The idea of a basic 'unity' of interests among all agriculturists glossed over the differential impact of material issues. Higher prices affected farmers on an individual basis: consequently the benefits of improvement in terms of trade were cornered by capitalist producers who monopolized commodity sales, whereas the burden of deteriorating terms of trade was invariably passed on to the poorer classes. However, the BKU's agenda was not limited to higher prices. It included a wide range of popular demands from which all farmers might benefit. These included better facilities for education, roads and employment, and the reservation of jobs for farmers. Though these were popular demands that helped the farmers' movement to marshall broad-based support, the BKU did not pursue them with the same vigour as higher prices or loan waiver.

The aspirations of farmers were further heightened by the critical national importance of food surpluses produced in this region. North India became the main source of food supply for the urban areas. This gave its farmers a bargaining power which their counterparts in western and southern India did not have at the national level. This power was augmented by the fact that the demands put forward by surplus producers in these regions were increasingly supported by small farmers who, for a variety of reasons, backed these agitations. Such agitations were more successful precisely in those regions where small and medium farmers were drawn in to expand the support base. This was the case in western UP where sugarcane was grown by medium as well as small farmers, all of whom were enthusiastic supporters of the BKU.

Cane growers were in the forefront of the BKU's movement for higher price. Since unrest was most pronounced in the sugarcane growing parts of western UP, the BKU focused attention primarily on higher prices of sugarcane and the waiver of loans made to cane cultivators. Their agitation and militancy was strengthened by the structure of cane cultivation in UP (Table 25.5). Cane was cultivated largely by medium and semi-medium holdings, and also to some extent by rich peasant households. This was evident from the large number of cultivators supplying cane to sugar mills: 25,000 to 30,000 in UP, compared to 3,500 to 4,000 cultivators in Maharashtra.[28] The political and economic clout of cane cultivators was considerbly enhanced by the patronage and backing given by Charan Singh to the demand for nationalization of sugar mills in UP.[29]

The 1960s and 1970s witnessed further improvement in the bargaining power of the cane grower vis-à-vis the sugar mill. This can be attributed to two factors: first, to the increased influence of rich farmers vis-à-vis the government; and second, to the emergence of the sugar cooperatives in other sugarcane growing states, a development which in general exercised an upward pressure on cane prices.[30] The terms of trade with respect to sugarcane improved in favour of sugarcane cultivators at a compound rate of 0.2 to 0.5 per cent and 3.3 to 3.5 per cent per annum respectively for the period from 1961-2 to 1977-8.[31] Much of this improvement occurred when terms of trade in general moved in favour of agriculture. As noted earlier, the terms of trade for agricultural commodities, however, deteriorated from 1976-7. Due to drought, the production of sugar decreased from 36.91 quintals in 1987 to 32.65 quintals in 1988, despite the fact that more sugarcane was crushed in 1988 than in the previous year. Poor rainfall

TABLE 25.5: Sugarcane Cultivation by Size-Class of Ownership Holding
1970-1 (Percentage Share)

Type of Holding	Size Class	All-India	UP	Mahrashtra (Hectares)
Marginal	0.0-0.5	–	6.8	2.1
Marginal	0.0-1.0	13.7	17.2	6.3
Semi-Medium	2.0-4.0	24.6	27.2	19.5
Medium	4.0-10.0	29.6	26.7	35.3
Large	10.0 & above	15.7	9.6	27.3

Source: All India Report on Agriculture Census, 1970-1, 1975.

brought down the sucrose content of sugarcane resulting in a recovery rate of only 8.12 per cent in 1988 as against 9.48 per cent in the previous year. As a result, priority was given to the enhancement of sugarcane prices, in order to offset the decline in sugarcane production owing to drought.

There is no doubt the BKU movement evoked a strong response from a large number of farmers in UP, where several hundred thousand farmers took part in the major protests. The enthusiasm generated by these agitations was impressive, as was the expression of solidarity. However, all this activity was concentrated in western UP, most notably in the districts of Meerut, Muzaffarnagar, Aligarh, Bijnor, Moradabad, Ghaziabad, Bulandshahr, and Saharanpur. The social base of the farmers' movement was accordingly centred in the districts dominated by Jat peasant proprietors.

Although the farmers' movement mobilized primarily on the basis of rural sector rather than class, economic differentiation is important to an understanding of the politics of the farmers' movement.[32] Class background determined the collective identities of leading actors and, as noted earlier, the BKU articulated the interests of surplus producers (accounting for the bulk of market sales) through highly specific and concrete demands, the interests of small producers being represented only in terms of vague demands for urban-rural parity. A small survey conducted in Meerut and Moradabad provides evidence for the argument that surplus producers who owned over 8 acre participated most actively in the farmers' movements.[33] This characterization is further confirmed by a another study, which found that in terms of membership and active participation, the BKU was dominated by rich and middle farmers, and more importantly that every rich farmer household in the five villages surveyed had taken part in the BKU agitation.[34] Among those surveyed, the supporters of the BKU were large producers with more than 8 acre of land and who hired labour to work their farms, while those with less than 8 acre depended on family labour.[35] The bulk of the workforce was made up of the landless, who were mostly dalits and Muslims. Interviews revealed considerable tension between the rural poor and rich Jat farmers. Frequent complaints were voiced about the heavy-handed methods used by the Jats to secure compliance and participation of the poorer sections of the peasantry in the farmers' movement.[36]

The BKU showed little concern for the specific problems faced by the rural poor, such as minimum wages, employment opportunities, house sites and harassment; minimum wages for agricultural labourers were not even mentioned in the list of 35 demands put forward by the BKU during the Meerut agitation. For peasant proprietors, the majority of landless Scheduled Castes were not members of the farming community, and therefore undeserving of notice. In the words of Charan Singh, 'if a man is landless he cannot be called a farmer'. The landless were the agricultural labourers, poor peasants, and sharecroppers whose interests were at variance with the farming community, especially the rich peasants.[37] It is hardly surprising, then, that the landless agricultural labourers reacted with apprehension to the consolidation of the affluent peasantry under the banner of the BKU, because they feared it would mean more harassment and oppression for them.

A striking feature of the UP farmers' movement was the low incidence of women's participation in the movement. The stance taken by the farmer's movement articulated in messages such as the abolition of dowry, limiting marriage expenses, discouraging drinking, taking action against husbands deserting or harassing wives, led to some women taking part in the earlier protests organized by the BKU. Their participation was, however, never an important feature of the movement, in contrast to the prominence of women in various Maharashtra agitations.[38] Women generally expressed sympathy for the difficulties of farmers, but they were not drawn into the activities or decision-making structures of the BKU. This was largely because of the conservative and traditional attitude of Jats towards women: though women work in the fields, there was no effort to alter the social conditions which hampered their participation in the movement, and no organized attempt to involve them in mobilizations. Many women were thus prevented by the social constrictions arising from the dominant patriarchal norms of the western UP society from participating in politics. Accordingly, the farmers' movement was not the best vehicle for the empowerment of women, since for women to be able to engage in public activity, they must have some control over their lives. In western UP, the autonomy and options of women were limited by social, cultural, and religious structures that confined women and dictated a customary social subservience to men in their everyday lives.[39]

The economic and social contradictions in the BKU movement were obscured ideologically by a peasant ideology which articulated issues in a populist style.[40] The BKU presented an urban bias view, arguing that the development process was systematically biased against the countryside and that this is deeply embedded in the political structure and bureaucracy which neglected the legitimate interests of farmers. Such populism emphasized the contradiction between the rural agricultural and urban industrial sectors, rather than the differences between classes in the countryside. In this vein Tikait claimed that his struggle was not confined to the acceptance of the BKU charter of demands, it was also a movement to safeguard the honour, dignity, and self-respect of all kisans, irrespective of caste or class.[41] The BKU variety of populism highlighted the moral character of the movement, and is summed up in the following words of Tikait: 'No dispute can ever be solved satisfactorily by legality, it can be settled only through truthfulness. The kisan must go on protesting in the hope that "some day sense will dawn on an insensitive state"'.[42] Within this framework, the farmers' movement was much more than just a protest against the government: it was a crusade that mobilized kisan power in order to convince government about the justness of the farmers' cause and the concomitant primacy of agriculture. The BKU leadership spoke a language that invoked elements of Charan Singh's discourses on agriculture. He deprecated the 'urban bias' of planning and heavy industrialization, and held it responsible for the diversion of resources away from agriculture. The present leadership, in a somewhat similar vein, blamed the city-based government for the problems faced by the farmers. Hence the imperative nature of the entire farming community mobilizing to oppose the privileged position of the urban industrial sector.

The emphasis on developing the rural economy created a political space in which prosperity in the countryside could be promoted by highlighting the common interests of all rural families, from rich capitalist producers to poor peasants. The BKU made much of its concern for the farming community as a whole. In this framework, the well-being of farmers was linked to higher prices for their produce: unremunerative prices affected not just rich peasants but also the small and middle peasants who grew cash crops. All rural producers, then, had a shared interest in demanding the principle of parity of prices, expansion of credit facilities, and remission of loans. In short, populism as practised by the BKU promoted the development of a non-class social consciousness by instilling and reinforcing in the ranks of the peasantry the traditional self-perception of an undifferentiated commodity producer.

All this is not to suggest that the BKU's populism succeeded in creating a groundswell of opposition to the Congress government's rural policies. Over the years, the rich and middle farmers of UP, as elsewhere in India, enjoyed an 'extremely comfortable accommodation with the ruling party',[43] helped in no small measure both by the non-existence of agricultural taxation and by the shelving of serious attempts at land reforms. Further, there was little evidence to show that agriculture suffered from neglect at the hands of the Congress government at centre or state level. After all, Congress was the party of India's Green Revolution, and Indira Gandhi was the chief architect of agricultural policies in the 1960s and the consequent boom in agricultural production. Even in the 1990s, the UP government's expenditure on the rural sector was substantial and the net share of agriculture was 51 per cent of the state's national domestic product in 1977-8.[44] Moreover, the rural sector commanded considerable influence in the polity. Not only did the majority of UP's legislators at the time come from a rural background, but the mobilization of farmers led to an enhancement of rural pressure in the polity and a corresponding boost to the self-confidence of farmers.

The alienation of the surplus producers from the Congress in this context was more political than economic. It gained momentum with the formation and victory of the Janata Party in 1977, which foregrounded agrarian ideology and policy. As the new agrarian interests became key players in the Janata coalition, they challenged the Nehruvian project favouring industry, the professional classes, and the cities.[45] The alienation of this surplus-producing rural class from the cultural milieu of urban areas created a major social dichotomy in north India, in that their sense of alienation was heightened by a perception that government was not interested in establishing a rational price regime, principally because of the urban dominated politics.

In several states the farmers' movements went on to pose a serious challenge to Congress dominance. The rural appeal and breadth of their support played a vital part in the defeat of the Congress in Karnataka and Andhra Pradesh Assembly elections in 1982. The Shetkari Sangathana was credited with significantly reducing the margin of victory of many Congress candidates in the 1984 parliamentary elections in Maharashtra, as also in the assembly elections held two months later. The BKU backed the National Front, which won a decisive victory over the Congress in UP in 1989, and thus played a significant role in the overthrow of the Rajiv Gandhi government in 1989.

Caste, Communalism, and the Decline of the BKU

Despite such wide support and political clout the UP farmers' movement floundered and declined. The most important reason for this decline was the drastic shift in political discourse. From the late 1980s the political agenda in UP was dominated by Hindutva politics.[46] The national momentum gained by Hindutva paralleled the progressive exhaustion and decline in activity on the farmers' front so the question becomes one of why this was the case.

The political significance and durability of the farmers' movement depended in part on its ability to forge a network of support by transcending the short-term interests of the elites of the movement. The challenge before the farmers' movement was to create the necessary conditions so that a spectrum of rural producers believed they shared economic interests and political outlooks. Initially, the BKU was able to do this. Its early success lay in highlighting a composite picture of the possibilities and influences that could shape agrarian relations: sectoral growth and peasant proprietorship as a counterforce to agrarian radicalism. Tikait's political hallmark was not so much in placing an emphasis on issues and policies shared by everyone as in creating a perception that remunerative prices and low input costs were a collective good for the entire countryside. However, in the ultimate analysis these ideological calculations were sufficiently contradictory and ambiguous, and interpretations remained subject to the influence of differing ideologies and interests. The principal constraint stemmed from the nature of ethnic identities and interests. Farmers' politics were very much based on caste, ethnicity, and religion which divided the countryside. Rural sectoral interests were overwhelmed by social cleavages. Farmers' assertion in this sense was inevitably self-limited.[47] Since it was differentiated and divided on the basis of class, caste, community, and religion, rural power articulated by the farmers' movement could not become a cohesive force united in the pursuit of sectoral interests.

At its peak, some observers felt that the BKU movement could negate the communal politics of the Rashtriya Swayamsevak Sangh-Bhartiya Janata Party-Vishwa Hindu Parishad (RSS-BJP-VHP) combine, as was done in Maharashtra by the Shetkari Sangathana. The Shetkari Sangathana seemed to many to be the only force capable of halting the growth of the Shiv Sena in small towns and rural areas, and the farmers' movement was the most popular opposition to growing communal forces.[48] In UP this impression was fostered by the absence of any communal disharmony in the Meerut agitation of early 1988. This was further borne out by the presence of cross-communal networks, the use of plural religious symbols, and the strong support for the BKU among Muslims. The demographic composition of western UP with a large and visible Muslim presence, contributed a lot to the BKU's cross-community network and need for communal unity. The population of Muslims in western UP was higher than their population at the all-India level, and their proportion in districts like Muzaffarnagar, Meerut, Moradabad, and Bijnor was particularly high. Consequently, the BKU invested special efforts in promoting communal harmony in Meerut which had been destroyed by the communal massacre in May 1987.

This cross-community support was bolstered by the BKU's campaign against the abduction and murder of a Muslim girl in Muzaffarnagar district. This incident snowballed into a major agitation as Tikait marched with thousands of farmers to the banks of the Ganga Canal, and demanded that the government recover Naiyma. Following the recovery of Naiyma's body, hundreds of thousands of farmers gathered near the canal to protest against her murder.[49] This particular agitation helped the BKU to shore up its support among Muslims. As *The Times of India* observed:

The mere act of thousands of Hindus squatting on the banks of a canal at Bhopa to seek redressal of a Muslim grievance is remarkable in itself. While this does not necessarily mean that communal prejudices are being consciously combated, it does powerfully demonstrate that there is a common code of social morality that guides rural society—a reality that urban politicians are usually unable to grasp.[50]

These anti-communal exertions ultimately did not amount to very much, mainly because of the BKU's general adherence to a strategy and politics based on existing non-economic cleavages of caste, religion, and ethnicity. From the very beginning, therefore, the mobilization of farmers was influenced and bolstered by the communal structure of western UP. The caste distribution of the region, like its communal composition, was unique because of the high concentration of Jats in western UP. The latter comprised nearly 40 per cent of the population in Meerut, Muzaffarnagar, Saharanpur, and Bijnor districts of western UP. Due to their numerical preponderance as well as their control over a sizeable proportion of land, Jats dominated both the politics and economy of the region. In the districts where the farmers' movement was particularly strong, the legacy of the *bhaichara* system still prevails among the Jats.[51] The Rajputs and Tyagis in this region also cultivated their own land and considered themselves to be the Jats' equal in status. Many of these peasants were linked by ties of caste and kinship and this helped to establish a rough correspondence between caste and class in western UP: hence the bulk of BKU support comes from Jats and other landholding castes. Caste support, however, was not unique to the BKU: the support of most such movements was located in the landholding dominant castes.[52] However, what distinguished the BKU from other farmers' organizations was the powerful district-level organizational structure of the Union. The BKU functioned on the basis of collective leadership provided by members of 'a community of near equals'[53] inspired by the coparcenary traditions of the *bhaichara* system in the region. The Sisauli Panchayat, the fulcrum of the grass roots decision-making structure, was itself an extension of the Jat *khap* councils, a form of caste panchayat which has existed for 500 years as the administrative apparatus of the Jat community.[54]

There is no doubt that caste, clan, and kinship ties helped in embedding and institutionalizing the BKU in the local society and polity of the region. There were however obvious limits and contradictions in such a pattern of mobilization. The process of propagating the message through Jat councils might have been an effective method in appealing to Jats, but it also deepened existing prejudices and hardened vertical loyalties of caste and community. As a result, the social composition of the BKU's main support base was essentially limited to Jats; accordingly the organization found it extremely difficult to sustain its support among the backward castes, and even more difficult to build bridges with the lower castes and classes. This failure to transcend communal identity and organization can explain the problems encountered by the farmers' organization in sustaining a broad-based support across castes and communities.

The farmers' movement in UP ran into difficulties on the issue of caste, especially the policy of reservation for the backward castes initiated by the Janata Dal government. The Janata Dal government reserved 27 per cent of government posts in the central government for the backward castes.[55] In addition, the UP government raised the reserved quota for OBCs to 12 per cent. However the upper castes who dominated the bureaucracy and public institutions were extremely hostile to it. Not surprisingly, reservations polarized the backward and upper castes throughout the state, and UP saw the outbreak of widespread violence.[56] Everywhere the upper castes mobilized powerful resistance to the Mandal Commission recommendations and this plunged the already split Janata Dal government at the centre into a serious crisis of survival. As it excluded Jats from its purview, the BKU was hostile to the new reservation package. Vehemently criticizing caste-based reservation, the BKU countered by advocating an economic criterion for job reservation which would have enabled the dominant castes—including the Jats—to benefit from reservation. The notable feature of the anti-Mandal agitation was its strong support in the western UP districts of Ghaziabad, Mathura, Bulandshahr, and Moradabad where the BKU held sway. The BKU backed the anti-Mandal agitation in UP, Haryana, and Delhi, which set the stage for the eruption of major conflicts and violence culminating in the fall of the Janata Dal government in October 1990. The disorder in UP from August 1990 to June 1991 contributed to the fall of the Janata Dal government at the centre as well as in UP: championed and nurtured by the BJP, the BKU, and the Congress, the anti-Mandal agitation played a crucial part in dislodging the central government. From October 1990 onwards, the anti-Mandal agitation slid into communal violence between Hindus and Muslims, intensifying social conflicts and confrontations between various groups and identities.[57]

The anti-Mandal agitation not only made visible all the pre-existing social divisions and tensions but also showed up the fragility of the attempted Hindu unity. Mandal was seen as antithetical to the construction of a composite, unified Hinduism: for the BJP, therefore, the political fallout of Mandal was damaging. As a party that was trying to project the notion of an undifferentiated Hindu society. The issue of caste-based reservations was problematic because it undermined the basis of Hindu consolidation, a problem compounded because the BJP had only recently made inroads among the backward castes in north India. The Ayodhya movement launched by the Hindu right very quickly managed to shift the political discourse from economy and reservation to Hindu nationalism and cultural identity, thereby offsetting the divisive impact of the Mandal factor. In this way the caste politics of the Janata Dal was displaced by the communal politics of Hindutva, which offered a language and vocabulary for the transformation of caste conflict into religious unity. The appeal of Hindutva's temple movement was strongest in UP because all the three disputed shrines—Ayodhya, Mathura and Varanasi—are located there. The Ram Janmabhoomi controversy was the most effective source of mass mobilization in recent times, because of its emotive appeal highlighted by a direct conflict with the Babri Masjid, a symbol of Muslim identity. The Ayodhya symbol worked not only because of an intrinsic attachment to Rama in the land of *Aryavarta*, but also because the symbol simultaneously provided both a rallying counter-ideology against the divisiveness of caste and an incorporating framework that was capable of mobilizing Hindus as an undifferentiated community.

The growth area of this movement was western and central UP, where it made strong inroads into rural areas. In western UP, where growth was shaped by the commercialization of agriculture and the rapid expansion of small towns, such as Bulandshahr, Khurja, Aligarh, Meerut, and Moradabad, there appeared to be a significant coincidence of rapid socio-economic growth and an increase in communalism.[58] Commercial growth predominated over industrial growth, though small-scale industry has expanded phenomenally in the small towns: in the 1970s, for example, the growth of Khurja was due to the rapid growth of the pottery industry. Khurja's economy took off because of rising levels of consumer-oriented demand, both for 'ethnic' pottery and for small inexpensive pottery used in kiosks and tea stalls in small towns, a process which created a new class of small industrial entrepreneurs.

Urban expansion was also connected to the commercialization of agriculture in western UP. New forms of commercial agriculture closely related to towns emerged, blurring the dividing line between urban and rural, with agro-based industries dominating and forming a rural-urban nexus. Agriculture and agro-based industries became prominent even in the urban areas, suggesting a close techno-economic link between agriculture and industry which accelerated the pace of urbanization. This is why most western UP towns looked like overgrown market-towns without a strong manufacturing base by the 1990s. With the rural and urban sectors reciprocally oriented towards each other, and with the growth of a rural middle class, towns began cashing in on the significant increase of the rural elite's purchasing power, fuelled by a consumer boom in the 1980s.

This pattern of combined rural/urban development in western UP was, however, not without its contradictions, which, when accompanied by a general rise in aspirations, opened up spaces vulnerable to communalization by the early 1990s.[59] There was a major expansion of the petite bourgeoisie, noted above, which the BJP could then identify as its political base. For example, the new petite bourgeoisie among urban Jats which includes traders, shopkeepers, brick-kiln owners—all with strong connections in villages—were won over by the RSS and BJP.

However, the rise of small towns and Hindu communalism were not directly connected, rather, the former in the region was conducive to the emergence of the latter in that the two histories intersected in significant ways. Accordingly, although neither the growth of a class nor urbanization per se generated communalization, their combined development in a specific conjuncture, in which particular forms of political mobilization and electoral calculation were crystallizing, dangerously reoriented many kinds of conflicts into Hindu-Muslim antagonisms. In this respect, a significant phenomenon was the incorporation of hitherto peaceful towns and surrounding rural areas into the ambit of communal violence. As the intensity of communal politics grew, there was a marked increase in communal violence and rioting associated with it. The escalation of violence during the rath yatra was greatest in UP.[60] More significantly, western UP was the area of maximum concentration. Thus Meerut, Bijnor, Bulandshahr, Saharanpur, Aligarh, Agra, and Etah witnessed all of the major riots—all these were BKU strongholds, and were clearly affected by communalization.

Another communal organization, the VHP, garnered its major support in western UP. Thus the largest number of participants at the Virat Hindu Sammelan[61] hosted by the VHP in June 1990—the first in UP— came from western UP.[62] Through the activities of such organizations, Hindutva ideology penetrated Jat-dominated villages. What is noteworthy is that sustained communal propaganda fractured the mixed ideological and syncretic traditions of UP.

The Hindu Right gained enormously from its ties with the VHP and the numerous social, cultural, and religious organizations associated with the RSS, which appeared to link the party with the traditional values and concerns of Hindu popular culture. It used these ties to heighten the friction between the state and the public arena, increasingly dominated by the RSS-

VHP through its congregational politics linking the home, the street, and the temple.[63] This new style of politics was specifically built around religious festivities requiring public participation and culminating in processions winding through major streets and towns. Congregational politics in UP filled the streets with festivals, *jagrans* and *yatras*. These celebrations were essential for a takeover of public spaces, previously the domain of the anti-Mandalites through their street theatre, and before that controlled by the *dharnas, gheraos,* and *rasta rokos* of the BKU. Hence the methods and appeal of the farmers was displaced and marginalized by the emotional and political appeal of Hindutva. Its totalizing ideology, aggressive chauvinism, and the massive communal violence which accompanied its ascendancy in UP politics left little space for other types of struggles and confrontations with the state. Until 1989 the farmers' movement operated in the public arena with formidable advantages. It could count on the support of political parties because of its avowedly non-party stance. Its steady politicization from then diminished its influence considerably. Initially the BKU was caught between the rivalries of different Janata Dal factions, besides their claim to be devoted to agriculture conflicted with Tikait's claim to be the sole spokesman of UP's farmers. The BKU then found itself arraigned against Yadav, the chief minister of UP, who prevented it from holding a kisan panchayat in Lucknow in July 1990 to press farmers' demands on the state government.[64] Tikait was arrested and his supporters lathi-charged in Lucknow and Barabanki jail. The BJP leaders were quick to extend full support to the farmers, thus further widening the gulf between farmers and the Janata Dal. This assumed significance in the context of the growing confrontation and turmoil over the Ayodhya issue in the state. Many of the BKU's supporters were clearly attracted to the Ayodhya campaign: indeed, the western districts dispatched a large number of *kar sevaks*[65] to Ayodhya. Many of them returned to their districts as heroes who had been able to penetrate the massive security forces deployed to protect the Babri Masjid. Some *kar sevaks* were killed in the police firing and became the symbolic fountainhead of mobilization against the state which was prepared to sacrifice Hindu lives to protect the disputed shrine. Another factor that pushed the farmers' movement more and more towards the upper castes was their shared hostility against Dalits. Frequent Jat-Dalit conflicts in western UP had helped the Bahujan Samaj Party (BSP) to establish a base among the Scheduled Castes threatened by the social dominance of landed castes in the region. These contradictions might well have encouraged the BKU to combine with the BJP in a trade-off, in order to gain the latter's support in their conflict with the Dalits.

The autonomy of BKU was further undermined by reports of Tikait's decision to enter into an informal alliance with the BJP in the 1991 parliament and state assembly elections in UP. As a result, the BJP performed extremely well in BKU strongholds, in contrast to the major losses suffered by Janata Dal in these areas; it is worth recalling that after his estrangement with the Janata Dal, Tikait warned that without the support of the farmers, the Janata Dal could win no more than a handful of seats in UP.[66] So it is not surprising that from a commanding position of 50 per cent of the popular vote in UP in 1989, and a 100 per cent success rate in seats contested, the Janata Dal and Samajwadi Janata Party slipped to 37.4 per cent of the popular vote and a success rate of just one-third of the seats contested. By contrast, a combination of ideological activity by the BJP-VHP-RSS combine followed by violence and rioting played a decisive role in the BJP victory in 1991. In western UP, the BJP won 11 of 17 parliamentary seats—all in riot-hit towns, except for Saharanpur and Khurja. In the Rohilkhand region of western UP, the BJP won 7 out of 10 seats, again winning in all 3 riot hit towns— Bijnor, Rampur, and Badaun.[67]

Although the BJP on its own garnered much of this electoral support, the BKU's endorsement helped the party in establishing its credentials among the farmers who might not otherwise have been sufficiently inspired by the BJP's obsession with the Rama Mandir alone. Whereas in the 1991 election there was no indication that agrarian interests could overcome the pull of caste and religious identities, in the past it was from this area, and from the intermediate agrarian classes of western UP, that Charan Singh fashioned a succession of agrarian political formations to provide the Janata Dal with much of its strength in UP. Even the new alliance forged by the Samajwadi Party and the BSP in the 1993 assembly elections failed to gain support in western UP which emerged as the chief bastion of the BJP, in contrast to eastern UP, where this alliance made major inroads in BJP strongholds. To sum up, the election results in western UP indicate that the BJP managed to bring about substantive changes in the political agenda; even though it did not manage to alter the caste-class alliance in the western region of UP, it managed to change cross-communal networks through a sharpening of Hindu-Muslim polarization. When these identities began to dominate the political agenda, they could obstruct a sectoral or even populist construction of rural interests.

It could be argued that voter choices may have very little to do with their preference for higher prices and loans.[68] In other words, a farmer who may have participated in rural price agitation may have cast his/her vote on ethnic consideration. The second point is the role of the BKU elite in influencing farmers' voting choices. Interviews with the local elite and BKU leaders in Muzaffarnagar district, for example, show that they supported the BJP in order to express their aversion to and repugnance of the Janata Dal's reservation policy and Yadav's refusal to allow the construction of the Rama Mandir at the disputed site.[69]

Conclusion: Ideological Convergences

Whatever the assessment of the public discourse and the subjective inclinations of the leading actors of the farmers' movement, the objective response to Hindutva was marked by silence; there was no evidence of a counter-campaign to halt its expansion. This does not warrant the conclusion that the BKU was actively supporting the Hindutva politics, but there did seem to be an ambivalence towards it, and a reluctance to confront.[70] This was not unusual: the ambivalence was shared by all the major political formations. Arguably it could be interpreted as a pragmatic acceptance of the hegemony of Hindutva in UP at the time, rather than a positive espousal of its politics. Nevertheless, it suggests that the farmers' movement failed to find an enduring basis in the sphere of social movements or social thinking. An important reason is that the farmers' movement did not contest the social field being taken over by communal politics which was consciously seeking to sharpen religious identities, reinterpret conflicts, and reshape institutions. Communal ideologies could flourish in the absence of counter-ideologies and movements. The refusal of the farmers' leadership to give precedence to their economic interests over ascriptive ethnic identities seriously constrained the sustainability of the movement.

The growth of Hindutva politics and the communal upsurge in UP in the late 1980s and early 1990s clearly overtook the farmers' movement. The BKU's politics and strategy may however have also increased ethnic energies conducive to a more acute communalization of political discourse. The adherence to a populist-ethnic register reinforced the space for the growth of the political right. More crucially, such a framework of identity projects and represents issues and interests in a non-class manner, as both the BKU and BJP have done. The BKU chose not to construct or present its interests in economic terms. This was because economic interests defined as better prices and subsidies did not affect or benefit all segments equally, and consequently the economic contradictions which in material terms divided rich and poor farmers in the BKU were deflected ideologically by a populism which simply demanded a better deal for the countryside from the state. In a similar vein, Hindutva projected an undifferentiated Hindu community oppressed and threatened by the 'pseudo-secularism' of the state and its 'appeasement' of Muslims, and demanded a better deal for the Hindu community as a whole. Both ideologies highlighted political symbols and forms which generated and reinforced undifferentiated notions of a community of commodity producers or Hindus simply on grounds of being rural-not-urban and Hindus-not-Muslims. In this sense the language employed by the ideologies of agrarianism or Hindutva converged by explicitly placing rural-agrarian in opposition to urban-industrial, or the majority in opposition to minority interests. Both claimed to speak for the collective good of the entire agricultural economy/community/nation. Despite the very different ideological provenance of the two movements, the terms of discourse joining together classes, castes, and communities shared a political framework which accepted the basic parameters of the system even as they called for some changes within it.

Notes and References

1. 'Surplus-producing' farmers refers to those well-to-do farmers who have a genuine surplus to sell after meeting their own requirements (that is, distress sellers are excluded). These farmers account for the bulk of total sales because they command the bulk of the area under cultivation, and they comprise roughly the top three pentiles of holdings ranked by area.

2. On various aspects of farmers movements see D.N. Dhanagare, 'An Apolitical Populism', *Seminar*, no. 352, 1988, pp. 24-31; C. Lenneberg, 'Sharad Joshi and the Farmers: The Middle Peasant Lives', *Pacific Affairs*, vol. 61, no. 3, 1988, pp. 446-64; M.V. Nadkarni, *Farmers' Movements in India*, Delhi: Allied Publishers, 1987; G. Omvedt, 'New Movements', *Seminar*, no. 352, 1988, pp. 39–44; G. Omvedt, 'Peasants, Dalits, and Women: Democracy and India's New Social Movements?', paper presented at a workshop on 'Social Movements, State and Democracy' organized by the Delhi University Group on Politics of Developing Countries and the Indian Statistical Institute, Sociology Group, New Delhi, 5-8 October 1992; L.I. Rudolph and S.H. Rudolph, *In Pursuit of Laxmi: The Political Economy of the Indian State*, Delhi: Orient Longman, 1987. Farmers have carried out agitations in various states, and staged massive rallies in Delhi.

3. Much of BKU's initial support was built through its advocacy of farmers grievances on electricity supply. The BKU got a shot in the arm after power rates were raised in August 1986, from Rs. 22.50 to Rs. 30. Added to this were the perennial problems faced by the farmers in dealing with the Uttar Pradesh State Electricity Board. The transformers are often burnt out, and farmers have to bribe officials to expedite repairs. The UP government's insistence that farmers should pay electricity dues or face cuts in power supply generated strong resentment against the government. Tikait quickly seized the initiative, urging farmers to ignore the UPSEB's directive. The non-payment campaign was taken to villages, with BKU activists succeeding in persuading farmers not to pay electricity dues. It is easy to understand why this was so. A regular power supply for tubewells is crucial to the growth of the highly capital intensive agriculture in western UP.

Though tubewells are owned and operated by rich farmers, small farmers too have a stake in power supply, because they have to rent tubewells for irrigation. This is the one issue that influenced all the farmers to join the numerous agitations launched by the BKU, *The Hindustan Times,* 2 April 1987.

4. Zoya Hasan, 'Self-Serving Guardians: Formation and Strategy of the Bharatiya Kisan Union', *Economic and Political Weekly*, vol. 24, no. 45, 2 December 1989, pp. 2663–70.

5. The Lok Dal won 85 seats in the 1984 Assembly elections, only nine weeks after the landslide victory of the Congress in the Lok Sabha elections held in the wake of Indira Gandhi's assassination. In 1989 the Janata Dal won the Assembly elections and formed the government in UP.

6. *The Tribune*, 10 February 1988.

7. S.S. Gill and K. Singhal, 'Farmers Agitation: Response to Development Crisis of Agriculture', *Economic and Political Weekly*, vol. 19, no. 40, 1984, pp. 1728–32.

8. *The Times of India*, 2 February 1989.

9. D. Gupta, 'Country-Town Nexus and Agrarian Mobilization: Bharatiya Kisan Union', *Economic and Political Weekly*, vol. 23, no. 51, 1988.

10. Rudolph and Rudolph, *In Pursuit of Laxmi.*

11. *Economic and Political Weekly*, 8 September 1980.

12. J.R. Westley, *Agriculture and Equitable Growth: The Caste of Punjab/Haryana*, London: Westview Press, 1986.

13. Ibid.

14. Towards the end of British rule in India the rural economic structure of UP was marked by extreme inequality in the ownership of land and means of production. Inequality in the distribution of landownership was most marked in central and eastern UP. In the central districts 11 per cent of zamindars owned three quarters of the land; the pattern of ownership was slightly less uneven in eastern UP where approximately 11 per cent of zamindars owned 61 per cent of the area. By contrast the great majority in both these areas owned holdings of less than 5 acre, accounting for 4 per cent of the land. In comparison, in western UP, about 5 per cent of large zamindars owned 51 per cent of the land, the 45 per cent of zamindars who had holdings below 5 acre accounting for 4 per cent of the land. More notably, western UP was dotted with a substantial class of rich and medium landowners: 36 per cent owned holdings of 5-25 acre and 18 per cent of the area, while another 13 per cent owned farms of 25-100 acre and 13 per cent of the area. See B. Singh and S. Misra, *A Study of Land Reforms in UP*, Calcutta: Oxford Book Co., 1984, pp. 215–17.

15. In 1970-1, 54 per cent of the acreage was controlled by peasants with minimum holdings of 7.5 acre. See P. Brass, 'The Politicization of the Peasantry in a North Indian State', *Journal of Peasant Studies*, vol. 8, no. 1, 1980, pp. 3-36. A study of Meerut highlighted the dominary of capitalist producers and rich peasants, who constituted 7.69 per cent of households and controlled the largest land area (47-53 per cent). The middle peasants who formed 20.44 per cent of the households, controlled 39.3 per cent of the land area. See J. Singh, *Capitalism and Dependence: Agrarian Politics in Western Uttar Pradesh 1951-1991*, Delhi: Manohar, 1992.

16. Government of Uttar Pradesh, *Statistical Abstract: Uttar Pradesh, 1980-1*, Lucknow: Economics and Statistics Division, State Planning Institute, 1986.

17. Zoya Hasan and U. Patnaik, 'Aspects of the Farmers' Movement in Uttar Pradesh in the Context of Uneven Growth of Capitalist Agriculture', *Social Change and Political Discourse in India*, ed. T.V. Satyamurthy, Delhi: Oxford University Press, 1997.

18. Kripa Shankar, *Land Transfers: A Case Study*, Delhi: Gian Publishing House, 1990.

19. Ibid., pp. 41-4.

20. Ibid., p. 44.

21. Government of India, *All-India Report on Agricultural Census, 1970-1*, New Delhi: Ministry of Agriculture and Irrigation, 1992.

22. The section on food production is based on Hasan and Patnaik, 'Aspects of the Farmers' Movement in Uttar Pradesh'.

23. Ibid.

24. Through the fair price shops of the public distribution system in cities and towns foodgrains and some manufactured necessities like sugar and fuel are sold to one quarter of the total population at low prices subsidized by government.

25. According to estimates for the 1980-1 wheat crop, the price index for agricultural products as percentage of that for manufactured products declined from 100.7 per cent in 1974-5 to 87.6 per cent in 1977-80, *Economic and Political Weekly*, 8 September 1990.

26. A. Mitra, *Terms of Trade and Class Relations*, London: Frank Cass, 1977.

27. Nadkarni, *Farmers' Movements in India*; V.K.R.V. Rao, *India's National Income 1950-1980*, Delhi: Sage, 1983.

28. S. Baru, *The Political Economy of Indian Sugar: State Intervention and Structural Change*, Delhi: Oxford University Press, 1990.

29. Charan Singh, *Land Reform in UP and the Kulaks*, Delhi: Vikas Publishing House, 1981.

30. Baru, *Political Economy of Indian Sugar*, p. 82.

31. Ibid., p. 173.

32. According to estimates for the 1980-1 wheat crop, the price index for agriculture products as percentage of that for manufactured products declined from 100.7 per cent in 1974-5 to 87.6 per cent in 1977-80. For more details see *Economic and Political Weekly*, 8 September 1990. Much of the analysis of farmers' movements adheres to the view that it was a movement of the middle peasantry. See Lenneberg, 'Sharad Joshi and the Farmers', and Omvedt, 'Peasants, Dalits, and Women', for an analysis of the Maharashtra farmers movement, and Rudolph and Rudolph, *In Pursuit of Laxmi* for the farmers' movements as a whole.

33. A small survey was conducted in two villages in Meerut and Moradabad districts just after the Meerut agitation of January-February 1988. The village in Meerut had a tradition of peasant proprietorship, while the village in Moradabad had a zamindars background. The stratified sample covered 15 per cent of households for every castes and class in the two villages. I am grateful to Jagpal Singh for his help in carrying out the survey.

34. A. Kant, 'Agrarian Mobilization in Western Uttar Pradesh: A Case Study of the Bharatiya Kisan Union', M.Phil. dissertation, School of Social Sciences, Jawaharlal Nehru University, 1990. The domination of the rural rich in the BKU is also stressed by Singh, *Capitalism and Dependence*.

35. The table below shows the presence of a high proportion of agricultural labourers in Saharanpur, Muzaffarnagar, Meerut, Bulandshahr, Aligarh and Bijnor districts. All these districts have experienced rapid capitalist development.

Districtwise Number of Total Marginal and Small Holdings (1980-1)
and Agricultural Labourers (1981) (Thousands)

Districts	Total (All Holding Groups)	Small (1-2 ha)	Marginal (Below 1 ha)	Agricultural Labourers
Saharanpur	255	49	144	224
Muzaffarnagar	249	45	147	182
Meerut	235	46	138	145
Ghaziabad	161	31	102	63
Bulandshahr	244	52	137	111
Aligarh	252	55	132	129
Mathura	162	37	69	65
Agra	235	52	125	75
Mainpuri	347	61	248	50
Etah	319	60	213	64
Bijnor	219	46	117	127
Moradabad	378	77	227	92
Rampur	148	31	92	37
Bareilly	331	61	221	78
Badaun	408	75	274	50
Shahjahanpur	354	65	242	58
Pilibhit	170	36	104	41
Farrukhabad	373	53	284	57
Etawah	287	54	191	58

Source: Statistical Diary, Uttar Pradesh, 1986.

36. There has been an intensification of Jat-scheduled caste conflicts in Meerut and Muzaffarnagar in 1989-90. The worst incident took place in Bhopal in Muzaffarnagar, in September 1989, after a labourer refused to work for a Jat farmer belonging to the BKU. The clash ended up in firing which killed 4 persons and injured 24. Jats were backed by the BKU, and scheduled castes by the BMU. See *The Hindustan Times*, 28 September 1989.

37. T.J. Byres, 'Charan Singh 1902-87: An Assessment', *Journal of Peasant Studies*, vol. 8, no. 2, 1988, pp. 139–89.

38. G. Omvedt, 'The Farmers Movement in Maharashtra', *A Space Within the Struggle*, ed. I. Sen, Delhi: Kali for Women, 1990.

39. L.J. Calman, *Towards Empowerment: Women and Movement Politics in India*, Boulder, CO: Westview Press, 1992.

40. Dhanagare, 'Apoliticist Populism'.

41. *Navbharat Times*, 8 February 1989.

42. *The Times of India*, 9 August 1989.

43. I. Duncan, 'Party Politics and the North Indian Peasantry: The Rise of the BKU in UP', *Journal of Peasant Studies*, vol. 16, no. 1, 1988.

44. Westley, *Agriculture and Equitable Growth*.

45. Rudolph and Rudolph, *In Pursuit of Laxmi*, p. 335.

46. *Hindutva* is a contemporary right-wing movement of Hindu self-assertion, for Hindu rights and Hindu nationhood.

47. A. Varshney, 'Self-Limited Empowerment: Democracy, Economic Development and Rural India', *Journal of Development Studies*, vol. 29, no. 4, 1993, pp. 177–215.

48. Omvedt, 'Peasants, Dalits, and Women'.

49. *The Hindustan Times*, 28 September 1989.

50. *The Times of India*, 9 August 1988.

51. *Bhaichara* refers to a system where the management and distribution of land is structured by exclusive customs and traditions of a particular community. The *bhaichara* system prevailed throughout the Jat dominated regions of western UP. In Meerut, for example 40 per cent of land came under *bhaichara* in 1940.

52. Omvedt, 'New Movements'.

53. Gupta, 'Country-Town Nexus'.

54. M.C. Pradhan, *The Political System of the Jats of Northern India*, Bombay: Oxford University Perss, 1986. The Sisauli Panchayat was the main decision-making body of the BKU: it met every month in Sisauli village, Muzaffarnagar district.

55. The Janata Party government appointed the Backward Classes Commission in December 1978, headed by Bindeshwari Prasad Mandal, popularly known as the Mandal Commission. The Commission identified castes as socially and educationally backward and recommended reservation of 27 per cent jobs for them in Central government.

56. For details on the anti-Mandal agitation see People's Union of Democratic Rights (PUDR), *Disputed Passages: Report on Law, Reservations and Agitations*, Delhi: PUDR, 1990.

57. A rath yatra is a pilgrimage or large-scale procession, the object of which is to put across a religious message. L.K. Advani, President of the BJP, undertook a rath yatra in September-October 1990, traversing several states in order to mobilize support for the construction of the Rama Mandir in Ayodhya. The course of the rath yatra was marked by massive communal violence, culminating in Advani's arrest and the fall of the Janata Dal government in November 1990. Between the rath yatra and the 1991 elections, three phases of tension and rioting can be identified. The first phase, starting in the wake of the anti-Mandal agitation, took the form of tension on the route of the rath yatra. This phase ended in considerable rioting when Advani was arrested and some *kar sevaks* were killed in police firing. In the first week of November, 34 towns in UP were under curfew along with 36 across the country. The second phase started after the fall of the Janata Dal government and was followed by another round of violence which lasted from the beginning of December till the end of January 1991. It was concentrated in UP with western UP being the area of maximum concentration. The third phase of rioting began in March 1991 with elections imminent, and continued well until elections in May. For more information on this phase, see Chakravarti et al., 'Khurja Riots 1990: Understanding the Conjuncture', *Economic and Political Weekly*, vol. 27, no. 18, 1992, pp. 951–65. Similarly, the two months preceding the 1989 elections witnessed riots in 55 places across nine states. See PUDR, *Disputed Passages*.

58. The analysis of the link between commercialization and communalism in western UP draws upon the research and information I collected along with Uma

Chakravarti, Prem Chowdhuri, Pradip Dutta, Kumkum Sangari and Tanika Sarkar. See Chakravarthi et al., 'Khurja Riots 1990'.

59. Chakravarthi et al., 'Khurja Riots 1990'.

60. See note 57 for more details on the rath yatra.

61. Virat Hindu Sammelan was a large-scale congregation of Hindus organized at the behest of the VHP.

62. *Frontline*, 14–17 August 1990.

63. Chakravarthi et al., 'Khurja Riots 1990'.

64. The BKU's differences with the BJP government emerged because the latter did not allow the BKU to hold its panchayat in Lucknow. The BJP government asserted its authority twice within a short span of five months, and in effect subdued the BKU. Tikait had to abandon plans to hold the panchayat in Lucknow in order to avoid confrontation. See *The Statesman*, 10 February 1992.

65. *Kar.seva* is the work a devotee is expected to do as a part of his obligation to a religious shrine or place of worship.

66. *Frontline*, 14–17 August 1990.

67. Chakravarthi et al., 'Khurja Riots 1990', p. 963.

68. Varshney, 'Self-Limited Empowerment'.

69. In-depth interviews of the local elite were conducted in Muzaffarnagar district in September 1993. Some of the information and analysis on the growth and impact of the BJP in western UP is based on these interviews. I am grateful to Ajay Kant, Ph.D. scholar in the Centre for Political Studies, Jawaharlal Nehru University for his help in conducting the interviews.

70. The analysis of the relationship between Hindutva and the farmers' movement is limited to the period until the 1991 elections. The chapter does not analyse developments after June 1991.

Index

discrimination 5, 394, 448–9
groups xiv, 10, 13, 32, 42, 51, 57, 122, 159, 195, 199, 239, 334, 351, 363, 366, 381, 385, 391–2, 403, 448, 450, 454, 483, 485
identities
  politicization of 469
lower xi, xiii, xvi, xix–xxi, 4–5, 10, 12, 20, 33, 42, 50–2, 54, 70–1, 76, 109, 110, 114, 132–3, 136, 141, 202, 218, 230, 239–40, 243, 313, 340, 342, 358, 360, 363, 368, 394–5, 400, 406, 431–2, 443–52, 454–5, 457–62, 467–70, 472–8, 483–5, 509
marginalized 107
mobilization 57, 396, 458, 475, 484
  limitations of 396
order 36
origins 54
parties xvii, xxi, 238–40, 319, 447, 458, 461–2, 467–9, 474–5, 485
political and administrative importance of 50
politics xxi, 42, 133, 342, 443, 448, 451, 454, 456, 459, 467–8, 472, 477, 483, 485, 510
power xxi, 406
system xiii, 32, 35, 39, 42, 201–2, 252, 354, 368, 449–50, 470
  hierarchical 39
underprivileged 46
upper xi, xii, xix–xxi, 4–6, 20, 33, 49, 51–2, 57, 70–3, 75, 106, 109–12, 115–16, 118, 127–8, 133–4, 136–8, 142, 205, 217, 238–40, 243, 288, 293–4, 316, 349–50, 354, 356–60, 362, 366–7, 379–80, 382, 385–91, 394, 396, 398–402, 405–6, 431–2, 439, 445–56, 459–61, 467–70, 472–8, 509, 512
caste versus class 51
caste versus community 51
central budgetary outlays 10
Central Educational Institutions
  (Reservation in Admission) Bill 2006 113
central government
  failure of 68
centralization 23–4, 67–8, 77, 80, 85–6, 138, 154, 433

structures of 77
centralization of power 67, 85–6, 433
Centrally Sponsored Government Schemes 10–12
Central Plan Assistance 96
central resources 72
Centre for the Study of Developing Societies (CSDS) 341, 443
Centre-State xiii, 65–8, 70, 72, 75, 86, 89, 92–3, 95, 97, 321
  conflicts 66
  distribution of powers 66
  relations 65–8, 70, 86, 89, 93–5
    fundamental renegotiation of 68
    restructuring of 95
Chamars 354, 358, 367, 382, 452
Chatterjee, N.C. 249
Chatterjee, Partha 157, 255
chauvinism 147, 512
  aggressive 512
Chhattisgarh 9, 25, 66
Chidambaram, P., Finance Minister 74
child marriage 33, 161, 213
  abolishing 33
children 33, 38–9, 161, 184, 196, 213, 223, 238, 246, 258, 268, 296, 334, 456, 458, 486
  adoption of 238
  labour 38–9
China xii, 3, 40, 322, 468
Chinmayananda, Swami 18
Chowdhary, Shefali 349
Christians 32, 54, 202–3, 214, 230, 252, 452
citizenship xvi, 17, 27, 31, 33, 49, 135–6, 159, 175, 214, 251, 253, 256–7
  equal xvi, 33, 159, 175, 214
  secular 31
City Congress Committee (CCC) 299
Civil Disobedience Movement 288, 290–1, 294–9, 301, 303–5, 362–3
civil servants 5, 52, 460, 474
civil society xvi, xxi, 12, 67, 71, 116–17, 144, 157, 174–5, 182, 332, 341, 429, 466, 483
  expansion of xxi
clashes 9, 115
  violent 9
class
  accommodation 350, 366